THE LEGITIMACY OF INVESTMENT ARBITRATION

International investment arbitration remains one of the most controversial areas of globalisation and international law. This book provides a fresh contribution to the debate by adopting a thoroughly empirical approach. Based on new datasets and a range of quantitative, qualitative and computational methods, the contributors interrogate claims and counterclaims about the regime's legitimacy. The result is a nuanced picture of many of the critiques lodged against the regime, whether they be bias in arbitral decision-making, close relationships between law firms and arbitrators, the absence of arbitrator diversity, or excessive compensation. The book comes at a time when several national and international initiatives are under way to reform international investment arbitration. The authors discuss and analyse how the regime can be reformed and how a process of legitimation might occur.

DANIEL BEHN is Senior Lecturer (Associate Professor) in International Dispute Resolution and Director of Graduate Studies, Centre for Commercial Law Studies, Queen Mary University of London; and Associate Research Professor II, PluriCourts Centre of Excellence, University of Oslo, where he leads the PITAD project. He is Co-Chair of the Academic Forum on Investor-State Dispute Settlement (which supports the UNCITRAL WG III reform process) and an Associate Editor of the *Journal of World Investment and Trade*.

OLE KRISTIAN FAUCHALD is Professor at the Faculty of Law, University of Oslo; and Research Professor at the Fridtjof Nansen Institute. He is a Coordinator at the PluriCourts Centre of Excellence, University of Oslo, where he also leads the Norwegian Research Council funded project, *Responses to the Legitimacy Crisis of International Investment Law* (LEGINVEST).

MALCOLM LANGFORD is Professor of Public Law and Director of the Centre of Excellence for Experiential Legal Learning (CELL), Faculty of Law, University of Oslo. He was Chair of the Academic Forum on Investor-State Dispute Settlement (which supports the UNCITRAL WG III reform process) (2019-2021) and is Co-editor of the Cambridge University Press book series, Globalization and Human Rights. Langford is also a Fellow at the PluriCourts Centre of Excellence, where he leads the Norwegian Research Council funded project, *Compliance Politics and International Investment Disputes* (COPIID).

STUDIES ON INTERNATIONAL COURTS AND TRIBUNALS

General Editors
Andreas Føllesdal, University of Oslo
Geir Ulfstein, University of Oslo

Studies on International Courts and Tribunals contains theoretical and interdisciplinary scholarship on legal aspects as well as the legitimacy and effectiveness of international courts and tribunals.

Other books in the series:

Mads Andenas and Eirik Bjorge (eds.) *A Farewell to Fragmentation: Reassertion and Convergence in International Law*

Cecilia M. Bailliet and Nobuo Hayashi (eds.) *The Legitimacy of International Criminal Tribunals*

Amrei Müller with Hege Elisabeth Kjos, (eds.) *Judicial Dialogue and Human Rights*

Nienke Grossman, Harlan Grant Cohen, Andreas Follesdal and Geir Ulfstein (eds.) *Legitimacy and International Courts*

Robert Howse, Hélène Ruiz-Fabri , Geir Ulfstein and Michelle Q. Zang (eds.) The Legitimacy of International Trade Courts and Tribunals

Theresa Squatrito, Oran Young, Andreas Føllesdal and Geir Ulfstein (eds.) *The Performance of International Courts and Tribunals*

Marlene Wind (ed.) *International Courts and Domestic Politics*

Christina Voigt (ed.) *International Judicial Practice on the Environment: Questions of Legitimacy*

Freya Baetens (ed.) *Legitimacy of Unseen Actors in International Adjudication*

Martin Scheinin (ed.) *Human Rights Norms in 'Other' International Courts*

Shai Dothan *International Judicial Review: When Should International Courts Intervene?*

Daniel Behn, Szilárd Gáspár-Szilágyi, Malcolm Langford (eds.) Adjudicating Trade and Investment Disputes: Convergence or Divergence?

Silje Langvatn, Mattias Kumm, Wojciech Sadurski (eds.) *Public Reason and Courts*

THE LEGITIMACY OF INVESTMENT ARBITRATION

Empirical Perspectives

Edited by

DANIEL BEHN
Queen Mary University of London
University of Oslo

OLE KRISTIAN FAUCHALD
University of Oslo

MALCOLM LANGFORD
University of Oslo

CAMBRIDGE
UNIVERSITY PRESS

University Printing House, Cambridge CB2 8BS, United Kingdom

One Liberty Plaza, 20th Floor, New York, NY 10006, USA

477 Williamstown Road, Port Melbourne, VIC 3207, Australia

314–321, 3rd Floor, Plot 3, Splendor Forum, Jasola District Centre, New Delhi – 110025, India

103 Penang Road, #05–06/07, Visioncrest Commercial, Singapore 238467

Cambridge University Press is part of the University of Cambridge.

It furthers the University's mission by disseminating knowledge in the pursuit of education, learning, and research at the highest international levels of excellence.

www.cambridge.org
Information on this title: www.cambridge.org/9781108837583
DOI: 10.1017/9781108946636

© Cambridge University Press 2022

This publication is in copyright. Subject to statutory exception and to the provisions of relevant collective licensing agreements, no reproduction of any part may take place without the written permission of Cambridge University Press.

First published 2022

A catalogue record for this publication is available from the British Library.

Library of Congress Cataloging-in-Publication Data
Names: Behn, Daniel, 1974– editor. | Fauchald, Ole Kristian, editor. | Langford, Malcolm, editor.
Title: The legitimacy of investment arbitration : empirical perspectives / edited by Daniel Behn, Queen Mary University of London; Ole Kristian Fauchald, University of Oslo, PluriCourts; Malcolm Langford, University of Oslo.
Description: [Cambrdige, United Kingdom] : Cambridge University Press, [2021] | Series: Studies on international courts and tribunals | Includes bibliographical references and index.
Identifiers: LCCN 2020058317 (print) | LCCN 2020058318 (ebook) | ISBN 9781108837583 (hardback) | ISBN 9781108931212 (paperback) | ISBN 9781108946636 (epub)
Subjects: LCSH: Investments, Foreign (International law) | International commercial arbitration.
Classification: LCC K3830 .L44 2021 (print) | LCC K3830 (ebook) | DDC 346/.092––dc23
LC record available at https://lccn.loc.gov/2020058317
LC ebook record available at https://lccn.loc.gov/2020058318

ISBN 978-1-108-83758-3 Hardback

Cambridge University Press has no responsibility for the persistence or accuracy of URLs for external or third-party internet websites referred to in this publication and does not guarantee that any content on such websites is, or will remain, accurate or appropriate.

CONTENTS

List of Figures   viii
List of Tables   x
Notes on Contributors   xii

1. Introduction: The Legitimacy Crisis and the Empirical Turn   1
DANIEL BEHN, OLE KRISTIAN FAUCHALD, MALCOLM LANGFORD

2. The International Investment Regime and Its Discontents   39
DANIEL BEHN, OLE KRISTIAN FAUCHALD, MALCOLM LANGFORD

PART I.   Process Legitimacy: Independence and Impartiality

3. Testing Cognitive Bias: Experimental Approaches and Investment Arbitration   85
SERGIO PUIG, ANTON STREZHNEV

4. The Influence of Law Firms in Investment Arbitration   100
RUNAR HILLEREN LIE

5. Arbitrator Challenges in International Investment Tribunals   133
CHIARA GIORGETTI

6. Dissents in Investment Arbitration: On Collegiality and Individualism   159
DAPHNA KAPELIUK

CONTENTS

PART II.   Process Legitimacy: Legal Reasoning

7. Foreign Investors, Domestic Courts and Investment
    Treaty Arbitration   171

    SZILÁRD GÁSPÁR-SZILÁGYI

8. Ensuring Correctness or Promoting Consistency: Tracking
    Policy Priorities in Investment Arbitration through Large-
    Scale Citation Analysis   230

    WOLFGANG ALSCHNER

9. Fair and Equitable Treatment: Ordering Chaos
    through Precedent   256

    FLORIAN GRISEL

PART III.   Output Legitimacy

10. The West and the Rest: Geographic Diversity and the
    Role of Arbitrator Nationality in
    Investment Arbitration   283

    MALCOLM LANGFORD, DANIEL BEHN, MAXIM USYNIN

11. Mixing Methodologies in Empirically Investigating
    Investment Arbitration and Inbound
    Foreign Investment   315

    SHIRO ARMSTRONG, LUKE NOTTAGE

12. Double Jeopardy? The Use of Investment Arbitration
    in Times of Crisis   365

    CÉDRIC DUPONT, THOMAS SCHULTZ AND MERIH ANGIN

13. Who Has Benefited Financially from Investment Treaty
    Arbitration? An Evaluation of the Size and Wealth
    of Claimants   394

    GUS VAN HARTEN, PAVEL MALYSHEUSKI

14. Explaining China's Relative Absence from Investment
    Treaty Arbitration   424

    FREDRIK LINDMARK, DANIEL BEHN, OLE KRISTIAN
    FAUCHALD

PART IV. Legitimation Strategies

15. Does International Arbitration Enfeeble or Enhance Local Legal Institutions? 467

CATHERINE R. ROGERS, CHRISTOPHER R. DRAHOZAL

16. Learning from Investment Treaty Law and Arbitration: Developing States and Power Inequalities 501

MAVLUDA SATTOROVA, OLEKSANDRA VYTIAGANETS

17. Legitimation through Modification: Do States Seek More Regulatory Space in Their Investment Agreements? 531

TOMER BROUDE, YORAM Z. HAFTEL, ALEXANDER THOMPSON

Index 555

FIGURES

1.1 Growth in the ISDS caseload: pending versus concluded cases (1987–2020)   3
2.1 Signed IIAs (1980–2019)   43
2.2 Bilateral ISDS relationships in BITs, FTAs and MITs (1966–2019)   45
2.3 Unique versus all bilateral ISDS relationships in IIAs (1966–2019)   46
2.4 All known ISDS cases by year of registration (1,126 as of 1 January 2020)   53
2.5 Bilateral ISDS relationships and all known treaty-based ISDS cases   54
2.6 Compensation ratios for all known treaty-based ISDS cases (1997–2020)   56
2.7 All known ISDS case outcomes by investor win across time (1997–2020)   57
2.8 Known treaty-based ISDS cases by economic sector (1997–2020)   59
2.9 'Legitimacy', 'investment' and 'arbitration' scholarship (2000–2020)   63
3.1 Sample experimental vignette showing manipulated elements   93
3.2 Estimated effects of claimant/respondent country development conditional on outcome   97
4.1 The full network between arbitrators and law firms   128
4.2 A partition of the network of arbitrators and law firms   129
4.3 Network between top arbitrators and law firms   129
5.1 Arbitration challenges – variation in outcomes by institution   140
7.1 Initiation of domestic and ITA cases   198
8.1 The growth of outward citations   241
8.2 Exemplary treaty network connected through citations   242
8.3 Treaty-citation network of top 10 IIAs with most citing awards   247
8.4 Share of self-citations for NAFTA and ECT awards over time   249
8.5 Citations ordered by underlying treaty similarity   252
8.6 Mean similarity of IIAs connected through citations (excluding self-cites)   253
9.1 Three tales of FET   267
10.1 Investor–state arbitration cases registered by year (1987–2018)   288
10.2 Distribution of Western and non-Western appointments per year   298
10.3 Distribution of Western and non-Western new entrant arbitrators by year   299
10.4 Type of arbitrator appointment   300

viii

LIST OF FIGURES

11.1 Annual total FDI outflows from OECD: 1985–2014   330
12.1 Number of investment arbitrations claims filed per year   374
14.1 Ratio of number of ITA cases to number of BITs (up to 1 August 2019)   432
14.2 Stocks of Chinese inward and outward FDI 2007–2017 (US$ million)   435
14.3 Judicial corruption in China 1970–2017 based on V-Dem data   451
14.4 Executive corruption in China 1970–2017 based on V-Dem data   453
14.5 Public sector corruption in China 1970–2017 based on V-Dem data   454
17.1 Average annual SRS ISDS in 2,785 IIAs, 1959–2016   540
17.2 SRS ISDS on Model BITs of India, the Netherlands, the United States and Germany   543
17.3 Annual number of renegotiated IIAs, 1971–2017   545
17.4 Average of SRS ISDS change in renegotiated IIAs, 1994–2015   547
17.5 The cumulative number of IIA terminations, 2000–2018   549
17.6 Number of terminated IIAs for the top seven terminating countries   550

TABLES

2.1 Treaty-based bilateral ISDS relationships by WBIGs 49
2.2 Investment protection through bilateral and unilateral consent to ISDS by WBIGs 51
2.3 All known treaty-based ISDS cases by outcome (1997–2020) 55
2.4 All known treaty-based ISDS cases by institution (1997–2020) 58
2.5 Distribution of all known treaty-based ISDS cases by WBIGs 61
4.1 Top 25 actors in the ISDS network ranked by HITS (hub) 119
4.2 Direct and indirect reappointments sorted by firms' total number of cases 121
4.3 Direct and indirect reappointments sorted by countries' total number of cases 123
4.4 Top 25 law firms' appointment of top 25 arbitrators sorted by number of firms' cases 124
5.1 Success rates of arbitrator challenges in investor–state arbitration 138
5.2 Summary of challenge procedures 148
6.1 Jurisdiction type of chair and frequency of dissents 167
7.1 References to domestic cases 185
7.2 Domestic cases appealed 189
7.3 Domestic cases by disputing parties 191
7.4 Domestic cases by subject-matter 192
7.5 Domestic cases won or lost by the investors at all levels 195
7.6 Domestic cases won or lost by the investors at different levels 195
7.7 Absolute ignorance about ITA 197
7.8 Length of domestic proceedings 201
7A.1 United States 215
7A.2 Canada 219
7A.3 Hungary 224
7A.4 Romania 227
8.1 Few IIAs have produced many final awards 245
8.2 Top citing and top cited IIAs 246
8.3 Most influential IIAs (in terms of attracting inward citations) based on their position in the treaty citation network 247
8.4 Share of references to awards rendered under the same treaty 248
8.5 Similarity of IIAs connected by citations 252

LIST OF TABLES

10.1 Regional distribution of arbitrators based on citizenship 296
10.2 Regional distribution of appointments based on citizenship 297
10.3 Nature of appointing authority: parties vs. institution (not including ICSID annulment cases) 301
10.4 Non-Western arbitrators by citizenship 302
10.5 Non-Western arbitrators by dominant residence 303
10.6 Panel composition and outcomes (by citizenship) 306
10.7 Summary statistics for regression analysis 308
10.8 Regression analysis 310
10.9 Dissents by arbitrator and outcome 311
10.10 Investor success rates by nationality 312
11.1 Definitions of dependent and control variables 328
11.2 The effects of BITs and specific provisions with system GMM estimator 333
11.3 Effects of MFN combined with ISDS in BITs 335
11.4 Sensitivity tests for different periods and host state groups 336
11.5 Effects of signed BITs on FDI (FE and PPML estimators) 353
11.6 Effects of ISDS1 and ISDS2 (FE and PPML estimators) 355
11.7 Sensitivity analysis with alternative time periods and country groups 359
11.8 Conditional effects of MFN and ISDS in BITs over different time periods 360
11.9 The FDI impact of PRI and alternative governance indexes 361
11.10 Countries covered by the FDI data set 362
12.1 Economic crisis variable 385
12.2 Ordinal logistic regression results for all countries 386
12.3 Negative binomial regressions results for all countries 388
12.4 Negative binomial regressions results for all countries excluding the cases with US investors 390
12.5 Negative binomial regressions results for all countries excluding the cases with primary sector 392
13.1 Aggregate ordered compensation 403
13.2 Forum-shopping 405
13.3 The Yukos cases 408
13.4 Size of claimant 409
13.5 Aggregated compensation including costs 411
13.6 Larger cost award cases 412
14.1 Distribution of Chinese ITA cases initiated after 2006 433
14.2 Chinese inward FDI stocks in 2012 435
14.3 Chinese inward FDI flows by economic sector 437
15.1 Summary statistics 491
15.2 Linear regression models with change in WGI rule-of-law rating as dependent variable 493
15.3 Fixed-effects models with WGI rule-of-law rating as dependent variable 495
15.4 Fixed-effects models with Fraser Institute Legal System Component Ratings as dependent variables 496
17.1 Categories and values of SRS ISDS 536

CONTRIBUTORS

Volume Editors

DANIEL BEHN, Queen Mary University of London and University of Oslo (d.behn@qmul.ac.uk)

Daniel Behn is Senior Lecturer (Associate Professor) in International Dispute Resolution and Director of Graduate Studies, Centre for Commercial Law Studies, Queen Mary University of London; and Associate Research Professor II, PluriCourts Centre of Excellence, University of Oslo, where he leads the PITAD project. He is Co-Chair of the Academic Forum on Investor-State Dispute Settlement (which supports the UNCITRAL WG III reform process) and an Associate Editor of the *Journal of World Investment and Trade*. Behn's research is data-driven and empirically orientated, applying quantitative, network-based, computational, and psychometric methods to the study of international courts and tribunals. He is the recent winner of the John H. Jackson Prize for Best Article in the Journal of International Economic Law.

OLE KRISTIAN FAUCHALD, University of Oslo (o.k.fauchald@jus.uio.no)

Ole Kristian Fauchald is Professor at the Faculty of Law, University of Oslo; and Research Professor at the Fridtjof Nansen Institute. He is a Coordinator at the PluriCourts Centre of Excellence, University of Oslo, where he also leads the Norwegian Research Council funded project, *Responses to the Legitimacy Crisis of International Investment Law* (LEGINVEST). His fields of research are international investment law, international and domestic environmental law, and international trade law. He has been guest researcher at Peking University during the academic year 2006–2007 and at the United Nations University for Peace, Costa Rica, during 2018–2019.

MALCOLM LANGFORD, University of Oslo (malcolm.langford@jus.uio.no)

Malcolm Langford is Professor of Public Law and Director of the Centre of Excellence for Experiential Legal Learning (CELL), Faculty of Law, University of Oslo. A lawyer and social scientist, his publications span international investment law, human rights, international development, comparative constitutionalism, technology and the politics of the legal profession. He was Chair of the Academic Forum on Investor-State Dispute Settlement (which supports the UNCITRAL WG III reform process) (2019-2021) and is Co-editor of the Cambridge University Press book series, Globalization and Human Rights. Langford is also a Fellow at the PluriCourts Centre of Excellence, where he leads the Norwegian Research Council funded project, *Compliance Politics and International Investment Disputes* (COPIID). His awards include the John H. Jackson Prize for Best Article in the Journal of International Economic Law and the European Society of International Law Young Scholar Prize.

Chapter Authors

WOLFGANG ALSCHNER, University of Ottawa (wolfgang.alschner@uottawa.ca)

Wolfgang Alschner is Associate Professor at the University of Ottawa, Faculty of Law. He holds a BA degree in International Relations from the University of Dresden, an LLB degree from the University of London, a Master of Law from Stanford Law School, as well as two degrees (a Master in International Affairs and a PhD) from the Graduate Institute of International and Development Studies. He is an empirical legal scholar specialised in international economic law and the computational analysis of law.

MERIH ANGIN, Koç University (mangin@ku.edu.tr)

Merih Angın is an Assistant Professor in the International Relations Department of Koç University. Previously, she held postdoctoral fellowships at the Weatherhead Center at Harvard University and the Blavatnik School of Government at the University of Oxford; and was a visiting scholar at the Mortara Center for International Studies at Georgetown University. She holds a PhD in International Relations/Political Science from the Graduate Institute of International and Development Studies, an MSc in International Relations from METU, and a bachelor's in

Economics from Bilkent University. Her research interests include: international political economy, international organizations, international development, investment arbitration, migration, quantitative methods, agent-based modeling, machine learning, artificial intelligence and computational social sciences.

SHIRO ARMSTRONG, Australian National University (shiro.armstrong@anu.edu.au)

Shiro Armstrong is an economist and Associate Professor at the Crawford School of Public Policy. He is Director of the Australia-Japan Research Centre, Editor of the East Asia Forum, Director of the East Asian Bureau of Economic Research and Research Associate at the Center on Japanese Economy and Business at the Columbia Business School. He holds BEcon, BActS, MA degrees and a PhD degree from Australian National University. Dr Armstrong's research interests include Sino-Japan economic and political relations, East Asian economic integration, International trade and foreign direct investment, and East Asian economies.

TOMER BROUDE, Hebrew University of Jerusalem (tomerbroude@gmail.com)

Tomer Broude is the Bessie and Michael Greenblatt, QC, Chair in Public and International Law at the Faculty of Law and Department of International Relations and Academic Director of the Minerva Center for Human Rights at the Hebrew University of Jerusalem. He holds a BA from the Department of International Relations, and an LLB from the Faculty of Law at the Hebrew University of Jerusalem, and a Doctor of Juridical Science degree from the University of Toronto. He specialises in public international law and international economic law, particularly international trade and investment, human rights, dispute settlement, development and cultural diversity.

CHRISTOPHER DRAHOZAL, University of Kansas (drahozal@ku.edu)

Chris Drahozal is John M. Rounds Professor of Law at the University of Kansas School of Law. Previously, he practised law with Sidley and Austin in Washington, DC, and served as a law clerk for Chief Judge Charles Clark of the United States Court of Appeals for the Fifth Circuit, Justice Byron R. White of the United States Supreme Court, and Judge

George H. Aldrich of the Iran–United States Claims Tribunal in The Hague, The Netherlands. Dr Drahozal obtained his BA degree in Economics from Washington University and a law degree from University of Iowa College of Law. His research focusses on the law and economics of dispute resolution, particularly arbitration.

CÉDRIC DUPONT, Graduate Institute (cedric.dupont@graduateinstitute.ch)

Cédric Dupont is Director of Executive Education and a Professor of International Relations and Political Science at the Graduate Institute of International and Development Studies. In addition to that, Professor Dupont is a Senior Research Fellow of the Berkeley Asia-Pacific Economic Cooperation Study Center (BASC) at the University of California at Berkeley. His research focuses on international political economic issues, both at the global and regional levels, on the problem of international cooperation, and international negotiation processes. Dr Dupont holds a PhD degree from the Graduate Institute of International and Development Studies.

SZILÁRD GÁSPÁR-SZILÁGYI, Keele University (s.gaspar-szilagyi@keele.ac.uk)

Szilárd Gáspár-Szilágyi is Lecturer in Law at Keele University School of Law. Previously, he was a Postdoctoral Fellow at PluriCourts, University of Oslo, focusing on EU and international investment law and policy. He holds a PhD from Aarhus University (Denmark) and a two-year LLM from Maastricht University. He taught or conducted research at Vienna University, University of Amsterdam, The Hague University, Michigan Law School and the Centre for EU External Relations Law (TMC Asser Institute, The Hague). He regularly publishes on issues relating to EU and international investment law, EU external relations law, and the domestic application of international law in the EU legal order.

CHIARA GIORGETTI, University of Richmond (cgiorget@richmond.edu)

Chiara Giorgetti is Professor of Law at the Richmond Law School. She holds a JD degree from University of Bologna School of Law, a Master of Science degree in Development Studies from the London School of Economics and Political Science, and LLM and JSD degrees from the Yale University Law School. Her previous work experience includes international arbitration practice in Washington, DC and Geneva;

xvi NOTES ON CONTRIBUTORS

United Nations posts in New York and Somalia; and a clerkship at the International Court of Justice in The Hague.

FLORIAN GRISEL, King's College London (florian.grisel@csls.ox.ac.uk)

Florian Grisel is an Associate Professor of Socio-Legal Studies at the University of Oxford. Previously, he was a Reader in Transnational Law at King's College London and a Research Fellow at the Centre National de la Recherche Scientifique (CNRS), Université Paris-Ouest La Défense Nanterre. He obtained a BA/MA degree from Sciences Po Paris, an MPA degree from Columbia University, an LLM degree from Yale Law School and MA/PhD from Université Paris 1 Panthéon-Sorbonne. His research focuses on the evolution of international arbitration and the emergence of judicial institutions outside the state.

YORAM HAFTEL, Hebrew University of Jerusalem (yoram.haftel@gmail .com)

Yoram Haftel is Professor and Giancarlo Elia Valori Chair in the Study of Peace and Regional Cooperation at the Department of International Relations, Hebrew University of Jerusalem. He obtained a BA in Economics and International Relations, a Master in International Relations and European Studies Program from the Hebrew University of Jerusalem, as well as MA and PhD degrees from the Department of Political Science, Ohio State University. His research agenda touches on the sources, design and effects of international organisations and agreements, security cooperation within regional economic organisations and overlapping regionalism as well as the politics of investment treaty ratification and renegotiation.

GUS VAN HARTEN, Osgoode Hall Law School (gvanharten@osgoode.yorku .ca)

Gus van Harten is Associate Dean (Academic) and Professor at Osgoode Hall Law School. He holds a BA degree from the University of Guelph, an LLB degree from York University Osgoode Hall Law School, a Master in Environmental Studies degree from York University, and a PhD degree from the London School of Economics and Political Science. His research interests include administrative law, international investment law and arbitration, international monetary law and policy, and inquiries and investigations.

NOTES ON CONTRIBUTORS

DAPHNA KAPELIUK, Goldfarb Seligman (daphna.kapeliuk@goldfarb.com)

Daphna Kapeliuk is partner in the Commercial and International Litigation Department at Goldfarb Seligman Law Offices. Previously, she worked as a Senior Lecturer at Radzyner School of Law, Interdisciplinary Center, Herzliya. She holds a law degree from the Hebrew University of Jerusalem, an LLM degree from Katholieke Universiteit Leuven, and a Doctor of Judicial Science degree from Tel Aviv University. Kapeliuk specialises in the field of private international law, and international and domestic arbitration.

RUNAR LIE, University of Oslo (r.h.lie@jus.uio.no)

Runar Lie is PhD Fellow at the PluriCourts Centre of Excellence, University of Oslo. He holds a law degree from the University of Oslo and has previously worked as an entrepreneur and developer. As a core participant in the LEGINVEST research project, Lie uses empirical and computational methods to study the behavior of the actors in the international investment arbitration system. He was recently awarded the John H. Jackson Prize for Best Article in the *Journal of International Economic Law*.

FREDRIK LINDMARK, University of Oslo (f.lindmark@jus.uio.no)

Fredrik Lindmark is Legal Adviser at Norwegian Industrial Property Office. He has a law degree from the University of Oslo, combined with exchange and research stays at the Renmin University of China. During his studies, Lindmark conducted research on Chinese and international commercial law, and Chinese dispute settlement mechanisms.

PAVEL MALYSHEUSKI, Lockyer + Hein (pmalysheuski@lhlaw.ca)

Pavel Malysheuski is Associate Lawyer at Lockyer + Hein. He holds a common law degree from York University Osgoode Hall Law School, together with degrees in civil law and international law from Belarus, as well as an undergraduate degree in nuclear physics. In addition to his legal practice, Pavel serves as an instructor in the Lawyer as Negotiator Program at Osgoode Hall Law School, teaching law students the theory and practice of negotiation.

xviii   NOTES ON CONTRIBUTORS

LUKE NOTTAGE, University of Sydney (luke.nottage@sydney.edu.au)

Luke Nottage is Professor of Comparative and Transnational Business Law, University of Sydney School of Law, and Co-Director of Australian Network for Japanese Law. Dr Nottage holds an LLM degree from Kyoto University and BCA, LLB, PhD degrees from Victoria University of Wellington. His research interests focus on arbitration, contract law, consumer product safety law and corporate governance, with a particular interest in Japan and the Asia-Pacific.

SERGIO PUIG, University of Arizona (spuig@email.arizona.edu)

Sergio Puig is Professor of Law at the James E. Rogers College of Law, University of Arizona. His previous academic track includes positions as lecturer and teaching fellow at Stanford University – School of Law and Duke University – School of Law. Professor Puig holds a law degree from Instituto Tecnológico Autónomo de México – ITAM (México), and two degrees (Master and Doctor of the Science of Law, respectively) from Stanford Law School.

CATHERINE ROGERS, Bocconi University (catherine.rogers@unibocconi.it)

Catherine Rogers is Full Professor of Law at Bocconi University and the Professor of Ethics, Regulation and the Rule of Law at Queen Mary, University of London. Before entering academia, Professor Rogers practised international litigation and arbitration in New York, Hong Kong and San Francisco. She has an LLM degree from Yale Law School, a JD degree from University of California at Hastings College of Law and a BA from University of California at Berkeley. Her scholarship focuses on the convergence of the public and private in international adjudication, the intersection of markets and regulation in guiding professional conduct, and on the reconceptualisation of the attorney as a global actor.

MAVLUDA SATTOROVA, University of Liverpool (m.sattorova@liver pool.ac.uk)

Mavluda Sattorova is Reader in Law at Liverpool Law School. She is also a director of the Liverpool Economic Governance Unit (LEGU) and a convenor of the Asian Society of International Law interest group on International Investment and Economic Law. Dr Sattorova obtained a PhD in Civil Law from the Tashkent State Institute of Law, Diploma in

Jurisprudence (with Distinction) from the Samarqand State University, as well as an LLM and a PhD from the University of Birmingham. She specialises in international economic law with particular focus on international investment law and investor-state arbitration. Her most recent work examines the impact of investment treaty law on national policy-making and governance.

THOMAS SCHULTZ, King's College London (thomas.schultz@kcl.ac.uk)

Thomas Schultz is Professor of Law at King's College London, Professor of International Arbitration at the University of Geneva, Visiting Professor of International Law at the Graduate Institute of International and Development Studies in Geneva, Co-Director of the Geneva Center for International Dispute Settlement (CIDS), and founder and Editor-in-Chief of the Journal of International Dispute Settlement. He was previously a Swiss National Science Foundation Research Professor in international law at the Graduate Institute of International and Development Studies, and a Swiss National Science Foundation Ambizione Fellow at the same institution. He has made contributions to the diversification of approaches and a greater opening of the field of dispute settlement to other disciplines. He has received the Jubilee Prize of the Swiss Academy of Humanities and Social Sciences.

ANTON STREZHNEV, New York University (as6672@nyu.edu)

Anton Strezhnev is CDS-Moore-Sloan Data Science Fellow at the New York University Center for Data Science. He holds BSFS in International Politics from Georgetown University, School of Foreign Service and a PhD degree from Harvard University, Department of Government. His research focuses on quantitative methods (causal inference; experimental design; measurement and latent variable models; network and text analysis), international political economy (international organisations; trade and investment law), and empirical legal studies (judicial behaviour; political economy of private law).

ALEXANDER THOMPSON, Ohio State University (thompson.1191@osu.edu)

Alexander Thompson is Professor of Political Science and a Faculty Affiliate of the Mershon Center for International Security Studies at Ohio State University. He holds a BA degree in International Relations from Connecticut College, as well as MA and PhD degrees in Political

Science from the, University of Chicago. His research is in the area of international relations, with a focus on the politics of international organizations and international law.

MAXIM USYNIN, University of Copenhagen (maksim.usynin@jur.ku.dk)

Maxim Usynin is a Postdoctoral researcher at CEPRI - Centre for Private Governance, University of Copenhagen. Maxim holds a bachelor degree in law from the Saint Petersburg State University, a master degree in law from the Russian School of Private Law, two LLM degrees in Public International Law and Maritime Law, respectively, from the University of Oslo, and a PhD in Law from the University of Copenhagen. From 2015 to the present, he has worked on the LEGINVEST project and as a core member of the investment tribunals research group at the PluriCourts Centre of Excellence, University of Oslo.

OLEKSANDRA VYTIAGANETS, Birmingham City University (o.vytiaga nets@gmail.com)

Oleksandra Vytiaganets is PhD Fellow at the Birmingham City University School of Law. She holds bachelor and master law degrees (with distinction) from the Yaroslav the Wise National Law University and a LLM degree (with distinction) from the University of Liverpool. Her PhD research examines the impact of the international investment regime on the development of tobacco control legislation. She is a qualified Ukrainian lawyer. Her previous working experience includes working as a legal advisor to MP Babak in the Ukrainian Parliament. Currently, she practices international litigation and arbitration in the UK.

1

Introduction: The Legitimacy Crisis and the Empirical Turn

DANIEL BEHN[*], OLE KRISTIAN FAUCHALD[**] AND
MALCOLM LANGFORD[***]

1.1 Introduction

The development of the modern investment treaty regime represents one of the most remarkable and swift expansions of international law in the post-war period. In just 30 years, the regime has developed from a small subsect of international law to one of its most prominent, with over 3,500 signed treaties[1] and over 1,100 investor-state arbitrations registered.[2] The significance of the regime is attributable to the largely bilateral treaty network, and to the tremendous growth in the use of the investor–state dispute settlement (ISDS) mechanisms embedded in the vast majority of all international investment agreements (IIA) currently in force.[3]

---

[*] Associate Professor (Senior Lecturer) in International Law, Queen Mary University of London; Associate Research Professor, PluriCourts, University of Oslo. This book and this chapter was supported by the Research Council of Norway through its Centres of Excellence Funding Scheme, project number 223274: PluriCourts: Centre for the Study on the Legitimate Roles of the Judiciary in the Global Order. The editors would also like to recognize and thank Maxim Usynin for his assistance with this volume, but also more generally for his hard work, dedication and loyalty to numerous projects over the years.

[**] Professor of Law and PluriCourts Coordinator (2012), Department of Public and International Law, University of Oslo; Research Professor, Fridtjof Nansen Institute.

[***] Professor of Public Law and Director of CELL, Department of Public and International Law, University of Oslo; Co-Director, Centre on Law and Social Transformation, University of Bergen and CMI.

[1] UNCTAD IIA Navigator <investmentpolicy.unctad.org/international-investment-agreements> data through 1 January 2020.

[2] PITAD database <pitad.org> data to 1 January 2020.

[3] UNCTAD IIA Navigator (n. 1). See ch. 2 for our updated mapping of ISDS clauses in IIAs. See also Joachim Pohl, Kekeletso Mashigo and Alexis Nohen, 'Dispute Settlement Provisions in International Investment Agreements: A Large Sample Survey' *OECD Working Papers on International Investment 2012/02* (96% of the 1,660 BITs surveyed contained ISDS language).

The ISDS[4] system – the focus of this volume – provides ad hoc, one-off international arbitration for prospective disputes that can be initiated by an individual or corporate foreign investor against the state hosting its investment. Starting with the first treaty-based ISDS case in 1987,[5] it has grown from a few cases into a sprawling network of international adjudication, which we analyse closely in the following chapter. As Figure 1.1 indicates, we have seen an upwards growth trajectory over the past two decades with the past five years flattening off at about 80–100 new treaty-based ISDS cases being registered annually. Given that treaty-based ISDS cases take an average of 3.74 years from registration to final award[6] and that about a third of all cases are settled or discontinued,[7] approximately 40–50 final awards are currently being rendered each year,[8] and 400 treaty-based ISDS cases are pending at any given time.[9]

Putting this evolution in comparative perspective, it is difficult to find other areas of international legal practice that have generated such a caseload in both quantity and case complexity in a relatively short period of time.[10] For example, the World Trade Organization (WTO) and its state-to-state Dispute Settlement Understanding (DSU) generated a comparable caseload to the investment treaty regime in the late 1990s and 2000s, but by 2012 new ISDS cases were outpacing WTO cases three to

---

[4] The term ISDS can be used to label the provisions in an IIA that permit foreign investors to initiate claims against states hosting their investments for alleged breaches of the investment protections standards provided in the relevant IIA. ISDS can also refer to individual arbitrations brought according to an ISDS provision in an investment treaty (and ISDS can be even broader, including contract or foreign direct investment law (FDI) law-based arbitrations against states or state entities; or even non-arbitral processes between investors and states such as mediation or conciliation). For the purpose of this chapter, we will use ISDS to refer primarily to the individual arbitration cases that arise directly out of an investment treaty. In addition to ISDS, such cases are also variously interchangeably called investment treaty arbitration, investor–state arbitration, international arbitration, investment arbitration, or international investment arbitration.

[5] *Asian Agricultural Products* v. *Sri Lanka* (ICSID Case No. ARB/87/3), Award, 27 June 1990, based on the United Kingdom–Sri Lanka BIT (1980).

[6] Daniel Behn, Tarald Berge, Malcolm Langford and Maxim Usynin, 'What Causes Delays in Investment Arbitration' (2019) *PluriCourts Working Paper*.

[7] PITAD (n. 2).

[8] Ibid.

[9] Ibid.

[10] As of 1 January 2020, a total of 751 cases were concluded with 373 cases pending (1,126 ISDS cases registered). Cases are listed by the year registered and whether the case has concluded (a final award rendered or case settled or discontinued). Post-award proceedings are not considered.

INTRODUCTION: THE LEGITIMACY CRISIS

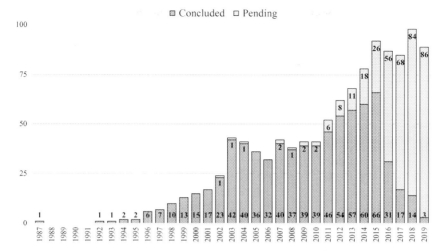

Figure 1.1 Growth in the ISDS caseload: pending versus concluded cases (1987–2020)[1]

[1] PITAD database <pitad.org> data to 1 January 2020.

one.[11] With many supporters,[12] it remains one of the most actively litigated areas of international law today. Moreover, as the caseload grew – over the past few decades – a considerable amount of jurisprudence through arbitral awards has emerged as well as an entirely new industry of investment arbitration experts, practitioners, government officials, and academics.[13]

---

[11] As of 1 January 2020, ISDS cases almost double those of the WTO. The WTO records 593 disputes compared with 1,126 ISDS cases registered. For WTO cases see WTO DSU <wto.org/english/tratop_e/dispu_e/dispu_status_e.htm>.

[12] See Sadie Blanchard and Charles N. Brower, 'From "Dealing in Virtue" to "Profiting from Injustice:" The Case against "Re-statification" of Investment Dispute Settlement' (2014) 55 *Harvard Int'l L. J. Online*; EFILA, 'A Response to the Criticism against ISDS' <efila.org/wp-content/uploads/2015/05/EFILA_in_response_to_the-criticism_of_ISDS_ final_dft. pdf>.

[13] Malcolm Langford, Daniel Behn and Runar Lie, 'The Revolving Door in International Investment Arbitration' (2017) 20(2) *JIEL* 301; Andrea Bianchi, 'Epistemic Communities in International Arbitration', in Federico Ortino and Thomas Schultz (eds.), *Oxford Handbook of International Arbitration* (Oxford University Press, 2020); Emmanuel Gaillard, 'Sociology of International Arbitration' (2015) 31(1) *Arbitration International* 1; Sergio Puig, 'Social Capital in the Arbitration Market' (2014) 25(2) *EJIL* 387; Moshe Hirsch, 'The Sociology of International Investment Law', in Douglas et al. (eds.), *The Foundations of*

4 DANIEL BEHN ET AL.

This growth, however, has not come without a cost. ISDS cases are and have been controversial. As a decentralized system of one-off dispute settlement decided by party-appointed arbitrators who are typically tasked with balancing the private interests of a foreign investor from the global North against the public interests of a state in the global South, it is little wonder that the ISDS system has been embroiled in a legitimacy crisis for nearly 20 years now with virtually every aspect of the system being challenged and critiqued.[14] Less critical responses to the legitimacy crisis tend to focus on the desirability of specific targeted reforms from inside the system, making claims about the evolutionary nature of international legal practice and how the system can and does become more legitimate over time.[15] Stronger critiques of the system tend to target

International Investment Law: Bringing Theory into Practice (Cambridge University Press, 2014).

[14] Charles N. Brower, Charles H. Brower and Jeremy Sharpe may be the have been the first to write an article on the topic with 'The Coming Crisis in the Global Adjudication System' (2003) 19(4) *Arbitration International* 415. That piece is followed by three articles specific to NAFTA: Charles H. Brower, 'Structure, Legitimacy and NAFTA's Investment Chapter' (2003) 36 *Vanderbilt Journal of Transnational Litigation.* 37; Ari Afilalo, 'Towards a Common Law of International Investment: How NAFTA Chapter 11 Panels Should Solve Their Legitimacy Crisis' (2004) 17 *Georgetown International Environmental Law Review* 51; Ari Afilalo, 'Meaning, Ambiguity, and Legitimacy: Judicial (Re-)construction of NAFTA Chapter 11' (2005) 25 *Northwestern Journal of International Law and Business* 279. Susan D. Franck puts the legitimacy crisis squarely in the title: 'The Legitimacy Crisis in Investment Treaty Arbitration: Privatizing Public International Law through Inconsistent Decisions' (2005) 73 *Fordham Law Review* 1521, and Gus Van Harten's book, *Investment Treaty Arbitration and Public Law* (Oxford University Press, 2007) is the first book-length critique of arbitration as a legitimate means for resolving public law disputes. Then come the regime critics: M. Sornarajah, 'A Coming Crisis: Expansionary Trends in Investment Treaty Arbitration', in Karl P. Sauvant (ed.), *Appeals Mechanism in International Investment Disputes* (Oxford University Press, 2008); and regime supporters, Charles N. Brower and Stephan W. Schill, 'Is Arbitration a Threat or a Boom to the Legitimacy of International Investment Law' (2008–9) 9 *Chicago Journal of International Law.* 471; and in 2010, Michael Waibel and colleagues published *The Backlash against Investment Arbitration: Perceptions and Reality* (Kluwer, 2010).

[15] Chester Brown and Kate Miles (eds.), *Evolution in Investment Treaty Law and Arbitration* (Cambridge University Press, 2011); Andrea Bjorklund, 'The Role of Counterclaims in Rebalancing Investment Law' (2013) 17(2) *Lewis and Clark Law Review* 461; Alec Stone Sweet and Florian Grisel, 'The Evolution of International Arbitration: Delegation, Judicialization, Governance', in Mattli and Dietz (eds.), *International Arbitration and Global Governance: Contending Theories and Evidence* (Cambridge University Press, 2014); Daniel Behn 'Legitimacy, Evolution, and Growth in Investment Treaty Arbitration: Empirically Evaluating the State-of-The-Art' (2015) 46 (2) *Georgetown Journal of International Law* 363; Alec Stone Sweet and Florian Grisel, *The Evolution of International Arbitration: Judicialization, Governance, Legitimacy* (Oxford University Press, 2017).

broader, more systemic issues that are less likely to be reformed from within over time. This type of critical perspectives about the regime is often characterized by systemic claims, for example that ISDS is afflicted by varying degrees of bias,[16] is excessively costly and lengthy,[17] with

[16] Susan D. Franck, 'Foreign Direct Investment, Investment Treaty Arbitration, and the Rule of Law' (2007) 19(2) *Pac. McGeorge Global Bus. & Dev. L. J.* 337; David Branson, 'Sympathetic Party-Appointed Arbitrators: Sophisticated Strangers and Governments Demand Them' (2010) 25(2) *ICSID Rev.* 367; Gus Van Harten, 'Arbitrator Behaviour in Asymmetrical Adjudication: An Empirical Study of Investment Treaty Arbitration' (2012) 50(1) *Osgoode Hall L. J.* 211; Stavros Brekoulakis, 'Systemic Bias and the Institution of International Arbitration: A New Approach to Arbitral Decision-Making' (2013) 4(3) *JIDS* 553; Gus van Harten, *Sovereign Choices and Sovereign Constraints: Judicial Restraint in Investment Treaty Arbitration* (Oxford University Press, 2013); Nathan Freeman, 'Domestic Institutions, Capacity Limitations, and Compliance Costs: Host Country Determinants of Investment Treaty Arbitrations 1987–2007' (2013) 39(1) *International Interactions* 54; Susan D. Franck, 'Conflating Politics and Development: Examining Investment Treaty Outcomes' (2014) 55 *VJIL* 13; Cédric Dupont and Thomas Schultz, 'Do Hard Economic Times Lead to International Legal Disputes? The Case of Investment Arbitration' (2014) 19(2) *Swiss Political Science Review* 564; Daniel Behn (ibid.); Thomas Schultz and Cédric Dupont, 'Investment Arbitration: Promoting the Rule of Law or Over-Empowering Investors? A Quantitative Study' (2015) 25(4) *EJIL* 14; Susan D. Franck and Lindsey Wylie, 'Predicting Outcomes in Investment Treaty Arbitration' (2015) 65 *Duke L. J.* 459; Gus Van Harten, 'Arbitrator Behaviour in Asymmetrical Adjudication (Part Two): An Examination of Hypotheses of Bias in Investment Treaty Arbitration' (2016) 53(2) *Osgoode Hall L. J.* 540; Cédric Dupont, Thomas Schultz and Merih Angin, 'Political Risk and Investment Arbitration: An Empirical Study' (2016) 7(1) *JIDS* 136; Alec Stone Sweet et al., 'Arbitral Lawmaking and State Power: An Empirical Analysis of Investor-State Arbitration' (2017) 8(4) *JIDS* 579; Daniel Behn and Malcolm Langford, 'Trumping the Environment? An Empirical Perspective on the Legitimacy of Investment Treaty Arbitration' (2017) 18(1) *JWIT* 14; Julian Donaubauer, Eric Neumayer and Peter Nunnenkamp, 'Winning or Losing in Investor-to-State Dispute Resolution: The Role of Arbitrator Bias and Experience' (2017) *Kiel Working Paper No. 2074*; Krzysztof Pelc, 'What Explains the Low Success Rate of Investor-State Disputes?' (2017) 71(3) *International Organization* 559; Daniel Behn, Tarald Laudal Berge, and Malcolm Langford, 'Poor States or Poor Governance? Explaining Outcomes in Investment Treaty Arbitration' (2018) 38(3) *Northwestern Journal of International Law and Business* 333; Mavluda Sattorova, *The Impact of Investment Treaty Law on Host States: Enabling Good Governance?* (Hart, 2018); Silvia Steininger, 'What's Human Rights Got to Do with It? An Empirical Analysis of Human Rights References in Investment Arbitration' (2018) 31(1) *Leiden J. Int'l L.* 33; Gus Van Harten, 'Leaders in the Expansive and Restrictive Interpretation of Investment Treaties: A Descriptive Study of ISDS Awards to 2010' (2018) 29(3) *EJIL* 504.

[17] Susan D. Franck, 'Rationalizing Costs in Investment Treaty Arbitration' (2011) 88(4) *U. Wash L. Rev.* 769; Albert Jan van den Berg, 'Time and Costs: Issues and Initiatives from an Arbitrator's Perspective' (2013) 28(1) *ICSID Rev.* 218; Adam Raviv, 'Achieving a Faster ICSID', in Jean Kalicki and Anna Joubin-Bret (eds.), *Reshaping the Investor-State Dispute Resolution System: Journeys for the 21st Century* (Brill, 2015), 653; Susan D. Franck, *Arbitration Costs: Myths and Realities in Investment Treaty Arbitration* (Oxford University Press, 2019); Sergio Puig, 'Contextualizing Cost-Shifting: A Multi-Method Approach' (2019) 58(2) *VJIL* 261; Daniel Behn and Ana Maria Daza, 'The Defense Burden in Investment Arbitration?' (2019) *PluriCourts Working Paper.*

conflicting and inconsistent jurisprudence,[18] a lack transparency and diversity in decision-making,[19] a system that rewards private over public interests;[20] and that all told, these aspects among others demonstrate that

[18] Ole Kristian Fauchald, 'The Legal Reasoning of ICSID Tribunals: An Empirical Analysis' (2007) 19(2) *EJIL* 301; Jeffrey Commission, 'Precedent in Investment Treaty Arbitration: A Citation Analysis of Developing Jurisprudence' (2007) 24(2) *J. Int'l Arb.* 129; Gabrielle Kaufmann-Kohler, 'Arbitral Precedent: Dream, Necessity or Excuse' (2007) 23 *Arb. Int'l* 357; Yas Banifatemi, 'Consistency in the Interpretation of Substantive Investment Rules: Is It Achievable?' in Roberto Echandi and Pierre Sauvé (eds.), *Prospects in International Investment Law and Policy: World Trade Forum* (Cambridge University Press, 2013); Thomas Schultz, 'Against Consistency in Investment Arbitration', in Zachary Douglas, Joost Pauwelyn and Jorge Viñuales (eds.), *The Foundations of International Investment Law: Bringing Theory into Practice* (Oxford University Press, 2014); Katharina Diel-Gligor, *Towards Consistency in International Investment Jurisprudence: A Preliminary Ruling System for ICSID Arbitration* (Brill, 2017); Damien Charlotin, 'The Place of Investment Awards and WTO Decisions in International Law: A Citations Analysis' (2017) 20(2) *JIEL* 279; Mark Feldman, 'Investment Arbitration Appellate Mechanism Options: Consistency, Accuracy, and Balance of Power' (2017) 32(3) *ICSID Rev.* 528; José E. Alvarez, *Boundaries of Investment Arbitration: The Use of Trade and European Human Rights Law and Investor-State Disputes* (Juris, 2018); Niccolò Ridi, 'The Shape and Structure of the "Usable Past": An Empirical Analysis of the Use of Precedent in International Adjudication' (2019) 10(2) *JIDS* 200.

[19] Eugenia Levine, 'Amicus Curiae in International Investment Arbitration: The Implications of an Increase in Third-Party Participation' (2011) 29(1) *Berkeley J. Int'l L.* 200; Sergio Puig (n. 13); Susan D. Franck et al., 'The Diversity Challenge: Exploring the "Invisible College" of International Arbitration' (2015) 53 *Col. J Transnt'l L.* 429; Emilie M. Hafner-Burton and David G. Victor, 'Secrecy in International Investment Arbitration: An Empirical Analysis' (2016) 7(1) *JIDS* 61; Langford, Behn and Lie (n. 13); Lucy Greenwood, 'Tipping the Balance: Diversity and Inclusion in International Arbitration' (2017) 33(1) *Arb. Int'l* 99; Michael Waibel and Yanhui Wu, 'Are Arbitrators Political: Evidence from International Investment Arbitration' (2017) *Working Paper*; Jansen Calamita and Elsa Sardinha, 'The Bifurcation of Jurisdictional and Admissibility Objections in Investor-State Arbitration' (2017) 16(1) *LPICT* 44; Luke Nottage and Ana Ubilava, 'Costs, Outcomes and Transparency in ISDS Arbitrations: Evidence for an Investment Treaty Parliamentary Inquiry' (2018) 21(4) *Int. Arb. L. Rev.* 111; James Crawford, 'The Ideal Arbitrators: Does One Size Fit All?' (2018) 32(5) *Am. U. Int'l L. Rev.* 100; Taylor St. John et al., 'Glass Ceilings and Arbitral Dealings: Gender and Investment Arbitration' (2018) *PluriCourts Working Paper*; James Devaney, 'An Independent Panel for the Scrutiny of Investment Arbitrators: An Idea Whose Time has Come?' (2019) 18(3) *LPICT* 366; Malcolm Langford, Daniel Behn and Runar Lie, 'Computational Stylometry: Predicting the Authorship of Investment Arbitration Awards', in R. Whalen (ed.), *Computational Legal Studies: The Promise and Challenge of Data-Driven Research* (Edward Elgar, 2020), 53–76; Thomas Schultz and Niccolò Ridi, 'Arbitration Literature', in Schultz and Ortino (eds.), *Oxford Handbook of International Arbitration* (Oxford University Press, 2020), ch. 1.

[20] Jose E. Alvarez, 'The Return of the State' (2011) 20 *Minnesota Journal of International Law* 223; Kyla Tienhaara, 'Regulatory Chill and the Threat of Arbitration: A View from Political Science', in Chester Brown and Kate Miles (eds.), *Evolution in Investment Treaty*

INTRODUCTION: THE LEGITIMACY CRISIS

the game is rigged against poorer states, stifling economic development, not promoting it.[21]

From the early 2000s onwards, this mountain of critical scholarship and civil society reports[22] on the legitimacy crisis could be placed in two broad categories: critiques of the investment treaties and their substantive rules; and critiques of the process of resolving investment disputes, that is, ISDS.[23] By the mid-2010s, both sets of critiques reached a degree of maturity, as the debate on the legitimacy of ISDS moved clearly into the public sphere, and a diverse group of states – from South Africa, India and Venezuela to the United States (US) and the Czech Republic – initiated unilateral and bilateral reforms to substantive and procedural provisions of their IIAs. This policy reform movement turned multilateral in the late 2010s with UNCTAD's initiation of an Investment Policy Framework for Sustainable Development in 2015,[24] the Proposals for Amendment of the ICSID Rules,[25] and the emergence of UNCITRAL Working Group III (WG III) on ISDS Reform in 2017.[26] The systemic and multilateral reform projects that had seemed so politically

---

Law and Arbitration (Cambridge University Press, 2011); Pia Eberhardt and Cecilia Olivet, *Profiting from Injustice: How Law Firms, Arbitrators, and Financiers are Fueling an Investment Arbitration Boom* (Transnational Institute, 2012).

[21] Lauge N. Skovgaard Poulsen and Emma Aisbett, 'When the Claim Hits: Bilateral Investment Treaties and Bounded Rational Learning' (2013) 65 *World Politics.* 273; M. Sornarajah, *Resistance and Change in the International Law on Foreign Investment* (Cambridge University Press, 2015); Lauge N. Skovgaard Poulsen, *Bounded Rationality and Economic Diplomacy: The Politics of Investment Treaties in Developing Countries* (Cambridge University Press, 2015); Peter Nunnenkamp, 'Biased Arbitrators and Tribunal Decisions against Developing Countries: Stylized Facts on Investor-State Dispute Settlement' (2017) 19 *J. Int'l Dev.* 851.

[22] See Stephan W. Schill, 'W(h)ither Fragmentation? On the Literature and Sociology of International Investment Law' (2011) 22(3) *EJIL* 875; Thomas Schultz and Niccolò Ridi, 'Arbitration Literature', in Thomas Schultz and Federico Ortino (eds.), *Oxford Handbook of International Arbitration* (Oxford University Press, 2020), ch. 1.

[23] We analyse this literature closely in Chapter 2.

[24] Launched at the Financing for Development Conference in Addis Ababa, 2015 <investmentpolicy.unctad.org/investment-policy-framework>.

[25] See ICSID, *Volume 3: Proposals for Amendment of the ICSID Rules – Working Paper*, August 2018, paras. 302–5.

[26] For a brief history, see Malcolm Langford, Gabrielle Kaufmann-Kohler, Michele Potestà and Daniel Behn, 'UNCITRAL and Investment Arbitration Reform: Matching Concerns and Solutions – An Introduction' (2020) 21(2–3) Journal of World Investment and Trade 167. The United Nations Commission on International Trade Law (UNCITRAL) Working Group III can, according to its mandate, work on all issues relating to the settlement of investment disputes, but not on the substantive rules provided in existing IIAs. UNCITRAL, 'Report of Working Group III (Investor–State Dispute Settlement

infeasible[27] became a possibility once again.[28] Regardless of what is achieved, at a minimum, the mandate of WG III provides a signal that a transition from a crisis period to a multilateral reform period could be occurring.[29]

While most critique of ISDS has been normative and doctrinal in nature, empirical research has been central in identifying and measuring the significance of certain concerns. Assisted by the empirical turn in international legal scholarship about a decade ago,[30] there is now a critical mass of empirical legal scholars and social scientists focusing

Reform) on the work of its thirty-fourth session (Vienna, 27 November–1 December 2017)', UN Doc. No. A/CN.9/930/Rev.1 (19 December 2017). The ISDS reform process emerged gradually in 2015, when the UNCITRAL Secretariat commissioned a study to the Geneva Center for International Dispute Settlement (CIDS) to review whether the *Mauritius Convention on Transparency* could provide a useful model for possible reforms in the field of ISDS. See Gabrielle Kaufmann-Kohler and Michele Potestà, *Can the Mauritius Convention Serve as a Model for the Reform of Investor-State Arbitration in Connection with the Introduction of a permanent investment tribunal or an Appeal Mechanism? Analysis and Roadmap* (CIDS, 2016) <uncitral.org/pdf/english/CIDS_Research_Paper_Mauritius.pdf>. In 2017, the UNCITRAL Secretariat commissioned a further study from CIDS: see Gabrielle Kaufmann-Kohler and Michele Potestà, *The Composition of a Multilateral Investment Court and of an Appeal Mechanism for Investment Awards* (CIDS, 2017) <uncitral.org/pdf/english/workinggroups/wg_3/CIDS_Supplemental_Report.pdf>.

[27] Many previous post-Second World War attempts to multilaterize the international investment law did not produce binding treaties, including: the Havana Charter (1948); the Abs-Shawcross Draft Convention on Investments Abroad (1959); Louis B. Sohn and Richard R. Baxter, 'Draft Convention on the International Responsibility of States for Injuries to Aliens' (1961) 55(3) *AJIL* 548; the OECD Draft Convention on the Protection of Foreign Property (1967); the OECD Draft Multilateral Agreement on Investment (1998).

[28] In addition, there are at least two other major initiatives: the ICSID Rule Amendment Project <icsid.worldbank.org/en/amendments>; and the Energy Charter Treaty Modernization Project <energychartertreaty.org/modernisation-of-the-treaty>.

[29] Feldman (n. 18); Stephan W. Schill, 'Reforming Investor–State Dispute Settlement: A (Comparative and International) Constitutional Law Framework' (2017) 20(3) *JIEL* 649; Stone Sweet and Grisel (n. 15); Sergio Puig and Gregory Shaffer, 'Imperfect Alternatives: Institutional Choice and the Reform of Investment Law' (2018) 112(3) *AJIL* 361.

[30] See Susan D. Franck, 'Empirical Modalities: Lessons for the Future of International Investment' (2010) 104 *ASIL Proceedings* 33; Gregory Shaffer and Tom Ginsburg, 'The Empirical Turn in International Legal Scholarship' (2012) 106(1) *AJIL* 1; Sergio Puig, 'Recasting ICSID's Legitimacy Debate: Towards a Goal-Based Empirical Agenda' (2013) 36(2) *Fordham International Law Journal* 465; Christopher Drahozal, 'Empirical Findings on International Arbitration: An Overview', in Thomas Schultz and Federico Ortino (n. 16), ch. 27; Wolfgang Alschner, Joost Pauwelyn and Sergio Puig, 'The Data-Driven Future of International Economic Law' (2017) 20(2) *JIEL* 217.

INTRODUCTION: THE LEGITIMACY CRISIS 9

specifically on investor-state arbitration: a substantial increase over a virtually non-existent field of study as late as 2004,[31] when almost all empirical research on the regime was still focused on measuring the effects of investment treaties,[32] and the few early empirical pieces on ISDS that did emerge were hampered by small sample size. Today, this critical mass of empirical legal scholars and social scientists[33] focusing on

[31] Before 2010, there were only a few scholars empirically assessing ISDS, Franck (n. 14); Susan D. Franck, 'The Nature and Enforcement of Investor Rights under Investment Treaties: Do Investment Treaties Have a Bright Future?' (2005) 12 *University of California Davis Journal of International Law and Politics* 47; Van Harten (n. 14); Commission (n. 18); Fauchald (n. 18); Susan D. Franck, 'Development and Outcomes of Investment Treaty Arbitration' (2009) 50(2) *Harvard Int'l L. J.* 436; José Alvarez and Kathryn Khamsi, 'The Argentine Crisis and Foreign Investors: A Glimpse into the Heart of the Investment Regime', in Karl Sauvant (ed.), *Yearbook on International Investment Law and Policy 2008/2009* (Oxford University Press, 2009); Kathleen S. McArthur and Pablo A. Ormachea, 'International Investor-State Arbitration: An Empirical Analysis of ICSID Decisions on Jurisdiction' (2009) 28(3) *The Review of Litigation* 559; David Schneiderman, 'Judicial Politics and International Investment Arbitration: Seeking an Explanation for Conflicting Outcomes' (2010) 30 *Northwestern Journal of International Law and Business* 383.

[32] Early studies on the investment treaty regime were researched primarily by political scientists focused on flows of FDI and their relation to IIAs. In fact, it appears to have been so focused on those aspects that it was not until 2014 when that first ISDS-related study took place: Beth Simmons, 'Bargaining over BITs, Arbitrating Awards: The Regime for Protection and Promotion of International Investment' (2014) 66(1) *World Pol.* 12. Pre-2010 empirical studies on investment treaties tended to focus on how treaties would bring more capital to the Global South: Mary Hallward-Driemeier, *Bilateral Investment Treaties Attract Foreign Direct Investment? Only a Bit . . . and They Could Bite* (World Bank, 2003); Peter Egger and Michael Pfaffermayer, 'The Impact of Bilateral Investment Treaties on Foreign Direct Investment' (2004) 32(4) *Journal of Comp. Econ.* 787; Eric Neumayer and Laura Spess, 'Do Bilateral Investment Treaties Increase Foreign Direct Investment to Developing States?' (2005) 33(10) *World Dev.* 1567; Tom Ginsburg, 'International Substitutes for Domestic Institutions: Bilateral Investment Treaties and Governance' (2005) 25(1) *Int'l Rev. L. Econ.* 107; Jeswald W. Salacuse and Nicholas P. Sullivan, 'Do BITs Really Work: An Evaluation of Bilateral Investment Treaties and Their Grand Bargain' (2005) 46 *Harvard Int'l L. J.* 67; Zachary Elkins, Andrew T. Guzman and Beth Simmons, 'Competing for Capital: The Diffusion of Bilateral Investment Treaties, 1960–2000' (2006) 60(4) *Int'l Org.* 811; Jason Yackee, 'Bilateral Investment Treaties, Credible Commitment, and the Rule of (International) Law: Do BITs Promote Foreign Direct Investment?' (2008) 42(4) *Law & Soc. Rev.* 805; UNCTAD, 'The Role of International Investment Agreements in Attracting Foreign Direct Investment to Developing States' (2009) *UNCTAD Series on International Investment Policies for Development*; Jennifer Tobin and Susan Rose-Ackerman, 'When BITs Have Some Bite: The Political-Economic Environment for Bilateral Investment Treaties' (2010) 6 *Rev. Int'l Orgs.* 1.

[33] Examples include the use of empirics to support a theoretical claim (by political scientists): Poulsen and Aisbett (n. 21), and the use of empirics to test changes in treaty design

ISDS reflects the emergence of a burgeoning field: scholars have already used a range of methods and approaches – quantitative,[34] qualitative,[35] longitudinal,[36] surveys,[37] interviews,[38] archival,[39] network[40] and computational[41] – to analyse the ISDS system, probe its origins, its functioning and effects, and to address doctrinal questions.

The effects of this empirical turn are clear in a number of the debates on ISDS. For example, quantitative and economic research assessing potential pro-investor bias,[42] excessive damages awards,[43] correctness

(by legal scholars): Wolfgang Alschner, 'The Impact of Investment Arbitration on Investment Treaty Design: Myth versus Reality' (2017) 42(1) *Yale J. Int'l L.* 1.

[34] See above (nn. 16–20).

[35] Martins Paparinskis, *The International Minimum Standard and Fair and Equitable Treatment* (Oxford University Press, 2013); Jonathan Bonnitcha, *Substantive Protection under Investment Treaties: A Legal and Economic Analysis* (Cambridge University Press, 2014); Caroline Henckels, *Proportionality and Deference in Investor-State Arbitration: Balancing Investment Protection and Regulatory Autonomy* (Cambridge University Press, 2015); David Collins, 'Loss Aversion Bias or Fear of Missing Out: A Behavioural Economics Analysis of Compensation in Investor–State Dispute Settlement' (2016) 8(3) *JIDS* 460.

[36] Malcolm Langford and Daniel Behn, 'Managing Backlash: The Evolving Investment Arbitrator?' (2018) 29(2) *EJIL* 551; Schultz and Dupont, Promoting the Rule of Law (n. 16).

[37] Franck et al. (n. 19); see also Maria Laura Marceddu, 'What's Wrong with Investment Arbitration?' Reforming International Investment Arbitration, ISDS Academic Forum, PluriCourts Centre for Excellence (LEGINVEST) and the Forum for Law and Social Science, University of Oslo, 1–2 February 2019.

[38] Stavros Brekoulakis et al., 'Impartiality and Personal Values in Arbitral Decision-Making', research project at Centre for Commercial Law Studies, Queen Mary University of London, 2019–2023; Todd Tucker, 'Inside the Black Box: Collegial Patterns on Investment Tribunals' (2016) 7(1) *JIDS* 183.

[39] Taylor St John, *The Rise of Investor-State Arbitration: Politics, Law, and Unintended Consequences* (Oxford University Press, 2018).

[40] Puig (n. 13); Langford, Behn and Lie (n. 13).

[41] Wolfgang Alschner, 'Correctness of Investment Awards: Why Wrong Decisions Don't Die' (2019) *LPICT* 345; Malcolm Langford, Runar Lie and Daniel Behn, 'Computational Stylometry: Predicting the Authorship of Investment Arbitration Awards', in Ryan Whalen (ed.), *Computational Legal Studies: The Promise and Challenge of Data-Driven Research* (Edward Elgar, 2020), 53; Wolfgang Alschner and Dmitriy Skougarevskiy, 'Can Robots Write Treaties? Using Recurrent Neural Networks to Draft International Investment Agreements', in Bex (ed.), *Legal Knowledge and Information Systems: JURIX 2016* (IOS Press, 2016), p. 119.

[42] Franck et al. (n. 19).

[43] Daniel Behn, 'Performance of Investment Treaty Arbitration', in Squatrito et al. (eds.), *The Performance of International Courts and Tribunals* (Cambridge University Press, 2018); Jonathan Bonnitcha and Sarah Brewin, *Compensation under Investment Treaties: Best Practices* (IISD, 2019); see also Diane Desierto, 'ICESCR Minimum Core Obligations

of decisions[44] and double hatting by arbitrators as legal counsel have been foregrounded.[45] The centrality of empirical perspectives has only accelerated in light of the problem-centric mandates of UNCTAD's Investment Policy Framework for Sustainable Development and UNCITRAL WG III. In assessing the desirability in addressing concerns surrounding excessive costs and duration, correctness and consistency of awards, and arbitral diversity and independence – and reforms to address them – the process in UNCITRAL WG III has relied increasingly on empirical research and called for new studies.[46]

The primary aim of this volume therefore is to interrogate empirically this legitimacy crisis and attempts by the regime to legitimate itself. Across a range of issues, the authors contribute new empirical findings, test old ones, experiment with new methods, cover new themes, and analyse the implications for debates and reform efforts.

The book also serves three other purposes. First, we seek to provide a theoretical justification for the use of empirical data and methods to test normative claims. Empirical (and doctrinal) analyses of legitimacy are rarely framed and inflected by the dominant theories of legitimacy within political and legal philosophy. We therefore seek to contribute to the broader literature on the legitimacy of international courts and tribunals by organizing the contents around prominently used categories of legitimacy.[47] Framing the research agenda in this way allows us also to assess more

---

and Investment: Recasting the Non-expropriation Compensation Model during Financial Crises' (2012) 44(3) *GW Int'l L. Rev.* 473.

[44] Alschner (n. 41).

[45] Malcolm Langford, Daniel Behn and Runar Lie, 'The Ethics and Empirics of Double Hatting', *ESIL Reflection* (2018).

[46] Beginning with the establishment of an Academic Forum on ISDS to work alongside WG III, a Concept Paper project original led by Gabrielle Kaufmann-Kohler, Michele Potestà and George Bermann, and later with Daniel Behn and Malcolm Langford, has so far produced fourteen reports, all drawing on empirical data. The reports are available at <jus.uio.no/pluricourts/english/projects/leginvest/academic-forum/papers>. See the empirical survey report: Daniel Behn, Malcolm Langford and Laura Létourneau-Tremblay, 'Empirical Perspectives on Investment Arbitration: What Do We Know? Does It Matter?' *Academic Forum on ISDS Concept Paper* (2020). Additional subject-matter specific reports include, *inter alia*: Stavros Brekoulakis and Catherine Rogers, 'Third-Party Financing in ISDS: A Framework for Understanding Practice and Policy', *Academic Forum on ISDS Concept Paper* (2019); Malcolm Langford, Daniel Behn and Maria Chiara Malaguti, 'The Quadrilemma: Appointing Adjudicators in Future Investor-State Dispute Settlement', *Academic Forum on ISDS Concept Paper* (2019).

[47] For an overview, see Andreas Føllesdal, 'Survey Article: The Legitimacy of International Courts' (2020) *Journal of Political Philosophy* <onlinelibrary.wiley.com/doi/pdf/10.1111/jopp.12213>.

rigorously our current empirical understanding of different legitimacy issues and where the need for future research lies. Thus, while the book can contribute to the current public policy debate over reform of the international investment regime,[48] it also provides an alternative template for the design of future empirical studies that investigate normative critique.

Second, we bring together a leading group of empirical legal scholars working on ISDS today to consolidate the empirical scholarship. Drawing on a range of social science theories, the authors theorize, conceptualize and interrogate the regime, deploy new and diverse methods and analytics, and advance a future research agenda. Importantly, given the rapid expansion and proliferation in arbitrations and accompanying actors, the ability of scholars to analyse broader patterns and develop generalizable findings, regardless of method, has been considerably enhanced.

Finally, many of the volume's chapters use a new and comprehensive data source for empirical research. As a somewhat diffuse, decentralized and often non-transparent system of international adjudication, the empirical study of ISDS has always been plagued by access to information and data. In order to overcome some of these limitations, a significant number of chapter authors in this volume have taken advantage of a newly developed comprehensive database on IIAs and ISDS created as part of a long-term research project at the PluriCourts Centre for Excellence: the PluriCourts Investment Treaty and Arbitration Database (PITAD).[49]

The remainder of the chapter proceeds as follows. Section 1.2 introduces the different types of legitimacy (normative, sociological, legitimation) and discusses how and to what extent empirical research can contribute to legitimacy claims in the context of historical and contemporary debate. Section 1.3 introduces the different chapters of the book, which is structured largely according to legitimacy categories. We conclude with some reflections on the overall themes and ways forward for empirical research.

1.2 Assessing Legitimacy Claims Empirically

One of the fundamental problems with the use of vague or broad normative conceptions, such as justice, fairness, and legitimacy, is that

---

[48] One of the features of many studies in the book is their nuanced conclusions: for example, studies using data on particular phenomena to find that some legitimacy claims are more relevant than others, or finding that the incidence of certain problematic aspects in ISDS is variable.

[49] PITAD (n. 2).

they – by their very nature – defy precise meaning. A further complication is that the breadth of these concepts permits their mobilization in popular discourse to advance general and sweeping claims. The result is that, in evaluating legitimacy critiques that arise out of the discourse on ISDS, the term legitimacy is often used as marker symbolizing dissatisfaction with a particular regime or legal order rather than articulating a particular normative conception of legitimacy. It risks therefore being either an 'empty signifier'[50] or ideational short-hand; glossing over the 'bewildering thicket of legitimacy challenges'.[51] Thus, when one says that ISDS is in a 'legitimacy crisis', the first question to ask is whether the term is being used to identify particular normative dilemmas in regard to its claims to authority, articulate a comprehensive moral critique of ISDS, or express a general dissatisfaction with the regime because it has been perceived as unfair or unjust by a certain set of actors.

For our purposes, we wish to move away from the use of legitimacy as a general term and instead focus on particular aspects of legitimacy (and legitimation) as they are expressed in the discourse and structured in theory. To give some depth to what we are talking about when evaluating specific legitimacy claims in the context of ISDS, we take a brief tour through the jungle of legitimacy definitions. We distinguish between normative (including legal) and sociological legitimacy; and between legitimacy and legitimation. Yet, ontology is not enough. In this volume, we seek to connect empirical inquiry with the various legitimacy claims lodged for and against the regime.

1.2.1 Normative and Sociological Legitimacy

There is no authoritative or generally accepted definition of legitimacy. However, one typology is common. Legitimacy is conceptualized as either normative (including legal legitimacy) or sociological. *Normative legitimacy* concerns the rightness of an institution's exertion of power. In the context of global governance institutions, Buchanan and Keohane define it as:

> the right to rule, understood to mean both that institutional agents are morally justified in making rules and attempting to secure compliance with them and that people subject to those rules have moral, content-independent reasons to follow them and/or to not interfere with others' compliances with them.[52]

---

[50] Claus Offe, 'Governance: An "Empty Signifier?"' (2009) 16(4) *Constellations* 550.
[51] Føllesdal (n. 47), 16.
[52] Alan Buchanan and Robert Keohane, 'The Legitimacy of Global Governance Institutions', in Rudolf Wolfrum and Volker Röben (eds.), *Legitimacy in International Law* (Springer, 2008), p. 25.

Legitimacy is thus a set of moral standards by which an institution or regime is judged or justified.

In the context of law and legal institutions, normative legitimacy may also carry claims about legal authority. In this respect *legal legitimacy* may be defined as a 'property of an action, rule, actor or system which signifies a legal obligation to submit to or support that action, rule, actor or system'.[53] While there may be discussions over the 'legal validity' of such a rule, the point for this species of normative legitimacy is that a discussion of legitimacy begins with legal obligation.[54]

Some go further and claim that the concept of normative legitimacy should be chiselled down to legal legitimacy when discussing law and its institutions, worrying that a broad normative approach is too demanding or even too permissive. The latter notion is clear in Abi-Saab's attack on the use of normative legitimacy assessments: 'I would discard from the discourse of legitimacy any attempt to use it as a means to dodge or get around the law; as a passé-droit, a licence trumping legality or a "justification" of its violation.'[55]

However, assessing the broader normative legitimacy of an institution represents a long tradition in political thought and practice, often forming the basis for policy and legal proposals or calls for adjudicative deferentialism or activism in the case of courts, and captures certainly the broad range of critiques directed at the ISDS regime – which are moral, legal or both. Moreover, normative legitimacy provides an important external assessment of an institution's ability to impose its legal (interpretive and coercive) authority. In any case, positive law remains consistently and highly relevant to two constituent elements of normative legitimacy: the fundamental role of consent in international law and process constraints on jurisdiction and legal reasoning. Any application of normative legitimacy needs to take seriously the existence of legal mandates and jurisdictional constraints. In the field of ISDS, part of the debate is precisely concerned with the scope of both the legal mandate and procedure. This underscores a more general point about the need to

---

[53] Christopher Thomas, 'Uses and Abuses of Legitimacy in International Law' (2014) 34(4) *Oxford J. Legal Studies* 729, 735.

[54] Ibid., 735–8.

[55] Georges Abi-Saab, 'The Security Council as Legislator and as Executive in Its Fight against Terrorism and against Proliferation of Weapons of Mass Destruction: The Question of Legitimacy', in Wolfrum and Röben (n. 52), 116.

separate out the different elements of legitimacy and the object and subject of legitimacy to which we return below.

Sociological legitimacy, as distinct from normative legitimacy, is a conception of legitimacy that is behavioural or descriptive. It asks whether 'the governed' believe and accept that an institution has, or maintains, the power to rule over them. In this Weberian sense, one asks whether individuals affirm 'a system of authority' and lend it 'prestige', such that obedience may follow.[56] This type of legitimacy is descriptive in the sense that its purpose is to empirically catalogue belief systems of those subject to a particular legal system, set of rules or institution. It does not claim to evaluate whether those beliefs are normatively justified. For sociological legitimacy, it may be important to identify which actors or audiences are the targets of a particular institution's legitimacy – which can include 'both state and societal actors, from government elites to ordinary citizens', representing different 'constituencies'.[57] Moreover, sociological legitimacy may relate to general or specific aspects of adjudication (e.g. ISDS generally or a particular decision or aspect of ISDS related rules of procedure); whether beliefs are stable or not; and whether there are particular background conditions for the formation of beliefs.[58]

In the field of law, sociological legitimacy is often unavoidable.[59] As Buchanan and Keohane state, 'The perception of legitimacy matters, because, in a democratic era, multilateral institutions will only thrive if they are viewed as legitimate by democratic publics.'[60] A modest body of literature has engaged with the sociological legitimacy of various national and international courts.[61] Efforts to measure it in the decentralized field of international investment law and arbitration have struggled, although some surveys and experiments,[62] and media and document content

---

[56] Max Weber, *The Theory of Social and Economic Organization* (Free Press, 1964), p. 382.

[57] Jonas Tallberg and Michael Zürn, 'The Legitimacy and Legitimation of International Organizations: Introduction and Framework' (2019) 14(4) *Rev. Int'l Orgs.* 581.

[58] James Gibson, Gregory Caldeira and Vanessa Baird, 'On the Legitimacy of National High Courts' (1998) 92(2) *Am. Pol. Sci. Rev.* 343, 351; and updated results in James Gibson, 'The Legitimacy of the U.S. Supreme Court in a Polarized Polity' (2007) 4(3) *J. Emp. Legal Studies* 507.

[59] Tallberg and Zürn (n. 57).

[60] Alan Buchanan and Robert Keohane, 'The Legitimacy of Global Governance Institutions' (2006) 20(4) *Ethics and International Affairs* 405, 406.

[61] On international courts, see the overview in Erik Voeten, 'Public Opinion and the Legitimacy of International Courts' (2013) 14(2) *Theor. Inq. Law* 411. On domestic courts, see e.g. Gibson, Caldeira and Baird (n. 58) and Gibson (n. 58).

[62] Marceddu (n. 37).

analysis, have sought to provide a quantitative character to evidence on beliefs about ISDS.[63]

International lawyers and international relations scholars sometimes conflate normative and sociological conceptions. It could be argued that the two go together in practice and that the former is a proxy for the latter (e.g. if an institution is normatively legitimate it is likely to be accepted as legitimate in a sociological sense). However, this approach is questionable: actor beliefs may diverge significantly from the results of a principle-based analysis. This divergence is often apparent, if not acute, for judges and arbitrators. In their decisions or reasoning, the need to build sociological legitimacy (e.g. through greater deference to a state) may come at the cost of normative legitimacy (e.g. ensure consistency in deference towards states), and vice versa.

Nonetheless, following Habermas and others, it is important to underline that sociological perspectives can sharpen normative claims.[64] If, contrary to normative expectations, an institution or regime is unable to maintain legitimacy in practice, those very expectations may require reconsideration. A sociological perspective can therefore heighten awareness of the real as opposed to imagined powers of institutions and 'inform judgments about alternative pathways to legitimate rule'.[65] Legitimacy beliefs may also produce indirect moral effects. As Føllesdal notes, an enhanced sociological legitimacy for an international court or tribunal can improve compliance, which 'may affect its actual *normative* legitimacy, enabling states to prevent free riding on agreed rules'.[66] Likewise, sociological legitimacy is not entirely free from normative notions. The framing of sociological legitimacy is dependent or 'conceptually parasitic' on some a priori conception of normative legitimacy.[67]

With that said, the main focus of this volume will be to respond to normative legitimacy claims – in other words, is the critique of ISDS justified? Yet, a secondary focus is sociological, and this dimension of

---

[63] Langford and Behn (n. 36).

[64] Jurgen Habermas, *Communication and the Evolution of Society* (Beacon Press, 1979), p. 205.

[65] Bruce Gilley, *The Right to Rule: How States Win and Lose Legitimacy* (Columbia University Press, 2009), p. xiii.

[66] Føllesdal (n. 47), 6.

[67] Daniel Bodansky, 'Legitimacy in International Law and International Relations', in Dunoff and Pollack (eds.), *Interdisciplinary Perspectives on International Law and International Relations* (Cambridge University Press, 2013), p. 327.

legitimacy is covered in three respects. First, many chapters take a departure point in beliefs. Second, some of the normative chapters explore how beliefs might shift with greater normative awareness. Third, the final part of the book is devoted to how sociological legitimacy might be enhanced – in others words through legitimation, to which we now turn.

1.2.2 Legitimacy and Legitimation

The terms legitimacy and legitimation are obviously interrelated but they require slightly different starting points. *Legitimacy* is a moral perspective or sociological belief but *legitimation* refers explicitly to the process by which actors 'come to believe in the normative legitimacy of an object'.[68] In some cases, this process is a result of an explicit legitimation strategy; while in other cases, it is neither deliberate nor controllable, for example an institution gains or loses legitimacy 'as the product of the unconscious replication of pervasive legitimacy narratives'.[69] A significant body of social science literature is thus concerned with identifying legitimacy beliefs (e.g. based on self-interest, normative approval, and comprehensibility), studying strategies for 'gaining, maintaining, and repairing legitimacy'[70] and parsing their dimensions such as 'intensity (strength), tone (direction), and narratives (content)'.[71]

Legitimation is inherently a dynamic concept. Legitimacy assessments, whether normative or sociological, often contain a relatively static version of the object at hand: the legitimacy of a regime or institution is viewed at one point in time. Legitimation, however, generally refers to a diachronic process, typically as a strategic response to identified legitimacy deficits. Legitimation studies are often concerned with processes and interventions that increase or decrease institutional legitimacy across time, using methods ranging from process tracing to qualitative interviews and surveys and quantitative and computational analysis. For example, scholars have scrutinized whether investment arbitrators have sought to maintain the legitimacy of the regime by collectively producing decisions that are more favourable to state respondents, such

---

[68] Thomas (n. 53), 742.
[69] Ibid.
[70] Mark C. Suchman, 'Managing Legitimacy: Strategic and Institutional Approaches' (1995) 20(3) *Academy of Management Review* 571, 572.
[71] Tallberg and Zürn (n. 57), 589.

as reducing the number of claims won, mitigating damages, or exercising caution in high-profile ISDS cases.[72]

While the modes of assessment between legitimacy and legitimation are distinct, it is not unusual for there to be overlap between evaluations of the legitimacy of an institution and the legitimation processes it engages in. To assess the legitimation processes of a regime requires that one evaluates these processes in terms of its 'targets' (who or what is the target of efforts to increase or decrease the legitimacy of a particular institution?), 'purposes' (for what purpose does the institution seek to enhance its legitimacy?) and 'audiences' (which actors hold relevant beliefs?). Once the target, purposes and audience for legitimation has been identified, it becomes easier to determine the factors that contribute to or detract from an institution's legitimacy in a particular context and what strategies might be more effective.

Given the focus of this volume, it is the various institutions and procedures constituting elements of ISDS that are the *targets* of legitimacy. Within ISDS, there are a number of ways that the focus can be disaggregated. This includes arbitrators, arbitration institutions, substantive provisions of treaties, and rules of procedure.

The *purpose* of legitimation may be diverse. We may take as a starting point that the core purpose that legitimacy may serve for ISDS is to influence disputing parties to voluntarily comply with decisions. To many, the purpose could extend further. It can include the willingness of third parties affected by the outcomes of ISDS (e.g. local populations, employees and the investors' home states) to accept and respect the conclusions of an ISDS tribunal; acceptance by relevant actors (e.g. national or international courts, tribunals and enforcement institutions) of the analytical approaches, interpretations and conclusions of ISDS as authoritative and controlling; and saving the entire system from systemic backlash.

In the case of ISDS, the *audiences* are many and diverse. There are multiple actors who are either required to comply with their rules and rulings or possess particular interests in their design and functioning. While core actors are those who should directly comply with the ruling of a tribunal – that is, the specific host state and investor in a particular ISDS dispute – there may be a variety of other relevant actors that are not direct parties to a particular dispute. These might include, *inter alia*,

---

[72] Langford and Behn (n. 36).

other states hosting foreign investments, the home states of investors, specific institutions and entities within home states and host states, transnational actors such as specific groups of investors, legal experts, quantum experts, intergovernmental political and adjudicative institutions, NGOs, and entities that advise states and investors.

While the main focus of this volume is in responding to normative legitimacy claims within a broader sociological setting, the final part of this volume contains three chapters assessing legitimation of different aspects of the system for different purposes (see section 1.3). Moreover, some of the specific legitimacy chapters (e.g. chapters 7 and 10) also address legitimation strategies.

1.2.3 Empirical Assessments: Approaches, Possibilities and Limitations

It is one thing to categorize legitimacy concepts; it is another to measure them empirically. This applies to both normative and sociological approaches. The empirical challenges are fourfold: construct validity, data collection, choice of theory and method, and interpretation of results.

The first challenge is *construct validity*, which concerns concretizing and operationalising the abstract moral notion or hidden social phenomenon of legitimacy. For normative forms of legitimacy, this requires reducing complex and contestable concepts in legitimacy debates such as 'independence', 'transparency', 'diversity' or 'interpretive activism' into something measurable.

In this volume, authors spend considerable time in trying to operationalize and justify methods for identifying 'bias' (chapter 3), 'rule of law' (chapter 8) and 'conflict of interest' (chapter 13). Even simpler concepts require difficult choices. For example, do we treat as similar developing countries facing an ISDS claim if they range from low income to upper middle income countries according to the World Bank Income Groups (see chapter 2)? Or in determining the effect of the 'nationality' of arbitrators on decision-making, should a 'non-Western' national with long-term residence in the 'West' be categorized as Western or not (see chapter 10)? Likewise, when is a foreign investor small, medium, large or extra-large given all have multi-million-dollar revenue streams (chapter 13)?

The same challenge applies in measuring sociological legitimacy, where Tallberg and Zürn note that '[a]s a product of internal processes of cognition and recognition, legitimacy is less readily observable than many other phenomena in world politics, such as wars and treaties.'[73] In this volume, we are faced with operationalizing concepts like 'backlash', 'strategy' and 'outcome'. Nonetheless, we know that these subjective belief systems can be identified and measured in a similar manner to the objective data points on wars and treaties, albeit the effort to collect such data is daunting and time consuming. In the field of international relations, the most common forms of seeking to identify beliefs are through surveys and survey experiments, political communication and political behaviour – as Armstrong and Nottage draw on in their mixed methods appraisal of support for ISDS (Chapter 11).[74]

The second challenge relates to data collection. All forms of empirical research on ISDS have historically been hampered by the international investment regime's default positions on confidentiality and decentralization. This difficult terrain has meant that data collection has been built on physical and digital sleuthing as much as traditional methods of collection and systemization of legal decisions and orders. In the last few years, however, ISDS databases can claim to include almost all treaty-based cases, even if not all awards and other arbitration-related documents are available.[75] We estimate, for example, that PITAD[76] – based on comments we have received from three arbitral institutions (see chapter 2) – currently only fails to account for a small universe of approximately fifty to sixty 'known unknown' treaty-based ISDS cases. There are also 'unknown unknown' cases that may range from ten to thirty.[77]

One important challenge is the lack of data on non-ICSID contract – and FDI law-based ISDS cases. Access to information regarding such cases is essential when exploring many legitimacy-related issues, in particular since countries that provide consent to ISDS through FDI laws

---

[73] Tallberg and Zürn (n. 57), 596.

[74] See above (n. 61–63).

[75] ITAlaw <italaw.com> is the main text-based database for treaty-based arbitration. The ICSID Cases Database <icsid.worldbank.org/en> includes a broader range of cases based on FDI laws and contracts, but does only cover those administered by ICSID. International Arbitration Database <arbitration.org> seems to include all kinds of ISDS cases, but its specific coverage remains somewhat unclear. More numerically oriented databases include PITAD (n. 2) and UNCTAD ISDS Navigator <investmentpolicy.unctad.org/investment-dispute-settlement>. This brief and selective overview does not include commercial or project-specific databases.

[76] PITAD (n. 2).

[77] In the early days of the practice of the system, the universe of completely below-the-radar cases was considered to be significantly higher than today.

tend to have low numbers of IIAs (see chapter 2) and since investors frequently have the option of basing ISDS claims on FDI laws or contracts rather than on IIAs. Difficulties in identifying contract and FDI law ISDS cases and their underlying awards has resulted in a 'spotty' cluster of known cases. There are also serious selection bias issues at play: the awards in such cases will almost exclusively enter the public domain through set-aside petitions in the courts of the seat or through enforcement actions in the courts of third states. These cases, all concerning post-award litigation, thus represent not only a small subset of the overall caseload, but a very particular one: that is, those typically with flaws and compliance problems.[78] These scattered and often buried awards thus continue to present challenges for the quality and expansion of ISDS databases.

Many empirical questions require access to other types of materials – which might include background or contextual factors for a tribunal decision (typically fact-based inquiries), motivations and characteristics of the various stakeholders and actors (arbitrators, foreign investors, law firms, valuation experts, industry experts, and the arbitral institutions themselves), or the effects of ISDS awards on either the system as a whole or on a particular respondent state facing enforcement actions against it in a third state (typically looking at questions of compliance and impact). Some data of this nature has been collected, for example the characteristics of arbitrators – their gender, nationality, education and professional background. Some research projects are also using ambitious experimental methods to identify the operation of cognitive biases in decision-making (chapter 3), while others seek to map the breadth and diversity of personal values among ISDS decision-makers using value surveys, interviews, and psychometric testing.[79]

However, even as the methods advance and data improves, challenges remain when researching legitimacy issues associated with ISDS. These include the problems that arise when basic information regarding the caseload of a global regime requires state-specific collection of

---

[78] Luke Eric Peterson at IAReporter <iareporter.com> has constructed a new dataset that has a large collection of non-ICSID FDI law and contract cases.

[79] Stavros Brekoulakis et al. (n. 38). This project develops a new theoretical understanding for the assessment of impartiality among different types of party-appointed adjudicators. Empirical methods, psychometric testing, interviews, textual content analysis and surveys are used to create new variables and measures that, when combined with more traditional socio-demographic data, can help us better understand how panel dynamics, personal value diversity, cognitive biases and various other institutional biases influence decision-making processes and outcomes in ISDS.

information, requiring the use of localized qualitative and quantitative methods and process tracing across all states. No other international judicial regime requires such intensive research, which explains why empirical scholarship on both the pre-litigation and the post-litigation phases in ISDS cases still lags behind significant studies elsewhere.[80]

The third challenge is choice of *method*. Much research on the ISDS regime has been of the doctrinal variety[81] although it is diversifying. Social science methods are employed increasingly, with greater attention being paid to issues of case selection and research design.[82] To be sure, doctrinal or traditional methods carry certain advantages in answering claims about the legitimacy crisis. Scholars are able to obtain a relatively fine-grained understanding of the actual development of the jurisprudence. For example, jurisprudential scholarship suggests a small but discernible capability of ISDS tribunals to respond reflexively to certain aspects of critique against the system: such as in the areas of environmental protection and broader issues of sustainable development;[83] in relation to indirect expropriation;[84] fair and equitable treatment;[85] full protection and

---

[80] See Laurence Helfer and Erik Voeten, 'International Courts as Agents of Legal Change: Evidence from LGBT Rights in Europe' (2014) 68(1) *Int'l Org.* 77; Courtney Hillebrecht, *Domestic Politics and International Human Rights Tribunals: The Problem of Compliance* (Cambridge University Press, 2014); Hyeran Jo and Beth A. Simmons, 'Can the International Criminal Court Deter Atrocity?' (2016) 70(3) *Int'l Org.* 443; Øyvind Stiansen, 'Directing Compliance? Remedial Approach and Compliance with European Court of Human Rights Judgments' (2019) *Br. J. Political Sci.* <doi.org/10.1017/S00071234190002921-9>.

[81] For a good example of a doctrinal survey of the jurisprudence in ISDS, see Rudolf Dolzer, 'Fair and Equitable Treatment: Today's Contours' (2014) 12(1) *Santa Clara J. Int'l L.* 7.

[82] See e.g. Jorge Viñuales, 'Foreign Investment and the Environment in International Law: Current Trends', in Kate Miles (ed.), *Research Handbook on Environment and Investment Law* (Edward Elgar, 2019), p. 12; Wolfgang Alschner and Kun Hui, 'Missing in Action: General Public Policy Exceptions in Investment Treaties', in Lisa Sachs, Lise Johnson and Jesse Coleman (eds.), *Yearbook on International Investment Law and Policy 2018* (Oxford University Press, 2019), ch. 21.

[83] Marie-Claire Condonier Segger, Markus W. Gehring and Andrew Newcombe (eds.), *Sustainable Development in World Investment Law* (Kluwer, 2011); Behn and Langford (n. 13); Viñuales (ibid.).

[84] Caroline Henckels, 'Indirect Expropriation and the Right to Regulate: Revisiting Proportionality Analysis and the Standard of Review in Investor-State Arbitration' (2012) 15(1) *JIEL* 223.

[85] Dolzer (n. 81).

security;[86] most-favoured-nation treatment;[87] or on the definition of an investment;[88] but also in studies showing how certain ISDS tribunals have ignored advances in seeming preference for maintaining the status quo.[89] These studies all demonstrate the potential for the use of more medium-N doctrinal research on the development of the jurisprudence in ISDS and how those doctrinal advances (or lack thereof) are modifying any trends away on legitimacy questions is also significant.[90]

Nonetheless, doctrinal methods suffer from various disadvantages. Their breadth is limited – in terms of description, generalization and information; as is their depth in terms of explanatory and predictive power. Moreover, even when legal texts provide seeming answers to legitimacy questions, a doctrinal approach can be misleading. For example, the legal discourse in awards may have no material consequences on actual decision-making.[91] Thus, a multimethod approach that harnesses the power of different methods is to be preferred.

In this volume, the trio of quantitative, qualitative and computational methods are deployed and sometimes together in a single chapter. *Quantitative* approaches permit broader description, identification of patterns, and testing for correlation through probabilistic logic.[92] With the use of controls and theory-driven testing, insight can also be gained on causation. The types of quantitative methods vary. They can range from simple descriptive statistics and binary correlations (chapters 5 and 6) to multivariate regression analysis on awards datasets and experimental surveys (chapters 3 and 11). However, quantitative methods have their clear limitations, especially their reliance on a numeric

---

[86] Stanimir A. Alexandrov, 'The Evolution of the Full Protection and Security Standard', in Meg Kinnear et al. (eds.), *Building International Investment Law: The First 50 Years of ICSID* (Kluwer, 2016), p. 319.

[87] Julie A. Maupin, 'MFN-Based Jurisdiction in Investor-State Arbitration: Is There Any Hope for a Consistent Approach' (2011) 14(1) *JIEL* 157.

[88] Van Harten (n. 14), 251.

[89] Jeffrey Waincymer, 'Balancing Property Rights and Human Rights in Expropriation', in Pierre-Marie Dupuy, Francesco Francioni and Ernst-Ulrich Petersman (eds.), *Human Rights in International Investment Law and Arbitration* (Oxford University Press, 2009), p. 275; Henckels (n. 84), 237.

[90] Thomas Keck, 'Medium-N Methods' in David Law and Malcolm Langford (eds.), *Research Methods in Constitutional Law: A Handbook* (Edward Elgar, 2020).

[91] Shai Danziger et al., 'Extraneous Factors in Judicial Decisions' (2011) 108(17) *Proceedings of the National Academy of Sciences of the United States of America* 6889.

[92] James Mahoney and Gary Goertz, 'A Tale of Two Cultures: Contrasting Quantitative and Qualitative Research' (2006) 14(3) *Pol. Anal.* 227.

simplification of complex phenomena and the challenge of controlling for multiple causal influences.

Focusing on a smaller number of cases, actors or objects, *qualitative* methods permit a deeper analysis of the context and explanation for different legal phenomena – whether case background, complexity of adjudicative reasoning and cultures. While a significant body of qualitative research is deductive and theory-driven,[93] much is inductive and operates with a different logic – seeking to find necessary and sufficient conditions rather than probabilistic relationships. The result is that qualitative approaches often contribute to theory and hypothesis development. In practice, qualitative methods are difficult to categorise but range from participant observation and interviews (chapter 11), to small to medium-N surveys, document content analysis (chapter 16), process tracing, and broader use of qualitative data to support theoretical propositions or hypotheses. Such qualitative studies might suffer from weaknesses from limited generalizability to risks of bias in case selection.

Computational methods are the new kid on the block and have rapidly made their presence felt in international economic law.[94] These methods represent a fusion of quantitative and qualitative methods – treating text as complex numerical patterns. They offer new techniques in prediction, text and network analysis, and computational power enables quicker analysis of a greater range of material and data. Existing data-driven research on ISDS and investment treaties has sought to map networks of citations,[95] arbitrators and counsel,[96] predict the authorship of arbitral awards[97] and the outcome of treaty negotiations between states.[98] In this volume, chapter 4 uses computational methods to map and probe the

---

[93] Langford, Behn and Lie (n. 13); Siri Gloppen, 'Courts and Social Transformation: An Analytical Framework', in Roberto Gargarella, Pilar Domingo and Theunis Roux (eds.), *Courts and Social Transformation in New Democracies: An Institutional Voice for the Poor?* (Ashgate, 2006), ch. 2.

[94] Alschner, Pauwelyn and Puig (n. 30).

[95] Niccolo Ridi, 'Approaches to External Precedent: The Invocation of International Jurisprudence in Investment Arbitration and WTO Dispute Settlement', in Szilard Gáspár-Szilágyi , Daniel Behn and Malcolm Langford, *Adjudicating Trade and Investment Disputes: Convergence or Divergence?* (Cambridge University Press, 2020), p. 121.

[96] Langford, Behn and Lie (n. 13).

[97] Langford, Lie and Behn, 'Computational Stylometry' (n. 19).

[98] Wolfgang Alschner and Dmitriy Skougarevskiy, 'Can Robots Write Treaties? Using Recurrent Neural Networks to Draft International Investment Agreements', in Floris Bex and Serena Villata (ed.), *Legal Knowledge and Information Systems: JURIX 2016* (IOS Press, 2016), p. 119.

relationship between arbitrators and law firms. However, these methods also face their challenges – especially in discerning meaning rather than pattern in text, and explaining rather than predicting.

Finally, some methodological approaches seek to combine different methods, so-called mixed methods.[99] Methods can be combined *sequentially* (e.g. a regression analysis followed by case studies to test causality) or *concurrently* (e.g. a survey instrument with quantitative and qualitative questions). There are of course limitations in commensurability – ensuring that the methods can speak to each other and reveal convergence or divergence in data collection, results or findings. However, from a pragmatic perspective, mixed methods often provide a more sophisticated understanding of complex phenomena (chapters 4, 11 and 14).

The final challenge is interpretation of results. Caution should be exercised in discerning and communicating any empirical result, and each study should be judged on its own assumptions, strengths and limitations. More importantly, it should be viewed as part of a longer 'academic conversation'.

A quick example might help illustrate this point. There has been a perception (belief) that ISDS is illegitimate because there is a structural bias in favour of foreign investors winning a disproportionate number of claims against less developed states. To test this empirically, we would be interested in evaluating whether, in fact, foreign investors do win a disproportionate number of such cases against less developed states (higher win ratio than against developed states), and if there are any legitimate reasons (e.g. poor levels of governance or fact-specific circumstances) that can explain such differences. The trajectory of existing research on potential structural bias against developing states can take Franck's study from 2009 as a starting point. Using data up to 2007, she found that the development status of the respondent state did not have a statistically significant relationship with the final outcome of a case on the merits,[100] and in 2014, with more data, she argued that the result continued to hold when controlling for the level of democracy within a particular respondent state.[101]

---

[99] Abbas Tashakkori and John Creswell, 'Exploring the Nature of Research Questions in Mixed Methods Research' (2007) 1(3) *J. Mixed Methods Research* 207, 211.

[100] Franck, 'Development and Outcomes' (n. 31) but see also Gus Van Harten, 'Fairness and Independence in Investment Arbitration: A Critique of Susan Franck's Development and Outcomes of Investment Treaty Arbitration' (2011) *Osgoode Hall Law School of York University Research Paper.*

[101] Franck, 'Conflating Politics and Development' (n. 16).

However, examining a much larger dataset covering all cases up through 2017 and with a focus on the role of democratic governance, Behn, Berge and Langford found the reverse. They identified a strong statistically significant correlation between foreign investor wins and the development status of a particular respondent state (whether as a continuous or categorical variable);[102] and that the pattern generally persists when controlling for almost all types of democratic governance indicators, except one.[103] These findings are reinforced by Sattorova's qualitative case studies on ISDS which show that 'there is a significant current within the international arbitration community that favours the vision of investors as victims of corrupt governments and thus downplays their role in normalizing and entrenching weak governance in developing states.'[104]

Yet, and alternatively, Strezhnev advances and tests a different theory for why poorer states may lose more frequently than wealthier states. He finds evidence that poorer states settle 'weaker' cases more frequently than wealthier states thus skewing the statistics on foreign investor success rates upwards in poorer states.[105] Thus, the conclusion to be drawn here is that any empirical analysis of a legitimacy critique in ISDS will likely be no simple endeavour and will require multiple studies across time that employ synthetic theories and use different methods; and even then the results will likely be very nuanced.

1.3 Forms of Legitimacy and Overview of the Book

We now turn from legitimacy theory and empirical approaches to how both are applied in this book. Legitimacy assessments can be framed and disaggregated in multiple ways within and across different disciplines and traditions.[106]

---

[102] Behn, Berge and Langford (n. 14). The interesting nuance uncovered by this study is that it appears that the correlation between foreign investor success and respondent state development status is driven by foreign investors having very low success rates in cases against respondent states with a high development status rather than foreign investors having very high success rates against respondent states with a low development status.

[103] Ibid. Controlling for a property protection strength variable wiped out most of the effect of a state's economic development status.

[104] Sattorova (n. 16), 138–40, 165.

[105] Anton Strezhnev, 'Why Rich Countries Win Investment Disputes: Taking Selection Seriously' (2017) *Working Paper*. The argument is that the system is anti-developing state, which is different than stating that the system is pro-investor as argued above. One additional consideration is that the empirical classification of 'strong' and 'weak' cases is very hard to establish in an 'objective' manner.

[106] For different perspectives on disaggregating normative legitimacy, see Føllesdal (n. 47); Mark Thatcher and Alec Stone Sweet 'Theory and Practice of Delegation to Non-Majoritarian Institutions' (2002) 25(1) *West European Politics* 1; Daniel Bodansky,

INTRODUCTION: THE LEGITIMACY CRISIS

However, it is not particularly controversial to disaggregate normative legitimacy into three elements: consent, process and output.

Consent legitimacy primarily focuses on issues of the original basis and authority of an institution or regime. We propose that this form of legitimacy refers to the constitutive process for establishing and maintaining institutions or regimes. In contemporary international law, this type of legitimacy might refer to the establishing of a treaty regime covering a specific area of governance. A treaty, such as an IIA, might lack consent legitimacy if certain states were coerced into signing it or if the treaty authorizes actions that its parties never envisioned.[107] Equally, there may be consent legitimacy issues arising out of the scope of the delegation of authority that a state gives to third party adjudicators, such as ISDS arbitrators.

Process legitimacy generally refers to assessments of the process(es) by which rules, decisions and actions are made, applied, or interpreted. In the context of ISDS, arbitral tribunals may be, or be viewed as, legitimate if they fulfil certain criteria such as independence, impartiality, transparency, accountability, judicial restraint and due process or contribute to more effective participation (commonly referred to as standards of procedural justice or fairness) or to standards of decision-making and legal reasoning.[108] However, issues relating to efficiency or the lack thereof may also raise issues of legitimacy. For example, are arbitrator challenge procedures legitimate if they are disproportionately disruptive to the progress of the case? Are there any legitimacy concerns with the costs of arbitral tribunals? What about the evidentiary standards and assurances of equality of arms between the parties?

Output legitimacy generally refers to the instrumental or substantive justifications (purposes) for an institution or regime; and how outcomes from decision-making processes are to be evaluated. Different aspects of output may be relevant, ranging from the negative (e.g. the avoidance of 'extreme injustice')[109] to the positive (e.g. the fulfilment of a moderate range of public goods),[110] through to optimal and just outcomes.[111] For our purposes, output legitimacy in the context of ISDS will generally require evaluation of whether the resolution of cases produces just effects

---

'The Legitimacy of International Governance: A Coming Challenge for International Environmental Law?' (1999) 93(3) *AJIL* 596.

[107] See discussion of economic coercion in Elkins, Guzman, Simmons (n. 32).

[108] Bodansky (n. 103).

[109] Buchanan and Keohane (n. 60), 44.

[110] Gilley (n. 65).

[111] Fabienne Peter, 'Political Legitimacy', *Stanford Encyclopedia of Philosophy* (2010, revised 2017) <plato.stanford.edu/entries/legitimacy/>.

for both the system of adjudication and the parties to particular disputes. Are the results in terms of allocation of costs and benefits normatively legitimate? Are particular outcomes or effects legitimate? Output legitimacy can also refer to general effects of ISDS on the justifications for entering into IIAs in the first place: for example, the extent to which it provides protections for investments in exchange for increased flows of FDI.

To be sure, there is some overlap across the three elements. Moreover, there is a question as to how these various elements of legitimacy might be balanced against each other through the application of legitimation strategies. For example, if there are legitimacy deficits identifiable with aspects of ISDS, can improvements in process legitimacy be used to cure aspects relating to a decision's lack of grounding in state consent? Likewise, might deficits in ISDS's process legitimacy be balanced against outputs or outcomes that are normatively sound in terms of their legitimacy? This question is at the heart of the debate over the mandate for the UNCITRAL WG III process: which seeks explicitly to bolster the system's legitimacy through procedural reforms. However, critics claim this mandate is insufficient to address both normative and sociological legitimacy concerns.[112]

While consent, process and output are the common theoretical categories, the contributions to this volume generally fall into the latter two; although many have implications relating to consent legitimacy. The layout of this book is therefore structured around three main themes: process legitimacy, outcome legitimacy, and legitimation strategies. These three parts of the book follow an empirical overview of the state of affairs with ISDS and the legitimacy crisis in chapter 2, which provides an empirical departure point for the book with a quantitative and qualitative analysis of: (1) states' exposure to ISDS through consent in treaties and investment legislation; (2) the operation of the ISDS regime in practice and (3) the academic discourse regarding the legitimacy of ISDS.

1.3.1   *Process Legitimacy: Independence and Impartiality*

In this volume, we split process legitimacy into two major themes: legitimacy concerns relating to concepts of *independence and impartiality* of adjudicative bodies; and legitimacy concerns relating to *legal*

---

[112] See Gus Van Harten, Jane Kelsey and David Schneiderman, 'Phase 2 of the UNCITRAL ISDS Review: Why "Other Matters" Really Matter' (2019) *Osgoode Hall Legal Studies Research Paper* 2; and discussion of debate in Langford, Kaufmann-Kohler, Potestà and Behn (n. 26).

reasoning. In the first part on independence and impartiality, the four studies address: (1) possible cognitive biases in arbitral decision-making; (2) the role that law firms play in repeat arbitral appointments; (3) challenges to arbitrators and the accompanying procedural rules and (4) how incidents of dissent relate to claims of independence.

Even if arbitrators are subject to intensified scrutiny, significant concerns remain regarding their impartiality. In 'Testing Cognitive Bias: Experimental Approaches and Investment Arbitration' Puig and Strezhnev provide an account of ways that experimental methods can be used to uncover and identify decision-making biases. Investment arbitration tribunals derive their legitimacy from different normative, sociological and political processes than standing courts. In great part, these tribunals rely on tacit norms of behaviour among arbitration professionals. Understanding what factors affect how arbitrators make decisions in these kinds of adjudicative settings is essential in assessing critiques concerning the quality or correctness of their decisions and especially their independence and impartiality. This chapter describes a promising alternative empirical strategy that utilizes survey experiments conducted on arbitration professionals to test bias claims. It discusses also how researchers can design experimental vignettes to mimic specific aspects of the arbitration process that are difficult to observe or manipulate in the real world context.

Legitimacy concerns are an essential element in the selection of the arbitral tribunal. In 'The Influence of Law Firms in Investment Arbitration' Lie starts with Dezalay and Garth's pioneering study that applied Bourdieu's concept of social capital to the arbitration market, revealing how certain groups established and maintained their status within the market. His study asks the following: What are the actual relationships between the most influential arbitrators and the most influential law firms in the system and how might these relationships create real or perceived conflicts of interest issues for the ISDS system? This chapter answers these research questions with mixed methods: using integrated network, statistical and doctrinal analyses. By utilizing this combination of doctrinal and data-driven approaches, Lie provides insights into how the law firms have gained a central position in the ISDS network by establishing strong relationships with leading arbitrators. He points out that the top law firms have positioned themselves as 'gatekeepers' to the ISDS system, in particular in terms of distribution of cases among potential arbitrators and the acceptance of new arbitrators, and discusses possible impacts on the perceived independence and legitimacy of the ISDS system.

Parties' dissatisfaction with the tribunals' composition increasingly results in formal challenges to individual arbitrators. In 'Arbitrator Challenges in International Investment Tribunals' Giorgetti tells us that, once rare in proceedings of international tribunals, challenges to investment arbitrators are increasingly common. Using data from different arbitral institutions up through 2019, she finds a remarkable upsurge in the number of arbitrator challenges from 2010 to the present. On the one hand, many challenges may be of a purely tactical character, designed by the parties – typically the respondent state – to delay proceedings or pressure a party to settle or withdraw a complaint. On the other hand, many arbitrators may be legitimately vulnerable to challenges; and the increase in number may suggest that the system is or should take more seriously concerns around repeat appointments by the same party, double hatting, and issue conflicts. This chapter argues that arbitrator challenges may in fact contribute to the legitimacy of the adjudicative process by ensuring in practice that independence and impartiality is maintained; and signalling to prospective arbitrators and their appointers the risks of non-disclosure or certain types of appointments.

Arbitrators might voice their sympathy for the perspectives of one of the parties to the dispute by formulating dissenting opinions. In 'Dissents in Investment Treaty Arbitration: On Collegiality and Individualism' Kapeliuk starts with one of the more enduring criticisms of international arbitration and its legitimacy: that parties can appoint 'their' arbitrator unilaterally. The striking lack of dissents and their asymmetry when they occur – usually by the losing party appointed arbitrator – raises questions over whether arbitrators act independently and impartially in relation to the party that appointed them; and the very concept of party-appointed arbitrators is by itself contrary to traditional notions of judicial impartiality. This chapter investigates whether a background in civil law, as opposed to common law where dissent is a more familiar phenomenon, could explain the absence of arbitral dissents. Using PITAD data on both dissents and arbitrator background, the chapter explores this potential causal factor. Her findings, that differences in background seem unrelated to frequency of dissents, lends some support to the view that the relationship between an arbitrator and the appointing party is a main driver of dissenting opinions.

1.3.2 Process Legitimacy: Legal Reasoning

The book's second part on process legitimacy focuses on due process and legal reasoning. We provide three studies on: (1) the often hidden and unexpected role of domestic courts in investment disputes before they reach an international arbitration tribunal; (2) the effect of informal citation networks on the consistency of arbitral decisions and (3) the stabilizing effect of a system of informal precedent on the fair and equitable treatment (FET) standard.

In general, we assume that there have been extensive discussions and formal procedures between investors and public authorities prior to the materialization of an ISDS case. This context is arguably essential for fully understanding the legal arguments of the parties, the reasoning of the tribunal, and ultimately the legitimacy of the system. In 'Foreign Investors, Domestic Courts and Investment Treaty Arbitration' Gáspár-Szilágyi notes that supporters of ISDS put forward several major justifications for its continued existence, including in particular that disputes are *denationalized*, thus keeping foreign investors out of domestic courts that lack *independence*, are less *efficient*, or are *biased* against foreigners. The justification that ISDS obviates a role for the host state's domestic courts strengthens a perception that foreign investors proceed directly to the international sphere. This chapter asks why investors do resort to the courts of the host state *prior* to an ISDS case. Looking at two states with transitional judiciaries and two states with well-functioning judiciaries, the author uncovers rich data on the impressive scope of claims brought by foreign investors in the host states where they are investing; and Gáspár-Szilágyi concludes with some reflections on the role of domestic litigation in legitimation of ISDS.

It can be argued that within a largely bilateral and contractual treaty regime – which to some extent characterizes international investment law – tribunals should focus on resolving the conflict that triggered the ISDS case, paying more attention to ensuring correctness and less to consistency and predictability. In 'Ensuring Correctness or Promoting Consistency: Tracking Policy Priorities in Investment Arbitration through Large-Scale Citation Analysis' Alschner identifies concerns about investment arbitration tribunals treating like cases differently – consistency problems – and different cases the same – correctness problems. Using empirical citation analysis, he looks at an *observable* selection of what a tribunal considers to be 'relevant' precedent to reveal that tribunals are more concerned with consistency than correctness. However, this is contrary to what states consider the policy priority in ISDS reform debates. As a result, he finds an apparent mismatch between the hierarchy of policy preferences voiced by states in the ISDS reform process and what tribunals do. States can resolve that mismatch by hard-coding their policy preferences into institutional design. He argues that as part of the ISDS reform, states should thus make the ordering between correctness and consistency considerations explicit when delegating adjudicatory authority to future ISDS institutions.

Tribunals face significant challenges when seeking consistency in their interpretations of IIAs, in particular where states have provided limited guidance in the treaty text. In 'Fair and Equitable Treatment: Ordering Chaos through Precedent?' *Grisel* provides an empirical account of doctrine in investment arbitration by tracing the effect that a small number of seminal cases have on maintaining a certain level of consistency in the interpretation of the FET standard. The FET standard and its interpretation by arbitral tribunals has been blamed for giving foreign investors carte blanche to sanction governments over broad swathes of policy. It is said to be lacking any common definition and that it is a vague and ambiguous catch-all term. This chapter provides a rigorous qualitative and quantitative empirical assessment of citations and their role in the development of the FET standard consistently by tribunals across time. Based on the in-depth exploration of FET case law the author find that three landmark cases have a de facto *stare decisis* effect of reconciling competing interpretations and ultimately providing a relatively consistent standard.

1.3.3 Output Legitimacy

The third part on output legitimacy provides five chapters that empirically assess various aspects of the consequences of states' consent to ISDS: (1) how geographic diversity among arbitrators in ISDS cases remains a problem from the perspective of perceived legitimacy but less so normative legitimacy; (2) whether and how ISDS provisions have (not) contributed to improved foreign investment and the costs to host states of consent to ISDS; (3) how some states may have to endure a double sanction when investment arbitration is used as a remedy in a time of crisis; (4) how large-scale foreign investors have prevailed disproportionately well over small-scale foreign investors in ISDS cases across time and (5) to what extent the Chinese approach to ISDS provides investors with adequate and effective remedies for resolving investment disputes, and whether it might contribute to combat corruption.

In responding to criticisms such as those discussed in chapters 3 and 4, significant efforts have been taken, in particular by arbitration institutions, to increase the diversity of arbitrators. In 'The West and the Rest:

Geographic Diversity and the Role of Arbitrator Nationality in Investment Arbitration' Langford, Behn and Usynin start with the critique that ISDS is not geographically diverse, a common refrain in the legitimacy crisis discourse. In this chapter, the authors look to determine: (1) if dominant place of residence and not nationality may be a better indicator of geographic difference; (2) whether there is a lack of geographical diversity in ISDS cases and why it matters and (3) whether more geographically representative tribunals would affect outcome in ISDS cases? On the issue of dominant residence versus nationality, the overall number of non-Western arbitrators in the system drops from 35% to 25% due to a sizable number of non-Western arbitrators living in the West. On issues of perceived legitimacy, 74% of those adjudicating ISDS cases are from Western states and this is problematic for the perceived legitimacy of the system because 80% of ISDS cases are against non-Western respondent states. However, the issue becomes more complicated when examining the effect on outcomes. The authors find that the absence of geographic representativeness can favour Western home and host states, especially when the chaiman of the tribunal is from the West. However, possibly due to a high degree of institutionalization and socialization of arbitrators in the system, it does not appear at present that arbitrator nationality has a significant effect on outcomes.

The voluminous literature on the benefits of IIAs in terms of increasing flows and stocks of investment indicates that there is no 'one size fits all' in terms of treaty design and effects. In 'Mixing Methodologies in Empirically Investigating Investment Arbitration and Inbound Foreign Investment' Armstrong and Nottage provide a key response to legitimacy concerns over investment arbitration by pointing to whether or not it produces material benefits. Through a mixed methods approach, the authors revisit the vexed question of whether offering treaty-based ISDS protections leads to significant increases in inbound FDI. The chapter examines the synergies and tensions involved with: (1) econometric research of the impact of ISDS provisions on inbound FDI; (2) qualitative research on investor and host state practices and attitudes and (3) framing and presenting research questions and findings, especially in light of social psychological research on cultural risk cognition. They conclude that whatever the results that emerge from empirical research findings, the form of presentation will determine whether they will be accepted by the public or fall victim to growing polarisation in perceptions and positions.

In recent years, ISDS has increasingly been employed by investors in the aftermath of a variety of crises, ranging from economic meltdown to inter-state war. In 'Double Jeopardy? The Use of Investment Arbitration in Times of Crisis' Shultz and Dupont focus on investment arbitration as a means of last resort that occurs as a response to the realization of two types of shock towards foreign investors – one from severely dysfunctional governance at the national level and the other from an economic crisis. Using an original dataset that includes investment claims filed under the rules of all arbitration institutions as well as ad hoc arbitrations, the authors test links between governance, economic crises and investment arbitration; and they find that poor governance, understood as corruption and lack of rule of law, has a statistically significant relation with investment arbitration claims, but economic crises do not when considered separately. Yet, bad governance and economic crises considered together are a good predictor of when countries will get hit by investment arbitration claims. Their findings are of great significance to important questions regarding outcome legitimacy, in particular whether ISDS produces legitimate outcomes if used to redress or mitigate severe governance deficiencies, and whether its use in the context of economic crises hurts countries in great difficulty and thereby undermines efforts to ensure mutually beneficial economic recovery.

Even if ISDS is resource demanding and time consuming, a relatively diverse group of investors has initiated ISDS cases and thereby indicated a strong belief that they might benefit from the regime. In 'Who has Benefited Financially from Investment Treaty Arbitration? An Evaluation of the Size and Wealth of Claimants' Van Harten and Malysheuski make the observation that the legitimacy of ISDS appears to depend in part on an expectation that it benefits smaller businesses, not just large multinationals and the super-wealthy. This chapter collects data on size and wealth of the foreign investors that have brought claims and received monetary awards due to ISDS. Categories for the size and wealth of foreign investors are compared to the size of damage awards, which helps determine that the primary beneficiaries in ISDS cases have been companies with annual revenue exceeding USD one billion and individuals with net wealth in excess of USD 100 million. The main finding is that the beneficiaries of ISDS-ordered financial transfers, in the aggregate, have overwhelmingly been wealthy individual investors and large companies – and especially extra-large companies. They also note that the awards gained by small companies are not so different from their legal costs.

The distribution of benefits from ISDS is not only related to the decisions of tribunals, but also to the interaction between investors and public authorities prior to the arbitration. In 'Explaining China's Relative Absence from Investment Treaty Arbitration' Lindmark, Behn and Fauchald explore whether the absence of ISDS cases against China means that investors are deprived of adequate and effective remedies for resolving investment disputes. While ISDS might be an effective tool for foreign investors against less powerful states, it is a less potent means for securing investors' interests against powerful countries, such as China. Based on a unique dataset of all Chinese IIAs, the authors find that the low number of ISDS cases against China up until 2007 can be better explained by jurisdictional limitations. In more recent years, the continued reluctance among foreign investors to bring cases can be explained only partially by the unequal power relationship between foreign investors and Chinese authorities. The authors find that the administrative review procedures required under Chinese IIAs prior to the establishment of arbitral tribunals promote dispute resolution that accommodate the joint interests of investors and public officials directly involved with the establishment and operation of the investment. Such non-transparent procedures allow parties to keep corrupt practices away from public scrutiny. In view of the high level of corruption in domestic courts, the authors argue that ISDS will be more easily available and is likely to prevent corruption if the administrative review requirement is removed.

1.3.4   *Legitimation Strategies*

The fourth and final part of the book includes three chapters looking empirically at strategies employed to enhance the legitimacy of ISDS. The chapters focus on: (1) how investment arbitration can promote the development of local legal institutions; (2) how states learn and develop capacity in the field of international investment law and arbitration and (3) how such capabilities are used to renegotiate the ISDS provisions in their BITs.

Since one of the main purposes of ISDS is to substitute for dysfunctional domestic judiciaries, one should expect the impact of ISDS on domestic judiciaries to be positive when assessing the legitimacy of the former. Indeed, the positive effects on domestic rule of law is one of the major output legitimacy claims of ISDS supporters. In 'Does International Arbitration Enfeeble or Enhance Local Legal Institutions?'

Rogers and Drahozal examine the critique that investment arbitration instead undermines or hampers the development of national legal institutions. By providing a forum for foreign investors separate and distinct from local courts, critics argue, ISDS removes any incentive for foreign investors to promote the development of local legal institutions. This chapter sets out an account of how investment arbitration might affect development of local legal institutions, in particular international commercial arbitration and, perhaps, domestic arbitration. The authors find that while both the number of investment agreements and investment arbitration proceedings to which a state is a party is negatively related to the rule of law in the state, the presence of an indicator for support for international commercial arbitration – adoption of the UNCITRAL Model Law on International Commercial Arbitration – essentially offsets that negative relationship.

As exemplified by the OECD negotiations of the Multilateral Agreement on Investment, developing countries have for a long time been regarded as 'rule-takers' rather than 'rule-makers', and they are still perceived as such despite multiple efforts at enhancing their performance. In 'Learning from Investment Treaty Law and Arbitration: Developing States and Power Inequalities' Sattorova and Vytiaganets show how the interaction of developing states with investment treaty law and arbitration constitutes an important, albeit often less visible, part of the ongoing debate about the legitimacy of the investment treaty regime and its ISDS provisions. Even a cursory overview of the literature on legitimacy of international investment law reveals that developing states and their concerns are frequently lumped together under the broader rubric of investment treaty law as a threat to national sovereignty and a constraint on state capacity to regulate in the public interest. By focusing on the formal equality between contracting state parties and the reciprocal nature of international investment agreements (IIAs), they argue that such narratives tend to mask the presence of power disparities, which considerably shape the involvement of developing states in the creation, diffusion, and internalization of investment treaty law. The authors seek to counter these narratives by drawing on new empirical data to expose a range of structural, normative and institutional power inequalities that currently shape the various stages of developing states' participation in the international investment regime. By using the optics of power and focusing on how developing states learn from and internalize investment treaty law, the chapter peers behind the formal structures of investment treaties and ISDS to identify the underlying processes and

INTRODUCTION: THE LEGITIMACY CRISIS

actors and to question the legitimacy of the prevailing norms and institutional arrangements. Their principal argument is that a meaningful reform of ISDS is impossible without addressing power inequalities in negotiating the norms constituting a global investment treaty regime.

Finally, traditionally essential strategies when renegotiating IIAs has been to provide (broader) consent to ISDS and negotiate more precise substantive provisions. In 'Legitimation through Modification: Do States Seek More Regulatory Space in Their Investment Agreements?' Broude, Haftel and Thompson claim that states unhappy with BITs and with the arbitration mechanisms under them should make efforts to insert, renegotiate or remove ISDS provisions. This chapter is based on a dataset on renegotiated and terminated BITs. The initial evidence indicates that states have not made a systematic effort over the years to recalibrate their BITs for the purpose of preserving more regulatory space. In fact, most renegotiations either leave ISDS provisions unchanged or render them more investor-friendly. Nevertheless, they find that this is beginning to change, as recent renegotiations are more likely to circumscribe ISDS in ways that preserve more state regulatory space.

1.4   Concluding Thoughts

The international investment arbitration regime emerged in the late 1990s as a leading symbol of economic globalization.[113] Its trajectory since then has followed many of the ups and downs of the neo-liberal economic order. Some claim that it strengthens economic growth, rule of law and peaceful interstate relations; others that it favours global financial elites, enhances power asymmetries between the Global North and South, and is built on a non-transparent and obtuse transnational legal order of powerful arbitrators.

The individual chapters presented in this volume sought to address empirically many of the critiques advanced against ISDS using a wide range of social scientific and data-driven tools. The answer to the question of legitimacy is mixed, whether on process or output legitimacy. Some chapters demonstrate clear legitimacy problems, others the opposite, while many provide a nuanced picture of the critiques and the need for a critical understanding of how we interpret findings. The final chapters point to some ways forward for the regime's legitimation.

---

[113] Yves Dezalay and Bryant Garth, *Dealing in Virtue: International Commercial Arbitration and the Construction of a Transnational Legal Order* (Chicago University Press, 1996).

We hope that the framing of the contributions within a centuries old political and legal discourse on legitimacy contributes to contextualizing and enhancing our understanding of how we research, analyse and interpret legitimacy in the context of international investment law in general and ISDS in particular. We hope also that the broad range of approaches to empirical research presented in this volume will inspire cooperation among social scientists (including legal scholars), and contribute to improving the quality of empirical research on the functions and roles of international courts and tribunals.

This volume seeks also to provide a comprehensive starting point for the empirical study of ISDS in the years to come. The chapters of this book demonstrate how the empirical study of legitimacy can advance our understanding of how ISDS works and how empirical evidence about the functioning of ISDS can assist in responding to many of the normative claims lodged for and against the use of ISDS in its past 25 years.

2

The International Investment Regime and Its Discontents

DANIEL BEHN*, OLE KRISTIAN FAUCHALD** AND MALCOLM LANGFORD***

2.1 Introduction

The sprawling nature of the international investment regime and the accompanying backlash and so-called legitimacy crisis defies most doctrinal and qualitative attempts at description. The international investment agreement (IIA) network is global in reach and decentralized in nature, investor–state dispute settlement (ISDS) is based on different procedural mechanisms and ad hoc proceedings in multiple jurisdictions, and the accompanying epistemic community and chorus of critique is populated with multiple actors and interests. It is a distinct universe. Fragmented and largely non-institutionalized, understanding it requires multiple methods in order bring all strands of its practice together, identify patterns, and to give justice to its contemporary nature and character.

Moreover, this assemblage of law, institutions and actors, is constantly changing. While the number of new treaties has declined, the number of cases continues to grow. The result is that much of the debate on the regime risks being based on outdated data and information. For example, Schultz and Dupont contest the idea that ISDS can be easily placed in a neo-colonial context or category given the rapid increase in ISDS cases filed against developed states in recent years.[1] Likewise, recent studies

---

* Associate Professor (Senior Lecturer) in International Law, Queen Mary University of London; Associate Research Professor, PluriCourts, University of Oslo. This chapter was supported by the Research Council of Norway projects number 223274 and 276009 (LEGINVEST).

** Professor of Law and PluriCourts Coordinator, University of Oslo; Research Professor, Fridtjof Nansen Institute.

*** Professor of Public Law and Director of CELL, University of Oslo; Co-Director, Centre on Law and Social Transformation, University of Bergen and CMI.

[1] Thomas Schultz and Cédric Dupont, 'Investment Arbitration: Promoting the Rule of Law or Over-Empowering Investors? A Quantitative Study' (2015) 25(4) *EJIL* 114.

show distinct differences between how cases are decided according to the ICSID Convention and UNCITRAL Arbitration Rules, whether in outcomes, duration and actors involved – yet many empirical analyses are or were still based only on ICSID cases.[2] Historiographies of the debate can become equally obsolete. Over time, critiques of the system have shifted from regime to regime, state to state, and institution to institution, with new issues and concerns emerging and fading.

In this chapter, we therefore seek to provide a survey of the state-of-the-art about the entire investment regime and discourse from a quantitative and qualitative perspective. We ask: What is the state of ISDS in investment treaties? What is the pattern of ISDS arbitration across time? What is the nature of the legitimacy crisis in ISDS? And finally, what is the ISDS regime doing to survive the storm?

The chapter proceeds as follows. Section 2.2 maps consent to arbitration in the modern international investment law regime, not on a generic per signed bilateral investment treaty (BIT) basis, but rather on the basis of bilateral and unilateral ISDS relationships up to 1 January 2020. The purpose is to foreground more precisely the exposure that a state has and the opportunities that investors have in regard to future ISDS disputes.

Section 2.3 moves from sketching the legal framework for the ISDS regime to a description and overview of the default dispute settlement system in IIAs: investment treaty arbitration and its over 1,100 registered cases up to January 2020. This section provides a quantitative overview of ISDS cases as based on approximately 20 variables most frequently discussed in the discourse, *inter alia*: case outcome, rules, institution, parties, economic sector and legal basis.

Section 2.4 then moves to trace and analyse the discontents with ISDS regime up to January 2020. From a largely qualitative perspective, we then chart where the legitimacy crisis in the current ISDS came from, how it developed and what particular events may have triggered reform efforts and self-regulation from within. We identify five discrete periods that are marked by shifts in the intensity of, and focus on, the legitimacy crisis in ISDS: beginning, building, maturity, reflection and reform.

---

[2] For a critique of sample selection, see Malcolm Langford, Daniel Behn and Runar Lie, 'The Revolving Door in International Investment Arbitration' (2017) 20(2) *JIEL* 301; Daniel Behn, Tarald Laudal Berge and Malcolm Langford, 'Poor States or Poor Governance? Explaining Outcomes in Investment Treaty Arbitration' (2018) 38(3) *Nw. J. Int'l L. & Bus.* 333.

THE INVESTMENT REGIME AND ITS DISCONTENTS   41

In section 2.5, we provide a concluding perspective on the dynamics of the ISDS regime today. We include a brief overview of the scholarship that has focused on the recursive or reflexive effect that the legitimacy critique has had on the pattern of positive evolutionary changes to ISDS in the past few years.

To be sure, all this analysis is only current at the date of publication. Whether it is the investment treaty regime, ISDS or the debate, it will continue to metamorphize – not least due to multilateral reform processes. But we hope that the chapter provides a snapshot in time in the year 2020 and underscores the importance of basing future empirical research on the 'actually existing' regime.

2.2   Mapping Exposure and Access to Investor–State Dispute Settlement

The complexity of international investment law is a key reason for the rise in empirical attempts to map the investment treaty ecosystem. One field of research focuses on the substantive features of the treaties. Using traditional quantitative methods, scholars have coded systematic features of the regime[3] and analysed, for example, the evolution of treaty drafting.[4] Others have used computational methods to analyse the textual patterns in drafting[5] and changes over time.[6] For example, Alschner and Panford-Walsh find that the NAFTA 2.0 treaty (USMCA) 'does not usher in a new era in the design of trade agreements' and despite the

---

[3] See UNCTAD International Investment Agreements (IIA) Navigator <investmentpolicy.unctad.org/international-investment-agreements>; Design of Trade Agreements (DESTA) <designoftradeagreements.org>; and the Electronic Database of Investment Treaties (EDIT) <wti.org/institute/news/500/new-desta-dataset-project-launched>. The latter is a new systematic and comprehensive database on IIAs, including available texts in one single language (English) and format (XML).

[4] Tarald Berge and Wolfgang Alschner, 'Reforming Investment Treaties: Does Treaty Design Matter?' *Investment Treaty News* (17 October 2018) <iisd.org/itn/2018/10/17/reforming-investment-treaties-does-treaty-design-matter-tarald-laudal-berge-wolfgang-alschner>: 'if we are mainly concerned with the risk of investment arbitration claims, clarifying the language of substantive clauses, adding new flexibilities or reining in arbitrator discretion is not necessarily a panacea. What seems to matter is the actual presence of substantive obligations and how many investors these obligations cover.'

[5] Wolfgang Alschner et al., 'Champions of Protection? A Text-as-Data Analysis of the Bilateral Investment Treaties of GCC Countries' (2016) 5(3) *Int'l Review of Law*.

[6] Wolfgang Alschner, 'Locked in Language: Historical Sociology and the Path Dependency of Investment Treaty Design', in Moshe Hirsch and Andrew Lang (eds.), *Edward Elgar Research Handbook on the Sociology of International Law* (Edward Elgar, 2017), ch. 17.

'Trump administration's anti-TPP rhetoric and actions' – it borrows 'more than half its text' from the Trans-Pacific Partnership (TPP).[7]

Another field of research focuses on the presence of *ISDS provisions* in IIAs, which can serve different purposes. Prior to the IIAs we have today, the history of treaty-based protection of foreign direct investment (FDI) goes back to the mid-1700s. However, the protection of foreign investors' rights through treaties combined with consent to ISDS emerged only after the Second World War.[8] Research on these provisions ranges from seeking to understand the emergence of and variation among ISDS provisions in IIAs, to testing whether the presence of such provisions affect FDI and the domestic rule of law. The extent to which states sign on to IIAs containing ISDS provisions is particularly relevant to trace trends in their policy choices regarding the negotiation and design of IIAs. In this section, we describe and analyse the presence of ISDS provisions in IIAs. Our starting point is the traditional one – as set out in figure 2.1[9] – the number of signed IIAs per year.

The current regime of IIAs was negotiated during the periods of decolonization and emergence of new states and economies in Eastern Europe and Asia. Unlike many other international legal regimes, the current version of international investment law is built on a network of 2,901 signed bilateral investment treaties (BITs), 384 signed regional[10] and bilateral free trade agreements with investment chapters (FTAs) and seven multilateral investment treaties (MITs)[11] that provide private

---

[7] Wolfgang Alschner and Rama Panford-Walsh, 'How Much of the Transpacific Partnership is in the United States-Mexico-Canada Agreement?' *Ottawa Faculty of Law Working Paper No. 2019-28*.

[8] Ole Kristian Fauchald and Daniel Behn, 'World Peace and International Investment: The Role of Investment Treaties and Arbitration', in Cecilia Bailliet (ed.), *Research Handbook on International Law and Peace* (Edward Elgar, 2019), 182, 191 and 202–5. See also Kate Miles, *The Origins of International Investment Law: Empire, Environment, and the Safeguarding of Capital* (Cambridge University Press, 2013).

[9] UNCTAD IIA Navigator (n. 3), data at 1 January 2020.

[10] Prominent examples of treaties in force include: North American Free Trade Agreement (NAFTA) (1994); Dominican Republic-Central American Free Trade Agreement (DR-CAFTA) (2005); Comprehensive and Progressive Agreement for Trans-Pacific Partnership (CPTPP) (2018), replacing the TPP; US-Mexico-Canada Agreement (USMCA) (2020) replacing NAFTA.

[11] Arab League Investment Agreement (1980); Agreement on Promotion, Protection and Guarantee of Investment among Member States of the Organisation of the Islamic Conference (OIC Agreement) (1981); Commonwealth of Independent States Investor Rights Convention (Moscow Convention) (1992); Energy Charter Treaty (ECT) (1998) 2080 UNTS 95; Association of South-East Asian Nations Comprehensive Investment

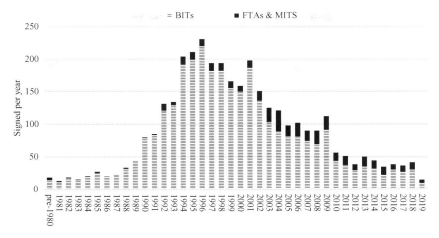

Figure 2.1 Signed IIAs (1980–2019)

foreign investors with beneficiary rights aimed at the protection of their investments abroad.[12] While each IIA is a stand-alone treaty with considerable textual diversity, agreements typically include similar standards of investment protection, including ISDS provisions.

Figure 2.1 shows the extent to which states have engaged in the drafting and signing of new IIAs the past four decades. The first of the current generation of IIAs was signed between Germany and Pakistan in 1957. By 1980, states had signed a total of 179 IIAs. Figure 2.1 indicates a bell-shaped curve and shows that the major expansion of IIAs occurred in the immediate post–Cold War period followed by a decline in the last two decades. The rapid expansion of IIAs following the collapse of the Soviet Union in the late 1980s coincided with a consolidation of the neoliberal economic world order aimed at promoting market liberalization through increased cross-border trade and foreign capital flows, the so-called 'Washington Consensus'.

The *signature-based* mapping provides an important policy perspective on states choices regarding the negotiation, conclusion and content of IIAs. While states are bound under the Vienna Convention on the Law of Treaties (VCLT) not to frustrate the objectives of signed but unratified treaties, it is

---

Agreement (ASEAN Agreement) (2009); ECOWAS Supplementary Act on Investments (2008); SADC Investment Protocol (2010).

[12] UNCTAD IIA Navigator (n. 9).

clear that a signed IIA – absent relatively unique 'provisional application' provisions such as in the Energy Charter Treaty (ECT) – will not provide a basis for consent to ISDS.[13] For the purpose of mapping access to ISDS, the *only* relevant legal mapping is one that is *ratification-based* and includes only IIAs that are both ratified and provide access to ISDS.[14]

In the remainder of this section, we will proceed with the complex task of mapping the IIA universe as seen through this ratification prism based on bilateral ISDS relationships. Thereafter, we supplement this picture by adding unilateral consent to ISDS through domestic FDI legislation. There exists no such mapping to date. Our primary objective is to establish a baseline for analyses of a states' exposure and investors' access to ISDS.

It took more than a decade from the signing of the first BIT until the first treaty with consent to ISDS entered into force – the BIT between Italy and Chad entered into force in September 1969.[15] Given that not all IIAs are ratified or provide consent to ISDS, and that many FTAs and MITs include multiple state parties, counting IIAs on the basis of a signed treaty could both overestimate and underestimate global exposure to ISDS, respectively. We therefore move our unit of analysis from the number of signed IIAs to the number of bilateral ISDS relationships in force. Starting with the universe of all signed IIAs, we first remove the 642 IIAs (20%) that have not yet entered into force.[16] Next, we remove all IIAs in force that do not provide consent to ISDS, which is approximately 10% in BITs and 70% in FTAs.[17] This reduces our initial IIA universe from 3,291 to approximately 2,000. Next, we count the number of bilateral ISDS relationships established by MITs and distribute them according to the year in which the bilateral ISDS relationship came into force (not necessarily the same as the year in which the treaty entered into force).

---

[13] An ISDS tribunal's *rationae temporis* jurisdiction is often based on disputes arising after the underlying treaty enters into force. Further, in a somewhat embarrassing series of events, an ISDS recently dismissed a case for lack of jurisdiction after determining there was insufficient proof that the IIA – upon which the ISDS case was brought – ever entered into force. See Lisa Buhmer, 'Analysis: In Besserglik v. Mozambique, arbitrators found insufficient evidence that the Mozambique-South Africa BIT ever entered into force' *IA Reporter* (19 November 2019).

[14] UNCTAD IIA Navigator (n. 9).

[15] It is possible that consent to ISDS was included in an earlier BIT, i.e. the BIT between Egypt and Kuwait (1966), but the text remains unavailable. Consent to ISDS was also included in a BIT between the Netherlands and Indonesia signed in 1968, but this treaty did not enter into force until 1971.

[16] UNCTAD IIA Navigator (n. 3), data at 1 January 2019.

[17] Ibid.

THE INVESTMENT REGIME AND ITS DISCONTENTS 45

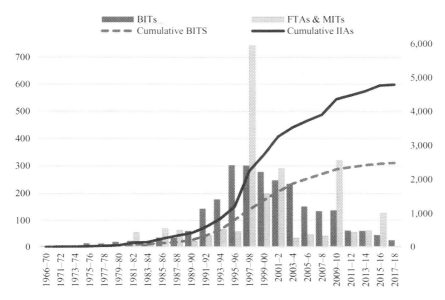

Figure 2.2 Bilateral ISDS relationships in BITs, FTAs and MITs (1966–2019)

Figure 2.2[18] presents all bilateral ISDS relationships established through IIAs since 1966. This includes all treaties in force that include consent to ISDS, demonstrating that FTAs and MITs together establish almost the same number of bilateral ISDS relationships as BITs (due to many of them being multilateral treaties). Five major multilateral treaties[19] establish nearly 2,500 bilateral ISDS relationships alone.[20]

---

[18] Ibid. There is some uncertainty regarding consent to ISDS in a number of IIAs since the texts of 163 IIAs in force are unavailable. We have gained access to some of these treaties and made our best qualified guess regarding consent to ISDS for the remaining IIAs based on the practice among treaty parties at the relevant time. When in doubt, we have counted the ISDS relationship (this is the reason why our numbers go back to 1966 despite our finding that the first BIT with ISDS consent entered into force in 1969).

[19] These are (bilateral ISDS relationships in brackets): the ECT (1,272); OIC Treaty (351); Arab Investment Agreement (210 which significantly overlap with the OIC Agreement); the 2008 ECOWAS Supplementary Act on Investments (105); and the 2010 SADC Investment Protocol (91). The number of parties for the respective treaties are 51 (ECT), 27 (OIC), Arab (21), 15 (ECOWAS) and 14 (SADC), but the figure for bilateral relationships for the ECT is reduced by three (from 1275 to 1272) due to Russia's withdrawal in 2009.

[20] Four overlapping ISDS relationships can be found among Eastern European and Central Asian states. Investors from Belarus, Kazakhstan, Kyrgyzstan and Tajikistan might have the opportunity to choose among four IIAs.

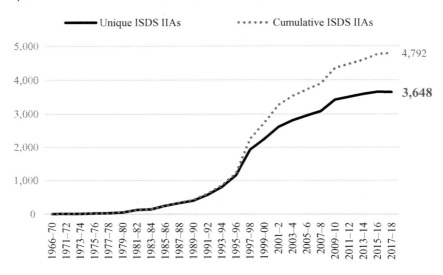

Figure 2.3 Unique versus all bilateral ISDS relationships in IIAs (1966–2019)

Figure 2.2[18] also shows the remarkable impact of the entry into force of the ECT in 1998 – establishing almost 750 new bilateral ISDS relationships.[21] Combined, all IIAs had established 4,792 bilateral ISDS relationships as the beginning of 2019. Counting this way includes overlapping bilateral ISDS relationships, which has occurred since 1988 and spiked with the entry into force of ECT in 1998. In order to correct for this, figure 2.3 counts only the establishment of *new* bilateral ISDS relationships over time. By the beginning of 2019, the number of *unique* bilateral ISDS relationships had reached 3,648.

Figure 2.3[22] also shows how the *aggregate* number of new bilateral ISDS relationships is markedly higher (the dotted line) than the number of *unique* bilateral ISDS relationships, illustrating the increasing existence of overlapping bilateral ISDS relationships. Currently, IIAs establish more than 1,100 overlapping bilateral ISDS relationships. This means that an investor may have no IIA, one IIA or a choice of two, three and even four IIAs for resolving investment disputes with a specific host state.[23] This

---

[21] We acknowledge that the ECT is sector-specific and therefore limited in its scope of application.
[22] UNCTAD IIA Navigator (n. 16).
[23] See n. 20 above. Three caveats about overlapping ISDS relationships should be noted: (1) not all overlapping treaties are identical in the levels and scope of protection provided; (2)

phenomenon represents an infrequently discussed form of 'treaty shopping'.[24] However, while we have seen a number of cases invoking a BIT and the ECT or a BIT and the OIC Treaty, foreign investors typically invoke only one treaty per case; and there is not a single known ISDS case of a foreign investor losing a case under one treaty and then bringing an identical claim under a different treaty.

Figure 2.3 takes account of terminated ISDS relationships.[25] Such termination caused the number of unique bilateral ISDS relationships to fall for the first time, from 3,655 in 2016 to 3,648 by the end of 2018. Treaty termination with no intent to renegotiate a newer treaty is a recent phenomenon.[26] We note that approximately 200 intra-EU BITs will be terminated as a consequence of the *Achmea* judgment from the Court of Justice of the EU (CJEU), and we therefore expect there to be a downward trend in bilateral ISDS relationship in the near future – but it will not be a dramatic drop.[27]

To put things in perspective, the theoretical number of bilateral ISDS relationships is 19,503 based on 198 possible treaty parties.[28] The current number of ISDS relationships thus represents 19% of the potential. This is in general a relatively low rate of saturation. However, it tells us little about the pattern of saturation, including variations in exposure and

---

overlapping treaties did not enter into force at the same time and (3) not all overlapping treaties provide the same levels of access to ISDS.

[24] For the classic notion of treaty shopping, see e.g. Julien Chaisse, 'The Treaty Shopping Practice: Corporate Structuring and Restructuring to Gain Access to Investment Treaties and Arbitration' (2015) 11(2) *Hastings Bus. L. J.* 225.

[25] Overall, treaty termination comes as part of recent efforts by states to modify or reform their existing IIAs and not as a trend towards regime exit. This is the case for Bolivia, India, Indonesia, Czech Republic, Poland, Italy, Russia and South Africa. See Daniel Behn, 'Performance of Investment Treaty Arbitration', in Theresa Squatrito et al. (eds.), *The Performance of International Courts and Tribunals* (Cambridge University Press, 2018), p. 77.

[26] Only Ecuador has made a complete exit from the regime by terminating all treaties with access to ISDS. For a more detailed discussion on regime exit, see e.g. Malcolm Langford, Daniel Behn and Ole Kristian Fauchald, 'Backlash and State Strategies in International Investment Law', in Thomas Gammeltoft-Hansen and Tanja Alberts (eds.), *The Changing Practices of International Law: Sovereignty, Law and Politics in a Globalising World* (Cambridge University Press, 2018), p. 70.

[27] European Commission, *Statement – EU Member States Agree on a Plurilateral Treaty to Terminate Bilateral Investment Treaties* <ec.europa.eu/info/publications/191024-bilat eral-investment-treaties_en>.

[28] Potential treaty parties include all member states of the United Nations (UN) (193) and five other economies that have undertaken obligations under IIAs (Hong Kong, Kosovo, Macau, Palestine and Taiwan).

access to ISDS in light of the global economy and FDI stocks. There are six states with more than 100 bilateral ISDS relationships; and that list is considerably regional in nature, consisting of Western European states and China.[29]

In order to further explore such patterns, we shall proceed to examine the distribution of bilateral ISDS relationships among groups of states. The first feature we examine is the relationship between ISDS exposure and a state's development status. One recurrent question concerning the legitimacy of the investment treaty regime is its implications for economic development (see discussion in chapter 1 of this volume). We can observe first that the average number of treaties in each of the World Bank's Income Groups (WBIGs)[30] varies significantly. At the bottom of table 2.1, we see that high income states account for almost half (44%) of all bilateral ISDS treaty-based relationships, while low income states only account for 9%. However, the intra-WBIGs exposure is much more complex and varied.

Table 2.1 shows in detail the distribution of bilateral ISDS treaty-based relationships based on World Bank Income Groups (WBIGs) as of the end of 2018. Each entry indicates for each dyad the (1) number of ISDS relationships; (2) potential number of ISDS relationships (within parentheses) and (3) saturation of ISDS relationships in percentage terms. Thus, in dyads for high income states, there are 706 ratified treaties with ISDS exposure out of total 1,830 possible, resulting in a saturation rate of 40%. At the other end of the scale, the lowest saturation level is between upper middle income states and low-income states (8%).[31]

---

[29] There are 6 states with more than 100 unique bilateral ISDS relationships: United Kingdom (115), Switzerland (113), Germany (112), France (111), China (110) and the Netherlands (108).

[30] World Bank Income Groups (WBIGs), which are frequently used in statistical studies on economic development are based on GNI (gross national income) per capita and are used to determine states' lending eligibility. They are calculated using the World Bank atlas method, essentially a way of smoothening out the impact of fluctuations in prices and exchange rates on the state-year estimates. In practice the World Bank applies a conversion factor that averages a state's exchange rate for a given year and the two preceding years, while adjusting for differences in rates of inflation between the state and a basket of developed state economies. Economies are split into four categories: (1) low income; (2) lower middle income; (3) upper middle income and (4) high income. The thresholds between each category vary by year. See generally World Bank Country and Lending Groups <datahelpdesk.worldbank.org/knowledgebase/ articles/906519-world-bank-coun try-and-lending-groups>.

[31] We find a more diverse distribution of bilateral ISDS relationships when including FTAs and MITs than we did when only using BITs: see Daniel Behn, Ole Kristian Fauchald and

THE INVESTMENT REGIME AND ITS DISCONTENTS 49

Table 2.1 Treaty-based bilateral ISDS relationships by WBIGs[1]

	High income	Upper middle income	Lower middle income	Low income
High income	706 (1,830) *(38.6%)*	1,009 (3,599) *(28.0%)*	603 (2,867) *(21.0%)*	205 (1,891) *(10.8%)*
Upper middle income		282 (1,711) *(16.5%)*	329 (2,773) *(11.9%)*	137 (1,829) *(7.5%)*
Lower middle income			126 (1,081) *(11.7%)*	166 (1,457) *(11.4%)*
Low income				75 (465) *(16.1%)*
Total and% of parties to ISDS treaties[2]	3,229 *(44.4%)*	2,039 *(28.0%)*	1,350 *(18.6%)*	658 *(9.0%)*

[1] UNCTAD IIA Navigator (n. 16).

[2] The total number of individual state parties is 7,276.

Table 2.1 also shows that, based on consent to ISDS through IIAs, low and lower middle income states are on average significantly less exposed to ISDS than are high and upper middle income states. However, table 2.1 and the underlying data only provide a general departure point for further research on state exposure to ISDS. A further and equally important factor to explore is the extent to which states have provided unilateral consent to ISDS through domestic FDI laws. Where such consent is provided, it applies to investments from *all* other states (unless specific exemptions are included in the legislation). This means that consent provided through domestic FDI laws creates access to ISDS for investors from all other states and that such consent will only be reciprocal where another state has provided similar consent in its own legislation.

Malcolm Langford, 'A Global Public Good? An Empirical Perspective on International Investment Law and Arbitration', in Massimo Iovane et al. (eds.), *The Protection of General Interests in Contemporary International Law: A Theoretical and Empirical Inquiry* (Oxford University Press, forthcoming 2021).

Drawing on a recently created dataset,[32] we can identify 31 states which have FDI laws in place that provide some degree of protection[33] to investors combined with consent to ISDS.[34] As information about domestic FDI laws may be unreliable – in particular whether amendments have been passed, the legislation still is in force, and the translated version is accurate – our data may contain errors. Further research is needed to clarify the level of investor protection in investment legislation. Nevertheless, this dataset and our findings in table 2.2 show the importance of taking into account FDI laws when assessing states' exposure to ISDS.

Table 2.2 includes unilateral consents to ISDS that both are and are not reciprocated by other states' unilateral consents. We therefore distinguish between states that provide consent to ISDS and states that benefit from such consent. We count only consents that are additional to those included in IIAs. The states providing unilateral consents through FDI laws establish 358 new bilateral (reciprocal) ISDS relationships and 4,438 unilateral ISDS relationships. This brings the total number of consents to ISDS for inward investment to 12,408. The saturation of this type of consent is 32%, which is much higher than for the bilateral ISDS relationships in IIAs alone (19%). This underlines the importance of unilateral consent to ISDS in domestic FDI laws.

When we look at the distribution of consents, the pattern is interesting, if not dramatic, from a legitimacy perspective. First, low income

---

[32] Tarald Laudal Berge and Taylor St John, 'Asymmetric Diffusion: World Bank "Best Practice" and the Spread of Arbitration in National Investment Laws' (2020) *Rev. of Int'l Pol. Economy* <doi.org/10.1080/09692290.2020.1719429>.

[33] We acknowledge that FDI law investment protections can be much more curtailed than under IIAs. For example, there is no instance of an ISDS case brought according to an FDI law when an IIA was also available for the investor to invoke. See PITAD database <pitad.org>, data at 1 January 2020.

[34] WBIGs (n. 30); UNCTAD Investment (FDI) Law Navigator <investmentpolicy.unctad .org/investment-laws> data at 1 January 2020: Afghanistan (2002, low income), Albania (1993, upper middle), Belarus (2013, upper middle), Benin (1990, low), Burkina Faso (1995, low), Burundi (2008, low), Cabo Verde (1993, lower middle), Cameroon (1990, lower middle), Democratic Republic of Congo (2002, low), Côte d'Ivoire (1995, lower middle), El Salvador (1999, lower middle), Gambia (2010, low), Georgia (1996, upper middle), Ghana (1994, lower middle), Guinea (1987, low), Guyana (2004, upper middle), Honduras (2011, lower middle), Jordan (1995, upper middle), Kyrgyzstan (2003, lower middle), Liberia (2010, low), Madagascar (2008, low), Mali (1999, low), Mongolia (2013, lower middle), Nepal (1992, low), Nigeria (1995, lower middle), Sierra Leone (2004, low), Somalia (1987, low), South Sudan (2009, low), Syria (2007, low), Timor-Leste (2005, lower middle) and Togo (1989, low).

Table 2.2 *Investment protection through bilateral and unilateral consent to ISDS by WBIGs*[1]

			States consenting to ISDS		
Benefiting state	High income	Upper middle income	Lower middle income	Low income	No and % of beneficiaries
High income	1,412 (3,660) *(38.6%)*	1,173 (3,599) *(32.6%)*	1,079 (2,867) *(37.6%)*	1,075 (1,891) *(56.8%)*	4,739 *(38.2%)*
Upper middle income	1,009 (3,599) *(28.0%)*	801 (3,422) *(23.4%)*	814 (2,773) *(29.4%)*	1,007 (1,829) *(55.1%)*	3,631 *(29.3%)*
Lower middle income	603 (2,867) *(21.0%)*	532 (2,773) *(18.9%)*	664 (2,162) *(30.7%)*	810 (1,457) *(55.6%)*	2,609 *(21.0%)*
Low income	205 (1,891) *(10.8%)*	277 (1,829) *(15.1%)*	424 (1,457) *(29.1%)*	523 (930) *(56.2%)*	1,429 *(11.5%)*
No and % of consents	3,229 *(26.0%)*	2,783 *(22.4%)*	2,981 *(24.0%)*	3,415 *(27.5%)*	1,2408 *(31.8%)*

[1] WBIGs (n. 30); UNCTAD IIA Navigator (n. 16); UNCTAD FDI Law (n. 34). We have excluded states for which we were in doubt of whether the FDI law provided unconditional consent, and we have not taken into account countries that previously consented to ISDS and subsequently withdrew that consent (examples include Kazakhstan (1994–2003) and Mauritania (2003–12)). Each entry contains the following information: number of ISDS relationships, potential number of ISDS relationships (within parentheses), and saturation of ISDS relationships – 100 being complete saturation (within parentheses).

states have undertaken very high levels of commitments when compared to all other income groups – more than 55% on average. Secondly, the percentage of benefiting low income states is much lower than any other income group. It is striking that high income states benefit the most from commitments by low income states – saturation as high as 57% – while at the same time having made the lowest number of commitments in relation to low income states – saturation as low as 11%. We also see that while low income states score highest regarding share of commitments undertaken (28%), they score significantly lower than other states in terms of benefiting from the commitments of others (12%).

The above mapping provides a solid basis for re-examining our understanding of what constitutes the ISDS regime. It requires a new lens. Our findings highlight the importance of researching how a broader range of consent to ISDS affects the bargaining power and vulnerability of states at different levels of development. Moreover, the mapping opens new research questions. One key example is attempts to explore whether and to what extent (threat of) ISDS contributes to 'regulatory chill' in host states. Such issues cannot be addressed without taking into account all consents to ISDS, not only those contained in BITs. Our mapping of exposure to ISDS is not complete, however. One significant challenge remains regarding the mapping of states' consent to ISDS through contracts. Extensive research cooperation is needed in order to carry out such mapping.

2.3 Mapping the ISDS Regime

In this section, we turn to the invocation of the ISDS provisions mapped in the previous section and chart their increased use across time. Considering the focus of this volume and its underlying thesis on the utility of using empirical methods to address normative critiques, we provide an empirical overview of the subject-matter of this volume (ISDS cases), but in the context of establishing a baseline on where the normative critiques on the legitimacy of ISDS originate.

An interesting aspect of the development of the ISDS system is just how young it is as a means of resolving foreign investment disputes. Even as of 1 January 2020, with 1,126 treaty-based ISDS cases registered, the system has been actively used for less than three decades. As the investment treaty regime entered the decade of the 1990s, there were 400 established ISDS relationships (figure 2.3) and the use of an ISDS provision in

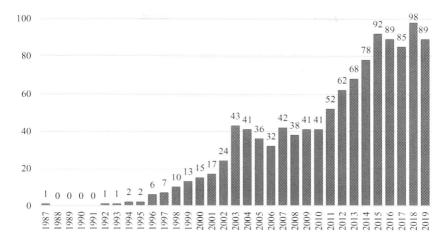

Figure 2.4 All known ISDS cases by year of registration (1,126 as of 1 January 2020)[1]

[1] PITAD database <pitad.org>, data at 1 January 2020. In the database, the 1,126 cases based on IIAs are complemented by a further 157 ICSID cases based on contracts (131) and domestic FDI laws (26). However, the ICSID contract and FDI law cases are not included here.

an IIA had only happened once.[35] In the 1990s, there is a dramatic increase in the entry into force of IIAs around the globe, with approximately 175 new bilateral ISDS relationships being established per year. However, for ISDS, the 1990s still remained a period of relative dormancy (figure 2.4). However, in what seems to be a ten to fifteen-year time lag between the marked uptick in the establishment of new ISDS relationships to the marked uptick in the registration of new treaty-based arbitrations (figure 2.5), the early 2000s put ISDS on the map as a form of international adjudication that still remained exceptional, but was certainly no longer the untested remedy it was just a decade before.

By the mid-2000s, approximately 40 cases per year were being registered and these were almost exclusively administered by ICSID. In the approximately 15 years since then, the annual number of newly registered cases rose to an average of about 70 cases per year in the early 2010s, and to an average of about 90 today (figure 2.4). A relatively new development is that the upwards growth trajectory that the ISDS regime has experienced in the past 20 years, may be plateauing at around 90 since 2015. A related feature

[35] *Asian Agricultural Products* v. *Sri Lanka* (ICSID Case No. ARB/87/3), Award, 27 June 1990, based on the United Kingdom–Sri Lanka BIT (1980).

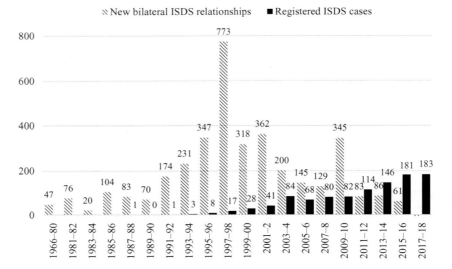

Figure 2.5 Bilateral ISDS relationships and all known treaty-based ISDS cases[1]

[1] PITAD database <pitad.org>; UNCTAD IIA Navigator (n. 16).

to its growth trajectory is the system's newness, with approximately two-thirds of all ISDS cases having been initiated in just the past decade; and about 40% in the past five years. As will be discussed, the initiation of ISDS cases raised a variety of legitimacy concerns for different actors – including resource use, vulnerabilities of targeted states, chilling effects on domestic policies, and consequences of future awards.

As the outcome of these cases have emerged, new legitimacy issues also appeared, including from compensation levels, risk of new cases, and effective restrictions on regulatory autonomy. As of 1 January 2020, of the 1,126 cases, 756 (67%) have been concluded – that is, discontinued, settled or decided by a tribunal (table 2.3). This leaves about 370 pending ISDS cases. For the past decade, the ratio of concluded-to-pending cases has been relatively constant at about three to one. In regard to awards rendered, fairly steady numbers can be observed in the past five years. Due to the structure of the ISDS system, including how long ISDS cases take to conclude[36] and how many cases are settled or discontinued, approximately 40 to 50 ISDS awards are currently rendered per year.

[36] Treaty-based ISDS cases take an average of 3.75 years to complete from registration to final award. Daniel Behn, Tarald Berge, Malcolm Langford and Maxim Usynin, 'What Causes Delays in Investment Arbitration' (2019) *PluriCourts Working Paper*.

THE INVESTMENT REGIME AND ITS DISCONTENTS 55

Table 2.3 *All known treaty-based ISDS cases by outcome (1997–2020)*[1]

Outcome Category	No.	Outcome Category	No.
Settled/discontinued	210	Discontinued	77
		Settled	133
Investor loses	284	Investor loses on jurisdiction	131
		Investor loses on merits	153
Investor wins	262	Investor partial win	124
		Investor full win	138
Case pending	370		
Total	**1126**		

[1] PITAD database <pitad.org>. Final awards on the merits are assessed as either a full win or a partial win. A full and partial win are determined based on whether the claimant-investor – in a holistic assessment of the case – was made whole by the arbitral tribunal in light of the claims presented, and not categorized according to the ratio of amount claimed and awarded or the number of successful claims.

There is a broad variety of ways to classify the outcome of cases. Here, we focus on investors' success rates. Table 2.3 shows that we can identify at least three categories of successful cases: settlements (133); partial win on the merits (124); and full win on the merits (138). Together, these categories indicate that investors have some degree of success in approximately 58% of all concluded cases.[37] However, we know very little about the results in settled cases – they might range from results where the investor is worse off than when initiating the case to significant improvements on the investor's situation. If we omit the settled cases, we find that the results in the decided cases are relatively even: investors have succeeded at least partially in 48% of cases decided (262 out of 546), and states have successfully defended 52% of cases (284 out of 546).

These outcome statistics show also that of all the ISDS cases reaching a final award, 24% are dismissed for lack of jurisdiction (131 out of 546 cases). In other words, three out of four eligible ISDS cases (i.e. those that do not settle or are discontinued) are assessed on the merits. If the case advances to the merits, though, investor success rates jump to 63% (262 out of 415 cases). In regard to investor win rates, partial wins and full wins are awarded in almost equal proportion (slightly more full wins,

[37] Taking out the known discontinued cases, this leaves us with a total of 679 cases decided or settled. If one includes settled cases as at least a partial win, then the overall success percentage for investors is 58%.

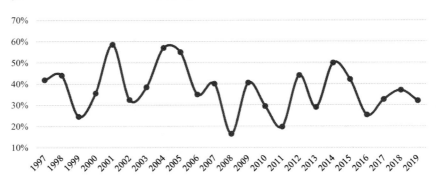

Figure 2.6 Compensation ratios for all known treaty-based ISDS cases (1997–2020)[1]

[1] PITAD database <pitad.org>. The compensation ratio is the amount claimed by an investor at the beginning stage of the dispute and the amount awarded when an investor succeeds on the merits in a final award. This ratio does not include the reductions in quantum by annulment committees, nor does it include the five ISDS cases where the investor succeeded on the merits but was awarded nothing in damages.

table 2.3). We also know that the average amount awarded in cases where investors succeed is about 38% of what the investors claim; and interestingly this number has been very consistent across time (figure 2.6).[38]

These outcomes, though, are dynamic. In the early years, investors almost always were successful at the jurisdiction stage and enjoyed high rates of success at the merits phase.[39] The win–loss ratios changed though over time (figure 2.7). The percentages for an investor win seem to have stabilized between 40% and 50% over the past decade – declining further since 2010 and then rising again from 2017.[40] More markedly, there has been a downward trend in regard to investors' ability to move beyond the jurisdictional phase where success rates have dropped to about 70% in recent years (figure 2.7). The trends towards stabilization might be due to the increasing number of treaty-based ISDS cases decided per year, but also the critique as we shall discuss in section 2.5.

The above numbers need to be accompanied by qualifications. In terms of reliability, the coding of the PITAD database includes some non-objective assessment such as on partial or full investor wins and could be subject to contestation despite having been coded by at least two coders for

---

[38] Malcolm Langford and Daniel Behn, 'Managing Backlash: The Evolving Investment Arbitrator?' (2018) 29(2) *EJIL* 551.
[39] Langford and Behn (n. 38).
[40] See detailed analysis in Langford and Behn, ibid

THE INVESTMENT REGIME AND ITS DISCONTENTS 57

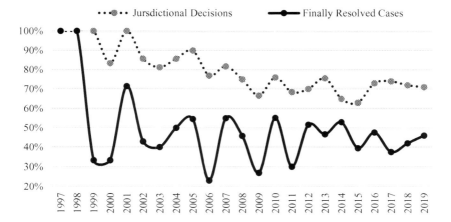

Figure 2.7 All known ISDS case outcomes by investor win across time (1997–2020)[1]

[1] PITAD database <pitad.org>. This graph shows two categories: first, it shows just jurisdictional decisions in all cases (bifurcated and non-bifurcated cases); and, second, finally resolved cases, which includes cases rendering a final award (i.e. investors achieve partial or full win, the states successfully defend, or the case is dismissed on jurisdiction).

reliability.[41] Further, we know that in 73% of all decided cases, the final award is publicly available, which leaves a little over a quarter that are not publicly available, and where PITAD relies on secondary information about outcomes.[42] Additionally, there are some missing cases which are obviously not included here, estimated as between 60 and 90 ISDS cases based on comments provided by the Permanent Court of Arbitration (PCA), the Arbitration Institute of the Stockholm Chamber of Commerce (SCC) and the International Chamber of Commerce (ICC) Court of Arbitration.[43]

Looking beyond treaty-based ISDS cases, we should also mention that we know little about ISDS cases based on FDI laws and contracts. The only institution that has publicized the existence of such cases is the ICSID, which has administered 28 FDI law- and 129 contract-based cases. The fact that other arbitration institutions are non-transparent in terms of the existence of such cases means that the relative importance and distribution over time among treaty-, FDI law-, and contract-based ISDS cases remain unknown. As might be inferred from the distribution

---

[41] See PITAD database <pitad.org>, coding information available on the PITAD website.
[42] Such as IAReporter <iareporter.com> and Global Arbitration Review <globalarbitrationreview.com>.
[43] PITAD database <pitad.org> and chapter 1 of this volume.

DANIEL BEHN ET AL.

Table 2.4 *All known treaty-based ISDS cases by institution (1997–2020)*[1]

Institutional Type	No.	%	Institutional Type (with Disaggregation of Non-ICSID Types)	No.	%
ICSID	620	55.1	ICSID	620	55.1
Non-ICSID	506	44.9	Ad hoc	217	19.2
			Permanent Court of Arbitration (PCA)	168	14.4
			Stockholm Chamber of Commerce (SCC)	70	6.2
			International Chamber of Commerce (ICC)	38	2.1
			London Court of International Arbitration (LCIA)	6	1.5
			Other	7	1.5
Total	**1126**	**100**	**Total**	**1126**	**100**

[1] PITAD database <pitad.org>.

of treaty-based cases among arbitration institutions (table 2.4), there is reason to assume that the numbers of FDI law- and contract-based ISDS cases are much higher than the numbers from ICSID might suggest. This lack of transparency remains a significant legitimacy concern.

While ICSID administered a vast majority of early ISDS cases and remains for many as synonymous with ISDS, the past ten years has seen a marked increase in the diversification of arbitral institutions administering treaty-based ISDS cases,[44] with ICSID losing market share year by year. For example, of the 89 new cases registered in 2019, ICSID registered 38 cases or 42%, significantly lower than its overall share of cases (55%). There are two explanations for this phenomenon. The first is that the PCA has become a viable alternative institution because, even though not named in treaties, the PCA will administer disputes according to the UNCITRAL arbitration rules. The second and less significant alternative institution is the SCC, which is listed as a choice in a number of BITs but

---

[44] The choice of arbitral institution for treaty-based arbitration is frequently restricted by the ISDS provisions in IIAs. Often drafted in a list format, foreign investors can make a choice when registering a case. Typically, the list will include ICSID arbitration, ad hoc arbitration according to the UNCITRAL arbitration rules and much less frequently the choice of a commercial arbitral institution such as the SCC, ICC or LCIA.

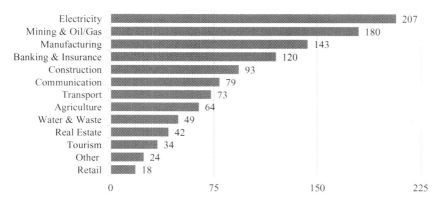

Figure 2.8 Known treaty-based ISDS cases by economic sector (1997–2020)[1]

[1] PITAD database <pitad.org>.

most importantly was included as an option in the ECT, which is by far the most frequently used treaty in ISDS cases.

This trend towards institutional diversification has a parallel in terms of the type of cases being brought. Figure 2.8 shows the distribution of the cases according to economic sectors. Historically, the extractive industries (mining and oil and gas) and other types of investments with high sunk costs were the most frequent sectors in ISDS cases. Such cases also had a particularly high investor success rate.[45] Cases within these sectors frequently raise significant legitimacy concerns, inter alia, due to the effects such investments can have for vulnerable populations in the host state. While the extractive industries and electricity sector still hold the largest share of cases by economic sector, there has been considerable diversification in the past decade with increasing numbers of manufacturing, banking and construction disputes.

Contrary to the above trends towards diversification, there has been a trend towards concentration in terms of IIAs invoked. We have seen a significant increase in resort to multilateral investment agreements, such as the ECT (149 cases) and the OIC Investment Agreement (17 cases), some investment chapters in FTAs, including the NAFTA (68 cases) and the DR-CAFTA (15 cases), as well as some frequently invoked BITs: e.g. the Argentina-US BIT (23 cases). Remarkably, these five IIAs just mentioned account for almost a quarter of all registered ISDS cases. Overall, the number of unique IIAs invoked in ISDS is a somewhat more diverse

---

[45] Langford and Behn (n. 38).

number, with a total of 382 IIAs having been invoked as of 1 January 2020; but this still leaves 80% of the IIAs in force without any cases, and the majority of the 382 treaties invoked have only been used once. The number of IIAs that have been subject to an award (i.e. not pending, settled or discontinued) drops the number of IIAs down to 189.[46]

The uneven use of treaties is also reflected in a strong asymmetry in the range of states that engage in ISDS. This topic has been at the core of significant legitimacy criticism directed towards ISDS. Investors from 95 different home states have initiated treaty-based ISDS cases. Few of these investors are repeat players, and many home states have only had investors initiate one ISDS claim. Despite this diversification, more than half of all ISDS cases (630) have been initiated by 656 investors from one of six states: United States (US) (225), followed by the Netherlands (119), the United Kingdom (UK) (107), Germany (75), Spain (68) and France (62). Some cases (those based on MITs for example) can brought by investors from more than one state, which accounts for number of cases and number of investors not being equal.

There is higher diversity in terms of those being sued. There have been 118 different respondent states in ISDS cases. All but 30 of these have been sued more than once, with 23 sued more than ten times. Six states have been respondents in 339 cases (30%). While some of the clustering of states can be explained by particular events (Argentina – 86) or policy choices (Venezuela – 68 and Spain – 58), others are less obvious as to why they have attracted so many claims (Egypt – 49, the Czech Republic – 40 and Poland – 38).

Finally, it is important to point out that, even today, treaty-based ISDS tends to be overwhelmingly initiated by investors from home states with a higher development status than that of the respondent host state – if we use the WBIGs[47] as the indicator. While 727 cases (65%) have been initiated by investors from states in a higher WBIG than the corresponding respondent state it is suing, only 37 cases (3%) exist where the investor's home state was in a lower WBIG than the respondent state (table 2.5). Moreover, 974 cases (86%) have been brought by investors from high income states (table 2.5). On the respondent side of the dispute, the development status of states is distributed somewhat more evenly, with the highest percentage (43%) of respondent states falling in the upper middle income group. However, low income states have only to a very limited degree of participated in treaty-based ISDS at all, with

[46] PITAD database <pitad.org>.
[47] WBIGs (n. 30).

THE INVESTMENT REGIME AND ITS DISCONTENTS   61

Table 2.5 Distribution of all known treaty-based ISDS cases by WBIGs[1]

		Claimant-investor home state				
		High income	Upper middle income	Lower middle income	Low income	Sum
Respondent state	High income	305 *26.9%*	21 *1.9%*	8 *0.9%*	0 *0.0%*	334 *29.1%*
	Upper middle income	405 *36.2%*	53 *4.7%*	8 *0.9%*	0 *0.0%*	466 *43.0%*
	Lower middle income	236 *20.9%*	55 *4.9%*	4 *0.2%*	0 *0.0%*	295 *26.8%*
	Low income	28 *2.9%*	3 *0.2%*	0 *0.0%*	0 *0.0%*	31 *3.1%*
Sum		974 *86.3%*	134 *11.9%*	20 *2.0%*	0 *0.0%*	1126 *100.0%*

PITAD database <pitad.org>.

no case being initiated by their investors and having acted as respondent in only 31 cases (3%). These asymmetries are sharpened, as discussed in Chapters 1 and 10, by the higher loss rates for developing states.

2.4 Charting the Legitimacy Discourse

2.4.1 Overview

The ISDS system has gone from infancy through adolescence to maturity, and, in doing so, has brought with it – almost from the very beginning – an undercurrent of critical commentary as to its legitimacy. This sustained criticism, which was partly a continuation of previous discourses on IIAs, has precipitated a backlash from many states and a wide array of stakeholders,[48] which in turn has resulted in what is commonly referred to as a legitimacy crisis.[49] It has become a defining feature of the regime

---

[48] See the overview in Langford, Behn and Fauchald (n. 26).

[49] Possibly as a result of Franck's aptly titled piece in 2005. Susan D. Franck, 'The Legitimacy Crisis in Investment Treaty Arbitration: Privatizing Public International Law through Inconsistent Decisions' (2005) 73 *Fordham Law Review* 1521.

as its use has increased dramatically from the mid-2000s and in turn has motivated efforts towards reform. In some ways, the emergence of the ISDS regime is a classic story of the growth of an inter-state system that brings with it a number of unintended consequences and is followed by a backlash that is likely to lead to significant reform or even collapse.

It is also important to recall that while treaty-based ISDS is new, disputes between foreign investors and states hosting their investments is not. States have been subject to third-party adjudicators in various fora for decades, albeit often based on contracts. Further, it is not that past international disputes involving foreign investors have not been uncontroversial, they have; and often involving violence as well, whether in the colonies or in war or through gunboat diplomacy. What is rather striking is that the recent *institutionalization* of peaceful dispute settlement mechanisms in the form of treaty-based ISDS would so decisively be seen as a step backwards. What is it about the rise of treaty-based ISDS that has transformed the discourse so dramatically; and especially so in an era marked by the proliferation of international courts and tribunals generally?

In this section, we chart the evolution of the legitimacy discourse – in regard to treaty-based ISDS, and how it has affected the evolution of the ISDS regime over time. We want to see what the crisis looks like across time and map it according to a number of rationally structured periods. We begin by providing a rough overview of the academic literature and its engagement with the legitimacy crisis discourse over the entire time period. Figure 2.9 provides a visualization, indicating that the scholarship on the legitimacy of ISDS emerged slowly at the beginning of the millennium and accelerated dramatically towards the end of the first decade.

While the legitimacy discourse on ISDS in the academic literature is about dispute settlement processes, it is significantly impacted by, and often changes course as a result of, particular events or 'lightning rod' cases. This is not an unusual phenomenon in general. It is often the case in both international and domestic legal systems that change or development of the law – or outcry from both the public and elites – is triggered by particular events or high-profile cases. Thus, while the legitimacy discourse on ISDS has been shaped by a range of cases and other events (e.g. reactions from states through treaty reforms, anti-globalization movements or civil society critiques on the use of ISDS), time and again we see single cases shaping the way that the discourse has developed across distinct periods of time. These high-profile or lightening rod cases, while not necessarily representative of the overall caseload, have always enjoyed a

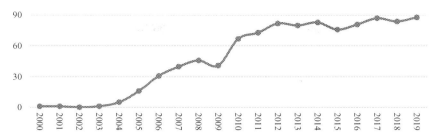

Figure 2.9 'Legitimacy', 'investment' and 'arbitration' scholarship (2000–2020)[1]

[1] Using specified Boolean search terms in Google Scholar we were able to identify the general upwards trend in use of the words 'legitimacy', 'investment' and 'arbitration' together in academic writings. While there is significant overlap – mostly where similar versions are printed in different fora – it is clear that there were no references to a single article using those three keywords prior to 2004 and that there does appear to be a spike in references between 2009 and 2010. However, one should not read too much into later rises as it is inevitable that the search terms will grab largely unrelated articles that merely cite an earlier article that includes the three keywords in its title.

high degree of influence over the discourse due to the symbolic value that comes to be attached to them. All high-profile cases have in common in that they are representative examples of one or more aspect of the regime whose legitimacy is being questioned.[50]

The evolution of the legitimacy discourse can be thus analysed through responses to specific *events* (especially cases in this context) and general *discourse* – and they are often mutually reinforcing. Several events tend to trigger discussions of legitimacy: investor threats of litigation, initiation of cases, the awards of tribunals, and state negotiation and denunciation of treaties. Such activities have contributed to increased awareness about the regime and its real and perceived legitimacy deficits. However, one should be aware of the limitations in seeking to empirically assess legitimacy claims in the context of ISDS at the systemic level by looking at specific cases. These events or cases may be mere anecdotal evidence for or against a particular claim about the legitimacy of ISDS that was

[50] A few examples include: *Philip Morris Asia* v. *Australia* (UNCITRAL), PCA Case No. 2012-12, Award on Jurisdiction, 17 December 2015; *Vattenfall II* v. *Germany* (ICSID Case No. ARB/12/12), Pending; and the Yukos cases, *Yukos Universal (Isle of Man)* v. *Russia* (UNCITRAL), PCA Case No. AA 227, Award, 18 July 2014; *Hulley Enterprises (Cyprus)* v. *Russia* (UNCITRAL), PCA Case No. AA 226, 18 July 2014; *Veteran Petroleum (Cyprus)* v. *Russia* (UNCITRAL), PCA Case No. AA 228, Award, 18 July 2014.

already percolating below the surface. They provide some evidence of discourse and debates surrounding ISDS, but cannot be relied upon as definitive. In order to ensure that high-profile cases are not used anecdotally to represent a general phenomenon, it is important to look at what any high-profile case tends to symbolize, and engage in the type of empirical research that is exhibited in this volume.

Moving to a more detailed chronology, we provide in the remainder of the section a historical narrative about the intertwined development of the practice and discourse of ISDS, which essentially maps along the same trajectory as figure 2.9, with what we argue are five distinct periods that have emerged over the past 30 years in the life-cycle of the legitimacy crisis in ISDS: precursor, building, maturity, reflection, reform. The first period can be pegged to when the first treaty-based ISDS case registered in 1987 and running to the mid-1990s ('the precursor'); the second building legitimacy crisis period starts with the early NAFTA cases and runs until about 2003 ('building legitimacy crisis'); the third begins with reforms to US policy and runs from 2004 until the Public Statement in 2010 ('maturing legitimacy crisis'); the fourth period sees a fully developed set of critiques against ISDS but also a new push towards 'mega-regionals'[51] and runs from about 2011–2016 ('reflective legitimacy crisis); and a fifth starts in about 2017 with UNCTAD's sustainable development initiative and the start of UNCITRAL WG III ('from crisis to reform').

2.4.2 The Precursor with Few Specific Concerns (1987–1994)

There was almost a 20-year gap between the signing of the first BIT with ISDS and the first ISDS case.[52] In this initial period, ICSID registered eight cases and three final awards were rendered in these cases by the end of 1994. In addition, there were two non-ICSID cases registered and no

---

[51] These included the TPP (later the CPTPP), the Transatlantic Trade and Investment Partnership (TTIP), the Regional Comprehensive Economic Partnership Agreement (RCEP) and all new post-Lisbon EU FTAs with investment chapters such as, *inter alia*, agreements with Canada (CETA), Singapore, Vietnam, Mercosur and Mexico.

[52] The modern international investment regime began primarily in the post-WWII period as a response to decolonization through the signing of BITs between capital-exporting states and capital-importing states. The ICSID Convention was signed in 1965, and while the first ICSID arbitration (a contract-based claim) was filed in 1972: *Holiday Inns and others* v. *Morocco* (ICSID Case No. ARB/72/1), and settled, the first treaty-based ISDS case was registered in 1987 and decided in 1990: *Asian Agricultural Products* v. *Sri Lanka* (ICSID Case No. ARB/87/3), Award 27 June 1990, based on the United Kingdom–Sri Lanka BIT (1980).

final awards were rendered in these cases by the end of 1994. This early period creates almost no caseload with only a few cases registered annually until the beginning of the 2000s.

The 1990s were more significant for treaty signing than litigating. There was the explosion of IIA signing directly following the fall of the Soviet Union, which would in turn provide the basis for many future ISDS cases. Additionally, the 1990s were significant for the international investment regime and for the first anti-globalization movement that followed. In 1994 alone, the WTO was established, the ECT was signed and NAFTA entered into force.

2.4.3 Rumblings – A Building Legitimacy Crisis (1995–2003)

In this second period, ICSID registered 101[53] cases and 24 final awards were rendered in these cases by the end of 2003. In addition, 35 non-ICSID cases were registered and 14 final awards rendered in these cases by the end of 2003.[54] Almost all of the 38 final awards were rendered in the period 2000 to 2003 (figure 2.4). Among the final awards, 27 were based on BITs, ten were based on the NAFTA and one was based on the ECT.

The early part of the 2000s saw some of the first ISDS cases that raised significant controversies. First, a number of cases were raised against developed states under NAFTA, of which some provided the catalyst for the NAFTA Free Trade Commission's interpretive note on the minimum standard of treatment and transparency of proceedings in 2001.[55] Secondly, several early NAFTA cases from this period raised significant concerns regarding the relationship between IIA standards and environmental policy measures;[56] and high success rates for investors in these

---

[53] This number covers all cases that are administered by ICSID, including those in which UNCITRAL's procedural rules have been applied (these cases are registered as ICSID cases but are given a reference number with UNCT instead of ARB or ARB(AF)). PITAD database <pitad.org>.

[54] Nine of these cases had no institutional affiliation, four were administered by the SCC, and one by the Cairo Regional Center for International Commercial Arbitration (CRCICA). Ibid.

[55] *Notes of Interpretation of Certain Chapter 11 Provisions,* NAFTA Free Trade Commission (31 July 2001), see Gabrielle Kaufmann-Kohler, 'Interpretive Powers of the Free Trade Commission and the Rule of Law', in Frédéric Bachand (ed.), *Fifteen Years of NAFTA Chapter 11 Arbitration* (Juris, 2011), pp. 175, 181–5.

[56] See Ole Kristian Fauchald, 'International Investment Law and Environmental Protection', in Ole Kristian Fauchald and David Hunter (eds.), *Yearbook of International Environmental Law*, Vol. 17 (Oxford University Press, 2006), pp. 3, 11–25.

cases caused great concern about how ISDS cases might chill efforts to protect the environment.[57] Thirdly, a high number of cases were initiated during this period in response to the Argentine economic crisis of 2001, a number of which still remain pending as of 2020.[58] Finally, this period saw some controversial examples of inconsistent case law, in particular exemplified by the *SGS* cases – which comprised of two tribunals that came to different interpretations of the umbrella clauses in the relevant BITs;[59] as well as the *Lauder* and *CME* cases – in which two awards were issued on essentially the same subject-matter in which the tribunals came to very different conclusions.[60]

More broadly, there was an attempt by the OECD to host the negotiations on a Draft Multilateral Agreement on Investment (MAI) that ended in failure in 1998, which – together with NAFTA – marked the start of an area in which IIAs could no longer be negotiated without the scrutiny of a broad range of interested parties.[61] Moreover, the aim of launching a new round of trade negotiations (called the Millennium Round) in the WTO, which would include negotiations of investment issues, failed in Seattle in 1999; and all investment issues were subsequently side-lined at the start of the Doha Round.[62] These failed multilateral negotiations relating to investment issues shifted the successive discourse back onto the largely bilateral network of IIAs and the increasing number of

---

[57] Daniel Behn and Malcolm Langford, 'Trumping the Environment? An Empirical Perspective on the Legitimacy of Investment Treaty Arbitration' (2017) 18(1) *JWIT* 14.

[58] See José Alvarez and Kathryn Khamsi, 'The Argentine Crisis and Foreign Investors. A Glimpse into the Heart of the Investment Regime', in Sauvant (ed.), *Yearbook on International Investment Law and Policy 2008–2009* (Oxford University Press, 2009), p. 379; William Burke-White and Andreas von Staden, 'Investment Protection in Extraordinary Times: The Interpretation and Application of Non-Precluded Measures Provisions in Bilateral Investment Treaties' (2009) 48 *VJIL* 307.

[59] *SGS* v. *Pakistan* (ICSID Case No. ARB/01/13), Award 6 August 2003; *SGS* v. *Philippines* (ICSID Case No. ARB/02/6), Award 29 January 2004.

[60] *Lauder (US)* v. *Czech Republic* (UNCITRAL), Award 3 September 2001; *CME (Netherlands)* v. *Czech Republic* (UNCITRAL), Partial Award 13 September 2001 and Final Award 14 March 2003. See Susan D. Franck, 'The Legitimacy Crisis in Investment Treaty Arbitration: Privatizing Public International Law through Inconsistent Decisions' (2005) 73 *Fordham L. Rev.* 1521; Andrea Bjorklund, 'Private Rights and Public International Law: Why Competition Among International Economic Law Tribunals is Not Working' (2007–08) 59(2) *Hastings L. J.* 241.

[61] OECD, Draft Multilateral Agreement on Investment Negotiating Text <oecd.org/invest ment/internationalinvestmentagreements/multilateralagreementoninvestment.htm>.

[62] The decision to address the 'Singapore Issues' (of which investment was one) in the Doha Ministerial Declaration (WT/MIN(01)/DEC/1, paras. 20–2) was not followed up at subsequent ministerial meetings.

THE INVESTMENT REGIME AND ITS DISCONTENTS 67

ISDS cases that would follow. For example, one can easily see from figure 2.1 that the signing of new IIAs went into a sharp and steady decline at the beginning of the new millennium, followed by a sharp and steady rise in new ISDS cases being registered per year during the same period (figure 2.4).

Overall, this second period sent some signals, rumblings of discontent – through treaty development, a few lightning rod cases, and a small emerging critical scholarship and general commentary – that ISDS had some shortcomings that, if not properly managed, could produce unjust and illegitimate results.

2.4.4 A Maturing Legitimacy Discourse (2004–2010)

The third period is where we see the emergence of a legitimacy crisis discourse in the academic literature (figure 2.9).[63] The emerging literature focused on four topics: (1) expansive interpretation of the rights of investors; (2) implications stemming from the jurisprudence about the policy space of public authorities to regulate environmental policy; (3) a state's freedom to act in times of economic crises and (4) the need to take measures to ensure a consistent jurisprudence. Much of the literature in this period concerned the question of whether there was a crisis and how to define it,[64] but also in categorizing what ISDS itself should be defined as.[65] Moreover, most of the literature was written by legal scholars – there were few contributions from

---

[63] Charles N. Brower, Charles H. Brower and Jeremy Sharpe, 'The Coming Crisis in the Global Adjudication System' (2003) 19(4) *Arbitration International* 415; Susan D. Franck, 'The Legitimacy Crisis in Investment Treaty Arbitration: Privatizing Public International Law through Inconsistent Decisions' (2005) 73 *Fordham Law Review.* 1521; Gus Van Harten, *Investment Treaty Arbitration and Public Law* (Oxford University Press, 2007); M. Sornarajah, 'A Coming Crisis: Expansionary Trends in Investment Treaty Arbitration', in Karl Sauvant (ed.), *Appeals Mechanism in International Investment Disputes* (Oxford University Press, 2008); Charles N. Brower and Stephan W. Schill, 'Is Arbitration a Threat or a Boom to the Legitimacy of International Investment Law' (2008–09) 9 *Chicago Journal of International Law.* 471; David Caron, 'Investor-State Arbitration: Strategic and Tactical Perspectives on Legitimacy' (2009) 32 *Suffolk Transnat'l L. Rev.* 513; Michael Waibel et al., *The Backlash Against Investment Arbitration: Perceptions and Reality* (Kluwer, 2010).

[64] Devashish Krishan, 'Thinking About BITs and BIT Arbitration: The Legitimacy Crisis That Never Was', in Todd Weiler and Freya Baetens (eds.), *New Directions in International Economic Law: in Memoriam Thomas Waelde* (Brill, 2010).

[65] Gus Van Harten and Martin Loughlin, 'Investment Treaty Arbitration as a Species of Global Administrative Law' (2006) 17(1) *EJIL* 121; Benedict Kingsbury and Stephan Schill, 'Investor-State Arbitration as Governance: Fair and Equitable Treatment, Proportionality and the Emerging Global Administrative Law' *NYU School of Law Public Law Research Paper No. 09-46* (2009).

political scientists and hardly any from other disciplines.[66] The critiques of the ISDS regime frequently focused on the general claim that ISDS implied a privatization of public disputes through processes and practices derived from international commercial arbitration.[67]

The late 2000s brought to light a number of latent critiques about ISDS: that it has a problematic incentivization structure that results in targeting of particular states and economic sectors; that the characteristics of ISDS procedures are biased against developing states and favour powerful investors; that a system of adjudication based on party-appointed arbitrators is unsuitable for public law disputes; that ISDS is not sufficiently transparent and inclusive of third-party participation; that ISDS directly or indirectly prevents states from implementing measures in the public interest (regulatory chill); that the costs to litigate an ISDS case is unsustainable; that ad hoc tribunals with no appellate mechanism would produce inconsistent and incoherent awards across time; that ISDS tribunals do not sufficiently balance investor rights with other areas of international law such as human rights or environmental protection; that there are significant challenges regarding compliance with arbitral awards; and that ISDS protects foreign investors' rights with no corresponding responsibilities.[68]

From 2004 up to the end of the decade, the annual number of cases filed per annum stabilized at around 40 (figure 2.4). From 2004 to 2009, a total of 271 treaty-based ISDS cases were registered and 94 final awards were rendered;[69] and the cases were distributed over most of the world (but already also seen to be targeting particular geographic areas and marked by an almost complete absence in Asia), covering a wide array of subject-matters. The final awards were overwhelmingly based on BITs (76), some were based on NAFTA (12), and the ECT (7) starts to produce

---

[66] See Chapter 1 of this volume. This is a reference to the ISDS regime specifically, not the investment treaty regime. One of the first pieces specifically focused on the effect of ISDS cases does not come until relatively late in the legitimacy crisis discourse: Lauge N. Skovgaard Poulsen and Emma Aisbett, 'When the Claim Hits: Bilateral Investment Treaties and Bounded Rational Learning' (2013) 65 *World Pol.* 273.

[67] Bjorklund (n. 60).

[68] Langford and Behn (n. 38).

[69] The numbers are as follows: nine in 2004; nine in 2005; 13 in 2006; 19 in 2007; 21 in 2008; and 23 in 2009. These numbers do not include cases where a decision on jurisdiction was followed by settlement or discontinuance of the case (in total 17 cases). PITAD database <pitad.org>.

THE INVESTMENT REGIME AND ITS DISCONTENTS 69

its first awards in this period.[70] The cases continued to be administered mostly by ICSID (69), but four other arbitration institutions were also active (12),[71] and a number of ad hoc cases were decided by tribunals without institutional affiliation (13).

There are a number of ISDS cases decided during this period that are important in their own right, but some also come to symbolize particular critiques of the system and catalyse state response, either by starting to redesign their treaties or shifting their litigation strategies. This third period most importantly starts to see awards rendered as a result of the Argentinian economic crisis,[72] and these cases produced a large amount of commentary.[73] While this commentary largely focused on whether and to what extent a state of necessity could excuse the Argentinean acts, it also generated a debate that had been percolating: the perception that ISDS is biased in favour of foreign investors.[74] Other lightning rod cases initiated or resolved during this period include cases against Venezuela following the passage of various nationalization laws;[75] the *Aguas del Tunari* case against Bolivia[76] that sparked the infamous water wars of

---

[70] The first award rendered under the ECT was based both on a BIT and the ECT: *Plama Consortium* v. *Bulgaria* (ICSID Case No. ARB/03/24), Award 27 August 2008.

[71] These include two LCIA cases, six SCC cases, one ICC case and three PCA cases.

[72] *CMS Gas Transmission* v. *Argentina* (ICSID Case No. ARB/01/8), Award 12 May 2005; *Azurix* v. *Argentina* (ICSID Case No. ARB/01/12), Award 14 July 2006; *Siemens* v. *Argentina* (ICSID Case No. ARB/02/8), Award 6 February 2007; *Enron and Ponderosa Assets* v. *Argentina* (ICSID Case No. ARB/01/3), Award 22 May 2007; *LG&E Energy* v. *Argentina* (ICSID Case No. ARB/02/1), Award 25 July 2007; *Sempra* v. *Argentina* (ICSID Case No. ARB/02/16), Award 28 September 2007; *BG Group* v. *Argentina* (UNCITRAL), Award 24 December 2007; *Continental Casualty* v. *Argentina* (ICSID Case No. ARB/03/9), Award 5 September 2008; *National Grid* v. *Argentina* (UNCITRAL), Award 3 November 2008. Not all of the awards involving Argentina were connected to the measures it took in response to the economic crisis.

[73] See e.g. Alvarez and Khamsi (n. 58); Burke-White and von Staden (n. 58).

[74] While Argentina lost most of the cases that were concluded during the period, it also developed a large in-house capacity in defending itself. Many Argentinean cases dragged on for more than a decade, and Argentina refused to comply with the final awards rendered against it. Eventually a number of deals were struck to settle outstanding debts in relation to a number of final awards but not before causing concern about the limits on the automatic enforcement of ICSID awards.

[75] *ConocoPhillips* v. *Venezuela* (ICSID Case No. ARB/07/30), pending; *Eni Dación* v. *Venezuela* (ICSID Case No. ARB/07/4), settled; *Venezuela Holdings and others* v. *Venezuela* (ICSID Case No. ARB/07/27), Award 9 October 2014; *CEMEX Caracas Investments* v. *Venezuela* (ICSID Case No. ARB/08/15), settled; *Holcim, Holderfin and Caricement* v. *Venezuela* (ICSID Case No. ARB/09/3), settled.

[76] *Aguas del Tunari* v. *Bolivia* (ICSID Case No. ARB/02/3), Decision on jurisdiction 21 October 2005.

Cochabamba; and the *Foresti* case against South Africa that attacked legislation seeking to correct apartheid-era policies.[77]

In each of these situations, the sued state modified its approach to the ISDS regime in varying degrees, which in turn sent signals to stakeholders and the academic community that in some ways the *status quo* was not sustainable. In 2007, following the registration of the *Foresti* case, South Africa conducted a full and comprehensive review of its IIA policy, which resulted in a 2009 announcement that it would generally be refraining from entering into new IIAs, it would terminate existing IIAs and offer renegotiation on the basis of a new model, and it would adopt a new Foreign Investment Act that would provide clear domestic remedies for investors.[78] Also during this period, a perception began to emerge that the international investment regime unfairly targeted Latin American states.[79] While none of the major cases against Venezuela, Ecuador or Bolivia[80] were decided during this period, the upsurge in ISDS cases being filed had a significant signalling effect for the legitimacy discourse. These cases led to the denunciation of the ICSID Convention by Bolivia in 2007, Venezuela in 2009 and Ecuador in 2012.

Turning to scholarly discourse, the tail end of the third period is marked by significant signals from academia, primarily exemplified by the *Public Statement on the International Investment Regime* (Public Statement). The Public Statement was signed by 76 academics, and states the following:

> We have a shared concern for the harm done to the public welfare by the international investment regime, as currently structured, especially its hampering of the ability of governments to act for their people in response to the concerns of human development and environmental sustainability ... Investment treaty arbitration as currently constituted is not a fair, independent, and balanced method for the resolution of investment disputes and therefore should not be relied on for this purpose. There is a strong moral as well as policy case for governments to withdraw from investment treaties and to oppose investor-state arbitration, including by refusal to pay arbitration awards against them

---

[77] *Piero Foresti and others* v. *South Africa* (ICSID Case No. ARB(AF)/07/01), Award 4 August 2010.

[78] *Bilateral Investment Treaty Policy Framework Review* Republic of South Africa, Department of Trade and Industry (2009) <info.gov.za/view/DownloadFileAction?id= 103768>.

[79] Catherine Titi, 'Investment Arbitration in Latin America: The Uncertain Veracity of Preconceived Ideas' (2014) 30(2) *Arb. Int'l.* 357.

[80] Eight cases were filed between 2005 and 2010. PITAD database <pitad.org>.

where an award for compensation has followed from a good faith measure that was introduced for a legitimate purpose. [81]

Overall, scholarly literature changes in character and intensity during the period. Criticism of the regime begins to move away from legalistic discussions of particular legal rules or the outcomes in particular cases and towards macro-critiques of the legitimacy of the regime.[82] By the late 2000s, critiques of the regime have moved away from a treaty-based policy discourse about whether IIAs deliver on their intended promise of increasing FDI flows to destination states, to a case-based policy discourse on the problems arising out of the increasing annual caseload of ISDS cases.[83] In focusing on the ISDS disputes themselves, the first series of critical views started to spread about the types of states being sued, who is bringing these suits, what is their development status, and if there is a correlation.

2.4.5 Reflective Legitimacy Crisis (2011–2016)

A fourth period is identifiable as including the following: (1) a significantly increasing number of ISDS cases initiated and decided; (2) a proliferation of annulment proceedings; (3) an intensification of the legitimacy discourse among scholars, including the emergence of literature that questioned or strengthened the empirical basis for claims regarding legitimacy and increasing focus on means to remedy legitimacy deficits and (4) shifts in state policy towards IIAs, including a significant

---

[81] *Public Statement on the International Investment Regime* (31 August 2010) <osgoode.yorku .ca/ public-statement/documents/Public%20Statement%20%28June%20201129.pdf>.

[82] See overview in Behn, Fauchald and Langford (n. 26).

[83] For the econometric-based scholarship arising from the early treaty-based policy focus, see footnote 32 in Chapter 1 of this volume; and for the later case-based scholarship, see Susan D. Franck, 'The Nature and Enforcement of Investor Rights under Investment Treaties: Do Investment Treaties Have a Bright Future?' (2005) 12 *University of California Davis Journal of International Law and Politics* 47; Ole Kristian Fauchald, 'The Legal Reasoning of ICSID Tribunals: An Empirical Analysis' (2007) 19(2) *EJIL* 301; Jeffrey Commission, 'Precedent in Investment Treaty Arbitration: A Citation Analysis of Developing Jurisprudence' (2007) 24(2) *J. Int'l Arb.* 129; Gabrielle Kaufmann-Kohler, 'Arbitral Precedent: Dream, Necessity or Excuse' (2007) 23 *Arbitration International* 357; Olivia Chung, 'The Lopsided International Investment Law Regime and Its Effect on the Future of Investor-State Arbitration' (2007) 47 *VJI* 953; Susan D. Franck, 'Foreign Direct Investment, Investment Treaty Arbitration, and the Rule of Law' (2007) 19(2) *Pac. McGeorge Global Bus. & Dev. L. J.* 337; Susa For an example of the earlier discourse on investment flows, see n D. Franck, 'Development and Outcomes of Investment Treaty Arbitration' (2009) 50(2) *Harvard Int'l L. J.* 436.

DANIEL BEHN ET AL.

reduction of the signing of IIAs (Figure 2.1) and the emergence of the EU as an IIA negotiator following the entry into force of the Lisbon Treaty.[84]

Arguably, the practice of ISDS reached maturity during this period. ISDS tribunals overwhelmingly recognized such arbitration as being carried out in the context of public international law, and a significant body of experienced arbitrators and lawyers emerges. It can also be argued that the academic legitimacy discourse is reaching maturity.[85] The period sees a dramatic increase in new publications on the legitimacy crisis from 2011.[86] The discourse increasingly focuses on exploring the extent to which claims regarding lack of legitimacy are rooted in realities or myth; and seeks possible solutions to lack of normative legitimacy. There is also a critical, but more sympathetic narrative that emerges during this period. It claims that any legitimacy crisis is a healthy part of a new regime, and that the 'growing pains' or 'adolescence crisis' was

---

[84] The Lisbon Treaty conferred competence to the EU in the area of foreign direct investment for the first time. This new competence has manifested through the initiation of a number of FTAs with investment chapters at the EU level. Treaty of Lisbon Amending the Treaty on European Union and the Treaty Establishing the European Community (Treaty of Lisbon), 13 December 2007, 2007/C 306/01.

[85] See generally Thomas Schultz and Niccolò Ridi, 'Arbitration Literature', in Thomas Schultz and Federico Ortino (eds.), *Oxford Handbook of International Arbitration* (Oxford University Press, 2020), ch. 1.

[86] Susan D. Franck, 'Rationalizing Costs in Investment Treaty Arbitration' (2011) 88(4) *U. Wash. L. J.* 769; Gus Van Harten, 'Arbitrator Behaviour in Asymmetrical Adjudication: An Empirical Study of Investment Treaty Arbitration' (2012) 50(1) *Osgoode Hall L. J.* 211; Stavros Brekoulakis, 'Systemic Bias and the Institution of International Arbitration: A New Approach to Arbitral Decision-Making' (2013) 4(3) *JIDS* 553; Gus van Harten, *Sovereign Choices and Sovereign Constraints: Judicial Restraint in Investment Treaty Arbitration* (Oxford University Press, 2013); Nathan Freeman, 'Domestic Institutions, Capacity Limitations, and Compliance Costs: Host Country Determinants of Investment Treaty Arbitrations 1987–2007' (2013) 39(1) *International Interactions* 54; Susan D. Franck, 'Conflating Politics and Development: Examining Investment Treaty Outcomes' (2014) 55 *VJIL* 13; Cédric Dupont and Thomas Schultz, 'Do Hard Economic Times Lead to International Legal Disputes? The Case of Investment Arbitration' (2014) 19(2) *Swiss Political Science Review* 564; Daniel Behn, 'Legitimacy, Evolution, and Growth in Investment Treaty Arbitration: Empirically Evaluating the State-of-the-Art' (2015) 46(2) *Georgetown Journal of International Law* 363; Thomas Schultz and Cédric Dupont, 'Investment Arbitration: Promoting the Rule of Law or Over-Empowering Investors? A Quantitative Study' (2015) 25(4) *EJIL* 14; Susan D. Franck and Lindsey Wylie, 'Predicting Outcomes in Investment Treaty Arbitration' (2015) 65 *Duke L. J.* 459; Gus Van Harten, 'Arbitrator Behaviour in Asymmetrical Adjudication (Part Two): An Examination of Hypotheses of Bias in Investment Treaty Arbitration' (2016) 53(2) *Osgoode Hall L. J.* 540; Cédric Dupont, Thomas Schultz and Merih Angin, 'Political Risk and Investment Arbitration: An Empirical Study' (2016) 7(1) *JIDS* 136.

completely normal, and, if properly responded to, would eventually lead the regime on an evolutionary path towards legitimacy.[87]

The fourth period indicates a further increase in the number of ISDS cases initiated per year, which stabilizes at more than 70 (figure 2.4). This period sees 441 new ISDS cases registered, as well as a significant increase in the number of awards rendered, stabilizing at around 25 per year, in total 158 final awards over the six-year period.[88] As in previous periods, the awards were overwhelmingly based on BITs (124), but we nevertheless see more diversity in the legal bases of the cases. The number of awards based on NAFTA remains stable (11), the number of awards based on the ECT increases significantly (16), and other multilateral treaties appear as legal bases in ten cases.[89] The number of awards in cases against OECD states decreases from 46 in the previous period to 12 in this period. The diversification of institutional affiliation was significant, with ICSID administering less than two-thirds of ISDS cases (102), the PCA (31) emerges as a significant alternative to ICSID, and the remaining cases being divided between three other institutions (12)[90] and ad hoc tribunals without any institutional affiliation (13). We also see a sharp increase in the percentage of losing parties using the ICSID annulment process – from 26% (23 out of 88 eligible ICSID awards) in the previous period to 45% (54 out of 118 eligible ICSID awards) in the fourth period.

Several lightning rod ISDS cases come to a conclusion. Many Chavez-era nationalization cases against Venezuela are fully or partially

---

[87] Chester Brown and Kate Miles (eds.), *Evolution in Investment Treaty Law and Arbitration* (Cambridge University Press, 2011); Andrea Bjorklund, 'The Role of Counterclaims in Rebalancing Investment Law' (2013) 17(2) *Lewis and Clark Law Review* 461; Alec Stone Sweet and Florian Grisel, 'The Evolution of International Arbitration: Delegation, Judicialization, Governance', in Walter Mattli and Thomas Dietz (eds.), *International Arbitration and Global Governance: Contending Theories and Evidence* (Cambridge University Press, 2014), ch. 2; Behn, ibid.

[88] The numbers are as follows: 27 in 2010; 18 in 2011; 29 in both 2012 and 2013; 32 in 2014; and 23 in 2015. These numbers do not include cases where a decision on jurisdiction was followed by settlement or discontinuance of the case (in total six cases). PITAD database <pitad.org>.

[89] These include four cases based on DR-CAFTA, three cases based on the Moscow Convention, and one case based on the OIC Investment Agreement and the Arab League Investment Agreement, respectively. Three cases were based on both a BIT and the ECT.

[90] These include SCC (eight), Moscow Chamber of Commerce and Industry (MCCI) (two), and CRCICA (one).

74 DANIEL BEHN ET AL.

concluded,[91] the 50 billion USD award is rendered in the *Yukos* cases,[92] natural resource-related cases against Ecuador are fully or partially concluded (including the *Chevron II* case),[93] mass claims cases against Argentina are settled,[94] the *Philip Morris cases* against Australia and Uruguay are both decided in favour of the states.[95] All of these cases, like the high-profile cases before, have made essential contributions to material shifts in states' policy towards the international investment regime. Without detailing each example, the effect of some these cases will be briefly charted.

In 2011, after being sued by Philip Morris, the Gillard government in Australia announced that no future IIA with Australia would include ISDS provisions.[96] While there are still a limited number of states responding with IIA reforms in response to an ISDS claim against them, this period increasingly shows state responses are a product of watching and learning from other states. However, states during this period also move towards new reform proposals focused on ISDS-related issues, such as transparency, exhaustion of domestic remedies, appeals mechanisms and selection of arbitrators. For example, the Czech Republic initiated an internal policy review, mutually terminated treaties with Italy and Ireland, and renegotiated 17 other treaties that all limited access to ISDS.[97] Romania, Poland,

---

[91] *ConocoPhillips* v. *Venezuela* (ICSID Case No. ARB/07/30), pending; *Gold Reserve* v. *Venezuela* (ICSID Case No. ARB(AF)/09/1), Award 22 September 2014; *Venezuela Holdings and others* v. *Venezuela* (ICSID Case No. ARB/07/27), Award 9 October 2014.

[92] *Yukos Universal (Isle of Man)* v. *Russia* (UNCITRAL, PCA Case No. AA 227), Award, 18 July 2014; *Hulley Enterprises (Cyprus)* v. *Russia* (UNCITRAL, PCA Case No. AA 226), Award 18 July 2014; *Veteran Petroleum (Cyprus)* v. *Russia* (UNCITRAL, PCA Case No. AA 228), Award 18 July 2014.

[93] This is a case initiated by Chevron and based on a claim that Ecuador denied justice to Chevron by permitting a lawsuit in Ecuadorian courts that resulted in an 18 billion USD (reduced to nine billion USD) verdict against Chevron for environmental damage. *Chevron II* v. *Ecuador* (UNCITRAL, PCA Case No. 2009-23), pending.

[94] *Abaclat and others* v. *Argentina* (ICSID Case No. ARB/07/5), pending; *Giovanni Alemanni and others* v. *Argentina* (ICSID Case No. ARB/07/8), discontinued; *Ambiente Ufficio and others* v. *Argentina* (ICSID Case No. ARB/08/9), discontinued.

[95] *Philip Morris Asia* v. *Australia* (UNCITRAL), PCA Case No. 2012-12, Award on jurisdiction and admissibility, 17 December 2015; *Philip Morris Brands* v. *Uruguay* (ICSID Case No. ARB/10/7), Award 16 July 2016.

[96] *Gillard Government Trade Policy Statement: Trading Our Way to More Jobs and Prosperity*, November 2011, Australian Government, Department of Foreign Affairs and Trade.

[97] Kathryn Gordon and Joachim Pohl, 'Investment Treaties over Time: Treaty Practice and Interpretation in a Changing World', *OECD Working Paper on International Investment* (2015).

THE INVESTMENT REGIME AND ITS DISCONTENTS   75

Indonesia and India also sought full-scale reform of their IIAs; the latter two states, having terminated all of their existing BITs, are attempting renegotiation.[98] Finally, the negotiations between the EU and the US on the Transatlantic Trade and Investment Partnership (TTIP) partly stuck on whether or not to include ISDS, which was primarily driven by the uneasiness about the regime in Europe after Germany was sued for a second time by Vattenfall in regard to its nuclear phase-out policies.[99] This phenomenon is reminiscent of the anti-regime sentiment that arose in the US and Canada after the early NAFTA cases.[100]

On the other hand, while some states were attempting to limit ISDS, other states were producing new agreements with ISDS provisions. The phenomenon of the 'mega-regionals' occurs during this period with the beginning of negotiations between Pacific Rim states (including the US but not China) for the TPP. Moreover, negotiations for the Regional Comprehensive Economic Partnership (RCEP) amongst almost all South and East Asian states was launched, and efforts to develop a TTIP between the EU and US were making progress.[101] In terms of bilateral treaties, the EU emerged as an IIA negotiator with third states following the entry into force of the Lisbon Treaty[102] and sought to negotiate and sign new FTAs with investment chapters (including with Brazil, Canada, India, Indonesia, Japan, Singapore and Vietnam). Brazil started signing new IIAs (but with no ISDS provisions) after famously refusing to ratify any of their

---

[98] See overview in Behn, Fauchald and Langford (n. 26); Tom Jones, 'Poland Threatens to Cancel BITs', *Global Arbitration Review* (26 February 2016). Indonesia's process commenced with its formal notification to the Dutch Embassy of its intention to terminate the BIT on its expiry on 1 July 2015. See Leon Trakman and Kunal Sharma, 'Indonesia's Termination of the Netherlands–Indonesia BIT: Broader Implications in the Asia-Pacific', *Kluwer Arbitration Blog* (21 August 2014).

[99] See *Vattenfall II* (n. 50).

[100] Charles H. Brower, 'Structure, Legitimacy and NAFTA's Investment Chapter' (2003) 36 *Vanderbilt Journal of Transnational Litigation* 37; Ari Afilalo, 'Towards a Common Law of International Investment: How NAFTA Chapter 11 Panels Should Solve Their Legitimacy Crisis' (2004) 17 *Georgetown International Environmental Law Review* 51; Ari Afilalo, 'Meaning, Ambiguity, and Legitimacy: Judicial (Re-)construction of NAFTA Chapter 11' (2005) 25 *Northwestern Journal of International Law and Business* 279.

[101] Mention of the TTIP was included in the US president's state of the union address, and an announcement of new talks by the European Commission president came the day after.

[102] See the Lisbon Treaty (n. 84).

previously signed agreements from the 1990s;[103] and Australia reversed their anti-ISDS policy and signed the TPP in February 2016.[104]

2.4.6 From Crisis to Reform (2017–2020)

In January 2017, a new President entered office in the US and immediately called an end to US involvement in the TPP and the TTIP. He also led an effort to renegotiate the NAFTA, including some aspects of its Chapter 11 on investment. The result is the USMCA, which keeps ISDS provisions for Mexico and the US but not Canada. The TPP agreement also re-emerged as the CPTPP and maintains ISDS options in the investment chapter of the agreement but with numerous limiting provisions. One of the only 'mega-regionals' surviving into 2017, the RCEP announced that there would be no ISDS in the agreement: a direct reversal of the negotiating positions at an earlier stage.

Overall, then, the past three years have seen any excitement about mega-regionals and conventional ISDS provisions in treaties dissipate. Rather, the EU has emerged as the most active player in the evolution of investment treaties and ISDS, often sending differing signals in relation to the international investment regime. On the one hand, the EU is concluding a new generation of FTAs with investment chapters, but at the same time the new treaties do not include traditional ISDS provisions. Instead, the EU has envisioned an investment court system (ICS) in its agreements to replace traditional ISDS. The EU, not content with limiting its ideas to its own treaties, has also sought to develop a multilateral investment court (MIC) through the work of UNCTIRAL WG III, which was given a mandate in 2017 to work specifically on the reform of ISDS.

While the number of state-specific reform efforts begins to wane during this period, the CJEU's 2018 Achmea decision now requires all EU Member States to terminate all of the BITs that they have amongst themselves (i.e. all intra-EU BITs).[105] Also in 2018, the Dutch government – a state with a portfolio of treaties with very robust investment

---

[103] Pedro Martini, 'Brazil's New Investment Treaties: Outside Looking...Out?' *Kluwer Arbitration Blog* (15 June 2015).

[104] Australia also ratified an FTA with Korea that included strong ISDS provisions, see *Korea-Australia FTA* (12 December 2014) <dfat.gov.au/trade/agreements/kafta/official-documents/ Pages/default.aspx>.

[105] *Slovak Republic* v. *Achmea BV*, C-284/16, 6 March 2018.

protections – released a new model BIT that rolls back many of those protections, although it is not clear whether the new model BIT could be used to renegotiate existing BITs or if that competence is exclusively with the EU now. Finally, one state succeeded in an exit strategy that no other state has managed. Ecuador became the first state to completely exit from the international investment regime.

In terms of lightning rod cases, the most predominant that are yet to be fully decided is the *Vattenfall II* case[106] against Germany and the more than 75 ECT cases relating to solar subsidies against Spain, the Czech Republic and Italy continue to be decided, but with not.[107] All of these so-called intra-EU ECT cases are doubly important in the sense that the status of using the ECT for intra-EU cases was not resolved by *Achmea*, and so uncertainty remains.

The biggest shift from 2017 onwards, however, is the fairly widespread agreement that some change to the ISDS regime is required. While some institutions (such as UNCTAD's Investment Policy Framework for Sustainable Development and the ICSID Rule Amendment Project) and some treaties (such as the ECT Modernization Project) are seeking reform, the most significant is the one at UNCITRAL in its WG III on the Reform of ISDS. From around early 2017 when UNCITRAL was given this mandate, it appears that the life cycle of the legitimacy crisis in ISDS has reached a consensus point on the need to move away from the *status quo*. What exactly those reforms will produce remains unknown in 2020, but it appears that the UNCITRAL process will continue up until at least 2024.

Peering dimly into the immediate future, our estimation is that the legitimacy crisis will persist in ISDS so long as it exists at all. However, there is some optimism about the various reform projects that have emerged; and while the next three or four years will not see major structural changes, it is possible that in a decade or more, the ISDS regime as we recognize it today will be replaced with something entirely different. Yet, many previous attempts at multilateralization of investment law and arbitration have failed, and so may these initiatives as well. And regardless of reforms, there are nearly 400 pending ISDS cases; and

---

[106] *Vattenfall II* (n. 50).

[107] PITAD database <pitad.org>; see also Daniel Behn and Ole Kristian Fauchald, 'Governments under Cross-fire: Renewable Energy and International Economic Tribunals' (2015) 12(2) *Manchester J. Int'l Econ. L.* 117.

the ISDS regime, despite nearly two decades of pummelling, has emerged surprising resilient.[108] The current system of ISDS continues to produce about 90 ISDS cases a year, and generating such a caseload supports an entire ISDS industry of arbitrators, institutions, lawyers and experts. In any event, we hope that any new period will see an even more informed discourse on ISDS.

2.5 Concluding Perspectives: The Dynamics of the Regime

After tracking the rise of ISDS and its critics, it is natural to conclude by asking whether the relationship is unidirectional. Does the critique rebound on arbitration? Some argue that the legitimacy crisis in investment treaty arbitration is merely a – *crise de croissance* – 'growing pains',[109] and as the system matures, it will evolve and adapt into a more legitimate, consistent and effective form of international adjudication. Dupont and Schultz argue that investment arbitration can follow Easton's theory whereby the input of 'key actors (namely states, investors, arbitrators and arbitration institutions)' is transformed into 'output (namely arbitral awards taken in the aggregate), with feedback loops from output to input, leading to or calling for adjustments or other reactions from these actors'.[110]

Many expect or expected that the principal change would come through unilateral and bilateral substantive treaty reform.[111] However, the material reforms to the treaties discussed above have so far had little impact on ISDS. Few cases have been litigated under the new treaties that seek to expand regulatory autonomy or restrict certain investor rights.[112] According to Berge and Alschner, the average age of a treaty that grounds jurisdiction for an ISDS claim is close to 20 years.[113] Moreover, studies

---

[108] On China's strategy, see Kate Hadley, 'Do China's BITS Matter? Assessing the Effect of China's Investment Agreements on Foreign Direct Investment Flows, Investor's Rights, and the Rule of Law' (2013) 45 *Geo. J. Int'l L*. 255.

[109] Andrea Bjorklund, 'Report of the Rapporteur Second Columbia International Investment Conference: What's Next in International Investment Law and Policy?', in Jose Alvarez et al. (eds.), *The Evolving International Investment Regime: Expectations, Realities, Options* (Cambridge University Press, 2011), p. 219.

[110] Cédric Dupont and Thomas Schultz, 'Towards a New Heuristic Model: Investment Arbitration as a Political System' (2016) 7(1) *JIDS* 3.

[111] Julian Arato, Chester Brown and Federico Ortino, 'Parsing and Managing Inconsistency in ISDS' (2020) 21 *JWIT* 220.

[112] Langford and Behn (n. 38).

[113] Berge and Alschner (n. 6).

THE INVESTMENT REGIME AND ITS DISCONTENTS 79

have found that respondent states have failed to avail themselves of new public policy exceptions in their arguments, and arbitral tribunals have ignored the new provisions or adopted interpretations reducing their impact.[114] Thus, treaty-based responsiveness will need time or more extensive reform.

A second potential arena for change is arbitrators themselves. There may be strong motives for arbitrators to evolve their behaviour in response to external critique. From the perspective of a *logic of consequence*, adjudicators will seek to optimize their goals within a constrained context.[115] Empirical and doctrinal scholarship suggests that the CJEU[116] and the WTO dispute settlement body[117] are sensitive to member state opinion, especially larger or more powerful states. The extent to which this applies in a decentralised system with ad hoc cases is partly doubtful. ISDS arbitrators can escape state critique, as it cannot be channelled against a permanent body or secretariat.[118] However, they may still incur material and reputational 'costs'. As a collective, arbitrators may be concerned about the enhanced risk of non-compliance, greater exits from the regime, or fewer or weaker treaties. At the individual level, arbitrators may be concerned about their reputation and chances of future appointment.[119] This may be enhanced if they experience challenges to their appointment, reversal through annulment procedures,[120] set-asides in domestic courts, or criticism by their colleagues or scholars.

---

[114] Wolfgang Alschner and Hui, Kun, 'Missing in Action: General Public Policy Exceptions in Investment Treaties', in Lisa Sachs et al. (eds.), *Yearbook on International Investment Law and Policy* (Oxford University Press, 2018), ch. 21.

[115] Lee Epstein and Jack Knight, 'Reconsidering Judicial Preferences' (2013) 16 *Ann. Rev. Pol. Sci.* 11.

[116] Olof Larsson and Daniel Naurin, 'Judicial Independence and Political Uncertainty: How the Risk of Override Affects the Court of Justice of the EU' (2016) 70(2) *Int'l Org.* 377; Mark Pollack, *The Engines of European Integration: Delegation, Agency, and Agenda Setting in the EU* (Oxford University Press, 2003).

[117] Cosette Creamer, 'Between the Letter of the Law and the Demands of Politics: The Judicial Balancing of Trade Authority within the WTO', *Working Paper* (2015).

[118] Malcolm Langford, Cosette Creamer and Daniel Behn, 'Regime Responsiveness in International Economic Disputes', in Szilard Gáspár-Szilágyi, Daniel Behn and Malcolm Langford (eds.), *Adjudicating Trade and Investment Disputes: Convergence or Divergence?* (Cambridge University Press, 2020), p. 244.

[119] Studies of domestic judges that are subject to reappointment processes reveal higher levels of strategic behaviour amongst this group. See Stefanie A. Lindquist, 'Judicial Activism in State Supreme Courts: Institutional Design and Judicial Behavior', (2017) 28 (1) Stanford L. & Pol. Rev. 61.

[120] Anne van Aaken, 'Control Mechanisms in International Investment Law', in Zachary Douglas et al. (eds.), *The Foundations of International Investment Law: Bringing Theory into Practice* (Cambridge University Press, 2014), 409.

Such strategic behaviour may be strengthened by a *logic of appropriateness*.[121] Shifts in stakeholder discourse may shape the 'background ideational abilities'[122] of arbitrators as they become exposed to or participate in the legitimacy debate. The crisis may also affect their 'foreground discursive abilities' and the space in which they 'communicate critically about those institutions, to change (or maintain) them'.[123] Arbitrators, arbitration institutions and lawyers may consciously evolve a new culture concerning appointment politics and decision-making. Consciously or unconsciously, new social norms emerge.

The evidence on a reflexive change by arbitrators and other stakeholders, however, is equally mixed. Doctrinal research points to an evolution of the jurisprudence, such as proportionality analysis in indirect expropriation cases,[124] but the development is partial and jurisprudence remains contradictory in some areas.[125] Empirical methods show that a sizeable sample of arbitrators themselves have acknowledged that they engage in strategic behaviour when writing decisions.[126] Stone Sweet and Grisel argue that the citation patterns of arbitrators reveal a judicial-like consciousness.[127] However, the effect on actual decision-making is mixed. Lie finds a partial change in arbitral language – reflecting

---

[121] On this empirical conundrum, see Alexandra Gilles, 'Reputational Concerns and the Emergence of Oil Sector Transparency as an International Norm' (2010) 54 *Int'l Stud. Q.* 103.

[122] Vivien A. Schmidt, 'Discursive Institutionalism: The Explanatory Power of Ideas and Discourse' (2008) 11 *Ann. Rev. Pol. Sci.* 303.

[123] Ibid. 304.

[124] See e.g. *Tecmed* v. *Mexico* (ICSID Case No. ARB (AF)/00/2), Award 29 May 2003, para. 122.

[125] David Schneidermann, 'Legitimacy and Reflexity in International Investment Arbitration: A New Self-Restraint' (2011) 2 *JIDS* 471; Jeff Waincymer, 'Balancing Property Rights and Human Rights in Expropriation', in Pierre-Marie Dupuy et al. (eds.), *Human Rights in International Investment Law and Arbitration* (Cambridge University Press, 2009), 275; Caroline Henckels, 'Indirect Expropriation and the Right to Regulate: Revisiting Proportionality Analysis and the Standard of Review in Investor-State Arbitration' (2012) 15(1) *JIEL* 223.

[126] In a survey conducted at an ICCA Congress, 262 international arbitrators, which included a subset of 67 with experience in ISDS, were asked whether they considered future re-appointment when deciding cases. A remarkable 42% agreed or were ambivalent. Given the sensitive nature of the question, it is arguable that this figure is understated. Susan D. Franck et al., 'International Arbitration: Demographics, Precision and Justice' (2015) *ICCA Congress Series No. 18, Legitimacy: Myths, Realities, Challenges* 33.

[127] Alec Stone Sweet and Florian Grisel, *The Evolution of International Arbitration: Judicialization, Governance, Legitimacy* (Oxford University Press, 2017).

discursively concerns with state regulatory autonomy – although a much greater change amongst counsel in their arguments.[128] Two of the authors of this chapter found that the significant drop in claimant-investor success across time can only be partly linked to changes in arbitral behaviour.[129]

Thus, the future of ISDS is difficult to predict. Even the ambitious procedural reforms proposed in the UNCITRAL WG III would take a long time to work through the system – requiring most likely each dyad of litigant states to have accepted the relevant procedural innovation.[130] The most likely scenario is a slowly evolving system – driven by external critique and incremental legal reforms – in which empirical evidence will be more necessary than ever in parsing claims and determining which types of reforms may be most appropriate in a changing political landscape.

---

[128] Runar Lie, 'A Self-Constituting Society of Law', *Pluricourts Working Paper 2020*.

[129] Langford and Behn (n. 38).

[130] Anthea Roberts and Taylor St John, 'UNCITRAL and ISDS Reform: Visualising a Flexible Framework', *EJIL: Talk!* (24 October 2019); Stephan W. Schill and Geraldo Vidigal, 'Designing Investment Dispute Settlement à la Carte: Insights from Comparative Institutional Design Analysis' (2019) 18(3) *LPJCT* 314.

PART I

Process Legitimacy

Independence and Impartiality

3

Testing Cognitive Bias: Experimental Approaches and Investment Arbitration

SERGIO PUIG* AND ANTON STREZHNEV**

3.1 Introduction

Most courts pre-date the questions that come before them, and decide a series of cases over a period of time. Most judges are selected through mechanisms that do not depend on the will of the litigating parties and sit on the bench for a series of cases, no matter how they vote in or decide a particular case. In contrast, international investment tribunals are established to hear individual disputes and are composed after most or all relevant facts of the case have already occurred. Investment arbitrators – the adjudicators deciding these cases – are appointed based on direct input and participation of the parties in the litigation and may or may not be reappointed, very often depending on their performance and decision.

Chiefly as consequence of this feature, international investment tribunals derive their legitimacy (or lack thereof) from unique normative, sociological and political processes. In great part, these tribunals rely on tacit norms of behavior among arbitration professionals. Understanding such tacit norms and what factors affect how arbitrators make decisions in investment disputes is essential to characterizing the broader function of the international investment law regime. In fact, arbitrator behavior is at the center of a number of current crucial debates surrounding the legitimacy of investment arbitration: Are arbitrators political? Are decisions or arbitrators biased towards the parties that appoint them? Is investment arbitration a pro-claimant or pro-respondent regime? Or, do arbitrators perceive investment arbitration as fair and balanced?

Among the most important challenges to empirically assessing these important debates is the difficulty of finding credible empirical designs.[1]

---

* Professor of Law, James E. Rogers College of Law, University of Arizona.
** Center for Data Science, New York University.
[1] Adam S. Chilton and Dustin Tingley, 'Why the study of international law needs experiments' (2013) 52(1) *Columbia Journal of Transnational Law* 173.

Empirical studies of arbitration using observational data exist, but are often limited in the sorts of inferences they can make. This is partly the result of the fact that some governments and international organizations have been slow to recognize the importance of transparency and the publication of key aspects of the process for such assessment.[2] The challenges will remain essential unless governments and institutions realize the ways in which limited available information affects empirical research in the field and adopt coordinated action to address this matter. The UNCITRAL Transparency Convention is a good first step that should be followed by further action, possibly within the new UNCITRAL reform process.[3] Moreover, observational designs will always have difficulty in making causal claims as there is always a risk that an association between a treatment and outcome of interest may be driven by some third, unmeasured, common cause.

As a way to overcome some of these challenges, in this chapter we describe a promising alternative empirical strategy that utilizes survey experiments conducted on arbitration professionals. This strategy is not a substitute, but a complement to observational data. However, it can be an effective way to overcome the limitations with data that we discuss below and expand our knowledge of implicit and explicit biases, political preferences, and attitudes of arbitrators as well as strategic choices of arbitration professionals that define the contours of investment arbitration.

As we explain further, researchers in the field can design experimental vignettes to mimic specific aspects of the arbitration process that are difficult to observe or manipulate in the real world. As an example, we present an overview of a survey experiment designed to assess how different legal and non-legal aspects of a dispute influence how arbitrators allocate costs – a question in which arbitrators typically have a high degree of discretion. After explaining this approach, we elaborate on some of the benefits and drawbacks of survey experiments and how empirical legal scholars can incorporate experiments into a broader research agenda.

---

[2] Ibid. at 210–11. See also the discussion in the preceding chapter.

[3] On the reform process, see Anthea Roberts, 'Incremental, Systemic and Paradigmatic Reform of Investor-State Arbitration' (2018) 112(3) *American Journal of International Law* 412. On the convention, see United Nations Convention on Transparency in Treaty-based Investor-State Arbitration (New York, 2014) (the 'Mauritius Convention on Transparency') <uncitral.org/uncitral/en/uncitral_texts/arbitration/2014Transparency_Convention.html>.

Before proceeding, an important point is in order: Good empirical research requires data, a suitable method and meaningful researchable questions that can be assessed empirically and can yield generalizable lessons. While some empiricists may have a preference for some methodological approaches, the decision whether to rely on experimental or observational (qualitative or quantitative) data in an empirical analysis should be based primarily on the nature of the research questions and the analysis intended. And when appropriate, a combination of methodologies may be the most powerful research tool. In this context, survey experiments may allow researchers to better understand relevant heuristics and biases of individual decision-makers, but are less effective in explaining how institutions aggregate individual preferences into observed outcomes as we elaborate in the final section of this chapter.[4]

Moreover, interdisciplinary empirical research should not be inaccessible to lawyers nor an exclusive territory for social scientists. Lawyers not trained in modern statistical methods can participate in very practical ways. Whether assisting social scientists in creating useful variables or measurements that reflect the complexity of the law in action, or designing and executing case studies to understand a social phenomenon in context without losing sight of the details and nuances that the more standardized survey approach neglects, lawyers should embrace, and not shy away from, empiricism.[5]

3.2 Empirical Research in International Investment Law

3.2.1 Lines of Research in the Field

Increasingly investment arbitration has been criticized as an illegitimate regime. While some scholars perceive the regime as a mechanism against opportunistic actions by weak states, many others believe it is a mechanism that over-empowers rich investors.[6] In this debate, what exactly is the role of the system of arbitration and the arbitrators who decide such cases hinges on important empirical evidence.

---

[4] Krin Irvine, David A. Hoffman and Tess Wilkinson, 'Law and Psychology Grows Up, Goes Online, and Replicates' (2018) 15(2) *Journal of Empirical Legal Studies* 320.

[5] Jason W. Yackee, 'Do States Bargain over Investor-State Dispute Settlement? Or, toward Greater Collaboration in the Study of Bilateral Investment Treaties' (2014) 12(1) *Santa Clara Journal of International Law* 277.

[6] For a discussion on different framings, see Sergio Puig and Anton Strezhnev, 'The David Effect and ISDS' (2017) 28(3) *European Journal of International Law* 731.

Consider the view of investment arbitration as a neo-colonial tool. For one, if the main function of the investor–state arbitration is indeed to allow developed states to exploit developing countries, then one would expect to see most cases brought by investors from developed countries against governments of developing countries. As explained by Shultz and Dupont, 'the hypothesis of the neo-colonial function is plausible, for instance, if a large part of arbitration claims is filed by investors from developed countries against governments of developing countries'.[7]

Conversely, if investment arbitration indeed helps to deter opportunistic behavior by public authorities, we should see a correlation between BITs with investment arbitration provisions with some measures of political risk, or at least corporations should consider investment arbitration as playing a major role in their companies' investing decisions abroad. Key scholarly works provide important yet inconclusive evidence to settle this quasi-constitutional debate.[8] However, there are complex methodological issues that limit the causal inferences that can be made from observational data, as we now explain.

3.2.2 Research on Biases and Its Limitations

Among the most important challenges with research in investment arbitration and arbitrator behavior is the difficulty in assigning a causal interpretation to observed associations in the data. This can be the result of a lack of a viable outcome measure, the presence of selective censoring of some outcomes due to early settlement, and non-random assignment of arbitrators to disputes.

Take, for instance, the debate over bias in the system. Some scholars and practitioners who claim bias often point to arbitrators' votes (or dissenting/separate opinions) as a principal indicator of arbitrator bias.[9]

---

[7] Thomas Schultz and Cédric Dupont, 'Investment Arbitration: Promoting the Rule of Law or Over-empowering Investors? A Quantitative Empirical Study' (2014) 25(4) *European Journal of International Law* 1147.

[8] Jason W. Yackee, 'Do Bilateral Investment Treaties Promote Foreign Direct Investment? Some Hints from Alternative Evidence' (2010) 51(2) *Virginia Journal of International Law* 396; Todd Allee and Clint Peinhardt, 'Delegating Differences: Bilateral Investment Treaties and Bargaining over Dispute Resolution Provisions' (2010) 54(1) *International Studies Quarterly* 1; Todd Allee and Clint Peinhardt, 'Contingent Credibility: The Impact of Investment Treaty Violations on Foreign Direct Investment' (2011) 65(3) *International Organization* 401.

[9] See Alan Redfern, '2003 Freshfields Lecture – Dissenting Opinions in International Commercial Arbitration: The Good, the Bad and the Ugly' (2004) 20(3) *Arbitration International* 223; Eduardo Silva Romero, 'Brèves observations sur l'opinion dissidente',

But these are imperfect indicators at best. For one, looking at individual votes in particular may obscure the true effects of arbitrators' biases. While votes are individual, decisions are not; both parties to the litigation appoint an arbitrator. As a result, some practitioners have explained that compromises or 'bartering' happens within tribunals and are often reflected in many complicated aspects of the case, for instance, the wording of decisions, the nature of violations identified, or the amount of damages awarded.[10]

This sole point should make scholars empirically looking at investment arbitration pause and carefully determine what is actual evidence of biases other than votes or damages awarded. At the very least, one should conclude that voting records and final outcomes are of limited use, especially if strategic behavior and compromises on the part of arbitrators are as common as anecdotal evidence suggests.

On top of compromises, there are other issues that can make the use of easily observed outcomes such as voting, win/loss ratio or damages awarded even more problematic from a methodological point of view. Selection effects complicate reliable inferences at many stages of the arbitration process. First, investors choose which cases they will bring, and in some instances there might be counter-claims from the government that could make the investor want to abandon the case. Hence, as in any other field of litigation, it is likely that aggravated investors file cases 'when they predict that the judges will favor them' and face limited risk.[11] Therefore, as explained by Posner and de Figueiredo, the pool of observations may not contain those cases where an arbitrator will more easily vote *against* investors.[12] Conversely, because litigation is costly, parties have incentives to settle prior to a final award when the outcome is

---

in *Les arbitres internationaux* (Société de législation compare, 2005), p. 179; cf. Giorgio Sacerdoti, 'Is the Party-Appointed Arbitrator a "Pernicious Institution"? A Reply to Professor Hans Smit' (2011) 35 *Columbia FDI Perspectives* 1, arguing that 'empirical evidence from the rejection disqualification requests confirms that the great majority of arbitrators are serious professionals', <academiccommons.columbia.edu/doi/10.7916/D8FR04H1>.

[10] Mark Kelman, Yuval Rottenstreich and Amos Tversky, 'Context-Dependence in Legal Decision Making' (1996) 25(2) *Journal of Legal Studies* 287 (describing effects of 'compromise' and 'contrast' behavior on jury decision-making); Sergio Puig, 'Blinding International Justice' (2016) 56(3) *Virginia Journal of International Law* 647, 661, 672–5 (explaining different forms of bias in ISDS).

[11] Eric A. Posner and Miguel de Figueiredo, 'Is the International Court of Justice Biased?' (2005) 34(2) *Journal of Legal Studies* 599, 613.

[12] Ibid.

relatively certain.[13] In international arbitration, particularly in investment arbitration, a great number of cases settle or are terminated prior to final adjudication – around 33 per cent – very often in financial terms impossible to know for researchers. This poses a selection problem in addition to the measurement problem of unobserved settlements. Pretrial bargaining results in a pool of final awards that does not necessarily reflect the overall distribution of cases filed. The observed equilibrium win rate of respondent versus claimant provides little information about whether the institution is systematically biased in favour of one side or the other. Finally, arbitrators themselves are not exogenously assigned to disputes.

Moreover, investment arbitration takes place in a fluid environment where investors can often choose among different dispute settlement options, many times in settings with restrictive policies regarding information disclosures and transparency: for example, commercial arbitration settings.[14] Like settlements, forum shopping may exacerbate selection issues as it can confound dispute forum with case quality and party representation – two difficult variables to control for. Combined, the selection issues resulting from filing and settlement as well as strategic choices by litigants like forum-shopping make it challenging to answer many important empirical questions using observed outcomes alone.

3.2.3 Survey Experiment as an Empirical Strategy

Many of the critical causal questions in investment arbitration are difficult to evaluate using heavily confounded observational evidence. However, some of the issues noted above can be overcome with experimental designs – rightly the 'gold standard' of social science research.[15] By randomly manipulating the relevant causal variables – for example,

---

[13] George L. Priest and Benjamin Klein, 'The Selection of Disputes for Litigation' (1984) 13 (1) *Journal of Legal Studies* 1.

[14] Richard H. Kreindler, 'Parallel Proceedings in Investment Arbitration: A Practitioner's Perspective', in Michael Waibel et al. (eds.), *The Backlash against Investment Arbitration – Perceptions and Reality* (Kluwer, 2010) (arguing that forum shopping in ISDS is inevitable).

[15] Chilton and Tingley (n. 1), 215: 'Random assignment of [treatment] solves the selection problem because random assignment makes [treatment] independent of potential outcomes.'

the appointing party in a dispute – experiments break the link between the variable of interest and all other unobserved confounding variables.

Survey experiments, which embed manipulations in survey questions in order to evaluate their effects on subsequent responses, provide a way of looking inside the decision-making processes of a specific arbitrator. In particular, experiments can yield important evidence to assess the role of specialization, that is, whether investment arbitrators make 'better' decisions or are subject to similar impulses than domestic judges, members of an international court, or international commercial arbitrators – all possible alternatives to investment arbitration. To be sure, these types of question are very complex, to say the least.[16] Leaving aside problems of what an unbiased application of the law actually means,[17] judges operate in different legal and institutional contexts that create an array of incentives that may result in behaviors often associated with 'bias'. However, by experimentally manipulating the factors that might affect a particular decision, survey experiments can assess the relevance of legal and 'extra-legal' variables in environments where these factors are not themselves subject to selection bias.

3.3 An Experiment on How Arbitrators Allocate Costs

3.3.1 Design of the Experimental Survey

To illustrate how survey experiments can help test hypotheses about arbitrator behavior, we conducted a survey of investment arbitration professionals. Within this survey, we embedded a vignette that asked survey respondents to evaluate a hypothetical arbitration scenario. The vignette asked survey respondents to imagine that they were appointed to an investment arbitration tribunal and briefly outlined the dispute, including the tribunal's decision on the merits. It then asked respondents

---

[16] See e.g. Gregory C. Sisk, Michael Heise and Andrew P. Morriss, 'Charting the Influences on the Judicial Mind: An Empirical Study of Judicial Reasoning' (1998) 73(5) *New York University Law Review* 1377, 1487–93. See Stephen J. Choi, G. Mitu Gulati and Eric A. Posner, 'What Do Federal District Judges Want? An Analysis of Publications, Citations, and Reversals' (2010, revised 2014), *University of Chicago Law & Economics, Olin Working Paper No. 508, New York University Law & Economics Research Paper No. 10-06,* 24, <ssrn.com/abstract=1536723>.

[17] Michael D. Goldhaber, 'The Global Lawyer: Arbitration without Legitimacy', *Law.com,* 7 June 2013, <law.com/americanlawyer/almID/ quoting Catherine Rogers as stating, 'no study can control for the correct legal outcome'.

about whether, and to what extent, the losing party in the dispute should compensate the legal costs of the winner.

Four elements of the vignette were randomly and independently manipulated for every respondent: the party that appointed the arbitrator, the income level of the respondent and of the claimant's home country, and the outcome of the dispute. Figure 3.1 shows an example vignette, highlighting the four areas where the vignette texts differed across respondents.

In the experimental survey, the claimant firm could either be headquartered in a high income or middle income economy, while the respondent country could be a middle income or a low income country.[18] Survey respondents could be told that they were appointed: (1) by the respondent, (2) by the claimant, (3) by the agreement of the litigating parties or (4) by an unknown party.[19] The tribunal's ruling could also take on four different conditions: (1) respondent expropriated the claimant's property (claimant wins dispute), (2) respondent did not expropriate the claimant's property (respondent wins dispute), (3) the dispute is outside the tribunal's jurisdiction (respondent wins, but not on the merits) and (4) the claimant's claims are manifestly without merit (respondent wins conclusively). In our design, each of the 64 unique combinations of the four treatment variables had an equal probability of appearing to a survey respondent and each respondent's treatment vignette was generated independently of the others.

Experiments that assign multiple randomized treatment conditions to each subject are often known as 'factorial' designs. In a 'fully factorial' design, where all possible combinations are assigned to at least one respondent, researchers can make comparisons across any two unique profiles. However, finding a sample size sufficient to estimate vignette-specific effects for moderately sized factorial experiments (such as this one) is often difficult. In our experiment, a total of 257 valid responses were received in the original experiment (plus a few responses that appeared to have a mistaken click and that were considered in the

---

[18] Since investment arbitration claimants tend to be from wealthier capital exporters and respondents tend to be developing countries, we omitted the 'low income claimant' and 'high income respondent' conditions in order to keep the total number of treatments reasonable given our sample size.

[19] In the last case, the treatment condition simply read: 'You were appointed to the tribunal'. This is what some authors call 'blind appointment'.

> Imagine an investor-state dispute being conducted under the 2006 Arbitration Rules of the International Centre for Settlement of Investment Disputes (ICSID). The claimant is a firm headquartered in a **[high income economy]**. The respondent is a country classified by the World Bank as a **[middle income economy]**.
>
> The claimant alleged that the respondent violated the provisions of a bilateral investment treaty to which the respondent is a party. Among other arguments, the claimant argued that the investor and its investments had been treated unfairly and that ultimately the respondent expropriated the claimant's investment located within the respondent's territory. The underlying dispute concerns an infrastructure project undertaken by the claimant under a concession contract with a governmental agency. The respondent argued in response that the claimant had violated provisions of the contract and that the investors received all compensation to which they were entitled.
>
> You were appointed to the tribunal **[by the respondent]**. After careful consideration of the facts of the case, the tribunal unanimously decided that **[the respondent unfairly treated and wrongfully expropriated the claimant's investment and that the claimant is entitled to compensation]**.
>
> In their submissions on costs, both parties have requested that the other party bear the costs of the proceedings in full, including legal fees and expenses. Counsel for both parties behaved professionally and ethically during the proceedings.

Figure 3.1   Sample experimental vignette showing manipulated elements

analysis to avoid inducing bias). As an integral part of the experimental design, each of the 64 unique combinations ($4 \times 4 \times 4$) of the four treatment variables had an equal probability of appearing and each treatment vignette was generated independently of the others. Because profiles were randomized, each profile appeared only one out of 64 times on average.[20] This makes it difficult to compare each unique vignette to another unique vignette as very few respondents received any one treatment vignette. Indeed, four of the 64 possible vignettes had only a single assigned respondent.

While we are unable to reliably estimate the effects of each unique vignette, thus accounting for all possible interactions across the treatments, this is not the quantity of interest. Rather, researchers using a factorial design with many attributes are typically interested in testing hypotheses relating to a *single attribute* of the vignette (e.g. the effect of being appointed by the respondent rather than the claimant). Conjoint analysis techniques provide one way of analyzing a factorial experiment

---

[20] Since many online survey experiments do not know the exact subject pool ex-ante and randomly assign treatments as respondents opt-in to the experiment, blocking respondents and obtaining exact uniformity in treatment assignment is often impossible.

94 SERGIO PUIG AND ANTON STREZHNEV

in order to estimate separate effects for each 'attribute' of a vignette. This strategy, originally developed in the field of market research for analyzing consumer preferences, has broader use within the social sciences for researchers studying how individuals make decisions when presented with a choice along multiple attributes.[21]

All this means that as long as each element of the vignette is manipulated independently, the general intuition behind experiments and randomization still holds. We can obtain unbiased estimates of the average effect of a change in a single attribute by taking the difference-in-means of the outcome between the individuals receiving a vignette with one level of the attribute and individuals receiving the other (control) level.[22] Higher-order interactions with the other treatments can be safely ignored (in terms of bias) since, by design, those treatments are independently assigned.

After presenting the survey respondents with the vignette, we asked them to state how they thought the parties' legal costs should be apportioned in the dispute. Survey respondents could choose to have the one party reimburse all or some of the other party's legal costs or have each party pay their own costs. We then asked respondents to briefly discuss the reasoning behind their decision.

Focusing on a single narrow decision like cost allocation highlights one advantage of experimental designs in studying complex legal decision-making processes by isolating a discrete choice. However, the decision to have arbitrators rule on costs was also made for practical purposes. Any experimental vignette has to strike a balance between detail and length. Respondents need enough detail in order to give realistic and reasonable responses. But if the vignette is too long, respondents will simply not have the time to participate in the experiment. We chose not to have respondents decide on the merits of the case (which may be more directly relevant to debates over bias) primarily because giving respondents enough information would have likely required arbitrators to spend hours on a vignette, a difficult demand given respondents' (e.g. international lawyers') busy schedules. We also want to maintain some

---

[21] See Paul E. Green, Abba M. Krieger and Yoram (Jerry) Wind, 'Thirty Years of Conjoint Analysis: Reflections and Prospects' (2001) 31(3 supplement) *Interfaces* 56, for an overview of conjoint methods in market research; and Jens Hainmueller, Daniel J. Hopkins and Teppei Yamamoto, 'Causal Inference in Conjoint Analysis: Understanding Multidimensional Choices Via Stated Preference Experiments' (2013) 22(1) *Political Analysis* 1, for an introduction to conjoint methods within the social sciences.

[22] Ibid.

sparsity in the vignette in order for our treatments to not get buried in a long list of minutiae. Having arbitrators decide on cost allowed us to abstract the question of which party was successful on the merits (making it one of the treatments) and instead have arbitrators rule on a more straightforward question.

Additionally, we wanted to choose an outcome that would not be over-determined by legal variables. Cost allocation in investment arbitration, particularly in disputes using the ICSID arbitration rules cited in the vignette, is an area where little formal or informal guidance exists for arbitrators.[23] Arbitrators have substantial discretion in whether and to what extent parties should cover opponents' costs. As a result, we might expect the effects of extra-legal factors to be magnified when considering the specific issue of cost allocation, effects that might be masked in raw observational data.

We recruited respondents via e-mail. We collected publicly available contact information of arbitrators and lawyers specializing in arbitration from a variety of internet sources (such as the websites of arbitration institutes). Expecting a rather high rate of non-response due to time constraints and wanting to ensure a reasonable sample size, we not only contacted individuals who work in investment arbitration, but also those specializing in commercial arbitration more broadly. Given that investment arbitration inherits much of its structure from private arbitration, we considered that commercial arbitrators still had the requisite expertise to provide reasonable answers to the vignette. The choice of who to recruit is an important experimental design question that requires researchers to strike a balance between targeting the population of interest and obtaining a sufficiently large sample. While an ideal survey would have polled exclusively arbitrators who have served on investment tribunals, this was unfeasible for our experiment given resource constraints. Nevertheless, we found that respondents who took our survey were a reasonably good representation for the overall community of arbitrators, and much better than a non-expert sample.

---

[23] Susan D. Franck, 'Rationalizing Costs in Investment Treaty Arbitration' (2011) 88(4) *Washington University Law Review* 769. But see John Y. Gotanda, 'Awarding Costs and Attorneys' Fees in International Commercial Arbitration' (1999) 21(1) *Michigan Journal of International Law* 1, 1–20 (discussing international arbitral rules generally); Noah Rubins, 'The Allocation of Costs and Attorney's Fees in Investor-State Arbitrations' (2003) 18(1) *ICSID Review* 109, 109–10.

3.3.2 Brief Analysis and Discussion of Results

We received a total of 270 complete responses to our survey conducted during the fall of 2015. However, our total sample size was reduced to 257 after removing all respondents who failed the 'attention check' embedded in the experiment. Attention checks are often used when conducting surveys to detect respondents who are simply answering at random and not paying attention to the vignette. Eliminating respondents that fail attention checks is a commonly used method of improving estimation efficiency by reducing measurement noise.[24] In contrast to a typical attention question, our attention check was implied by the way we asked the cost allocation question. Depending on the treatment assigned in the vignette, some of the outcome options are not logical. Respondents who were not paying careful attention to the vignette may have chosen to have the winning party reimburse the loser, an outcome that does not make sense in the arbitration context.

Overall, we find that arbitrators tend to render more favourable cost decisions to the party that appointed them. Being appointed by the winning party causes a statistically significant ($p < 0.05$) increase of approximately 20 percentage points in the probability that the arbitrator will have the loser pay all of the costs of the dispute. The magnitude of this effect is comparable to the effect of a claimant being ruled 'manifestly without merit' rather than simply losing the dispute. Notably, there is no statistically significant difference between the two groups in the probability that the arbitrator chooses to have the parties split the costs of the dispute. What the experimental results suggest is that arbitrators do tend to have a predisposition towards the party that appointed them, but that bias operates within the constraints of legal norms. Arbitrators who would have adopted a 'fall where they may' approach to litigation costs do not appear more likely to cost shift when appointed by a party that would benefit from reimbursement. However, given that an arbitrator chooses to have the losing party pay part of the winner's legal costs, the winning party's appointee will tend to have the loser reimburse a greater amount.

In addition to appointer effects, we find that arbitrators also tailor cost awards depending on the economic status of the respondents and claimants. Figure 3.2 plots the average effects of assigning a different respondent or

---

[24] Daniel M. Oppenheimer, Tom Meyvis and Nicolas Davidenko, 'Instructional Manipulation Checks: Detecting Satisficing to Increase Statistical Power' (2009) 45(4) *Journal of Experimental Social Psychology* 867.

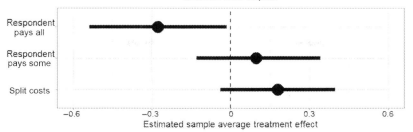
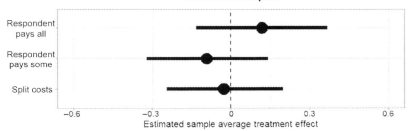
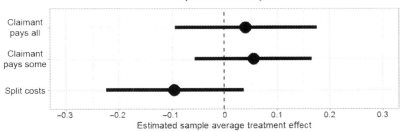
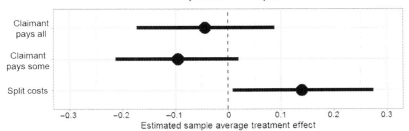

Figure 3.2 Estimated effects of claimant/respondent country development conditional on outcome
Lines denote 95% bootstrapped confidence intervals. N = 257

claimant home country income level on cost allocation. Among claimants that win the dispute, claimants with higher expected resources (those from high income rather than middle income countries) are less likely to have their full costs reimbursed. Likewise, when the respondent wins the dispute, low income respondents are more likely to have at least part of their costs reimbursed. Interestingly, we find null effects on average for the losing party. Arbitrators tend to allocate costs in a way that attempts to counterbalance some resource disparities among the parties, but in a way that tends to compensate the winning rather than losing party.

In separate discrete papers, we explore each of the different effects found in our experiment and its relationship with the current debates over the legitimacy of investment arbitration.[25] We believe this is one of the most comprehensive studies done on this important population, and its implications are important for a field in which empirical research can present the explained challenges.

3.4 Conclusion: The Future and Limitations of Experimental Approaches to Investment Arbitration

Experimental surveys can be a methodological complement to the problem of assessing behavior in a world confounded by selection effects, unknown outcome distribution due to settlement and forum shopping as well as multiple challenges in comparing disputes, non-random selection of arbitrators, and consensus decision-making processes, etc. Experiments can address some of the resulting selection effects and measuring errors and can be purposefully used to address some questions of empirical research in a complex environment of investment arbitration. Hence, the future of the inclusion of this among the empirical strategies to study investment arbitration is optimistic.

There are, of course, many obvious limitations to the survey experiments in this field – others are not so obvious. For one, the real world can be much more complex than the discrete controlled environment in which experimental surveys are implemented. Moreover, unless researchers use a more realistic setting that replicates the deliberation and discussion of the tribunal our proposed methodology is unable to

---

[25] Puig and Strezhnev (n. 6), 731 (discussing biases, equity and legitimacy in ISDS). See also Sergio Puig and Anton Strezhnev, 'Affiliation Bias in Arbitration: An Experimental Approach' (2017) 46(2) *The Journal of Legal Studies* 371 (providing evidence of affiliation bias).

assess how exactly preferences of individual arbitrators affect outcomes of the arbitration tribunal, a collective and collaborative body. This is not only a limitation of survey experiments, but a general concern with experiments on individual actors who act within organizations that have its own norms, rituals and tacit procedures.

Finally, the profession of arbitration is a casebook example of how socialization among professionals may affect the entire field. In essence, arbitration takes place in a close-knit community of legal actors and repeat-players who interact routinely. Hence, arbitrators rely on different signals and respond to complex impulses that drive their career advantage. The close-knit nature of the community and thick social structure pose important challenges to generalizing from single-shot experiments. Nevertheless, empirical research and especially survey experiments can help to improve investment arbitration, its legitimacy and its role in our global governance system.

4

The Influence of Law Firms in
Investment Arbitration

RUNAR HILLEREN LIE[*]

4.1 Introduction

'Grand old men'[1] is a common description in scholarly research on the actors in the investor–state dispute settlement (ISDS) system.[2] The term[3] was coined by Dezalay and Garth in their comprehensive empirical study of the international arbitration community.[4] Their pioneering work, based on a large number of interviews with arbitrators and counsel, generated valuable insights into the social and professional networks that constitute the international arbitration system. The study applied Bourdieu's concept of social capital[5] to the arbitration market, revealing how certain groups established and maintained their standing within the system through means of informal networks. The book revealed that these networks were primarily formed by highly educated, mature men, who had received their appointments based on reputation and social

---

[*] PluriCourts, University of Oslo. Research for this chapter has been funded by the Norwegian Research Council through project no. 276009 – Responses to the legitimacy crisis of international investment law.

[1] Yves Dezalay and Bryant G. Garth, *Dealing in Virtue: International Commercial Arbitration and the Construction of a Transnnational Legal Order* (University of Chicago Press, 1996), p. 34.

[2] See e.g. Chiara Giorgetti, 'Who Decides Who Decides in International Investment Arbitration' (2013) me>35(2) *University of Pennsylvania Journal of International Law* 431; Sergio Puig, 'Social Capital in the Arbitration Market' (2014) 25(2) *European Journal of International Law* 387; Malcolm Langford, Daniel Behn and Runar Hilleren Lie, 'The Revolving Door in International Investment Arbitration' (2017) 20(2) *Journal of International Economic Law* 301; Catherine A. Rogers, 'The Vocation of the International Arbitrator' (2005) 20(5) *American University International Law Review* 957.

[3] Dezalay and Garth (n. 1), 34.

[4] Ibid.

[5] Pierre Bourdieu, 'The Forms of Capital', in John Richardson, *Handbook of Theory and Research for the Sociology of Education* (Greenwood, 1986), p. 241.

networks built over long, distinguished careers. The network was indeed made up of 'grand', 'old', and, at the time, exclusively 'men'.[6] It is one where appointments are traded between the members of the 'club',[7] and where education, previous experience and status within the network determines who is assigned to the most favourable arbitral positions.

Although Dezalay and Garth's work addressed the arbitration community as a whole, rather than the ISDS system specifically, they described many of the critical elements of what would in the latter decades be components of the legitimacy crisis. In the two decades since it was published, their work has prompted further scholarly debate on the intricate institutional mechanisms of the ISDS system. Some scholars have stressed the lack of geographical, educational and socio-economic diversity among the arbitrators,[8] others have scrutinised the significant male bias in ISDS.[9] The networks and entanglements between individual arbitrators has been mapped,[10] while recent work has investigated the practice of 'double hatting', that is individuals acting as both arbitrators and counsel within the system.[11]

This chapter will likewise investigate the networks and social capital of the ISDS system, building on the studies cited above. However, there is a vital difference to previous work: the present study considers not the individual arbitrators, but the networks and relationships between *individual arbitrators and law firms* that they work with and against, with the goal of illuminating what relevance such relationships have for questions of conflicts of interest, and, as an extension, the perceived legitimacy of the system. By building on the PluriCourts Investment Treaty and

---

[6] According to the PluriCourts Investment Treaty and Arbitration Database (PITAD), <pitad.org/index#welcome>, the first female arbitrator was appointed in 1999.

[7] Dezalay and Garth (n. 1), 10.

[8] Susan D. Franck et al., 'The Diversity Challenge: Exploring the "Invisible College" of International Arbitration' (2015) 53(3) *Columbia Journal of Transnational Law* 429.

[9] Taylor St John et al., 'Glass Ceilings and Arbitral Dealings: Explaining the Gender Gap in Investment Arbitration', (2018) *PluriCourts Working Paper*; Giorgetti (n. 2).

[10] Puig (n. 2); Langford, Behn and Lie (n. 2).

[11] Nassib G. Ziadé, 'How Many Hats Can a Player Wear: Arbitrator, Counsel and Expert?' (2009) 24(1) *ICSID Review* 49; Philippe Sands, 'Conflict and Conflicts in Investment Treaty Arbitration: Ethical Standards for Counsel', in Chester Brown and Kate (eds.), *Contemporary Issues in International Arbitration and Mediation* (Cambridge University Press, 2012), 19, 28; Behn, Langford and Lie (n. 2).

Arbitration Database (PITAD),[12] which details the involvement of 996 law firms and over 4,000 individuals in the ISDS system, the aim of this chapter is to increase the current insight into the influence and power of law firms in ISDS networks.

The overarching aim of this study is thus: first, to analyse the extent to which law firms can influence and come into potential conflicts of interest with arbitrators in the ISDS system, especially through arbitrator selection processes; second, to analyse how effectively the current conflict of interest rules protect against conflicts between arbitrators and law firms; and, finally, to consider what can be done to reform these rules to protect the ISDS system against such influence.

Specifically the chapter will address the following research questions: What are the actual relationships between the most influential arbitrators and the top law firms, and how might these relationships create real or perceived conflict of interest issues for the ISDS system? To further illuminate these relationships, how can the significance and influence of law firms in the ISDS be identified, mapped and measured, and to what effect?

This chapter seeks to answer these research questions through integrated network, statistical and doctrinal analyses. By utilising this combination of doctrinal and data-driven approaches, this chapter will provide insights into how the law firms influence the ISDS system, particularly in relation to arbitrators, their selection, and the possible impacts on conflicts of interest.

4.2 Conflict of Interest in ISDS

From the outset, it is important to note that this chapter does not seek to evaluate how the law firms *themselves* are subject to conflict of interest rules;[13] rather I discuss whether a conflict of interest can arise through the *arbitrators' relationships with law firms.* In this section, I will primarily discuss general conflict of interest issues, as the current rules and cases do not consider law firms specifically. However, a general discussion is relevant as the challenges raised against arbitrators may be comparable to the potential conflicts of interest embedded in the relationship between arbitrators and law firms.

---

[12] PITAD (n. 6).

[13] Examples from case law include: *Hrvatska Elektroprivreda, d.d.* v. *Republic of Slovenia,* ICSID Case No. ARB/05/24, Order Concerning the Participation of Counsel, 6 May 2008; *Rompetrol Group N.V.* v. *Romania,* ICSID Case No. ARB/06/3, Decision of the Tribunal on the Participation of a Counsel, 14 January 2010.

4.2.1 The Challenge of Law Firms in ISDS

Before delving in to the legal regulations governing conflict of interest, I will briefly outline the role of law firms in the ISDS system. The perceived primary actors in the system are the parties and the arbitrators. The parties will normally consist of a private individual or company on the claimant side, and a sovereign state on the other. The arbitrators, which usually vary from one to three, decide the dispute with binding effect. Beyond these primary actors, we find supporting groups that have become important actors in the increasingly complex system. The most important actors, beyond the aforementioned, are the legal counsel and their adherent law firms. Legal counsel is in practice a prerequisite of the system and litigating a case without counsel is almost unheard of.

Because of the increase in caseloads over the last twenty years, the role of specialised law firms in providing legal counsel has become increasingly important. Law firms largely fall into seven categories: firms consisting of a sole counsel; boutique firms; barrister chambers; local specialised firms (or in many cases local representatives); international Global 100 legal firms; and, finally, specialised legal teams from governments' interior departments.[14] The increased complexity and size of the system requires expert knowledge both of case matter and procedural routines.[15]

The law firms' involvement in ISDS may be briefly summarised through the following timeline:

1. Evaluating the potential of a case, either after being approached by a client, or by approaching a potential client.
2. Preparing briefs and documents for the case.
3. Presenting clients with a choice of potential arbitrators.
4. Litigating the case.
5. Advising on annulment and enforcement proceedings.

This chapter will focus on step 3 – the choice of arbitrator. The arbitrator's views on substantive law, jurisdiction, procedural matters, as well as the arbitrator's relative standing and influence over the other arbitrators on the tribunal, may tilt the outcome of a case in one direction or the

---

[14] Rodrigo P. Lazo, 'Systems of Legal Defence Used by Latin American Countries in Investment Disputes' (2016) 17(4) *Journal of World Investment and Trade* 562.

[15] Gary Born, *International Commercial Arbitration* (Kluwer Law International, 2014), 2847.

other.[16] We can see from the PITAD database that 629 arbitrators have been appointed within the ISDS system at the time of the data extraction for this study.[17] Choosing the right arbitrator from this pool is part of the law firm's value proposition. However, law firms' influence on arbitral selection arguably constitutes a potential source of conflict of interest: by selecting the right arbitrator, the firm may potentially influence the outcome of the case. Furthermore, it is up to any given arbitrator to accept or decline an appointment, thus a counsel's relationship with an arbitrator may facilitate a client in acquiring the arbitrator that they desire.[18]

This chapter assumes a fundamental premise in all its further argumentation: that arbitrators when conducting arbitrations are to *some* degree influenced by factors other than the black letter of the law. In the general discourse on legal bodies, researchers have argued that legal practitioners are indeed human, and that factors other than law and jurisprudence may have an impact on their decisions.[19] In his 2012 article, Sands, himself a participator in the ISDS system, agreed with the premise that arbitrators may be affected by external circumstances; and as an example presented a compelling argument that when mixing roles, particularly switching between being an arbitrator and a counsel ('double hatting'), a certain bias ensues, even if it is unconscious and un-reflected.

As described in the introduction, Dezalay and Garth introduced the idea of informal networks and social capital as key factors in the arbitral selection process. In 2003, Ginsburg critiqued the focus on social capital in the arbitration market. He argued that a greater emphasis should be placed on how arbitrators utilise network effects to create both insiders and outsiders through the creation of informal networks that share certain key properties.[20] Puig expanded on this idea by applying social network analysis on the currently available data of arbitrators in the ICSID system.[21] In his paper, he illustrates how Ginsburg's networks

---

[16] Claudia T. Salomon, 'Selecting an International Arbitrator: Five Factors to Consider' (2002) 17(10) *Mealey's International Arbitration Report*.

[17] This chapter is based on case law until the end of 2016.

[18] Born (n. 15), 1680.

[19] Sands (n. 11); Shai Danziger, Jonathan Levav and Liora Avnaim-Pesso, 'Extraneous Factors in Judicial Decisions' (2011) 108(17) *Proceedings of the National Academy of Sciences of the United States of America* 6889; Adam N. Glynn and Maya Sen, 'Identifying Judicial Empathy: Does Having Daughters Cause Judges to Rule for Women's Issues?' (2015) 59(1) *American Journal of Political Science* 37.

[20] Tom Ginsburg, 'The Culture of Arbitration' (2003) 36 *Vanderbilt Journal of Transnational Law* 1335.

[21] Puig (n. 2).

may be expressed and quantified using social network mapping. Specifically, Puig shows how social capital is distributed in a network of arbitrators. This capital may influence both arbitrator selection, and perhaps the choices arbitrators make.[22] While social capital is difficult to quantify, *network capital*, that is the aggregate of social capital embedded in the ties and relations between actors in the system, can to some extent be quantified through various network analyses. As Puig's study was restricted to arbitrators in ICSID cases, it did not address other actors that affect the system. As part of a study to quantify the extent of 'double hatting', Langford, Behn and Lie, applying data from PITAD, expanded on Puig's work to include a more comprehensive list of cases, as well as including expert witnesses, secretaries, and, perhaps most importantly for this study – legal counsel.[23] To capture the relative imoportance of each role and relationship they developed a weighting matrix that factors in both the perceived social capital of the actor and distance of each relationship, and utilising this with analytical algorithms, we could rank every member of the system in terms of network capital.[24]

It is worth noting that both the Puig and Langford, Behn and Lie studies focused exclusively on the individuals of the arbitration system, whether in their roles as arbitrators, counsel, witnesses or secretaries. Simultaneously, Segal-Horn and Dean have argued the rise of what they categorise as *super-elite law firms*.[25] According to the authors, a small selection of Anglo-American firms has through a mixture of international mergers and strategic expansions established themselves as a new category of elite law firms. By expanding on these previous analyses of ISDS actors, this chapter will attempt to identify how law firms in general, and the super-elite law firms in particular, are gaining influence in the ISDS by continuingly increasing their aggregated network capital.

This network capital may provide preferential access to the ISDS community. In a working paper, St John et al. express how the system's preference for network capital, or, in their words, 'preference for historical experience' creates an effect where the inflow of new arbitrators is very limited.[26] While the focus of the paper is on the gender balance of

---

[22] Ibid.
[23] Behn, Langford and Lie (n. 2).
[24] Ibid.
[25] Susan Segal-Horn and Alison Dean, 'The Rise of Super-Elite Law Firms: Towards Global Strategies' (2011) 31(2) *The Service Industries Journal* 195.
[26] St John et al. (n. 9).

ISDS, their argument that these preferences cement existing structures is highly relevant for the present study.

Moreover, in 2012 Schultz and Kovacs reproduced Dezalay and Garth's study, 15 years later.[27] They claim that the social capital of the arbitrator was a lesser driver for arbitrator selection, and suggested that their perceived skills and experience have become the most important factors in arbitrator selection. It could be argued that this reflects a shift away from the personalised value of social capital, to the more distributed network capital. Highly pertinent to the focus in this chapter, the authors make an interesting finding in the paper: 'Non-association with a law firm' was identified as one of the weakest selection criteria when counsel was selecting an arbitrator to nominate.[28] This indicates that counsel do not appear to be concerned whether arbitrators are associated with a law firm, indicating a potential lack of awareness of conflict of interest issues related to law firms.

An illustration of the conflict of interest issue is the double hatting phenomenon. Langford, Behn and Lie quantified the phenomenon and found double hatting to be frequent and accepted throughout the ISDS system.[29] The actors of the system are, in other words, possibly so used to the tight-knit structure of ISDS that they do not see it as a significant problem. This might further explain the empirical analysis conducted by Giorgetti in her chapter,[30] where she identifies that there have been only 84 challenges out of a total of 1,620 appointments in the ICSID system.[31] Of these 84, only four resulted in the forced dismissal of the arbitrator. While other institutions/rules have higher dismissal rates,[32] this is still a remarkably low number. It should be noted that the count of four may not reflect the reality of the system, as, according to Giorgetti, 30% of challenges resulted in some sort of alteration to a tribunal's composition. One could speculate whether arbitrators, either by accepting that a conflict existed, or by wanting to avoid any perception of conflict, resigned voluntarily.[33] Nonetheless, if we consider that either four (0.2% of all appointments) or 25 (30% of 84 challenges, or 1.5% of all appointments) resulted in changes caused by conflict of interest, this number is still low.

---

[27] Thomas Schultz and Robert Kovacs, 'The Rise of a Third Generation of Arbitrators? Fifteen Years after Dezalay and Garth' (2012) 28(2) *Arbitration International* 161.

[28] Ibid.

[29] Behn, Langford and Lie (n. 2).

[30] Chiara Giorgetti, 'Arbitrator Challenges in International Investment Tribunals', Chapter 5 of the present volume; Puig (n. 2), 405.

[31] Includes ICSID cases and ICSID annulments up to 2015.

[32] Giorgetti (n. 30) points out that 22% of challenges under UNCITRAL rules succeed.

[33] Ibid.

Rogers argues that in the eyes of the system's participants, ethics have moved from a peripheral issue to being one of the most prominent subjects of discussion within the arbitral institutions. She contends that the community has recognised that self-regulation is necessary in maintaining the legitimacy of the system.[34]

4.2.2 The Legal Frameworks of ISDS Cases

The system of ISDS is a beast of many heads. It lacks formal coherence, and its mechanisms of conflict resolution are regulated by a myriad of international conventions, municipal laws and formal and informal principles.[35] While the agreements vary based on their signatories, as well as the time of signing, they exhibit many of the same qualities and provisions.

The bilateral investment treaty (BIT) – the dominant underlying legal instrument – does not directly specify the applicable rules. Rather it will list different types of arbitration that are available to the claimant. In a large number of BITs, the party is offered a choice between submitting their arbitration to the International Centre for Settlement of Investment Disputes (ICSID), and participating in ad-hoc arbitration according to the United Nations Commission on International Trade Law (UNCITRAL) arbitration rules. If the party chooses the ICSID path, the applicable rules will be those of the ICSID Convention, and the ICSID Arbitration Rules in most cases. If a party chooses the ad-hoc path, the UNCITRAL arbitration rules will apply. In addition, parties may by agreement apply further legal or ethical frameworks such as the International Bar Association's (IBA) Guidelines on Conflicts of Interest.[36]

If one is to summarise the rules on conflict of interest, the most appropriate word would perhaps be 'sparse'. Each set of rules (e.g. ICSID,[37] UNCITRAL,[38] ICC[39]) have their own regulations that address

---

[34] Catherine A. Rogers, *Ethics in International Arbitration* (Oxford University Press, 2014), p. 5.

[35] Born (n. 15), 124.

[36] IBA Guidelines on Conflicts of Interest in International Arbitration, Adopted by Resolution of the IBA Council on Thursday 23 October 2014 (IBA Guidelines).

[37] The ICSID Rules have operative and substantive regulations with equal wording to the Convention, hence I have chosen to discuss only the Convention. Please note that several cases discussed below refer to the rules.

[38] The UNCITRAL Arbitration Rules have been subject to multiple revisions. In the jurisprudence below both the 2010 and the 1976 rules have been applied.

[39] International Chamber of Commerce (ICC) Arbitration Rules (2017), Article 14(1); see also Stockholm Chamber of Commerce (SCC) Arbitration Rules (2017), Article 15(1).

how and under what circumstances a party may challenge an arbitrator, and how the remaining arbitrators should handle this challenge.

While the regulations vary slightly in their wording, including at what threshold violation is likely to result in dismissal, they are uniformly brief and clearly leave substantive discretion to the tribunal or institution applying the rules. In addition to the regulations mentioned above, there are several procedural variations between the different sets of rules that will not be discussed further here.[40]

In recent years, several newer BITs and model agreements have introduced innovations within the regulations on conflict of interests. These include clauses that restrict double hatting, increase transparency, and introduce enhanced requirements of disclosure on the part of arbitrators.[41] The ongoing UNCITRAL Working Group III is further discussing these issues in their ongoing reform efforts.[42]

4.2.3 Case Law

While the legal frameworks regulating conflicts of interest are rather sparse and broadly worded, interpretations made by various tribunals may offer some insight into the depth of the rules. It should be noted that each tribunal in ISDS is independent of all others: there are no binding precedents,[43] and no clear and binding hierarchy of authority. As the tribunals are composed of skilled legal practitioners, it is however common for them to seek coherence in the interpretation of law.[44] Tribunals tend to cite and reference other tribunals when they make decisions, so, while there is no formal rule of precedence, there appears to be an informal drive for convergence.

While the last decade has shown a significant increase in arbitrator challenge requests,[45] only a handful of challenges have resulted in the

---

[40] Giorgetti (n. 30).

[41] See e.g. the Netherlands model BIT (2018) and the Indian model BIT (2016).

[42] See e.g. UNCITRAL working papers A/CN.9/WG.III/WP.151 and A/CN.9/WG.III/WP.152.

[43] Born (n. 15), 3822; Rogers (n. 34), 317.

[44] Rogers (n. 34).

[45] For a general overview, see Catherine A. Rogers and Idil Tumer, 'Arbitrator Challenges: Too Many or Not Enough?' in Arthur W. Rovine (ed.), *Contemporary Issues in International Arbitration and Mediation: The Fordham Papers 2014* (Brill: 2015); Born (n. 15), 1895; Baiju S. Vasani and Shaun A. Palmer, 'Challenge and Disqualification of Arbitrators at ICSID: A New Dawn?' (2015) 30(1) *ICSID Review* 194.

removal of an arbitrator.[46] This should not lead to the conclusion that failed challenges indicate the absence of conflicts; rather this may be the result of a relatively high threshold set forth in the current legal frameworks.[47] Certain types of conflict are repeatedly raised by the parties and dismissed by the tribunals. This suggests that the concerns should at minimum be taken into consideration when formulating future rules.

The tribunals in *AWG* v. *Argentina* and *National Grid* v. *Argentina* agree that the term 'justifiable doubt' in UNCITRAL Article 10(1) maintains that the standard must be based on an objective stance.[48] Under the ICSID Convention, the standard is again objective.[49] In addition, these facts must satisfy the 'manifestly' standard – a requirement of clarity set forth in Article 14(1).[50] However, there is variation in the tribunals' stance on whether the rules require alleged facts proven by objective evidence. While the tribunal in *ConocoPhillips* v. *Venezuela*[51] argues that objective evidence must be provided, a later challenge in the same case argues that the ICSID Convention does not require actual proof.[52]

The IBA Guidelines can serve as a voluntary agreement, which the parties may choose to incorporate. No BIT agreements nor any of the major institutional legal frameworks currently incorporate the IBA Guidelines. The IBA Guidelines assign a set of general principles determining when a relationship or action constitutes a conflict of interest, and what types of relationship require disclosure. There is currently little empirical information on the extent of the IBA Guidelines being applied

[46] Giorgetti (n. 30); Rogers and Tumer (n. 45); Born (n. 15).

[47] Giorgetti (n. 30).

[48] *AWG Group Ltd* v. *Argentine Republic*, UNCITRAL Case, Decision on the Proposal for the Disqualification of a Member of the Arbitral Tribunal, 22 October 2007; *National Grid plc* v. *Argentine Republic*, LCIA Case No. UN 7949, Decision on the Challenge to Mr Judd L. Kessler, 3 December 2007.

[49] For example, *Repsol, S.A. and Repsol Butano, S.A.* v. *Argentine Republic*, ICSID Case No. ARB/12/38, Decision on the Proposal for Disqualification of Francisco Orrego Vicuña and Claus von Wobeser, 13 December 2013; *Abaclat and Others* v. *Argentine Republic*, ICSID Case No. ARB/07/5, Decision on the Proposal to Disqualify a Majority of the Tribunal, 4 February 2014.

[50] *SGS Société Générale de Surveillance S.A.* v. *Islamic Republic of Pakistan*, ICSID Case No. ARB/01/13, Decision on Claimant's Proposal to Disqualify Arbitrator, 19 December 2002; *Alpha Projektholding GmbH* v. *Ukraine*, ICSID Case No. ARB/07/16, Decision on Respondent's Proposal to Disqualify Arbitrator Dr Yoram Turbowicz, 19 March 2010.

[51] *ConocoPhillips Petrozuata B.V., ConocoPhillips Hamaca B.V. and ConocoPhillips Gulf of Paria B.V.* v. *Bolivarian Republic of Venezuela*, ICSID Case No. ARB/07/30, Decision on the Proposal to Disqualify L. Yves Fortier, QC, Arbitrator, 27 February 2012.

[52] Ibid; Decision on the Proposal to Disqualify a Majority of the Tribunal, 5 May 2014.

in the ISDS system. However, parties in practice never incorporate these into their agreements. [53]

While not directly incorporated, tribunals have made statements on the applicability of the IBA Guidelines.[54] In an arbitral challenge on the case of *SARL* v. *Gabon*, the tribunal indicated that the guidelines have an indicative value,[55] while the tribunal in *Alpha Projektholding* v. *Ukraine* attain that they have a certain value in light of their frequent arbitral use and their relation to the UNCITRAL and ICSID rules.[56] Yet, in *Urbaser* v. *Argentina* the tribunal explicitly points out that while the IBA Guidelines may provide inspiration, they may not be considered part of the legal basis for any decisions (unless agreed upon by the parties), as they are not part of the ICSID Convention.[57] Several other tribunals appear to recognise this duality,[58] that while the IBA Guidelines may provide valuable inspiration, they are not an authoritative legal source.[59]

There are several decisions that deal with the relationship between arbitrators and firms. The issue that perhaps comes closest to this question arose in the cases involving the London-based barrister chambers, Essex Court Chambers. In *Hrvatska* v. *Slovenia*, the tribunal considered a challenge in which the chair arbitrator (Williams) and one party's counsel (Mildon) had 'door tenancy' in the same chambers (Essex Court Chambers). The tribunal concluded that no 'hard-and-fast' rule bars the phenomenon, however it argued that there is 'no absolute rule to the opposite effect'. The tribunal is therefore critical of the lack of disclosure and argues that this is an 'error of judgement'.[60] It should be noted that barrister chambers are not analogous to law firms. The members of a chamber are sole practitioners who share certain facilities

---

[53] Born (n. 15), 1840; Rogers (n. 34); Rogers and Tumer (n. 45).

[54] Born (n. 15); Rogers and Tumer (n. 45).

[55] *Participaciones Inversiones Portuarias SARL* v. *Gabonese Republic*, ICSID Case No. ARB/08/17, Decision on the Proposal to Disqualify an Arbitrator, 12 November 2009.

[56] *Alpha* v. *Ukraine* (n. 50).

[57] *Urbaser S.A. and Consorcio de Aguas Bilbao Bizkaia, Bilbao Biskaia Ur Partzuergoa* v. *Argentine Republic*, ICSID Case No. ARB/07/26, Decision on Claimants' Proposal to Disqualify Professor Campbell McLachlan, Arbitrator.

[58] For example, *Universal Compression International Holdings, S.L.U.* v. *Bolivarian Republic of Venezuela*, ICSID Case No. ARB/10/9, Decision on the Proposal to Disqualify Prof. Brigitte Stern and Prof. Guido Santiago Tawil, Arbitrators.

[59] For example, *Abaclat* v. *Argentina* (n. 49); *ConocoPhillips* v. *Venezuela* (n. 51); *Blue Bank International Trust (Barbados) Ltd* v. *Bolivarian Republic of Venezuela*, ICSID Case No. ARB 12/20, Decision on the Parties' Proposals to Disqualify a Majority of the Tribunal.

[60] *Hrvatska* v. *Slovenia* (n. 13). The challenge in this case was actually against the counsel.

and are not financially dependent on each other. Regardless, the tribunal argues that such a relationship may be susceptible to accusations of favouritism, and that this may compromise the integrity and legitimacy of the process and final award.[61] We can observe that the tribunal urges an 'abundance of caution', where full disclosure is presented as an ideal. The tribunal's identification that the integrity and legitimacy of the ruling may be compromised, or at least be questioned, goes to the core of this chapter's key questions. Even though the relationship here in question is *prima facie* rather innocuous, it may prompt a reasonable observer's 'justifiable doubt' as to the legitimacy of the process.

In another challenge, the tribunal in *Saint-Gobain* v. *Venezuela*[62] discusses the potential dismissal of an arbitrator (Bottini), as he has had previous employment in Argentina's legal team. The tribunal argues that as long as the relationship is disclosed, no manifest conflict ensues; but the case raises relevant points. The challenge was raised on the basis that the arbitrator was previously employed by another state. This implies that parties have an impression that all states have certain shared interests, and that to work for one state can potentially bias an arbitrator in favour of all states. This impression may likewise be applicable for law firms when they work for both states and claimants at the same time. While they may not have direct conflicts, as they do not represent the same states, an impression that all states somehow have shared interests persists. As with the previous example, states, as barrister chambers, are not law firms, and would not have the same instructional authorities, nor the potential for information sharing or direct financial interests as individuals in a law firm may have. With this still in mind, I argue that if we accept the argumentation from the previous example, the mere appearance of bias may limit the legitimacy of the tribunal's decision.

The issue of close relationships between arbitrators and parties/parties' counsel has been subject to multiple (albeit unsuccessful) challenges. In *Tidewater* v. *Venezuela*, Stern, one of the most central arbitrators, and one of two 'formidable women'[63] in the ISDS system, was challenged on

---

[61] Ibid., paras. 20ff.
[62] *Saint-Gobain Performance Plastics Europe* v. *Bolivarian Republic of Venezuela*, ICSID Case No. ARB/12/13, Decision on Claimant's Proposal to Disqualify Mr Gabriel Bottini from the Tribunal under Article 57 of the ICSID Convention, 27 February 2013.
[63] Puig (n. 2), 410.

the basis that she had received three appointments by the same party in other cases.[64] The tribunal found no grounds for dismissal, pointing out Stern's partaking in several unanimous decisions against the party that appointed her, and thereby indicating her independence. Stern has been the subject of challenges based on similar circumstances – in *Electrabel v. Hungary* the claimant remarked upon Stern's continuing relationship with both Hungary and the law firm Arnold & Porter. The tribunal specifically claims that these issues are not sufficient to demonstrate a conflict of interest either by themselves or together.[65] Additionally, the tribunal remarks that the complaining party required 30 pages of descriptions to make their case – hence, in the tribunal's opinion, not fulfilling the 'manifest' requirement in the ICSID rules.

In the context of this chapter, the last comment raises an interesting observation – the tribunal appears to argue that the 'manifest' threshold requires a relation to be clear, easily described and distinguishable.[66] However, such relations are frequently entangled and convoluted. Yet, the tribunal in this example, as well as several others dealing with parallel issues,[67] seem to agree that the mere existence of relationships is not sufficient to put an arbitrator in a state of conflict to establish a conflict.

I would, however, argue that the current rules fail to account for the questions of general legitimacy. While the tribunal's observation of Stern's independence in the above case may be accurate,[68] the case illustrates the question of whether the current rules are sufficient to safeguard the system's perceived legitimacy. The complex web of relations that exist within the ISDS system warrants, in my opinion, a broader discussion on how to untangle and evaluate entwined relationships between law firms and arbitrators.

---

[64] *Tidewater Inc., Tidewater Investment SRL, Tidewater Caribe, C.A., et al.* v. *Bolivarian Republic of Venezuela*, ICSID Case No. ARB/10/5, Decision on Claimants' Proposal to Disqualify Professor Brigitte Stern, Arbitrator, 23 December 2010.

[65] *Electrabel S.A.* v. *Republic of Hungary*, ICSID Case No. ARB/07/19, Decision on the Claimant's Proposal to Disqualify a Member of the Tribunal, 25 February 2008.

[66] Ibid.

[67] For example, *İçkale İnşaat Ltd Şirketi* v. *Turkmenistan*, ICSID Case No. ARB/10/24, Decision on Claimant's Proposal to Disqualify Professor Philippe Sands, 11 July 2014; *Universal Compression* v. *Venezuela* (n. 58).

[68] *Electrabel* v. *Hungary* (n. 65).

4.2.4 Concluding Remarks

The point most relevant to the objective of this chapter is that the legal frameworks regulating conflict of interest address the relationship between law firms and arbitrators only indirectly. In several cases, repeat appointments by the same law firms have been one of the underlying reasons why arbitrators were challenged. In most instances, the concern is related to arbitrators being repeatedly appointed by the same party. In the following analysis, I will investigate whether law firms form increasingly close relationships with certain arbitrators by repeatedly selecting the same individuals to arbitrate their clients' cases.

In this chapter, I argue that neither the underlying rules, nor the current jurisprudence, sufficiently reflect the potential scope of this issue. In the following section, I illustrate that the relationships between leading arbitrators and law firms are more comprehensive than a doctrinal analysis may project. While there are several legitimate and well-founded reasons for law firms reusing known arbitrators, including knowing the arbitrators' quality of work, their position on issues, personal chemistry, work ethic and so forth, a concern remains that frequent interactions may create the potential for conscious and unconscious allegiances, arbitrator bias, increased leniency and sympathy, or antipathies against other actors or opinions, or at the very least the perceptions that such issues are present.

4.3 Empirical Methods

As the current case law and regulations provide only a cursory glance into potential areas of conflict of interest, I utilise various analytical strategies to illuminate the research questions from an empirical perspective: quantitative studies of law firms' choice of arbitrators; and network analysis to determine the interconnections between the firms and arbitrators in the network. While each method provides a complementary perspective on the overarching objective, each method also poses some challenges that must be addressed. In the following, I explain the methods as well as the scope and caveats of this chapter. The empirical basis of the study is data from PITAD.[69]

---

[69] PITAD (n. 6). This article is based on data validated up to the end of 2016. While newer data is available, I have chosen to utilise the same dataset as Behn, Langford and Lie

4.3.1 Calculating Relations – Statistical and Network Analysis

The empirical analysis contains two integrated studies. The primary study is a computational empirical analysis of the frequency of arbitral reappointment by the leading law firms. In this empirical analysis, I investigate how often the top 25 law firms appoint the top 25 arbitrators, compared to a baseline of a simulated random assignment process. To establish this baseline, I have implemented an algorithm that takes all arbitrators who have two cases or more (and as such could be considered 'qualified'), and assigned them randomly to available arbitral positions. This exercise is repeated 100,000 times for each year between 2000 and 2016. For selecting the top 25 arbitrators Langford, Behn and Lie's ranking is applied, while to establish the top 25 law firms a network analysis of the law firms, based on the same framework as these authors, is developed.[70]

Network analysis has proved to be a useful tool in legal studies, providing new and quantifiable insights into otherwise complex and convoluted data.[71] In network analysis, all data is represented in one of two core elements: nodes and ties. Nodes represent entities such as people, firms, countries or cases. Ties represent and describe the relationship between the nodes.[72] Examples of ties may be working relationships between individuals (nodes), or a law firm's (node) involvement in a case (node). Ties may be uni- or bi-directional – indicating a one-way or reciprocal relationship.

Graphs are usually analysed through visual mapping tools, a computational method called graph traversal, and various index generating algorithms such as PageRank, centrality, HITS rating, etcetera.[73] By using various algorithms on the networked data, it is through rankings

---

(n. 2), to provide the reader with a comparable set of data. Preliminary review of data available after 2016 does not appear to significantly change the results of this analysis.

[70] Behn, Langford and Lie (n. 2).

[71] Ibid.; Puig (n. 2); Katherine J. Strandburg et al., 'Law and the Science of Networks: An Overview and an Application to the "Patent Explosion"' (2007) 21 *Berkeley Technology Law Journal* 1293.

[72] Brian v. Carolan, *Social Network Analysis and Education: Theory, Methods and Applications* (Sage Publications, 2013), p. 43.

[73] Ibid; Stefan Dobrev, Rastislav Královič and Euripides Markou, 'Online Graph Exploration with Advice', in Even G. Halldórsson et al. (eds.), *Structural Information and Communication Complexity* (SIROCCO, 2012); Lecture Notes in *Computer Science*, vol. 7355 (Springer, 2012), p. 267; Sergey Brin and Lawrence Page, 'The Anatomy of a Large-scale Hypertextual Web Search Engine' (1998) 30(1–7) *Computer Networks and ISDN Systems* 107; Jon M. Kleinberg, 'Hubs, Authorities, and Communities' (1999) 31 (4es) *ACM Computing Surveys*; Heyong Wang et al., 'Estimating the Relative Importance of Nodes in Social Networks' (2013) 21 *Journal of Information Processing* 414.

and relative scores still possible to interpret patterns and information from the processed graphs. One such algorithm is graph traversal, which forms the basis for the network analysis. This is a computational method of 'walking' the graph: visiting each node; recording and correlating its data and then using its ties to determine the nodes relationships. In most cases, the traversal will compute the graph from every possible entry point.[74] A second method of network analysis is applying index-generating algorithms. By counting and compounding the ties between nodes, key metrics are made available. These include PageRank, centrality, and various other eigenvector algorithms.[75] To enhance the comparability with Langford, Behn and Lie's article, I likewise use the HITS (hub) score for the rankings.[76]

It should be noted that most graph-related scoring is relative rather than absolute. Any comparison should as such not be based on the absolute numbers presented, but rather it should use the ranked positions to compare the variations between this chapter and other rankings.[77]

An important differentiation between simple descriptive statistics and the utilisation of graphs is the way data is regressively processed. Most of the scoring[78] presented in section 4.6 does not calculate scores based only on a single dimension for a single entity (e.g. ranks by the number of cases per firm), but regressively counts every possible pathway, from every possible perspective, in relation to every other node in the system.[79] This way of scoring captures in other words not merely the node itself, but its place and importance in relation to every other node.

4.3.2 Scope and Caveats

Four caveats deserve comment. Firstly, the methods and analyses I utilise in this chapter should be seen in the context of its overarching goal; to examine how law firms potentially influence the ISDS system through arbitrator selection; and how effectively the conflict of interest rules protect

---

[74] Dobrev, Královič and Markou (n. 73); Wang et al. (n. 73).

[75] Dobrev, Královič and Markou (n. 73); Wang et al. (n. 73); Brin and Page (n. 73); Kleinberg (n. 73).

[76] Christian Collberg et al., 'A System for Graph-Based Visualization of the Evolution of Software', in Stephan Diehl (ed.), *Proceedings of ACM Symposium on Software Visualization* (SoftVis, 2003), p. 77; Behn, Langford and Lie (n. 2).

[77] Wang et al. (n. 73).

[78] See Section 4.1 on ranking the law firms. Examples of such algorithms are HITS, centrality, etc.

[79] Wang et al. (n. 73).

the integrity of the ISDS system against such influence. The purpose is therefore not to provide a comprehensive understanding of conflict of interest in general, nor how the rules would apply in specific situations. For a general overview of the rules for conflict of interest I will refer to other scholars' work on the subject.[80]

Secondly, in the present study, I do not consider chronological changes in the dataset. As ISDS is more than 40 years old, analysing it as synchronous may generate some unfortunate inaccuracies, yet preliminary analysis of limited timeframes do not make significant impact to the results.

Thirdly, the use of data-driven analyses, especially when based on non-exhaustive data, also raises source-critical concerns.

Finally, due to the system's confidential nature,[81] this chapter is based on a non-exhaustive dataset. It is beyond the scope of this chapter to evaluate each case in detail, and, even if this was achievable, most of the internal deliberations and actions are not found in official documents, and would thus still create gaps in our understanding of the cases.

However, with these caveats in mind, the use of quantitative data analysis in legal studies is still of significant value. As I seek to demonstrate throughout this chapter, data-driven approaches offer new perspectives and methods, advancing our understanding of the complex, entangled networks in the world of international arbitration.

4.4 Expanding the Perception of Law Firms' and Arbitrators' Relationships through Network and Statistical Analysis

To address the research questions, I will now turn to empirical and network analysis to create a clearer picture of the relationships between arbitrators and law firms. The first analysis investigates the network capital of law firms in relation to the leading arbitrators. By establishing the relative influence of each law firm in the network as whole, I create a top-list for firms.[82] This data is applied in the second analysis to quantify the relations between the top firms and leading arbitrators.

---

[80] For example, Rogers (n. 34); Giorgetti (n. 30); Born (n. 15), ch. 12.

[81] Cecily Rose, 'Questioning the Role of International Arbitration in the Fight against Corruption' (2014) 31(2) *Journal of International Arbitration* 183, 185; Christoph Schreuer, 'The Future of Investment Arbitration', in Arsanjani et al. (eds.), *Looking to the Future: Essays on International Law in Honor of W. Michael Reisman* (Brill, 2011), p. 787.

[82] Mirroring the approach of Langford, Behn and Lie (n. 2).

4.4.1 Network Ranking of Law Firms and Individuals

Building on studies from the last two decades that offer a sociological perspective on ISDS,[83] I will in this analysis explicitly challenge the assumption that arbitrators alone have agency in decision-making within the ISDS system. Most of the cited studies have focused on the arbitrators, based on an underlying assumption that these are the main actors in the structure.[84]

In the current enquiry, I have reproduced Behn, Langford and Lie's analysis with one modification: I have collated individual counsel into collective nodes representing their associated law firms, to create a top 25 list not only of individuals, but of the *most influential actors, regardless of the actors being individuals or firms.*

4.4.1.1 Adapting Behn, Langford and Lie's Approach

Ranking law firms based on their influence is a tricky matter. As Langford, Behn and Lie argue, it is necessary to differentiate forms of relationships within the system. I build on the assumption that a certain hierarchy is embedded in the ISDS system.[85] As I am collating multiple individuals into a single abstract entity (i.e. the law firm), a question is how the individuals' scores should be calculated. A particular challenge is the fact that there are large discrepancies in how official documents record the counsel on a given case. While some cases record scores of counsel, others only list lead counsel. To address this bias, I apply a conservative stance where only the most influential counsel, based on the individual scoring from Langford, Behn and Lie's study, in each case from each firm is counted. Additionally, it can be argued that by collating individual counsel into collective nodes, we can better consider the aggregated influence and information within the node.

As with the list of top 25 arbitrators from Langford, Behn and Lie, I use multiple metrics to rank the law firms, namely the HITS hub score, PageRank and a weighted number of outgoing ties. Each of the three variables measure the network influence in slightly different ways. The weighted number of outgoing ties is the most conservative measure, including only the first-degree interactions weighted by importance.

---

[83] See e.g. Puig (n. 2); St John et al. (n. 9); Langford, Behn and Lie (n. 2); Dezalay and Garth (n. 1).

[84] Puig (n. 2); Langford, Behn and Lie (n. 2).

[85] Langford, Behn and Lie (n. 2).

There is a direct correlation between the number of ties and the number of cases a law firm has been involved in. The two former scores, however, take the whole network into account, estimating the importance of the nodes' relations not only to their closest neighbour, but to the network as a whole.

Crafting such a ranking encompasses some trade-offs regarding accuracy at the individual level. Nonetheless, I argue that this is offset by an improved overall perception of the system, observing law firms as an aggregate, rather than unrelated individuals.

After analysing both arbitrators and the collated law firms in the ISDS system, Table 4.1 presents an alternate ranking for the most influential actors in the system. The list includes six firms, two government ministries and seventeen individuals. Sixteen of the individuals are arbitrators, while one works primarily as a tribunal secretary. The law firms/government ministries are highlighted in table 4.1.

Several results prompt further comment. The influence, that is, the network capital, of the top law firms is comparable to the top arbitrators. While the firms and government ministries do not rank at the very top of the list, their continued presence throughout indicates that their influence is on par with the leading arbitrators. The firms are based, or have significant presence in London, New York or Washington, DC, they work for both claimants and respondents, and all have litigated a significant number of ISDS-cases. Furthermore, all the top-ranked firms are on the Global Arbitration Review (GAR) 100 or Global 100 lists, indicating that the super-elite firms are procuring significant influence in the ISDS system. The two government ministries, Argentina and Venezuela, are both frequent litigants. Consequently, these states have arguably been able to acquire network influence by internalising large parts of their litigation teams.

Finally, while arbitrators populate the top of the list, when we compare the results to Langford, Behn and Lie's list, there are internal shifts in the ranking of the arbitrators' influence. Stern is in my calculation the most influential actor in the system, improving her rank from third to first place. Kaufmann-Kohler's influence is slightly reduced from first to second. In general, arbitrators who frequently work with the most influential firms tend to improve their rankings compared to other arbitrators, a point I will develop further below.

Summing up, the results presented here constitute a useful alternate perspective to counting individual counsel. First, it considers the aggregate of the internal relationships within a firm, where internal

INFLUENCE OF LAW FIRMS

Table 4.1 *Top 25 actors in the ISDS network ranked by HITS (hub)*[1]

Rank	Langford, Behn and Lie (all individuals)	Langford, Behn and Lie (arbitrators only)	
1	3	2	Brigitte Stern
2	1	1	Gabrielle Kaufmann-Kohler
3	–	–	**Freshfields Bruckhaus Deringer**
4	2	4	Yves Fortier
5	5	6	Francisco Orrego Vicuña
6	4	3	V. V. Veeder
7	–	–	**King & Spalding**
8	–	–	**White & Case**
9	–	–	**Government Ministry Argentina**
10	7	5	Charles Brower
11	13	7	Albert Jan van den Berg
12	19	14	Piero Bernardini
13	–	–	**Arnold & Porter**
14	16	12	Marc Lalonde
15	11	8	Bernard Hanotiau
16	14	13	J. Christopher Thomas
17	22	15	Juan Fernández-Armesto
18	15	9	Karl Heinz Böckstiegel
19	–	–	**Government Ministry Venezuela**
20	–	21	Rodrigo Oreamuno
21	–	–	**Foley Hoag**
22	24	10	Vaughan Lowe
23	–	11	David Williams
24	20	–	Gonzalo Flores
25	–	–	**Shearman & Sterling**

[1] The table including HITS (hub), PageRank and Degrees out (weighted) can be downloaded from <pitad.org/assets/LIE_The_Influence_of_Law_Firms_in_ISDS_Tables_and_Illustrations .pdf>.

redistribution of influence must be expected to be relatively accessible. Second, it challenges a tribunal's perception that relationships should merely be considered on an individual-to-individual basis, rather than recognising that firms can to some extent have inherent agency beyond the sum of the individuals that form them.

This analysis should, however, be considered as an addition to, rather than a replacement of, earlier work. By observing the rankings together, we can see how the inclusion of law firms as separate entities shifts and nuances the results. Seeing the ISDS system from both an individual and an institutional perspective allows us to observe a more complex network of influence, which is not being sufficiently addressed in the current legal discourse.

4.4.2 The Relationships between the Law Firms and Arbitrators

Having in the previous section established the firms' and arbitrators' general ranks of influence in the network of actors, I will in this section analyse how often the top law firms appoint the leading arbitrators for cases litigated by the firms. Table 4.2 shows all *direct reappointments* (i.e. the party-appointed arbitrators, also known as 'wing' arbitrators by the top 25 law firms in terms of number of cases. The table is sorted by the number of cases per law firm, and provides the average number of reappointments for the firm.

Two results from this analysis deserve further discussion. First, the average number of reappointments, while not insignificant, is still fairly low. At an average of 1.38 appointments and with a max of 2.15, firms are to an extent varying their selection of arbitrators. Yet, when we consider the most frequent reappointments (see online version of Table 4.2), a different picture emerges. Some of the top firms reappoint the same arbitrators in up to six different cases. While six reappointments of the same arbitrator by the same firm may not necessarily constitute an inappropriately close relationship, given the duration, scale and financial benefits such appointments entail, further discussion is warranted.

Moreover, the number of repeat appointments described above should be seen in relation to the baseline of random selection of arbitrators. Between the years 2000 and 2016 any given arbitrator has on average 0.28 reappointments with the highest random chance at 0.38. Comparing this to the figures for law firm-realted appointments of an average of 1.38, maximum of 2.15 and over six reappointments we can observe a large discrepancy between a random sample and the actual choices of the

Table 4.2 *Direct and indirect reappointments sorted by firms' total number of cases*[1]

Name of firm	Type of firm	No. of cases	Avg no. of *direct* reappointments	Avg no. of *indirect* reappointments
Freshfields	GLOBAL 100	85	1.57	1.45
White & Case	GLOBAL 100	71	1.48	1.39
King & Spalding	GLOBAL 100	66	1.68	**1.54**
Allen & Overy	GLOBAL 100	46	1.32	1.44
Arnold & Porter	GLOBAL 100	43	1.55	1.27
Curtis Mallet	GLOBAL 100	43	1.62	1.27
Shearman & Sterling	GLOBAL 100	41	1.46	1.42
Foley Hoag	GAR 100	35	**2.15**	1.21
Sidley Austin	GLOBAL 100	35	1.73	1.26
Matrix Chambers	Barrister Chambers	35	1.38	1.26
Debevoise & Plimpton	GLOBAL 100	28	1.14	1.16
Essex Court Chambers	Barrister Chambers	26	1.18	1.25
Derains & Gharavi	GAR 100	24	1.29	1.21
Covington & Burling	GLOBAL 100	23	1.23	1.24
Cleary Gottlieb	GLOBAL 100	23	1.40	1.30
Weil Gotshal & Manges	GLOBAL 100	22	1.62	1.24
Dechert	GLOBAL 100	21	1.14	1.32
Clifford Chance	GLOBAL 100	21	1.12	1.08
Todd Weiler	Sole – OECD	20	1.00	1.00
Latham & Watkins	GLOBAL 100	19	1.17	1.17
Baker McKenzie	GLOBAL 100	19	1.31	1.27
Squire Patton Boggs	GLOBAL 100	18	1.88	1.25
DLA Piper	GLOBAL 100	18	1.07	1.17
Winston & Strawn	GLOBAL 100	17	1.09	1.13
Quinn Emanuel	GLOBAL 100	16	1.07	1.06
Volterra Fietta	GAR 100	16	1.20	1.05

[1] Extended versions of the table, including names of the three most frequently reappointed arbitrators, can be downloaded from <pitad.org/assets/LIE_The_Influence_of_Law_Firms_in_ISDS_Tables_and_Illustrations.pdf> (see table 2 for direct appointments and table 3 for indirect appointments).

parties. Certain arbitrators from the top of Behn, Langford and Lie's top 25 list occur frequently in this analysis. The most frequently used and reappointed arbitrator appears to be Stern. Other frequent appearances include Thomas, Fortier and Kaufmann-Kohler.

The analysis in table 4.2 also details the reappointment of tribunal chairs. This category is primarily made up of appointments where the parties agree on chair selection, but also includes a limited number of appointments where the institutions or wing arbitrators have made or suggested a choice for chair. As the individual party only has limited influence and right of refusal, rather than full control over the appointment, I refer to this as *indirect reappointments*.

The selection of arbitrators is slightly more varied for this group, with a result of 1.25 (i.e. each arbitrator is indirectly reappointed 1.25 times by the same law firm on average). The maximum number of repeat appointments is also lower than in the direct appointments, reaching a ceiling at four. As with the previous analysis we see many actors from the top 25 list, including Fortier, Veeder, Crawford and Kaufmann-Kohler.

In table 4.3, I present similar data for the top ten government ministries in terms of number of cases. Government ministries are slightly more prone to reappointments with an average of 1.49 (with a maximum of two) for direct and 1.29 (with a maximum of 1.67) for chair appointments. Similar to the private firms, governments reappoint the same arbitrator six times when appointing directly, but surpass private firms with six chair reappointments (compared to four). This result is slightly surprising, as one might expect private law firms to be more aggressive when it comes to creating and maintaining close relationships.

Finally, I have explored what happens when we consider the relationship between the top 25 law firms and the top 25 arbitrators (Table 4.4). As these two groups of actors account for a significant share of appointments, their continuing interactions are of particular interest when evaluating the impact such engagements have on conflicts of interest, and the perception of system-wide legitimacy. Given their significant network capital, and broad involvement, any perception of conflicts of interest would have impact on a large number of cases, and as such on the legitimacy of the system as a whole.

First, I have examined the *share of appointments* assigned by the firms to the arbitrators. The top 25 law firms assign on average 41% of their direct arbitral appointments (i.e. wing arbitrators) to top 25 arbitrators. A similar pattern is present with indirect appointments, where 40% of arbitral appointments on average is assigned to the top 25 arbitrators.

INFLUENCE OF LAW FIRMS 123

Table 4.3 *Direct and indirect reappointments sorted by countries' total number of cases*

Country	No. of cases	Avg no. of *direct* reappointments	Avg no. of *indirect* reappointments
Argentina	69	**2.00**	**1.67**
Venezuela	42	1.85	1.47
Spain	32	1.37	1.21
Egypt	28	1.77	1.19
Ecuador	22	1.60	1.41
United States	22	1.00	1.08
Canada	21	1.21	1.08
Mexico	17	1.13	1.17
Ukraine	13	1.50	1.31
Czech Rep.	12	1.50	1.33

[1] Extended versions of the table, including names of the three most frequently reappointed arbitrators, can be downloaded from <pitad.org/assets/LIE_The_Influence_of_Law_Firms_in_ISDS_Tables_and_Illustrations.pdf> (see table 4 for direct appointments and table 5 for indirect appointments).

Thus, there seems to be a trend of law firms preferring top 25 arbitrators for their tribunals.

Second, I have considered the *number of arbitrators* that have received appointments by each of the top 25 firms. On average, the firms either directly or indirectly appointed or approved 14 of the top 25 most influential arbitrators. The top five firms have worked with 20 of the 25 arbitrators; while the leading firm on the list, *Freshfields Bruckaus Deringer* alone has been involved in appointing 22 of the top 25 arbitrators. While this number must be seen in the context of the number of cases these firms are involved in – having more cases naturally leads to a greater use of arbitrators in general – it is clear from the data above that the larger firms maintain close and active relationships with elite arbitrators.

4.4.3 Conclusions

With these analyses in mind, three clear patterns emerge. First, the network analyses indicate strong and consistent relationships between the leading law firms/states and the top 25 arbitrators in the ISDS system.

Table 4.4 *Top 25 law firms' appointment of top 25 arbitrators sorted by number of firms' cases*

Name of firm	No. of cases	% of *direct* reapp. of top 25 arbs. (%)	% of *indirect* reapp. of top 25 arbs. (%)	Avg no. of *indirect* reapps.
Freshfields	**85**	41	33	**22**
White & Case	71	34	37	21
King & Spalding	66	46	34	19
Allen & Overy	46	42	43	18
Arnold & Porter	43	38	42	20
Curtis Mallet	43	24	30	15
Shearman & Sterling	41	37	45	17
Foley Hoag	35	38	29	14
Sidley Austin	35	62	44	17
Matrix Chambers	35	32	41	15
Debevoise & Plimpton	28	40	39	15
Essex Court Chambers	26	54	43	15
Derains & Gharavi	24	39	41	13
Covington & Burling	23	50	39	12
Cleary Gottlieb	23	43	50	14
Weil Gotshal & Manges	22	38	48	13
Dechert	21	47	22	11
Clifford Chance	21	38	48	9
Todd Weiler	20	27	29	6
Latham & Watkins	19	43	52	14
Baker McKenzie	19	29	42	9
Squire Patton Boggs	18	38	**57**	13
DLA Piper	18	53	35	8
Winston & Strawn	17	42	33	11
Quinn Emanuel	16	53	44	12
Volterra Fietta	**15**	41	33	**10**

Second, state employed lawyers and private firms seem to be operating under the same pattern. Third, each of the leading law firms has contributed to the appointment – and hence contributed to the professional interest – of up to 80% of the top 25 arbitrators.

When I identified the top 25 influential agents in section 4.1, I noted that arbitrators who frequently work with the most influential law firms tend to improve their rankings compared to other arbitrators. The cause for this is in part the model itself, as arbitrators obtain fewer connections when all counsel are collated into single law firm entities. However, actors working with influential firms may also benefit from the firms' collective network capital. This observation can be transferred to the present discussion: the top 25 firms and the top 25 arbitrators to some extent form close relationships; the benefits of which I will now explore.

4.5 Discussion – Grand Old Women and Men and Their Friends at the Firm?

The aim of this chapter is to discuss and expand on the suggested hegemony of the 'grand old women and men' of the ISDS system. Through empirical and network analyses, I have throughout this chapter implicitly questioned whether the correct phrase should be 'grand old women and men and their friends at the firm'.

In the doctrinal analysis, I explored the brevity of regulations and case law on law firms and the relationships they cultivate with arbitrators. I highlighted the substantial threshold that such relationships must meet to be perceived as conflicts of interest, and how tribunals address individual connections while regulation on firms–arbitrator relations are nearly absent.

In the network and statistical analysis, I illustrated how law firms have gained a central position in the ISDS network, and that through frequent reappointments they build in theory and most likely in practice strong relationships with the leading arbitrators.

I will now address two larger issues that will be the subject of in-depth discussion. First, I explore how network capital may elevate law firms to a position of de facto gatekeepers, which potentially exposes them to situations where conflicts of interest may intrude. Second, I apply the results from the network and empirical analyses to shed light on how the influential actors appear to reproduce and even cement their influence in the system, and how such cementation may cause conflicts of interest and issues of perceived legitimacy unaddressed by the current legal regulations.

126 RUNAR HILLEREN LIE

4.5.1 Access to Gatekeepers

Previous studies of social and network capital in the arbitration world argue that individuals with a higher capital may have greater influence on tribunals.[86] This presumes that an arbitrator with higher social capital can draw on this capital in the arbitration, as one of several factors influencing the proceedings. Building on this premise, it would be strategic for a party to select a wing arbitrator with higher social capital than the chair and opposite wing arbitrator. If we accept the premise that arbitrator selection is a key component of success in arbitration, does this shape how clients are able to access certain arbitrators; and, if so, does this make law firms the gatekeepers of the ISDS system?

In practice, achieving an advantage through arbitrator selection requires two things: first, the party needs sufficient knowledge of each arbitrator's network and social capital; and, second, it requires access to a wing arbitrator with these characteristics. For both issues, the party's best strategy would arguably be to go through a top 25 law firm. Consequently, I argue that the top law firms have uniquely positioned themselves as gatekeepers in the ISDS system.

The basic trait that allows the top firms to become gatekeepers is their knowledge of the arbitrators and the system. Previous research provides insight into arbitrator selection,[87] but the academic discourse is likely to be less accessible to infrequent users of the system. Therefore, the ability to pick the 'right' arbitrator is a key asset of top law firms. The empirical and network analyses demonstrate how top firms are uniquely situated to provide such guidance. The analysis shows how the top firms have first-hand experience with the vast majority of top arbitrators. I additionally found that the top law firms selected top 25 arbitrators for almost 40% of their appointments (out of an available pool of at least 629 possible arbitrators). Furthermore, the anlaysis showed how several arbitrators are awarded multiple appointments by the same law firm.

The absence of successful challenges indicates that these relationships, at least as perceived by the tribunals in considering these challenges, do not cross the threshold for impropriety. From the firms' perspective, the

---

[86] Dezalay and Garth (n. 1); Puig (n. 2).

[87] Dezalay and Garth (n. 1); Schultz and Kovacs (n. 27); Puig (n. 2); St John et al. (n. 9); Behn, Langford and Lie (n. 2).

relationships between firms and arbitrators may be motivated by innocuous reasons such as shared experience; a certain level of trust; and strong working relationships. Given the arbitrators' time constraints as well as their existing relationships with firms, arbitrators may choose to almost exclusively work with firms they have experience with, thus cementing these firms as the arbitrators' gatekeepers.[88]

When changing the perspective from the law firms and clients to that of the arbitrators, the recognition of a small number of law firms as key gatekeepers may create incentives for arbitrators to maintain stable relationships with the firms, perhaps even at the expense of perceived independence. Such perceptions, whether perceived or real, may, when unaddressed, create challenges to the legitimacy of ISDS. In the following section, I continue this discussion, with a focus on how these firms appear to participate in, and benefit from, the closed loop-nature of the ISDS system.

4.5.2 Closed Loops

In their working paper, St John et al. illustrate that the selection of arbitrators is significantly limited by historical selection bias. Each year only 11% of arbitral appointments are awarded to new entrants, while the remaining 89% are awarded to individuals who have had at least one previous arbitral appointment.[89] They see this as a hurdle for gender equality within the system. The paper underlines that, unless the system undergoes fundamental structural changes, gender equality will not be achieved this century. The 'closed loop', that is, self-electing and self-reproducing nature of the system, is a frequent item for criticism and is reflected by descriptions of the system as 'an old boys club' or 'club for rich white men'. When considering St John et al.'s argument in light of the findings of this chapter, I argue that the self-reproducing phenomenon does not apply solely to arbitrators but describes the system in general.

This closed loop phenomenon is further reflected in the distribution of cases between law firms. As a human services business, law firms

---

[88] There is no data available on how often or why a top 25 arbitrator rejects appointments. A study of such rejections could be a promising avenue of future research that may increase our understanding of the extent of law firms' influence.

[89] St John et al. (n. 9).

typically market themselves on expertise, experience, network and reputation, the latter being largely analogous to network capital. As law firms make gains in these areas, clients have stronger incentives to select these firms. This again gives the firm more ties into the network, making them more frequent selectors of arbitrators. This phenomenon is well illustrated in fgures 4.1–4.3 where we can see that the top firms form a core at the centre of the network together with the leading arbitrators.

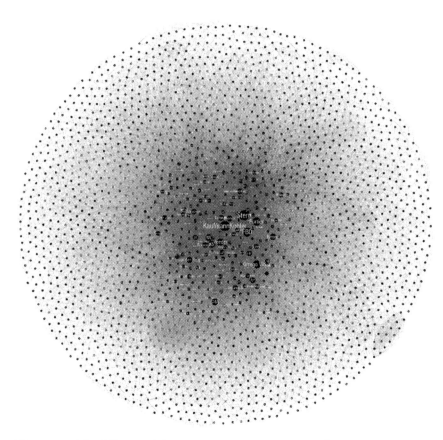

Figure 4.1 The full network between arbitrators and law firms[1]

[1] Electronic versions of figures that can be enlarged can be downloaded from <pitad.org/assets/LIE_The_Influence_of_Law_Firms_in_ISDS_Tables_and_Illustrations.pdf>.

INFLUENCE OF LAW FIRMS 129

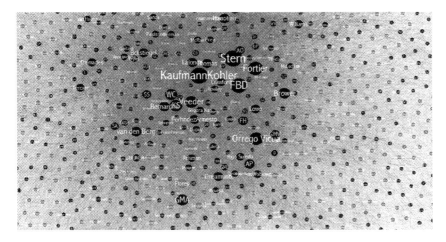

Figure 4.2 A partition of the network of arbitrators and law firms

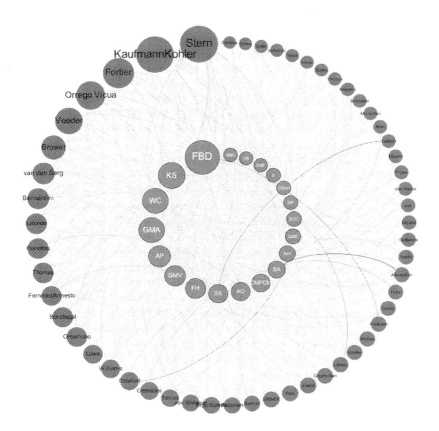

Figure 4.3 Network between top arbitrators and law firms

To summarise, we can describe the trajectory of the closed loop in the following manner:

1. top law firms appoint top 25 arbitrators, thereby strengthening these arbitrators' network influence;
2. in turn, making these arbitrators more attractive to clients and/or law firms;
3. this again exponentially increases the ties of a certain arbitrator, allowing the arbitrator further network capital; and
4. the arbitrators' increased network capital aggregates back into the law firm, making them more desirable for clients compared to firms with less network capital.

In other words, the closed loop is continually increasing the influence of the most influential law firms in the ISDS system.

4.5.3 Implications for Conflicts of Interest and Perceived Legitimacy

The objective of this chapter was stated in the introduction: first, to analyse the extent to which law firms can influence and come into potential conflict with arbitrators in the ISDS system, especially through arbitrator selection processes; and, second, to analyse how effectively the current conflict of interest rules protect against conflicts between arbitrators and law firms and what can be done to reform these rules to protect the ISDS system against such influence.

This has proved to be a challenging task, partly due to the vague formulation of the rules and partly because challenges due to law firm influence seem largely absent from case law. I have argued that this absence is not a result of an absence of conflicts, but rather a result of a high and narrowly defined threshold of impropriety, and a system of rules that were not designed to address the influence of law firms. As I have argued throughout the analysis, law firms' influence within the system is significant and widespread. I have further argued that this influence appears to have structural causes and consequences.

By combining the effects of an ever-strengthening mechanism of closed loops and increasing influence of the leading law firms, we can surmise that the frequency of reappointment of leading arbitrators by the leading law firms is likely to increase. From a legitimacy standpoint this may be perceived as a hindrance to arbitrators' independence and create a fertile ground for situations that could be perceived as conflicts of interest.

While I do not contend that the close-knitted relationships between law firms and arbitrators is necessarily unethical in nature, I do claim that it is problematic that the issue is sparsely addressed in current discourse. Additionally, the fact that parties challenge arbitrators on the grounds of their close relationships with counsel reveals a dissonance between current legislation and the perception among the actors in the ISDS system. In many cases, the number of connections that directly or indirectly entangle law firms and arbitrators may appear incidental on the level of the individual arbitrator, but, nonetheless, for the system as a whole it may create impediments to the perceived independence and legitimacy.

4.6 Concluding Remarks

In a personal statement made to a faculty member at the University of Oslo, a senior arbitrator expressed dissatisfaction with a recent interview. During the last decade, ISDS has received a vast amount of of criticism by the media, academia and states. The impression of a system with 'grand old men' and backroom dealings has been prevailing. While the system's critics are often vocal, the system itself has many defenders, and the ISDS mechanism is incorporated in many newer trade agreements. The findings in this chapter may prove to support some of the critical viewpoints. In many ways, the ISDS system functions like a closed-loop system; there are many entanglements between its key actors; and there is a blurring of lines between the actors. The data presented in this chapter indicate that law firms are significant contributors to this closed-loop system. By empirically mapping the extent of law firms' involvement, we can more accurately assess the extent of their influence, and the potential consequences this has for arbitrators' independence. Extending this through network analysis and an alternate ranking for the most influential actors in the system, including law firms, may make a future debate on these issues more informed. While these issues are likely going to be the subject of broad debate in the coming years, I find that the analysis showing that the top arbitrators and elite law firms form strong entwinements and relationships to be of most concern. This may very well lead to a system where the law firms become the gatekeepers of the top arbitrators, creating a 'closed loop' that continually increases the influence of law firms in the ISDS system. The lack of legal consideration of less transparent forms for networks and allegiances within the system poses a true challenge to the legitimacy and future of the ISDS mechanism.

5

Arbitrator Challenges in International Investment Tribunals

CHIARA GIORGETTI[*]

5.1   Introduction

On 22 July 2015, the Croatian daily newspaper *Večernji list* published transcripts and audio recordings of conversations between Dr Sekolec – an international arbitrator nominated by Slovenia as their national arbitrator in the international maritime border dispute between Slovenia and Croatia – and Slovenia's agent in the case, Ms Drenik. In their conversations, the arbitrator disclosed the preliminary conclusions of the Tribunal (which allegedly favoured Slovenia) and discussed ways to influence the other arbitrators in the panel by trying to introduce legal arguments that would sway the arbitrators.[1]

Following the revelation, Slovenia's Prime Minister announced that he had demanded and received the resignations of both individuals, and announced that the Slovenian Government had not known of the pair's communications. Slovenia then nominated French national Judge Abraham, President of the International Court of Justice (ICJ), as Dr Sekolec's replacement. Shortly thereafter, Croatian Prime Minister Zoran Milanović asked that the proceedings be suspended.[2] The arbitrator

---

[*] Professor of Law, Richmond Law School. I am glad to have the opportunity to thank Cassie Powell of the University of Richmond for her exquisite research assistance.

[1] In general, see Arman Sarvarian and Rudy Baker, 'Arbitration between Croatia and Slovenia: Leaks, Wiretaps, Scandal', *EJILTalk!*, 28 July 2015, <ejiltalk.org/arbitration-between-croatia-and-slovenia-leaks-wiretaps-scandal>. See also Press Releases from the PCA, <pcacases.com/web/view/3> and Patricia Živković, 'Severe Breaches of Duty of Confidentiality and Impartiality in the Dispute between Croatia and Slovenia: Is Arbitration Immune to Such Violations?' *Kluwer Arbitration Blog*, 29 July 2015, <arbitrationblog.kluwerarbitration.com/2015/07/29/severe-breaches-of-duty-of-confiden tiality-and-impartiality-in-a-dispute-between-croatia-and-slovenia-is-arbitration-immune-to-such-violations/>.

[2] 'Arbitration Between the Republic of Croatia and the Republic of Slovenia', PCA Press Release, 28 July 2015, <pcacases.com/web/sendAttach/1313>.

133

134 CHIARA GIORGETTI

appointed by Croatia, Professor Vukas, resigned from the Tribunal few days later, on 30 July 2015.[3] The day after, on 31 July, Croatia informed the Tribunal that it ceased to apply the Arbitration Agreement with Slovenia.[4] On 3 August, Judge Abraham resigned from the Tribunal and, 10 days later, Slovenia informed the Tribunal that it objected to Croatia's termination of the Arbitration Agreement as it believed that the Tribunal could continue the proceedings and had a duty to do so.[5] In September 2015, the President of the Tribunal and former President of the ICJ, Judge Guillaume, appointed Professor Michel to succeed Professor Vukas and Ambassador Fife to succeed Judge Abraham to 'consider the Parties' positions carefully.'[6] The reconstituted Tribunal

[3] 'Arbitration Between the Republic of Croatia and the Republic of Slovenia', PCA Press Release, 30 July 2015, <pcacases.com/web/sendAttach/1330>.

[4] 'Arbitration Between the Republic of Croatia and the Republic of Slovenia', PCA Press Release, 5 August 2015, <pcacases.com/web/sendAttach/1389>. Croatia requested the following note be posted on the website of the PCA: 'On 31 July 2015 Croatia informed the Arbitral Tribunal that, as a consequence of a material breach of the Arbitration Agreement committed by Slovenia and pursuant to Articles 60 and 65 of the Vienna Convention on the Law of Treaties, Croatia notified Slovenia with respect to termination of the Arbitration Agreement. Croatia also informed the Tribunal that, as of the date of the notification, 30 July 2015, Croatia ceased to apply the Arbitration Agreement', <pcacases .com/web/view/3>.

[5] 'Slovenia demands continuation of arbitration proceedings – Arbitral Tribunal clarifies further procedural steps', PCA Press Release, 19 August 2015, <pcacases.com/web/ sendAttach/1403>, setting out Slovenia's position and its request that the President of the Tribunal appoint the two missing arbitrators.

[6] 'Tribunal reconstituted by appointment of Norwegian and Swiss arbitrators, H.E. Mr. Rolf Fife and Professor Nicolas Michel', PCA Press Release, 25 September 2015, <pcacases .com/web/sendAttach/1468> stating that: 'Following the resignation of Professor Budislav Vukas (on 30 July 2015) appointed by Croatia, and the successive resignations of Dr. Jernej Sekolec (on 23 July 2015) and Judge Ronny Abraham (on 3 August 2015) appointed by Slovenia, the Tribunal had invited each Party to appoint a replacement arbitrator. No appointment was made by Croatia. Slovenia informed the Tribunal on 13 August 2015 that, "in order to preserve the integrity, independence and impartiality of the Arbitral Tribunal and the ongoing proceedings, it will refrain from appointing a member of the Tribunal to replace Judge Abraham". Instead, Slovenia requested "the President of the Arbitration Tribunal, Judge Gilbert Guillaume, in exercise of his powers under Article 2, paragraph 2, of the Arbitration Agreement, to appoint a member of the Arbitration Tribunal". Article 2, paragraph 2 of the Arbitration Agreement provides that, "[i]n case that no appointment has been made within [15 days], the respective member shall be appointed by the President of the Arbitral Tribunal". Since neither Party made an appointment within 15 days after the resignation of Professor Vukas and Judge Abraham, it fell to the President to appoint the remaining two members of the Tribunal. Professor Michel was appointed to succeed Professor Vukas on the Tribunal, and Ambassador Fife was appointed to succeed Judge Abraham. Further Proceedings – The Tribunal now intends to consider the Parties' positions carefully, including in respect

requested further briefs from both parties in December 2015[7] and held additional hearings in March 2016.[8] On 30 June 2016, the Tribunal issued a unanimous Partial Decision holding that the arbitration will continue and that the remedial actions undertaken were sufficient to ensure the continuation of the case. The Tribunal found no reason why its future decisions would be affected by past events, for which the present members of the Tribunal were not responsible, and noted the Tribunal's duty to deliver procedural fairness to both Parties, which would not be achieved by putting the case on hold.[9]

In addition to the unusual entertainment value, this story highlights more serious and fundamental issues: (1) the high degree of trust parties put in the hands of arbitrators chosen to resolve important international disputes; (2) the fundamental role played by ethics in international arbitration (and foremost of independence and impartiality) and (3) the immeasurable damage that international arbitration as an institution and those involved in it can suffer when blatant cases of ethics violations occur.

Though clear-cut ethical violations such as the one highlighted above are rare, this situation underscores the fundamental importance of having robust ethical rules in international dispute resolution. More specifically, the case also highlights the paramount importance of securing the independence and impartiality of arbitrators throughout the selection and arbitration process, as well as the essential importance that clear mechanisms of challenges and recusals of arbitrators can offer in securing a form of control for parties in the proceedings.

This chapter analyses the rules, reasons and results of arbitrator challenge requests under several applicable sets of arbitration rules, and in so doing it offers three ways to assess challenges procedures empirically. Section 5.2 introduces the issue by presenting new data related to the number and success rate of challenges under several procedural rules,

---

of the effect of Croatia's stated intention to terminate the Arbitration Agreement and in respect of the possible implications for the present proceedings of the events reportedly underlying Croatia's decision. In this regard, the Tribunal may invite further submissions from the Parties on questions of fact and law as may be necessary'.

[7] 'Arbitration between the Republic of Croatia and the Republic of Slovenia', PCA Press Release, 2 December 2015, <pcacases.com/web/sendAttach/1541>, stating that that Tribunal sets d,ates for further submissions.

[8] Ibid.

[9] 'The Croatia and Slovenia Show Will Go On', *Global Arbitration Review*, 30 June 2016.

with the goal of providing a general picture of challenges proceedings and their outcome. Section 5.3 examines the rules applicable to challenges procedures in some of the most used international arbitration rules with the aim of assessing variation. Section 5.4 reviews the main reasons for challenges and assesses comprehensively the final results. Section 5.5 concludes.

5.2 Challenges of Arbitrators: An Analysis of Available Data

In the last few years, in parallel to the increased use of investor–state arbitration as a dispute resolution mechanism, arbitrator challenges have also become increasingly common in these proceedings. This has also resulted in a heightened interest in challenges procedures and the outcome of such challenges.[10] Little comprehensive data is available, however, on the prevalence of challenges and their outcomes. Trying to address this gap, this section provides an initial review of available data on challenges in investor–state arbitration.

An important caveat applies to the availability of data. Due to the confidentiality rules often applicable in these arbitrations, not all cases are public. At times, the reasoning of the arbitrator challenge decisions remains confidential, while the holding is public. At other times, even the existence of a case (and thus the challenge) may remain confidential. Thus, the data available in this section shows a partial figure of a wider picture. Nonetheless, while calling for more transparency, it is instructive to review available data to assess claims and perceptions about challenges.

This section focuses on challenges at ICSID and at the PCA, the two forums where most investor–state arbitrations are resolved and for which more data is available.

Challenge requests have generally increased in the last decades, in parallel with the growth of investor–state arbitration. For example, the first case at ICSID where an arbitrator challenge was filed was *Amco v. Indonesia*, a case filed in 1982. At the time, 20 cases had been filed

---

[10] See e.g. Karel Daele, *Challenges and Disqualification of Arbitrators in International Arbitration* (Kluwer Law International, 2012), Chiara Giorgetti (ed.), *Challenges and Recusals of Judges and Arbitrators in International Courts and Tribunals* (Brill, 2015) and Maria Nicole Cleis, *The Independence and Impartiality of ICSID Arbitrators* (Brill, 2017).

since the first ICSID case in 1972. The next challenge, *Pey Casado v. Chile,* was filed 16 years after *Amco,* in 1998. As of June 2019, 76 known decisions on arbitrator challenges have been rendered, 52 of which have come since 2010.[11]

Overall, challenges requests remain unusual. At ICSID, for example, of the total 1,620 appointments of arbitrators and ad hoc annulment committee members between 1972 and September 2014, only 84 have been challenged. This is only 5% of all appointments.[12] When challenges happen, however, they are rather disruptive, as the proceeding is normally suspended until the challenge is resolved, causing delays and additional expenses.[13]

As table 5.1 shows, the success rate of challenges is also quite low. Of 84 arbitrators who were challenged under the ICSID Convention, only four were upheld. At the PCA, 34 arbitrators in investor–state arbitration cases were challenged as of the end of 2018. Seven of these challenges were upheld. By way of comparison, at the International Chamber of Commerce (ICC) Court of Arbitration, as of end 2014, there have been 66 challenges in 43 arbitrations, four of which were upheld.[14]

Broadly, these results also seem to signal that the success rate of challenges may vary according to the rules applied to the challenges. Thus, while less than 5% of the cases (four cases out of 84) were upheld at ICSID, about 20% were upheld under the UNCITRAL rules (seven cases out of 34).[15] Different challenges success rates can, of course, be explained by a variety of reasons. The reasons for a challenge, the strength of the case, and the positions of the parties, all play a role in

---

[11] Meg Kinnear and Frauke Nitschke, 'Disqualification of Arbitrators under the ICSID Convention and Rules', in Chiara Giorgetti (n. 10), 34–79. For the same and careful analysis on ICC data, see Loretta Malintoppi and Andrea Carlevaris, 'Challenges of Arbitrators, Lessons from the ICC', in Chiara Giorgetti (n. 10), 140–63. For the data on PCA administered arbitrations, see PCA, Annual Report 2018, p. 16; for a detailed analysis, Sarah Grimmer, 'The Determination of Arbitrator Challenges by the Secretary-General of the Permanent Court of Arbitration', in Chiara Giorgetti (n. 10), 80–114.

[12] Kinnear and Nitschke, ibid., 34–7.

[13] Note that under the proposed new ICSID rules, the filing of a challenge will not automatically suspend proceedings.

[14] Malintoppi and Carlevaris (n. 11).

[15] Note that similar percentages are also found at the SCC. See Karel Daele, 'Investment Treaty Arbitration: Similar Challenge, Different Outcome', *Global Arbitration Review,* 21 March 2012, stating that 'A study of challenges under the rules of the Arbitration Institute of the [SCC], which apply the same disqualification standard as the UNCITRAL Rules, yield similar statistics. In those, 30 to 40 per cent of the challenges made in the last twenty years have been upheld'.

Table 5.1 *Success rates of arbitrator challenges in investor–state arbitration*

Institution	No. challenges	Challenge Outcome
ICSID (as of Sept 2014)[1]	84	60 resulted in determination, of which – 56 were rejected – 4 were upheld 21 arbitrators resigned 3 withdrawn/ discontinued
PCA 1976 and 2010 UNCITRAL Rules (as of end 2018)[2]	34	28 resulted in determination, of which –21 were rejected – 7 were upheld 5 arbitrators resigned 1 withdrawn

[1] Kinnear and Nitschke (n. 11), 34–7.

[2] Annual Report 2018 (n. 11), p. 16 and Grimmer (n. 11), 80–114.

the success of a challenge. That said, it is worth noting the difference in success rates according to the different rules. As explained in detail in the next section, there are some significant differences between the rules, both substantially in terms of the standard of review that applies to consider the challenges and procedurally in terms of who decides the challenge. These may explain in part the different outcomes.

Importantly, the success rate of challenges procedures does not describe the full picture. In fact, a significant number of arbitrators decided to resign from the Tribunal once challenged, without waiting for the results of the procedure. This may signal different issues, which remain necessarily hypothetical. Resignation may be the result of a desire of an arbitrator not to disrupt the proceedings and withdraw from a case when one of the parties has lost trust in him or her. It may also be the consequence of a perceived legitimate challenge likely to succeed, which the arbitrator recognizes as such. Whatever the reason, challenges procedures may alter the composition of the tribunals irrespective of the result of the challenge itself, as they often result in the resignation of the challenged arbitrator. For example, under the ICSID procedure, while only four decisions upheld the request of disqualification of an arbitrator, in 21 of the 84 cases (25%), the arbitrator resigned before the challenge was resolved. At the PCA using the UNCITRAL Rules, five of the 34 arbitrators (15%) resigned before the procedure was finalized. Differently to what we found when looking at final results of challenges, which show that disqualification is rarer under the ICSID Rules, resignations seem to be more common in ICSID and less prevalent under UNCITRAL at the PCA.

It is significant to underline that challenge procedures result in an alteration of the members of the tribunal, and thus in the composition of the tribunal, in about 30% of the cases, in both ICSID and at the PCA using UNCITRAL Rules.[16] Figure 5.1 shows variation in outcome in the two forums. When adding challenges that result in removal of an arbitrator to challenges where the arbitrator decides to resign prior to the issuance of a decision on the challenge, therefore, filing a challenges procedure is likely to result in a change of the composition of the tribunal members in over 30% of cases. This is an important finding, including for counsel contemplating a challenge. In unscrupulous hands, this may also have the perverse effect of encouraging spurious challenges, in the hope of succeeding altering the bench regardless of the merits of the disqualification proposals.

Challenges are overwhelmingly initiated by respondent. The reasons for this vary. Of course, respondents' challenges may be due solely to the choice of arbitrator nominated by claimant. That said, respondent is typically in a defensive position and the proceedings may have caught the respondent by surprise. Challenges may signal a novel, concrete interest in the arbitration. They may also be used tactically to delay proceedings. Respondents have brought 71% of all challenges in ICSID cases (60 of the 84 challenges), while claimants filed only 29% (24 of the 84 challenges).[17] Similarly, of the 24 challenges filed in investor–state arbitrations for determination by the Secretary-General of the PCA, only five were submitted by a claimant, about 21%.[18]

Interestingly, consideration of who appointed the challenged arbitrators also matters in the analysis, as significant discrepancies exist. In ICSID, respondents brought all of the challenges against claimant-

---

[16] Kinnear and Nitschke (n. 11), 37.
[17] Ibid., 41–2.
[18] Grimmer (n. 11), 82–3.

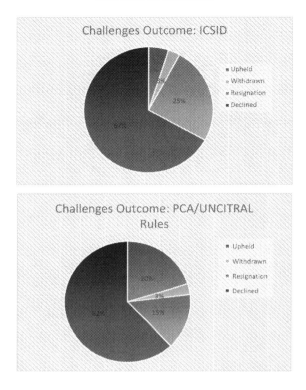

Figure 5.1 Arbitration challenges – variation in outcomes by institution

appointed arbitrators. Respondents also brought eight of the 27 challenges against respondent-appointed arbitrators, four of the five challenges against arbitrators who were jointly appointed, and 11 of the 15 challenges against ICSID-nominated arbitrators.[19] Similarly, at the PCA in the 1976–2015 period, 24 challenges were submitted to the Secretary-General for determination in investor–state arbitrations. Seventeen of these challenges were submitted by the respondent against the arbitrator appointed by claimant, while only five challenges were submitted by claimant against an arbitrator appointed by respondent. Respondent also challenged the president twice, and the entire tribunal – including the arbitrator it appointed – once.[20]

[19] Kinnear and Nitschke (n. 11), 42.
[20] Grimmer (n. 11), 82–3.

Similarly, in certain cases more than one arbitrator may be challenged. For example, at the PCA in the 1976 to 2015 period, 28 challenge requests were submitted to the Secretary-General for determination in the context of 17 arbitrations.[21] Similarly, at ICSID the 84 disqualifications proposal filed as of September 2014 related to 57 different individuals. Fifty-six of the 84 cases related to a single arbitrator, while 28 cases challenged the majority or the entirety of the tribunal.[22] In some cases, parties challenged more than one arbitrator at a time; in other cases, parties tried to disqualify the same individual more than once. For example, Mr Fortier was challenged seven times in the course of the *ConocoPhillips* v. *Venezuela* arbitration, always unsuccessfully.[23] Challenges of one arbitrator may produce a chain effect as other members are challenged by the opposing or same party. For example, at the PCA, more than one member of a tribunal was challenged in seven of the 24 challenges filed in investor–state arbitrations decided by the PCA Secretary-General, and in four of those cases, challenges were initiated by one side against the arbitrator appointed by the other side within one month of a challenge.[24] Similarly, in one case, when challenging the entire tribunal, a respondent also challenged the arbitrator that it had appointed.[25]

5.3 Removing Arbitrators: Applicable Rules

The section above highlights available data detailing the number of challenges cases filed at ICSID and at the PCA and explains the data relating to challenges. It is now interesting to review the main differences that exist among the rules often applied in resolving arbitrator challenges in international investment arbitrations, as well as some cases in which these rules were applied.

The selection of arbitrators and the possibility of challenging that selection is a fundamental factor that contributes to the perceived legitimacy of each member of the arbitral tribunal. As seen above, once rare in proceedings of international tribunals, in parallel to the increased use

---

[21] Ibid., 83. This number includes four non-investor–state arbitrations.

[22] Kinnear and Nitschke (n. 11), 36–7.

[23] *ConocoPhillips Petrozuata B.V., ConocoPhillips Hamaca B.V. and ConocoPhillips Gulf of Paria B.V. v. Bolivarian Republic of Venezuela,* ICSID Case No. ARB/07/30. See Cleis (n. 10), 74–7.

[24] Grimmer (n. 11), 83.

[25] Ibid., 82–3.

of investor-state arbitration as a dispute resolution mechanism, challenges have of late become more common.[26] On the one side, repeat appointments and potential personal, professional and case- or issue-specific conflicts result in more reasons for parties to suspect possible partiality or lack of independence of an arbitrator.[27] Challenges procedures can be an important control mechanism to ensure the legitimacy of the international investment arbitration process. Challenges provide a remedy to the possible abuse of the arbitration process by a party through its right to appoint an arbitrator. On the other side, however, tactical or unmeritorious challenges are also on the rise, and are used by parties to delay proceedings, obtain tactical advantages and minimize possible disadvantages. Partasides, for example, argues that parties can have four reasons to launch a tactical challenge: (1) delay proceedings; (2) send a warning to the challenged arbitrator; (3) drive the arbitrator into making a mistake and create a reason to challenge and (4) push the arbitrator to resign.[28]

It is therefore important to examine and explain the most commonly used challenge rules, with an eye to identifying the different elements that may strengthen or undermine the legitimacy of the members of the tribunal and of the arbitration process generally. Grounds for challenging an arbitrator are generally limited to an alleged lack of the qualities needed to be an arbitrator, which most often revolve around lack of independence and impartiality. The proper applicable standards differ and the applicable rules should be closely examined when considering a challenge.[29]

---

[26] For example, of the 84 challenges filed at ICSID up to September 2014, all but two were filed after 2000. See Karel Daele, *Challenge and Disqualification of Arbitrators in International Arbitration* (Kluwer, 2012), pp. 515, 527 (table of cases). Kinnear and Nitschke, (n. 12), 35.

[27] Luke Sabota, 'Repeat Arbitrator Appointments in International Investment Disputes' in Giorgetti, (n. 10); Romain Zamour, 'Issue Conflicts and the Reasonable Expectation of an Open Mind: The Challenge Decision in Devas v. India and Its Impact', in Chiara Giorgetti (n. 10); *Burlington Resources, Inc. v. Republic of Ecuador*, ICSID Case No. ARB/08/5, Decision on the Proposal or Disqualification of Professor Francisco Orrego Vicuña, 13 December 2013. The arbitrator was challenged because, *inter alia*, he had been nominated by claimant's counsel eight times.

[28] See Costantine Partasides, 'The Art of Selecting the Right Arbitrator' Lecture, London School of Economics, 9 November 2011, <lse.ac.uk/lse-player?id=1252>.

[29] See generally Chiara Giorgetti, 'Challenges of International Investment Arbitrators: How Does It Work and Does It Work?' (2013) 7(2) *World Arbitration and Mediation Review* 303.

ARBITRATOR CHALLENGES   143

This section explains and compares the challenges rules that most often apply in investor–state disputes; those of ICSID, UNCITRAL, the SCC and the ICC.

5.3.1   The ICSID Convention and Arbitration Rules

Challenges procedures under ICSID are quite unique.[30] Article 57 of the ICSID Convention provides that a party may propose the disqualification of an arbitrator 'on account of any fact indicating a manifest lack of the qualities' required to be nominated.[31]

Challenges under ICSID must be filed with the Secretary-General 'promptly' and in any case before the proceedings are declared closed.[32] The Secretary-General then transmits the challenge to the members of the Tribunal and notifies the other party. If the challenge relates to a sole arbitrator or the majority of the tribunal, the file is transmitted to the Chairman of the ICSID's Administrative Council The challenged arbitrator is then invited to give explanations to the tribunal or the Chairman. Where the decision rests with the tribunal, its remaining members consider and vote on the challenge. Only if the remaining members are equally divided or if the disqualification proposal pertains to the majority of the tribunal, the Chairman of the Administrative Council decides on the challenges, using his or her best effort to make a decision within 30 days after he or she has received the proposal. Pending the decision, the proceedings are suspended. The fact that decisions are taken by the tribunal's remaining members in most cases is unique in investment arbitration, and has been rightly criticized.[33] The

---

[30] See generally James Crawford, 'Challenges to Arbitrators in ICSID Arbitration', in David D. Caron et al. (eds.), *Practising Virtue: Inside International Arbitration* (Oxford University Press, 2015), p. 596.

[31] ICSID Convention, art. 57: 'A party may propose to a Commission or Tribunal the disqualification of any of its members on account of any fact indicating a manifest lack of the qualities required by paragraph (1) of Article 14. A party to arbitration proceedings may, in addition, propose the disqualification of an arbitrator on the ground that he was ineligible for appointment to the Tribunal under Section 2 of Chapter IV'.

[32] ICSID Arbitration Rule 9, detailing the procedure to be taken.

[33] On this issue, see Noah Rubins and Bernhard Lauterburg, 'Independence, Impartiality and Duty of Disclosure in Investment Arbitration', in Christina Knahr et al. (eds.), *Investment and Commercial Arbitration – Similarities and Divergences* (Eleven Int'l Pub, 2009), p. 163, noting that 'The ICSID's unique system for adjudicating arbitrator challenges raises interesting questions. Are a challenged arbitrator's colleagues on the tribunal likely to remove him [or her] in light of the personal and professional connections between them? It would seem that an arbitral institution (like the ICC or the SCC

144 CHIARA GIORGETTI

concern is that arbitrators could be reluctant to disqualify a co-arbitrator. In the history of ICSID, co-arbitrators upheld a challenge only twice.[34]

In ICSID's practice, the term 'manifest' required to uphold a challenge has generally been strictly applied to mean '"obvious" or "evident" and highly probable, not just possible'.[35] In *ConocoPhillips* v. *Venezuela*, for example, the Tribunal rejected the disqualification proposal of an arbitrator and recalled that ICSID decisions recognized that the term 'manifest' in Article 57 of the Convention meant 'obvious' or 'evident' and highly probable, and not just possible. Indeed, it imposed a relatively heavy burden on the party proposing disqualification that the manifest lack of the required qualities to sit as an arbitrator had to appear from objective evidence.[36] This has established a high threshold under ICSID.

However, recent practice seems to adjust the understanding of 'manifest' so that it comes closer to other commonly used challenges rules. In *Blue Bank* v. *Venezuela*, for example, the Chairman of the ICSID Administrative Council interpreted the manifest standard differently.[37] In the case, Venezuela had challenged the claimant-appointed arbitrator

---

Board) would have more interest than co-arbitrators in carefully scrutinizing alleged conflicts of interest, given the systemic and reputational risks that such conflicts implicate.'

[34] *Caratube International Oil Company LLP and Devincci Salah Hourani* v. *Republic of Kazakhstan*, ICSID Case No. ARB/13/13 and *Big Sky Energy Corporation* v. *Republic of Kazakhstan*, ICSID Case No. ARB/17/22.

[35] *ConocoPhillips Company et al.* v. *Bolivarian Republic of Venezuela*, ICSID Case No. ARB/07/30, Decision on the Proposal to Disqualify L. Yves Fortier, QC, Arbitrator, 27 February 2012, para. 56.

[36] Ibid. Similarly, other ICSID Tribunals deciding proposals for the disqualification of members of the arbitral tribunal confirmed that the term manifest meant 'obvious' or 'evident' and that such a finding would require 'obvious evidence' of a state of mind lacking independence or impartiality. For a well-reasoned explanation and summary, see *Sociedad General de Aguas de Barcelona S.A. and Vivendi Universal S.A* v. *Argentina*, ICSID Case No. ARB/03/19, Decision on the Proposal for the Disqualification of a Member of the Arbitral Tribunal, 22 October 2007, concluding at para. 28 that it 'agree [d] with earlier panels which have had to interpret and apply Article 57 that the mere existence of some professional relationship with a party is not an automatic basis for disqualification of an arbitrator or Committee member. All the circumstances need to be considered in order to determine whether the relationship is significant enough to justify entertaining reasonable doubts as to the capacity of the arbitrator or member to render a decision freely and independently.'

[37] *Blue Bank Int'l and Trust (Barbados) Ltd* v. *Bolivarian Republic of Venezuela*, ICSID Case No. ARB/12/20, Decision on the Parties' Proposals to Disqualify a Majority of the Tribunal, 12 November 2013, paras. 22–6. In the case, the respondent had challenged the arbitrator appointed by claimant because of his partnership in the Madrid office of

alleging that the international law firm in which he was a partner also represented a client against Venezuela in another investment arbitration, albeit from a different office. The Chairman applied 'an objective standard based on a reasonable evaluation of the evidence by a third party' and interpreted the word 'manifest' in the ICSID Convention 'as meaning "evident" and "obvious" and relating to the ease with which the alleged lack of qualities can be perceived'.[38] Hence, the Chairman upheld the challenge while staying within the boundaries set in Article 57 of the Convention.

The ICSID Rules on arbitrator challenges show two distinctive features: challenges are decided by the unchallenged arbitrators when only one arbitrator is challenged, and the standard of review. Both of these features can and have been criticized for causing the high threshold for ICSID challenges compared with other major arbitral rules. Does the low number of successful challenges – only five in the entire ICSID history – show that these procedures are excessively strict? Does the system of requiring the two unchallenged arbitrators to decide on the fate of a fellow arbitrator create impossible conundrum? What about having the Chairman of the Administrative Council always deciding challenges under the Convention? Would the same person – who also sits as the President of the World Bank and has always been a US national – guarantee consistency? These are key questions when assessing challenges under ICSID.

5.3.2 The UNCITRAL Arbitration Rules

Under UNCITRAL Rules, a party that intends to challenge an arbitrator must send a notice of the challenge within fifteen days after it has been notified of the appointment of the arbitrator or after having learned of the circumstances giving rise to the challenge.[39] The notice of challenge and its reasons are communicated directly to the other party, the arbitrator who is challenged, and to the other arbitrators. If, within 15 days from the date of the notice, the parties have not agreed on the challenge or the challenged arbitrator has not withdrawn, the party making the challenge may pursue the challenge by seeking, within thirty days from the date of

---

Baker and McKenzie. At the time, Baker and McKenzie also represented claimant in another case against Venezuela through its offices in New York and Caracas.

[38] For a critical analysis of this case, see Baiju S. Vasani and Shaun A. Palmer, 'Challenge and Disqualification of Arbitrators at ICSID: A New Dawn?' (2015) 30(1) *ICSID Review* 194.

[39] UNCITRAL Rules (2010), art. 13.

146 CHIARA GIORGETTI

the challenge notice, a decision on the challenge from the appointing authority.

Under UNCITRAL Rules, arbitrators may be challenged 'if circumstances exist' that give rise to 'justifiable doubts' as to the impartiality or independence of an arbitrator.[40] The standard in this case is very different from the ICSID 'manifest lack' standard and it is generally interpreted as a requirement that a 'reasonable and informed third party' would have justifiable doubts as to the impartiality of the challenged arbitrator.[41] Note that a party can challenge the arbitrator it appointed only for reasons the party learnt about after the appointment was made.

The combination of the justifiable doubts threshold with the fact that challenges decisions are taken by the appointing authority seems to provide a less strict approach to challenges than the ICSID approach examined above because the decision is taken from a neutral authority and not the remaining arbitrators and because the standard does not require the difficult 'manifest' evidence. That said, all challenges are highly fact-dependent and a discretion on how to interpret the circumstances surrounding challenges remains.

5.3.3   The SCC Arbitration Rules

Under SCC Rules, a party may challenge an arbitrator if there are circumstances which 'give rise to justifiable doubts as to the arbitrator's impartiality or independence' or if the arbitrator does not possess the qualifications agreed by the parties.[42] Any challenge procedure must be submitted in writing to the Secretariat within fifteen days from when the circumstances became known to the party. A failure to challenge within the allotted time constitutes a waiver of the right to make the challenge. The Secretariat then notifies the parties and the arbitrators of the challenge and gives them all an opportunity to submit a comment on the

---

[40] UNCITRAL Rules (2010), art. 12(1) stating that: '1. Any arbitrator may be challenged if circumstances exist that give rise to justifiable doubts as to the arbitrator's impartiality or independence. 2. A party may challenge the arbitrator appointed by it only for reasons of which it becomes aware after the appointment has been made.'

[41] See, for example, *Vito G. Gallo* v. *Government of Canada*, NAFTA/UNCITRAL Case, Decision on the Challenge to Mr J. Christopher Thomas, QC, 12 October 2009, holding that that a 'reasonable and informed third party' would have had justifiable doubts about Mr Thomas' impartiality and independence as an arbitrator when also acting as an adviser to NAFTA non-disputing party Mexico.

[42] SCC Rules, art. 15.

challenge. If the other party agrees on the challenge, the arbitrator must resign.[43] In all other cases, the Board of Directors of the SCC Arbitration Institute makes the final decision on the challenge.[44]

5.3.4 The ICC Arbitration Rules

ICC Rules provide that a challenge to an arbitrator, 'whether for an alleged lack of impartiality or independence, or otherwise', must be filed with the Secretariat in writing specifying the facts and circumstances on which the challenge is based.[45] Challenges must be made within thirty days from the appointment or confirmation of the arbitrator, or from the date when the party making the challenge was informed of the facts and circumstances. The Secretariat then offers the opportunity to the arbitrator concerned, the other arbitrators, and the parties to comment in writing. It is for the ICC International Court of Arbitration to rule on the admissibility and, at the same time, if necessary, on the merits of a challenge.[46]

With the exception of the provisions of the ICSID Convention, challenges procedures are mostly the same in terms of applicable threshold and deciding authority, but vary in the details, including in the timing of the request and to whom the request should be filed (see table 5.2).

5.4 Removing Arbitrators: Reasons to Challenge

As explained above, arbitrators are challenged when they lack the qualities to sit as arbitrators. This happens when at least one of the parties does not believe they are independent and impartial anymore. In practice, lack of impartiality and independence is alleged when several different situations occur. Reasons employed to challenge arbitrators can be broadly divided into three categories: (1) familiarity with other participants in the proceedings; (2) reasons linked to the conduct of

---

[43] Ibid.

[44] Ibid. See also SCC Rules, art. 16 (Release from Appointment). Note that LCIA Rules also provide that arbitrators can be challenged if circumstances exist that give rise to justifiable doubts as to their independence and impartiality. Challenges must be filed in writing to the LCIA Secretariat within fifteen days from the establishment of the tribunal or from the moment in which the party became aware of the circumstances justifying the challenge. The LCIA Court decides on the challenge in writing. Since 2006, the decisions related to challenges are published in a suitably redacted form. See LCIA Rules, art. 10.

[45] ICC Rules, art. 14.

[46] For analysis of ICC data, see Malintoppi and Carlevaris (n. 11).

Table 5.2 *Summary of challenge procedures*

Rules	To whom to file the request?	When to submit	Who decides?	Reasons for challenge
ICSID	The ICSID Secretary-General	'Promptly' and in any case before the proceedings is declared closed.	The remaining members of the tribunal if only one arbitrator is challenged. The Chair of the AC if the remaining members are equally divided or if the majority or sole arbitrator is challenged.	Any fact indicating a manifest lack of the qualities required to be nominated.
UNCITRAL	The other party, the arbitrator who is challenged, and to the other arbitrators.	Fifteen days after appointment of the arbitrator or after learning of the circumstances giving rise to the challenge.	If parties do not agree within time-limit and arbitrator has not withdrawn, the appointing authority.	If circumstances give rise to justifiable doubts as to the arbitrator's impartiality or independence.
SCC	The Secretariat	Within fifteen days from when the circumstances became known to the party.	If the other party agrees on the challenge, the arbitrator must resign. Otherwise, the Board of Directors of the SCC Arbitration Institute.	If circumstances 'give rise to justifiable doubts as to the arbitrator's impartiality or independence' or the arbitrator does not possess the qualifications agreed by the parties.
ICC	The Secretariat	Within thirty days from the appointment or confirmation of the arbitrator, or from the date when the party making the challenge was informed of the facts and circumstances.	ICC International Court of Arbitration rules on the admissibility and, at the same time, if necessary, on the merits of a challenge.	Challenges can be submitted for an alleged lack of impartiality or independence or otherwise.

proceedings and (3) statements made by the arbitrators on issues related to the dispute. Each category is examined below. Note that it is quite common for parties to raise more than one ground in an arbitrator challenge.

5.4.1 Familiarity with Other Participants in the Proceedings

The most common situations to challenge an arbitrator arise from some kind of familiarity among participants in the proceedings. This can be due to professional or personal relationship between the arbitrator and some other actor in the arbitration, including because of previous contacts, repeat appointments and different roles played in arbitration. Some form of familiarity was the reason for challenges in 25 ICSID cases, for example.[47] These situations include: arbitrators having acted as co-counsel with one of the counsel in the arbitration; repeat appointments of an arbitrator by the same party or the same counsel; professional contacts between the arbitrator and counsel or party; long-term personal relationship between an arbitrator and counsel or party; and the existence of financial interests or link with one of the parties. More specifically, some of the reasons that resulted in the initiation of challenges proceedings include: the merger of law firms, the assumption of partnership or adviser role; multiple appointments of an arbitrator by the same party or counsel; financial interest or link to one of the parties; the fact that the arbitrator and counsel previously acted as co-counsel; professional contacts between the arbitrator and counsel; family links between the arbitrator and counsel for a party; personal animosity between an arbitrator and counsel; and double hatting (i.e. acting as counsel and arbitrator in related proceedings).[48]

Several examples of such situations exist. For example, in *Gallo v Canada,* a NAFTA case decided under UNCITRAL (1976) Rules, the claimant filed a challenge after learning that the professional situation of respondent-appointed arbitrator Mr Thomas had changed since his appointment.[49] Specifically, Mr Thomas had agreed to advise Mexico, a non-disputing party under NAFTA, on legal matters, which could

---

[47] See generally Cleis (n. 10), 56, stating that 'an overwhelming majority' of ICSID challenges was based on pre-existing familiarity with another participant in the proceeding.

[48] See generally Kinnear and Nitschke (n. 11) and Grimmer (n. 11).

[49] *Vito G. Gallo* v. *Government of Canada*, NAFTA/UNCITRAL Case, Decision on the Challenge to Mr J. Christopher Thomas, QC, 14 October 2009.

include international investment arbitration. The appointing authority deciding the challenge concluded that from the point of view of a 'reasonable and informed third party' there would be justifiable doubts about Mr Thomas' impartiality and independence as an arbitrator. He was therefore directed to choose whether to continue to advise Mexico, or continue to serve as an arbitrator. Mr Thomas resigned as arbitrator a few days after the decision. This is an interesting case in which the appointing authority in adopting a 'reasonable and informed' third party view was cautious and feared the possibility that future conflict could be created as the position of the arbitrator changed. It is also interesting that the arbitrator could choose which assignment he wanted to retain.

Similarly, in *ICS* v. *Argentina,* another case applying UNCITRAL (1976) Rules and decided under the Argentina–United Kingdom bilateral investment treaty (BIT), the respondent challenged the claimant-appointed arbitrator alleging that a conflict of interest existed because the arbitrator and his firm were concurrently representing claimants in another long-running investment treaty proceeding against Argentina.[50] The appointing authority found that that circumstance put the arbitrator, Mr Alexandrov, in a situation of adversity towards Argentina, a situation that was often a source of justified concerns that the appointing authority believed should in principle be avoided. The appointing authority noted that the case at hand was not merely a case in which an arbitrator's firm was acting adversely to one of the parties in the dispute, but it was a case in which the arbitrator had personally and recently acted adversely to one of the parties to the dispute.[51] The authority therefore held that the conflict was 'sufficiently serious to give rise to objectively justifiable doubts as to Mr Alexandrov's impartiality and independence'.[52] Thus, although there was no reason to doubt the arbitrator's personal intention to act impartially and independently, the claimant had to appoint another arbitrator.[53] This case also applies a justifiable doubts standard to ensure that a possible – not demonstrated – animosity might create difficulties between the tribunal and the parties and thus undermine the proceedings.

---

[50] *ICS Inspection and Control Services Ltd (United Kingdom)* v. *Republic of Argentina*, PCA Case No. 2010-9, Decision on Challenge to Arbitrator, 17 December 2009, para. 1.
[51] Ibid., para. 4.
[52] Ibid., para. 2.
[53] Ibid., para. 5.

The question of the relationship between arbitrator and counsel was also addressed in *Blue Bank* v. *Venezuela*, a case filed under the Barbados–Venezuela BIT and decided under ICSID procedural rules.[54] In the case, the respondent filed a request to disqualify the claimant's appointed arbitrator, Mr Alonso,[55] and the claimant filed a request to disqualify the respondent's appointed arbitrator, Dr Torres-Bernardez.[56] Thus, as provided by ICSID Rules, the Chairman of Administrative Council decided the challenge. In its proposal for the disqualification, Venezuela argued that Mr Alonso's interests were adverse to its interests because his firm, Baker and McKenzie, represented interests against Venezuela, and Mr Alonso was a partner and co-manager of Baker and McKenzie's global arbitration practice.[57] Venezuela questioned in particular Mr Alonso's position as a Managing Partner of the Litigation and Arbitration Department at Baker and McKenzie in Madrid and as Member of Steering Committee of Baker and McKenzie's International European Dispute Practice Group and the fact that Baker and McKenzie represented the claimant in *Longreef* v. *Venezuela* through its offices in New York and Caracas.[58] The Chairman of the Administrative Council upheld the challenge against Mr Alonso on those undisputed facts and the similarity of the issues between the two ICSID cases against Venezuela, and held that a reasonable third party would find an appearance of lack of impartiality in Alonso's judgment.[59]

In the same case, the claimant proposed disqualification of Dr Torres-Bernardez based on repeat appointments by Argentina and Venezuela when represented by the former Attorney General of Argentina; and on his alleged systematic findings in favour of States.[60] Dr Torres-Bernardez resigned from the Tribunal after submitting his remarks on the challenge[61] and the Chairman of the Administrative Council accordingly dismissed the challenge.

---

[54] *Blue Bank International and Trust (Barbados) Ltd* v. *Bolivarian Republic of Venezuela*, ICSID Case No. ARB 12/20, Decision on the Parties' Proposals to Disqualify a Majority of the Tribunal, 12 November 2013.
[55] Ibid., para. 7.
[56] Ibid., para. 10.
[57] Ibid., para. 27.
[58] Ibid., paras. 22–3.
[59] Ibid., paras. 66–9.
[60] Ibid., paras. 45–6.
[61] Ibid., para. 51.

Repeat appointments have also been the subject of several disqualification requests. In the practice of investment tribunals, what seems to matter is not the number of cases in which an arbitrator has sat, but rather the proximity – both legally and factually – of the specific cases examined.

In *Caratube* v. *Kazakhstan*, for example, the issue at stake was the similarities of two cases in which the challenged arbitrator sat and to which he was appointed by the same State.[62] In the case, Caratube and Mr Devincci Salah Hourani, a US national, filed a claim against Kazakhstan in 2013 at ICSID. The claimants appointed Professor Laurent Aynès as arbitrator and the respondent appointed Mr Bruno Boesch. The parties then jointly nominated Dr Laurent Lévy to act as president of the tribunal. In 2014, the claimants submitted a request for disqualification of Mr Boesch, alleging that he manifestly could not be 'independent and impartial' because he was serving as arbitrator appointed by Kazakhstan in another related case, *Ruby Roz* v. *Kazakhstan*.[63] The claimants identified similarities between *Ruby Roz* and *Caratube* and asserted that both claims relied on essentially the same factual allegations with respect to acts and omissions and pattern of conduct. Additionally, the claimants argued that several individuals who submitted witness statements in *Ruby Roz* would also likely submit witness statements in *Caratube*.[64] The claimants also asserted that Mr Boesch had been appointed as arbitrator by the same firm, Curtis, Mallet-Prevost, Colt and Mosle, in numerous cases including *Caratube* and *Ruby Roz*, which also created a potential conflict.[65]

In a first for ICSID, the two unchallenged arbitrators upheld the challenge,[66] and agreed with the claimants that *Ruby Roz* arose out of the same factual context as *Caratube* and concluded that the case exhibited an imbalance because of Mr Boesch's involvement with *Ruby Roz* and that Mr Boesch could not be expected to 'to maintain a "Chinese wall" in his own mind'.[67] Though they explained that they did not

---

[62] *Caratube International Oil Company LLP and Mr Devincci Salah Hourani* v. *Republic of Kazakhstan*, ICSID Case No. ARB/13/13, Decision on the Proposal for Disqualification of Mr Bruno Boesch, 20 March 2014, para. 62.

[63] *Ruby Roz Agricol* v. *Kazakhstan*, UNCITRAL contract case, Award on Jurisdiction, 1 August 2013.

[64] *Caratube* (n. 62), paras. 24–6.

[65] Ibid., para. 30.

[66] Ibid., para. 111.

[67] Ibid., para. 75.

question Mr Boesch's moral character, his actual impartiality, or his honesty,[68] they concluded that 'a third party would find that there is an evident or obvious appearance of lack of impartiality or independence based on a reasonable evaluation of the facts in the present case'.[69] At the same time, the arbitrators found that multiple appointments by the same firm alone did not constitute an objective circumstance that would demonstrate the arbitrator's inability to exercise independent and impartial judgment in the case at hand.[70]

This decision is quite unique and also shows the challenges faced by both parties and the deciding authority when assessing challenges. What is the difference between knowledge that is useful for an arbitrator to have to exercise his or her function and knowledge that may create conflict? If the factual pattern of the cases are the same, could they have been run in parallel?

These important cases show the difficulties in applying the standards for challenges. They also highlight the importance that the deciding authorities give to the view of 'an objective and informed third party' and thus the weight that the perception plays in challenges proceedings – that arbitrators are seen as impartial and independent.

5.4.2 Reasons Linked to the Conduct of Arbitrators during the Proceedings

Other reasons for bringing challenges are linked to the behaviour of arbitrators during the proceedings. This was the reason in five cases

---

[68] Ibid., para. 64.

[69] Ibid., para. 91.

[70] Ibid., para. 109. Also holding at para. 107 that: 'The Unchallenged Arbitrators agree with the two remaining arbitrators in *Tidewater* that the mere fact of Mr. Boesch's prior appointments as arbitrator by Curtis, Mallet-Prevost, Colt and Mosle LLP, one of which was made on behalf of the Respondent in the Ruby Roz arbitration, does not, without more, indicate a manifest lack of independence or impartiality on the part of Mr. Boesch. Absent any other objective circumstances demonstrating that these prior appointments manifestly influence his ability to exercise independent judgment in the present arbitration, they do not on their own justify Mr. Boesch's disqualification'; and nonetheless observing at para. 108 that: 'Be it only said that the Unchallenged Arbitrators are impressed in particular by the fact that there exists a sufficient number of potential arbitrators for an appointment to be made without any appearance being given of an existing link, real or suspected, between the arbitrator and the appointing party and its counsel. And conversely, that it is quite natural that a party and its counsel will wish to appoint the "best" arbitrator available for a given case and that prior experiences with that potential arbitrator are of course adequate to give that assurance'.

154 CHIARA GIORGETTI

brought at ICSID, in which arbitrators' conduct was found to be wanting and demonstrating a lack of independence and impartiality.[71] These include certain procedural or jurisdictional decisions. Four of the five cases were dismissed.

The challenge in *Burlington* v. *Ecuador,* which was upheld on issues of arbitrator's conduct during proceedings, tackled also issues concerning repeat appointments of the same arbitrator by counsel and duties of disclosure. The case, applying the ICSID Rules and decided under the Ecuador–US BIT, was decided by the Chairman of ICSID's Administrative Council after the two remaining co-arbitrators failed to reach a decision on the challenge.[72] Several years after the beginning of the proceedings, counsel for the respondent learnt from a news report that the claimant-appointed arbitrator, Mr Vicuña, had been appointed multiple times by counsel, Freshfields Bruckhaus Deringer, acting for other claimants. Mr Vicuña was asked to disclose all of his appointments in cases in which Freshfields acted as counsel, and particularly any cases accepted after signing his disclosure declaration as well as compensation paid in those proceedings.[73] Proceedings in the main case were suspended and challenges proceedings were initiated, in which all parties, including Mr Vicuña, were given the opportunity to provide written statements, as a result of which Ecuador learnt that Mr Vicuña had been nominated by claimant's counsel eight times. On the issue of multiple appointments and duty of disclosure, the Chairman of ICSID's Administrative Council found that the respondent 'had sufficient information to file its Proposal for Disqualification of Mr Vicuña on the basis of repeat appointments and non-disclosure of such appointments well before it did' and thus held those issues were time-barred.[74]

Differently, the Chairman found that the issue of arbitrator's conduct during proceedings had been timely raised. On this issue, the Chairman analysed in particular the following paragraph in the arbitrator's written statement:

> Lastly there are some ethical assertions that cannot be left unanswered. Dechert admonishes this arbitrator to resign on ethical grounds as if Dechert's views were proven correct. This is certainly not the case. Moreover, the real ethical question seems to lie with Dechert's

---

[71] See generally Cleis (n. 10), 53–4.
[72] *Burlington* (n. 27), para. 16.
[73] Ibid., para. 4.
[74] Ibid., para. 75.

submissions and the handling of confidential information. To the best of this arbitrator's knowledge the correspondence concerning disclosure and other matters in *Pan American* v. *Bolivia* is part of the confidential record of that case. Dechert is in the knowledge of such correspondence as counsel for Bolivia, but it does not seem appropriate or ethically justified that this information be now used to the advantage of a different client of Dechert, a use that in any event should be consented to by the other party to that case.[75]

The Chairman found that in his reply to the challenge, the arbitrator had made comments that did 'not serve any purpose in addressing the proposal for disqualification or explaining circumstances relevant to the allegations'.[76] He thus decided to uphold the challenge finding that a third party undertaking a reasonable evaluation of this statement would conclude it 'manifestly evidences an appearance of lack of impartiality' with respect to Ecuador and its counsel.[77]

This was the first and only case in which a challenge was upheld as a consequence of the behaviour of an arbitrator during the proceedings. In other cases, challenges pertaining to decisions taken by the arbitral tribunal during the proceedings, which were found to be adverse to the challenging parties, failed. Deciding authorities concluded that more evidence of impartiality and independence of an arbitrator than making what a party considers an adverse decision, was needed. For example, in *Abaclat*, Argentina complained that the two arbitrators had issued a majority award without the dissenting opinion of the remaining arbitrator, had rejected an urgent request for provisional measures, had allegedly limited Argentina's right to defence and had prejudged some of the issues. The parties requested a recommendation by the Secretary-General of the PCA, as required under the applicable rules, and the final decision was taken by the Chairman of ICSID's Administrative Council, who held that the finding of a lack of independence and impartiality of arbitrators 'requires evidence other than the making of a decision which is considered to be adverse to one party, or, indeed wrong in law or insufficiently supported by reasons' because an arbitrator is not bound to make rulings that are 'mutually acceptable to both parties or which are

---

[75] Ibid., para. 79.
[76] Ibid.
[77] *Burlington* (n. 27), para. 80.

156   CHIARA GIORGETTI

neutral in their effects as against both of the parties'.[78] It is the arbitrator's very job to make decisions based on her or his judgement and assessing competing claims. The arbitrator cannot be removed for exercising this function.

5.4.3 Statements Made by the Arbitrators on Issues Related to the Dispute

Statements related to the disputes made by arbitrators can also lead to challenges. These include statements made in prior awards and decisions, outside the context of a decision or award (informal remarks), or in academic writings which may provide the impression that the arbitrator has developed an issue conflict. Arbitrators are expected to have an open mind, and such statements may raise concerns.

In the ICSID arbitration of *Urbaser* v. *Argentina*, for example, the claimants challenged the appointment of Dr McLachlan as respondent-appointed arbitrator because of the views he had expressed in his scholarly publications on two questions claimants considered crucial to the arbitration.[79] The claimants alleged that Dr McLachlan had therefore prejudged essential elements of the conflict that was the object of the arbitration.[80] The two unchallenged arbitrators disagreed with the claimants and held that the scholarly opinions expressed by Dr McLachlan did not meet the threshold of 'presenting an appearance' that he would not be prepared to hear and consider the position of the parties 'with full independence and impartiality'.[81]

Issue conflict was also addressed in *Devas* v. *India*, a case brought in an PCA administered UNICTRAL artibtration arising out of the India–Mauritius BIT.[82] The respondent challenged the arbitrator appointed by the claimants, Mr Vicuña and the presiding arbitrator Mr Lalonde,

---

[78] *Abaclat and Others* v. *Argentine Republic*, ICSID Case No. ARB/07/5, Recommendation Pursuant to the Request by ICSID on the Respondent's Proposal for the Disqualification of Arbitrator, 19 December 2011, para. 83.

[79] *Urbaser S.A. and Consorcio de Aguas Bilbao Bizkaia, Bilbao Biskaia Ur Partzuergoa* v. *Argentine Republic*, ICSID Case No. ARB/07/26, Decision on Claimants' Proposal to Disqualify Professor Campbell McLachlan, Arbitrator, 12 August 2010, para. 20.

[80] Ibid., paras. 23–4.

[81] Ibid., para. 58.

[82] *CC/Devas (Mauritius) Ltd, Devas Employees Mauritius Private Ltd and Telecom Devas Mauritius Ltd* v. *India*, PCA UNCITRAL, Decision on the Respondent's Challenge to the Hon. Marc Lalonde and Prof. Francisco Orrego Vicuña, 30 September 2013.

alleging a lack of impartiality. The challenge was decided by the President of the ICJ, Judge Tomka, as the appointing authority under the applicable rules. The respondent argued that the two challenged arbitrators 'strongly held and articulated positions' in the case on a controversial legal standard which would give rise to justifiable doubt as to their impartiality.[83] Specifically, the respondent referred to decisions by three ICSID tribunals chaired by Mr Vicuña, and in two of which Mr Lalonde served as co-arbitrator, as well a chapter in a book written by Mr Vicuña after the decisions were issued, in which he reiterated his position on the legal question at issue (the question of an essential security interest).[84] Judge Tomka first noted that it was not surprising that the two challenged arbitrators had decided consistently in the ICSID cases because those tribunals had applied the same provision to similar facts.[85] Judge Tomka then specifically assessed the relevance of the chapter written by Mr Vicuña and concluded that it showed that:

> ... his view remained unchanged. Would a reasonable observer believe that the Respondent has a chance to convince him to change his mind on the same legal concept? Professor Orrego Vicuña is certainly entitled to his views, including to his academic freedom. But equally the Respondent is entitled to have its arguments heard and ruled upon by arbitrators with an open mind. Here, the right of the latter has to prevail.[86]

For that reason, he upheld the request for disqualification of Mr Vicuña, while he rejected the proposed disqualification of Mr Lalonde.[87]

As this case-review emphasizes, challenges have been brought in a variety of situations and the deciding authorities have always very carefully reviewed the facts and avoided broad general conclusions. In fact, the few decisions in which an arbitrator has been removed are rare and generally based on very clear facts.

5.5   Conclusion

This chapter offered an empirical analysis of challenges of arbitrators from three different perspectives: first, it provides and discusses data on challenges cases prevalence and outcome to paint a general picture; it

[83] Ibid., para. 17.
[84] Ibid., paras. 19 and 22.
[85] Ibid., para. 59.
[86] Ibid., para. 64.
[87] Ibid., paras. 64, 66–7. On this decision, see in general, Zamour (n. 27).

then focuses on procedure and compares the rules applicable to challenges under ICSID, UNCITRAL, the ICC and the SCC. Finally, it more substantively assesses some of the circumstances that may lead parties to file challenges.

In so doing, we highlighted some issues and possible directions for further research. First, while challenges remain rare, and accepted challenges are even rarer, initiating a challenge procedure can still result in the alteration of membership of the tribunal in about 30% of cases. Challenges are overwhelmingly filed by respondents, often challenging more than one arbitrator, at times even the one appointed by them. There can be a variety of reasons for this, including the fact that respondents often arrive late to the proceedings, they are often in an antagonistic position vis-à-vis the process, may want to assert their presence, and may use challenges more aggressively, also to delay proceedings.

Secondly, our analysis showed that, among the rules applicable to challenges, ICSID stands out both in terms of who decides and the review standards that are applied. Given the existing reform process in investment arbitration, this anomaly could be discussed and possibly addressed, for example through the Rules Amendment process occurring at the time of writing.

Finally, the chapter some of the reasons for challenges and determined that they vary substantially and that authorities have based their decisions on detailed analyses of the facts and circumstances of each case. However, with the growing interest and scrutiny of international arbitration, challenges procedures will become increasingly important because of their relevance in ensuring the continued independence of arbitrators: ensuring a balanced approach – which keeps in mind the interests of both parties – will continue to be fundamental.

6

Dissents in Investment Arbitration: On Collegiality and Individualism

DAPHNA KAPELIUK[*]

6.1 Introduction

A colleague of mine, who regularly serves as an arbitrator in large international commercial and investment arbitrations, once remarked to me that in all the arbitrations he had chaired there had not been any dissents. The colleague, who received his legal training in a civil law country, stressed that dissents should not be allowed in arbitration since they undermine the authority of the award by revealing the differences among the members of the tribunal that arise during deliberations. He added that when he chairs a tribunal, he does all that he can to prevent an arbitrator from issuing a dissenting opinion. In line with the civil law tradition, he argued that collegiality requires that the members of the tribunal should work together to reach a unanimous decision, and, in the event that no agreement can be reached, the dissenting arbitrator should accept the majority's opinion and refrain from expressing his own opinion. This, he added, is how justice should be done – issuing an award by a unified tribunal.

There are broadly two approaches towards dissents – one which embraces dissents, which I term the individualist, and the other which encourages unanimity among the members of the tribunal by way of issuing a single unanimous decision, which I term the collegial. According to the individualist approach, individual opinions, including dissents, help produce better awards since the majority has to consider each point of the opinion and relate to it. Additionally, they encourage the expression of the individual voices of each arbitrator on the panel and

---

[*] Partner, Goldfarb Seligman, Law Offices, Israel <daphna.kapeliuk@goldfarb.com>. The author wishes to thank Sadri Saieb and Karim El Chazli of the Swiss Institute of Comparative Law for providing valuable library resources, as well as Mai Arlowski for excellent research assistance.

serve as guiding tools to the parties in understanding inter-panel dynamics. According to the collegial approach, any individual opinion, and especially a dissenting opinion, breaks collegiality and weakens the authority of the award. Additionally, they also break the confidentiality of deliberations as they reveal the disagreements between the panel members and thus create uncertainty.

The individualist approach is well rooted in the common law tradition, in which judges are encouraged to state their own opinion and render individual opinions (dissenting opinions in case they disagree with the majority, separate opinions when the judge supports the operative part of the judgment but not with its reasons, or concurring opinions). In the words of former US Supreme Court Justice Hughes on dissents: 'dissenting opinions enable a judge to express his individuality. He is not under the compulsion of speaking for the court and thus of securing the concurrence of a majority. In dissenting he is free-lance.' In contrast, the civil law tradition embraces collegiality and judges are generally perceived as a unified voice of the state. The idea of secrecy of deliberations is strongly emphasized and the results of the voting among the individual judges are not disclosed. Thus, since the idea of consensus is of special importance, individual opinions are generally not part of the decision-making process.

This study focuses on individual opinions rendered by arbitrators in investment arbitration tribunals composed of two party-appointed arbitrators and a chair. The study evaluates whether in panels composed of a chair who earned his or her legal education in a country which embraces individualism in its judiciary, there are fewer individual opinions than in panels composed of a chair whose legal education is from a collegial jurisdiction. The study also evaluates whether individuals who received their legal education in an individualist jurisdiction tend to issue more individual opinions than those who received their legal education in a collegial jurisdiction.

6.2 Appointing Arbitrators

The opportunity of disputing parties to select their arbitrators has been considered to be one of the major advantages of arbitration over public court adjudication. While in court adjudication the parties are assigned judges without having any control over their identity, in arbitration, the parties are free to select their own adjudicators. This characteristic has been described as 'the most important single factor' in arbitration,[1] or, as one author suggested, as something that 'is more akin to a marriage proposal than a phone call to see a movie'.[2] Arbitrations are usually heard by a single arbitrator or by a panel composed of three arbitrators.

The current system for appointing arbitrators in investment arbitrations is usually that of two party-appointed arbitrators and a chair. In investment treaties, as well as under procedural rules (e.g. ICSID and UNCITRAL Rules), the claimant-investor is to select one arbitrator, the respondent-State to appoint the second, and the parties, the co-arbitrators or a third party (e.g. the Chairman of the Administrative Council of ICSID under the ICSID Rules or the Secretary-General of the Permanent Court of Arbitration under the UNCITRAL Rules) shall select the chair of the Tribunal.

It is the sense of participation in the arbitration process that has engendered criticism by scholars who have questioned the legitimacy of unilateral appointments.[3] These scholars have expressed the concern that even though all arbitrators are required to act independently and impartially,[4] the very concept of party-appointed arbitrators is by itself contrary to traditional notions of judicial impartiality.[5] As stated by one author who questioned the ability of a party-appointed arbitrator to exercise independent judgment, 'why would any party have confidence in an arbitrator selected by its unloved opponent?'[6] Indeed, since each party selects an arbitrator in the hope that he will hold in his favour, the other party may have reasons to be suspicious of that appointment. This has led one author to question whether 'party-appointment leads to "moral hazard" because those who appoint want to win and those who want to be appointed want the income that appointment brings.'[7] As

---

[1] Yves Dezalay and Bryant G. Garth, *Dealing in Virtue: International Commercial Arbitration and the Construction of a Transnational Legal Order* (Chicago University Press, 1996), p. 8 fn. 6.

[2] David Branson, 'Sympathetic Party-Appointed Arbitrators: Sophisticated Strangers and Governments Demand Them' (2010) 25(2) *ICSID Review* 367, 381.

[3] Detlev F. Vagts, 'The International Legal Profession: A Need for More Governance?' (1996) 90(2) *American Journal of International Law* 250, 258.

[4] As the major arbitration rules require: see e.g. AAA Commercial Arbitration Rules, rule 17; ICDR Arbitration Rules, art. 7; ICC Arbitration Rules, arts. 7.1–7.2.

[5] See e.g. Yuval Shany, 'Squaring the Circle? Independence and Impartiality of Party-Appointed Adjudicators in International Legal Proceedings' (2008) 30(3) *Loyola of Los Angeles International and Comparative Law Review* 473.

[6] Jan Paulsson, 'Moral Hazard in International Dispute Resolution' (2010) 25(2) *ICSID Review* 339, 348.

[7] Branson (n. 2), 381.

162   DAPHNA KAPELIUK

supporting evidence for the problematic aspect of unilateral appointments, commentators have argued that 'the statistics show that dissenting opinions are almost universally issued in favour of the party that appointed the dissenter'.[8]

Once the arbitrators are selected and the tribunal is constituted, the arbitration proceedings begin. Typically, the proceedings are comprised of a written phase followed by an oral one, where evidence is submitted to the tribunal. Upon completion of the pleadings by the parties, the tribunal moves to the deliberation stage in order to decide the dispute. The decision-making process in arbitration tribunals is composed of two intertwined processes: the individual process, whereby each arbitrator arrives at a decision on the dispute; and the collective process, by which the panel members deliberate together, consider the views of their colleagues and agree on the award.

It may well be that during deliberations the arbitrators have similar views on the dispute and agree on how it is to be decided. In this case, they render a unanimous award. Unlike judges, who are assigned majority opinions to write, in arbitration typically it is the chair of the tribunal who writes a draft of the award and circulates it between the members of the tribunal for their comments. Once the arbitrators agree on the draft, the award is issued.

It is not uncommon, however, that the arbitrators disagree with respect to some issues pertaining to the dispute, or even regarding the ultimate decision. In this case, the role of the chair of the arbitration tribunal, who 'performs a different role than the party-appointed arbitrator' is of particular importance.[9] It is in these instances that his or her ability to lead the arbitrators into an acceptable solution comes into play,[10] especially since he or she can 'influence the style' of the arbitration.[11] It is at this stage that the chair may try to exert influence on the

---

[8] See e.g. Alan Redfern, 'Dissenting Opinions in International Commercial Arbitration: The Good, the Bad and the Ugly' (2004) 20(3) *Arbitration International* 223–42; Albert Jan van den Berg, 'Dissenting Opinions by Party-Appointed Arbitrators in Investment Arbitration', in Arsanjani, Cogan, Sloane and Wiessner (eds.), *Looking to the Future: Essays on International Law in Honor of W. Michael Reisman* (Brill, 2010), pp. 821, 824; Paulsson (n. 6), 348–9.

[9] Claudia T. Salomon, 'Selecting an International Arbitrator: Five Factors to Consider' (2002) 17(10) *Mealey's International Arbitration Report* 2, 3.

[10] Thomas E. Carbonneau, 'The Exercise of Contract Freedom in the Making of Arbitration Agreements' (2003) 36 *Vanderbilt Journal of Transnational Law* 1189, 1211–12.

[11] Urs Martin Laeuchli, 'Civil and Common Law: Contrast and Synthesis in International Arbitration' (2007) 62(3) *Dispute Resolution Journal* 81, 82.

arbitrators, so that they agree on an acceptable solution. The more the chair is of the opinion that dissents are undesirable, the more pressure he or she may put on an arbitrator who disagrees with the majority. During the bargaining phase, the chair may be more lenient towards concessions in the award in order to avoid an eventual split between the members of the tribunal. However, it may well be that, notwithstanding such efforts, the chair is unsuccessful in bridging the differences between the arbitrators, and eventually one arbitrator will issue a dissenting opinion.

From an economic perspective, during the decision-making process the arbitrators incur two types of costs – external and internal.[12] The external costs refer to costs of an arbitrator who disagrees with the ultimate decision, but during the deliberations gives in and agrees with the co-arbitrators. Internal costs are those incurred by the arbitrators who have to be flexible in order to adopt a single unified decision. A unanimity rule has the largest internal costs.[13] A majority rule, by contrast, has greater external costs.

The perceptions of arbitrators towards dissents may affect their behavior within the tribunal and their tendency to issue dissenting opinions. An arbitrator whose perception on judicial decision-making is that dissents should not be allowed will try to reach an acceptable solution with the other members of the tribunal. By contrast, an arbitrator who perceives dissents as a normal course of the decision-making process, may be less responsive to bridging the gaps with his colleagues, and, as a result, stick to his individual opinion. One of the reasons for these differing views may be the arbitrators' legal tradition with respect to dissents in judicial decision-making.

6.3   Dissenting in Collegial Panels: On Collegiality and Individualism

6.3.1   *The Market Pressures of Arbitrators*

Disputing parties often select an arbitrator due to his or her perceived predisposition to a party type (investor or state) and its legal position. The party-appointed arbitrator plays an especially important role, since

---

[12] Alberto Alvarez-Jimenez, 'The WTO Appellate Body's Decision-Making Process: A Perfect Model for International Adjudication' (2009) 12(2) *Journal of International Economic Law* 289, 292–3.

[13] Ibid., 293.

he or she often serves as a translator of the legal arguments of the appointing party.[14] However, the party-appointed arbitrator is expected to act independently and impartially.[15] Thus, while the party-appointed arbitrator understands well that a party selected him or her with a desire that he or she renders a decision favourable to that party's claim, the arbitrator ultimately acts under the duties of integrity, independence, and impartiality. Notwithstanding these duties, the legitimacy of unilateral appointments has been questioned by some authors, who argue that the very concept of party-appointed arbitrators may conflict with the notion of arbitrators' independence and impartiality.[16]

Arbitrators who sell dispute resolution services to disputing parties compete in the market for business, just like any other service provider.[17] This competition takes place with respect to any position in an arbitration tribunal, that of a sole arbitrator, a party-appointed arbitrator, or a chair of the tribunal. Scholars have expressed concern over the practice of tribunals composed of a chair and party-appointed arbitrators. They argue that a party-appointed arbitrator, whose income depends on his or her appointment to hear a case and who wishes to increase the likelihood of being reappointed by the appointing party or a party of its type in future disputes, may be predisposed to vote in its favour.[18] As one author suggested, 'an arbitrator may perceive that his award is likely to have an impact on his own acceptability, that is, on the probability of his being appointed again.'[19] In investment arbitrations, at least from the perspective of the investor (who may not be a repeat player, as compared to a host state), the incentive is not directly related to reappointment by the same party, but, more broadly, to future appointments by the same

---

[14] Andreas F. Lowenfeld, 'The Party-Appointed Arbitrator in International Controversies: Some Reflections' (1995) 30(1) *Texas International Law Journal* 59, 65; see also Seth H. Lieberman, 'Something's Rotten in the State of Party-Appointed Arbitration: Healing ADR's Black Eye That Is "Nonneutral Neutrals"' (2004) 5 *Cardozo Journal of Conflict Resolution* 215, 222.

[15] M. Scott Donahey, 'The Independence and Neutrality of Arbitrators' (1992) 9(4) *Journal of International Arbitration* 31, 39.

[16] See e.g. Shany (n. 5), 473.

[17] For an expanded analysis on the market for arbitrators and the parties' opportunity to select their arbitrators, see Daphna Kapeliuk, 'Collegial Games – Analyzing the Effect of Panel Composition on Outcome in Investment Arbitration' (2012) 31(2) *The Review of Litigation* 267.

[18] Shany (n. 5), 483.

[19] See e.g. Allan Scott Rau, 'Integrity in Private Judging' (1997) 38(2) *South Texas Law Review* 485, 522.

type of party – investors or host states. That is, an arbitrator appointed to an ICSID arbitration may wish to increase the likelihood of being appointed in future arbitrations by the same type of party – investors or host states. Indeed, some arbitrators are known to be predominantly repeatedly appointed by investors, while others are being mostly appointed by host states.

6.3.2 The Dynamics of Collegial Panels: On Unanimity and Dissents

The process of arbitral decision making in collegial panels is composed of two interconnected phases: individual and collegial.[20] In the individual phase, each panel member arrives at a decision on the dispute, or at least at an inclination to decide the dispute one way or another. In the collegial phase, which focuses on the dynamics within the panel, the arbitrators deliberate and engage in bargaining in order to arrive at an agreement on the award.

During the deliberation, the arbitrators consider the factual and legal arguments advanced by the parties in order to decide the dispute. From an economic perspective, each arbitrator weighs the costs and benefits that his decision might engender and chooses a voting strategy that will increase his utility.[21] A party-appointed arbitrator motivated by creating a reputation for being impartial might decide the dispute differently from an arbitrator who has an incentive to be reappointed in future disputes by the same party or by the same type of party as the one appointing him. From this perspective, a party-appointed arbitrator, who joins the members of the panel in a decision against the party that appointed him or her, has to consider the effects of his or her decision for future appointments. Similarly, a dissenting party-appointed arbitrator has to weigh the costs and benefits that his or her dissent might produce. The arbitrator will dissent when he or she expects the benefits of breaking from unanimity to exceed the costs this action might engender.[22]

In the collegial phase, the dynamics between the members of the tribunal in reaching a decision are of great importance. Arbitrators may adopt different decision patterns based on their perceptions

---

[20] For an analysis of the dynamics of collegial panels, see Kapeliuk (n. 17).

[21] Daphna Kapeliuk, 'The Repeat Appointment Factor: Explaining Decision Patterns of Elite Investment Arbitrators' (2010) 96(1) *Cornell Law Review* 48, 58.

[22] Lee Epstein, William M. Landes and Richard A. Posner, 'Why (and When) Judges Dissent: A Theoretical and Empirical Analysis' (2011) 3(1) *Journal of Legal Analysis* 101.

regarding the costs and benefits of dissents. When an arbitrator considers that collegiality should be maintained at any costs, he or she will refrain from dissenting. When he or she is of the opinion that the costs of breaking collegiality are smaller than the costs of joining the majority, he or she may prefer to issue a dissenting opinion. Likewise, when an arbitrator is of the opinion that issuing an individual opinion increases the quality of the decision or the process, he or she may wish to write his or her own opinion irrespective of that of the other members of the tribunal.

Dissents do not impose costs on the dissenting arbitrator only, but also on the other members of the tribunal.[23] These costs involve the majority's efforts to justify the award in light of the dissenting opinion.[24] The majority may incur reputational costs when the dissenting arbitrator criticizes the award harshly.[25] When the costs that the majority has to incur because of the dissent exceed the benefits of rendering a majority award, the arbitrators may be more lenient towards the dissenting arbitrator.[26] In this respect, the chair of the arbitration tribunal plays an important role. The chair's perception on the desirability of dissents may have an effect on the majority's flexibility with respect to the resolution of the dispute.

Arbitrators who adopt the individualist approach may behave differently within the panel and in reaching the ultimate decision on the dispute than arbitrators who adopt the collegial approach. Those who follow the individualist approach may be more inclined to issue individual opinions and less responsive to reaching compromises within the panel. In contrast, those who follow the collegial approach may be more lenient and make concessions during the decision-making process.

6.4 Methodology and Results

This study evaluates whether in panels chaired by an arbitrator whose legal training is from an individualist jurisdiction there are more dissents

---

[23] On the costs of dissent in public courts, see Stephen J. Choi and G. Mitu Gulati, 'Trading Votes for Reasoning: Covering in Judicial Opinions' (2008) 81(4) *Southern California Law Review* 735, 746.

[24] Josuha B. Fischman, 'Decision-Making under a Norm of Consensus: A Structural Analysis of Three-Judge Panels' (2008), paper presented on the First Annual Conference on Empirical Legal Studies, published on *SSRN*, see <doi.org/10.2139/ssrn.912299>.

[25] Epstein, Landes and Posner (n. 22).

[26] Richard A. Posner, *How Judges Think* (Harvard University Press, 2008), p. 33.

Table 6.1 *Jurisdiction type of chair and frequency of dissents*

| Jurisdiction Type – Chair | Dissent | | |
	No individual opinion	Individual opinion	Total
Collegial	134	46	180
Individualist	315	72	387
Total	449	118	567

than in panels chaired by an arbitrator whose legal training is from a collegial jurisdiction. For the purpose of this study the jurisdictions will be divided into two types – those that allow issuing dissenting opinions in their courts, which I name 'individualist jurisdictions', and those that do not allow dissents, which I name 'collegial jurisdictions'.[27]

Building on data provided from PluriCourt's PITAD database (updated until 30 May 2019) the research identified 567 investment arbitration cases in which a three-member arbitration tribunal rendered an award (awards on jurisdiction and/or award on merits). Of the 567 cases, there was an individual opinion in 118 cases (dissenting, concurring or separate). Of the 118 cases, in nine cases two arbitrators rendered an individual opinion, in two cases the chair rendered an individual opinion, and in one case the chair and a party-appointed arbitrator each issued an individual opinion.

As seen in Table 6.1, of the 567 cases, arbitrators who received legal education in collegial jurisdictions chaired 180, and arbitrators who received legal education in individualist jurisdictions chaired 387. Party-appointed arbitrators issued a dissenting opinion in 46 of the 180 arbitrations chaired by an arbitrator from a collegial jurisdiction (25.56 per cent), and in 72 of the 387 arbitrations chaired by an arbitrator from an individualist jurisdiction (18.6 per cent). The results of a Pearson's Chi-square Test of Independence revealed that there was no statistically significant relationship between the legal jurisdiction of the chairman and individual opinions ($\chi^2(2) = 3.6018$; p = 0.0577; n = 567).

The study further assessed whether there is a tendency of party-appointed arbitrators who received their legal education in individualist jurisdictions to issue individual opinions more often than those who

---

[27] Information regarding country classification is available from the author upon request.

received their legal education in collegial jurisdictions. There were 421 individuals who acted as party-appointed arbitrators. Of the 421 individuals, 105 received their legal education in a collegial jurisdiction and 316 in an individualist jurisdiction. The average of individual opinions rendered by party-appointed arbitrators from an individualist jurisdiction was 7.32 per cent, while the average of individual opinions rendered by party-appointed arbitrators from a collegial jurisdiction was 5.36 per cent. The results of a T Test were t = 0.76 p = 0.4499, which were not significant.

Not surprisingly, all dissenting arbitrators favoured the party that selected them (except for the individual opinions rendered by the chair). These arbitrators, who have signaled their type through their dissenting opinion, were obviously not in agreement with the majority and have not succeeded in convincing the other arbitrators to agree with them.

6.5   Conclusions

The selection of the optimal arbitrators is a delicate task. Since arbitral decision-making in arbitration panels is a collegial enterprise, the arbitrators' perceptions regarding collegiality and individualism may affect their behavior within the tribunal.

The results of this study demonstrate that the legal training of the chair or of the party-appointed arbitrators, be it a collegial jurisdiction or an individualist jurisdiction, does not affect their tendency to issue individual opinions. This may be explained by the international character of investment treaty arbitrations. Further research should evaluate whether there are other characteristics relating to chairs and party-appointed arbitrators that may affect their behavior in this respect. Once these characteristics are singled out, the legitimacy of dissents could be evaluated.

PART II

Process Legitimacy

Legal Reasoning

7

Foreign Investors, Domestic Courts and Investment Treaty Arbitration

SZILÁRD GÁSPÁR-SZILÁGYI[*]

7.1 Introduction

Supporters of investment treaty arbitration (ITA) and international investment law (IIL) put forward several major justifications for the establishment[1] and continued existence of the investment treaty regime and ITA:

1. investment treaty arbitration *depoliticizes* the dispute, in the sense that 'governments are less likely to intervene diplomatically in disputes where investors have access to treaty-based investor-state arbitration';[2]
2. investment treaty arbitration ensures that investor-state disputes are *denationalized*, thus investors will not be subjected to domestic courts

---

[*] Lecturer in Law at Keele University School of Law. This work was partly supported by the Research Council of Norway through its Centres of Excellence funding scheme, project number 223274. I would like to thank Ole Kristian Fauchald, August Reinisch, Daniel Behn, Dr Maxim Usynin and Silje Hermansen for their useful comments on earlier drafts.

[1] For an overview of the justifications to have ISA, see Gus van Harten, 'Five Justifications for Investment Treaties: A Critical Discussion' (2010) 2(1) *Trade, Law and Development* 1. For a historical overview of the beginnings of investor–state arbitration and ICSID, see Taylor St John, *The Rise of Investor-State Arbitration* (Oxford University Press, 2018), pp. 20–2. She finds that: (a) there was little initial demand for ISDS from investors; (b) the ICSID Convention 'did not emerge as an optimal institutional solution'; (c) 'ICSID officials influenced states' decisions to delegate in their investment treaties' and (d) exiting from ISDS is hard.

[2] See Geoffrey Gertz et al., 'Legalization, Diplomacy and Development: Do Investment Treaties De-politicize Investment Disputes?' (2018) 107 *World Development* 239; see also Leon Trakman and Kunal Sharma, 'Jumping Back and Forth between Domestic Courts and ISDS: Mixed Signals from the Asia-Pacific Region', in Steffen Hindelang and Markus Krajewski (eds.), *Shifting Paradigms in International Investment Law* (Oxford University Press, 2018); St John (n. 1), 102.

172   SZILÁRD GÁSPÁR-SZILÁGYI

that lack *independence*, are less *efficient*, or are *biased* against foreigners;[3] and

3. investment treaties *promote* investments.[4]

Recent, predominantly empirical studies have cast a shadow of doubt on justifications (1) and (3).[5] However, the justification that ITA ensures that investor–state disputes are *denationalized* has received less empirical attention. Investment law literature has mainly focused on the purpose of ITA for bypassing domestic courts, on 'fork-in-the-road' (FITR) clauses, and on introducing an exhaustion of local remedies requirement. Empirical studies that concern the role of domestic courts in IIL have mainly focused on the post-award phase, more specifically on issues surrounding the domestic enforcement and setting aside of international arbitral awards.[6]

This chapter, however, departs from these approaches and asks a novel question, which to my knowledge has yet to be discussed in an empirical way in legal academia: Why *do* or *should* investors resort to the courts of the host country *prior* to ITA? The question has an empirical and a normative angle to it and can be broken down into three sub-questions that inform the structure of the chapter:

1. Do investors rely on domestic courts prior to ITA?

---

[3] See Van Harten (n. 1), Section IV.B; Mavluda Sattorova, 'Return to the Local Remedies Rule in European BITs? Power (Inequalities), Dispute Settlement, and Change in Investment Treaty Law' (2012) 39(2) *Legal Issues of Economic Integration* 223, 226–30.

[4] See UNCTAD, 'The Role of International Investment Agreements in Attracting Foreign Direct Investment to Developing Countries' (2009) UNCTAD Series on International Investment Policies for Development; Kevin P. Gallagher, 'Do Investment Agreements Attract Investment? Evidence from Latin America', in Karl P. Sauvant and Lisa E. Sachs (eds.), *The Effect of Treaties on Foreign Direct Investment: Bilateral Investment Treaties, Double Taxation Treaties, and Investment Flows* (Oxford University Press, 2009); Jason W. Yackee, 'Bilateral Investment Treaties, Credible Commitment, and the Rule of (International) Law: Do BITs Promote Foreign Direct Investment?' (2008) 42(4) *Law & Society Review* 805; Rudolph Dolzer, 'The Impact of International Investment Treaties on Domestic Administrative Law' (2005) 37 *New York University Journal of International Law and Politics* 953, 953–4.

[5] See Gertz (n. 2); Catharine Titi, 'Are Investment Tribunals Adjudicating Political Disputes? Some Reflections on the Repoliticization of Investment Disputes and (New) Forms of Diplomatic Protections' (2015) 32 *Journal of International Arbitration* 261.

[6] To name a few: Julien Fouret (ed.), *Enforcement of Investment Treaty Arbitration Awards: A Global Guide* (Globe Law and Business, 2015); Kaj Hobér and Nils Eliasson, 'Review of Investment Treaty Awards by Municipal Courts', in Katia Yannaca-Small (ed.), *Arbitration under International Investment Agreements* (Oxford University Press, 2010), ch. 24; Gaëtan Verhoosel, 'Annulment and Enforcement Review of Treaty Awards: To ICSID or Not to ICSID' (2008) 23(1) *ICSID Review* 119.

INVESTORS, COURTS AND INVESTMENT ARBITRATION   173

2. If they do, why do they rely on domestic courts?
3. Should investors rely on domestic courts?

This study also comes at a crucial point in IIL, when various international actors are aiming to reform ITA and to alleviate some of the legitimacy concerns faced by ITA. The European Union (EU) has included bilateral investment courts in some of its recent international investment agreements (IIAs) – that have yet to fully enter into force – and the Council of the EU authorized the European Commission to negotiate a convention setting up a Multilateral Investment Court (MIC).[7] From 2017 onwards, UNCITRAL's Working Group III is also looking into possible ways to reform investor–state dispute settlement.[8] Nonetheless, neither the EU's proposals, nor the UNCITRAL sessions have considered whether or not investors do or should rely on domestic courts prior to initiating international arbitration. Knowing whether or not foreign investors rely on domestic courts prior to ITA and how such cases unfold can help us better understand the motivations of investors for launching international arbitration. Furthermore, this analysis can also add to the discussion on whether domestic courts should first handle disputes between foreign investors and the host states, given their alleged better understanding of the local context when balancing the rights of investors and other public policy concerns. This in itself might increase the perceived legitimacy of the international investment law system.

Following the introduction and the description of the methodology, the chapter is structured into three main parts, so as to reflect the three research questions: an initial empirical-descriptive part (section 7.3), followed by an empirical-analytical part (section 7.4) and a normative part (section 7.5). Section 7.3 tackles four main issues:

1. whether investors rely on domestic courts if given the chance to pursue ITA;
2. the extent to which foreign investors appeal against the judicial decisions of domestic courts;
3. the types of domestic cases that foreign investors bring and against whom; and
4. the success rate of foreign investors before the domestic courts of each country.

---

[7] Council of the EU, 'Negotiating Directives for a Convention Establishing a Multilateral Court for the Settlement of Investment Disputes', 20 March 2018; UNCITRAL, WG III, 'Investor-State Dispute Settlement Reform', <uncitral.un.org/en/working_groups/3/investor-state>.
[8] UNCITRAL Working Group III, 'Investor-State Dispute Settlement Reform' (ibid.).

174 SZILÁRD GÁSPÁR-SZILÁGYI

The issues are then further refined with the help of four hypotheses that are tested by contrasting two countries that have *well-developed judiciaries* (the United States and Canada) with two countries possessing *transitional judiciaries* (Hungary and Romania).

Section 7.4 then focuses on why investors might choose to rely or not rely on the domestic courts of the host state. With the help of data gathered for both sections 7.3 and 7.4, as well as academic literature, it is argued that investors might choose to resort to domestic courts because domestic disputes are quite different compared to their international counterparts. The remedies sought by the investors and the subject-matter of the disputes can play an important role in choosing domestic courts. The data also shows that investors commenced almost all Canadian and United States ITA cases pursuant to the widely known North American Free Trade Agreement (NAFTA) Chapter 11 and on average ITA cases in all four countries were initiated a decade after the entry into force of the IIA. Thus, it is hard to argue that investors chose domestic courts because of ignorance towards ITA, as they or their legal counsel should have known about ITA. Furthermore, ITA is often a measure of last resort, as it can seriously affect the relationship between the investor and the host state. As to why investors might choose not to rely on domestic courts, section 7.4 also looks at the existence of FITR clauses, the average length of the domestic proceedings in question compared to the length of ITA cases, and the possible perception of the investors that domestic courts might be biased against them.

The normative part of the chapter (section 7.5) then discusses whether investors should first resort to domestic courts, by only focusing on those arguments that can be backed up by the data gathered and the conclusions reached in the empirical parts.

7.2 Delimitation, Theory and Methodology

7.2.1 Setting the Framework

When a foreign investor alleges that a host-state breached its obligations towards the investor, it can resort to the following *legal* remedies:[9]

1. bring a case before a *domestic court* and base its claim(s) on domestic law *and/or* standards found in the IIA *and/or* the contract with the host State;

---

[9] I do not discuss diplomatic protection or political pressure that the home state might exert on the host state. See Gertz (n. 2); Jeswald W. Salacuse, *The Law of Investment Treaties* (Oxford University Press, 2nd ed., 2015), pp. 396–9.

2. bring a claim before an ITA tribunal and invoke *IIL standards* found in the underlying IIA and investment awards; or
3. bring a claim before an ITA tribunal and rely on *domestic law/the contract*, depending on the applicable law to the dispute, either by way of contract, domestic law or due to the provisions of the IIA.[10]

This chapter focuses on the first possibility, namely, cases brought before domestic courts in which the investor relies on domestic law, the contract with the host state or IIL norms in order to obtain a specific remedy.

Concerning the ITA cases, the study only considered concluded international arbitral cases, not pending ones. However, not all concluded cases are followed by an award. In some cases, the investors opted not to continue the case, while in others the disputing parties settled the dispute. In such cases, I took into account the notices of arbitration, orders of discontinuance, or settlement agreements (if available), because some of them referred to prior domestic court proceedings.[11] Furthermore, some international arbitral documents were not publicly available.[12]

Regarding the domestic cases, as one of the aims of the chapter is to elucidate what happens in domestic courts *prior to* ITA proceedings, the analysis *excludes* domestic court proceedings concerning the enforcement or setting-aside of ITA awards, since they occur *after* the ITA proceedings. The chapter also does not discuss provisional measures that national courts should adopt based on the request of an ITA tribunal. Furthermore, the research *does not* consider administrative proceedings because other domestic authorities, such as various agencies, or bureaus handle them, not domestic courts. Hence, it is often difficult to get access to such cases and investors can most often challenge the outcome of such proceedings before domestic courts.

---

[10] See Hege Elisabeth Kjos, *Applicable Law in Investor State Arbitration* (Oxford University Press, 2013), ch. 5, p. 162; St John (n. 1), 8–9.

[11] For example, *Domtar Inc.* v. *United States*, UNCITRAL, Notice of Arbitration and Statement of Claim (16 April 2007); *GL Farms LLC and Carl Adams* v. *Canada*, UNCITRAL, Notice of Arbitration (6 May 2006).

[12] Not public: *AES Summit Generation Ltd* v. *Hungary (AES I)*, ICSID No. ARB/01/04, Settlement Agreement (3 January 2002); *EDF International SA* v. *Hungary*, UNCITRAL, Award (4 December 2014); *Edenred SA* v. *Hungary*, ICSID Case No. ARB-13/2, Award (13 December 2016).

176 SZILÁRD GÁSPÁR-SZILÁGYI

7.2.2 Research Questions and Hypotheses

7.2.2.1 Do Foreign Investors Rely on Domestic Courts If Given the Chance to Pursue ITA?

The justification that ITA ensures that investor–state disputes are *denationalized* has not received empirical attention. According to Salacuse, 'depending on the country involved', local courts might not be independent from the host government, they might be prejudiced towards foreign investors, local courts might not have the expertise to apply complex principles of international law, and often have inefficient procedures in place.[13] Yet, none of these allegations are backed up by empirical evidence, with the exception of the highly publicized and often used example of a Canadian funeral company not being treated in an impartial manner by local courts in Mississippi.[14]

Some of the more recent discussions on the role of domestic courts in handling investor–state disputes have occurred in the context of the EU concluding far-reaching trade agreements with investment chapters.[15] Much of the discussion, however, was centred on whether domestic courts are capable of applying international investment law. According to Bronckers, 'it is sometimes felt that domestic courts ... tend to defer too much to their national administrations regarding international law', possibly because domestic courts do not feel comfortable applying international law.[16] He furthermore argues that, even in the EU, a third of EU Member States are perceived to perform badly when it comes to the independence and efficiency of domestic courts.[17]

The reliance on domestic courts might present other obstacles as well. For example, in countries where the launching of a case is conditioned by the payment of a court fee that represents a percentage of the damages claimed, the payment of such a fee on a multi-million or even billion-dollar claim can pose significant obstacles.[18] Furthermore, in case the IIA includes a 'fork-in-

---

[13] Salacuse (n. 9), 397–8.

[14] *Loewen Group, Inc. and Raymond L. Loewen* v. *United States of America*, ICSID Case No. ARB(AF)/98/3. Salacuse (n. 9), 397, refers only to this domestic case (397); so does Sattorova (n. 3), 228.

[15] Marco Bronckers, 'Is Investor-State Dispute Settlement (ISDS) Superior to Litigation before Domestic Courts? An EU View on Bilateral Trade Agreements' (2015) 18 *Journal of International Economic Law* 655, 655–7.

[16] Ibid., 661.

[17] Ibid., 671.

[18] I would like to thank Professor August Reinisch for bringing this to my attention. In Romania, all legal or natural persons must pay a 'judicial tax' (*taxă judiciară de timbru*)

the-road' clause, the ITA tribunal might dismiss a subsequent claim, if there is identity of the parties and of the facts, and the legal norms embedded in the IIA were already invoked in the domestic court proceedings.[19]

In light of the above, one would expect that investors would rather resort to ITA than domestic courts, as a means to denationalize their disputes with the host states and to ensure that their disputes are not heard by partial and inefficient domestic courts. Furthermore, advocates for ITA also argue that domestic remedies in 'developing and transition states, and even in developed countries, are inadequate because they take much too long [time], [and domestic courts] are biased, are corrupt, or are otherwise unreliable'.[20] Thus, one would expect that the more problems the domestic judiciary faces, the more likely it is that foreign investors will prefer to circumvent domestic courts and opt for ITA. In other words, we may hypothesize that:

(H1) *foreign investors will circumvent domestic courts if given the option to pursue ITA; and*

(H2) *foreign investors will more likely circumvent domestic courts in states with transitional judiciaries than in states with highly developed judiciaries.*

In order to test these hypotheses, I looked at how often domestic court cases preceded the international arbitral cases. I took into account references to prior domestic cases in the international awards, settlement agreements, and notices of arbitration. If such documents often referred to prior domestic court cases, then it indicates that the investors chose to pursue domestic remedies even if they had the option to go straight to international arbitration. However, if the documents show that investors rarely/never pursued domestic remedies before initiating international arbitration, then this supports H1.

---

when initiating a domestic case, the value of which depends on the value of the claim and whether it is quantifiable or not in a monetary way. For example, for a claim with a value above 250,000 lei (approx. 54,000 euros) the claimant must pay 6,105 lei (approx. 1,300 euros) plus 1% of the value exceeding 250,000 lei. See OUG 80/2013 privind taxele judiciare de timbru, Art. 3 complementing Art. 197 of the Code of Civil Procedure.

[19] George K. Foster, 'Striking a Balance between Investor Protections and National Sovereignty: The Relevance of Local Remedies in Investment Treaty Arbitration' (2011) 49 *Columbia Journal of Transnational Law* 201, 206; Christoph Schreuer, 'Interaction of International Tribunals and Domestic Courts in Investment Law' (2011) *Contemporary Issues in International Arbitration and Mediation: The Fordham Paper 2010*, 78–9.

[20] Van Harten (n. 1).

When estimating the extent to which investors resort to domestic courts, I took into account two factors. First, *the option to pursue ITA had to exist when the investor brought the domestic case*, meaning that the IIA – based on which the investor initiated international arbitration – had to have entered into force prior to the launching of the domestic proceedings. It is for this reason that the tables annexed to this chapter include the entry into force of the IIA, the date on which the domestic case was filed, and the date on which the domestic court decision was rendered. Second, *the international documents must be available.* Not all arbitral awards are public or investors sometimes discontinue a case without any available documents, making it difficult to know whether investors initiated prior domestic cases.

7.2.2.2 To What Extent Do Foreign Investors Appeal against the Decisions of Domestic Courts?

The second question follows from the first one. If foreign investors do in fact resort to domestic courts, are they able/willing to pursue multiple levels of adjudication? One could argue that this will depend on the level of trust that foreign investors have in the domestic judicial system, the available domestic judicial avenues/remedies, and how efficiently domestic courts can handle appeals or other forms of recourse. It follows that investors operating in countries with highly developed judiciaries would appeal more often a lower court's decision, because they trust the system and they know that the extra time and money spent on the appeal can result in a fair decision for them. Furthermore, in a more efficient system the likelihood of obtaining a swift settlement of the appeal is higher. Conversely, investors operating in countries with transitional judiciaries would appeal less often, because they do not trust the impartiality or efficiency of the system and they would rather spend the extra time and money on international arbitration. Thus, we may hypothesize that:

(H3) *investors operating in countries with transitional judiciaries appeal less than those in countries with highly developed judiciaries do.*

In order to test this hypothesis I needed to identify the levels at which the investors pursued their domestic cases and the rate of their appeals. Because the references in the ITA documents were often partial or done in a haphazard way, I checked all references to domestic cases in national databases. This resulted in the finding of a number of prior domestic cases not mentioned in the ITA documents. A lower rate of appeals in the two transitional judiciaries would strengthen H3.

The annexed tables mark a case at first instance with '1', at second instance with '2', and at third instance with '3'. These numbers mark the levels in a specific case and not the levels of the courts in the domestic court hierarchy.[21]

7.2.2.3 What Types of Cases Do Foreign Investors Bring and against Whom?

The third question looks at the types of domestic cases that involve foreign investors, from the perspective of their subject-matter and the disputing parties. The purpose is to better understand how foreign investors act before domestic courts, which might then point to possible reasons why they choose to pursue their claims domestically prior to pursuing international remedies.

I first took into consideration the subject-matter of the domestic cases. When classifying the types of cases in the annexed tables, I used the classification in the domestic systems. There are two main reasons for this. First, what some countries might classify as a commercial dispute others might classify as an 'economic' dispute. Furthermore, even in the same country the same dispute can be classified differently, depending on whether the court before which the case is launched categorizes cases in a specific way.[22] Second, classifying domestic cases from four countries with varied judicial systems would inadvertently introduce discretionary criteria, subject to criticism.

Furthermore, I also looked at who initiated the domestic cases and against whom. It is expected that investors bring most domestic cases against various public authorities, agencies or government bodies. However, it might also happen that investors will be the respondents or they will bring cases against private actors.

7.2.2.4 What Is the Success Rate of Foreign Investors before the Domestic Courts of the Host State?

One of the justifications for having ITA is to ensure that foreign investors are not subjected to domestic courts that are biased against them. Court

---

[21] For example, Romania has four levels of courts: trial courts (*judecătorii*), tribunals (*tribunale*), courts of appeal (*curți de apel*), the Supreme Court/High Court of Cassation (*Înalta Curte de Casație și Justiție*), plus the Constitutional Court (*Curtea Constituțională*). Even though a tribunal ranks above a trial court, it will often be the court of first instance due to the nature of the claim (the amount of money involved, the litigating parties, etcetera).

[22] For example, the domestic cases referenced in *Gavazzi v. Romania* are classified as commercial disputes by the Bucharest Court of Appeals and heard by their Commercial Section (VI), while the Romania Supreme Court heard the cases via its Civil Section (II). Marco Gavazzi and Stefano Gavazzi v. Romania, ICSID Case No. ARB/12/25, Decision on Jurisdiction, Admissibility and Liability (21 April 2015).

180   SZILÁRD GÁSPÁR-SZILÁGYI

bias is difficult to test and it is not limited to domestic courts.[23] The purpose of this question is *not to test actual bias*. This would require not only interviews, but also large-scale comparisons between domestic cases involving foreign investors and local investors. The latter would be a difficult task due to the large number of local companies with foreign or partial foreign ownership. Instead, it is argued that a low success rate before domestic courts might create the *perception* among investors that domestic courts are biased against them. This can happen at two different stages. First, if counsel has information that foreign investors lose more domestic cases than they win, this might inform the investor not to rely on domestic courts but pursue ITA, where the chances of bias might be lower. Second, a foreign investor might *perceive* domestic courts as being biased against it in an individual case, if it loses all or most cases before the local courts. This in turn might give the investor an extra reason to commence international arbitration. Furthermore, if the argument were correct that less developed judiciaries will disfavour foreign investors, then one would expect a higher investor loss rate in transitional judiciaries as opposed to highly developed judiciaries. Therefore, the expectations are that:

(H4) *foreign investors will have a lower success rate in domestic courts and that this will be more pronounced in transitional judiciaries.*

In order to test the hypothesis I looked at how often investors won or lost a domestic case. The hypothesis is strengthened if the win–loss ratio of foreign investors is lower in domestic courts, and this is more pronounced in the two transitional judiciaries. I coded the outcome of the domestic cases in the following way. A 'loss' ('L') occurs when the court rejected the action of the claimant or found in favour of the respondent. This could be a higher court dismissing an appeal of the investor when the investor lost at the lower level, a higher court finding in favour of the other disputing party when the investor won at the lower court, a lower court denying a motion of the investor or a domestic court finding in favour of a local entity. 'Wins' ('W') on the other hand are counted when the court agreed fully with the claim of the foreign investor, while a 'partial win' ('PW') occurs when the investor managed to obtain only part of what it was claiming. I counted the wins and losses separately at every level of the domestic proceedings. This way, certain

---

[23] For studies on bias in international courts, see Eric A. Posner and Miguel F. P. de Figueiredo, 'Is the International Court of Justice Biased?' (2005) 34(2) *Journal of Legal Studies* 599; and Erik Voeten, 'The Impartiality of International Judges: Evidence from the European Court of Human Rights' (2005) 102(4) *American Political Science Review* 217.

INVESTORS, COURTS AND INVESTMENT ARBITRATION   181

differences might be found between lower and higher courts, which can explain why investors end up resorting to ITA after having gone through all levels of the domestic judiciary.

7.2.3   Selecting the Countries

When selecting the states for the study I took into account several criteria. First, in order to test some of the expectations (H2, H3 and H4) I chose two states with *well-established judiciaries*, Canada and the United States, and two states with post-Communist, *transitional judiciaries*, Hungary and Romania. Canada and the United States can be considered as *highly developed judiciaries*, with the occasional, highly publicized exceptions, such as *Loewen v. United States*.[24] Conversely, Hungary and Romania have transitioned from a communist regime to a market economy and joined the EU in 2004 and 2007. However, just because they became members of the EU does not mean that their judiciaries and those of other EU Member States have not received criticism from various regional and EU bodies. For example, the '2017 EU Justice Scoreboard' conducted on EU Member States found that, in Hungary and Romania, slightly more than a third of companies had a negative perception of local courts. The two main motives raised were interference and pressure from the government/politicians and from economic interests.[25] Furthermore, Romania is still under the European Commission's 'cooperation and verification mechanism' (CVM) which is meant to assist the country in the fields of judicial reform, corruption and organised crime.[26] In the case of Hungary, the 2018 Sarghentini Report of the European Parliament has been highly critical towards the Hungarian Government's tactics to undermine the rule of law and the independence of the judiciary.[27] Therefore, for the purposes of this chapter, Hungary and Romania are classified as *transitional judiciaries*.

---

[24] *Loewen* v. *USA* (n. 14).

[25] European Commission, 'The 2017 EU Justice Scoreboard' (2017) 37–8, <ec.europa.eu/info/sites/info/files/justice_scoreboard_2017_en.pdf>.

[26] European Commission, 'Cooperation and Verification Mechanism for Bulgaria and Romania', <ec.europa.eu/info/policies/justice-and-fundamental-rights/effective-justice/rule-law/assistance-bulgaria-and-romania-under-cvm/cooperation-and-verification-mechanism-bulgaria-and-romania_en>.

[27] European Parliament, 'Report on a proposal calling on the Council to determine, pursuant to Article 7(1) of the Treaty on European Union, the existence of a clear risk of a serious breach by Hungary of the values on which the Union is founded' (Sarghentini Report), 2017/2131(INL), <europarl.europa.eu/sides/getDoc.do?type=REPORT&reference=A8-2018-0250&language=EN>.

182 SZILÁRD GÁSPÁR-SZILÁGYI

Second, in order to gather any meaningful statistics, I had to select countries that were respondents in a significant number of ITA cases (10–20).

Third, when searching for and analysing domestic court cases one also needs to consider the *linguistic limitations*.

7.2.4 Selecting the Cases

The first step was to identify the ITA cases initiated by foreign investors against the selected countries. In the second step, I identified the references within the ITA documents to prior domestic cases. The third step entailed finding the referenced domestic cases in national databases or court registries. In the fourth step, I coded the retrieved domestic cases for various variables so as to test the hypotheses.

The sources for the ITA cases were the PluriCourts Investment Treaty and Arbitration Database (PITAD)[28] Italaw, and Investment Policy Hub. In total, the data collected for the four countries includes 57 concluded ITA cases, 46 of which were deemed as relevant. This represents slightly less than 10% of the total number of concluded ITA cases at the end of 2017. The annexed tables include 18 ITA cases against the United States,[29] 20 against Canada, ten against Hungary, and nine against Romania. I then had to consider whether (a) the IIA – based on which the investor initiated the ITA – had entered into force prior to the initiation of the domestic cases and (b) the availability of the ITA documents. Therefore, the dataset used for the statistical calculations is slightly different. In the case of the United States, I had to exclude *Mondev* v. *United States*,[30] *Loewen* v. *United States*[31] and the domestic cases to which they referred to, because the investors launched the domestic cases at first instance *prior* to the entry into force of NAFTA on 1 January 1994. I further excluded six international cases from the US dataset for which there were no available documents.[32] In the case of

---

[28] With special thanks to Daniel Behn and Maxim Usynin for allowing me to use PITAD.

[29] I counted *Apotex I* and *II* separately, even though the two proceedings were joined. This is because they refer to different domestic court proceedings that preceded the arbitration. On the other hand, the five *Stanford Ponzi Scheme* cases were counted as one.

[30] *Mondev International Ltd* v. *United* States, ICSID Case No. ARB(AF)/99/2, Award (11 October 2002).

[31] *Loewen* v. *United States* (n. 14).

[32] Excluded: *Baird* v. *United States, Canfor* v. *United States, CANACAR* v. *United States, Doman Industries* v. *United States, Kenex* v. *United States, Victims of the Stanford Ponzi Scheme* v. *United States*, Notices of Intent (28 and 29 December 2012).

INVESTORS, COURTS AND INVESTMENT ARBITRATION   183

Hungary, of the ten ITA cases, three were not public[33] and were therefore excluded from the dataset.

The final dataset thus included ten ITA cases against the United States, 20 against Canada, seven against Hungary and nine against Romania. It also needs to be mentioned that all the ITA cases against Canada and the United States, with the exception of one case,[34] were initiated under NAFTA. The picture is more diverse for Hungary and Romania, as investors commenced ITA under a variety of IIAs, such as intra-EU bilateral investment treaties (BITs) the Energy Charter Treaty (ECT) and BITs with non-EU states.

Once I found a reference to a domestic case in the international ITA documents (awards, settlement agreements and notices of arbitration), I then had to retrieve the cases from domestic databases or from domestic courts. During the searches in domestic databases, I would sometimes find further domestic cases (often lower court decisions) that were not referenced in the ITA documents. In total 80 prior domestic cases were included in the study. Even if this number might seem low, the results for the four countries show striking similarities that support meaningful observations.

Gathering the domestic cases posed several challenges. Some domestic cases were hard to identify because the ITA documents would reference them in a haphazard way. Often, relevant domestic case identifiers – such as the names of the disputing parties, the names of domestic courts, or the date of the domestic decisions – were lacking.[35] Domestically incorporated businesses often had a different name than the shareholders that initiated the international cases[36] and some arbitral awards would simply mention that the investors pursued domestic remedies, without providing any specific information about the domestic proceedings.[37] Furthermore, researching domestic court cases also required an understanding of the domestic legal systems and their search engines. Canadian and Hungarian search engines allowed for searches in all court

---

[33] See (n. 12).

[34] *Victims of the Stanford Ponzi Scheme* v. *United States*, Notices of Intent (28 and 29 December 2012).

[35] An example to the contrary is *Marco Gavazzi and Stefano Gavazzi* v. *Romania*, ICSID Case No. ARB/12/25, Decision on Jurisdiction, Admissibility and Liability (21 April 2015), paras. 77–9.

[36] For example, in *GL Farms* v. *Canada*, GL Farms filed the notice of arbitration, but a local subsidiary – the Georgian Bay Milk Company – brought one of the domestic proceedings: *GL Farms* (n. 11).

[37] *Telenor Mobile Communications AS* v. *Republic of Hungary*, ICSID Case No. ARB/04/15, Award (13 September 2006), paras. 25 and 47.

184 SZILÁRD GÁSPÁR-SZILÁGYI

cases in these countries, while the United States and Romanian search engines often only concerned specific courts or certain levels of the judiciary. In the case of Romania, I obtained five court decisions by personally petitioning the Bucharest Tribunal (*Tribunalul București*) and the Bucharest Court of Appeals (*Curtea de Apel București*).[38] Furthermore, some of the older cases lacked a digital format, or I only gained partial access to other cases, while certain decisions were redacted for sensitive/confidential data.

7.3   Assessing the Four Countries

7.3.1   Do Foreign Investors Rely on Domestic Courts If Given the Chance to Pursue ITA?

I hypothesized that foreign investors will circumvent domestic courts if given the option to pursue ITA (H1) and that they will more likely circumvent domestic courts in states with transitional judiciaries than in states with highly developed judiciaries (H2).

As Table 7.1 illustrates, the results are more nuanced than the hypotheses suggest. If I count all ITA cases that referred to *any type* of domestic cases, then 70% of the ITA cases against the United States made references to prior domestic court proceedings. This number is 55% for Canada, 86% for Hungary, and 78% for Romania.

These numbers change slightly when taking into account those references which are made to *relevant* domestic cases. Thus, the ITA cases against Canada – compared to the other three countries – referred to both Canadian *and* United States domestic court cases. Of the 11 (55%) ITA cases referencing domestic court proceedings, seven referred only to Canadian cases,[39] two referred to both Canadian and US cases,[40] and two

---

[38] *D.C. Patriciu/Rompetrol* v. *Serviciul Român de Informații*, Bucharest Court of Appeals, Civil Section III, Decision No. 1 of 9 February 2009 (File No. 12770/3/2006); *Rompetrol Group NV* v. *PÎCCJ*, Bucharest Tribunal, Criminal Section I, Decision No. 860 of 29 June 2006 (File No. 12139/3/2006); *PÎCCJ* v. *D.C. Patriciu*, Bucharest Court of Appeals, Criminal Section I, Decision of 10 April 2006 (File No. 10352/3/2006); *AVAS* v. *SC C.M.E.I.E. SRL*, Bucharest Court of Appeals, Commercial Section VI, Decision No. 430 of 8 October 2007 (File No. 7341/3/2003); *AVAS* v. *SC C.M.E.I.E. SRL*, Bucharest Tribunal, Section VI Civil, Decision No. 3145 of 5 May 2006 (File No. 7341/3/2003).

[39] *Chemtura* v. *Canada, Eli Lilly* v. *Canada, Great Lakes Farms* v. *Canada, Mobil Investments* v. *Canada, St Marys* v. *Canada, UPS* v. *Canada, Pope & Talbot* v. *Canada.*

[40] *AbitibiBowater* v. *Canada*, ICSID Case No. UNCT/10/1, Consent Award (15 December 2010); *Detroit International Bridge Company (DIBC)* v. *Canada*, PCA Case No. 2012-25, Award on Jurisdiction (2 April 2015).

INVESTORS, COURTS AND INVESTMENT ARBITRATION 185

Table 7.1 *References to domestic cases*

State	ITA cases (no.)	ITA cases referring to *any type of* domestic cases		ITA cases referring to *relevant* domestic cases	
		no.	%	no.	%
US	10	7	70.0	7	70.0
Canada	20	11	55.0	8	40.0*
Hungary	7	6	85.7	5	71.0
Romania	9	7	77.8	6	66.7
Total/Average	**46**	**31**	**67.4**	**26**	**56.5**

* This rises to 47% if I exclude the three discontinued ITA cases.

referred only to US cases.[41] Thus, I excluded the two ITA cases that referred only to US domestic cases. Another reason for excluding one of the ITA cases, *Mesa Power* v. *Canada*,[42] is that the three domestic US cases referenced in the award occurred during the investor–state arbitration, but prior to the handing down of the award. Furthermore, they concerned the investors' efforts to secure evidence via domestic courts for the ongoing NAFTA Chapter 11 arbitration. Of the seven ITA cases referring only to Canadian cases, I excluded *Pope & Talbot* v. *Canada* because the award referred to *other* producers challenging domestic measures before Canadian courts, without giving further details regarding these cases.[43] It follows that eight (40%) ITA cases referred to at least one Canadian case in which the foreign investor was involved. In the case of Canada, the lower number of ITA cases that refer to relevant domestic cases might be a result of a higher number of ITA cases that were discontinued, but for which some international documents are available. Thus, if I were to exclude the three discontinued ITA cases then 47% of Canadian ITA cases refer to domestic ones (eight out of 17).

As for Hungary, the award in *Electrabel* v. *Hungary*[44] referred to a prior case brought before the General Court of the EU. Thus, I excluded

---

[41] *Mesa Power Group LLC* v. *Canada*, PCA No. 2012-17, Award (24 March 2016); *SD Myers* v. *Canada*, UNCITRAL (1976).

[42] *Mesa Power* v. *Canada* (ibid.). See annexes, table 3, 'Canada.'

[43] *Pope & Talbot Inc.* v. *Canada*, UNCITRAL, Award on the Merits of Phase 2 (10 April 2001), para. 183.

[44] *Electrabel SA* v. *Hungary*, ICSID Case No. ARB/07/19, Award (25 November 2015), para. 36 with reference to T-179/09, *Dunamenti Erőmű* v. *Commission of the European Communities*, General Court of the EU.

186 SZILÁRD GÁSPÁR-SZILÁGYI

it since it did not arise before Hungarian courts. For Romania,[45] I ended up excluding *Micula* v. *Romania I* because it mentions a decision of the Constitutional Court of Romania that was initiated by other parties, not the Micula brothers.[46]

The above data weakens the first hypothesis according to which (H1) *foreign investors will circumvent domestic courts if they have the option of pursuing ITA*. Contrary to expectations, in the case of the United States, Hungary, and Romania, approximately 70% of all ITA cases were preceded by prior domestic cases. In Canada, this number (40%) is lower than in the other three countries. As mentioned, if I discount the three discontinued cases, then it rises to 47%. The data weakens H2 as well. In the two transitional countries, Romania and Hungary, the percentage of ITA cases preceded by domestic cases was equally high as in the United States and higher than in Canada. This seems to indicate that foreign investors will resort to domestic courts if the domestic judiciary is relatively well functioning, regardless of whether it is highly developed or transitional.

Without yet going into the reasons of why investors might or might not have relied on domestic courts (see section 7.4), it should be mentioned that there is no standard way of referencing domestic cases in ITA documents. Domestic cases are often referenced or mentioned in a haphazard way, which suggests that some ITA documents might simply not refer to prior domestic cases, even if they existed. I found only two ITA cases (out of the 46) in which the tribunals specifically mention that the investors *did not* resort to domestic courts.[47]

7.3.2 To What Extent Did Foreign Investors Appeal against the Decisions of Domestic Courts?

Next, I looked at the levels of adjudication the investors resorted to during the domestic proceedings in order to test the hypothesis that

---

[45] *Noble Ventures Inc.* v. *Romania*, ICSID Case No. ARB/01/11, Award (12 October 2005), paras. 88, 113 and 168. This case only mentioned the existence of domestic court proceedings, without providing further details.

[46] *Ioan Micula et al.* v. *Romania*, ICSID Case No. ARB/05/20, Award (11 December 2013), para. 376.

[47] *AES Summit Generation Ltd et al.* v. *Hungary*, ICSID Case No. ARB/07/22, Award (23 September 2010), paras. 6.5.3 and 9.3.65; *Ömer Dede and Serdar Elhüseyni*, ICSID Case No. ARB/10/22, Award (5 September 2013), paras. 142–3.

INVESTORS, COURTS AND INVESTMENT ARBITRATION   187

(H3) *investors operating in countries with transitional judiciaries appealed less than those in countries with highly developed judiciaries did.*

The datasets for this question included all domestic cases commenced prior to the initiation of the ITA, even if the domestic case was initiated prior to the entry into force of the ITA. I have chosen this approach because we are interested in knowing whether investors can correct the decisions of lower courts and whether this might be affected by the level of development of the judiciary. The domestic cases are counted separately at each level of adjudication.

The dataset included 16 domestic cases (three before state courts,[48] the rest before federal courts[49]) for the United States, 17 for Canada (23 of which were brought before Canadian courts and four before US courts), 12 for Hungary, and 25 for Romania.[50] I have excluded one case from the US dataset[51] and managed to get full access to 11 cases, including the various domestic decisions, opinions, judgments referenced in the arbitral awards.[52] In the Hungarian dataset three of the domestic cases referenced in *Accession Mezzanine v. Hungary*[53] and *Emmis v. Hungary* overlapped.[54] From the Canadian dataset I excluded the three US cases

---

[48] In Mississippi and Nebraska.

[49] District Courts, Courts of Appeal, and the Supreme Court.

[50] Decision 9227/2005 of the Supreme Court of Romania (*Înalta Curte de Casație și Justiție*) – referenced in *Awdi* v. *Romania*, ICSID Case No. ARB/10/13, Award (2 March 2015) – referred to almost a dozen prior domestic cases between the investors and various state bodies or agencies. Thus, the total number of domestic cases could be higher than 26.

[51] In *Methanex* v. *US* only the USDC for the Central District of California was mentioned and I could not identify the case.

[52] This was mostly due to state court databases (State of Mississippi Judiciary <courts.ms .gov/newsite2/index.php>; State of Nebraska Judicial Branch <supremecourt.nebraska .gov/>), Westlaw, and the subscription based PACER system for federal courts not including electronic versions of older files from the early or mid-1990s. Nonetheless, I still managed to get useful information on the types of cases, the parties or the case outcome from the ITA awards, older newspapers or from partial online access. The domestic proceedings referenced in *Methanex* could not be fully identified due to the lack of sufficient case identifiers. Nonetheless, for the purposes of this section we at least know the level of the court before which the case occurred.

[53] *Accession Mezzanine Capital LP et al.* v. *Hungary*, ICSID Case No. ARB/12/3, Award (17 April 2015).

[54] Hungarian online Collection of Court Cases (Bírósági Határozatok Gyűjteménye, <birosag.hu/ugyfelkapcsolati-.284"/>portal/birosagi-hatarozatok-gyujtemenye>). The reference in *ADC* v. *Hungary* to the invalidation of a public tender by the Metropolitan Court of Budapest (Fővárosi Törvényszék) did not result in a fully identifiable domestic case. Nevertheless, the arbitral award included useful information on the outcome of the

188   SZILÁRD GÁSPÁR-SZILÁGYI

that concerned the securing of evidence for the ongoing NAFTA Chapter 11 arbitration. In the case of Romania, I excluded the domestic case referenced in *Micula* v. *Romania I*, as it was launched by other parties, and I had full access to 17 domestic court decisions. For the rest of the cases I managed to gather significant data by having partial access to them or from the international awards.

As table 7.2 illustrates, in all four countries investors regularly appealed first instance cases and often ended up before the highest courts. For the United States and Canada the rate of appeal for first instance cases is 40% and 54% respectively, while 30% and 31% of the cases reached the highest courts. In the case of Hungary and Romania, the number of appealed first instance cases (80% and 82%) and those that reached the highest courts (80% and 64%) are significantly higher.[55]

These findings weaken the third hypothesis (H3). Investors in the two transitional judiciaries actually appealed more often than investors in the highly developed judiciaries did, and they reached the highest courts of the land more often. The lower rates of appeals and highest court cases in the United States and Canada might be a result of greater court costs or the difficulty of reaching the highest courts in non-unitary states, such as reaching the US Supreme Court.[56]

Thus, it seems that investors are willing to pursue multiple levels of domestic adjudication, regardless of whether the judiciary is transitional or highly developed. These findings also lend support to the conclusions in section 3.1, that investors are confident enough to use the domestic courts of highly developed judiciaries, as well as those of countries with transitional judiciaries. The possibility to appeal might also influence the decision of investors to resort to domestic courts, since the higher courts can correct possible errors of the lower courts, a possibility not yet present in international investment law.[57]

---

case, its type and the date the court delivered its decision: *ADC Affiliate Ltd et al.* v. *Hungary*, ICSID Case No. ARB/03/16, Award (2 October 2006), para. 203. The award in *Telenor* v. *Hungary* only referred to the existence of Hungarian court cases, without providing more details: *Telenor Mobile Communications A.S.* v. *Republic of* Hungary, ICSID No. ARB/04/15, Award (13 September 2006), paras. 25 and 47.

[55] In the case of Hungary, the lower number of domestic cases might cause more significant statistical variation.

[56] See United States Courts, 'Supreme Court Procedure', <uscourts.gov/about-federal-courts/educational-resources/about-educational-outreach/activity-resources/supreme-1>.

[57] Unless one counts the ICSID annulment proceedings and the Appellate Bodies of the yet to be operational investment courts in EU bilateral IIAs.

Table 7.2 *Domestic cases appealed*

State	Total no. of domestic cases identified		No. of cases at first instance		First instance cases appealed %		First instance cases reaching highest court %	
US	16		10		40%		30%	
	State	Federal						
	3	13						
CA	27		All*	Just CA	All	Just CA	All	Just CA
	Provincial	Federal	17	13	41.2%	54%	23.5%	30.8%
	7	20						
HU	12**		5		80.0%		80%	
RO	25		11		82.0%		64%	
Total	**80**		**All**	**Just CA**	**All**	**Just CA**	**All**	**Just CA**
			43	**39**	**55.8%**	**61.5%**	**41.%**	**46.1%**

* 'All' includes both US and Canadian domestic cases referenced in ITA cases against Canada. 'Just CA' includes only the Canadian ones.

** Three domestic cases overlap in two separate ITA cases.

7.3.3 What Types of Cases Do Foreign Investors Bring and against Whom?

Unlike in the previous sub-section, I did not count the domestic cases at every single level of adjudication. Instead, I counted a case as 'one' even if it went through several levels of domestic courts, because the dispute *ratione materiae* will not change and *ratione personae* it is important to know who resorted to the domestic courts first: the investor or the state. I also included the domestic cases in *Mondev* v. *United States* and *Loewen* v. *United States* because we are mostly interested in the subject-matter and the disputing parties to the cases. For Canada, I included both Canadian and US cases referenced in the ITA documents, excluding the three US domestic cases on securing evidence for NAFTA arbitration. Thus, the dataset includes ten domestic cases for the United States, 16 for Canada, four for Hungary and 13 for Romania. It must also be mentioned that an ITA case can refer to several different types of domestic cases (criminal and civil) initiated by both the investor and the state.[58]

As expected (table 7.3) most of the domestic cases were initiated by investors (84%) against some form of emanation of the state or state-controlled commercial entity. In the case of Canada, it is interesting to note that 19% of the cases were brought by investors against other contracting parties. These are part of the string of cases brought by Eli Lilly against other private competitors for patent infringement. Romania is a curious outlier. Only 62% of the domestic cases were initiated by the investors. Various state bodies initiated the rest of the cases (civil and criminal) against the investors, such as the National Anticorruption Agency (DNA), the Romanian Information Services (SRI), the Authority for State Assets Administration (AVAS), or the Financial Guard (Garda Financiară).

Things also get interesting when considering the subject-matter of the cases. Looking at the total number of domestic cases (table 7.4) in the four countries, civil, commercial/economic and judicial/administrative review cases are almost even in number, followed by intellectual property (IP) cases, criminal cases and one case involving international trade matters. The disputes included contractual breaches, patent infringements, challenges to domestic legislation, criminal charges brought against the investor, and even the refunding of cash-deposits from US authorities in an anti-dumping case.[59]

---

[58] See for example, *Rompetrol Group NV* v. *Romania*, ICSID Case No. ARB/06/3 (6 May 2013).

[59] See *Tembec Inc.* v. *United States*, US Court of International Trade, 441 F. Supp. 2d 1302.

Table 7.3 *Domestic cases by disputing parties*

State	Domestic cases	Disputing parties (no./ %)											
		Investor claimant		Investor defendant		State claimant		State defendant		Priv party claimant		Priv party defendant	
US	10	9	90.0%	1	10.0%	1	10.0%	9	90.0%	0	0	0	0
CA	16	15	94.0%	1	6.0%	0	0	12	75.0%	1	6.0%	3	19.0%
HU	4	4	100%	0	0	0	0	4	100%	0	0	0	0
RO	13	8	61.5%	5	38.5%	5	38.5%	8	61.5%	0	0	0	0
Total/Avg	**43**	**36**	**83.7%**	**7**	**16.3%**	**6**	**13.4%**	**33**	**76.7%**	**1**	**2%**	**3**	**7.0%**

Table 7.4 *Domestic cases by subject-matter*

State	Domestic cases	Subject-matter (no.)						
		Civil	IP	Com./ econ.	Int. econ.	Jud. or admin. rev.	Crim.
US	10	5	2	1	1	1	N/A
CA	16	2	5	2	N/A	7	N/A
HU	5*	1	N/A	4	N/A	N/A	N/A
RO	13	3	N/A	4	N/A	2	4
Total	**44**	**11**	**7**	**11**	**1**	**12**	**4**

* The domestic case referenced in *ADC* v. *Hungary* mentioned the subject-matter of the case but not the disputing parties.

What strikes the eye in the case of Canada – in comparison to the other countries – is the high percentage of cases involving the judicial review of various measures of government institutions/bodies/agencies. What is also remarkable is the dialogue between Canadian and US courts. For example, the Superior Court of Quebec accepted the petition of *AbitibiBowater Inc.* and recognized the bankruptcy proceedings initiated before the US courts.[60] In Hungary, the 'economic' cases concerned public tenders, while the IP cases – present only in Canada and the United States – mainly concerned patent infringements.

The domestic cases in Romania are peculiar for two reasons. First, a number of civil and commercial cases relate to the wave of privatizations of formerly state-owned companies following the fall of Communism. For example, the Lebanese-American investors – brothers Awdi Hassan and Awdi Mehdi – initiated a string of real estate cases which they eventually lost. The local courts ordered the Romanian authorities to return the title of the properties given to the two investors to the previous owners, who were dispossessed by the Communist authorities. The Awdi brothers also faced criminal charges for money laundering and tax evasion that resulted in lengthy prison sentences. Second, compared to the other countries, four out of the 13 Romanian cases were of a criminal nature, such as money laundering, tax evasion or bribery. For example,

[60] *AbitibiBowatr Inc. et al.*, Superior Court of Quebec in Canada, 2009 QCCS 6459. No. 500-11-036133-094, Amended Initial Order (22 April 2009).

the local investor in *EDF* v. *Romania* alleged that it had to bribe Romanian officials in order to get certain concessions at the Bucharest Otopeni International Airport.[61] The investor did not manage to prove the solicitation of the bribe in a criminal case before the Bucharest Tribunal, later appealed to the Bucharest Court of Appeals.[62] In *Rompetrol* v. *Romania*,[63] the Dutch incorporated *Rompetrol NV* had as its main shareholder the late Romanian businessman Dinu Patriciu. Interestingly, in his personal capacity or by representing the Netherlands incorporated company, he managed to win two domestic criminal cases.[64] Furthermore, in a set of civil cases that went up to the Supreme Court of Romania, he managed to obtain civil damages from the Romanian Information Services for the secret wiretapping conducted against him.

Some important conclusions can be drawn from this data. First, domestic cases that involve foreign investors can cover any type of subject-matter and investors actively bring cases against multiple state bodies and their measures, as well as other private parties. This means that states might find themselves on the opposite end of an international arbitral claim, even pursuant to domestic cases that involved only private actors. For example, Eli Lilly brought a string of cases before Canadian courts against its competitors, claiming patent infringement. The Canadian courts ended up annulling the patents of the investor on the ground that the patents did not meet the domestic law's requirement to be 'useful'. The investor then brought an arbitral claim, alleging that the Canadian courts have expropriated its patents and they did not apply the minimum standards of treatment. Second, claimants can also find themselves in the respondent's position, either in cases brought by other private parties or by the state. The latter cases in Romania were of a criminal nature. On the one hand, criminal cases against the investor might prompt investors to initiate ITA on the basis that the criminal cases against them might breach the fair and equitable treatment standard. They might also evidence tactics to intimidate the investor, such as the afore-mentioned secret wiretappings. On the other hand, as the case

---

[61] *EDF (Services) Ltd* v. *Romania*, ICSID Case No. ARB/05/13, Award (8 October 2009), paras. 221–37.

[62] *SC EDF ASRO SRL et al.* v. *DNA*, Bucharest Court of Appeals, Decision 1388 of 27 September 2007 (File No. 390004/3/2006); *SC EDF ASRO SRL et al.* v. *DNA*, Bucharest Tribunal, Criminal Section 2, Decision of 31 May 2007.

[63] *The Rompetrol Group NV* v. *Romania* (n. 58).

[64] See annexes, table 4 'Romania'.

194   SZILÁRD GÁSPÁR-SZILÁGYI

of the Awdi brothers illustrates, some investors acquire or conduct their investment via fraudulent means, which should prompt investment tribunals to better scrutinize investor claims and whether the investments were made through fraudulent means, such as bribing local officials.

7.3.4   What Was the Investors' Success Rate in Domestic Courts?

It was hypothesised that (H4) *foreign investors will have a lower success rate in domestic courts and that this will be more pronounced in transitional judiciaries.*

The relevant dataset for the United States included 15 domestic cases, out of 17 referenced in the ITA cases. I excluded the domestic cases referenced in *Methanex* v. *United States* and in *Grand River Enterprises* v. *United States* since there was not enough information about their outcome. The dataset for Hungary included nine domestic cases (three overlapped), while the one for Canada[65] included 26. For Canada I excluded the aforementioned US cases to secure evidence and the cases referenced in *St Marys* v. *Canada*, because the Canadian branch of the investor withdrew its application for judicial review before the Federal Court of Canada.[66] Therefore, this withdrawal could not be classified as either a loss or a win. For Romania, I counted 24 cases.

As table 7.5 illustrates, in the United States the investors lost in 12 out of 15 domestic cases (80%); they won twice (13%), and had a partial win once (7%).[67] In Canada, out of the 26 domestic cases, the investors lost in 19 cases (73%), won in nine cases (31%), and had a partial win in one case before the Ontario Superior Court of Justice.[68] It is also worth

---

[65] Out of the 32 domestic cases referenced in the ITA documents, 25 were brought before Canadian courts and seven before US courts. Out of the 32 cases, I could fully identify 30. One case referenced in *Chemtura Corporation* v. *Canada*, UNCITRAL, Award (2 August 2010), para. 160 could not be fully identified, while the *Pope & Talbot* v. *Canada* award only mentioned the existence of domestic proceedings brought by other producers.

[66] *St Marys VCNA LLC* v. *Canada*, UNCITRAL, PCA, Consent Award (29 March 2013), p. 7.

[67] In *Lafayette Places* v. *Boston* (referenced in *Mondev* v. *United States*) the Suffolk Superior Court held that even though the Boston Planning and Development Agency (the respondent) breached the contract with the investor, the municipal authority was immune under the Massachusetts Tort Claims Act. I counted this outcome as a partial win. *Lafayette Places* v. *Boston RDA*, Suffolk Superior Court, PACER No. 9284CV01664, Judgment on Jury Verdict of 18 August 1995.

[68] *HMQ (Canada)* v. *Canadian Transit Company*, Ontario Superior Court of Justice, 2012 ONSC 1219.

Table 7.5 *Domestic cases won or lost by the investors at all levels*

State	Domestic cases	Outcome for investors at *all* levels						
		Win		Loss		Partial Win	
US	15	2	13.3%	12	80.0%	1	6.7%
CA	26	6	23.0%	19	73.0%	1	3.8%
HU	9	5	55.5%	4	44.5%	N/A	N/A
RO	24	8	33.3%	14	58.3%	2	8.6%
Total	**74**	**21**	**28.4%**	**49**	**66.2%**	**4**	**5.4%**

Table 7.6 *Domestic cases won or lost by the investors at different levels*

State	Domestic cases at levels			Investor *losses* at different levels					
	1st	2nd+3rd	3rd	only 1st		2nd+3rd		only 3rd	
US	9	6	2	6	66.7%	6	100%	2	100%
CA	15	11	4	10	66.7%	9	81.8%	4	100%
HU	3	6	3	1	33.3%	3	50.0%	2	66.6%
RO	10	14	5	5	50.0%	9	64.3%	5	100%
Total	**37**	**37**	**14**	**22**	**59.4%**	**27**	**72.3%**	**13**	**92.3%**

mentioning that half of the losses concern the patent infringement cases launched by Eli Lilly before Canadian courts. In Hungary, out of the nine fully identifiable domestic cases, the investors won five (55 per cent) and lost four of them (45 per cent). In Romania, out of the 24 domestic cases, the investors lost in 14 cases (58 per cent), won in eight cases (33 per cent) and had a partial win in two cases (9 per cent).

The data becomes more revealing if we look at the investors' success rate at different levels of the domestic proceedings (table 7.6). Thus, in all four countries the rate of investor losses increases as investors resort to higher domestic courts. Out of a total of 37 first instance cases investors lost 59 per cent, which increases to 72 per cent if we count only the second and third instance cases. When counting only the third instance cases investor losses increase to 92 per cent.

The data partly supports the first part of the hypothesis that *foreign investors have a lower success rate in domestic courts*; investors lost more cases in the United States, Canada and Romania, while in Hungary investors won slightly more cases than they lost. However, the data does not support the second part of the hypothesis (H5) that *the lower success rates are more prevalent in the transitional judiciaries.* In both Hungary and Romania, investors on average won more cases than in the United States and Canada.

It is somewhat surprising that investors lost more cases in the two countries with well-developed judiciaries compared to the two countries with transitional judiciaries. This suggests that an investor's chances of winning a domestic case is not necessarily linked to whether the domestic judiciary is very well developed or still in transition. The question is whether the same holds true for countries where the judiciary faces severe problems.

The high loss-rate and the increase of losses before the higher courts also has important implications for how investors *perceive* the domestic courts and why investors eventually chose to resort in ITA. This issue is handled in more detail in section 7.4.2.2.

7.4 Why Would Investors Rely (or Not) on Domestic Courts?

The results for the four countries show similarities that require some further analysis into why investors might rely (or not) on domestic courts. I shall focus on those arguments that can be backed up by the data.

7.4.1 Why Would Investors Rely on Domestic Courts?

The data shows that in all four countries a considerable percentage of investors relied on domestic courts prior to ITA. Before continuing, it has to be pointed out that in cases in which the investor was the passive disputing party, the answer is quite obvious: investors had to resort to domestic courts to defend themselves. In the following paragraphs we are more interested in knowing why investors, as the active disputing party, chose to bring a case before domestic courts.

7.4.1.1 Investors Did Not Know about ITA and Its Advantages; or Should They Have Known?

One could argue that investors (or their counsel) initiated domestic cases instead of ITA because they did not know about the latter avenue or they did not know about its advantages.

ITA became more widely known in the last two decades. According to Behn's empirical study conducted on 878 ITA cases, investors initiated

Table 7.7 *Absolute ignorance about ITA*

Country	Number of years after IIA's entry into force when domestic case filed	
	First instance (year)	All cases (year)
US	11.12	11.27
Canada	13	13.48
Hungary	20	21.5
Romania	10.28	11.05
Average	**12.7**	**13.57**

90% of the ITA cases after 2000, while 42% were filed between 2012 and 2017.[69] His data indicates that ITA has gone through a considerable growth trajectory and there might be a learning curve involved. In the selected countries, however, it has to be nuanced more whether investors knew or should have known about ITA or its advantages.

First, some IIAs and the remedies under them are better known than others. Thus, it is hard to argue that investors and their legal counsel did not know *at all* about ITA under well-known international treaties, such as NAFTA, which was the basis for all investor claims against Canada and the United States, with the exception of one case. Thus, even if the investors or their counsel did not know about NAFTA Chapter 11 arbitration, they should have known! Second, there might be a *learning curve* involved for ITA and its advantages. Let us look at two sides of this argument: absolute ignorance about ITA as a remedy (they did not know about ITA at all) and relative ignorance about the benefits of ITA (they knew about ITA, but not about its advantages).

Concerning the argument of *absolute ignorance* about ITA, one could argue that the investor or counsel might not have known about ITA if the domestic dispute occurred shortly after the IIA came into force. Thus, I have looked at the average number of years that have passed from the entry into force of the IIA until the date of filing of the domestic cases (see table 7.7). When looking at the filing of *only first instance* cases, the average is 11 years for the United States, 13 for Canada, 20 for Hungary and 10 for Romania. When looking at all domestic cases –

---

[69] Daniel Behn, 'Performance of Investment Treaty Arbitration', in Theresa Squatrito et al. (eds.), *The Performance of International Courts and Tribunals* (Oxford University Press, 2018), p. 89.

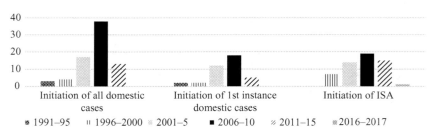

Figure 7.1 Initiation of domestic and ITA cases

regardless of the level of the case – these numbers are slightly higher at 11 years for the United States, 13 for Canada, 22 for Hungary and 11 for Romania. In other words, in all four countries on average more than a decade (even two) had passed between the entry into force of the IIA and the initiation of domestic proceedings. Thus, investors and their counsel should have known about ITA.

Relative ignorance about the benefits of ITA implies that investors and counsel knew about ITA, but not about its advantages. Thus, if investors indeed chose domestic courts because they did not know about the advantages of ITA, then in our examples one should see a decrease in domestic cases over time. As Behn argued, investors commenced most ITA cases after 2000. This would imply that the number of domestic cases has fallen after 2000. However, as figure 7.1 illustrates, most domestic cases at all levels and at first instance were filed after 2000. The initiation of domestic cases peaks in the period 2006–10 and then declines. One could argue that the learning curve occurred later towards the end of the first decade after 2000. However, this correlation is unfounded for two reasons.

First, with the decline in domestic cases one would expect investors to commence a higher number of ITA cases. Nevertheless, if we look at the periods in which investors initiated all the ITA cases against the four selected countries (figure 7.1, third set of columns), then we see that in the periods 2001–5, 2006–10 and 2011–15 roughly the same number of ITA cases were initiated, significantly higher than the ones initiated between 1995 and 2000. Thus, for these four countries there seems to be a learning curve for ITA after 2000, but it evens out between 2001 and 2015. Second, the domestic cases were initiated several years prior to the ITA cases. Thus, any correlation between the year in which domestic cases and ITA cases were initiated needs to take into account this time difference. Thus, the high peak of domestic cases initiated between

2006 and 2010 seems to translate into the relatively high number of ITA cases launched between 2011 and 2015. In conclusion, it is hard to argue that investors resorted to domestic courts because they did not know about ITA or its benefits. Furthermore, even if they did not know about them, the data indicates that counsel should have known about ITA and its advantages, especially for cases initiated in the last decade, when ITA has become more mainstream.

7.4.1.2 Domestic Disputes Are a 'Different Animal'

A more compelling reason as to why investors opt to use domestic courts concerns the type of domestic cases, compared to the international ones, and the remedies that investors want to obtain. In most cases the domestic dispute is different from the international one,[70] which in turn affects the remedies available to the investors and the adjudicatory mechanisms they can use to obtain those remedies. Thus, if an investor alleges, for example, that a competing firm infringed its patent or that the local patent authorities have not done enough to protect its intellectual property rights, then it makes more sense to bring first a patent infringement case before a domestic court. The remedy sought by the investor – stopping the infringement of a patent – is not even available in ITA, the main remedy of which is compensation. Similarly, if an investor does not win a public tender, the first logical choice is to have a domestic court set aside the initial tender, so it can be repeated and potentially awarded to the investor.

Furthermore, at this stage of the dispute, a domestic case is probably less costly, less time-consuming (see section 4.2) and the 'dispute' as such is not yet 'ripe' to go to international arbitration. Conversely, the international dispute will often entail some form of prolonged, serious or egregious treatment of the investor that could amount to a breach of the international standards of protection contained in the IIA. For example, an expropriation claim under an IIA is not 'ripe' if the host state has provided a mechanism for prompt, adequate and effective compensation, which the investor did not invoke.[71] An investor could also not argue for 'denial of justice' that amounts to a breach of the IIA's fair and equitable treatment (FET) standard, if it did not resort to domestic courts.[72]

---

[70] There are exceptions, when the international and the domestic disputes were the same. See Foster (n. 19), 265, with reference to *Pantechniki SA Contractors & Eng'rs* v. *Albania*, ICSID Case No. ARB/07/21, Award (30 July 2009).

[71] Foster (n. 19), 248.

[72] Ibid., 238.

7.4.1.3 Other Considerations

There are some further considerations for some of which I could not gather data, but which might also be relevant.

First, there might be a *financial motive* for using domestic courts. International arbitration often requires specialized, highly costly 'boutique' law firms and costly arbitrators in comparison to more resource-friendly domestic proceedings. Thus, counsel might advise the client to resort to domestic courts, especially if the client might not be in the position to cover the expenses of an international arbitration. Nonetheless, in the cases selected for this study the investors in the end were willing to spend the money on international arbitration.

Second, Dupont and Schulz have argued that ITA can seriously damage the investors' relationship with the host state and is 'often a cause for divorce'.[73] In this sense, ITA 'might be likened to a weapon of last resort'.[74] Behn's 2017 study also concluded that 'the majority of [ITA cases] appear to be claims of last resort'.[75] Therefore, a less high-profile domestic case might be a good first avenue to settle a dispute between the investor and the host state.

Third, investors might want to resort to domestic courts because they can appeal unfavourable decisions. As we have seen, in the selected countries investors could and did regularly appeal the decisions of lower courts. ITA, on the other hand, lacks an appellate mechanism, except for the ICSID annulment procedure and the appellate bodies of the investment courts included in recent EU IIAs, which have yet to fully enter into force. Thus, there is no possibility to correct an unfavourable ITA award.

7.4.2 Why Would Investors Not Rely on Domestic Courts?

The data shows that there are also a number of ITA cases that did not refer to prior domestic cases. This might be due to the inconsistent way investment tribunals reference domestic cases or because the investor did not seek domestic remedies and opted for ITA instead. We know that this was the case in at least two cases in which the tribunals specifically

---

[73] Cédric Dupont and Thomas Schultz, 'Do Hard Economic Times Lead to International Legal Disputes? The Case of Investment Arbitration' (2013) 19(4) *Swiss Political Science Review* 564, 565.

[74] Ibid.

[75] Behn (n. 69), 94–5.

Table 7.8 *Length of domestic proceedings*

State	Only 1st instance Average length in months	1st + 2nd, if 2nd is last instance Average length in months	1st + 2nd + 3rd, if 3rd is last instance Average length in months
US	24.95*	31.5	49.75
Canada	19.8	31.2	47.3
Hungary	9.66	N/A	22.7
Romania	14.9	14.75	58.4

* *Grand River* v. *King*, 783 F. Supp. 2d 516 inflates the US average as it lasted for 104.5 months.

mentioned that investors did not resort to domestic courts, even if domestic remedies existed.

7.4.2.1 Domestic Courts Are Less Efficient

One of the justifications to resort to ITA instead of domestic courts is the latter's lack of efficiency compared to international arbitration, which results in lengthier proceedings. Such a general statement needs to be nuanced.

Not all domestic court systems suffer from protracted and inefficient proceedings. The EU Justice Scoreboard found that in most EU Memeber States, the average length of civil, commercial and administrative cases at first instance was under 200 days, the major outliers being Cyprus and Portugal, with approximately 1,000 days and 700 days respectively.[76] These numbers are of course higher if one counts appeals, recourses or reviews. With this in mind, I looked at the length of the domestic proceedings selected for this analysis. The average length (see table 7.8) of all types of first instance proceedings was 25 months in the United States, 20 in Canada (excluding the US cases), ten in Hungary and 15 in Romania. The average length increases when looking at the length of proceedings that went through three levels of domestic adjudication, to 50 months in the United States, 47 in Canada, 23 in Hungary and 58 months in Romania.

Based on the data one could argue that in three of the analysed countries (United States, Canada and Romania) the length of domestic

---

[76] See European Commission (n. 25).

cases that have gone through three levels of courts – averaging four to five years – is excessive and investors will prefer faster and more efficient ITA. However, ITA is not that much different. Several studies have found that the average length of ITA cases is around four years,[77] with the occasional outliers such as *Grand River* v. *United States*,[78] which took almost seven years to conclude from the moment the notice of arbitration was sent until the final award was rendered. This period does not include possible set-aside proceedings, ICSID annulments or other domestic proceedings to enforce the award. The *Sedelmayer*, *Micula* and *Yukos* affairs are prime examples that many years will pass between the delivery of the award and the recovery of damages, if recovery is possible at all.

In conclusion, at least for transitional and highly developed judiciaries, the argument that domestic courts will take longer to solve a dispute than ITA is a weak one and should be used with caution when arguing against investors first resorting to domestic courts.

7.4.2.2 Investors Might Perceive Domestic Courts as Biased against Them

When combining the domestic cases in the selected countries, the data in section 7.3.4 is quite telling: investors lost roughly two-thirds of all domestic cases prior to ITA. With the exception of Hungary, where investors won slightly more cases, in the other three countries investors lost substantially more cases than they won. This has important implications on how investors *perceive* domestic courts.

First, counsel might argue that an overall high loss rate of foreign investors in domestic courts is a sign of systemic bias against foreign investors, which could be a reason for not relying on domestic courts. Second, in the individual cases a string of losses or losses before the high/highest courts can also provide a reason for the investor to pursue ITA. As the data indicates in table 7.6, the rate of investor losses increased in all four countries as investors reached the highest courts, from an average of 59 per cent losses at first instance to 59 per cent losses at third

---

[77] Anthony Sinclair, 'ICSID Arbitration: How Long Does It Take?' (2009) 4(5) *Global Arbitration Review* (115 ICSID cases, four years); Allen & Overy, 'Investment Treaty Arbitration: Cost, Duration and Size of Claims all Show Steady Increase' (2017), ISA (324 cases, 3.8 years); Joongi Kim, 'Streamlining the ICSID Process: New Statistical Insights and Comparative Lessons from Other Institutions' (2004) 11(1) *Transnational Dispute Management* (4.1 years).

[78] *Grand River Enterprises Six Nations, Ltd, et al. v. United States*, UNCITRAL.

INVESTORS, COURTS AND INVESTMENT ARBITRATION   203

instance. Thus, in the individual cases the investors who lost the highest court cases have exhausted all domestic remedies and these losses at last instance were most probably the reason why they resorted to ITA.

Interestingly, some investors resorted to ITA even when they won at the third level of adjudication. Thus, the investors in *Accession Mezzanine* v. *Hungary* and *Emmis* v. *Hungary* won the domestic cases before all three levels of the domestic courts. Nevertheless, they pursued international arbitration because other branches of the Hungarian State, following the favourable court decisions, enacted measures that had a detrimental effect on their investments. Furthermore, the higher number of domestic losses should not lead to the conclusion that there is *actual* bias against foreign investors in domestic courts. Testing actual bias in domestic courts is a complicated process that exceeds the scope of this chapter.

7.4.2.3   A 'Fork-in-the-Road' Clause Might Hinder Investors from Having Recourse to Domestic Courts

Some IIAs also include 'fork-in-the-road' (FITR) or 'no-U-turn' clauses. FITR clauses require the investor to decide whether it chooses domestic courts or ITA, prohibiting it to have recourse to the other forum once it has made its choice. 'No-U-turn' clauses forbid the investor to resort to domestic courts, once it has opted for ITA. 'While [FITR] clauses may discourage recourse to local courts, "no-U-turn" provisions do not have this effect'.[79] Thus, if an investor 'wishes to preserve its right to resort to international arbitration, it is likely to avoid [domestic] litigation'.[80] One would thus expect that the presence of an FITR clause in the IIA – under which ITA was initiated – would hinder the investor from bringing domestic cases. Therefore, I also looked at the presence of FITR clauses and whether investors had recourse to prior domestic litigation.

With the exception of the *Standford Ponzi Scheme* cases (discontinued), all the ITA cases against the United States and Canada were initiated under NAFTA. NAFTA does not contain an FITR clause, while its Article 1121 'no-U-turn' clause would not have any discouraging effect on investors bringing prior domestic cases.[81] In the case of

---

[79] UNCTAD, 'Investor-State Dispute Settlement' (2014) UNCTAD Series on Issues in International Investment Agreements III, <unctad.org/en/PublicationsLibrary/dia eia2013d2_en.pdf>, 86–7.

[80] Ibid., 87.

[81] For the differences between the NAFTA Article 1121 and FITR clauses, see Todd Weiler, *International Investment Law and Arbitration: Leading Cases from the ICSID, NAFTA,*

NAFTA it also has to be mentioned that under its statute of limitations clause[82] investors are barred from bringing a case if more than three years have elapsed from the moment when the investor/investment first acquired/should have acquired knowledge of the alleged breach. However, in the case of the ITA cases against the United States and Canada, investors were not barred from initiating arbitration by the statute of limitations clause, even if prior domestic cases existed. This lends support to the argument expressed in section 4.1.2, that the domestic disputes are different from the ITA disputes.[83]

In the ITA cases against Hungary, four cases were brought under the ECT, which includes an FITR clause in Annex ID. Of the four cases, two are not publicly available, while *AES* v. *Hungary II* did not refer to any domestic cases and *Electrabel* v. *Hungary* mentioned the prior existence of a case brought before the General Court of the EU but not the Hungarian courts. The two ITA cases for which information is available might suggest that the presence of the FITR clause in the ECT could have incentivized the investors not to resort to domestic courts and to choose ITA instead. However, such a conclusion is unfounded for two reasons.

First, three ITA cases against Romania were initiated under IIAs that included a FITR clause[84] and all three of them made references to prior domestic cases launched by the investor.[85] Thus, the presence of the FITR clauses has neither stopped the investors from relying on domestic courts, nor did it stop them from later resorting to arbitration.

Second, FITR clauses in practice often do not prevent investors from bringing ITA cases.[86] In order for this clause to properly operate, one would need identity of the facts, the disputing parties and the legal rules

---

Bilateral Treaties and Customary International Law (Cameron May, 2005), p. 313. See also Foster (n. 19), 249.

[82] NAFTA, Articles 1116(2) and 1117(2).

[83] There are exceptions, when the international and the domestic disputes were the same. See Foster (n. 19), 265, with reference to *Pantechniki* v. *Albania* (n. 70).

[84] *Awdi* v. *Romania* (US–Romania BIT, Article VI.3); *Noble Ventures* v. *Romania* (US–Romania BIT, Article VI.3); *Rompetrol* v. *Romania* (Romania–Netherlands BIT, Article 8.3).

[85] In *Noble Ventures* the tribunal mentions prior national cases without giving more detail, while in the other two cases various domestic cases were initiated by the investors and state bodies.

[86] UNCTAD (n. 79), 87.

invoked. In most cases, however, the domestic dispute is brought by a different legal entity than the international one, the facts of the domestic case differ, as well as the legal rules. Whilst in an ITA case the applicable law will mainly be formed by the underlying IIA, in domestic cases investors will mostly rely on domestic laws. As an illustration, I looked at the rules invoked in all the domestic cases – to which I had full access – to see whether or not investors might have invoked IIAs besides domestic law. I only found two domestic cases that referred to IIAs or their implementing legislation. In *Tembec* v. *United States*[87] before the US Court of International Trade (USCIT), which preceded the UNCITRAL arbitration in *Domtar* v. *United States* (tribunal not constituted), the domestic court referred to NAFTA. More specifically, the determination of an Article 1904 NAFTA Panel, in a case that concerned the liquidation of cash deposits given by non-US firms to the US authorities in an anti-dumping case. The USCIT concluded that the liquidation had to be made in accordance with the NAFTA Panel's decision. However, this case did not concern the usage of the NAFTA provisions pertaining to investment protection. The second case was *AVAS* v. *SC CMEIE SRL,* referenced in *Roussalis* v. *Romania*. In this case, the state agency (AVAS) argued that the Romanian tribunal lacked jurisdiction, because a BIT existed that provided for its own mechanism to solve investor–state disputes. The Bucharest Court of Appeals rejected this argument. It referred to Law 166/1997 implementing the Romania–Greece BIT which provided for international arbitration and the usage of local courts. The Court of Appeals concluded that it had jurisdiction to hear the case as the dispute was contractual, not treaty based, and the company involved was a Romanian company, registered in the country.[88] The Supreme Court of Romania also dismissed the state agency's arguments regarding the Court's lack of jurisdiction. It held that the company in question was a Romanian entity, therefore, the law implementing the BIT was not applicable to the dispute.[89]

In conclusion, the likelihood that in practice an FITR clause will prevent an investor from having recourse to domestic courts seems quite low.

---

[87] 441 F. Supp. 2d 1302.

[88] *AVAS* v. *SC C.M.E.I.E. SRL*, Bucharest Court of Appeals, Commercial Section VI, Decision 430 of 08.10.2007, File No: 7341/3/2003.

[89] *AVAS* v. *SC C.M.E.I.E. SRL*, Romanian Supreme Court, Decision 2090/2009 of 30.03.2009.

7.5 Should Investors First Resort to Domestic Courts?

The last part of the chapter takes a normative turn. The data shows that domestic courts in the four countries analysed are regularly involved in disputes that involve foreign investors and the host state and investors do not shy away from using domestic courts. This begs the question whether – at least between countries with highly developed or transitional judiciaries – BITs should include some form of mechanism that obliges investors to resort to domestic courts prior to initiating international arbitration and whether the future Multilateral Investment Court (MIC) should – at least in an optional manner – include an exhaustion of local remedies clause. As this topic has been widely debated in academia,[90] the next sections will only focus on some key arguments where the results of the previous analysis can be helpful.

Furthermore, one should not confuse the recourse to domestic courts prior to ITA with the exclusion of ITA in favour of domestic courts. The prior recourse to domestic courts should not create an underlying expectation that they are 'better' or 'superior'[91] to investment tribunals. Many of the world's international adjudicative systems have been set up to curb the abuses of domestic authorities. The European Convention on Human Rights (ECHR) system and the EU see their roots in post-WWII Europe. International Criminal Law has expanded following the atrocities of the 1990s in places such as the former Yugoslavia or Rwanda, while ITA was meant to curb the abusive behaviour of certain states against the property of foreign investors.[92]

7.5.1 Ensuring Increased Legitimacy of ITA and of a Future Multilateral Investment Court

Resorting to domestic courts prior to international adjudication is not an alien concept in international law. For example, the requirement to exhaust local remedies under the ECHR has 'had a remarkable success in socialising the regime's members into the logics of collective, transnational rights protection, and in enlisting participation in the

---

[90] See Sattorova (n. 2); Foster (n. 19); Matthew Porterfield, 'Exhaustion of Local Remedies in Investor-State Dispute Settlement: An Idea Whose Time Has Come' (2015) 41 *Yale Journal of International Law* 1.

[91] See Bronckers (n. 15), 655.

[92] See St John (n. 1).

Convention's expansionary dynamics'.[93] Thus, one could argue that relying on domestic courts prior to ITA could help address some of the legitimacy challenges faced by IIL and ITA, as well as help create a more legitimate MIC.[94] Without going into a detailed debate over the various concepts of legitimacy used in academia,[95] this section differentiates between normative and societal/perceived legitimacy.

From the perspective of *normative* legitimacy,[96] ITA tribunals and domestic courts have different sources for their legitimacy. In the case of ITA tribunals, the traditional view is that international institutions, including international adjudicative bodies, derive legitimacy from state consent or their legitimacy is linked to the processes they use to render their decisions.[97] More recently, some authors have argued that other bases for legitimacy should be included, based on procedural fairness that takes into account the interests of non-litigating parties, transparency and a minimum set of core human rights.[98] Whatever the exact source of the legitimacy of ITA tribunals, they exist in a normative system that is not fully developed; there is no clear hierarchy of norms and courts, the legal norms are often vaguely worded and there is no clear separation of powers.[99] Contrast this to those domestic courts that operate in an *État de droit*, courts which derive their normative legitimacy from national legal systems, in which there is more or less a clear separation of powers, a hierarchy of norms with a constitution on top, a hierarchy of courts, and a representative body(ies) tasked with the formation of new norms. This of course does not deny the existence of problems in countries where the domestic courts, either *de jure* or *de facto*, are not fully

---

[93] Helen Keller and Alec Stone Sweet (eds.), *A Europe of Rights: The Impact of the ECHR on National Legal Systems* (Oxford University Press, 2008), Part 1.

[94] See United Nations Commission on International Trade Law, WG III, 'Possible Reform of Investor-State Dispute Settlement (ISDS) – Cost and Duration' (2018) A/CN.9/WG.III/WP.153.

[95] On the various uses and concepts of legitimacy, see Nienke Grossman, 'Legitimacy and International Adjudicative Bodies' (2010) 41 *George Washington International Law Review* 107; Christopher A. Thomas, 'The Uses and Abuses of Legitimacy in International Law' (2014) 34(4) *Oxford Journal of Legal Studies* 729; Erik Voeten, 'Public Opinion and the Legitimacy of International Courts' (2013) 14(2) *Theoretical Inquiries in Law* 411.

[96] See Thomas (ibid.).

[97] Nienke Grossman, 'The Normative Legitimacy of International Courts' (2013–14) 86 *Temple Law Review* 61, 65–7.

[98] Ibid., 79.

[99] See Philip Allots, 'The Concept of International Law' (1999) 10 *European Journal of International Law* 31.

independent from other branches of the government and where serious 'rule of law' concerns exist.

As Foster notes, 'national courts are in the best position (at least as a general rule) to interpret and apply their own laws',[100] while Dodge argues that NAFTA Chapter 11 review 'tends to be less determinate, less accountable, less legitimate, and more intrusive on national sovereignty' compared to domestic courts.[101] Furthermore, compared to ITA tribunals, domestic courts 'may also be better suited than an international tribunal to make findings of fact if they have greater access to evidence'.[102] As the data illustrates, even if in two of the countries the domestic judiciary still faces problems, a separate branch of the government (the judiciary) handled the domestic cases, investors had access to all levels of adjudication (up to three levels), and local courts applied domestic laws adopted via the domestic constitutional process. Thus, one could argue that the domestic courts in question possess higher or at least better grounded normative legitimacy than ITA tribunals. Therefore, relying first on domestic courts might help increase the normative legitimacy of IIL and that of a future MIC.

If one looks at public/perceived legitimacy,[103] the situation is more complicated. Voeten's study finds that 'trust in international courts remains strongly correlated with trust in international and domestic institutions'.[104] Public attitudes towards courts are not static though. For example, in the early 1990s the case law of the European Court of Human Rights (ECtHR) and the ECHR 'provided a benchmark for European ideals, a brake upon post-totalitarian societies' backsliding and a sign of belonging to Western Europe'.[105] Nowadays, however, the perception of the ECtHR in ex-communist countries ranges from 'sparse criticism' in the Czech Republic to 'hostile criticism' in Russia.[106] Furthermore, in countries where there is a lack of trust in domestic

---

[100] Foster (n. 19), 262.
[101] William S. Dodge, 'Loewen v. United States: Trials and Errors under NAFTA Chapter Eleven' (2002) 52(2) *De Paul Law Review* 563, 570.
[102] Foster (n. 19), 262.
[103] See Voeten (n. 95); Armin von Bogdandy and Ingo Venzke, *In Whose Name? A Public Law Theory of International Adjudication* (Oxford University Press, 2014).
[104] Voeten (n. 95), 411, 414.
[105] Ľubomír Majerčík, 'Czech Republic: Strasbourg Case Law Undisputed', in Patricia Popelier et al. (eds.), *Criticism of the European Court of Human Rights* (Intersentia, 2016), p. 133.
[106] Ibid.

courts the public might look at international law and courts as the ones bringing justice where the national courts and authorities have failed. Nonetheless, do these arguments hold true for ITA?

The picture will differ depending on whose perspective one takes. On the one hand, investors could very well argue that domestic courts are biased; therefore, they need to resort to impartial international arbitration. Similar attitudes towards the prior recourse to domestic courts might also be shared by the home state of the investor, which would prefer its investor not to rely on the domestic courts of a party whose judiciary it cannot trust. On the other hand, critics of ITA – such as non-governmental organizations (NGOs) – have argued that any reform of ITA should include an exhaustion of local remedies clause, which 'will ensure that investment law will be again back on par with international human rights law and customary international law'.[107] Furthermore, the more recent public contestation of ITA within the EU – that involved academics, NGOs and members of civil society[108] – is a good example of the possible mistrust in and diminished social legitimacy of ITA.

In conclusion, compared to investment tribunals, some domestic courts might possess higher normative legitimacy and, depending on the perspective one takes, they might also possess higher public legitimacy. As Foster has argued, domestic courts may not be better than ITA in striking a balance between public policy concerns and the rights of investors. However, they are more legitimate and have a thorough understanding of the context in which a certain government measure was adopted.[109] After all, 'measuring private interests against broader societal, political and other considerations is the core task' of domestic courts.[110]

7.5.2   Investors Already Rely on Domestic Courts

The data paints a diverse picture in which – contrary to our expectations – investors rely on domestic courts prior to ITA cases. In three out

---

[107] Client Earth, 'Towards a More Diligent and Sustainable System of Investment Protection', 15 March 2017, p. 10, <documents.clientearth.org/wp-content/uploads/2017-03-15-towards-a-more-diligent-and-sustainable-system-of-investment-protection-ce-en.pdf>.

[108] Matthias Bauer, 'Manufacturing Discontent: The Rise to Power of Anti-TTIP Groups' (2016), Occasional Paper, *European Center for International Political Economy*, <ecipe.org/wp-content/uploads/2016/11/Manufacturing-Discontent.pdf>.

[109] Foster (n. 19), 249.

[110] Bronckers (n. 15), 666.

of the four countries roughly two-thirds of ITA cases were preceded by prior domestic cases. There are also instances in which the ITA cases do not refer to prior domestic cases and in two ITA cases investors purposely chose not to pursue domestic remedies. In other words, domestic courts already play a role in settling disputes between investors and host states. This data should not be surprising given the subject-matter of the domestic cases, the lower costs of domestic proceedings and the possibility of ITA claims upsetting the relationship between the investors and the host states. Furthermore, given the vast number of domestic companies owned by foreign investors, the existing ITA cases are only a tiny fraction of the overall disputes that occur between foreign investors and their host states.[111] Consequently, domestic courts will continue being one of the fora where investors will settle their disputes.

7.5.3 Protection of Sovereignty

The global legal landscape is now littered with a multitude of multilateral and regional courts. However, in recent years a certain 'court fatigue' has set in and the willingness of states to create new international courts is dwindling, coupled with a series of backlashes against international courts and the ISDS system, often fuelled by populist discourse to regain more 'sovereignty'.[112] On top of all these, 'states never enjoy having to defend themselves before an external body'.[113] Therefore, in the current climate it is doubtful whether states are willing to further limit their sovereignty and create a MIC. If a MIC has any chance of ever coming into existence, the drafters must reassure states that any limitations to their sovereignty will be minimal.

State fears over loss of sovereignty are not new and have been a contentious issue during the drafting of Article 17 of the Rome Statute for the International Criminal Court (ICC). These concerns were alleviated by allowing states to have the primary role in trying international crimes, giving the ICC a complementary role.[114] Following this example, states could be reassured that ITA or a future MIC shall protect their

---

[111] Behn (n. 69), 95.

[112] See Joost Pauwelyn and Rebecca J. Hamilton, 'Exit from International Tribunals' (2018) *Journal of International Dispute Settlement* 1.

[113] Jan Paulsson, 'The Power of States to Make Meaningful Promises to Foreigners' (2010) 1(2) *Journal of International Dispute Settlement* 341, 344.

[114] William A. Schabas, *The International Criminal Court: A Commentary on the Rome Statute* (Oxford University Press, 2016), p. 447.

sovereignty, if their courts are first given the chance to amend any wrongdoings towards investors. This could be done by assigning domestic courts the primary role in protecting the rights of foreign investors from state wrongdoings. If this avenue fails, then investors would still have the chance to bring an ITA claim.

7.5.4 What about Bias and Inefficiency?

As mentioned in section 7.2.2.1, advocates of ITA argue that investment treaty arbitration ensures that foreign investors are not subjected to biased and inefficient domestic courts.

One should not dismiss, of course, the very real concern that many legal systems still struggle to become an *État de droit*; the courts of many states are not fully independent, and their judiciaries face systemic deficiencies as also exemplified by the '2017 EU Justice Scoreboard' (see above, section 7.2.3). Whilst the data was not gathered to test actual bias, the higher loss ratio might create a perception amongst investors that the domestic courts are biased. If investors could prove the existence of actual bias in a case or the presence of systematic bias against them, then – in a fashion similar to Article 17 of the Rome Statute – the requirement to first go before the domestic court could be forgone if the investor proves that the domestic courts are 'unable' or 'unwilling' to handle their case.

Furthermore, one should also not presume that ITA is 'inherently' better than domestic courts because it is impartial. One of the often-raised criticisms of ITA is the perceived lack of independence and impartiality of arbitrators.[115] Most wing arbitrators are appointed by the disputing parties, which some could read as the arbitrators favouring their appointers. A recent study has also found a high-degree of 'double-hatting' amongst the most influential arbitrators.[116] Conversely, it can also be argued that, unlike domestic courts, ITA allows the disputing parties to appoint their arbitrators, ensuring that the tribunal is

---

[115] Sergio Puig and Anton Strezhnev, 'Affiliation Bias in Arbitration: An Experimental Approach' (2017) 46(2) *Journal of Legal Studies* 371; Susan D. Franck, et al. 'Inside the Arbitrator's Mind' (2017) 66(5) *Emory Law Journal* 1115.

[116] Malcolm Langford, Daniel Behn and Runar Lie, 'The Revolving Door in International Investment Arbitration' (2017) 20(2) *Journal of International Economic Law* 301.

composed of persons with sufficient ability to consider the case from the perspectives of the two disputing parties.

As regards the argument that domestic courts are inefficient, the data for the four countries has shown that the domestic proceedings on average lasted from four to five years in Canada, Romania and the United States, while this length was slightly under two years in Hungary. Knowing that ITA cases on average last four years, one should look at the 'domestic court inefficiency' justification through a more critical light.

7.6 Conclusions

To my knowledge, this is the first empirical study that focuses on domestic court proceedings between investors and host states, prior to the initiation of treaty-based investor–state arbitration. The choice of looking at two countries with highly developed judiciaries (the United States and Canada) and two countries with transitional judiciaries (Hungary and Romania) was meant to highlight that some expectations based on the level of development of a country's judiciary do not necessarily hold true. The data shows that investors often had recourse to the domestic courts in the selected countries prior to initiating ITA and that the transitional or highly developed character of the domestic judiciary does not condition the usage of domestic courts. Once investors choose to rely on domestic courts, they also regularly appeal lower court decisions to the highest courts of the land, and the transitional or highly developed character of the domestic judiciary does not influence the rate of appeals. In relation to subject-matter, the cases are very diverse and investors can also act as defendants, not just as claimants. Lastly, investors lost more cases than they won in three out of the four countries and, once again, the higher number of losses was not conditioned by the transitional nature of the domestic judiciary; rather the opposite.

This study has several broader implications. First, it can help better explain why investors actually choose to rely on domestic courts, even if they have the possibility of pursuing denationalized international arbitration. The data indicates that reliance on domestic courts in the selected countries was not a result of ignorance towards investment arbitration, but is more likely a result of the differences between the domestic and the international 'disputes', which in turn affects the available remedies and adjudicatory mechanisms. Second, one cannot argue that investors in the selected countries did not have access to domestic courts at multiple levels. However, the higher rates of losses might create the perception amongst investors that domestic courts are biased against them. The higher rates of investor losses do not, of course, prove actual bias. Third, given the highly diverse legal areas, as well as state and non-state measures that can subsequently form the basis of an international arbitral claim, states should be extra careful when signing up to IIAs as potentially any measure in any area of the law is challengeable internationally. Fourth, in the context of creating a multilateral investment court or reforming ITA, the study also helps develop arguments in favour of obliging investors first to resort to domestic courts, prior to ITA, at least when they invest in countries with highly developed or transitional judiciaries. The length of domestic cases in the selected countries was similar to the average length of ITA proceedings. Furthermore, due to the more solid normative grounding of domestic courts and the perception that ITA is also biased, relying on domestic courts prior to ITA might actually increase the legitimacy of ITA and that of international investment law.

~

Annexes

Explanations for all the tables

(1) **Case name/identifier:** 'Aw' – Award; 'TNC' – Tribunal not constituted; 'S' – Settled; 'D' – Discontinued. Also includes year when investor initiated arbitration

(2) **Date filing:** Day when the domestic case was filed; **Year Decision:** Day when the domestic court handed down its decision. Appears below 'Case Name' or 'Case Identifier'

(3) **Access:** Did the author have full access to the case? 'Y' – Yes; 'N' – No; 'P' – Partial access

(4) **Year after:** How many years after the entry into force of the IIA was the domestic court case filed?

(5) **Type of case:** How is the case classified in the domestic legal order? 'AR' – Administrative Review; 'B' – Bankruptcy; 'C' – Civil; 'CM' – Commercial; 'CR' – Criminal; 'E' – Economic; 'IP' – Intellectual Property; 'IE' – International Economic; 'JCR' – Judicial/Constitutional Review

(6) **Level:** The level of adjudication in the domestic system. '1' – first instance; '2' – second instance; '3' – third instance

(7) **Length:** Length of cases in months

(8) **Outcome investor:** 'L' – Loss; 'W' – Win; 'PW' – Partial win

Table 7A.1 *United States*

INTERNATIONAL LEVEL		DOMESTIC LEVEL								
Case name/identifier (1)	IIA	Case name (2) (Date filing/ decision)	Case identifier	Access (3)	Year after (4)	Court	Type (5)	Level (6)	Outcome investor (7)	Length months (8)
ADF v. US (2000) ICSID ARB(AF)/00/1 (Aw)	NAFTA 01.01.1994	N/A	N/A	N/A	N/A	N/A	N/A	N/A	N/A	N/A
Apotex v. US										
I **Apotex v. US (2010)** ICSID UNCT/ 10/2 (Aw)	NAFTA	*Apotex Inc. v. Pfizer Inc* 2006/ 10.10.2006	127 S.Ct. 379	Y	12	US Supreme Court	IP	3	L	max 10
		Apotex Inc. v. Pfizer Inc 2005/ 12.12.2005	159 F. App'x 1013, 2005 WL 3457408	N	11	USCA for the 2nd Circuit	IP	2	L	max 12
		Apotex Inc. v. Pfizer Inc 01.04.2004/ 03.01.2005	385 F. Supp. 2d 187 1:2004cv2539	Y	10	USDC South. District of New York	IP	1	L	8
II **Apotex v. US (2010)** ICSID UNCT/ 10/2 (Aw)		*Apotex Inc. v. FDA* 19.04.2006/ 06.06.2006	449 F.3d 1249 0:2006cvus05105	Y	12	USCA for Federal Circuit	IP	2	L	1.5
		Apotex Inc. v. FDA 05.04.2006/ 19.04.2006	2006 WL 1030151 1:2006cv00627	Y	12	USDC for District of Columbia	IP	1	L	0.5
III **Apotex v. US (2012)** ICSID ARB(AF)/ 12/1 (Aw)	NAFTA	N/A	N/A	N/A	N/A	N/A	N/A	N/A	N/A	N/A

Table 7A.1 (cont.)

INTERNATIONAL LEVEL		DOMESTIC LEVEL								
Case name/identifier (1)	IIA	Case name (2) (Date filing/ decision)	Case identifier	Access (3)	Year after (4)	Court	Type (5)	Level (6)	Outcome investor (7)	Length months (8)
Baird v. US (2002) (TNC)	NAFTA	N/A	N/A	N/A	N/A	N/A	N/A	N/A	N/A	N/A
Canadian Cattlemen v. US (2005) UNCITRAL (Aw)	NAFTA	N/A	N/A	N/A	N/A	N/A	N/A	N/A	N/A	N/A
Canfor v. US (2002) (prev. Canfor v. US, Tembec v. US, Terminal v. US) UNCITRAL (D)	NAFTA	N/A	N/A	N/A	N/A	N/A	N/A	N/A	N/A	N/A
CANACAR v. US (2009) UNCITRAL (TNC)	NAFTA	N/A	N/A	N/A	N/A	N/A	N/A	N/A	N/A	N/A
Doman Industries v. US UNCITRAL (TNC)	NAFTA	N/A	N/A	N/A	N/A	N/A	N/A	N/A	N/A	N/A
Domtar v. US (2007) UNCITRAL (TNC)	NAFTA	Tembec Inc. v. US 19.01.2005/ 13.10.2006	441 F. Supp. 2d 1302 No. 05-00028	Y	11	US Court of International Trade	IE	1	W	21
Glamis Gold v. US (2003) UNCITRAL (Aw)	NAFTA	Glamis v. Babbitt 14.04.2000/ 26.09.2000	3:2000cv00196	N	6	USDC for the District of Nevada	C	1	L	5.5
		Glamis v. US Dep. Int. 12.03.2001/ 13.11.2001	1:2001cv00530	Y	7	USDC for District of Columbia	C	1	W	8

Grand River v. US (2004) UNCITRAL (Aw)	NAFTA	*Grand River v. King* 01.07.2002/ 17.03.2011	783 F. Supp. 2d 516 1:2002cv05068	Y	8	USDC South. District of New York	C	1	L	104.5
		Kansas v. Grand River 2008/ 11.02.2008	No. 08C-000207	N	14	USDC for Kansas	C	1	N/A	max 2
Kenex v. US (2002) ICSID (TNC)	NAFTA	N/A	N/A	N/A	N/A	N/A	N/A	N/A	N/A	N/A
Loewen v. US (1998) ICSID ARB(AF)/98/3 (Aw)	NAFTA	*Loewen Group v. O'Keefe* 27.11.1995/ 24.01.1996	95-TS-01216	N	1	Mississippi Supreme Court	CM	2	L	2
		O'Keefe v. Loewen Group 1991/ 06.11.1995	91-67-423 1995 WL 777615	Y	−3	CC of First Judicial District of Hinds County	CM	1	L	max 59
Methanex v. US (1999) UNCITRAL (Aw)	NAFTA	N/A	Lacks identifiers	N	N/A	USDC for the Cent. Dist. of Calif.	N/A	N/A	N/A	N/A
Mondev v. US (1999) ICSID ARB(AF)/99/2 (Aw)	NAFTA	*Lafayette Pl. v. Boston* 1998/ 01.03.1999	119 S.Ct. 1112	Y	4	US Supreme Court	C	3	L	max 14
		Lafayette Pl. v. Boston 1997/ 20.05.1998	427 Mass. 509 1997-P-1925	Y	3	Massachusetts Supreme Judicial Court	C	2	L	max 16.5
		Lafayette Pl. v. Boston 16.03.1992/ 18.08.1995	96-1664-A 9284CV01664	Y	−2	Suffolk Superior Court	C	1	PW	max 39

Table 7A.1 (*cont.*)

INTERNATIONAL LEVEL		DOMESTIC LEVEL								
Case name/identifier (1)	IIA	Case name (2) (Date filing/ decision)	Case identifier	Access (3)	Year after (4)	Court	Type (5)	Level (6)	Outcome investor (7)	Length months (8)
TransCanada v. US (2016) ICSID ARB/16/21 (D) **Victims of the Stanford Ponzi v. US (2012)** (TNC)	NAFTA	*Thompson v. Heineman* 2015/ 09.01.2015	289 Neb. 798 S-14-158	Y	21	Nebraska Supreme Court	JCR	1	L	max 2
I **Nationals of Peru**	US-PE FTA	N/A	N/A	N/A	N/A	N/A	N/A	N/A	N/A	N/A
II **Fleitas**	US-UY BIT									
III **Moor**	US-CL FTA									
IV **Peruvian Victims**	US-PE FTA									
V **Guatemalan etc. Victims**	CAFTA- DR									

Table 7A.2 *Canada*

INTERNATIONAL LEVEL		DOMESTIC LEVEL								
Case name/identifier (1)	IIA	Case name (Date filing/decision)	Case identifier (2)	Access (3)	Year after (4)	Court	Type (5)	Level (6)	Outcome investor (7)	Length months (8)
AbitibiBowater v. Canada (2012) ICSID No. UNCT/10/1 (S)	NAFTA 01.01.1994	*AbitibiBowater Inc.* 2009/22.04.2009	500-11-036133-094	Y	15	Superior Court of Quebec in Canada	B	1	W	max 5
		AbitibiBowater Inc. 06.04.2009/18.12.2012	09-11296 (KJC)	Y	15	US Bankruptcy Court for Delaware	B	1	W	44
Centurion v. Canada (2009) PCA No. 2009-21 (D)	NAFTA	N/A	N/A	N/A	N/A	N/A	N/A	N/A	N/A	N/A
Chemtura v. Canada (2002) UNCITRAL, PCA (Aw)	NAFTA	*Crompton* Hearing 06.05.2003	Lacks identifiers	N	N/A	Federal Court of Canada	N/A	1	N/A	N/A
		Crompton v. Minister of Health and Agriculture 04.04.2001/04.05.2001	2001 FCT 435	Y	7	Federal Court of Canada	IP	1	L	1
Contractual Obligation Productions v. Canada (2005) UNCITRAL (TNC)	NAFTA	N/A	N/A	N/A	N/A	N/A	N/A	N/A	N/A	N/A
Detroit Int'l v. Canada (2011) PCA No. 2012-25 (Aw)	NAFTA	*CA v. Canadian T Co.* 2011/21.02.2012	2012 ONSC 1219	Y	17	Ontario Superior Court of Justice	AR	2	PW	max 14
		Canadian T Co. v. CA 31.12.2009/04.05.2011	2011 FC 515	Y	15	Federal Court	JCR	1	L	16
		Canadian T Co. v. CA 31.12.2009/04.05.2011	2011 FC 517	Y	15	Federal Court	AR	1	L	16

Table 7A.2 (*cont.*)

INTERNATIONAL LEVEL		DOMESTIC LEVEL								
Case name/identifier (1)	IIA	Case name (Date filing/decision) (2)	Case identifier (2)	Access (3)	Year after (4)	Court	Type (5)	Level (6)	Outcome investor (7)	Length months (8)
		Detroit Int'l Bridge v. CA 22.03.2010/01.12.2011	1:2010cv00476	Y	16	*USDC for the District of Columbia*	C	1	W	20
		Latin Americans for SED v AOFHA 01.11.2010/05.04.2012	858 F.Supp.2d 839 2:2010cv10082	Y	16	*US District Court for E.D. Michigan*	C	1	L	18
Dow AgroSciences v. CA (2009) UNCITRAL (S)	NAFTA	N/A	N/A	N/A	N/A	N/A	N/A	N/A	N/A	N/A
Eli Lilly v. Canada (2013) ICSID No. UNCT/14/2 (Aw)	NAFTA	*Eli Lilly v. Novopharm* 13.05.2013/16.05.2013	R-002, 2013 CanLII 26762 (SCC)	Y	19	Supreme Court of Canada	IP	3	L	0.1
		Eli Lilly v. Novopharm 09.12.2011/10.09.2012	C-147/R-035 2012 FCA 232	Y	17	Federal Court of Appeals	IP	2	L	9
		Eli Lilly v. Novopharm 06.06.2007/10.11.2011	C-146/R-016 2011 FC 1288	Y	13	Federal Court	IP	1	L	51
		Eli Lilly v. Novopharm 03.11.2009/21.07.2010	C-046/R-015 2010 FCA 197	Y	15	Federal Court of Appeals	IP	2	W	8.5
		Eli Lilly v. Novopharm 06.06.2007/05.10.2009	C-145/R-033 2009 FC 1018	Y	13	Federal Court	IP	1	L	28

		Eli Lilly v. *Teva Canada* 05.07.2011/08.12.2011	R-003, 2011 CanLII 79177 (SCC)	Y	17	Supreme Court of Canada	IP	3	L	5
		Eli Lilly v. *Teva Canada* 14.10.2010/05.07.2011	C-163/R-028 2011 FCA 220	Y	16	Federal Court of Appeals	IP	2	L	9
		Novopharm v. *Eli Lilly* 22.05.2008/14.09.2010	C-160/R-027 2010 FC 915	Y	14	Federal Court	IP	1	L	28
		Eli Lilly v. *Novopharm* 06.06.2007/05.11.2007	C-512/R-208 2007 FCA 359	Y	13	Federal Court of Appeals	IP	2	L	5
		Eli Lilly v. *Novopharm* 08.09.2005/05.06.2007	C-144/R-032 2007 FC 596	Y	11	Federal Court	IP	1	L	21
Ethyl Corp v. Canada (1997) UNCITRAL (Aw)	NAFTA	N/A	N/A	N/A	N/A	N/A	N/A	N/A	N/A	N/A
Gallo v. Canada (2007) PCA No. 55798 (Aw)	NAFTA	N/A	N/A	N/A	N/A	N/A	N/A	N/A	N/A	N/A
Great Lakes Farms v. Canada (2006) UNCITRAL (D)	NAFTA	*Allan* v. *Ontario* 2005/12.05.2006	M33165, C44066	Y	11	Court of Appeal for Ontario	JCR	3	L	max 8.5
		Allan v. *Ontario* 2003/29.07.2005	2005 CanLII 25770	Y	9	Ontario Superior Court of Justice, Div. Court	JCR	2	L	max 25
		Georgian Bay Milk v. *DFO* 2003/04.06.2003	2003 ONAFRAAT 17	Y	9	Ontario Agriculture, Food and Rural Affairs Appeal Tribunal	AR	1	W	max 5
Greiner v. Canada (2010) UNCITRAL (D)	NAFTA	N/A	N/A	N/A	N/A	N/A	N/A	N/A	N/A	N/A

Table 7A.2 (*cont.*)

INTERNATIONAL LEVEL		DOMESTIC LEVEL									
Case name/identifier (1)	IIA	Case name (Date filing/decision)	Case identifier (2)	Access (3)	Year after (4)	Court	Type (5)	Level (6)	Outcome investor (7)	Length months (8)
Longyear v. Canada (2014) UNCITRAL (S)	NAFTA	N/A	N/A	N/A	N/A	N/A	N/A	N/A	N/A	N/A
Merrill & Ring v. Canada (2006) ICSID No. UNCT/07/1 (Aw)	NAFTA	N/A	N/A	N/A	N/A	N/A	N/A	N/A		N/A
Mesa Power v. Canada (2011) PCA No. 2012-17 (Aw)	NAFTA	*In re app. of Mesa Power* 01.12.2011/13.07.2012	878 F.Supp.2d 1296 1:2011mc24335	Y	17	*US District Court for S.D. Florida*	IE	1	W	7.5
		In re app. of Mesa Power 14.11.2011/20.11.2012	2012 WL 6060941 2:11–mc–280–ES	Y	17	*US District Court for D. of New Jersey*	IE	1	PW	12
		In re app. of Mesa Power 14.11.2011/09.05.2012	3:11-cv-05510-JCS	Y	17	*US District Court for N.D. California*	IE	1	W	6
Mobil Inv'ts v. Canada (I) (2007) ICSID No. ARB(AF)/07/4 (Aw)	NAFTA	*Hibernia v. CA-NLOPB* 04.09.2008/19.02.2009	2009 CanLII 6794	Y	14	Supreme Court of Canada	AR	3	L	5.5
		Hibernia v. CA-NLOPB 2007/04.09.2008	2008 NLCA 46	Y	13	Supr. Court of Newfoundland and Labrador, Appeal	AR	2	L	max 18
		Hibernia v. CA-NLOPB 2005/22.01.2007	2007NLTD14	Y	13	Supr. Court of Newfoundland and Labrador, Trial	AR	1	L	max 25

SD Myers v. Canada **(1998)** UNCITRAL (Aw)	NAFTA	*Sierra Club* v. *E.P.A.* 27.03.1996/07.07.1997	No. 96-70223 118 F.3d 1324	Y	2	*US Court of Appeals, Ninth Circuit*	AR	1	W	15
Pope & Talbot v. Canada **(2000)** UNCITRAL (Aw)	NAFTA	N/A	N/A	N/A	N/A	Reference to other producers challenging domestic measures	N/A	N/A	N/A	N/A
St Marys v. Canada (2011) UNCITRAL, PCA (S)	NAFTA	*St Marys VCNA*	withdrawn	N/A	N/A	Federal Court of Canada	JCR	N/A	N/A	N/A
UPS v. Canada (2000) ICSID No. UNCT/02/1 (Aw)	NAFTA	*Dussault* v. *Customs and Revenue Agency* 15.06.2001/25.08.2003	2003 FC 973	Y	7	Federal Court	AR	1	L	26.5
Windstream Energy v. CA **(2013)** PCA No. 2013-22 (Aw)	NAFTA	N/A	N/A	N/A	N/A	N/A	N/A	N/A	N/A	N/A

US cases are marked with *italics*.

Table 7A.3 *Hungary*

INTERNATIONAL LEVEL		DOMESTIC LEVEL								
Case name/ identifier (1)	IIA	Case name (Date filing/ decision)	Case identifier (2)	Access (3)	Year after (4)	Court	Type (5)	Level (6)	Outcome investor (7)	Length months (8)
Accession **Mezzanine v. HU (2011)** ICSID ARB/12/3 (Aw)	UK-HU 28.08.1987	*ORTT* v. *Danubius* 2010/23.02.2011	Pfv.IV.21. 908/2010/6	Y	23	Supreme Court of Hungary (*Kúria*)	E	3	W	max 9
		ORTT v. *Danubius* 2010/14.07.2010	14.Gf.40. 119/2010/ 15	Y	23	Metro. Court of Appeals (*Fővárosi Ítélőtábla*)	E	2	W	max 6
		Danubius v. *ORTT* 02.11.2009/ 05.01.2010	7.G.41.820/ 2009/26	Y	22	Metro. Court of Budapest (*Fővárosi Törvényszék*)	E	1	W	2
ADC v. Hungary (2003) ICSID ARB/03/16 (Aw)	CY-HU 25.05.1990	N/A N/A/29.09.2005	Lacks identifiers	N	N/A	Metro. Court of Budapest (*Fővárosi Törvényszék*)	E	1	N/A	N/A
AES v. Hungary (I) (2001) ICSID ARB/01/04 (Aw) Not public	ECT 16.04.1998 UK-HU 28.08.1987	N/A	N/A	N/A	N/A	N/A	N/A	N/A	N/A	N/A
AES v. Hungary (II) (2007) ICSID ARB/07/22 (Aw)	ECT 16.04.1998	N/A	N/A	N/A	N/A	Investor did not seek domestic remedies	N/A	N/A	N/A	N/A
EDF v. Hungary (2014) UNCITRAL (Aw) Not public	ECT 16.04.1998	N/A	N/A	N/A	N/A	N/A	N/A	N/A	N/A	N/A
		N/A	N/A	N/A	N/A	N/A	N/A	N/A	N/A	N/A

Edenred **v. Hungary (2013)** ICSID ARB/13/21 (Aw) Not pub	FR-HU 30.09.1987									
Electrabel **v. Hungary** *(2007)* ICSID ARB/07/ 19 (Aw)	ECT 16.04.1998	N/A	N/A	N/A	N/A	Prior case brought before EU General Court	N/A	N/A	N/A	N/A
Emmis v. Hungary *(2011)* ICSID ARB/12/2 (Aw)	HU-NL 01.06.1988 HU-CH BIT 16.05.1989	*ORTT* v. *Sláger* 2010/23.02.2011	Pfv.IV.21.976/ 2010/6	Y	22/21	Supreme Court of Hungary	E	3	L	max 9
		ORTT v. *Sláger* 2010/14.07.2010	14.Gf.40.109/ 2010/12	Y	22/21	Metropolitan Court of Appeals	E	2	W	max 6
		Sláger v. *ORTT* 02.11.2009/ 19.01.2010	7.G.41.821/ 2009	Y	21/20	Metropolitan Court of Budapest	E	1	W	2
		ORTT v. *Danubius** 2010/23.02.2011	Pfv.IV.21.908/ 2010/6	Y	22/21	Supreme Court of Hungary	E	3	W	max 9
		ORTT v. *Danubius** 2010/14.07.2010	14.Gf.40.119/ 2010/15	Y	22/21	Metro. Court of Appeals	E	2	W	max 6
		Danubius v. *ORTT** 02.11.2009/ 05.01.2010	7.G.41.820/ 2009/26	Y	21/20	Metro. Court of Budapest	E	1	W	2
Telenor **v. Hungary (2004)** ICSID ARB/04/15 (Aw)	NO-HU 04.12.1992	N/A	N/A	N/A	N/A	HU courts mentioned. No reference to specific case	N/A	N/A	N/A	N/A
Vigotop **v. Hungary (2011)** ICSID ARB/11/22 (Aw)	CY-HU 25.05.1990	*Blum* v. *MNV* 16.07.2012/ 13.11.2012	Pfv.VI.21.317/ 2012/6	Y	22	Supreme Court of Hungary	C	3	L	4

Table 7A.3 (*cont.*)

INTERNATIONAL LEVEL			DOMESTIC LEVEL								
Case name/ identifier (1)		IIA	Case name (Date filing/ decision)	Case identifier (2)	Access (3)	Year after (4)	Court	Type (5)	Level (6)	Outcome investor (7)	Length months (8)
			Blum v. *MNV* 20.01.2012/ 13.06.2012	17.Pf.20.237/ 2012/10	Y	22	Metro. Court of Appeals	C	2	L	5
			MNV v. *Blum* 18.11.2009/ 16.12.2011	25.P.22597/ 2009/269	Y	19	Fejér County Court (*Fejér Megyei Bíróság*)	C	1	L	25

* overlap of domestic cases with domestic cases in Accession Mezzanine

Table 7A.4 *Romania*

INTERNATIONAL LEVEL		DOMESTIC LEVEL								
Case Name/ identifier (1)	IIA	Case name	Case identifier (2) (Date filing/decision)	Access (3)	Year after (4)	Court	Type (5)	Level (6)	Outcome investor (7)	Length months (8)
Awdi v. Romania (2010) ICSID ARB/10/13 (Aw)	RO-US 15.01.1994	*DIICOT v. Awdi Hassan & Awdi Mehdi ("CFR mesagerie")*	File 49772/3/2012 Decision No. 1489 10.03.2014/27.11.2014	Y	20	Bucharest Court of Appeals (*Curtea de Apel București*)	CR	2	PW	8.5
		DIICOT v. Awdi Hassan & Awdi Mehdi	File 49772/3/2012 21.12.2012/31.01.2014	Y	18	Bucharest Tribunal (*Tribunalul București*)	CR	1	L	13
		M.I.M.L. & S.S. v. Consiliul General al Mun. București	Decision No. 9227 2003/15.11.2005	Y	9	Romanian Supreme Court (*Înalta Curte de Casație și Justiție*) Numerous prior cases since 1997	C	3	L	max 23.5
		SC Rodipet SA v. Mun. Bistrița	Decision No. 823 21.01.2008/ 07.07.2008	Y	14	Const. Court of Romania (*Curtea Constituțională a României*)	JCR	3	N/A	5.5
Dede v. Romania (2010) ICSID ARB/10/22 (Aw)	RO-TR 08.07.2010	N/A	N/A	N/A	N/A	Did not resort to domestic courts	N/A	N/A	N/A	N/A
EDF v. Romania (2005) ICSID ARB/05/13 (Aw)	RO-UK 10.01.1996	*SC EDF ASRO SRL v. AIHC*	File 16421/3/2006 Decision No. 4834 09.05.2006/03.04.2008	P	10	Bucharest Tribunal, Civil Section VI	CM	1	L	23
				P	11		CR	2	L	1.5

INTERNATIONAL LEVEL		DOMESTIC LEVEL								
Case Name/ identifier (1)	IIA	Case name	Case identifier (2) (Date filing/decision)	Access (3)	Year after (4)	Court	Type (5)	Level (6)	Outcome investor (7)	Length months (8)
Micula **v. Romania (1) (2005)** ICSID ARB/05/20 (Aw)	RO-SE 01.04.2003	*Not brought by Micula*	Decision No. 130 of 01.04.2003			Constitutional Court of Romania				
Noble Ventures **v. RO** *(2001)* ICSID ARB/01/11 (Aw)	RO-US 15.01.1994	N/A	Lacks identifiers	N/A	N/A	National court cases only mentioned	N/A	N/A	N/A	N/A
Rompetrol v. Romania *(2006)* ICSID ARB/06/3 (Aw)	RO-NL 01.02.1995	*SRI v. D.C. Patriciu/ Rompetrol*	File 12770/3/2006 Decision No. 1475 26.05.2009/18.02.2011	Y	14	Romanian Supreme Court	C	3	L	20.5
		SRI vs D.C. Patriciu/ Rompetrol	File 12770/3/2006 Decision No. 1 17.08.2007/09.02.2009	Y	12	Bucharest Court of Appeals, Civil Section III	C	2	W	17.5
		D.C. Patriciu/ Rompetrol v. SRI	File 12770/3/2006 Decision No. 709 07.04.2006/11.05.2007	Y	11	Bucharest Tribunal, Civil Section VI	C	1	PW	13
		Rompetrol Group NV v PICCJ	File 12139/3/2006 Decision No. 860 04.04.2006/29.06.2006	Y	11	Bucharest Tribunal, Criminal Section I	CR	1	W	2
		State Prosecutor v D.C. Patriciu	File 10352/3/2006 Decision 03.04.2006/10.04.2006	Y	11	Bucharest Court of Appeals, Criminal Section I	CR	2	W	0.25

Roussalis v. *Romania* (*2006*) ICSID ARB/06/1 (Aw)	RO-GR 11.06.1998	*AVAS v SC C. M.E.I.E. SRL*	File 7341/3/2003 Decision No. 2090 18.02.2008/30.06.2009	Y	5	Romanian Supreme Court	CM	3	L	17.5
		AVAS v SC C.M.E.I.E. SRL	File 7341/3/2003 Decision No. 430 28.07.2006/08.10.2007	Y	8	Bucharest Court of Appeals, Commercial Section VI	CM	2	W	15
		AVAS v SC C.M.E.I.E. SRL	File 7341/3/2003 Decision No. 3145 2003/05.05.2006	Y	5	Bucharest Tribunal, Section VI Civil	CM	1	W	max 41
		APAPS (AVAS) v SC C.M.E.I.E. SRL	File 2230/1/2003 Decision No. 3397 11.03.2003/09.07.2003	Y	5	Romanian Supreme Court	C	3	L	4
		APAPS (AVAS) v SC C.M.E.I.E. SRL	Decision No. 351 11.2001/ 08.03.2002	N	N/A	Bucharest Court of Appeals, Civil Section	C	2	W	max 4.5
		APAPS (AVAS) v SC C.M.E.I.E. SRL	Decision No. 7886 23.04.2001/19.10.2001	N	N/A	Bucharest Tribunal	C	1	W	6
S&T Oil v. *Romania* (*2007*) ICSID ARB/07/13 (D)	RO-US 15.01.1994	N/A	N/A	N/A	N/A	N/A	N/A	N/A	N/A	N/A

8

Ensuring Correctness or Promoting Consistency? Tracking Policy Priorities in Investment Arbitration through Large-Scale Citation Analysis

WOLFGANG ALSCHNER[*]

8.1 Introduction

Current efforts to multilaterally reform international investor–state dispute settlement (ISDS) under the auspices of UNCITRAL have identified a perceived lack of consistency and of correctness of arbitral awards as two significant concerns contributing to the field's legitimacy crisis.[1]

Consistency relates to the coherence of interpretations and outcomes across ISDS decisions.[2] It is conceptually rooted in the rule-of-law idea that legal systems should treat like cases alike.[3] In the ISDS context, states are concerned that some tribunals treat like cases differently, resulting in unjustifiably inconsistent decisions, or unlike cases alike, resulting in

---

[*] Associate Professor, Common Law Section, University of Ottawa. I am grateful to Claudia Lach for her excellent research assistance and to the editors for their helpful peer review. This article also benefited from the SNSF project 'Convergence versus Divergence? Text-as-data and Network Analysis of International Economic Law Treaties and Tribunals' (Grant Number: 162379), which provided funding for the collection of citation data used in this article.

[1] UNCITRAL, Report of Working Group III (Investor-State Dispute Settlement Reform) on the work of its thirty-fifth session, 35th Session, 23–27 April 2018, New York, A/CN.9/935, paras. 20–38. See also Anthea Roberts and Zeineb Bouraoui, 'UNCITRAL and ISDS Reforms: Concerns about Consistency, Predictability and Correctness' *EJILTalk!* 5 June 2018, <ejiltalk.org/uncitral-and-isds-reforms-concerns-about-consistency-predictability-and-correctness/>.

[2] UNCITRAL, Report April 2018 (n. 1), paras. 20–1.

[3] See, e.g., Susan D. Franck, 'The Legitimacy Crisis in Investment Treaty Arbitration: Privatizing Public International Law through Inconsistent Decisions' (2004) 73 *Fordham Law Review* 1521, 1585; Harlan Grant Cohen, 'Lawyers and Precedent' (2013) 46 *Vanderbilt Journal of Transnational Law* 1025, 1035.

unjustifiably consistent outcomes undermining the system's legitimacy.[4] As a procedural attribute of decision-making, enhanced consistency would help to make awards seem more just, principled and legitimate, including to the losing party.[5] It would also improve predictability, legal certainty and efficiency for future litigants and treaty drafters.[6] Hence, promoting consistency has become one of the goals of ISDS reform.

Correctness, in turn, relates to the substantive quality of arbitrators' reasoning and the accuracy of outcomes.[7] It denotes that adjudicators get it 'right'. In the ISDS context, states are concerned that tribunals do not always correctly identify, interpret and apply the applicable law in ISDS and thus arrive at incorrect conclusions.[8] Similar to consistency, correctness has become a goal of ISDS reform because it is seen as making decision-making more just, principled and legitimate. However, it draws these attributes not from the procedure of following past practice, but from the accuracy of the individual, substantive judgment. Hence, while consistency is a systemic notion, correctness is a dispute-specific one.[9]

In the ISDS reform debate, ensuring dispute-specific correctness and promoting systemic consistency can be seen as two potentially conflicting policy goals. On the one hand, states have stressed that, since ISDS is based on more than 3,000 international investment agreements (IIAs), different treaties can warrant different interpretive outcomes; some inconsistency across decisions is hence justifiable and even necessary.[10] On the other hand, states agree that like cases should be treated alike in ISDS and that unjustifiably inconsistent arbitral decisions should be avoided.[11] To resolve that tension, states have imposed a clear hierarchy between both objectives in

---

[4] UNCITRAL, Report April 2018 (n. 1), paras. 21, 25. See also Report of Working Group Three, Academic Forum on ISDS, *Inconsistency of ISDS Decisions*, 30 January 2019, 4, <cids.ch/images/Documents/Academic-Forum/3_Inconsistency_-_WG3.pdf>.

[5] Irene M. Ten Cate, 'The Costs of Consistency: Precedent in Investment Treaty Arbitration' (2013) 51 *Columbia Journal of Transnational Law* 418, 448–55.

[6] UNCITRAL, Report April 2018 (n. 1), para. 24.

[7] Ibid., paras. 23–4; UNCITRAL, Note by the Secretariat, *Possible reform of investor-State dispute settlement (ISDS)*, 36th Session, 29 October–2 November 2018, A/CN.9/WG.III/WP.149, paras. 9–10, 24, 27.

[8] This definition of correctness is inspired by Anne De Luca, Mark Feldman, Martins Paparinskis and Catherine Titi, 'Responding to Incorrect Decision-Making in Investor-State Dispute Settlement: Policy Options', (2020) 21(2-3) *Journal of World Investment & Trade*, 374-409, published initially as the Report of Working Group Four, Academic Forum on ISDS, *Incorrectness of ISDS Decisions*, 5 April 2019.

[9] For background on the distinction, see Ten Cate (n. 5), 457.

[10] UNCITRAL, Report April 2018 (n. 1), paras. 21, 25.

[11] Ibid., paras. 24–5.

their UNCITRAL deliberations. They stressed that 'consistency should not be to the detriment of the correctness of decisions'.[12] In other words, on balance, states are more concerned about consistently incorrect arbitral decisions than inconsistent but correct ones.

In this contribution, I switch the focus from states to tribunals to assess to what extent this hierarchy of policy goals emerging from the state-led UNCITRAL process mirrors the implicit hierarchy of policy goals present in investor–state arbitration decisions. Put differently, do arbitral tribunals also care more about ensuring case-specific correctness? Or do they strive for promoting systemic consistency? Answering this question is important, because it enables us to compare the policy preferences of states and tribunals and, on that basis, allows us to better understand the potential causes of the current legitimacy crisis and to inform efforts to reform investment law.

I answer the question whether tribunals care more about ensuring correctness or promoting consistency by empirically investigating the similarity of treaties connected through precedent they cite. My argument is simple. Investment tribunals enjoy large discretion in the precedents they reference. This *observable* selection of what a tribunal considers to be 'relevant' precedent allows us to draw inferences about otherwise *unobservable* underlying policy goals that guide this choice. My argument is that a tribunal primarily concerned with *correctness* – it wants to get its interpretation 'right' in the specific case rather than contribute to any wider systemic jurisprudential debate – will build its interpretation closely around the specific language of the applicable IIA and will primarily cite cases relying on awards rendered under the *same treaty or highly similar IIAs*.

Vice versa, a tribunal keenly concerned with promoting *consistency* – it wants to interpret the applicable treaty so as to facilitate the emergence of a common interpretation in ISDS in order to enhance the predictability, legal certainty, and efficiency of the system more generally – will likely cite cases more liberally including those rendered under *more dissimilar IIAs*. We can thus draw inferences about the relative importance tribunals accord to correctness and consistency considerations in arbitral decision-making by assessing the similarity of treaties they cite through precedent.

I find that, contrary to states, arbitral tribunals tend to prioritize consistency over correctness considerations. Three out of four citations,

---

[12] Ibid., para. 26.

based on a dataset of more than 4,500 references, connect highly dissimilar IIAs. Hence, for most tribunals, treaty similarity is not a pertinent factor in the selection of relevant precedent. There are exceptions to this general trend. NAFTA tribunals, for instance, generally wear a 'NAFTA hat' when selecting precedent: they tend to exclude non-NAFTA decisions cited by the litigants and predominantly refer to prior NAFTA awards. In contrast, tribunals constituted under the Energy Charter Treaty (ECT) tend to wear an 'ISDS hat': they extensively rely on awards rendered under other IIAs and only cite ECT awards in 16 per cent of citations. Overall, ISDS tribunals tend to be consistency-driven in their choice of precedent, selecting prior awards liberally, including under highly dissimilar treaties, with a view to promoting systemic jurisprudential coherence, rather than being correctness-driven, limiting relevant precedent to awards rendered under the same or highly similar agreements with a view to ensuring treaty-specific interpretive accuracy.

As a result, there is an apparent mismatch between the hierarchy of policy preferences voiced by states in ISDS reform (correctness > consistency) and those implicitly expressed by the majority of tribunals through their choice of precedent (correctness < consistency). According to principal–agent theory, differing institutional incentives help explain this mismatch. States prefer treaty-specific correctness, because it limits the interpretive autonomy of tribunals and focuses attention on the terms of delegation in the applicable IIA. Tribunals, in turn, prefer systemic consistency, because it provides them with autonomy beyond the terms of delegation to develop the law for the benefit of the larger ISDS community. States can resolve that mismatch by hardcoding their policy preferences into institutional design. As part of the ISDS reform, states should thus make the ordering between correctness and consistency considerations explicit when delegating adjudicatory authority to future ISDS institutions.

This chapter is structured as follows. Section 8.2 develops an analytical framework that departs from the premise that precedent implies choice and that this choice, in turn, can reveal an implicit ordering of tribunals' policy preferences. Since each precedent connects two treaties, observations on what treaties tribunals choose to connect through citations allow us to infer what importance these tribunals attribute to correctness or consistency considerations. Section 8.3 introduces the dataset and methodology. Section 8.4 investigates the network of IIAs connected through precedent, quantifies the degree of similarity of treaties connected through citations, and draws inferences on the relative importance of correctness and consistency considerations. Finally, Section 8.5 links the resulting findings on the mismatch of preferences between states and tribunals to institutional design choices and suggests how ISDS reform can correct that mismatch.

8.2 The Choice of Precedent as an Expression of Tribunals' Policy Preferences

In international investment law, arbitral awards do not have a *stare decisis* effect – they are only binding on the parties to the dispute, but not on subsequent tribunals.[13] Legally speaking, tribunals are thus under no obligation to refer to prior awards. Yet parties and tribunals alike frequently use prior investment law jurisprudence to support their legal analyses.[14] Engaging with earlier investment awards is thus not a formal legal duty, but it is a widespread socio-legal practice.[15] As a socio-legal practice, the use and selection of precedent offers a window into the underlying motivations and preferences of ISDS tribunals.

8.2.1 Studying Preferences of Judicial Institutions through Citation Behavior

A growing scholarship has begun to study the citation behavior of international courts to draw inferences about the norms, values and motivations guiding actors in international litigation. Studies have investigated how references to a court's own decisions can reveal institutional strategies;[16] how citations to other international courts shed light on how

---

[13] See e.g. *Wintershall Aktiengesellschaft* v. *Argentine Republic, ICSID Case No. ARB/04/14*, Award, 8 December 2008, para. 194: '*stare decisis* has no application to decisions of ICSID tribunals ... The award of such tribunal is binding only on the parties to the dispute (Article 53 of the Convention) – not even binding on the State of which the investor is a national. Decisions and Awards of ad hoc ICSID tribunals have no binding precedential effect on successive tribunals, also appointed ad hoc between different parties.'; *Methanex* v. *United States of America*, Partial Award, 7 August 2002, para. 141: '[Prior awards] are not sources of law; and neither can be regarded as authority legally binding upon this Tribunal.'

[14] For an empirical study showing that tribunals extensively rely on prior awards, see Ole Kristian Fauchald, 'The Legal Reasoning of ICSID Tribunals – An Empirical Analysis' (2008) 19 *European Journal of International Law* 301.

[15] See Dolores Bentolila, *Arbitrators as Lawmakers* (Kluwer Law International, 2017), ch. 4.

[16] Yonatan Lupu and Erik Voeten, 'Precedent in International Courts: A Network Analysis of Case Citations by the European Court of Human Rights' (2012) 42 *British Journal of Political Science* 413; Wolfgang Alschner and Damien Charlotin, 'The Growing

a court or tribunal perceives itself in the larger field of public international law;[17] how decisions cited by an international judge give clues as to his or her policy preferences;[18] or how litigants use precedent to strategically influence jurisprudence.[19] In short, the citation behavior of courts and litigants can reveal underlying preferences, strategies and motivations.

To be sure, international investment tribunals, like judges generally, can have a range of different motivations for their actions only some of which may be related to policy preferences.[20] An investment tribunal may cite prior authorities for their legal merit, or because they have been put forward by the parties or because the same arbitrators sat on both cases. What investment tribunals are likely to not do, however, is to cite cases purely at random or to reference decisions that they consider inappropriate or irrelevant for the case at hand. Hence, while it may be difficult to pin down specific motivations, it is in keeping with the rational choice literature to assume that observable choices on precedent allow inferences about otherwise unobservable underlying preferences, motivations and worldviews of tribunals.

In the realm of international investment law, scholars have begun to use citation analysis to investigate how tribunals perceive their adjudicatory roles based on how they cite precedent. Suha Jubran-Ballan, for example, has done extensive empirical work to investigate whether tribunals cite differently depending on their institutional background.[21] She finds that investment tribunals constituted under the

---

Complexity of the International Court of Justice's Self-Citation Network' (2018) 29 *European Journal of International Law* 83.

[17] Gabrielle Marceau, Arnau Izaguerri and Vladyslav Lanovoy, 'The WTO's Influence on Other Dispute Settlement Mechanisms: A Lighthouse in the Storm of Fragmentation' (2013) 47 *Journal of World Trade* 481; Damien Charlotin, 'The Place of Investment Awards and WTO Decisions in International Law: A Citation Analysis' (2017) 20 *Journal of International Economic Law* 279.

[18] Jens Frankenreiter, 'The Politics of Citations at the ECJ – Policy Preferences of E.U. Member State Governments and the Citation Behavior of Judges at the European Court of Justice' (2017) 14 *Journal of Empirical Legal Studies* 813.

[19] Krzysztof J. Pelc, 'The Politics of Precedent in International Law: A Social Network Application' (2014) 108 *American Political Science Review* 547.

[20] Lee Epstein and Jack Knight, 'Reconsidering Judicial Preferences' (2013) 16 *Annual Review of Political Science* 11.

[21] Suha Jubran-Ballan, 'Investment Treaty Arbitration and Institutional Backgrounds: An Empirical Study' (2016) 34 *Wisconsin International Law Journal* 31; Suha Jubran-Ballan, 'How Institutions Matter: On the Judicial Reasoning of Investment Treaty Arbitration Awards' (2018) 41 *Houston Journal of International Law* 57.

ICSID Convention cite precedents significantly more frequently than other investment tribunals and concludes that ICSID tribunals are more judicialized, that is, they consider themselves more strongly as part of a larger legal system, than non-ICSID tribunals, which tend to view themselves more as independent ad hoc adjudicators tasked to solve a specific dispute.[22]

8.2.2 The Selection of 'Relevant' Precedent as Signal of Underlying Policy Preferences

The present contribution employs a similar research design. I argue that citation patterns can tell us something about the relative importance tribunals attach to consistency and correctness considerations as competing policy goals in ISDS. Investment tribunals constantly have to select 'relevant' precedents from the wider pool of available cases. Investment arbitration lacks *stare decisis* as well as cogent corrective mechanisms that tell a 'right' from a 'wrong' interpretation.[23] Absent formal constraints, tribunals' policy preferences, including the relative importance of consistency and correctness, then arguably guide their selection of relevant precedent.

On one extreme, a tribunal may have a strong preference for systematic consistency. By that I mean that it considers itself as an organ of the larger ISDS legal system with a duty to promote jurisprudential consistency in investment law. We would expect that such a tribunal with a preference for promoting consistency, figuratively wearing a 'general ISDS hat', considers all ISDS awards as *per se* relevant when selecting precedent since all ISDS awards form part of the corpus of the investment law 'system'. Conversely, they will pay less attention to treaty design differences when selecting precedent, because they assume that, notwithstanding differences in wording, all IIAs share a set of common

---

[22] Jubran-Ballan, 'How Institutions Matter' (ibid.), 79–84.

[23] UNCITRAL, Note by the Secretariat, Possible reform of investor-State dispute settlement (ISDS): Consistency and related matters, 36th session, 29 October–2 November 2018, A/CN.9/WG.III/WP.150, paras. 19–21. See also Malcom Langford, Cossette Creamer and Daniel Behn, 'Regime Responsiveness in International Economic Disputes', in Gáspár-Szilágyi, Behn and Langford (eds.), *Adjudicating Trade and Investment Disputes: Convergence or Divergence?* (Cambridge University Press, 2019). On potential dangers associated with the absence of control mechanisms, see Wolfgang Alschner, 'Correctness of Investment Awards: Why Wrong Decisions Don't Die' (2019) 18(3) *The Law and Practice of International Courts and Tribunals* 345.

ENSURING CORRECTNESS OR PROMOTING CONSISTENCY? 237

principles that are progressively fleshed out and developed through the harmonious interpretation of tribunals.

The tribunal in *Planet Mining* v. *Indonesia*, for instance, illustrates this ideal type tribunal well. It expresses a preference for interpretive consistency and considers prior awards to be relevant by default:

> The Tribunal ... is of the opinion that it must pay due consideration to earlier decisions of international tribunals. Specifically, it deems that, subject to compelling contrary grounds, it has a duty to adopt solutions established in a series of consistent cases. It further deems that, subject to the specific provisions of a given treaty and of the circumstances of the actual case, it has a duty to contribute to the harmonious development of investment law, with a view to meeting the legitimate expectations of the community of States and investors towards certainty of the rule of law.[24]

On the other extreme, a tribunal may have a strong preference for dispute-specific correctness. Accordingly, it will figuratively wear a 'treaty-specific hat' and consider its role to be the resolution of the specific dispute under the unique treaty rather than to contribute to a broader system of law. It will also likely use precedent more cautiously only considering awards as 'relevant' that interpreted the same or language highly similar to the treaty at hand. That is because it assumes that differences in wording between IIAs matter; they are the result of explicit choices by states and impose strict interpretive confines on tribunals. Conversely, it will exclude precedent under dissimilar third treaties as 'irrelevant', since such precedent could result in an incorrect interpretation of the applicable law.

This preference for correctness and the restrictive use of prior cases is best expressed in a dissenting opinion by Arbitrator Bernardo Cremades, who declared that '[t]he integrity of th[e] interpretative process must not be compromised by the pronouncements of other arbitral tribunals in their interpretation of different treaties in wholly unrelated factual and legal contexts'.[25] Arbitrator Pedro Nikken has expressed similar

---

[24] *Planet Mining Pty Ltd* v. *Republic of Indonesia*, ICSID Case No. ARB/12/14 and 12/40, Decision on Jurisdiction, 24 February 2014, para. 85 (footnote omitted). See similarly, *ADC Affiliate Ltd and ADC & ADMC Management Ltd* v. *Republic of Hungary*, ICSID Case ARB/03/16, Award, 2 October 2006, para. 293: 'cautious reliance on certain principles developed in [prior investment arbitration] cases, as persuasive authority, may advance the body of law, which in turn may serve predictability in the interest of both investors and host States'.

[25] *Fraport AG Frankfurt Airport Services Worldwide* v. *Republic of the Philippines*, ICSID Case No. ARB/03/25, Dissenting Opinion of Mr Bernardo M. Cremades, 16 August 2007, para. 7.5.

concerns: 'great caution is needed when identifying cases as alike, especially when dealing with factual issues ... and when, moreover, the BITs often contain significant differences despite their similarity'.[26] Some tribunals have also stressed the case-by-case nature of their mandate. The *SGS* v. *Philippines* tribunal, for example, stated that 'although different tribunals constituted under the ICSID system should in general seek to act consistently with each other, in the end it must be for each tribunal to exercise its competence in accordance with the applicable law, which will by definition be different for each BIT and each Respondent State'.[27]

Tribunals have therefore explicitly stated different worldviews as to their roles as interpreters and adjudicators and have indicated different preferences for consistency and correctness considerations, which they invoked to filter relevant precedent from existing case law. While for the consistency-driven *Planet Mining* tribunal a series of consistent cases is relevant *per se* and should be excluded only for cogent reasons, for the correctness-oriented Cremades, prior cases should be excluded *per se* unless they bear factual and legal similarity to the specific interpretation at hand.

On the basis of these examples we can formulate a more general argument, which can be tested empirically at scale: by looking at observable patterns of cited precedents we can detect tribunals' otherwise unobservable policy preferences for correctness versus consistency considerations in ISDS. Specifically, tribunals that predominantly cite awards rendered under the same or highly similar treaties tend to place more importance on correctness. In contrast, tribunals that cite awards rendered under very different treaties and that place little importance on treaty design differences tend to prioritize consistency considerations. Put differently, we can investigate whether tribunals err on the side of correctness or consistency by quantifying how similar or how different the treaties are they cite through precedent.

8.3 Methodology and Dataset

Based on the assumption that the explicit choice of precedent can reveal tribunals' implicit policy preferences, the remainder of the chapter will

---

[26] *AWG Group Ltd* v. *Argentine Republic*, UNCITRAL, Separate Opinion of Arbitrator Pedro Nikken, 30 July 2010, para. 24.

[27] *SGS Société Générale de Surveillance S.A.* v. *Republic of the Philippines,* ICSID Case No. ARB/02/6, Decision on Jurisdiction, 29 January 2004, para. 97.

investigate the citation behavior of investment tribunals. Specifically, it will quantify the similarity of IIAs linked through precedent to empirically assess to what extent treaty design differences matter for the selection of precedent and to draw inferences about the relative weight tribunals accord to consistency and correctness considerations in investor–state arbitration. This section begins the empirical assessment with a short disclaimer on the promises and limitations of empirical research before introducing the dataset and methodology.

8.3.1 Disclaimer on the Promises and Limitations of Empirical Research

Before proceeding to the analysis, it is important to acknowledge a number of simplifications and assumptions. Empirical research is most robust when targeted at 'small' questions. To be effective, empirics need a clearly defined research question limited in scope. The relative importance of correctness and consistency in ISDS, however, is a 'big' policy question that raises fundamental debates about the nature of ISDS as a mode for the ad hoc settlement of distinct disputes or as a system of law structuring the relations between foreign investors and states. The present research design thus simplifies a larger multi-dimensional policy debate – preferences for consistency or correctness in ISDS – to an empirically testable research question – how similar or different are the IIAs linked through citations? It assumes that assessing the latter is a credible way for revealing the former.

It furthermore involves methodological choices and dataset limitations. Empirical research often imposes definitions that place the world into conceptual boxes to focus the inquiry; it selects proxies that link abstract concepts to observable facts; and it relies on available datasets and methods that have shortcomings of their own. As a result, it does not reveal truths, but rather provides objectively verifiable evidence that needs to be evaluated and interpreted within the confines of the research design choices made. As explained below, the sample of citations is illustrative rather than representative or comprehensive and our findings need to be assessed with the limitations of the research design and data in mind.

In spite of these simplifications, assumptions and limitations, empirics can make a meaningful contribution to legal policy debates. By investigating specific claims about the purported state of the world, such as the relative weight accorded to consistency and correctness considerations, it

240 WOLFGANG ALSCHNER

can demonstrate contextual anecdotes as outliers or as representative examples, and reveal patterns otherwise neglected or unknown. It thereby enables evidence-based decision-making. Such contribution, even if seemingly technical, is thus ultimately beneficial for larger policy debates as it grounds them in a more solid factual basis.

8.3.2   The Dataset

According to UNCTAD, 942 treaty-based ISDS cases have been filed up to the end of 2018. [28] Of these, 401 cases have resulted in a final award. Yet, not all of these decisions are publicly available. To obtain publicly available awards, we scraped all treaty-based investment arbitration decisions, awards and opinions available on www.italaw.com until 31 January 2019. As decisions, we include awards on jurisdiction, merits or quantum, as well as concurring and dissenting opinions, but we exclude orders.

Subsequently, we used regular expressions to automatically extract citations from the footnotes of all decisions and identified the case thereby cited.[29] This procedure yields a dataset of 8,756 citations between treaty-based investment arbitration decisions. It comprises a total of 290 citing cases and 371 cited cases. Every citation in our database is a unique link between two ISDS decisions, meaning that if award A cites case B three times, this is counted only as one citation in the dataset between award A and case B.[30] Figure 8.1 provides an overview of the distribution of citations over time by plotting the number of outward citations per year.

In spite of its large scope, the dataset remains a convenience sample rather than the full population of ISDS cross-citations for several reasons. First, we only extracted citations from footnotes. A minority of awards, however, provides citations in the decision's full text, which we then did not capture. Second, some arbitral decisions in our dataset had to be made machine-readable through optical character recognition software.

---

[28] UNCTAD, Investment Policy Hub Statistics, <investmentpolicy.unctad.org>.

[29] For background on the dataset and data generation, see Wolfgang Alschner and Aleksander Umov, 'Towards an Integrated Database of International Economic Law (IDIEL) Disputes for Text-as-Data Analysis' (2016) CTEI Working Papers <graduateinstitute.ch/files/live/sites/iheid/files/sites/ctei/shared/CTEI/working_ papers/ CTEI-2016-08.pdf>.

[30] While we distinguish between individual awards, i.e. on jurisdiction or merits, on the side of citing cases, we only identify the target dispute on the side of cited cases, not the specific target decision, i.e. on jurisdiction or merits.

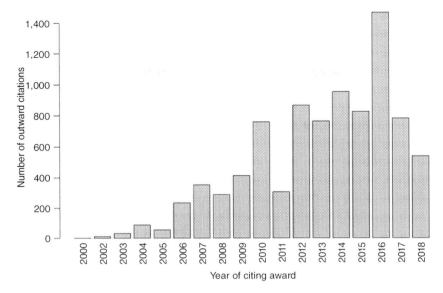

Figure 8.1 The growth of outward citations

Since this process creates errors (e.g. 'i' becomes 'l'), some footnotes may not have been identified as containing a reference. Finally, the process of linking the reference in a footnote to the specific ISDS case cited was automated through a similarity-based matching algorithm. We spot checked results, but cannot fully exclude the possibility of occasional errors where similar case names existed. Although the dataset is thus imperfect, it does provide an illustrative picture of the citing behavior of ISDS tribunals.

Finally, our dataset only provides us with the information that a citation occurs. It does not tell us whether the citation comes from the litigants or the tribunal, nor do we know whether the citing award endorses, rejects, distinguishes or neutrally describes the cited decision. To the extent possible, we will therefore supplement our quantitative analysis with targeted qualitative case analysis in order to provide better context and to make our findings more robust.

8.3.3 Building a Treaty-Citation Network

We are not primarily interested in the ISDS cases that cite or are cited, but rather in the investment treaties connected through these citations.

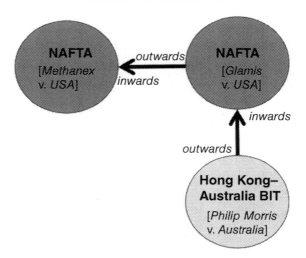

Figure 8.2 Exemplary treaty network connected through citations

As an illustration, consider the hypothetical constellation in Figure 8.2. Imagine the tribunal in *Philip Morris* v. *Australia*, decided on the basis of the Hong Kong–Australia BIT, cites *Glamis* v. *USA*, decided under NAFTA. Consequently, the citation between both disputes connects the Hong Kong–Australia BIT and NAFTA – for the former, it counts as outward, and, for the latter, it counts as inward citation. The tribunal in *Glamis* v. *USA*, in turn, may cite the decision *Methanex* v. *USA*, decided under NAFTA. This is a self-citation for NAFTA, that is, both an outward citation and inward citation for NAFTA.

For each of the 8,756 citations we thus determine the treaty under which the citing award was rendered as well as the treaty under which the cited case was decided.[31] In total, the dataset links 167 citing IIAs and 190 cited IIAs, which together form the treaty-citation network, which constitutes the basis of our analysis.

8.3.4 Quantifying Treaty Similarity

Finally, we quantify the similarity of every treaty pair linked through a citation. For that, we use the approach and dataset developed by Alschner

---

[31] All citations to non-treaty investment awards had been excluded ex ante from the dataset.

and Skougarevskiy.[32] Only English language IIAs are considered, since raw textual similarity measures cannot be meaningfully calculated across languages. Each investment treaty is represented through its constituent word components and the overlap of these components between a treaty pair is calculated. The resulting measure, formally known as Jaccard distance, reflects the treaty pair's textual similarity. If two treaties are identical (i.e. a self-citation), then the Jaccard distance will be 0. If two treaties are completely different, their Jaccard distance will be 1. Since not all cited or citing treaties are in English or are in the treaty dataset used, we were only able to calculate the treaty similarity for 4,531 citations or 52 per cent of the dataset. Systematically excluded thereby are decisions rendered under non-English treaties. While our results then only speak to the English language treaty universe, this should make our findings more conservative as citations across languages arguably make cases more dissimilar.

Admittedly, the textual similarity of two treaties is an imprecise measure to evaluate a citation. After all, two treaties may be very dissimilar generally, but share an almost identically worded provision that is the subject of the citation. At the same time, empirical research on investment treaties suggests that treaties vary in systematic ways: developed states have internally consistent treaty networks and act as rule-makers, while developing countries have internally inconsistent treaty networks and act as rule-takers.[33] Dissimilarity is thus typically not limited to specific clauses, but indicates varying underlying model agreements.[34] Moreover, even if the wording of two clauses is similar, the differences in the wider treaty context captured by the similarity measure will affect the interpretation of the clause as interpretive context under the Article 31 of the Vienna Convention on the Law of Treaties and may thus warrant a different interpretation. In conclusion, even though it is possible that a treaty similarity measure overstates the differences between specific treaty passages at issue in a citation, it should generally be correlated with how similar or different the underlying applicable law is.

---

[32] Wolfgang Alschner and Dmitriy Skougarevskiy, 'Mapping the Universe of International Investment Agreements' (2016) 19 *Journal of International Economic Law* 561.

[33] Ibid.

[34] Tarald Laudal Berge and Øyvind Stiansen, 'Negotiating BITs with Models. The Power of Expertise' (2016) PluriCourts Research Paper No. 16-13 <papers.ssrn.com/sol3/papers .cfm?abstract_id=2851454>.

8.4 Analysis: Quantifying the Preference for Correctness and Consistency

We are now ready to quantify the similarity of treaties connected by citations to draw inferences about the relative preference for correctness and consistency. To recall, the argument is that a propensity to cite the same or similar treaties indicates a preference for case-specific correctness; a propensity to cite dissimilar treaties indicates a preference for systemic consistency.

The following analysis is divided into four parts. Section 8.4.1 provides an overview of the ISDS treaty-citation network to set the relevant background. Section 8.4.2 evaluates the degree to which tribunals rely on precedent rendered under the *same* treaty. Section 8.4.3 tracks how similar or different IIAs are when tribunals rely on precedent under *other* treaties. Section 8.4.4 relates these findings to the preferences over correctness and consistency.

8.4.1 The ISDS Treaty-Citation Network

While tribunals enjoy large discretion in their selection of precedent, this selection necessarily depends on the pool of available awards. Therefore, we begin our analysis by describing the current state of the ISDS treaty-citation networks to provide relevant background. As we show, (1) litigation is concentrated in few IIAs and (2) therefore precedent is distributed unevenly across existing IIAs.

8.4.1.1 Few IIAs Have Many Disputes, Many IIAs Have Few Disputes

The vast majority of investment treaties have not given rise to an investment dispute. Litigation on ISDS is instead concentrated around a few central treaties. According to UNCTAD, by the end of 2018, only 401 investment treaties out of the more than 3,000 IIAs in existence have attracted litigation.[35] Slightly more than half of them, or 211 IIAs, have produced a final investment award.[36] Table 8.1 maps their distribution. Only two IIAs, NAFTA and the Energy Charter with 35 and 34 disputes

---

[35] The data was retrieved from the UNCTAD Investment Policy Hub in late May 2019 (n. 28).

[36] By final decision, we mean that UNCTAD marks it as 'Decided'.

ENSURING CORRECTNESS OR PROMOTING CONSISTENCY? 245

Table 8.1 *Few IIAs have produced many final awards*

# of treaties (and %)	# of disputes with final decision
2 (1)	> 10
6 (3)	10 ≥ 6
20 (9)	5 ≥ 3
34 (16)	2
149 (71)	1

respectively, have generated more than 10 disputes with a final decision. The vast majority of treaties that produced a final decision (71%) have only been litigated once.

8.4.1.2 Precedent Is Skewed towards Few IIAs

Since few treaties have attracted most disputes, only a minority of tribunals has the luxury of applying an IIA that has been interpreted before. In fact, only NAFTA and the Energy Charter with more than 30 decided disputes each have produced a corpus of awards that permits frequent self-citations. Most tribunals will have to look for precedent under other IIAs to inform their reasoning either because no precedent has been rendered under the same treaty or because the same interpretive issue has not yet arisen under the limited case law rendered under the same treaty. So to which IIAs do tribunals look when choosing precedent?

While tribunals look to a variety of IIAs when citing precedent, most precedent is concentrated in a few IIAs (see Table 8.2). The top-10 cited IIAs have attracted 50% of all inward citations. NAFTA awards have been cited most, with 15% of all inward citations. Based on the most citations for a single dispute, the Chile–Malaysia BIT is the most influential IIA whose 2004 award in *MTD* v. *Chile*[37] was cited by 130 other cases.

Turning to outward citations, the Energy Charter Treaty (ECT) has produced most outward citations. Yet, other agreements with fewer disputes have produced many citations as well. For instance, through the *Philip Morris* v. *Uruguay* case alone (comprising decisions on jurisdiction, merit and a dissenting opinion), the Switzerland–Uruguay BIT makes the top-10 list of most citing IIAs with 292 outward citations.

---

[37] *MTD Equity Sdn. Bhd. and MTD Chile S.A.* v. *Republic of Chile*, ICSID Case No. ARB/01/7, Award, 25 May 2004.

Table 8.2 *Top citing and top cited IIAs*

Top citing treaties	# outward citations	Top cited treaties	# inward citations
Energy Charter Treaty	729	NAFTA	1,274
Ecuador–USA BIT	538	Argentina–USA BIT	882
NAFTA	458	Energy Charter Treaty	440
Argentina–USA BIT	409	Argentina–France BIT	419
CAFTA	293	Ecuador–USA BIT	383
Switzerland–Uruguay BIT	292	Argentina–Germany BIT	239
Argentina–Spain BIT	228	Argentina–Spain BIT	222
Argentina–United Kingdom BIT	210	Egypt–United Kingdom BIT	215
Argentina–France BIT	203	Czech Rep.–Netherlands BIT	185
Argentina–Germany BIT	185	Netherlands–Venezuela BIT	176

These raw counts, however, only reveal part of the structure of the citation network. While it is impractical to visualize the entire citation network, Figure 8.3 provides a snapshot by displaying the top-10 citing IIAs and their connections. The graph reveals the unique position that NAFTA occupies. All treaties cite NAFTA cases extensively; even NAFTA cases cite primarily other NAFTA cases.

This centrality of NAFTA is furthermore affirmed through network measures. Table 8.3 shows the top authority scores calculated for the entire network. These scores quantitatively express the importance of a node in a network not only based on the number of connections it has, but also based on whether these connections come from nodes that, in their turn, have many connections. By that measure NAFTA is by far the most influential IIA in the ISDS citation network.

To conclude, since few IIAs have attracted most disputes, precedent is concentrated in a few IIAs that are often cited, because they have given rise to an abundant case law. To account for this asymmetric structure of the treaty-citation universe, we proceed in two steps. First, we concentrate on those IIAs that have attracted most litigation, that is, NAFTA and the ECT. Only tribunals based on these two IIAs had ample

Table 8.3 *Most influential IIAs (in terms of attracting inward citations) based on their position in the treaty-citation network*

Most influential IIAs	Authority scores
NAFTA	0.98
Argentina–USA BIT	0.15
Energy Charter Treaty	0.09
Ecuador–USA BIT	0.08
Argentina–France BIT	0.05

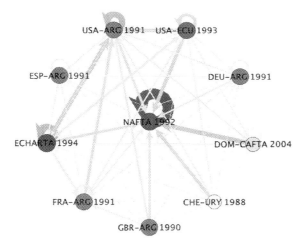

Figure 8.3 Treaty-citation network of top 10 IIAs with most citing awards

opportunity to self-cite. Since self-citations are a proxy for correctness, quantifying the degree of self-citation allows us to draw inferences about the preferences of these tribunals. Second, we turn to all disputes and quantify the similarity of treaties connected through citations.

8.4.2 Self-Citations: NAFTA Tribunals are about Correctness, ECT Tribunals Are about Consistency

Since few treaties have attracted most disputes, only tribunals under such heavily litigated agreements can extensively rely on precedent rendered

WOLFGANG ALSCHNER

Table 8.4 *Share of references to awards rendered under the same treaty*

	Outward citation		Inward citation	
Treaty name	Self-cite (%)	Other (%)	Self-cite (%)	Other (%)
NAFTA	63	37	22	78
Energy Charter Treaty	16	84	26	74

under the same treaty. We therefore concentrate on NAFTA and ECT, which have each produced more than 30 final decisions and thus present ample opportunities for self-citations. Yet, as Table 8.4 reveals, they display very different patterns.[38] When relying on precedent, NAFTA tribunals tend to wear a 'NAFTA hat', that is, they predominantly cite other NAFTA tribunals (63%) rather than tribunals constituted under other IIAs (37%). In contrast, ECT tribunals do not wear an 'ECT hat', that is, they tend to cite almost exclusively tribunals that have been constituted under other IIAs (84%) and only cite other ECT awards in a minority of outward citations (16%). Since ECT tribunals embed their decisions in ISDS jurisprudence more generally, they could be said to wear a 'general ISDS hat' when choosing precedent.

But can we infer different attitudes on correctness and consistency from this data or are the patterns we see a product of other determinants? For instance, time may explain the difference in self-citation patterns given that NAFTA's disputes started to proliferate already in the late 1990s, while disputes were only submitted to the ECT starting in the early 2000s. Differently put, perhaps NAFTA and ECT tribunals had to cite more NAFTA (and less ECT) decisions since these were the only awards in existence? Figure 8.4 tracks self-citation rates of both NAFTA and ECT tribunals over time based on the year of the citing award. Although self-citations of ECT tribunals did pick up as the ECT case law grew, they have fallen again since, whereas NAFTA's self-citation rates have been consistently high. So time is not the driving factor.

Another explanation could be that NAFTA is very different from all other investment agreements, while the ECT is relatively similar to other IIAs. The latter may thus not self-cite as much as NAFTA, but may cite IIAs highly similar to the ECT. Yet, when looking at the average

---

[38] For different numbers, but similar trends, see Niccolò Ridi, 'The Shape and Structure of the "Usable Past": An Empirical Analysis of the Use of Precedent in International Adjudication' (2019) 10 *Journal of International Dispute Settlement* 200.

ENSURING CORRECTNESS OR PROMOTING CONSISTENCY? 249

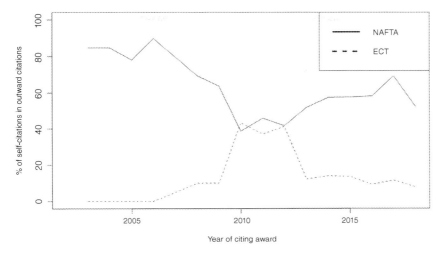

Figure 8.4 Share of self-citations for NAFTA and ECT awards over time

similarity to other treaties cited, both agreements show identical scores. Other IIAs cited by ECT and NAFTA share on average only 30 per cent of their text with the applicable IIA. Hence, the ECT is as dissimilar as NAFTA to the agreements that its tribunals cite when they are not relying on precedent rendered under the same agreement.

Finally, given that our citation data does not distinguish between party citations and the tribunal's citations, could this impact results? After all, NAFTA litigants may cite case law under NAFTA, but NAFTA tribunals could still base their decisions predominantly on non-NAFTA case law. While we cannot account for party versus tribunal submitted citations in our dataset, the above findings are corroborated by existing research as well as targeted case law analysis. Our results on the high self-citation rates in NAFTA litigation mirror the results of an earlier study by Jubran-Ballan.[39] She coded citations by hand, focused exclusively on merits awards, and excluded all citations advanced exclusively by the parties.[40] Hence, these high self-citation rates do seem to reflect a choice by NAFTA tribunals rather than NAFTA parties.

An analysis of specific awards also suggests that different attitudes towards consistency and correctness explain the difference in self-citation rates. NAFTA tribunals tend to accord considerable weight to

---

[39] Jubran-Ballan, 'How Institutions Matter' (n. 21), 88–92.
[40] Ibid.

the specific language of NAFTA in order to arrive at a correct interpretation. As a corollary, they are reluctant to admit precedent under third treaties with divergent wordings even where similar interpretive issues arise. This is perhaps best expressed in *Grand River* v. *USA*:

> The Parties' briefs and arguments cited awards in many other NAFTA and non-NAFTA investment cases. These often helped to illuminate legal issues presented by the present claims. Being rooted in their specific facts, NAFTA arbitral awards are not binding precedents (Article 1136(1)) of NAFTA). But on jurisdictional aspects, NAFTA awards are more relevant and appropriate than decisions in non-NAFTA investment cases.[41]

NAFTA tribunals generally use treaty design differences as a filter to narrow the field of relevant precedents. The *Cargill* v. *Mexico* tribunal, for example, explicitly rejected reliance upon the *Tecmed* award rendered under the Mexico–Spain BIT as precedent, because the BIT differed from NAFTA wording.[42] Similarly, other NAFTA tribunals have declined to consider precedents from third IIAs in relation to NAFTA's fair and equitable treatment provisions based on the fact that those treaties do not root the concept in customary international law.[43] Moreover, NAFTA tribunals seem less concerned about consistency in interpretation. The *Glamis* v. *USA* tribunal, for example, explicitly distinguished NAFTA arbitration from 'institutions with a closed docket of cases where consistency between the various claimants is often of paramount importance' and stated that 'a [NAFTA] tribunal may depart from even major previous trends [in case law]' and it should state reasons for doing so.[44]

In contrast, tribunals interpreting the Energy Charter Treaty have been more liberal in accepting precedent without distinguishing between underlying treaty sources. One of the *Yukos* tribunals, for instance, considered awards cited by the parties *per se* as 'relevant sources to consider in deciding the arbitrations'.[45] The *Energoalians* v. *Moldova*

---

[41] *Grand River Enterprises Six Nations, Ltd, et al.* v. *United States of America*, Award, 12 January 2011, para. 61.

[42] *Cargill, Incorporated* v. *United Mexican States*, ICSID Case No. ARB(AF)/05/2, Award, 18 September 2009, paras. 268, 280–1.

[43] *Glamis Gold Ltd* v. *United States of America* (2009), Final Award, 8 June 2009, para. 611: 'The Tribunal therefore holds that it may look solely to arbitral awards – including BIT awards – that seek to be understood by reference to the customary international law minimum standard of treatment, as opposed to any autonomous standard.'

[44] Ibid. fn. 7.

[45] *Hulley Enterprises Ltd (Cyprus)* v. *Russian Federation*, UNCITRAL, PCA Case No. AA 226, Final Award, 18 July 2014, para. 116.

tribunal was similarly open to accepting precedent 'to the extent it considered the findings stated in those arbitral awards to be convincing and applicable to this case.'[46] Hence, unlike in NAFTA, treaty design differences are not generally used as a filter to distinguish relevant from irrelevant precedent up front. At the same time, at least one ECT tribunal, *Khan Resources* v. *Mongolia*, stressed the heightened importance of ECT precedent over non-ECT awards: 'the Tribunal considers that it has a duty to take account of [ECT-based] decisions, in the hope of contributing to the formation of a consistent interpretation of the ECT.'[47]

This difference in the weight accorded to treaty design suggests that NAFTA and ECT tribunals differ in their attitudes towards correctness and consistency considerations. NAFTA tribunals wear a 'NAFTA hat' and use predominantly NAFTA precedents to interpret NAFTA. ECT tribunals tend to wear a 'general ISDS hat' and consider all precedent to be relevant *a priori* regardless of the treaty they are derived from. They tend to approach the interpretive task from a systemic perspective that privileges promoting consistency over ensuring a narrow treaty-specific textual correctness. NAFTA tribunals, in contrast, approach their interpretation from a treaty-specific perspective, placing emphasis on NAFTA's textual idiosyncrasies so as to ensure correctness rather than promote wider systemic consistency.

8.4.3 Similarity: Most Citations Connect Highly Dissimilar Treaties

Apart from NAFTA and the ECT, most ISDS tribunals are interpreting IIAs that have attracted little or no prior litigation and therefore they cannot rely on precedents rendered under the same agreement. So how much weight do they accord to treaty design differences in their choice of precedent when citing cases under other agreements?

In fact, most citations connect highly dissimilar treaties. Table 8.5 displays the variation of similarity of treaties connected through citations. A total of 642 citations, or 14% of all 4,531 citations in our dataset considered, are between awards rendered under the same IIA. Only 202 citations, or 4%, connect IIAs that share 75% or more of their text, and 303 citations, or 7%, connect IIAs that have at least 50% of their text in

---

[46] *Energoalians* v. *Republic of Moldova*, UNCITRAL, Award, 23 October 2013, para. 131.

[47] *Khan Resources Inc., Khan Resources B.V. and CAUC Holding Company Ltd* v. *Government of Mongolia*, UNCITRAL, Decision on Jurisdiction, 25 July 2012, para. 417.

Table 8.5 *Similarity of IIAs connected by citations*

Jaccard distance	Similarity	Share (%)
0	Identical	14
0 > 0.25	High	4
0.25 ≥ 0.5	Medium	7
0.5 ≥ 0.75	Low	12
0.75 ≥ 1	Very Low	12

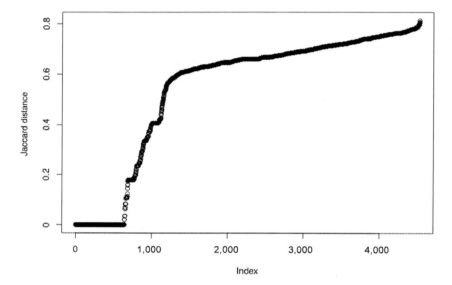

Figure 8.5 Citations ordered by underlying treaty similarity

common. The vast majority of citations, or 75%, links agreements that are very dissimilar, that is, have less than 50% of their text in common.

Figure 8.5 displays the same patterns visually. The x-axis ranks 4,531 citations by their textual distance and the y-axis displays the corresponding textual distance. The steep initial slope and the flat upper tail indicate that a minority of citations connect highly similar IIAs and that most awards connect extremely dissimilar treaties.

In the aggregate, ISDS tribunals thus appear to pay little weight to treaty design differences when choosing precedent. Excluding self-citations, the average treaty connected through a citation only has 36% of its text in common. As illustrated in Figure 8.6, this low rate of textual similarity of IIAs connected through citations has been relatively stable over time.

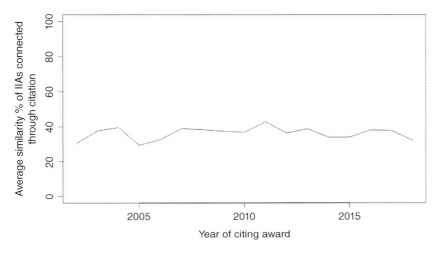

Figure 8.6 Mean similarity of IIAs connected through citations (excluding self-cites)

There is variation, however, as some tribunals accord more weight to treaty design similarities when assessing the relevance of prior cases than others. As highlighted in Table 8.5, 4% of citations connect highly similar treaties that have 75% or more of their text in common. The tribunal in *Kilic v. Turkmenistan*, for example, is particular sensitive to treaty design differences and very deliberate in its choice of precedent. Its 17 unique citations to other disputes link treaties that are 53% similar on average. The references to the disputes *Rumeli Telekom v. Kazakhstan* and *Sistem v. Kyrgyzstan* are particularly targeted, referencing the Turkey–Kazakhstan BIT and Turkey–Kyrgyzstan BIT, which share 98% and 97% of their text respectively with the Turkey–Turkmenistan BIT at issue. The *Kilic v. Turkmenistan* tribunal justified this choice explicitly:

> The Tribunal considers that whatever the merits (or otherwise) of the various authorities referred to by Claimant, they were concerned with different – and differently worded – provisions of other BITs. They cannot therefore be dispositive.[48]

Yet, as the statistics from Table 8.5 show, such citations to highly similar agreements are the clear minority. Most citations connect highly

---

[48] *Kilic Insaat Ithalat Ihracat Sanayi ve Ticaret Anonim Sirketi v. Turkmenistan*, ICSID Case No. ARB/10/1, Award, 2 July 2013, para. 7.1.3.

dissimilar agreements. This, in turn, suggests that tribunals tend not to consider treaty design differences in their choice of precedent.

8.4.4 Summary of Findings

If we accept the argument that the weight tribunals accord to treaty design differences when selecting relevant precedent is a proxy for their underlying policy preferences, then tribunals tend to err on the side of consistency, rather than correctness. The majority of tribunals pays little attention to treaty design differences and thus arguably prioritizes concerns of systemic consistency over case-specific correctness.

8.5 Conclusion: A Mismatch between State and Tribunal Policy Priorities

The foregoing analysis points to a mismatch of the policy priorities emerging from the state-led UNCITRAL deliberations and the tribunal-led ISDS practice. States value both consistency and correctness, but fear consistently incorrect decisions more than inconsistent yet correct ones. Tribunals, in contrast, seem to fear inconsistency more than incorrectness. While NAFTA tribunals and a minority of tribunals under other IIAs, such as the one in *Kilic* v. *Turkmenistan,* do pay close attention to treaty design differences when selecting precedent, the overwhelming majority of arbitral decisions tends to cite precedent liberally, including awards rendered under higher dissimilar IIAs. These awards thus implicitly prioritize systemic concerns of consistent interpretations across agreements over treaty-specific notions of correctness.

Future research is required to explain the variation between tribunals. For example, is Jubran-Ballan correct in asserting that institutional background (NAFTA versus non-NAFTA; ICSID versus non-ICSID) drives these policy preferences? Or is the composition of tribunals responsible for the variation we see? As for the mismatch between policy preferences of tribunals and states, I conclude by suggesting that principal–agent theory (PA theory) provides initial clues to explain the misalignment.

According to PA theory, states worry about agency slack when delegating interpretive and adjudicatory authority to tribunals.[49] They fear

---

[49] This use of principal–agent theory to understand incentives in delegation in ISDS is inspired by Florian Grisel and Alec Stone Sweet, 'Transnational Investment Arbitration:

that tribunals 'go rogue' and use the delegated authority to expand their autonomy beyond what contracting states intended. Tribunals, in turn, seek to retain and, if possible, expand their independence from their state principals. Applied to the ISDS context, the policy goal of consistency provides tribunals with a means to enlarge their autonomy. It allows them to consider systemic considerations going beyond the four corners of the IIA that delegated them authority. The policy goal of correctness, in contrast, reins in tribunals' discretion, because it reduces the interpretive analysis to the wording of the applicable treaty, that is, the original terms of delegation, and de-emphasizes systemic concerns. PA theory therefore offers a potential explanation for the mismatch between state and tribunal preferences: states want to curb agency slack by prioritizing correctness; tribunals seek more discretion and therefore prioritize consistency.

If policy preferences for consistency and correctness are indeed, at least in part, the result of the delegation set-up of ISDS, then institutional reform is required to address the mismatch. Curbing agency slack by tightening the terms of delegation has to be the goal of the reform in order to hard code states' priority of correctness over consistency into ISDS institutions. A number of possible reform options would create more effective state control mechanisms to address agency slack from more explicit *ex ante* terms of delegation, for example, that govern the choice of precedent, to *ex post* mechanisms, such as state commissions with a power to issue binding interpretations.[50] IIA reform would then seek to more closely align states' preferences with tribunals' incentives to avoid the mismatch between the policy goals of states and adjudicators revealed in this contribution.

---

from Delegation to Constitutionalization?' in Dupuy, Petersmann and Francioni (eds.), *Human Rights in International Investment Law and Arbitration* (Oxford University Press, 2009), p. 118; Anne van Aaken, 'Delegating Interpretative Authority in Investment Treaties: The Case of Joint Commissions' (2014) 11 *Transnational Dispute Management* (TDM) <transnational-dispute-management.com/article.asp?key=2045>.

[50] See Anne van Aaken, 'Control Mechanisms in International Investment Law', in Douglas, Pauwelyn and Viñuales (eds.), *The Foundations of International Investment Law: Bringing Theory into Practice* (Oxford University Press, 2014), p. 409. State committees are also discussed by Yuliya Chernykh, 'Assessing Convergence between International Investment Law and International Trade Law through Interpretative Commissions/Committees: A Case of Ambivalence?' in Gáspár-Szilágyi, Behn and Langford (n. 23).

9

Fair and Equitable Treatment: Ordering Chaos through Precedent?

FLORIAN GRISEL[*]

9.1 Introduction

In recent years, investment arbitration has been heavily criticized for its lack of transparency, its undemocratic foundations, and the legal uncertainty that it imposes on investors and states. The backlash seems to have reached fever pitch in the negotiations of several major trade treaties: the Transatlantic Trade and Investment Partnership (TTIP), the Comprehensive Trade and Economic and Trade Agreement (CETA), and the Trans-Pacific Partnership (TPP). At the core of this backlash lies a particularly heated debate surrounding the fair and equitable treatment standard (FET), which has increasingly served as the basis for claims brought by investors against states.[1] Over the past few years, for instance, the press has blamed the FET for giving investors carte blanche 'to sanction governments over everything from banning chemicals, withdrawing tax breaks or writing new environmental regulations',[2] for lacking any common definition,[3] and for being a 'vague and amorphous standard'.[4] In short, according to its critics, the FET is proof of how chaotic and unpredictable the system of investment arbitration can be.

---

[*] Associate Professor of Socio-Legal Studies, University of Oxford.

[1] See Alec Stone Sweet and Florian Grisel, *The Evolution of International Arbitration: Judicialization, Governance, Legitimacy* (Oxford University Press, 2017), ch. 4.

[2] Tom Bergin, 'Doubts over EU's Proposals for Saving US Trade Deal', Reuters, 16 June 2015, <reuters.com/article/2015/06/12/us-europetrade-ttip-idUSKBN0OS1UC20150612>.

[3] Amy Westervelt, 'Lawsuit against El Salvador Mining Ban Highlights Free Trade Pitfalls', *The Guardian*, 27 May 2015, <theguardian.com/sustainable-business/2015/may/27/pacific-rim-lawsuit-el-salvador-mine-gold-free-trade>: '[E]ach company and government has their own interpretation of what constitutes "fair and equitable"'.

[4] Simon Lester, 'Letter to the Editor: Foreign Investors', *The Economist*, 25 October 2014, <economist.com/news/letters/21627551-letters-editor>.

A second debate runs parallel to the FET discourse but focuses on the emergence of precedent in investment arbitration.[5] Advocates of legal orthodoxy would prefer to nip this trend in the bud. In their view, an arbitrator's mandate is limited to the cases he or she is called upon to resolve, and a system of binding precedent would only add to the chaos.[6] Some arbitrators share this resistance to precedent. A panelist in *Burlington* v. *Ecuador*, for example, considered it 'her duty to decide each case on its own merits, independently of any apparent jurisprudential trend'.[7]

Despite the vocal criticism of the FET and of precedent, as an empirical matter, both play highly influential roles in investment arbitration. Found in most bilateral investment treaties (BITs), the FET is one of the most heavily litigated provisions and a cornerstone of investor protections.[8] As my study and others have documented, tribunals are increasingly citing prior arbitral awards and considering previous tribunals' interpretations of various provisions.[9] In other words, investment arbitration is gaining a system of precedent without the formal norm of *stare decisis* that governs common law systems.

While the investment arbitration literature has lavished much attention on the FET and on precedent as separate matters, few scholars have focused on their emergence as dual and intertwined trends. This chapter aims to do just that. By tracing the citation and treatment of precedent within the FET case law, this study uses each as a lens for understanding the other. The FET is an ideal case study for the emergence of precedent as a tool of control in a decentralized system, of order within chaos. FET provisions are similarly worded across BITs such that FET

---

[5] Precedent in this chapter is defined as in Stone Sweet and Grisel (n. 1), 119: 'that stream of normative materials, issuing from past awards, that (a) parties plead in submissions and (b) tribunals rely upon when they justify either their awards or their approach to decision-making'.

[6] See e.g. W. Michael Reisman, '"Case Specific Mandates" versus "Systemic Implications": How Should Investment Tribunals Decide? The Freshfields Arbitration Lecture' (2013) 29(2) *Arbitration International* 131; Gilbert Guillaume, 'The Use of Precedent by International Judges and Arbitrators' (2011) 2(1) *Journal of International Dispute Settlement* 5, 16–18.

[7] *Burlington Resources Inc.* v. *Republic of Ecuador*, ICSID Case No. ARB/08/5, Decision on Liability, 14 December 2012, para. 187.

[8] Christoph Schreuer, 'Fair and Equitable Treatment in Arbitral Practice' (2005) 6(3) *Journal of World Investment and Trade* 357, 359.

[9] Tai Heng Cheng, 'Precedent and Control in Investment Treaty Arbitration' (2006) 30(4) *Fordham International Law Journal* 1014, 1016.

interpretations can apply across cases and be considered one body of case law. In addition, the language of FET provisions is open-textured and vague, forcing interpreters to fill in the gaps with their own definitions. The amorphous language also leaves arbitrators eager for guidance and justifications for their particular approach, which reliance on prior interpretations can provide. Finally, since the FET arises so frequently in claims by investors, it has spawned a large number of interpretations by various investment tribunals. As a result, by delving into the well-developed FET case law, one can see whether arbitrators invoke precedent and how they use prior interpretations to fashion a new standard of investor protection. This process is akin to the creation of judge-made standards in common law systems such as negligence in US tort law.[10]

Just as the FET illuminates the role of precedent in investment arbitration, studying the various strands of citations reveals different approaches to the FET, all competing for influence within the ad hoc, decentralized system. As discussed below, my study isolates three distinct interpretations of the FET, each of which can be traced back to a key precedent. Only by studying the pattern of citations can one fully understand the complexity and dissonance within this single standard and the trends of convergence and divergence over time. I hope to offer both a static but nuanced snapshot of the FET as it currently stands and a dynamic account of how certain interpretations come to dominate others. These insights into precedent and the FET help to make sense of what appears at first glance to be a system defined by chaos and to rebut the charges of intractable disorder levied against investment arbitration.

This study bridges the existing FET and precedent literatures and aims to fill in gaps left in both areas. At the same time, this analysis of FET engages with the systemic debates on investment arbitration that have plagued the system since its inception and received renewed attention in the global media. The current FET commentary divides into two strands. The first camp seeks to clarify the FET's contours[11] or even find a 'common theory' of FET[12] on the basis of existing cases. Contrary to

---

[10] Leon Green, 'The Negligence Issue' (1928) 37 *Yale Law Journal* 1029.

[11] See e.g. Rudolf Dolzer, 'Fair and Equitable Treatment: A Key Standard in Investment' (2005) 39 *The International Lawyer* 87; Rudolf Dolzer, 'Fair and Equitable Treatment: Today's Contours' (2014) 12(1) *Santa Clara Journal of International Law* 7; Schreuer (n. 8).

[12] See e.g. Kenneth Vandevelde, 'A Unified Theory of Fair and Equitable Treatment' (2010) 43(1) *New York University Journal of International Law and Politics* 43.

this first strand of research, this chapter focuses on the way in which competing interpretations of the FET emerge and how the case law converges or diverges. The second strand of research places the FET within a general understanding of foreign investment law, linking it with the development of global administrative law.[13] These strands will situate FET within a broader conception of foreign investment law, it will also use the standard to illustrate the dynamics and processes that drive this field rather than formulating a meta-theory of investment arbitration. This chapter bears no normative presumption: instead of taking a pro-investor or pro-state angle, its presentation of the various approaches to the FET provides a basis from which to assess criticism, both old and new, of its development.

In addition to contributing to the larger FET literature, the chapter also aims at contributing to the small, but growing, body of work on precedent in investment arbitration. Currently, insiders, mostly prominent arbitrators noting the use of precedent by tribunals, have written the vast majority of academic papers on this topic.[14] Only a few papers have begun to theorize about precedent in any general way.[15] This chapter roots all of its insights on precedential development in a quantitative and qualitative analysis of FET cases. It digs into the actual language of awards to show precisely how arbitrators are dealing with precedent, whether they are ignoring, following or distinguishing prior cases. From this analysis, I hope to flesh out the beginnings of a theory of precedent unique to investment arbitration and not as a diluted form of the *stare decisis* that governs common law systems.

This chapter differs from existing work in both substance and methodology. The research is based on an exhaustive review of all published investment awards up to 2014 that have set out an interpretation of the FET standard[16] and then focuses on three cases that have emerged as

---

[13] See e.g. Benedict Kingsbury and Stephan Schill, 'Public Law Concepts to Balance Investors' Rights with State Regulatory Actions in the Public Interest – the Concept of Proportionality', in Stephan W. Schill (ed.), *International Investment Law and Comparative Public Law* (Oxford University Press, 2010), p. 75; Stephan W. Schill, 'Fair and Equitable Treatment under Investment Treaties as an Embodiment of the Rule of Law' (2006) 5 *Transnational Dispute Settlement*.

[14] See e.g. Guillaume (n. 6); Gabrielle Kaufmann-Kohler, 'Arbitral Precedent: Dream, Necessity or Excuse? The 2006 Freshfields Lecture' (2007) 23(3) *Arbitration International* 357.

[15] See e.g. Cheng (n. 9); W. Mark C. Weidemaier, 'Toward a Theory of Precedent in Arbitration', (2009–10) 51(5) *William & Mary Law Review* 1895.

[16] The first draft of this chapter was prepared in the Spring of 2015, and the data is up-to-date as of September 2014.

260 FLORIAN GRISEL

guidelines and arguably as 'precedent' for the interpretation of FET: *Tecmed* v. *Mexico* (2003), *Waste Management* v. *Mexico* (2004) and *Occidental* v. *Ecuador* (2004).[17] After reviewing the FET case law, these three cases were selected for their authoritative value, which stems from both their distinctive and fully formed interpretations of FET and their frequent use by later tribunals. Among the most cited awards in all of investment arbitration, these three cases have become focal points in the ongoing effort to define investor protections in foreign investment law and were deemed by at least one prominent arbitrator to be 'authoritative precedents'.[18] By focusing on these three cases, it becomes possible to trace different lines of case law and explore how ad hoc, decentralized tribunals, contrary to popular belief, can coalesce around certain interpretations and how those approaches converge or diverge from others.

Each of these cases represents a different take on the FET. The *Tecmed* tribunal adopted a *subjective* interpretation in which fair and equitable treatment is measured against the 'basic expectations' held by the investor when making its investment.[19] By contrast, the *Waste Management* tribunal championed an *objective* interpretation enumerating state actions that amount to a breach of FET, such as conduct that is 'arbitrary, grossly unfair, unjust or idiosyncratic, is discriminatory and exposes the claimant to sectional or racial prejudice, or involves a lack of due process'.[20] Occupying a middle ground between *Tecmed* and *Waste Management*, the *Occidental* tribunal takes the 'stability of the legal and business framework' as the key factor to FET.[21]

This study relies on a review of all citations to the *Tecmed, Waste Management* and *Occidental* awards to 2014.[22] Citations were counted

---

[17] *Técnicas Medioambientales Tecmed, S.A.* v. *United Mexican States*, ICSID Case No. ARB (AF)/00/2; *Waste Management, Inc.* v. *United Mexican States (II)*, ICSID Case No. ARB (AF)/00/3; *Occidental Exploration and Production Company* v. *Republic of Ecuador (I)*, LCIA Case No. UN 3467.

[18] *International Thunderbird Gaming Corporation* v. *United Mexican States*, UNCITRAL/ NAFTA Case, Award, 26 January 2006, Separate Opinion of Thomas Wälde, paras. 30–1.

[19] *Tecmed* v. *Mexico* (n. 17), Award, 29 May 2003, para. 154.

[20] *Waste Management* v. *Mexico (II)* (n. 17), Award, 30 April 2004, para. 98.

[21] *Occidental* v. *Ecuador (I)* (n. 17), Award, 1 July 2004, paras. 190, 191. On the FET standard and regulatory stability, see Federico Ortino, 'The Obligation of Regulatory Stability in the Fair and Equitable Treatment Standard: How Far Have We Come' (2018) 21(4) *Journal of International Economic Law* 845.

[22] Citations to prior cases in decisions from ICSID annulment committees have not been included. However, some ad hoc decisions are discussed below in order to contextualize certain lines of interpretation.

only if they were sufficiently explicit, that is, when the tribunal referred to one of these cases by name no matter whether the arbitrators agreed or disagreed with the prior interpretation.[23] Citations that were either made implicitly in the tribunal's reasoning or set out solely in the parties' positions have been disregarded. To complement the quantitative empirical analysis, I have conducted a few micro case studies delving into the language of subsequent awards, focusing on how arbitrators are analogizing to, and distinguishing from, earlier cases. These micro case studies were selected because they provided particularly interesting examples of the ways in which the arbitrators referred to the three above cases. They are also useful in examining a sub-question posed by this research: whether individual arbitrators or the merits of particular interpretations are driving citation rates. To explore that issue, I try to highlight when the reasoning and reliance on prior interpretations relate to the backgrounds and predispositions of particular arbitrators, noting the relationship between citations and reappointment of the same arbitrators in later cases.

Based on the in-depth exploration of FET case law, my argument is three-fold. I first show how the high number of citations made to these three landmark cases demonstrates the emergence of precedent in an ad hoc, decentralized system that never boasted a norm of *stare decisis*. These dynamics of precedent are neither simple nor linear: they reflect complex evolutions based on competing narratives of the FET. By illustrating the formation of precedent within one body of case law in all its complexity, this picture captures the development of a system of precedent in investment arbitration. I then analyse how tribunals have treated competing interpretations, particularly their attempts to reconcile different approaches into an overarching interpretation and offer new focal points in the ongoing debate over the FET. Finally, I will note a fascinating recent phenomenon in investment arbitration: the latest generation of investment treaties has begun to incorporate and codify the dominant interpretations of the FET from key arbitral awards. This latest step of codification is sure to change the dynamics of interpretation and use of precedent by arbitral tribunals going forward, creating a continuous feedback loop between arbitrators and treaty drafters.

---

[23] Citations to cases in footnotes have also been counted.

262   FLORIAN GRISEL

9.2 Three Tales of FET

This study of the FET is based on three decisions – all rendered within a fourteen-month period. These decisions have adopted three different perspectives on the FET: *Tecmed* espoused a subjective standard based on investor expectations as the baseline against which state actions are to be assessed; *Waste Management* adopted an objective interpretation of the FET by enumerating specific state actions that constitute FET breaches; finally, *Occidental* sought to 'objectivize' *Tecmed*'s subjective interpretation by tying it to the 'stability of the legal and business framework' offered by the state. On the basis of the data presented in the appendix, I will analyse how each of these decisions has been, to varying extents, cited and discussed by subsequent tribunals.

9.2.1 Tecmed v. Mexico (2003)

The case of *Tecmed* v. *Mexico* arose out of an investment made by a Spanish company through local affiliates[24] for the operation of a waste landfill in Mexico. The dispute was prompted by a resolution from the Mexican environmental protection agency rejecting the application for renewal of an authorization to operate the landfill. Tecmed argued that the cancellation of the authorization breached the bilateral investment treaty between Spain and Mexico, international law, and Mexican law. Specifically, Tecmed argued *inter alia* that Mexico's actions breached Article 4(1) of the BIT, which provided that '[e]ach Contracting Party will guarantee in its territory fair and equitable treatment, according to International Law, for the investments made by investors of the other Contracting Party.'

Before assessing Tecmed's FET claim, the tribunal formulated its interpretation of this standard in broad terms. The fact that the tribunal wrestled with the amorphous language before dealing with the facts speaks to the need for reasoning and justification even in ad hoc dispute resolution. The attempt to define the standard generally is what gives rise to the possibility of precedent. The tribunal emphasized that the 'scope of the undertaking of fair and equitable treatment under Article 4(1) of the Agreement ... is that resulting from an autonomous interpretation',[25] thus implying that this interpretation was specific to the treaty in

---

[24] *Tecmed* v. *Mexico* (n. 17), Award, 29 May 2003, para. 4.
[25] Ibid., para. 155.

question. Despite this caveat, and as will be shown further below, the interpretation adopted by the *Tecmed* tribunal has shaped subsequent tribunals' views of the FET.

The *Tecmed* tribunal anchored the FET standard on investor expectations: a treatment is fair and equitable when it 'does not affect the basic expectations that were taken into account by the foreign investor to make the investment'.[26] The tribunal specified the nature of these expectations as follows:

> The foreign investor expects the host state to act in a consistent manner, free from ambiguity and totally transparently in its relations with the foreign investor, so that it may know beforehand any and all rules and regulations that will govern its investments, as well as the goals of the relevant policies and administrative practices and directives, to be able to plan its investment and comply with such regulations.[27]

The *Tecmed* tribunal therefore defined fair and equitable treatment in a *subjective* way: the determination of whether state actions are 'fair and equitable' ultimately depends on the expectations of the investors at the time of their investment. Of course, these expectations can stem from objective elements such as the regulatory framework at the time of the investment and the policy goals underlying the regulatory framework: an investor would expect 'the State to use the legal instruments that govern the actions of the investor or the investment in conformity with the function usually assigned to such instruments ...'.[28] But the notion of 'expectations' is flexible and open-ended so as to accommodate subjective considerations. By contrast, the *Waste Management* tribunal sought to determine objectively the types of state measures that breach fair and equitable treatment without regard to the expectations of investors.

9.2.2   Waste Management *v.* Mexico *(2004)*

The case of *Waste Management* v. *Mexico* arose out of a concession agreement entered into between Acaverde, a wholly owned subsidiary of Waste Management (a Delaware corporation) and the City of Acapulco. Under this agreement, Acaverde undertook to 'provide on an exclusive basis certain municipal waste disposal and street cleaning services in a

---

[26] Ibid., para. 154.
[27] Ibid.
[28] Ibid.

specified area of Acapulco'.[29] Shortly after the execution of the concession agreement, Acaverde faced numerous difficulties such as resistance from local groups that benefited from or provided competing services as well as non-payment of invoices by the City of Acapulco, which eventually led to the withdrawal of Acaverde from Acapulco.[30]

After Acaverde initiated proceedings in different fora,[31] Waste Management brought NAFTA proceedings before an arbitral tribunal, which dismissed its claims.[32] Waste Management then brought new NAFTA proceedings before a second arbitral tribunal, arguing that Mexico had breached its obligations under Articles 1105 and 1110 of NAFTA. Article 1105(1) of NAFTA provides that '[e]ach Party shall accord to investments of investors of another Party treatment in accordance with international law, including fair and equitable treatment and full protection and security.'

When assessing Waste Management's FET claim, the arbitral tribunal analysed Article 1105(1) in light of a prior interpretation of the Free Trade Commission[33] and NAFTA awards.[34] The arbitral tribunal noted that 'despite certain differences of emphasis [in different cases] a general standard for Article 1105 is emerging'.[35] Such an attempt to survey and synthesize the existing case law is characteristic of a common law system but rather unexpected of ad hoc tribunals. In its review of arbitral case law, the *Waste Management* tribunal limited itself to NAFTA awards and did not refer, at least explicitly, to the *Tecmed* award.

---

[29] *Waste Management* v. *Mexico (II)* (n. 17), Award, 30 April 2004, para. 41.

[30] Ibid., paras. 40–72.

[31] Acaverde initiated proceedings before the Mexican federal courts and before an arbitral tribunal. See ibid., para. 70.

[32] The first NAFTA tribunal dismissed Waste Management's claims on the basis that it had not validly waived its right to initiate or continue before any tribunal or court proceedings with respect to the state measures that are the object of the NAFTA claims. See *Waste Management, Inc.* v. *United Mexican States (I)*, ICSID Case No. ARB(AF)/98/2, Award, 2 June 2000.

[33] The NAFTA Free Trade Commission issued the following binding interpretation of Article 1105(1) on 21 July 2001: 'Article 1105(1) prescribes the customary international law minimum standard of treatment of aliens as the minimum standard of treatment to be afforded to investments of investors of another Party. The concepts of "fair and equitable treatment" and "full protection and security" do not require treatment in addition to or beyond that which is required by the customary international law minimum standard of treatment of aliens. A determination that there has been a breach of another provision of the NAFTA, or of a separate international agreement, does not establish that there has been a breach of Article 1105(1).'

[34] *Waste Management* v. *Mexico (II)* (n. 17), Award, 30 April 2004, paras. 91–8.

[35] Ibid., para. 98.

The tribunal's reference to the 'representations' made by the state to the investor – which would be the basis for the investor's expectations – may have been a subtle indication of its consideration of, and effort to, distinguish the interpretation laid out in *Tecmed* v. *Mexico*. The *Waste Management* tribunal laid out the following interpretation of Article 1105(1):

> ... the minimum standard of treatment of fair and equitable treatment is infringed by conduct attributable to the State and harmful to the claimant if the conduct is arbitrary, grossly unfair, unjust or idiosyncratic, is discriminatory and exposes the claimant to sectional or racial prejudice, or involves a lack of due process leading to an outcome which offends judicial propriety – as might be the case with a manifest failure of natural justice in judicial proceedings or a complete lack of transparency and candour in an administrative process. In applying this standard it is relevant that the treatment is in breach of representations made by the host State which were reasonably relied on by the claimant.[36]

The first sentence of the above paragraph reflects an *objective* interpretation of the FET standard, influenced by the traditional public international law reading of the FET.[37] However, inferring from the second sentence discussing representations made by the state and the investor's reasonable reliance, the tribunal might have felt compelled to respond to the *Tecmed* tribunal's highly influential subjective approach to the FET, though the *Waste Management* tribunal declined to name the case explicitly. On balance, the above interpretation leans more heavily towards an objective reading of the FET: the tribunal sets out specific state actions that constitute FET breaches and places only a secondary focus on the 'representations' made by the host state. By contrast, in *Tecmed*, the primary focus was on the investor's expectations, based in large part on representations made by the host state.

These two divergent approaches to the FET reveal contrasting value judgments in foreign investment law: the *Tecmed* approach is mainly seen as favouring investors, while *Waste Management* appears to protect the states. The identities of the arbitrators may also have played a role:[38] the president of the *Tecmed* tribunal (Naon) is predominantly a leading

---

[36] Ibid.

[37] See *L.F.H. Neer* v. *United Mexican States*, U.S.–Mexico General Claims Commission, Award, 15 October 1926.

[38] On this phenomenon, see Florian Grisel, 'Marginals and Elites in International Arbitration', in Federico Ortino and Thomas Schultz (eds.), *Oxford Handbook of International Arbitration* (Oxford University Press, 2020), ch. 10.

266 FLORIAN GRISEL

practitioner of international commercial arbitration,[39] while the president of the *Waste Management* tribunal (Crawford) is a leading practitioner of public international law.[40] In the wake of the rift created by these two awards, other tribunals have tried to reconcile the subjective and objective approaches by 'objectivizing' the subjective approach promoted in *Tecmed*. *Occidental* v. *Ecuador* presents one example of the attempt at reconciliation.[41]

9.2.3 Occidental v. Ecuador (2004)

Occidental, a US company, entered into a contract with PetroEcuador, an Ecuadorian State enterprise, for the exploration and exploitation of hydrocarbons in Block 15 of the Amazon. The dispute between Occidental and Ecuador arose out of the refusal of the Ecuadorian tax administration to reimburse the value-added tax (VAT) on the importation and local acquisition of goods and services used for the performance already accounted for in a participation formula set out in the contract. Occidental disagreed and argued, *inter alia*, that Ecuador had breached Article II(3)(a) of the BIT between the US and Ecuador by 'revoking preexisting decisions that were legitimately relied upon by the investor to assume its commitments and plan its commercial and business activities . . .'.[42] Article II(3)(a) provides that: '[i]nvestment shall at all times be accorded fair and equitable treatment, shall enjoy full protection and security and shall in no case be accorded treatment less favourable than that required by international law.'

In its discussion of the FET standard, the *Occidental* tribunal followed the interpretation laid out in *Tecmed*[43] but re-framed its definition of fair and equitable treatment in terms of 'stability' of the legal framework of the host state (rather than in terms of investor expectations). For instance, the *Occidental* tribunal referred twice to the requirement of 'stability and predictability' of the 'legal and business framework' for the

---

[39] Among other functions, Horacio Grigera Naon was the Secretary General of the ICC International Court of Arbitration from 1996 until 2001.

[40] James Crawford is currently a judge at the International Court of Justice, after teaching international law at Cambridge University for more than two decades.

[41] See also the discussion in *LESI, S.p.A. and Astaldi, S.p.A.* v. *Peoples Democratic Republic of Algeria (II)*, ICSID Case No. ARB/05/3, Award, 12 November 2008, para. 151.

[42] *Occidental* v. *Ecuador (I)* (n. 17), Award, 1 July 2004, para. 181.

[43] Ibid., para. 185.

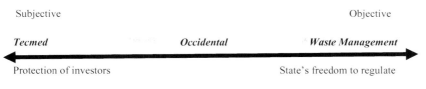

Figure 9.1 Three tales of FET

investment under international law,[44] to the 'obligation not to alter the legal and business environment in which the investment has been made'[45] and to the duty to ensure 'both the stability and predictability of the governing legal framework'.[46] The *Occidental* decision thus reinterprets the *Tecmed* standard objectively, by linking the investors' expectations to the stability and predictability of the framework underlying the investment. As such, the *Occidental* decision can be seen as an attempt to find middle ground between an objective approach to the FET as exemplified in *Waste Management* and a subjective approach as showcased in *Tecmed*.

Tecmed, Waste Management and *Occidental* can therefore be placed on a continuum from 'subjective' to 'objective'. This continuum also represents varying ideological values concerning the balance between investor protection and the states' freedom to regulate: the subjective approach prioritizes the protection of investors, while the objective approach stresses the state's freedom to regulate. These three tales of the FET – objective, subjective and a compromise – represent three points on the continuum that have polarized the debates on the FET (figure 9.1).

9.3 Dynamics of Precedent

The three strands of interpretation have helped structure the debates on FET before arbitral tribunals. Some tribunals have tried to compete with earlier interpretations by rejecting or synthesizing them. The polarizing effect of the *Tecmed, Waste Management* and *Occidental* awards among

---

[44] Ibid., paras. 190, 191.
[45] Ibid., para. 191.
[46] Ibid., para. 192.

arbitrators becomes apparent when reviewing the references made to these awards in subsequent cases. The patterns of citation to these three influential awards illustrate the 'fragmentary and gradual development' of the FET standard, as pointed out by the *Enron*[47] and *Sempra*[48] tribunals, which in many ways exemplifies the emergence of arbitrator-made law within investment arbitration. Because this development is 'fragmentary', however, these awards do not exhaust the possible interpretations of the FET. In fact, other precedents have emerged and vied for influence, either by rejecting outright one of the three dominant interpretations or by merging multiple definitions into an overarching understanding of FET. These non-linear, complex dynamics give insight into how control and order can arise organically from within what can be perceived as a chaotic system.

9.3.1 Three Strands of Case Law

Tecmed is undoubtedly the landmark FET case as it might have prompted other tribunals, including the *Waste Management* and *Occidental* tribunals, to position themselves vis-à-vis *Tecmed*'s interpretation of FET. In other words, other tribunals feel compelled to align or distance themselves from *Tecmed*, whether implicitly or explicitly. As the first attempt to define comprehensively the FET, *Tecmed* is a particularly powerful focal point, a status that is borne out in the citation rate to *Tecmed* in subsequent awards. According to the data, in the years after *Tecmed* was decided, it was unquestionably the dominant reference for the FET: before 2010, 21 out of 37 tribunals interpreting the FET cited *Tecmed*. Adding the cases after 2010 shows that *Tecmed*'s influence may have waned somewhat but remains significant: it has been cited by 36 of the 114 tribunals that have analysed the FET standard until 2014.

Waste Management, a NAFTA case, represents a competing authority on the FET standard. Looking at citation counts alone, *Waste Management* seems less influential than *Tecmed* as it was cited by twenty tribunals. *Occidental*, the compromise between the subjective and objective approaches, drew citations from nine tribunals. While one may have

---

[47] *Enron Creditors Recovery Corporation (formerly Enron Corporation) and Ponderosa Assets, L.P.* v. *Argentine Republic*, ICSID Case No. ARB/01/3, Award, 22 May 2007, para. 257.

[48] *Sempra Energy International* v. *Argentine Republic*, ICSID Case No. ARB/02/16, Award, 28 September 2007, para. 297.

expected this middle way to have attracted supporters from both the *Tecmed* and *Waste Management* camps, it in fact seems to be the least influential of the three. Note that the three awards were rendered at around the same time, one in 2003 and two in 2004, so they have all had about the same amount of time to garner citations.

Beyond looking at the raw citation rates, it is useful to isolate the role of arbitrator identity and repeat appointments.[49] In a system of precedent driven predominantly by those two factors, the vast majority of citations would come from arbitrators citing their own prior interpretations. That would nonetheless represent a system of precedent and indeed one unique to the institutional structure of dispute resolution by ad hoc panels. It also seems relevant to explore to what extent arbitrators are citing others' interpretations, presumably convinced by the strength of the legal reasoning or the ideological values embodied in the rationale. As an initial observation, one of the nine cases citing *Occidental* is *Enron* v. *Argentina*, whose tribunal was headed by the same president as in *Occidental* (Vicuña). The language in the two awards are remarkably similar, both emphasizing that 'a key element of fair and equitable treatment is the requirement of a "stable framework for the investment"'.[50] Similarly, the *Sempra* \ tribunal (also presided by Vicuña) referred to the 'legal and business framework under which the investment [i]s decided and implemented' as well as 'business certainty and stability'.[51] The identity of arbitrators, which is compounded by repeated appointment,[52] seems to have been key to the continued influence of *Occidental*.

Beyond looking at citation numbers and arbitrator identities, it is useful to review the weight and authority given to prior interpretations. Tribunals do not always cite prior cases to adopt the interpretations therein. For instance, *Tecmed*, the most cited case on FET, has occasionally raised controversy. In *MTD*, the tribunal cited *Tecmed* in support of its interpretation of FET.[53] Chile subsequently brought proceedings for

---

[49] On 'repeat appointments' in international arbitration, see Florian Grisel, 'Competition and Cooperation in International Commercial Arbitration: The Birth of a Transnational Legal Profession' (2017) 51(4) *Law & Society Review* 790, 811; Grisel (n. 38), ch. 10.

[50] *Enron* v. *Argentina* (n. 47), para. 260.

[51] *Sempra* v. *Argentina* (n. 48), para. 303.

[52] See Daphna Kapeliuk, 'The Repeat Appointment Factor: Exploring Decision Patterns of Elite Investment Arbitrators' (2010) 96 *Cornell Law Review* 47.

[53] *MTD Equity Sdn. Bhd. and MTD Chile S.A.* v. *Republic of Chile*, ICSID Case No. ARB/01/7, Award, 25 May 2004, para. 114.

270 FLORIAN GRISEL

the annulment of the award, where it argued that the arbitral tribunal manifestly exceeded its powers (one of the annulment grounds under Article 52 of the ICSID Convention) by relying on the interpretation of FET contained from *Tecmed*, which Chile called, with irony, the 'TecMed programme for good governance'.[54] In particular, Chile contrasted the *Tecmed* approach with the *Waste Management* approach.[55] Put differently, Chile did not seek reversal of the award on the basis that the tribunal relied on precedent in the absence of *stare decisis* but that the tribunal invoked the *wrong* precedent – an argument that presupposes at least to some extent the legitimacy of adopting prior interpretations. In a system without a formal vertical hierarchy among various tribunals, *Waste Management* holds just as much precedential weight as *Tecmed*, so Chile was perfectly within its right to lobby for the more favourable precedent.

The annulment committee was composed of prominent public international lawyers, with a former President of the ICJ (Guillaume) as President and the former President of the *Waste Management* tribunal (Crawford) as co-member. The committee first expressed its disagreement with the *Tecmed* standard:

> the TECMED Tribunal's apparent reliance on the foreign investor's expectations as the source of host State's obligations (such as the obligation to compensate for expropriation) is questionable. The obligations of the host State towards foreign investors derive from the terms of the applicable investment treaty and not from any set of expectations investors may have or claim to have. A tribunal which sought to generate from such expectations as set of rights different from those contained in or enforceable under the BIT might well exceed its powers, and if the difference were material might do so manifestly.[56]

However, the annulment committee rejected Chile's argument, in part because the MTD tribunal quoted *Tecmed* 'in support of this standard [of FET as discussed by the MTD tribunal], not in substitution for it'.[57] This reason implies that an ICSID tribunal does not manifestly exceed its powers when it relies on a prior case if it uses that case in support of its own reasoning and decision, and not as a substitute for its own determination. The committee also commended the MTD tribunal for defining

---

[54] *MTD* v. *Chile* (ibid.), Decision on Annulment, 21 March 2007, para. 66.
[55] Ibid., para. 66.
[56] Ibid., para. 67.
[57] Ibid., para. 70.

FET as 'treatment in an even-handed and just manner'[58] and for taking an objective approach similar to the one adopted in *Waste Management*. Again, the predispositions of public international lawyers seem to have weighed towards the right side of the continuum drawn above (i.e. towards an objective approach favouring the state's freedom to regulate). In addition, the chain of precedent seems to be linked to arbitrator identity, as one of the committee members in *MTD* v. *Chile* also presided over the tribunal in *Waste Management*.

Yet the *MTD* v. *Chile* story yields an even broader and more exciting insight: the annulment committee, the only institution situated above the decentralized ad hoc tribunals, began to create norms of precedent in two ways. First, it announced a kind of meta-norm of how tribunals should treat prior interpretations – they can only supplement but not supplant the tribunal's own rationale. Such a norm should force arbitrators to reflect on the merits of various precedents and justify their adoption or rejection of previous interpretations. Second, the committee elevated the precedential status of MTD's interpretation of the FET by praising its logic. It therefore appears that annulment committees can serve to organize and discipline the development of precedent, making the annulment decisions focal points in and of themselves.

9.3.2 New Contenders

Just as important as the awards approving prior interpretations are those that distinguish them. Some tribunals have disagreed with the dominant interpretation of the FET in *Tecmed*. For instance, in *Glamis Gold* v. *US*, a NAFTA case, the tribunal emphasized the specific character of the *Tecmed* interpretation and denied the existence of precedent in international arbitration, while pointing out that it had a duty to 'communicate its reasons for departing from major trends present in previous decisions'.[59] That language captures the intriguing paradox of denying the power of arbitral precedent: if precedent holds no weight because no tribunal is bound by any other, why do arbitrators feel the need to distinguish prior interpretations in the first place? The denial itself rather confirms the creeping influence of prior decisions. The *Glamis Gold* tribunal specified that its approach was 'partially apparent in this Award's evidentiary approach to the requirement of fair and equitable

---

[58] Ibid., para. 71.
[59] *Glamis Gold Ltd* v. *US*, NAFTA/UNCITRAL Case, Award, 8 June 2009, para. 8.

272 FLORIAN GRISEL

treatment under Article 1105'.[60] As a matter of fact, the tribunal denied that *Tecmed* had any relevance to the matter before it:

> Looking, for instance, to Claimant's reliance on *Tecmed v. Mexico* for various of its arguments, the Tribunal finds that Claimant has not proven that this award, based on a BIT between Spain and Mexico, defines anything other than an autonomous standard and thus an award from which this Tribunal will not find guidance.[61]

The tribunal's efforts to insulate *Tecmed* have not stopped many other tribunals from seeking guidance from *Tecmed*'s reasoning on FET and citing the award accordingly. That trend in and of itself is interesting. At this point, no tribunal's view on precedential authority appears to influence any other's view. Each panel of arbitrators is free to craft an approach to precedent applicable to that dispute and that dispute only. This kind of ad hoc approach to precedent lies somewhere between the rigid *stare decisis* of some legal systems and a completely decentralized scheme where each case is an island unto itself with no ties to earlier cases. Again, my view is that arbitrators, consciously or unconsciously, develop and use precedent in a way that conforms to the institutional design of investment arbitration.

Instead of directly rejecting a prior interpretation, other tribunals prefer to synthesize the three strands of case law and reconcile their interpretations. The tribunal in *Saluka* has evensucceeded in laying out a fourth strand of interpretation based on a mix of subjective and objective considerations. It should first be noted that the president in *Saluka v. Czech Republic*, a prominent public international lawyer (Watts), also served as Chile's legal expert in the *MTD* annulment proceedings, in which he harshly criticized the *Tecmed* interpretation.[62] Again, public international lawyers appear to fall on the right side of the continuum drawn above (towards an objective approach). In *Saluka*, the tribunal discussed the subjective approach, and cautiously recognized its potential relevance while emphasizing its limits. For instance, relying on the *Tecmed* award, the *Saluka* tribunal held that:

---

[60] Ibid., para. 8.

[61] Ibid., para. 610.

[62] *MTD v. Chile* (n. 53), Decision on Annulment, 21 March 2007, para. 66: 'The *TECMED* dictum is also subject to strenuous criticism from the Respondent's experts, Mr. Jan Paulsson and Sir Arthur Watts. They note, *inter alia*, the difference between the *TECMED* standard and that adopted in other cases, including one the Tribunal also cited in a footnote but without comment [Waste Management].'

The standard of 'fair and equitable treatment' is therefore closely tied to the notion of legitimate expectations which is the dominant element of that standard. By virtue of the 'fair and equitable treatment' standard included in Article 3.1 the Czech Republic must therefore be regarded as having assumed an obligation to treat foreign investors so as to avoid the frustration of investors' legitimate and reasonable expectations. . . .

This Tribunal observes, however, that while it subscribes to the general thrust of these and similar statements, it may be that, if their terms were to be taken too literally, they would impose upon host States obligations which would be inappropriate and unrealistic. Moreover, the scope of the Treaty's protection of foreign investment against unfair and inequitable treatment cannot exclusively be determined by foreign investors' subjective motivations and considerations.[63]

The *Saluka* tribunal then proceeded to re-balance the 'subjective' approach with 'objective' considerations, invoking both perspectives:

A foreign investment protected by the Treaty may in any case properly expect that the Czech Republic implements its policies bona fide by conduct that is, as far as it affects the investors' investment, reasonably justifiable by public policies and that such conduct does not manifestly violate the requirements of consistency, transparency, even handedness and non-discrimination. . . . Finally, it transpires from arbitral practice that, according to the 'fair and equitable treatment' standard, the host State must never disregard the principles of procedural propriety and due process and must grant the investor freedom from coercion or harassment by its own regulatory authorities.[64]

Saluka also raises fascinating questions about the dynamics and timing of precedential development: how and when do arbitrators decide to synthesize disparate strands of case law and why do they feel justified in doing so? Again, since no ad hoc tribunal has authority over any other, competing interpretations could theoretically run parallel to each other indefinitely, causing dissonance within the case law. The fact that the *Saluka* tribunal reconciled their divergence into a new interpretation that then gained influence should take those sceptical of investment arbitration by surprise. This dynamic shows that a decentralized, horizontal system of tribunals can organize its own precedent without any norms of *stare decisis*, vertical or temporal precedence, or formal appellate review, all of which anchor common law systems of precedent. From these

---

[63] *Saluka Investments B.V.* v. *Czech Republic*, UNCITRAL/PCA Case, Partial Award, 17 March 2006, paras. 302, 304.
[64] Ibid., paras. 307, 308.

developments one can begin to theorize about a self-governing regime of precedent adapted to the idiosyncracies of investment arbitration.

9.4 Dynamics of Codification

Finally, perhaps the most surprising trend of all is the possible codification of existing interpretations of the FET, as discussed in recent negotiations of major investment treaties. In most legal systems, it is not uncommon for the legislature to codify interpretations of a particular statute in subsequent revisions. In the case of a vaguely worded statute, the legislature likely intended for the courts to fill in the meaning based on varying circumstances. As the courts flesh out the statute through application to particular cases, the legislature may correct the courts' approach or even reject certain interpretations by amending the statutory language. This back-and-forth between legislature and court and between statutory law and judicial interpretation is part of an ongoing dialogue.

Could the same dynamic arise in investment arbitration? The FET is very much like a broadly worded statutory provision. The analogue for the legislature would be the drafters of treaties governing foreign investment. The counterpart to the judicial system would be the ad hoc arbitral tribunals and possibly the annulment committees. This analogy is more than theoretical. Article 8.10 of the Comprehensive Economic and Trade Agreement (CETA), the trade and investment agreement signed between the European Union and Canada, which was also the basis for negotiations of the Transatlantic Trade and Partnership Agreement (TTIP), reads as follows:

> Article 8.10: Treatment of Investors and of Covered Investments
>
> 1. Each Party shall accord in its territory to covered investments of the other Party and to investors with respect to their covered investments fair and equitable treatment and full protection and security in accordance with paragraphs 2 to 7.
> 2. A Party breaches the obligation of fair and equitable treatment referenced in paragraph 1 where a measure or series of measures constitutes:
>   a. denial of justice in criminal, civil or administrative proceedings;
>   b. fundamental breach of due process, including a fundamental breach of transparency, in judicial and administrative proceedings;
>   c. manifest arbitrariness;
>   d. targeted discrimination on manifestly wrongful grounds, such as gender, race or religious belief;
>   e. abusive treatment of investors, such as coercion, duress and harassment; or

FET: ORDERING CHAOS THROUGH PRECEDENT?

> f. a breach of any further elements of the fair and equitable treatment obligation adopted by the Parties in accordance with paragraph 3 of this Article.
>
> 3. The Parties shall regularly, or upon request of a Party, review the content of the obligation to provide fair and equitable treatment. The Committee on Services and Investment, established under Article 26.2.1(b) (Specialised committees), may develop recommendations in this regard and submit them to the CETA Joint Committee for decision.
>
> 4. When applying the above fair and equitable obligation, a tribunal may take into account whether a Party made a specific representation to an investor to induce a covered investment that created a legitimate expectation, and upon which the investor relied in deciding to make or maintain the covered investment, but that the Party subsequently frustrated. . . .

The approach adopted in Article 8.10 of the CETA resembles the *Saluka* tribunal's rebalancing of the FET in that it combines objective and subjective interpretations. Indeed, Article 8.10.3 of CETA clearly refers to the first strand of interpretation inspired by the *Tecmed* award. In this provision, the FET standard is framed in terms of 'representations' from the state that create 'legitimate expectations' for the investor. In addition, Article 8.10.2 of CETA codifies the second strand of interpretation stemming from the *Waste Management* award. That provision lists a series of state actions amounting to breaches of the FET standard, which are analogous to those listed in *Waste Management*: 'manifest failure of natural justice', 'lack of due process', 'arbitrary' or 'discriminatory' conduct.[65]

The similarities are too apparent to be mere coincidences. If treaty drafters are indeed incorporating existing interpretations from arbitral tribunals into new FET provisions, many new questions come naturally to mind. What are the states aiming to do – adopt interpretations wholesale, use them for guidance, or even correct the pro-investor or pro-state biases they see in the case law? How are states selecting the interpretations worthy of codification? How does codification then feed back into the exercise of interpretation? Note how much more detailed the CETA FET language is compared to the bare-bones amorphous standards found in most earlier BITs. The more specific the language,

---

[65] *Waste Management v. Mexico (II)* (n. 17), Award, 30 April 2004, para. 98.

the less leeway arbitrators have to say what the FET means. That textual specificity may be a sign that states are reining in the discretion originally delegated to arbitral tribunals. Relevant examples of this trend are Article 14.6.4 of the United States–Mexico–Canada Agreement (USMCA) and Article 9.8.4 of the Trans-Pacific Partnership (TPP) which explicitly carved out the *Tecmed* approach from the definition of FET.[66] Ironically, the feedback loop between codification and interpretation may in fact reduce the need to reach for precedent. As tribunals begin to decide future cases under this new generation of BITs, these questions will become ripe for further exploration.

[66] See e.g. USMCA, art. 14.6.4: 'For greater certainty, the mere fact that a Party takes or fails to take an action that may be inconsistent with an investor's expectations does not constitute a breach of this Article, even if there is loss or damage to the covered investment as a result.'

Appendix

Citations to the *Tecmed, Waste Management* and *Occidental* interpretations of FET in subsequent investment awards as of September 2014.

Técnicas Medioambientales Tecmed, S.A. v. *United Mexican States*, ICSID Case No. ARB(AF)/00/2:

1. *Occidental Exploration and Production Company* v. *Ecuador*, UNCITRAL/LCIA Case, Award, 1 July 2004, para. 185.
2. *CMS Gas Transmission Company* v. *Argentina*, ICSID Case No. ARB/01/8, Award, 12 May 2005, para. 279.
3. *MTD Equity Sdn. Bhd. and MTD Chile S.A.* v. *Chile*, ICSID Case No. ARB/01/7, Award, 25 May 2005, para. 114.
4. *Bayindir Insaat Turizm Ticaret Ve Sanayi A.S.* v. *Pakistan*, ICSID Case No. ARB/03/29, Decision on Jurisdiction, 14 November 2005, paras. 237, 240.
5. *Saluka Investments B.V.* v. *Czech Republic*, UNCITRAL/PCA Case, Partial Award, 17 March 2006, para. 302.
6. *Azurix Corp.* v. *Argentina*, ICSID Case No. ARB/01/12, Award, 14 July 2006, para. 371.
7. *LG&E Energy Corp. et al.* v. *Argentina*, ICSID Case No. ARB/02/1, Decision on Liability, 3 October 2006, para. 127.
8. *PSEG Global Inc. et al.* v. *Turkey*, ICSID Case No. ARB/02/5, Award, 19 January 2007, para. 240.
9. *Siemens A.G.* v. *Argentina*, ICSID Case No. ARB/02/8, Award, 6 February 2007, paras. 298, 299.
10. *Enron Corporation Pondesora Assets, L.P.* v. *Argentina*, ICSID Case No. ARB/01/3, Award, 22 May 2007, paras. 257, 262.
11. *Sempra Energy International* v. *Argentina*, ICSID Case No. ARB/02/16, Award, 28 September 2007, para. 297.
12. *Metalpar S.A. and Buen Aires S.A.* v. *Argentina*, ICSID Case No. ARB/03/5, Award, 6 June 2008, paras. 182, 184.
13. *Biwater Gauff (Tanzania) Ltd* v. *Tanzania*, ICSID Case No. ARB/05/22, Award, 24 July 2008, paras. 528, 600.

278   FLORIAN GRISEL

14. *Duke Energy Electroquil Partners et al.* v. *Ecuador*, ICSID Case No. ARB/
    04/19, Award, 18 August 2008, para. 339.
15. *Plama Consortium Ltd* v. *Bulgaria*, ICSID Case No. ARB/03/24, Award,
    27 August 2008, para. 176.
16. *National Grid P.L.C.* v. *Argentina*, UNCITRAL Case, Award, 3 November
    2008, para. 173.
17. *Jan de Nul N.V. and Dredging International N.V.* v. *Egypt*, ICSID Case No.
    ARB/04/13, Award, 6 November 2008, para. 186.
18. *LESI S.p.A. et Astaldi S.p.A.* v. *Algérie*, ICSID Case No. ARB/05/3, Award,
    12 November 2008, para. 151.
19. *Waguih Elie George Siag and Clorinda Vecchi* v. *Egypt*, ICSID Case No.
    ARB/05/15, Award, 1 June 2009, para. 450.
20. *Glamis Gold, Ltd* v. *USA*, NAFTA/UNCITRAL Case, Award, 8 June 2009,
    para. 610.
21. *Bayindir Insaat Turizm Ticaret Ve Sanayi A.S.* v. *Pakistan*, ICSID Case
    No. ARB/03/29, Award, 27 August 2009, para. 179.
22. *Ioannis Kardassopoulos and Ron Fuchs* v. *Georgia* , ICSID Cases No. ARB/
    05/18 and ARB/07/15, Award, 3 March 2010, para. 440.
23. *AES Summit Generation Ltd et al.* v. *Hungary*, ICSID Case No. ARB/07/
    22, Award, 23 September 2010, paras. 9-3-8, 9-3-40.
24. *Alpha Projektholding GMBH* v. *Ukraine*, ICSID Case No. ARB/07/16,
    Award, 8 November 2010, para. 420.
25. *Frontier Petroleum Services Ltd* v. *Czech Republic*, UNCITRAL Case,
    Award 12 November 2010, paras. 286, 287.
26. *Binder* v. *Czech Republic*, Ad hoc Case, Award, 15 July 2011, para. 446.
27. *El Paso Energy International Company* v. *Argentina*, ICSID Case No.
    ARB/03/15, Award, 31 October 2011, paras. 341, 342.
28. *White Industries Australia Ltd* v. *India*, UNCITRAL Case, Award,
    30 November 2011, paras. 10.3.5, 10.3.6.
29. *Spyridon Roussalis* v. *Romania*, ICSID Case No. ARB/06/1, Award,
    7 December 2011, para. 316.
30. *Oostergetel* v. *Slovak Republic*, UNCITRAL Case, Award, 23 April 2012,
    para. 222.
31. *Marion Unglaube and Reinhard Unglaube* v. *Costa Rica*, ICSID Cases No.
    ARB/08/1 and ARB/09/20, Award, 16 May 2012, para. 249.
32. *Toto Costruzioni Generali S.P.A.* v. *Lebanon*, ICSID Case No. ARB/07/12,
    Award, 7 June 2012, para. 152.
33. *Franck Charles Arif* v. *Moldova*, ICSID Case No. ARB/11/23, Award,
    8 April 2013, para. 538.
34. *Ioan Micula et al.* v. *Romania*, ICSID Case No. ARB/05/20, Award,
    11 December 2013, paras. 532, 534.

FET: ORDERING CHAOS THROUGH PRECEDENT? 279

35. *Gold Reserve Inc.* v. *Venezuela*, ICSID Case No. ARB(AF)/09/1, Award, 22 September 2014, para. 572.
36. *Antoine Abou Lahoud et al.* v. *Congo*, ICSID Case No. ARB/10/4, Award, 7 February 2014, para. 440.

Waste Management, Inc. v. *United Mexican States (II)*, ICSID Case No. ARB (AF)/00/3:

1. *Saluka Investments B.V.* v. *Czech Republic*, UNCITRAL/PCA Case, Partial Award, 17 March 2006, para. 302.
2. *Azurix Corp.* v. *Argentina*, ICSID Case No. ARB/01/12, Award, 14 July 2006, para. 370.
3. *LG&E Energy Corp. et al.* v. *Argentina*, ICSID Case No. ARB/02/1, Decision on Liability, 3 October 2006, para. 128.
4. *Siemens A.G.* v. *Argentina*, ICSID Case No. ARB/02/8, Award, 6 February 2007, paras. 297, 299.
5. *BG Group Plc* v. *Argentina*, UNCITRAL Case, Award, 24 December 2007, paras. 292, 294.
6. *Biwater Gauff (Tanzania) Ltd* v. *Tanzania*, ICSID Case No. ARB/05/22, Award, 24 July 2008, paras. 529, 565, 597, 601.
7. *National Grid P.L.C.* v. *Argentina*, UNCITRAL Case, Award, 3 November 2008, para. 173.
8. *Frontier Petroleum Services Ltd* v. *Czech Republic*, UNCITRAL Case, Award, 12 November 2010, para. 290.
9. *Merrill & Ring Forestry L.P.* v. *Canada*, NAFTA/UNCITRAL Case, Award, 31 March 2010, paras. 156, 199.
10. *Sergei Paushok et al.* v. *Mongolia*, UNCITRAL Case, Award on Jurisdiction and Liability, 28 April 2011, para. 625.
11. *Meerapfel Sohne A.G.* v. *République centrafricaine*, ICSID Case No. ARB/ 07/10, Award, 11 May 2011, para. 359.
12. *Binder* v. *Czech Republic*, Ad hoc Case, Award, 15 July 2011, para. 445.
13. *El Paso Energy International Company* v. *Argentina*, ICSID Case No. ARB/03/15, Award, 31 October 2011, para. 348.
14. *Oostergetel* v. *Slovak Republic*, UNCITRAL Case, Award, 23 April 2012, para. 225.
15. *Toto Costruzioni Generali S.P.A.* v. *Lebanon*, ICSID Case No. ARB/07/12, Award, 7 June 2012, para. 152.
16. *Railroad Development Corporation* v. *Guatemala*, ICSID Case No. ARB/ 07/23, Award, 29 June 2012, para. 219.
17. *Deutsche Bank A.G.* v. *Sri Lanka*, ICSID Case No. ARB/09/02, Award, 31 October 2012, para. 420.
18. *Ioan Micula et al.* v. *Romania*, ICSID Case No. ARB/05/20, Award, 11 December 2013, paras. 522, 524.

280 FLORIAN GRISEL

19. *Antoine Abou Lahoud et al.* v. *Congo*, ICSID Case No. ARB/10/4, Award, 7 February 2014, paras. 439, 440.
20. *Gold Reserve Inc.* v. *Venezuela*, ICSID Case No. ARB(AF)/09/1, Award, 22 September 2014, para. 573.

Occidental Exploration and Production Company v. *Republic of Ecuador (I)*, LCIA Case No. UN 3467:

1. *Saluka Investments B.V.* v. *Czech Republic*, UNCITRAL/PCA Case, Partial Award, 17 March 2006, para. 303.
2. *PSEG Global Inc. et al.* v. *Argentina*, ICSID Case No. ARB/02/5, Award, 19 January 2007, para. 240.
3. *Enron Corporation Pondesora Assets, L.P.* v. *Argentina*, ICSID Case No. ARB/01/3, Award, 22 May 2007, para. 257.
4. *Sempra Energy International* v. *Argentina*, ICSID Case No. ARB/02/16, Award, 28 September 2007, para. 297.
5. *Biwater Gauff (Tanzania) Ltd* v. *Tanzania*, ICSID Case No. ARB/05/22, Award, 24 July 2008, para. 530.
6. *Duke Energy Electroquil Partners et al.* v. *Ecuador*, ICSID Case No. ARB/04/19, Award, 18 August 2008, paras. 334, 339.
7. *Plama Consortium Ltd* v. *Bulgaria*, ICSID Case No. ARB/03/24, Award, 27 August 2008, para. 176.
8. *Frontier Petroleum Services Ltd* v. *Czech Republic*, UNCITRAL Case, Award, 12 November 2010, para. 334.
9. *El Paso Energy International Company* v. *Argentina*, ICSID Case No. ARB/03/15, Award, 31 October 2011, para. 344.

PART III

Output Legitimacy

10

The West and the Rest: Geographic Diversity and the Role of Arbitrator Nationality in Investment Arbitration

MALCOLM LANGFORD[*], DANIEL BEHN[**] AND
MAXIM USYNIN[***]

10.1 Introduction

'Stale, male and pale' is the epithet often applied to arbitrators that adjudicate investor–state disputes under international investment agreements (IIAs). Honing in on the feature of paleness, 74 per cent of arbitrators[1] and almost all of the top 25 'powerbrokers' hail from Western states.[2] Yet, the vast majority of claims in investor–state dispute settlement (ISDS) target developing and non-Western states,[3] and these states disproportionately lose.[4] The result is that the lack of geographic

---

[*] Professor of Public Law and Director of CELL, University of Oslo; Co-Director, Centre on Law and Social Transformation, University of Bergen and CMI.

[**] Senior Lecturer in International Law, Queen Mary University of London; Associate Research Professor, PluriCourts, University of Oslo. This chapter was supported by the Research Council of Norway through projects number 223274 and 276009.

[***] Postdoctoral researcher, CEPRI – Centre for Private Governance, University of Copenhagen.

[1] See Section 10.4 below.

[2] Malcolm Langford, Daniel Behn and Runar Lie, 'The Revolving Door in International Investment Arbitration' (2017) 20(2) *Journal of International Economic Law* 301–32; Sergio Puig, (2014) 'Social Capital in the Arbitration Market' 25 *European Journal of International Law* 387.

[3] Thomas Schultz and Cedric Dupont, 'Investment Arbitration: Promoting the Rule of Law or Over-Empowering Investors? A Quantitative Empirical Study' (2014) 25 *European Journal of International Law* 1147; Daniel Behn, Malcolm Langford and Ole Kristian Fauchald, 'Private or Public Good? An Empirical Perspective on International Investment Law and Arbitration,' in Massimo Iovane, Fulvio Palombino, Daniele Amoroso and Giovanni Zarra (eds.), *The Protection of General Interests in Contemporary International Law: A Theoretical and Empirical Enquiry* (Oxford University Press 2021), 91–118.

[4] Daniel Behn, Tarald Berge and Malcolm Langford, 'Poor States or Poor Governance? Explaining Outcomes in Investment Treaty Arbitration' (2018) 38(3) *Northwestern Journal of International Law & Business* 333–89.

diversity among the arbitrators sitting in judgment in these disputes continues to contribute to legitimacy concerns over the international investment regime and its dispute settlement process.[5] A system designed by the West,[6] dominated by the West, and producing pro-Western outcomes, has struggled, unsurprisingly, to maintain its mantle of universality. On its surface, it looks unmistakably neo-colonial.

While this critique of geographical homogeneity dates back more than a decade, it has gained traction in the past few years. Diversity is now central in various reform discussions about the future of the international investment regime,[7] especially through the UNCITRAL Working Group III reform process.[8] Proposals range from a greater institutionalization of arbitrator appointment to conversion of the current ad hoc dispute settlement process to a standing international court with tenured or quasi-tenured judges.[9] A major feature of this shift will focus on the types of adjudicators suited to sit on such a court, and it is highly likely that appointment requirements will destabilize the current distribution of nationality, gender and professional background.[10]

This chapter addresses two questions in the legitimacy debate on geographic diversity. The first is descriptive and concerns *representativity*, the

---

[5] Gabrielle Kaufmann-Kohler and Michele Potestà, *The Composition of a Multilateral Investment Court and of an Appeal Mechanism for Investment Awards*, CIDS Supplemental Report, 15 November 2017.

[6] Throughout the chapter, we focus on the distinction between Western states and non-Western states according to the main UN groupings. The Western group is comprised of the following states: Andorra, Australia, Austria, Belgium, Canada, Denmark, Finland, France, Germany, Greece, Iceland, Ireland, Israel, Italy, Liechtenstein, Luxembourg, Malta, Monaco, Netherlands, New Zealand, Norway, Portugal, San Marino, Spain, Sweden, Switzerland, United Kingdom and the United States. All other states are classified as non-Western.

[7] Anthea Roberts, 'UNCITRAL and ISDS Reforms: Concerns about Arbitral Appointments, Incentives and Legitimacy', *EJIL:Talk!* 6 June 2018.

[8] See Andrea K. Bjorklund, Daniel Behn, Susan Franck, Chiara Giorgetti, Won Kidane, Arnaud de Nanteuil and Emilia Onyema, 'The Diversity Deficit' (2020) 21(2–3) *Journal of World Investment and Trade* 410; Report of Working Group III (Investor-State Dispute Settlement Reform) on the work of its thirty-fifth session (New York, 23–27April 2018), AQ/CN.9/935, para. 70.

[9] United Nations Commission on International Trade Law (UNCITRAL), 'Report of Working Group III (Investor-State Dispute Settlement Reform) on the work of its thirty-fourth session (Vienna, 27 November–1 December 2017)', UN Doc. No. A/CN.9/930/Rev.1 (19 December 2017); Malcolm Langford, Michele Potestà, Gabrielle Kaufmann-Kohler and Daniel Behn, 'UNCITRAL and Investment Arbitration Reform: Matching Concerns and Solutions', (2021) 21(2–3), *Journal of World Investment & Trade* 167.

[10] James Crawford, 'The Ideal Arbitrator: Does One Size Fit All? (2018) 32(5) *American University International Law Review* 1003.

degree of asymmetry in appointments. We ask: What is the current level of geographic diversity? Who appoints non-Western nationals? Is it improving over time? And how is this picture affected when we disaggregate nationality by residence rather than citizenship? Drawing on our comprehensive PluriCourts Investment Treaty and Arbitration Database (PITAD) of all investment treaty arbitrations (including ICSID contract and foreign direct investment (FDI) law cases), we provide a comprehensive overview of appointment by citizenship[11] and dominant residence.[12]

The second question is correlative and concerns *bias*, the possible effect of the lack of geographic diversity. Would greater heterogeneity concretely matter for outcomes in investor–state arbitration? The current literature is equivocal. In an early paper on a limited sample of 47 investor–state arbitration cases, Franck found that the economic development status of the presiding arbitrators (who often carry the key deciding vote) did not affect outcomes for states in ISDS disputes according to their economic development status.[13] However, in a more recent paper on 231 ICSID cases, Waibel and Wu found that arbitrators from developing states were significantly more likely to favour respondent states (whether developed or developing) – although only on decisions concerning jurisdiction, not the merits.[14] Moreover, nationality may matter for perceived legitimacy. Using a dataset of all ICSID decisions, Puig and Strezhnev found that developing states that have lost an arbitration are less likely to seek annulment if a member of the arbitration panel hailed from the developing world.[15]

However, the effect of geographic diversity on outcomes requires further interrogation. In their study of the International Court of Justice (ICJ), Posner and de Figueredo found that ICJ judges were clearly more favourable to states with similar levels of democratic governance

---

[11] We define citizenship as the original citizenship of the arbitrator but we have also coded secondary citizenship (including where an arbitrator might hold dual nationality from birth).

[12] We define location of dominant residence as the primary place of domicile and work at the time the investment arbitration case was registered.

[13] Susan Franck, 'Development and Outcomes of Investment Treaty Arbitration' (2009) *50* (2) *Harvard International Law Journal* 435.

[14] Michael Waibel and Yanhui Wu, 'Are Arbitrators Political? Evidence from International Investment Arbitration', *Working Paper*, January 2017.

[15] Anton Strezhnev and Sergio Puig, 'Diversity and Compliance in Investment Arbitration: Future Directions in Empirical Research on Investment Law and Arbitration' (2019) LEGINVEST Conference, 31 January 2019, Oslo; see also Anton Strezhnev, 'Detecting Bias in International Investment Arbitration' (2016) *Working Paper*, finding a significant increase in claimants' wins when tribunal presidents are nationals of advanced economies and have worked in government.

and economic development.[16] This stark finding in one regime warrants further study elsewhere. Moreover, existing arbitral behaviour studies on geographic diversity have drawn on limited sample sizes and only one aspect of 'nationality', namely citizenship.

In this chapter, drawing again on PITAD, we go further than previous efforts in three respects. First, we analyse all investor–state arbitration cases,[17] including those conducted on a non-institutional basis according to the UNCITRAL rules and those held at arbitral institutions other than ICSID. Second, we introduce the dual approach to the definition of nationality: citizenship and location of dominant residence.[18] In previous research, we found that some of the most powerful and influential non-Western state nationals acting as arbitrators in investor–state arbitration have spent most of their professional career in the West (including their legal education). We are thus interested in seeing whether *dominant place of residence* may be more important than *passport(s)* in determining one's approach to the adjudication of disputes involving Western and non-Western states. Are non-Western state nationals less likely to be sceptical to interests of the West when they are residing in the West? Third, we examine the potential bi-directionality of arbitral preferences. We test not only whether non-Western arbitrators are more likely to award in favour of non-Western respondent states, but also whether this extends to non-Western corporate-claimants. In doing so, we seek to provide a diverse theoretical palette for thinking through the geographic effect on arbitral decision-making. With these findings, we can provide some estimates of the likely consequences of future appointment models and strategies proposed in the UNCITRAL reform process.

The chapter is structured as follows. Section 10.2 introduces investor–state arbitration and some of the debates around its legitimacy, with a particular focus on the issues of a non-Western/Western divide in the system. Section 10.3 theorizes about the likely effects of arbitrator citizenship; and Section 10.4 introduces the descriptive data on both types of national identity (citizenship and location of dominant residence). Using

---

[16] Eric Posner and Miguel de Figueiredo, 'Is the International Court of Justice Biased?' 34 *Legal Studies* (2005) 599.

[17] A total of 1,228 cases as of 1 August 2018.

[18] While usually the dominant place of residence coincides with the working address at the moment of case registration, the detailed explanation of the term follows in the methodology section below. See Section 10.4.1.

regression analysis with various controls, Section 10.5 analyses whether the citizenship and the location of dominant residence of arbitrators affects outcomes – the success rates for all respondent states and for non-Western respondent states. Section 10.6 concludes.

10.2 The International Investment Treaty Regime

The modern international investment regime can be described in multiple ways, but generally includes the international institutions and rules governing the regulation of trans-border investments. As described in the Introduction to this book,[19] it builds upon a network of various IIAs and gives foreign investors a number of substantive protections and rights, including, most importantly, access to ISDS. The most distinct feature of this regime is the proliferation of litigation: see Figure 10.1. An investor–state arbitration case arises when: a foreign investor alleges that the beneficiary rights they are granted under an IIA has been breached by the state hosting its investments; and, where there is a relevant ICSID arbitration clause, that a contract signed with the host state has been breached or that a domestic FDI law in a host state has been breached. It is the swift rise in the instances of investor–state arbitration over the past two decades that has led some to claim there is 'no other category of private individuals' that are 'given such expansive rights in international law as are private actors investing across borders'[20] prompting increasing scrutiny from a growing number of states, scholars and civil society actors.

Through PITAD, we have tracked and coded all known cases, a total of 1,228 cases as of 1 August 2018.[21] This figure includes all known treaty-based arbitrations (976 cases), ICSID contract and FDI law-based arbitrations (131 cases), and ICSID annulment committee proceedings (121 cases). The dataset would ideally include all international commercial arbitrations and all non-ICSID contract-based investment arbitrations, but given the default confidentiality of such processes, the data available remains far from complete or accessible. In any case, our dataset has a certain coherence. It covers all known cases whose legal claim is

---

[19] See the Introduction to this volume.
[20] Beth Simmons, 'Bargaining over BITS, Arbitrating Awards: The Regime for Protection and Promotion of International Investment' (2014) 66 *World Politics* 12, 42.
[21] PluriCourts Investment Treaty Arbitration Database (PITAD) as of 1 August 2018. For current data, see pitad.org.

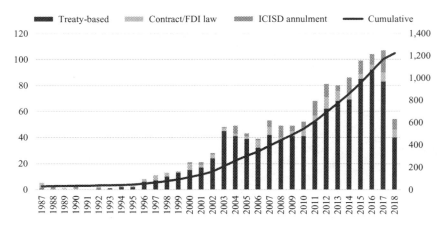

Figure 10.1 Investor–state arbitration cases registered by year (1987–2018)[1]

[1] PITAD (n. 21); 1,228 cases in total at 1 August 2018. Figure 10.1 starts in 1987 when the first treaty-based investment arbitration was registered. The first non-treaty-based investment arbitrations began in 1972. Between 1972 and 1986 there were 24 of this type of case (excluded from Figure 10.1).

procedurally or substantively based on an international treaty: whether through the ICSID Convention and/or various IIAs.

Not all of the cases have been concluded and claimant-investor success rates vary. Of the 1,107 investor–state arbitration cases registered as of 1 August 2018 (treaty-based and ICSID contract-based or FDI law-based), the outcomes are as follows:[22] 485 had reached a final conclusion (either on jurisdiction or the merits),[23] 367 cases remained pending, and an additional 255 were settled or discontinued. Of the finally concluded cases (428 treaty-based and 57 ICSID contract- or FDI law-based), claimant-investors won on the merits in 47.2 per cent of the cases and lost on jurisdiction or the merits in 52.8 per cent.

In addition, there have been 121 ICSID annulment committee cases registered (see also Figure 10.1). Under Article 53(1) of the ICSID Convention, a party may seek an annulment of their award on one of five narrow grounds. While these annulments concern existing ICSID cases, distinct arbitration panels are selected and therefore are included

[22] Ibid.
[23] A concluded case is one where the claimant-investor has either won on the merits or lost on jurisdiction or the merits. It does not include discontinued or settled cases.

as separate cases below in our analysis of arbitrator citizenship and location of dominant residence. Of these cases, 61 have been concluded, 34 remain pending and an additional 26 have either been settled or discontinued. Of the concluded annulments, only 22.9 per cent have resulted in a full or partial annulment.

Turning to the arbitrators, investor–state arbitration inherited the procedural setting of commercial arbitration. Typically, arbitral tribunals consist of three arbitrators who are appointed in a similar manner: each party to the dispute will appoint one of three arbitrators; and in many cases the parties (or the co-arbitrators) will jointly appoint the presiding arbitrator (or chair). While the default is that the parties will appoint the two wing arbitrators, the presiding arbitrator can be appointed by the parties, the wing arbitrators, by the institution hosting the arbitration, or even by a third party. For ICSID annulment committee cases, all three members are appointed by the President of the World Bank acting as a Chairman of the ICSID Administrative Council.

Of all the possible configurations for the appointment of arbitrators in investor-state arbitration, however, there is an underlying constant: all arbitrators are selected for a particular dispute on an ad hoc basis. This structure means that for every arbitration, there are individuals (either the parties, legal counsel representing the parties, arbitral institutions or co-arbitrators) that are making selection decisions for each of the 1,228 cases in our dataset.

10.3 Theorizing Nationality

The fact that the nationality of arbitrators features prominently in debates on the legitimacy of international investment arbitration is not surprising when one considers three core features of the system in practice. The first is that developing – all are also non-Western – states (defined as all but high-income states as categorized by the World Bank Income Groups (WBIGs)) are more frequently sued than developed states. Of the 1,107 registered cases (not including ICSID annulment cases), developing states are respondents in 74.6 per cent of the cases (and if one looks at whether the respondent state is non-Western, the percentage rises to 90.6 per cent of all cases).[24] The second is that the

---

[24] The caveat of these numbers being that developed states and Western states especially are only a small percentage of the overall number of states in the world and so it is not unsurprising that these states would constitute a smaller percentage of the caseload.

overwhelming majority of arbitrators appointed to decide these disputes are from Western and developed states (see further Section 10.4).[25] The third is that developing states (according to the lowest three WBIG categories) are two to three times more likely to lose than developed states – and this gap does not disappear when we control for most democratic governance indicators.[26]

Together, the first two features of the system naturally raise normative questions of *representativity*. Is it legitimate that Western, developed state arbitrators should dominate substantially in a system of adjudication that almost always sees a developing, non-Western state being sued? The latter two features, however, raise empirical questions of *bias*. Can the very low success rates of claimant-investors when suing Western states be accounted for by the nationality of the arbitrators sitting in those disputes?[27] Or, in the alternative, is it the comparably higher success rates of claimant-investors in cases against non-Western states attributable to the largely Western nationality of arbitrators? We focus on these two questions in this chapter using two vectors of nationality: citizenship and dominant residence. It is important, however, to consider first why nationality might (or might not) matter. We present a number of competing hypotheses.

10.3.1 Home Region Bias

The general arguments for why the nationality of adjudicators might affect international courts and arbitrations are diverse.[28] In the case of investor-state arbitration, three reasons might be important. First, and sociologically, arbitrators may possess a greater understanding of the challenges of their own state, region, income grouping or 'civilization' compared to others in complying with investment treaties; thus being 'more receptive to arguments for why a national legal system seemingly

---

However, with that said, the number of investment arbitration cases against developing states are still disproportionately higher than those cases against developed states and despite the fact that most investment flows are between developed states.

[25] Langford, Behn and Lie (n. 2).

[26] Behn, Berge and Langford (n. 4).

[27] Ibid.

[28] For an overview, see Erik Voeten, 'International Judicial Behaviour', in Cesare Romano, Karen Alter and Yuval Shany (eds.), *Oxford Handbook of International Adjudication* (Oxford University Press, 2015), pp. 550–68.

departs from international standard'.[29] Huntingdon argues that civilizational culture divide between the West and the rest is particularly important, differentiating 'communities of states based on persistent and frequently opposing beliefs and values' – with the non-Western/Western divide being the most important.[30] Second, and attitudinally, arbitrators may unconsciously reflect the policy preferences of their part of the world. Third, and strategically, certain arbitrators may signal a home region affinity or sensitivity for the purposes of signalling future appointments (especially those seeking appointments by respondent states). Thus, we can hypothesize:

H1.1 *Arbitrators will be more favourably disposed to the position of respondent states belonging to a similar regional grouping of Western or non-Western states (e.g. European or Latin American states) as the state in which they reside or have citizenship.*

This 'home region' bias hypothesis needs to be nuanced in a number of ways, however. The first is that several leading arbitrators from non-Western states reside and work in Western states (and received their education there); and this may affect their outlook or future appointment strategy. The second is that nationality may affect how arbitrators view the cause or position of the claimant-investor in the case – a growing share of claimants include foreign investors that are themselves from non-Western states. In these cases, for both strategic and ideological reasons, we might expect arbitrators to be more sensitive to the problems of corporations from their part of the world. On the basis of these observations on 'dominant residence' and the 'home state' of the corporation, we can add two additional home 'region' hypotheses:

H1.2 *Arbitrators will be more favourably disposed to the position of respondent states that have a similar regional grouping (Western or non-Western) with the region in which they reside.*

H1.3 *Arbitrators will be more favourably disposed to the position of foreign investors that come from their regional grouping (Western or non-Western) with the state in which they reside or have citizenship.*

---

[29] Ibid., 555.

[30] Wade Cole, 'When All Else Fails: International Adjudication of Human Rights Abuse Claims, 1976–1999' (2006) 84 *Social Forces* 1909–35, 1912 citing Samuel Huntington, *Clash of Civilizations and the Remaking of World Order* (Simon and Schuster, 1996), pp. 183–86.

10.3.2 The First Competing Hypothesis: No Bias

The principal alternative to the above hypotheses is that arbitrators are not swayed by their citizenship or where they reside. Drawing on *legal positivism*, we might therefore expect that arbitrators, according to their professional judgment, would seek to apply IIA provisions in good faith to the specific facts of the case. Accordingly, variation in arbitral behaviour could only be explained by differences between substantive rules in treaties, factual circumstances, and various conceptual positions taken by tribunals.[31] However, legal positivism is not alone in predicting expectable outcomes. An *attitudinalist* perspective of adjudicative behaviour would suggest the same predictable and trustee-based hypothesis: Adjudicators make decisions according to their sincere ideological attitudes and values (according to their 'personal judgment')[32] because they are relatively unconstrained by other actors, including states.[33]

As investment arbitrators represent a small group, often with experience in commercial arbitration, their overall positions regarding the interpretation of IIA commitments may be quite similar. This cadre may constitute a micro-civilization of their own. Moreover, the 'West/non-West' or 'Global North/South' divides are highly abstract geographical imaginaries that cover over deep ideological, political and military divisions between individual states, even when they are neighbours in the sub-region. Is a Colombian or Chilean arbitrator less likely or more likely than an American or Swiss arbitrator to evince empathy for Ecuador's politics towards foreign investors? Even a *strategic* perspective could suggest no bias if aspiring arbitrators from outside the West seek to gain acceptance, and thus follow the general norms of the investment arbitration community. Thus, we can hypothesise that:

H2 *Arbitrators will not be more favourably disposed to respondent states or foreign investors that come from their regional grouping (Western or non-Western), on the basis of citizenship or residence.*

---

[31] Jorge E. Viñuales, 'Too Many Butterflies? The Micro-Drivers of the International Investment Law System' (2018) 9(4) *Journal of International Dispute Settlement* 628.

[32] See generally Jeffrey Segal and Harold Spaeth, *The Supreme Court and the Attitudinal Model* (Cambridge University Press, 1993).

[33] Jeffrey Segal, 'Separation-of-Powers Games in the Positive Theory of Congress and Courts' (1997) 91 *The American Political Science Review* 1, 28.

10.3.3   The Second Competing Hypothesis: Reverse Bias

A final but under-considered theory of nationality is that the 'bias' may work in the opposite direction. Arbitrators from developing, non-Western states may be biased against – or ideologically indifferent to – states from their own part of the world for both sociological and strategic reasons. Familiarity with states similar to their own may make them more sceptical of the government's treatment of foreign investors' rights. Moreover, arbitrators may possess or gain greater legitimacy when they are more critical of states similar to their own. Within the logic of 'only hawks can make peace', arbitrators can avoid a critique of bias when they act against the affiliation expectation. Such an approach may also be strategic for future appointment. Developed, Western state arbitrators can signal their openness to the positions of non-Western respondent states, while non-Western arbitrators can signal the reverse. Indeed, the latter may be particularly important for emerging arbitrators from non-Western states seeking to break into the international arbitration market.[34] Building the symbolic capital of impartiality and professionalism may push younger non-Western state arbitrators to overcompensate (and favour foreign investors from Western states for example) and avoid open conflicts with other arbitrators (for example, preferring consensus decisions over dissent). Thus, we can hypothesize that:

H3 *Arbitrators will be more favourably disposed to respondent states or foreign investor home states that have a different status than their own (Western or non-Western state) on the basis of citizenship or residence.*

10.4   Descriptive Data

10.4.1   Coding Citizenship and Dominant Residence

In seeking to chart and analyse geographic diversity, we have used the following hierarchy of sources for the coding of citizenship and location of dominant residence fields. Citizenship can be multiple; and location of dominant residence can also be manifold but also can change across time. In this section, we define both terms and how they have been coded.

---

[34] Yves Dezalay and Bryant Garth, *Dealing in Virtue: International Commercial Arbitration and the Construction of a Transnational Legal Order* (University of Chicago Press, 1996).

The primary source is the specialized aggregators of arbitrator's profiles (ICSID database of arbitrators,[35] IAI Paris[36] and ASA Arbitration[37]). The information on citizenship and dominant residence provided in such aggregators was enough for the vast majority of arbitrators. In some cases, where the arbitrator was absent from the aggregators, her or his university or law firm profile served as secondary guidance. Lastly, in a few rare cases, where the profile information was scarce, the coding referred to the nationality mentioned by arbitral tribunals or it was deduced from the postal address of arbitrators. When sources for the assessment of nationality was not available in English, French, Russian or Scandinavian languages, automatic translation services such as Google Translate were utilized.

A particualr challenge in coding was that both citizenship and dominant residence can change over time. Arbitrators may acquire additional citizenship and shift between different offices and states. Therefore, the chapter adopts two different approaches to the coding of both fields. The coding of nationality focuses on latest information available about citizenship and does not specify the moment in time the arbitrator acquired any additional citizenship. The reason is a problem of obtaining data: the information about newly acquired citizenship is usually absent from the public records of arbitrator profiles. Therefore, while arbitrators could have acquired additional citizenship during their active professional careers, the coding includes only the latest and fullest account.

At the same time, information about the changes in dominant residence is typically present in the public records. Many of those who later became arbitrators typically changed residence during their studies abroad. Later in their career, they may also migrate between different offices and work simultaneously from two or more places. The chapter makes a choice by assessing the dominant residence of arbitrators at the time of case registration. The primary reference for dominant residence is the known working location of arbitrators during a specified period (that is, when the case was registered), based on the assumption that location of dominant residence coincides with the main working location of the

---

[35] *ICSID*, searchable database of*ICSID*, arbitrators, conciliators and ad hoc committee members, <icsid.worldbank.org/resources/databases/arbitrators-conciliators-ad-hoc-committee-members>.

[36] *International Arbitration Institute*, <iaiparis.com/index.asp>.

[37] *Swiss Arbitration Association*, database of Swiss and international specialists, <profiles.arbitration-ch.org/search>.

arbitrator. In situations where the working location of an arbitrator is unknown, the coding used their publicly known postal address for work-related correspondence or their known domestic residence. In only a few cases (approximately 10 cases), none of this information was available, so that the coding assumed that the primary citizenship of the arbitrator was also the same as the location of dominant residence.

Concerning the descriptive statistics, arbitrators typically had one citizenship and one location of dominant residence at the time of case registration (and in the majority of cases, these were the same). However, a number of arbitrators have two and more citizenships. A few also split time between two places of residence. In these cases, and given that they are a small minority, we have made every effort to determine the primary citizenship and the most likely location of dominant residence at the time of case registration. However, for completeness, all known citizenships and dominant residences have been coded and will be made available in the raw data released with this chapter; and a future iteration of the research will draw on the indicator for dual citizenship/residence (available at pitad.org).

10.4.2 Diversity of Arbitrators

As of 1 August 2018, there have been at least 695 individual arbitrators who have sat in at least one investor–state arbitration case. These 695 arbitrators account for 3,327 discrete appointments in 1,109 cases (including ICSID annulment cases as well). There remain 119 cases where either the arbitrators sitting in the case are unknown or where the tribunal has yet to be constituted. Of the individual arbitrators and their appointments, several findings about the geographic diversity can be drawn.

As can be seen from Table 10.1, the percentage of non-Western arbitrators that are – or have been – in the system at some point is 35 per cent. In other words, 241 of the 695 known arbitrators to have sat in at least one investor–state arbitration case have citizenship from states that are non-Western according to the UN groupings. The proportion of non-Western arbitrators with a single appointment and the percentage of non-Western arbitrators with multiple appointments is roughly the same. As Table 10.1 also shows, when non-Western state arbitrators are disaggregated into more specific regions, it is clear that the most dominant regional set of arbitrators are those coming from Latin America (either South America or Central America and the Caribbean). Combined, this group of non-Western arbitrators constitutes nearly half of all non-Western arbitrators in the system.

Table 10.1 *Regional distribution of arbitrators based on citizenship*

Region	1 Appt	More than 1	Total	%
South America	29	36	65	9
Central America & Caribbean	31	14	45	6
Eastern Europe & Central Asia	19	20	39	6
Middle East	18	18	36	5
South-East Asia	5	6	11	2
Sub-Saharan Africa	14	12	26	4
South Asia	7	4	11	2
East Asia	4	4	8	1
All Non-Western Regions	127	114	241	35
All Western Regions	238	216	454	65
All Regions	365	330	695	100
Non-West %	35%	35%		

The high percentage of arbitrators coming from Latin America provides an important insight into the overall distribution of non-Western arbitrators. Non-Western arbitrators are often appointed in cases involving respondent states from their home region: see Table 10.2. There is a high proportion of investment arbitration cases against Latin American states (302 cases) as compared to East Asian, South Asian and Sub-Saharan African states (201 cases combined). Thus, there is strong evidence of region-dependent appointment processes for non-Western arbitrators, suggesting they are view as 'local' rather than 'global' legal professionals.

While non-Western arbitrators do make up about one-third of all arbitrators in the system, there appear to be interesting segregations when looking at the number of appointments that this sub-set of arbitrators have received. First, while non-Western arbitrators are receiving multiple appointments (see discussion above), they do not obtain the high number of repeat appointments that would put them (save three – Stanimir Alexandrov, Rodrigo Oreamuno and the late Francisco Orrego Vicuña) on the list of top 25 arbitrator 'power brokers'.[38] The raw numbers also confirm that the repeat appointments of non-Western

---

[38] Behn, Berge and Langford (n. 4).

GEOGRAPHIC DIVERSITY & INVESTMENT ARBITRATION   297

Table 10.2 *Regional distribution of appointments based on citizenship*

Region	No. of appointments					
	Claimant	Resp.	Chair	Annul.	Total	%
South America	111	83	69	35	298	9
Central America & *Caribbean*	10	68	41	28	147	4
Eastern Europe & Central *Asia*	61	52	16	11	140	4
Middle East	30	44	22	25	121	4
South-East Asia	3	11	20	24	58	2
Sub-Saharan Africa	5	25	3	13	46	1
South Asia	3	23	8	6	40	1
East Asia	0	2	7	16	25	1
All Non-Western Regions	223	308	186	158	875	26
All Western Regions	779	687	787	194	2,452	74
All Regions	1,002	995	973	352	3,327	100
Non-West %	22%	31%	19%	45%		

arbitrators are comparably low: 35 per cent of all arbitrators in the system are non-Western but they have received only about a quarter of all appointments to date (see Table 10.2). Secondly, non-Western arbitrators tend to receive a higher percentage of appointments as respondent state wing arbitrators (and as ICSID annulment committee members), as compared to appointments as claimant-appointed or as presiding arbitrator.

10.4.3   Distribution and New Entrants over Time

Examining trends, we find that the percentage of annual appointments going to non-Western arbitrators has increased over time but that the rate of appointments has largely stabilized in the past six years. Looking at Figure 10.2, one can see that there were very few non-Western arbitrators in the system throughout the 1970s until the mid-1990s. However, there were not many appointments during this period going to either non-Western or Western arbitrators because of the very limited caseload. From about 1999, we see, however, a slight increase in the proportion of non-Western arbitrators.

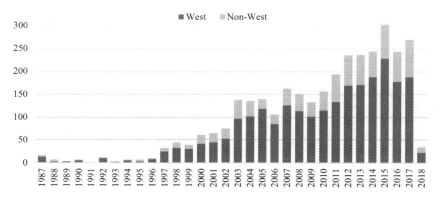

Figure 10.2 Distribution of Western and non-Western appointments per year[1]

[1] PITAD (n. 21); 3,255 (3,327 – 72) appointments at 1 August 2018. Figure 10.2 starts in 1987 when the first treaty-based investment arbitration was registered. The first non-treaty-based investment arbitrations began in 1972. Between 1972 and 1986 there were 72 appointments made (excluded from Figure 10.2).

Nonetheless and overall, the proportion of non-Western arbitrator appointments to Western arbitrator appointments is surprisingly consistent across time. The overall average of about 26 per cent of all appointments going to non-Western arbitrators breaks down to about the same percentage on a yearly basis as well. This means that there is little indication that there has been any significant increase in the proportion of non-Western arbitrator appointments in the period of its legitimacy crisis over the past eight to ten years.

Part of the reason why the proportion of non-Western arbitrator appointments has remained fairly consistent in the recent years is due to what we could call the 'prior experience norm' in investment arbitration.[39] This is the same justification as to why the proportion of female arbitrators in the system has not increased over time. The theory is that because there were few female and non-Western arbitrators receiving appointments in the early days of the system, these sub-sets of arbitrators will not increase because the vast majority of new appointments goes to arbitrators who have sat in previous cases. However, Figure 10.3 shows that the percentage of non-Western new entrants coming into the system

[39] Taylor St John, Daniel Behn, Malcolm Langford and Runar Lie, 'Glass Ceilings and Arbitral Dealings: Gender and Investment Arbitration', *Pluricourts Working Paper*, January 2018.

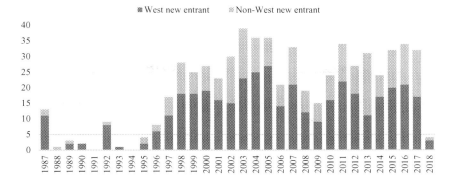

Figure 10.3 Distribution of Western and non-Western new entrant arbitrators by year[1]

[1] PITAD (n. 21); 643 (695 – 52) arbitrators at 1 August 2018. Figure 10.3 starts in 1987 when the first treaty-based investment arbitration was registered. The first non-treaty-based investment arbitrations began in 1972. Between 1972 and 1986 there were 52 arbitrators entering the system (excluded from Figure 10.3).

each year is higher than the overall percentage of non-Western arbitrators in the system (35 per cent). Over the past decade, there are approximately 30 new arbitrators coming into the system. While there is some yearly fluctuation, the number of non-Western new entrants is nearing 50 per cent annually. This provides a *small* reason for optimism regarding future increase of geographic diversity.

10.4.4 Panel Role and Appointing Body

As stated in Section 10.4.1 above, the percentage of non-Western arbitrators is clearly differentiated by the role they play in a particular arbitration. Overall, about 31 per cent of all respondent-appointed arbitrators are non-Western, 22 per cent are claimant-appointed and only 19 per cent are appointed as the influential, prestigious presiding arbitrator. See Figure 10.4. As is clear, the proportion of non-Western arbitrators obtaining appointments is significantly higher for respondent-appointees than for the two other roles.

Another interesting disributive consideration is to compare appointments by the parties with those of an appointing authority such as the institution administering the arbitration. Institutions appoint a non-Western arbitrator almost twice more frequently than her or his

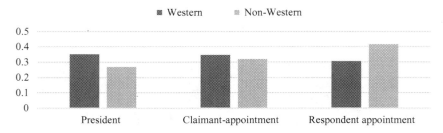

Figure 10.4 Type of arbitrator appointment

Western colleague (see Table 10.3: institutional appointments for non-Western/Western arbitrators give almost a double ratio). However, the overall numbers of appointments made by institutions still go to Western arbitrators 67 per cent of the time (the total number of institutional appointments is 111 to non-Western arbitrators and 223 to Western arbitrators for a total of 334 appointments).

10.4.5 Personal Identity of Arbitrators

Finally, we will briefly look at the number of appointments of the top 25 individual non-Western arbitrators according to their citizenship and their dominant residence. Looking at Table 10.4, it is obvious that there are several non-Western arbitrators with a significant number of appointments across time. The top ten non-Western arbitrators account for 292 appointments or an average of 29 appointments per arbitrator. These ten non-Western arbitrators alone account for nearly 10 per cent of all appointments in the system to date. Looking at the entire list, however, the distribution by region is quite restrictive, with no non-Western arbitrators from Sub-Saharan Africa and only one arbitrator from East Asia. The most represented region is Latin America with 11 of the top 25 non-Western arbitrators.

Looking at the list of top 25 arbitrators according to their location of dominant residence (see Table 10.5), several shifts occur. Seven of the top 25 non-Western arbitrators by citizenship are removed from the list due to the fact that these individuals actually reside in Western states. Interestingly, however, two prominent Western arbitrators (by citizenship) are added to the list (Christopher J. Thomas and Neil Kaplan) due to the fact that they reside in East or South-East Asia. Overall, the number of appointments going to the top ten arbitrators on this list

Table 10.3 *Nature of appointing authority: parties vs. institution (not including ICSID annulment cases)*

| | Non-Western Arb. | | | | Western Arb. | | | |
	Party	Inst.	Unknown	Total	Party	Inst.	Unknown	Total
Chair	44	81	60	185	324	210	251	785
Claim.-Appoint.	220	0	0	220	775	0	0	775
Resp.-Appoint.	200	30	56	286	518	13	152	683
Total	486	111	116	691	1617	223	403	2243
% of Total	69.3%	16.1%	15.6%	100%	72.1%	9.0%	17.9%	100%

Table 10.4 *Non-Western arbitrators by citizenship*

No.	Name	Citizenship	Region	Claim.	Resp.	Chair	Annul.	Total
1	Francisco Orrego Vicuña	Chile	South America	31	2	18	1	52
2	Stanimir Alexandrov	Bulgaria	Eastern Europe	1	43	4	3	51
3	Rodrigo Oreamuno	Costa Rica	Central America	0	16	14	6	36
4	Horacio Grigera Naón	Argentina	South America	30	2	2	0	34
5	Claus von Wobeser	Mexico	Central America	1	13	7	3	24
6	Eduardo Zuleta	Colombia	South America	4	2	12	6	24
7	Peter Tomka	Slovakia	Eastern Europe	0	6	8	6	20
8	Raúl Vinuesa	Argentina	South America	1	17	2	0	20
9	Guido Santiago Tawil	Argentina	South America	16	0	0	0	16
10	Ahmed El-Kosheri	Egypt	Middle East	1	5	5	4	15
11	Azzedine Kettani	Morocco	Middle East	0	0	4	9	13
12	Ibrahim Fadlallah	Lebanon	Middle East	8	4	1	0	13
13	Cecil Abraham	Malaysia	South-East Asia	0	0	3	9	12
14	Florentino Feliciano	Philippines	South-East Asia	0	4	3	5	12
15	Kamal Hossain	Bangladesh	South Asia	0	11	0	1	12
16	Michael Hwang	Singapore	South-East Asia	2	4	3	3	12
17	Eduardo Silva Romero	Colombia	South America	0	3	3	5	11
18	Teresa Cheng	Hong Kong	East Asia	0	0	4	7	11
19	Makhdoom Ali Khan	Pakistan	South Asia	0	2	3	5	10
20	Ricardo Ramírez Hernández	Mexico	Central America	1	2	2	4	9
21	Enrique Gómez Pinzón	Colombia	South America	6	0	2	0	8
22	Fali Nariman	India	South Asia	0	3	5	0	8
23	Georges Abi-Saab	Egypt	Middle East	0	9	0	0	8
24	Pedro Nikken	Argentina	South America	0	8	0	0	8
25	Yas Banifatemi	Iran	Middle East	2	3	3	0	8

Table 10.5 Non-Western arbitrators by dominant residence

No.	Name	Residence	Region	Claim.	Resp.	Chair	Annul.	Total
1	Francisco Orrego Vicuña	Chile	South America	31	2	18	1	52
2	Rodrigo Oreamuno	Costa Rica	Central America	0	16	14	6	36
3	Christopher Thomas	Singapore	South-East Asia	1	24	0	0	25
4	Claus von Wobeser	Mexico	Central America	1	13	7	3	24
5	Eduardo Zuleta	Colombia	South America	4	2	12	6	24
6	Raúl Vinuesa	Argentina	South America	1	17	2	0	20
7	Guido Santiago Tawil	Argentina	South America	16	0	0	0	16
8	Ahmed El-Kosheri	Egypt	Middle East	1	5	5	4	15
9	Azzedine Kettani	Morocco	Middle East	0	0	4	9	13
10	Cecil Abraham	Malaysia	South-East Asia	0	0	3	9	12
11	Florentino Feliciano	Philippines	South-East Asia	0	4	3	5	12
12	Kamal Hossain	Bangladesh	South Asia	0	11	0	1	12
13	Michael Hwang	Singapore	South-East Asia	2	4	3	3	12
14	Teresa Cheng	Hong Kong	East Asia	0	0	4	7	11
15	Makhdoom Ali Khan	Pakistan	South Asia	0	2	3	5	10
16	Enrique Gómez Pinzón	Colombia	South America	6	0	2	0	8
17	Fali Nariman	India	South Asia	0	3	5	0	8
18	Pedro Nikken	Argentina	South America	0	8	0	0	8
19	Álvaro Castellanos Howell	Guatemala	Central America	0	0	0	8	8
20	Francisco Rezek	Brazil	South America	0	4	3	0	7
21	Hugo Perezcano Diaz	Mexico	Central America	0	5	2	0	7
22	Cavinder Bull	Singapore	South-East Asia	0	0	5	2	7
23	Neil Kaplan	Hong Kong	East Asia	2	0	5	0	7
24	Hi-Taek Shin	South Korea	South-East Asia	0	0	4	2	6
25	Bohuslav Klein	Czech Republic	Eastern Europe	0	3	3	0	6

drops from 292 in the citizenship-based list to 237 in the dominant residence-based list.

10.5 Analysis

10.5.1 Research Design

How can we determine the influence of nationality on investment arbitration? Traditional doctrinal approaches may provide a fine-grained perspective but it is a demanding task if one wants to provide empirical grounding to these approaches. There are at least two hurdles interfering with the methodology. The first relates to the complexity of the term 'nationality'. The latter, as the chapter suggests, shall account not only for citizenship but also for the dominant residence of arbitrators. The second concerns the collegial pattern of decision-making, forcing one to account for all the individual members without knowing their personal views.[40] Given the aggregative nature of the research problem, it would require a 'qualitative large-N' approach, synthesizing patterns over a massive volume of awards. Moreover, the disadvantage of a doctrinal lens is that one may be simply tracking a 'subterfuge of verbiage' – doctrinal twists may only be loosely related to actual outcomes.[41] Thus, analysing the influence of citizenship and the dominant residence of arbitrators requires the full arsenal of empirical methods – qualitative, quantitative and computational. In this chapter, we use quantitative methods and focus on the potential influence of arbitrator citizenship and dominant residence on outcomes in investor–state arbitration. Its prime advantage is its focus on the largely concrete nature of decisions and remedies, which cannot be obscured by written reasoning or oral speech. In other words, the chapter prefers core factual data (such as citizenship, dominant residence and outcomes of awards) to the various secondary sources and by-products of the process, such as arbitrators' speeches and academic publications.

In this chapter, we focus on the final outcome at the merits stage and on jurisdictional decisions where jurisdiction is rejected. To ensure comparability across individual cases, we analyse only cases whose legal

---

[40] One earlier study relied on interviews in order to uncover the collegial patterns: see Todd Tucker, 'Inside the Black Box: Collegial Patterns on Investment Tribunals' (2016) 7 *Journal of International Dispute Settlement* 183.

[41] Malcolm Langford and Daniel Behn, 'Managing Backlash: The Evolving Investment Arbitrator?' (2018) 29(2) *European Journal of International Law* 551.

claim is treaty-based. Claims based exclusively on a contract or a host state's FDI law are excluded; discontinued or settled cases are also omitted, along with a further six cases where the identity of the arbitrators is unknown. With these conditions in place, and as at 1 August 2018, the dataset includes 422 *finally resolved* treaty-based arbitration cases. These include all known investment treaty arbitration cases where the claimant-investor wins on the merits or loses on jurisdiction or the merits. Of course, cases can also be sliced another way and Waibel and Wu analyse the discrete jurisdiction and merit decisions.[42] While this increases the sample size, we are unsure as to whether it captures the potential influence of citizenship – which may affect the case as a whole rather than particular legal determinations. In any event, our approach provides a useful complement.

One issue in coding outcomes in investment treaty arbitration is the measurement of how and to what degree a claimant-investor can be said to win at the jurisdiction or liability/merits stage of the dispute. Our database provides some nuance and makes a distinction between full wins and partial wins. This results in two different indicators. The first is Any Win (at least a partial win) and the second is Full Win (only full wins counted).[43] In this chapter, we conduct analysis for both outcome indicators although only results for the former are fully reported.[44] The Any Win indicator is the most reliable measure as distinguishing partial wins from full wins is dependent on discretionary assessments. It is also a strong analytical measure: failing to award anything to a claimant-investor is a stark outcome given the costs involved in litigating this type of international investment dispute. Table 10.6 shows the Any Win ratios based on distinctions between compositions of panel according to arbitrator nationality, from the fully Western panel (WWW) to the fully non-Western panel (OOO).

---

[42] See Michael Waibel and Yanhui Wu, 'Are Arbitrators Political? Evidence from International Investment Arbitration', *Working Paper*, January 2017.

[43] For *Any Win* (full and partials wins are coded as (1) and losses as (0)); and for a *Full Win* (full win coded as (1) and partial wins and losses as (0)). At the liability/merits stage, a full and partial win are not categorized according to the ratio of amount claimed and awarded or the number of successful claims. Rather, the distinction between full win and partial win is based on whether the claimant-investor – in a holistic assessment of the case – was made whole by the arbitral tribunal. At the jurisdiction stage, a full win is scored when no jurisdictional objections are sustained, and a partial win is scored where the jurisdiction of the tribunal is restricted in scope.

[44] Full results are available from the authors.

Table 10.6 *Panel composition and outcomes (by citizenship)*

Panel composition citizenship				Outcomes			
Category	Claimant	Chair	Resp.	Investor Any Win	Investor Loss	Win %	No Cases
1	W	W	W	113	93	54.9	206
2	W	O	W	11	23	32.4	34
3	O	W	W	24	23	51.1	47
4	W	W	O	51	40	56.0	91
5	W	O	O	2	6	25.0	8
6	O	W	O	9	8	52.9	17
7	O	O	W	3	4	42.9	7
8	O	O	O	6	7	46.6	13

W=Western, O=Non-Western

Eye-balling the trends, it is relatively clear that for many compositions there does not appear to be a difference in outcomes as compared with the overall win–loss rate in investment treaty arbitration – which hovers around 50 per cent. The overall outcome rate across all investment treaty arbitrations to date is 48.2 per cent in favour of claimant-investors. The most notable difference is in categories 2, 5, 7 and 8 in which there is a non-Western national as *presiding arbitrator*. Here foreign investor success rates are considerably lower and vary between 25 and 46 per cent Whether this is statistically significant and holds for dominant residence as well will be taken up in the next sub-section.

10.5.2 Operationalization

In seeking to test the nationality hypotheses, we have operationalized the first two home region bias hypotheses (H1.2 and H1.3) into three different models. Each model tests different ways in which nationality may be influential. The first, and following Franck, is the presence of a non-Western arbitrator in the most important role in arbitration – the presiding arbitrator. Given that the presiding arbitrator usually has the responsibility in drafting much of the award and presumably possesses the crucial swing vote, it is likely any nationality effect will be substantially transmitted in this role. The second model seeks to examine the potential influence of a non-Western arbitrator on the arbitral tribunal, regardless of which role they have. This model picks up any potential benefits of mere geographic diversity, which may have some effect on intra-panel discussions, framing and deliberations. The third model looks at each possible panel combination – it is more complex but is in essence a combination of the first two. Thus, we examine the eight different panel composition possibilities along the non-Western/Western binary ranging from a panel with only Western arbitrators (WWW) to a panel with only non-Western arbitrators (OOO). Here, we can see if particular panel compositions may swing more in one direction than others. Thus, does the presence of two non-Western arbitrators make a difference or is there a difference between having a non-Western arbitrator as a claimant-appointed wing rather than a respondent-appointed wing?

In order to avoid potentially misleading bivariate results for the correlation between these three indicators and investment treaty arbitration outcomes, we include also a set of controls for each model. The basic attributes are summarized in Table 10.7 alongside the independent variables. First, we include a dummy variable for treaty-based arbitration type, specifically *NAFTA-based* cases, *Energy Charter Treaty-based (ECT)* cases and *ICSID-administered* cases.[45] Second, we apply an *Extractive Case* dummy measuring whether the investment leading to a claim is in the extractive industries economic sector. These cases often involve varying degrees of nationalization with the dispute centring on levels of compensation not liability (and thus claimant-investors will be more likely to win). Third, we add a measure of *Law Firm Advantage* to control for the effect of the quality (or at least the expense) of legal counsel as measured by whether claimant-investors and respondent states retained counsel from a Global 100 law firm.[46] Fourth, we include a dummy variable for *State Learning* to control for the effect of previous exposure to investment arbitration. Fifth, to control for situations where specific events or circumstances create an artificially large caseload against a

---

[45] We include this dummy because NAFTA-based and ECT-based arbitrations are the most frequently used IIAs in investment treaty arbitration, while ICSID-administered arbitrations are based on a specific treaty (the ICSID Convention) with some specific structural features.

[46] See *American Lawyer,* <law.com/americanlawyer/sites/americanlawyer/2017/09/25/the-2017-global-100>. The dummy takes the value of (1) if only the claimant-investor counsel is from a Global 100 law firm; −1) if only the respondent state retains a Global 100 law firm; or (0) if both the claimant-investor and the respondent state both have the same type of law firm representing them.

Table 10.7 *Summary statistics for regression analysis*

Variable	Mean	Std. Dev.	Min.	Max.	Observations
Dependent					
Any Win	0.469	0.500	0	1	422
Full Win	0.225	0.418	0	1	422
Independent					
Chair (Citizenship-West)	0.832	0.375	0	1	422
Chair (Residence-West)	0.867	0.340	0	1	422
Non-West Presence (Citizenship)	0.514	0.500	0	1	422
Non-West Presence (Residence)	0.403	0.491	0	1	422
Panel Comp. (Citizenship WWW-OOO)	1.543	1.874	1	8	422
Panel Comp. (Residence WWW-OOO)	1.244	1.825	1	8	422
Controls					
Extractive Case	0.171	0.377	0	1	422
NAFTA Case	0.088	0.283	0	1	422
ECT Case	0.095	0.293	0	1	422
ICSID Case	0.621	0.486	0	1	422
Law Firm Advantage	−0.081	0.584	−1	1	421
Case Learning	9.384	10.007	1	55	422
Case Cluster	0.142	0.350	0	1	422
WBIG	1.986	0.798	0	3	422
Trend	12,723.3	6,816.401	1	25,000	422

respondent state in a short space of time, we use a *Case Cluster* dummy.[47] Sixth, we include a variable to capture GNI per capita (WBIGs) particularly since it has been found in previous work that respondent states with higher GNI per capita are less likely to lose.[48] Finally, we have included a cubic year trend variable in all models.

---

[47] This measure takes the value (1) if a respondent state has had five or more cases registered against it in a given year, and (0) otherwise.

[48] Behn, Berge and Langford (n. 4). Here, we have used WBIGs, but the results with the continuous GNI per capita variable were not different.

10.5.3 Regression Results

Table 10.8 presents the logit regression results for the three different models by arbitrator citizenship and location of dominant residence. The logit regression determines the probability that each variable contributes to a win for the claimant-investor. A positive coefficient means that the variable contributes to the likelihood of a claimant-investor winning something; a negative coefficient indicates an inverse relationship. Table 10.8 shows the results for Any Win for all claimant-investors, but we note that almost identical results are obtained when the dependent variable is a *FullWin*. The same occurs when we remove the 40 cases with Western states as respondents – in order to test whether Western arbitrators display different behaviour towards Western states compared to non-Western states.

Viewing the first model, the presence of a Western presiding arbitrator is correlated with a greater likelihood of a claimant-investor winning (39 per cent more likely) but the relationship is not statistically significant – although it is close to the zone of significance with a p-score of 0.165. However, in Model 1A, where non-Western arbitrators residing in the West are classified as Western, this correlation drops dramatically. Here, the group of Western' arbitrators are only slightly more likely to vote for respondent states. These two sets of results lead to a surprising and unanticipated outcome. Non-Western presiding arbitrators living in the West are most likely to favour a non-Western respondent state.

Turning to the second model, we see that the mere presence of a non-Western arbitrator anywhere on the panel is positively correlated with claimant-investor success. Notably, this is statistically significant for arbitrators whose dominant residence is not in the West. This possibly suggests a reverse bias but may be a result of different panel compositions.

In the third model, we examine which type of panel composition is most likely to favour claimant-investors when compared with a panel of all Western arbitrators, and the results confirm and clarify the divergent directions of the first two models. A panel with a non-Western presiding arbitrator follows the same pattern as Model 1. They are less likely to support claimant-investors as a whole, but panels with non-Western arbitrators living in their home regions are more likely to side with 'their' claimant-investors. The remainder of the panel compositions generally follow expected voting with one exception. Panels with non-Western respondent wings are more likely to vote in favour of claimant-investors.

Thus, we identify a partly reverse bias result when there is a non-Western arbitrator presence on the panel and when the respondent wing arbitrator is

Table 10.8 *Regression analysis*

Any Win	Controls	Model 1	Model 1A	Model 2	Model 2A	Model 3	Model 3A
		West Chair by Cit.	West Chair by Res.	Non-West Presence by Cit.	Non-West Presence by Res.	Panel Comp. by Cit.	Panel Comp. by Res.
Western Chair		0.387	−0.045				
Non-West Presence				0.048	0.413*		
Panel Comp., WWW as base							
WOW						−0.688	0.400
OWW						0.2015	0.515
WWO						0.258	0.655**
OWO						−0.626	−0.395
WOO						0.098	−0.243
OOW						−0.025	−0.211
OOO						0.0618	0.172
Controls							
ICSID Case	−0.224	−0.200	−0.221	−0.221	−0.217	−0.174	−0.207
NAFTA Case	−0.766*	−0.819*	−0.567	−0.587	−0.752	−0.755	−0.992
ECT Case	0.269	0.249	0.211	0.222	0.299	0.266	0.293
Extractive Case	0.495*	0.510*	0.397	0.396	0.374	0.424	0.372
Law Firm Adv.	0.372**	0.366**	0.403**	0.399**	0.394*	0.367*	0.350*
Case Learning	0.012	0.013	0.011	0.012	0.011	0.0122	0.013
Case Cluster	0.413	0.422	0.274	0.270	0.300	0.307	0.265
WBIG	−0.32**	−0.324**	−0.258*	−0.254*	−0.253*	−0.265*	−0.261*
Trend	−0.001	−0.001	−0.001	−0.001	−0.001	−.0000161	−.0000147
Constant	0.725	0.427	0.633	0.564	0.368	0.5424523	0.4000221
Sample Size	421	421	421	421	421	421	421

* Statistically significant at 0.10 level; ** Statistically significant at 0.05 level; *** Statistically significant at 0.01 level

GEOGRAPHIC DIVERSITY & INVESTMENT ARBITRATION   311

Table 10.9 *Dissents by arbitrator and outcome*

	Dissent by claim.-appointed arbitrator		Dissent by resp.-appointed arbitrator		
	Losing party arbitrator	Winning party arbitrator	Losing party arbitrator	Winning party arbitrator	Total
Non-Western	13	1	13	1	28 (37%)
Western	20	9	17	2	48 (63%)
Total	33	10	30	3	76

non-Western; and this might be explained when looking at the presence of dissents. Non-Western arbitrators dissent at greater proportions than Western arbitrators: see Table 10.9. They account for 37 per cent of all dissents and 41 per cent of dissents that side with that of the losing party; yet they account for only 26 per cent of all arbitrator appointments. In other words, it is not uncommon for a non-Western arbitrator to dissent in cases in which claimant investors win. However, examining only unanimous decisions and using a multinomial logit regression model that distinguishes unanimous from majority decisions, the result still holds. Non-Western respondent-appointed arbitrators are more likely to be on panels that favour claimant-investors. Our hypothesis for this finding is that it can be explained by their lack of experience. Their comparative lack of symbolic capital and practical knowledge of the system may affect their ability to influence the chair in comparison to well-established Western arbitrators – this is a hypothesis in need of further investigation.

10.5.4   *Claimant Investor Bias and Regional Analysis*

The final question concerns whether citizenship affects outcomes for claimant-investors if the party-appointed arbitrator is from the same state or the same part of the world[49] as the citizenship of the party that appointed her or him. The descriptive statistics in Table 10.10 set out the correlation between a non-Western arbitrator's home state/region and

---

[49] The chapter has earlier identified the following regions: South America; Central America & Caribbean; Eastern Europe & Central Asia; Middle East; South-East Asia; Sub-Saharan Africa; South Asia; East Asia. See Section 10.4.2.

Table 10.10 *Investor success rates by nationality*

	Claimant home state				Respondent host state				All cases	
	Same state		Same region		Same state		Same region			
All finally resolved cases										
Investor any win	24	31%	48	23%	29	40%	61	39%	234	32%
Investor loss	40	51%	79	37%	31	42%	59	38%	251	34%
Settled	8	10%	62	29%	9	12%	23	15%	163	22%
Discontinued	6	8%	22	11%	4	6%	12	8%	92	12%
Total	78		211		73		155		740	
All cases excluding settled and discontinued										
Investor any win	24	37%	48	38%	29	48%	61	51%	234	48%
Investor loss	40	63%	79	62%	31	52%	59	49%	251	52%
Total	64		127		60		120		485	

the outcomes for investors/states from those home states/regions. The results are the reverse of what are expected. Claimant-investors with a claimant-appointed arbitrator that shares the same home state/region are likely to do worse than are investors who choose arbitrators that come from other regions – although these arbitrators do tend to dissent more frequently when their party loses.

For respondent states, there is no correlation. This is interesting given that in other international courts there is a strong correlation between a judge's nationality and how she or he votes in regard to parties from their own states/regions. A multinomial logit regression of the eight possible combinations of Western and non-Western claimant-investor nationality, states and outcomes revealed similar correlations but none was statistically significant.

10.6 Conclusion and Prospects

The lack of geographic diversity among arbitrators sitting on international investment arbitration tribunals is a common refrain in the critiques of the regime for the international regulation of foreign investment. Our survey of 1,228 past and present investor–state cases show that arbitrators from outside the West represent a clear minority even though the overwhelming majority of cases concern respondent states that are non-Western. The appointment system has shown some signs of improvement on geographic diversity in recent years with high proportions of non-Western arbitrators coming into the system. A few of these are gaining multiple appointments. However, the system remains strongly marked by exclusiveness rather than inclusiveness, underlining legitimacy concerns. Non-Western arbitrators are mostly appointed by states as the respondent wing and much less likely to land the prestigious and influential role as presiding arbitrator. When they are nominated in this role, it is overwhelmingly by arbitral institutions and not by the parties or the co-arbitrators. Moreover, half of these non-Western arbitrators are from a single region: Latin America. The rest of the world is weakly represented, whether Eastern Europe, Asia, Africa or the Middle East.

Our statistical analysis shows, however, that nationality may not matter that much for actual outcomes – providing a wrinkle in legitimacy critiques. However, there is one sign of home region bias. Panels with non-Western presiding arbitrators tend to favour non-Western respondent states more than their counterparts. The result, nonetheless, lies just outside the zone of statistical significance. Moreover, the mere presence of non-Western arbitrators on a tribunal tends to increase the chance of a claimant-investor succeeding; and panels that include such arbitrators are more likely to be critical of claimant-investors from their own state/region. Thus, any change to the system that merely increases geographic diversity is unlikely to have material effects on outcomes. It may increase the regime's sociological legitimacy – and thus compliance or a lower likelihood of seeking annulment or appealing in a future review mechanism – but is unlikely on current trends (as at August 2018) to dramatically change the nature of outcomes. However, this prediction only applies to the current system of international investment with its myriad of constraints, incentives and cultures. Should we move to a multilateral investment court, as proposed by the European Union, it would be an open question as to whether nationality might play this subdued or negligible role in a new juridical landscape. In that respect, experiences from the ICJ, WTO and ECHR may be more relevant in predicting future trajectories.

11

Mixing Methodologies in Empirically Investigating Investment Arbitration and Inbound Foreign Investment

SHIRO ARMSTRONG AND LUKE NOTTAGE[*]

11.1 Introduction

This chapter illustrates the potential and challenges of mixing methods[1] in empirically investigating treaty-based investor–state dispute settlement (ISDS). It focuses on three issues raised by policy-makers and wider public discussion in recent years:

- Do ISDS provisions lead to more cross-border foreign direct investment (FDI)?
- Do investors need and (threaten to) use ISDS-backed protections when investing abroad?
- Does offering ISDS lead to excessive costs to host states, directly or (via 'regulatory chill') indirectly?

---

[*] Respectively, Associate Professor, Crawford School of Public Policy, Australian National University; Professor of Comparative and Transnational Business Law, University of Sydney. Updated version of a paper presented at the PluriCourts book project conference on 'Empirical Perspectives on the Legitimacy of International Investment Tribunals', Oslo University, 27 August 2015. We acknowledge helpful feedback from conference participants as well as Axel Berger. We are grateful to Dr Son Chu for superb research assistance and input regarding Section 11.2 of this chapter and the related Appendix A (prepared primarily by Armstrong). We also thank Luca Moretti and Angus Nicholas for general research and editorial assistance, especially regarding Sections 11.3 and 11.4 (prepared primarily by Nottage). Any and all errors throughout the chapter remain our own. This chapter also draws on support from an Australian Research Council Discovery Project (DP140102526) (2014–2018), jointly with Professors Jurgen Kurtz and Leon Trakman.

[1] For another recent mixed-method study, see Lauge N. Skovgaard Poulsen, *Bounded Rationality and Economic Diplomacy: The Politics of Investment Treaties in Developing Countries* (Cambridge University Press, 2015), reviewed in Luke Nottage, 'Rebalancing Investment Treaties and Investor-State Arbitration: Two Approaches' (2016) 17 *Journal of World Investment and Trade* 1015. See also, generally, e.g. James Mahoney and Gary Goetz, 'A Tale of Two Cultures: Contrasting Quantitative and Qualitative Research' (2006) 14 *Political Analysis* 227.

The first question is amenable to quantitative analysis, and Section 11.2 below sets out our approach to methodological challenges and some intriguing econometric results.[2] However, model specification and interpretation of results can benefit from qualitative (survey- or interview-based) research. That approach is also best suited to answering the latter two questions above. Yet there can be even more difficulties in carrying out such qualitative research, especially when it is supplemented by involvement in public inquiries into ISDS and investment treaties, as indicated in Section 11.3. By way of conclusion, Section 11.4 briefly identifies various heuristics and biases that seem to influence both proponents and opponents of ISDS. These too need to be factored into ongoing research, particularly in qualitative studies, and into effective presentation of empirical results.

Our chapter draws on a project investigating the three research questions, and others associated with ISDS such as its potential impact on governance in host states, with a particular focus on appropriate international investment dispute management for Australia in regional context.[3] The Australian Government's Productivity Commission was critical of ISDS when posing these questions in a 2010 Report.[4] Along with the first-ever ISDS claim filed against Australia (in 2011, by Philip Morris Asia regarding tobacco plain packaging legislation), arguably illustrating the costs of ISDS to host states,[5] the 2010 Report encouraged a centre-left coalition government to refuse to accept ISDS provisions in future treaties from 2011. Centre-right governments in power since 2013 have reverted to agreeing to ISDS on a case-by-case basis.[6] Yet Australia's experience has often been mentioned in the ongoing worldwide debates over ISDS.[7] Indeed, in October 2017 a new centre-left

---

[2] Replicating the study in Section 11.2 below but adding a more Asia-specific focus, finding similar results, see Shiro Armstrong 'The Impact of Investment Treaties and ISDS Provisions on FDI in Asia and Globally', in J. Chaisse and L. Nottage (eds.), *International Investment Treaties and Arbitration Across Asia* (Brill, 2018) p. 57.

[3] See Shiro Armstrong et al., 'The Fundamental Importance of Foreign Direct Investment to Australia in the 21st Century: Reforming Treaty and Dispute Resolution Practice' (2013) 13/90 *Sydney Law School Research Paper* <ssrn.com/abstract=2362122>.

[4] <pc.gov.au/inquiries/completed/trade-agreements/report>.

[5] See Jarrod Hepburn and Luke Nottage, 'A Procedural Win for Public Health Measures' (2017) 18 *Journal of World Investment and Trade* 307.

[6] Jurgen Kurtz and Luke Nottage, 'Investment Treaty Arbitration 'Down Under': Policy and Politics in Australia' (2015) 30(2) *ICSID Review* 465.

[7] In a recent comparative project <cigionline.org/series/investor-state-arbitration>, see e.g. Luke Nottage, 'Investor-State Arbitration Policy and Practice in Australia', in A. de

coalition government in New Zealand similarly announced that it would not agree to ISDS in its new treaties.[8] Empirically informed debates, inquiries and policy positions in Australia are also significant, particularly for major regional free trade agreements (FTAs) such as the Comprehensive and Progressive Agreement for Trans-Pacific Partnership (CPTPP, signed on 8 March 2018 but not yet fully in force)[9] and the Regional Comprehensive Economic Partnership (or 'ASEAN+6' FTA, under negotiation since late 2012).[10]

11.2 Methodology in Econometric Analysis of Foreign Investment

11.2.1 Empirical Literature Review

Quantitative empirical research into the effects on bilateral FDI from international investment agreements in general, and bilateral investment treaties (BITs) in particular, started to expand only from the late 1990s.[11]

Mestral (ed.), *Second Thoughts: Investor-State Arbitration between Developed Democracies* (Centre for International Governance Innovation, 2017) p. 377, abridged then updated in Luke Nottage, *International Commercial and Investor-State Arbitration: Australia and Japan in Regional and Global Contexts* (Elgar, 2021).

[8] Amokura Kawharu and Luke Nottage, 'Has ISDS Gone Rogue for Australia and New Zealand? CPTPP (C-3PO), RCEP (R2-D2) and Beyond' (2019) *Yearbook on International Investment Law and Policy 2017*, ch. 25.

[9] See <dfat.gov.au/trade/agreements/in-force/cptpp/Pages/comprehensive-and-progressive-agreement-for-trans-pacific-partnership.aspx>; and, regarding its predecessor (with a mostly similar investment chapter), Luke Nottage, 'The TPP Investment Chapter and Investor-State Arbitration in Asia and Oceania: Assessing Prospects for Ratification' (2016) 17(2) *Melbourne Journal of International Law* 313.

[10] See <https://www.dfat.gov.au/trade/agreements/not-yet-in-force/rcep>; and analysis of a draft investment chapter (leaked in late 2015) in Amokura Kawharu and Luke Nottage, 'Models for Investment Treaties in the Asian Region: An Underview' (2017) 34(3) *Arizona Journal of International and Comparative* Law 461.

[11] See studies surveyed in UNCTAD 'The Impact of International Investment Agreements on Foreign Direct Investment: An Overview of Empirical Studies 1998–2014' (September 2014); Jonathan Bonnitcha, Lauge N. Skovgaard Poulsen and Micgael Waibel, *The Political Economy of the Investment Treaty Regime* (Oxford University Press, 2017), especially at 158–64 (critically summarising 'quantitative studies on the impact of investment treaties on FDI'); and Joachim Pohl 'Societal Benefits and Costs of International Investment Agreements: A Critical Review of Aspects and Available Evidence', *OECD Working Paper on International Investment* 2018/01, <oecd-ilibrary.org/finance-and-investment/societal-benefits-and-costs-of-international-investment-agreements_e5f85c3d-en> especially at 16–31, also discussing some of the methodological difficulties mentioned in this chapter.

This was despite the fact that many BITs had been adopted before this, and signings in fact accelerated from the early 1990s.[12] The expanding research trajectory has been associated with the increasing availability of data on bilateral FDI at the aggregate country level, thanks to more unified and comprehensive data measurement and collection efforts by international and national investment authorities. Yet the data remains quite limited in that types of FDI and bilateral sectoral data are not widely available (as indicated towards the end of our Statistical Appendix), and there are many gaps in reporting.

Albeit with qualifications, such empirical studies estimating the impact of investment treaties on FDI can provide insights into the ongoing policy debate. Yet results vary in the existing empirical literature. While many studies find BITs help to increase FDI, other studies do not.[13] A closer examination reveals two important methodological issues that may have significant bearing on the findings and conclusions of such research.

First, there seems to be lack of agreement or consistency among researchers in adopting an analytical framework underlying the choice of an empirical model. While there exists a substantial body of theoretical literature on FDI, the majority of empirical studies have adopted the gravity-type model, which was developed for trade flows, to examine the determinants of FDI. The gravity model of trade suggests that trade is larger, the larger the countries trading and the closer they are. The popular application of the gravity model to FDI flows may be due to a fact that several key determinants of trade flows are similar to the determinants of FDI flows – this is because trade and FDI are deeply

---

[12] Poulsen argues that the acceleration among developing countries was driven by 'bounded rationality', namely 'motivated reasoning' that made them optimistically want and hope for investment treaties to result in more inbound investment, uncritically accepted evidence in favour of their pre-conception and discounting contrary evidence: Poulsen (n. 1), 17–18.

[13] UNCTAD 2014 (n. 11); Christian Bellak, 'Survey of the Impact of Bilateral Investment Agreements on Foreign Direct Investment', in Australian APEC Study Centre at RMIT (ed.), Current Issues in Asia-Pacific Foreign Direct Investment (2015), 70 <mams.rmit .edu.au/cwgz1keqt2r8.pdf>. See also recent econometric studies focusing on China or regionally for the Asia Development Bank, summarised in Luke Nottage, 'Rebalancing Investment Treaties and Arbitration in the Asian Region', in Mahdev Mohan and Chester Brown (eds.), *Regulation and Investment Disputes: Asian Perspectives* (Cambridge University Press, 2021). Finding a positive impact on FDI from India's (ISDS-backed) investment treaties but on a cumulative basis, see also Jaivir Singh, 'Indian Investment Treaty Practice: Qualitatively and Quantitatively Assessing Recent Developments' in Luke Nottage et al (eds.), *New Frontiers in Asia-Pacific International Arbitration and Dispute Resolution* (Wolters Kluwer, 2021) p. 287.

endogenous. Portes and Rey suggest that the gravity approach emerges naturally from theories of asset trade.[14] Blonigen notes that 'a gravity specification actually fits cross-country data on FDI reasonably well'.[15] But unlike trade flows that are determined by multiple-agent demand-side factors, FDI activities are driven by the behaviour of multinational enterprises (MNEs) motivated by at least two other factors: to gain market access in the face of trade frictions or barriers (horizontal FDI) and to access input cost differences as a part of a production process (vertical FDI).[16]

Accordingly, the Knowledge-Capital Model ('KCM')[17] has proven to be appropriate in accounting for distinct motivations of MNEs that can be tested empirically with available secondary data on GDP and resource endowments of a country. Therefore, a small number of studies have explicitly adopted the KCM in examining the BIT impact on FDI flows, among its key determinants. But complexity of the model variables and data quality issues often lead to unexpected coefficient signs in the KCM.[18] Nevertheless, it is important to take into account the additional impact of these determinants on the quantitative changes in FDI flows between countries in any empirical investigation of BIT impact. The complex theoretical background behind FDI flows suggests that the search for proper model specifications is still evolving, with the model selection also being driven by data quality and availability.

Second, the findings of significant effects of BITs on FDI seem to depend substantially on dealing with endogeneity problems in model estimation. A number of studies that found strong and significant effects of BITs on FDI face scrutiny for inadequately addressing endogeneity problems.[19] Empirical studies have identified two important causes of

---

[14] Richard Portes and Hélène Rey, 'The Determinants of Cross-Border Equity Flows' (2005) 65(2) *Journal of International Economics* 269, 275.

[15] Bruce A. Blonigen, 'A Review of the Empirical Literature on FDI Determinants' (2005) 33 (4) *Atlantic Economic Journal* 383, 393.

[16] Ibid.

[17] Developed by James R. Markusen, Anthony J. Venables, Denise Eby Konan, Kevin H. Zhang, 'A Unified Treatment of Horizontal Direct Investment, Vertical Direct Investment, and the Pattern of Trade in Goods and Services' (1996) 5696 *NBER Working Paper*, <nber.org/papers/w5696>; and James R. Markusen, 'Trade versus Investment Liberalization' (1997) 5696 *NBER Working Paper*, <nber.org/papers/w6231>.

[18] Blonigen (n. 15).

[19] Emma Aisbett, 'Bilateral Investment Treaties and Foreign Direct Investment: Correlation Versus Causation', in Sauvant and Sachs (eds.), *The Effect of Treaties on Foreign Direct Investment: Bilateral Investment Treaties, Double Taxation Treaties, and Investments Flows* (Oxford University Press, 2009) p. 395. She suggests that studies that fail to

320   SHIRO ARMSTRONG AND LUKE NOTTAGE

endogeneity affecting consistency of BIT impact estimation: reverse causality and omitted variables.

Reverse causality results from interdependence between the time-series nature of FDI flows and formation of BITs or FTAs. The conclusion of treaties between two countries in a particular year is in some cases more likely to result from the increased investment flows or substantial investment relations in previous years.[20] In addition, FDI flows are often path-dependent, leading to the potential problem of autocorrelation.[21] Omitted variables in bilateral FDI models arise from unobserved individual-country or country-pair effects or heterogeneity. These effects might be time-invariant or time-variant. For example, an increase in FDI flows and a decision on BIT participation may happen at the same time as the investment climate improves in a host country.[22]

In dealing with such endogeneity problems, there are two popular approaches: a fixed effects estimator with additional dummy variable controls and the dynamic panel estimator. Aisbett undertook a study adopting the first approach.[23] Apart from the Ordinary Least Squares ('OLS') fixed effects estimator, the endogenous adoption of BITs is controlled for by using three sets of dummies: (i) host-year dummies; (ii) source-year dummies and (iii) a country-pair time trend. With this approach to addressing endogeneity, Aisbett's study found that establishing a BIT does not have a significant impact on FDI flows between a source OECD country and a developing host country, despite the positive sign of estimated coefficients on BITs. While this approach might be effective in dealing with endogeneity problems in a panel data model of FDI flows, the final set of estimates is much less informative, with only the BIT coefficient remaining. Moreover, there could be a computational problem arising from estimating a large dataset with a long-time period and large number of country-pairs.[24] The use of a large number of

---

consider endogeneity problems tend to find a more significant and stronger impact from BIT provisions.

[20] UNCTAD 2014 (n. 11).

[21] Peter Egger and Michael Pfaffermayr, 'The Impact of Bilateral Investment Treaties on Foreign Direct Investment' (2004) 32(4) *Journal of Comparative Economics* 788; Jennifer L. Tobin and Susan Rose-Ackerman, 'When BITs Have Some Bite: The Political-economic Environment for Bilateral Investment Treaties' (2011) 6(1) *Review of International Organizations* 1.

[22] UNCTAD 2014 (n. 11).

[23] Aisbett (n. 19).

[24] Arjan Lejour and Maria Salfi, 'The Regional Impact of Bilateral Investment Treaties on Foreign Direct Investment', *CBP Discussion Paper 298* (2014), <econpapers.repec.org/paper/cpbdiscus/298.htm>.

MIXING METHODOLOGIES IN INVESTMENT ARBITRATION   321

dummy variables across multiple dimensions also runs the risk of reducing the variability in the data and therefore making it more difficult to estimate the statistical significance of the key coefficients of interest.

By contrast, the dynamic panel estimator (i.e. Generalised Method of Moments or 'GMM') has been adopted by some studies, particularly more recent ones. This estimation method appears to be effective in dealing with the dynamic nature of FDI and the endogenous formation of BITs by using instrumental variables. An advantage of this approach is its exploitation of lags of endogenous variables as instrumental variables, and correction for serial autocorrelation by using differenced forms of the estimation model. Such estimation results address the endogeneity problem of explanatory variables, particularly BITs.

Related to the problem of omitted variables, one important issue is whether and how the BIT impact is contingent or dependent on the FDI recipient countries' domestic business environment. Most studies examine the role of the domestic legal and policy environment in their empirical models with various proxies, such as a political risk index, a political constraint measure or an institutional quality index. Some studies take into account this factor through their interactions with BITs.[25] While the inclusion of a proxy for a country's domestic business environment is common and generally significant alongside the effect of the BIT, the role of BITs as a risk insurance device is less clear.[26] Contrary to a common expectation that BITs are more effective in attracting FDI in a more institutionally risky or politically unstable country,[27] BITs have been found to be associated with more inward FDI flows in countries that have a *better* domestic business environment, or to have little correlation with political and institutional regimes.[28]

Overall, some studies have found that the impact of BITs has become smaller over time. The underlying hypothesis is based on two reasons.

---

[25] See e.g. Rodolphe Desbordes and Vincent Vicard, 'Foreign Direct Investment and Bilateral Investment Treaties: An International Political Perspective' (2009) 37(3) *Journal of Comparative Economics* 372; Matthias Busse, Jens Königer and Peter Nunnenkamp, 'FDI Promotion through Bilateral Investment Treaties: More Than a BIT?' (2010) 146(1) *Review of World Economics* 147; and Tobin and Rose-Ackerman (n. 21).

[26] Jason Yackee, 'Bilateral Investment Treaties, Credible Commitment, and the Rule of (International) Law: Do BITs Promote Foreign Direct Investment?' (2008) 42(4) *Law & Society Review* 805.

[27] Eric Neumayer and Laura Spess, 'Do Bilateral Investment Treaties Increase Foreign Direct Investment to Developing Countries?' (2005) 3(1) *World Development* 31.

[28] Yackee (n. 26); Tobin and Rose-Ackerman (n. 21).

First, competition for FDI between countries has meant domestic legal and policy environments for investors – both foreign and domestic – have been improving over time. Second, there are competition effects from having more BITs. Given the tendency for more and more countries to protect rights of foreign investors by signing more BITs or FTAs, there has been more competition among countries to offer preferential treatments for the same sources of FDI, thus resulting in a decreasing marginal effect from such investment treaties.

Finally, there is a growing trend to focus on specific provisions in BITs to examine whether those aspects matter in influencing foreign investors' decisions to invest (and the scale of such investments) in a host country. Some efforts have been made to quantitatively assess the separate impact of BIT provisions on bilateral FDI. Much of that work has been made possible due to the contribution of international law scholars in assessing the contents of BITs to define and measure the strength of BITs and their specific provisions. Studies examining the detailed contents of BITs suggest significant variation in the degree of foreign investor protection and support depending on the particular provisions of each BIT.[29] Among common areas of negotiations found in BITs, those that attract the most attention in empirical studies are national treatment (NT), most favoured nation (MFN) and investor–state arbitration or ISDS mechanisms. The NT and MFN provisions appear to be most relevant when considering differences in BIT strength because they can embody important commitments relating to both the liberalisation and the protection of FDI.

In the first notable study of differentiated BIT impact, Yackee classified about 1,000 BITs between developing and major capital exporting countries in the period 1945–2002 into two categories, strong BITs and weak BITs, based on the strength of their dispute settlement provisions. The strong BITs are ones that provide investors from the capital exporting countries access to ISDS. These BITs contain prior consent from the host state to allow foreign investors to make claims to arbitration in a wide variety of treaty-related disputes.[30] More recently, Berger et al. extended the analysis of specific aspects of BIT strength and coverage to pre-

---

[29] Axel Berger et al., 'Do Trade and Investment Agreements Lead to More FDI? Accounting for Key Provisions Inside the Black Box' (2013) 10(2) *International Economics and Economic Policy* 247.

[30] Yackee (n. 26), 806, 813–14.

establishment NT and MFN clauses. In addition, the coverage of their study was broadened to investment chapters in FTAs.[31]

A subsequent study by Chaisse and Bellak contains the most comprehensive breakdown of BITs and the investment-related provisions of FTAs.[32] They carried out an assessment and coding of all-important provisions of such treaties based on degrees of liberalisation and protection for FDI. These provisions are: Definition of Investment, Admission versus Establishment, NT, MFN, Fair and Equitable Treatment, Direct and Indirect Expropriation, Free Transfer of Investment-related Funds, Non-economic Standards, ISDS, Umbrella Clause and Temporal Scope of Application. As a result, they constructed a database comprising a BIT index, called BITSel.[33] The BITSel can measure the overall strength of BITs for FDI protection by constructing a composite index of BITs using a factor analysis or principal component analysis.[34] Such an index arguably provides the most sophisticated measure currently available, but methodological problems arise from various measurement errors.[35]

Despite the widespread expectation that more liberal and/or protective provisions for investors would entail an increase in FDI into a host country, the findings of these studies also show contrasting evidence, with statistically insignificant or even some negative estimated coefficients for the variables representing the strong BIT provisions. Yackee found positive, but insignificant, estimated coefficients for both strong and weak BITs on bilateral FDI between capital exporting and capital

---

[31] Berger et al. (n. 29). FTA investment chapters, especially along US lines, tend to include fewer pro-investor features than the earlier generation of BITs on Western European templates: see e.g. Wolfgang Alschner, 'The Impact of Investment Arbitration on Investment Design: Myth versus Reality' (2017) 42 *Yale Journal of International Law* 1.

[32] Julien Chaisse and Christian Bellak, 'Do Bilateral Investment Treaties Promote Foreign Direct Investment?' (2011) 3(4) *Transnational Corporations Review* 3. See also Julien Chaisse and Christian Bellak, 'Navigating the Expanding Universe of International Treaties on Foreign Investment: Creation and Use of a Critical Index' (2015) 18(1) *Journal of International Economic Law* 79.

[33] See <webapp1.law.cuhk.edu.hk/bitsel/signup.php>.

[34] As adopted by Ho Thi Viet Nguyen, Cao Vinh and Lu Trang, 'The Impact of Heterogenous Bilateral Investment Treaties (BIT) on Foreign Investment (FDI) flows to Vietnam', *SECO/WTI Academic Cooperation Project Working Paper Series* 2014/03, <papers.ssrn.com/sol3/papers.cfm?abstract_id=2618451>.

[35] For a recent example of divergent results from the impact of ISDS-backed treaties on FDI flows depending on whether the OECD or Thai government data are used, see Jason Yackee, 'Do Investment Treaties Work – In the Land of Smiles?' in Chaisse and Nottage (eds.), *International Investment Treaties and Arbitration Across Asia* (Brill, 2018) p. 83.

importing countries, leaving him with inconclusive evidence for the theoretical hypothesis of BITs as credible commitment devices.[36] Berger et al. found overall a positive and significant effect from BITs containing ISDS provisions generally. However, when those were differentiated, neither weaker ISDS provisions (containing only partial pre-consent to arbitration) nor stronger provisions (more surprisingly) showed any significant effect – indeed, both types showed a small negative impact.[37] More recently, Berger et al. were unable to find conclusive evidence of a positive impact of BITs with ISDS on FDI flows, yet they found significant and positive effects from BITs on FDI more generally (without any specific provisions taken into account). In addition, they found significant FDI-enhancing effects of both BITs with and without pre-establishment NT.[38] Despite efforts to account for specific aspects of FDI liberalisation and protection of BITs, the inconsistency within the empirical evidence suggests that the high expectation of significant FDI-promoting effects of specific provisions of BITs may not be warranted.

Overall, researchers have been investigating various theoretical explanations for how BITs can affect FDI. Key econometric techniques have also been applied to address and overcome the potential problems associated with the panel structure of both FDI stock and flow data. The remaining potential problems appear to lie in the nature of data on FDI and BITs themselves. Particular problems are associated with the conceptualisation, measurement and collection of BIT data given the extent, coverage and strength of their specific clauses. The measurement errors in BIT indexing or scaling might be substantial. They are not easily addressed due to conceptual complexity as well as significant resources needed for data collection. Future quantitative studies are therefore constrained by the ongoing problems of availability and measurement errors at disaggregated levels for both FDI and BIT data, prompting some researchers to turn to more qualitative research on the impact of treaties on FDI decision-making and outcomes.[39]

In this context, the econometric work below is expected to generate additional evidence on the effects of BITs on FDI flows using

---

[36] Yackee (n. 26).

[37] Axel Berger, Matthias Busse, Peter Nunnenkamp and Martin Roy, 'More Stringent BITs, Less Ambiguous Effects on FDI? Not a Bit!' (2010) *WTO Staff Working Paper* ERSD-2010-10, <doi.org/10.30875/ec4fa856-en>.

[38] Berger et al. (n. 29).

[39] See e.g. some studies reviewed in Bonnitcha et al. (n. 11), 164–6; and Section 11.3 below.

the best available secondary data and most plausible methodology to address the endogeneity problem identified in the existing literature. Specifically, our study contributes to updating the existing empirical literature by:

1. examining the effects of specific ISDS provisions on FDI flows using the most recent available data on FDI and BITs; and
2. carrying out alternative sensitivity tests on the effects of BITs and specific provisions, especially ISDS.

11.2.2   Method

The BITSel database (as of 2015) was used for investigating the BIT impact on FDI, but using its disaggregated data rather than the composite index of BIT strength, for treaties signed or ratified over 1985–2014. Our analysis also develops a baseline model of global FDI flows to estimate a stable counterfactual that allows an initial estimation of the effect of BITs.

We rely on the KCM to model our empirical specifications, for two main reasons. First, as FDI flows are driven by the behaviour of MNEs, the KCM provides theoretical underpinnings that identify key economic determinants of FDI. An important feature of the KCM model is that it provides testable hypotheses on the relevance of the driving forces of different types of FDI.[40] Second, the KCM model can be considered as an expansion of the gravity-type model but accounting for additional economic determinants of FDI. As UNCTAD suggests, in the context of FDI determinants and the role of international investment agreements,[41] a wide range of factors can be divided into three main groups: (i) the policy framework for FDI; (ii) economic determinants and (iii) business facilitation activities. While BITs are identified as a determinant in the policy framework for FDI, economic determinants are considered to cover the factors that underlie all different motives for FDI: market-seeking, natural resource-seeking, efficiency-seeking and strategic asset-seeking investments. The gravity-type model is usually limited to trade flow determinants such as economic mass and trade and investment costs. By contrast, the KCM also includes resource endowment factors that are important motives for FDI flows.

---

[40]   Busse et al. (n. 25), 155.
[41]   UNCTAD 2014 (n. 11).

Based on the KCM, we use two empirical specifications:

$$(1) \ In\left(FDI_{ijt}\right) = \alpha_0 + \beta'X_{ijt} + \alpha_1 BIT_{ijt} + \lambda_t + \alpha_{ij} + \varepsilon_{ijt}$$
$$(2) \ In\left(FDI_{ijt}\right) = \alpha_0 + \beta'X_{ijt} + \alpha_1 ISDS1_{ijt} + \alpha_1 ISDS2_{ijt} + \lambda_t + \alpha_{ij} + \varepsilon_{ijt}$$

where FDI_{ijt} stands for bilateral FDI flows from country i to country j in year t. X_{ijt} represents a set of control variables. Variable BIT_{ijt} in specification (1) corresponds to a *signed* bilateral investment treaty between the source and host countries or an investment chapter in a signed FTA, which are either bilateral or multilateral. In addition, we compare the impact of *ratified* BITs in sensitivity tests below in Section 11.2.3. Variables $ISDS1_{ijt}$ and $ISDS2_{ijt}$ are used to examine the specific impacts of BITs without and with a strong ISDS mechanism respectively. An ISDS mechanism is limited to some form of Investor–State Arbitration, and does not include an investor–state conciliation process as it would not necessarily generate a binding outcome. More specifically, following BITSeL, ISDS1 is defined as a weak clause as the ISDS mechanism is subject to certain conditions (partial pre-consent), in contrast with ISDS2 which is without any conditions (full advance consent to ISDS).[42] Despite much wider coverage in the time period (from the earliest BITs to the year 2014) and types of investment provisions, the ISDS classification of BITs in BITSel appears to be less specific compared to the coding of BITs by Yackee,[43] which assigns three levels of protection for foreign investors in terms of ISDS provisions. However, testing Yackee's BIT coding against other

[42] This is the major distinction in practice, and therefore most likely to influence investment decisions, although further graduations are conceivable. For example, some ISDS clauses are arguably even weaker because the pre-consent is limited only to certain substantive rights such as determining the 'amount of compensation' for expropriation (although some tribunals have further interpreted specific treaty wording to allow ISDS also regarding whether or not expropriation occurred anyway), or NT (as in 2015 Australia–China FTA, with the further complication that the extent of NT commitments may not be fully reciprocal). Alternatively, a tribunal may interpret a treaty – even decades after signing – as not providing full pre-consent to ISDS, as occurred controversially in 2014 in an ICSID claim by an Australian investor against Indonesia: *Churchill Mining PLC and Planet Mining Pty Ltd* v. *Republic of Indonesia*, ICSID Case No. ARB/12/14 and 12/40. However, the tribunal may anyway find consent to ISDS on another basis (as in a mining licence from Indonesian authorities, in that case: Luke Nottage, 'Do Many of Australia's Bilateral Treaties Really Not Provide Full Advance Consent to Investor-State Arbitration? Analysis and Regional Implications' (2015) 1 *Transnational Dispute Management*). Anyway, such unexpected interpretations (also potentially impacting on other earlier Australian BITs with similarly worded ISDS clauses) are not likely to have influenced decisions on whether and how to invest.

[43] Yackee (n. 26).

coding strategies in the literature is beyond the scope of this chapter. Finally, λ_t is a set of year dummies, α_{ij} accounts for country-pair fixed effects and ε_{ijt} represents the error term.

Based on the KCM, a set of control variables is defined as in Table 11.1. This set includes standard gravity-type variables: economic size represented by the sum of GDP of two partners, and distance which proxies for trade or investment costs. In addition, differences in resource endowments between two investment partner countries are accounted for by several variables, including real capital stock, skilled and unskilled labour ratio, and land per capita ratio. We adopt a reduced form or baseline model with a few interaction terms.[44] Adoption of this baseline model allows us to reduce the problems of multicollinearity among many interaction terms in the full specification of the KCM,[45] and to include additional important control variables for FDI flows. One such determinant is the host country's institutional and political environment, which has been widely recognised in empirical studies as a concern for most foreign investors. Another important factor is the relative macroeconomic condition of the host country compared with the source country. We control for this factor by relative exchange rate between two partners. This measure is closely correlated with the inflation rate of the host country, a variable usually used in other studies.

The dependent variable is outward FDI *flows*, as commonly used in many studies for its advantage of being more responsive to FDI determinants and data properties, which are specific to year and price level.[46] By contrast, a significant measurement problem is the price-inconsistent accounting of FDI *stock*. Baltagi and others note that: 'FDI stocks have been criticized because they are historical cost positions measured at their book value [and] reflect prices of various years rather than constant or current dollar values.'[47] Finally, as the stock measure reflects the accumulation of FDI flows over time, it has the advantage of being less subject to fluctuations, but is strongly affected by a strong autocorrelation problem in the FDI data series.[48]

---

[44] As suggested by Badi H. Baltagi, Peter Egger and Michael Pfaffermayr, 'Estimating Models of Complex FDI: Are There Third-country Effects?' (2007) 140(1) *Journal of Economics* 260.

[45] Blonigen (n. 15).

[46] Andrew Kerner, 'Why Should I Believe You? The Costs and Consequences of Bilateral Investment Treaties' (2009) 53(1) *International Studies Quarterly* 73.

[47] Baltagi et al. (n. 44) 266.

[48] Aisbett (n. 19); Sinon Crotti, Tony Cavoli, a.nd John K. Wilson, 'The Impact of Trade and Investment Agreements on Australia's Inward FDI Flows' (2010) 49(4) *Australian Economic Papers* 259.

Table 11.1 *Definitions of dependent and control variables*

Variable	Expected sign	Definition
Lnflowfdi1		Log of FDI flows, measured in US$ million. Data is from the OECD's FDI Statistics for 1985–2014.
Lndist	+	Log of the great circle distance between capital cities of source (d) and recipient (i) countries. Data is from the CEPII Database.
Gt	+	$Gt = ln(GDP_{it}+GDP_{jt})$. Log of the sum of country d's and country i's GDP is measured in current or constant 2005 USD. (The World Bank's WDI Database.)
S_t	+	A measure of GDP similarity: $1 - S_i^2 - S_j^2$, where $S_i = GDP_{it}/(GDP_{it}+GDP_{jt})$ and $S_j = GDP_{jt}/(GDP_{it}+GDP_{jt})$.
K_t	+	$Kt = ln(K_{it}/K_{jt})$. Log of the ratio of source country (i) to destination country capital stock. Capital stock is measured in million 2005 USD. Capital stock is estimated using the perpetual inventory method. The data source is Penn World Table 8.1 Database.
Ht	+	$Ht(j) = ln(H_{it}/H_{jt})$. Log of the ratio of source country to destination country skilled labour. Skilled labour is defined by percentage of people with tertiary education completion. The primary data source for various types of skilled labour is the Barro and Lee's (2010) dataset on educational attainment. This dataset is available for 146 countries in the 5-year intervals from 1950 to 2010. The data on this variable in years within the 5-year intervals are interpolated.
Lt	–	$Lt(j) = ln(L_{it}/L_{jt})$. Log of the ratio of source country to destination country unskilled labour. Unskilled labour is defined by percentage of people without tertiary education completion. This is equal to 100 – the percentage of people with tertiary education completion as defined above.
N_t	–	$Nt(j) = ln(N_{it}/N_{jt})$. Log of the ratio of source country to destination country

MIXING METHODOLOGIES IN INVESTMENT ARBITRATION   329

Table 11.1 (*cont.*)

Variable	Expected sign	Definition
		natural resource endowment. Natural resource endowment is defined by land per capita. The data on land per capita is obtained from the World Bank's WDI database.
Gamma$_t$ **(Γ_t)**	+/–	Interaction term between G_t and K_t : $G_t K_t$
Phi$_t$ (Φ_t)	+/–	*Phi$_t$ (j)= Lndist * (Ht-Lt)* Interaction term between distance (*lndist*) and the difference in capital and unskilled labour ratios between source and destination countries. There are also three alternative proxies of this interaction term corresponding with three measures of unskilled labour.
PRI	+	The host country's political risk index, ranging from 0 to 100. The higher the index is, the better political condition the host country has. The data on this index is based on the International Country Risk Guide (ICRG) composite political risk measure.
lnEXR	–	Log of exchange rate, which is defined as the ratio of the source Log of exchange rate, which is defined as the source country's currency per one unit of the host country's currency. The lower the exchange rate, the higher the value of the source country's domestic currency. The data on a country's nominal exchange rates are obtained from the World Bank's WDI Database.

The FDI flows are outward FDI flows from 33 OECD countries to their host countries (listed in our Statistical Appendix at Table 11.9), both within and outside the OECD (and therefore into developed as well as developing economies). Further research might examine the impact of the growing outbound FDI from non-OECD economies, but data availability is challenging. Figure 11.1 shows the overall progression in OECD outflows from 1985 until 2014.

For our econometric analysis, instead of constructing a dependent variable as the share of FDI flows in a source country's total FDI flows

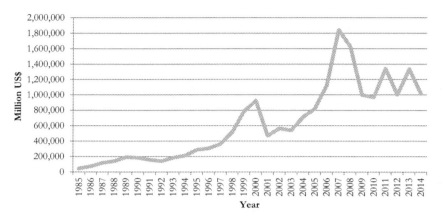

Figure 11.1 Annual total FDI outflows from OECD: 1985–2014.
Source: Authors' calculation based on OECD's FDI Data Set

in the period (year) t as found in many studies, we use a standard log form of FDI for the following reasons. First, while the share measure of FDI flows can reduce the impact of measurement error and price level change, our measure has a clear and straightforward interpretation of the impact of BITs and any other control variables on FDI flows, which is percentage change. By definition, FDI share is in ratio and percentage, so the BIT impact change on log of FDI share is a percentage change in the percentage share, which is quite ambiguous. Second, the change in share of FDI flows is harder to detect or identify due to competition effects among the host countries for the same source of FDI flows. This situation could happen when a source country signed (or ratified) BITs with two or more host countries at the same time. As the total share from a source country is 100 per cent, an increase in FDI flow share in one host country is associated with a decrease in that of another host country, thus even FDI flows into these countries may increase as a result of BIT conclusion.

Like many other studies, we consider negative FDI flows as zero flows. But we did not take the multiple year simple average for smoothing data. That process reduces the variation in the size of FDI flows from the source into the host countries, resulting in the more limited responses of FDI flows to any changes in the explanatory variables, particularly in the dummy variables as with the alternative measures of BITs. Consequently, the estimated size of coefficients might be reduced.

There also remain various other limitations with the data, as mentioned above. The FDI data cannot differentiate investment that may

MIXING METHODOLOGIES IN INVESTMENT ARBITRATION 331

derive from or induce corruption, and it is not easy to address this by adding anti-corruption treaties as a further variable. There is considerable variability in the scope of such treaties and even more in terms of their actual implementation.[49] Further factors potentially impacting on FDI flows include double-tax treaties,[50] and the implementation of broader legislation on international arbitration in the home state (potentially highlighting and improving enforcement of ISDS).[51] Future research can be expected to take into account such factors. Nonetheless, our econometric study provides some preliminary baseline results to inform such ongoing research.

11.2.3 Estimation Results from the Econometric Analysis

To identify the significance and magnitude of the impact of BITs in general and specific ISDS provisions in particular, we employ different estimation techniques. Initially, the potential endogeneity of BITs, ISDS1 and ISDS2 is ignored and a standard fixed effects (FE) model is used to obtain coefficient estimates.[52] Subsequently, the fixed effects Poisson Pseudo-Maximum Likelihood estimator (PPML) is used to deal with the observations that have zero values for FDI in the sample.[53] FDI flow data often has more zero value observations than trade flow data, due to missing observations, reporting errors and negative numbers. Finally, the dynamic Generalised Methods of Moments (GMM), or the system GMM estimator, is used to deal with the potential endogeneity problem of key variables of interest.

---

[49] The main distinction is between (UN) 'demand-side' and (OECD) 'supply-side' treaties, but even among developed countries adopting the latter there is significant variability in national laws and especially enforcement activity: Meg Beasley, 'Dysfunctional Equivalence: Why the OECD Anti-Bribery Convention Provides Insufficient Guidance in the Era of Multinational Corporations' (2015) 47(1) *George Washington International Law Review* 191. Indices of corruption perceptions, such as those from Transparency International, may not provide more traction given their reference groups and lack of variability over time.

[50] Professor Julien Chaisse has been building a dataset to conduct further research involving this variable (personal communication, 21 June 2016).

[51] For ongoing research on this point, see Catherine A. Rogers and Christopher R. Drahozal, 'Does International Arbitration Enfeeble or Enhance Local Legal Institutions?' Chapter 15 in this volume.

[52] The Hausman test was used to confirm its validity over the random effects model.

[53] Compared to trade data, FDI flow data often has more zeros observations than trade flow data, due to missing observations, reporting errors and negative numbers.

The initial results with FE and PPML estimation methods are explained in the Appendix. Those results give some evidence of positive effects of BITs and its specific provisions on FDI flows. While PPML is commonly considered to produce more consistent estimates than FE due to accounting for zeros observations, the inconsistency between the two sets of estimates for some variables might be due to endogeneity problems as identified in several recent studies. Therefore, we address this problem using the system GMM estimator and use its estimates as our preferred results for analysis, as given in Table 11.2. There are two sets of GMM estimates: one is for BIT as a single variable and one is for BIT divided into specific ISDS provisions contained within BITs. There are two model specifications: the baseline model and the model with the host country's political risk index (PRI) included.

These results show that FDI flows are path-dependent, as indicated by the positive and significant coefficients of FDI flows lagged by 1 and 2 years. This result is consistent with that of previous studies and confirms that the potential endogeneity of BITs is caused by simultaneity bias. There is some evidence that resource endowment differences matter for FDI flows and the coefficients have expected signs, although not all of them are significant. The GMM estimator accounts for the impact of past investments on current FDI flows, so some of the magnitudes of the coefficients are smaller than in the FE and PPML models given in our Statistical Appendix. The results also indicate the importance of the host country's domestic political environment in attracting FDI flows.

The main results illustrated by Table 11.2 are, first, that BITs do have a significant and positive impact on FDI flows. Interestingly, the magnitude of the BIT coefficient is about 0.33, equivalent to 38.4 per cent increase in the FDI flows for a country pair with BITs signed, considerably higher than expected (or than the FE and PPML estimates in the Appendix). Second, estimates of coefficients for the two specific provisions of key interest, ISDS1 and ISDS2, show positive effects as well (with a considerably higher magnitude for the ISDS1 coefficient compared with FE and PPML estimates in the Statistical Appendix).

The magnitude of BIT impact is reduced by the inclusion of the host country's PRI, implying that BIT impact indeed depends on the measure of political risk in the host country. Further examination of the impact of specific BIT provisions, ISDS1 and ISDS2, reveals a key finding. Both ISDS1 and ISDS2 show a significant positive impact on FDI flows. Counter-intuitively, however, BITs with the former (*weaker* or partial pre-consent) ISDS provisions appear to have a *stronger* impact on FDI flows (0.43 for ISDS1, compared with 0.22 for ISDS2).

MIXING METHODOLOGIES IN INVESTMENT ARBITRATION 333

Table 11.2 *The effects of BITs and specific provisions with system GMM estimator*

Dependent variable: Log(FDI flows)

	GMM (1)	GMM (2)	GMM (3)	GMM (4)
L.lnflowfdi1	0.54***	0.54***	0.57***	0.58***
	(0.05)	(0.08)	(0.06)	(0.09)
L2.lnflowfdi1	0.20***	0.19***	0.17**	0.17**
	(0.06)	(0.07)	(0.07)	(0.07)
Gt	0.31***	0.33***	0.31***	0.30***
	(0.04)	(0.06)	(0.04)	(0.07)
St	1.18***	1.19***	1.18***	1.12***
	(0.2)	(0.2)	(0.2)	(0.3)
lnEXR	−0.011**	−0.013*	−0.016**	−0.017**
	(0.006)	(0.007)	(0.007)	(0.007)
Kt	0.68**	0.80**	0.60**	0.70**
	(0.3)	(0.3)	(0.3)	(0.3)
Ht3	−0.0031	0.0091	0.0013	0.0097
	(0.02)	(0.02)	(0.02)	(0.02)
Lt3	−0.51***	−0.61***	−0.52***	−0.61***
	(0.2)	(0.2)	(0.2)	(0.2)
Nt	0.010	0.0068	0.0094	0.0057
	(0.01)	(0.010)	(0.010)	(0.009)
Gamma	−0.0056	−0.0069	−0.0024	−0.0032
	(0.008)	(0.008)	(0.007)	(0.008)
Phi3	−0.074***	−0.070***	−0.076***	−0.071***
	(0.02)	(0.02)	(0.02)	(0.02)
BIT	**0.33*** **	**0.32*** **		
	(0.1)	**(0.1)**		
PRI		**0.018*** **		**0.017*** **
		(0.003)		**(0.003)**
bit_ISDS1			**0.49*** **	**0.43*** **
			(0.2)	**(0.2)**
bit_ISDS2			**0.23*** **	**0.22*** **
			(0.1)	**(0.11)**
Constant	−7.84***	−9.71***	−7.58***	−8.91***
	(1.1)	(1.7)	(1.1)	(1.9)
N	12,880	12,645	12,880	12,645
Country-pairs	1,856	1,798	1,856	1,798
AB2 (p-value)	0.306	0.402	0.605	0.683
Hansen (p-value)	0.171	0.233	0.533	0.692
Instruments (lags)	172(2–4)	171(2–4)	221 (2–4)	216 (2–4)

Note: * $p < 0.10$, ** $p < 0.05$, ***$p < 0\ 01$; Standard errors are in brackets; AB2 is Arellano-Bond test for AR(2); Hansen is Hansen test of over-identification restrictions.
Source: Authors' calculation.

Given the diverging effects of BITs due to their different strengths in protecting investors, including with respect to the ISDS procedure, it is worth examining whether such effects are correlated with another important attribute of BITs: substantive treatment of FDI. BITs differ regarding specific provisions, including the definition of investment, admission rules, NT, MFN treatment, and fair and equitable treatment. While these provisions have been increasingly included in the substantive core of modern treaties, there is considerable variation in the strength of these provisions among existing BITs. For example, Berger et al. argue there can be three different NT modalities among BITs corresponding to levels of liberalisation in the admission of foreign investments at the pre-establishment phase of investment.[54] BITs can be differentiated by an MFN clause for the establishment phase if there are no NT provisions. In our analysis, the BITSel dataset used includes information on the NT and MFN clauses. As for the ISDS provisions, there are only two options used for determining the scope of application to investors, with MFN1 being limited or narrow and MFN2 being broad or more favourable to investors.

With the BITs between OECD home countries and their destination partner countries covered in the BITSel dataset, there is a strikingly high correlation between NT and MFN provisions in terms of their scope of application.[55] Therefore we focus just on MFN provisions with two levels of application or treatment for investors, to combine with the two categories of ISDS provisions, to classify BITs into four groups incorporating both substantive treatment and procedural protection aspects. The first group of BITs has weaker investor rights with both narrow MFN and ISDS clauses (MFN1*ISDS1 in Table 11.3). The second and third groups have a mix of narrow MFN and broad ISDS (MFN1*ISDS2), or broad MFN and narrow ISDS (MFN2*ISDS1). The fourth group has both broad MFN and ISDS provisions (MFN2*ISDS2). The GMM estimation results of variables for these four groups of BITs and the political risk index (PRI) are shown in Table 11.3.

This analysis shows that BITs with both limited (weak) MFN and ISDS clauses have the largest impact on the FDI flows from OECD countries to host partners. Counter-intuitively, BITs with broader and stronger MFN and ISDS clauses have a smaller effect on FDI flows. Yet combining stronger ISDS with weaker MFN shows somewhat more impact than vice versa, and the impact across all four combinations remains positive and

---

[54] Berger et al. (n. 29).

[55] Running the regressions in Table 11.3 using NT instead of MFN produces similar results.

Table 11.3 *Effects of MFN combined with ISDS in BITs*

	1985–2014
PRI	0.017***
	(0.003)
MFN1*ISDS1	**0.54***
	(0.2)
MFN1*ISDS2	0.36**
	(0.1)
MFN2*ISDS1	0.35*
	(0.2)
MFN2*ISDS2	**0.20***
	(0.09)

Note: * $p < 0.10$, ** $p < 0.05$, ***$p < 0.01$; Standard errors are in brackets.

Source: Authors' calculation.

significant. This result is consistent with the evidence above for the overall impact of BITs with ISDS1 compared with ISDS2, found in Table 11.2. Moreover, our finding of the impact of MFN provisions is broadly consistent with the evidence provided by Berger et al.,[56] who found that BITs without NT provisions have a positive and significant effect on FDI flows, but inclusion of MFN obligations in these BITs does not have any additional impact on the estimated coefficient. Overall, therefore, our estimation results above find that BITs as well as both types of ISDS protections impact positively on FDI, but that provisions with *weaker* rights or protections for investors have a *larger* effect on FDI compared to stronger rights or protections. This could be due to investors historically having been more impressed by a broader 'signalling' effect from states concluding investment treaties, without looking closely at the content of the ISDS provision.[57]

Our Statistical Appendix also suggests that, overall, the impact on FDI flows from treaty provisions may be diminishing over time. For example,

---

[56] Berger et al. (n. 29).

[57] This possibility, which merits more qualitative research, is mentioned by Luke Nottage and Jaivir Singh, 'Does ISDS Promote FDI? Insights from and for Australia and India' (November 2016) *Asia-Pacific Forum for International Arbitration Blog*, <afia.asia/2016/11/does-isds-promote-fdi-asia-pacific-insights-from-and-for-australia-and-india>.

Table 11.4 *Sensitivity Tests for Different Periods and Host State Groups*

Variable	Whole sample	Different periods		Host states	
		1985–2000	2001–14	OECD	Non-OECD
BIT (Signed)	**0.32*****	**0.37*****	**0.29**	**0.31****	**0.056**
	(0.1)	(0.10)	(0.2)	(0.1)	(0.1)
BITR (Ratified)	**0.48*****	**0.34****	**0.52****	**0.17**	**0.49****
	(0.1)	(0.2)	(0.3)	(0.2)	(0.2)
ISDS1_Signed	**0.43*****	**0.35***	**0.51****	**0.35***	**0.38***
	(0.13)	(0.19)	(0.21)	(0.2)	(0.2)
ISDS2_Signed	**0.23****	**0.33*****	**0.087**	**0.17**	**0.13**
	(0.11)	(0.099)	(0.29)	(0.2)	(0.2)
ISDSR1_Ratified	**0.42*****	**0.56****	**0.64*****	**0.45***	**0.58****
	(0.14)	(0.24)	(0.22)	(0.2)	(0.2)
ISDSR2_Ratified	**0.39****	**0.16**	**0.79***	**0.10**	**0.46***
	(0.20)	(0.18)	(0.44)	(0.3)	(0.2)

Notes: $* p < 0.10$, $** p < 0.05$, $*** p < 0.01$; standard errors are in brackets. Estimations are based on two-step System GMM with robust standard errors.

Source: Authors' calculation.

Table 11.8 (see Statistical Appendix) shows that the combination of (broader) MFN2 with (stronger) ISDS2 is significantly positive for 1985–2000 FDI flows but not for 2001–14 (although still positive when combined with MFN1 for the latter period). In addition, Table 11.4 shows that the impact from signed BITs is significantly positive for FDI but loses significance for 2001–14 flows, as does the impact from ISDS2 (but not ISDS1).

Such a shift might be explained by a general improvement in the host states' business environment providing encouragement for all foreign and indeed even local investors over that latter period, diminishing the impact of (especially stronger-form) investment treaties. However, this shift might also reflect a change towards less pro-investor treaty drafting from around the turn of the twenty-first century, as the United States updated its Model BIT and the United States as well as other (especially Asia-Pacific) countries began concluding BITs and (especially) FTAs drawing on that new template.[58]

---

[58] See generally e.g. Alschner (n. 31); Wolfgang Alschner and Dimitriy Skougarevskiy, 'Mapping the Universe of International Investment Agreements' (2016) 19(3) *Journal of International Economic Law* 531.

In addition, Table 11.4 reveals that it is worthwhile to compare patterns for *ratified* investment treaties, as well as whether or not the host country is also a member of the OECD. Looking at our entire sample, the impact on FDI flows from treaties that are ratified *in the same year* as signing is larger than for signed treaties. But the effect is larger and remains significant for such treaties ratified over 2001–14. In addition, when results are further broken down by host state group, we find that the impact from ratified BITs is significantly positive for FDI flows from OECD member states into non-OECD states (0.49) but not into other OECD states (0.17). Similarly, there is a positive albeit less significant impact on FDI flows from ISDS2 in such ratified treaties (0.46), but an even stronger impact from the ISDS1 (0.58). The impact of ISDS2 from signed treaties is insignificant when the host states are divided into either OECD or non-OECD groups, but becomes significant over the entire sample (0.23) although less so than that for ISDS2 in treaties ratified in the same year as signing (0.39).

Nonetheless, further regressions show that the relative effects become insignificant when we consider all ratified treaties, irrespective of how soon ratification occurred after signing.[59] The results are also not very robust in terms of host country grouping, as can be seen by the extended version of Table 11.4 reproduced as Table 11.7 in the Statistical Appendix. The latter shows, for example, that the impact from ISDS2 on FDI flows from OECD countries into 'less developed countries' is positive but insignificant even for treaties ratified in the same year of signing (0.29), despite being significant for FDI flows into non-OECD countries (as mentioned above: 0.46), which would include more middle-income countries. Overall, therefore, our econometric study still generates complex implications for policy-makers reassessing the historical impact of ISDS in order to decide whether and how to include different forms of such procedural provisions in future investment treaties.

11.3 Potential and Challenges for Qualitative Analysis of ISDS and Investment Treaties

The previous section has detailed the methodological challenges associated with quantitative analysis to test whether offering ISDS protections,

---

[59] Further, BITs that are ratified in the same year in which they are signed have the largest impact on FDI flows, followed by a positive impact from BITs that are ratified after one or two years. Yet BITs that are ratified three years after they have been signed instead have a negative impact on FDI flows.

of various intensity across different types of treaties, leads to greater inbound FDI. Our preliminary econometric results suggest that stronger protections do not necessarily lead to greater FDI flows, although the stronger form of ISDS still has some significant and positive impact. Particularly against such intriguing results, qualitative research can likely help tease out the complex interaction between treaty provisions and impact on foreign investment decisions. Qualitative research also has the advantage of allowing examination of sector-specific FDI patterns, which are not well captured by OECD data. It may also offer a better opportunity of examining the other two research questions set out in our Introduction, such as the extent to which outbound investors may in fact face discrimination or other adverse treatment in host states compared to local investors, and the scope for additional regulatory chill. However, qualitative research in this field presents its own methodological and practical challenges. This aspect of our project is complex and ongoing, and it is beyond the scope of this chapter to present even preliminary findings.

Methodological challenges are compounded as the existing qualitative research is quite varied, ranging from survey and/or interviews relating to a broader topic, through to narrower case studies. Thus, for example, Poulsen's interviews around 2009 suggested that various political risk insurers take little account of BITs (not just with ISDS) when determining the availability and pricing of insurance offered to outbound investors.[60] However, it is not very clear how many insurers were actually interviewed.[61] Critics have anyway argued that this was an 'unreliably small survey' to determine whether or not political risk insurers (and multinational corporations) discount BITs,[62] and highlighted some of Poulsen's own findings that they argue work against his conclusions.[63]

---

[60] Poulsen (n. 1).

[61] Ibid., 14 refers to a 'much larger sample' than an UNCTAD study of six insurers regarding Brazil (which reported mixed results), then refers to 'a selection of providers' in a Table (listing 39 insurers), but not all seem to be quoted in this paper.

[62] Charles Brower and Sadie Blanchard, 'What's in a Meme? The Truth about Investor-State Arbitration: Why It Need Not, and Must Not, Be Repossessed by States' (2014) 52 *Columbia Journal of Transnational Law* 689, 704.

[63] Ibid., 705, referring to the summary in Lauge Poulsen, 'Political Risk Insurance and Bilateral Investment Treaties: A View from Below' (2010) *Columbia FDI Perspectives*, they emphasise that (a) official insurers in France and Germany required a treaty (although Poulsen argues they were an exception), (b) the Multilateral Investment Guarantee Agency factor a BIT into insurance premiums, (c) MIGA considers a BIT a sufficient condition for coverage (although Poulsen argues that it is not a necessary

MIXING METHODOLOGIES IN INVESTMENT ARBITRATION   339

Another interesting qualitative study drew partly on in-depth interviews as well as electronic surveys for a PhD thesis submitted to the London School of Economics in 2014, but had a narrower target and adopted more of a case-study approach. Côté found little evidence of regulatory chill in Canada regarding measures to preserve public health and the environment, despite NAFTA Chapter 11 proceedings, nor among tobacco regulators across multiple countries. However, she was careful to note that this study focused on Canadian federal regulators, and obtaining access and information concerning tobacco control world-wide was more challenging.[64]

11.3.1 Survey- versus Interview-Based Research in Potentially Polarised Media Environments

The qualitative aspect of our own project aimed partly at revisiting Australia's Productivity Commission Report's view of World Bank research survey research that suggested, counter-intuitively, that foreign investors were favoured rather than disfavoured compared to local investors. One difficulty with the World Bank's study was its timing: conducted around 1999–2000.[65] That was before implementation of anti-bribery conventions and related national laws in OECD home states as well as host states.[66] As such regimes are enforced, foreign investors in

---

condition), (d) some private insurers weigh BITs when assessing insurance for very risky countries and (e) overall (by reverse analogy), BITs may be relevant to 'countries facing reputational hurdles' in attracting foreign investment. They also cite an OECD paper in 2008 for the proposition that other countries' official insurers consider BITs in their risk assessments. In addition, Mark Kantor (formerly counsel to the US political risks insurer and very familiar with MIGA as well as investment treaties in general) is sceptical about the generalization that political risks insurers take little account of investment treaty protections: see e.g. <youtube.com/watch?v=uX1od6amOwc> (from minute 30:20 to 46:15) and generally Mark Kantor, 'Comparing Political Risk Insurance and Investment Treaty Arbitration' (2014) *Transnational Dispute Management*.

[64] Christine Côté, *A chilling effect? The impact of international investment agreements on national regulatory autonomy in the areas of health, safety and the environment*, PhD thesis, London School of Economics and Political Science (2014) <etheses.lse.ac.uk/897>.

[65] Other issues including its aggregated nature – not focused on countries in the (now) most dynamic parts of the world economy, such as Asia. See further Armstrong et al. (n. 3), section 3.

[66] See generally <oecd.org/daf/anti-bribery/> and <unodc.org/unodc/en/treaties/CAC/>. Focusing on ex post rather than ex ante effects, however, international investment arbitration tribunals have arguably not dealt well with corruption allegations: Cecily

particular are likely to turn away from 'extra-legal' or outright 'illegal' means of controlling risks in (especially developing) host states, thus making it more likely that they will end up being disfavoured compared to local investors, who after all have more direct access to normal law-making processes.[67] More generally, investment treaty protections could substitute for past tendencies to safeguard foreign investment through bribery in host states. However, implementation of anti-corruption measures remains a slow process.[68]

The broader methodological point here is that if investment treaty protections need to be considered in the context of corruption and anti-bribery measures, interview-based research will be more effective than written or electronic surveys, and, even then, there will be confidentiality concerns among respondent firms or government officials. Such concerns are already significant, although Côté managed to obtain high response rates for her (admittedly short) surveys and especially for her interviews. In the latter respect she notes that this achievement was probably related to herself having been a former federal government official in Canada (responsible in fact for treaty negotiations).[69] Yet that personal history in itself raises some methodological issues, as outlined more generally below.

A further difficulty with qualitative interviews of current or likely outbound investors is that these constitute a very disparate group. They could vary depending, for example, on:

1. Whether part of a large and/or multinational group – which may have more leverage with host or home states, hence less scope for adverse treatment or need to invoke ISDS protections.[70]

Rose, 'Questioning the Role of International Arbitration in the Fight against Corruption' (2014) 31(2) *Journal of International Arbitration* 183.

[67] As mentioned in Section 11.2, econometric evidence confirms that political risks which are related to corruption and transparency have a significant impact on FDI flows.

[68] Examples include Australia's poor record in enforcing the OECD Convention (in force from 1999) and bribery scandals involving prominent Australian companies including in Asia. See e.g. <oecd.org/daf/anti-bribery/australia-oecdanti-briberyconvention.htm>; <smh.com.au/national/the-world-thinks-australia-should-lift-its-anticorruption-game-20160331-gnv9pz.html>; and generally, Beasley (n. 49).

[69] Côté (n. 64).

[70] Alternatively, they may be better able to plan their affairs to take advantage of investment protections. Interestingly, several known claims brought under Australian treaties are by mining companies within international corporate groups: *Churchill Mining PLC and Planet Mining Pty Ltd* (n. 42); *Tethyan Copper Company Pty Ltd* v. *Islamic Republic of Pakistan*, ICSID Case No. ARB/12/1.

2. The nature of their investments – suppliers of services may have less risk exposure than those committed to mining or infrastructure projects, involving long lead times, large fixed investments and more scope for community concerns, e.g. over environmental impact.[71]
3. The geographical reach of investments.

Large-scale surveys into the treatment by host states and/or impact of investment treaties in planning and implementing projects,[72] let alone in-depth interviews, become more difficult to conduct under such circumstances. Our project supplements these interviews, with a sample of large and smaller Australian investors (as well as some foreign investors into Australia), with more free-ranging seminars jointly with business and other concerned groups, incorporating a country- or region-specific emphasis.

We also attempted to complement the direct investigation of investor perceptions and practices by asking officials what they think of those, including delicate issues such as the extent to which investors may still be 'managing' their overseas investment risk exposure by engaging in bribery. Interviews are more likely to be revealing than surveys in this respect, as well as in examining questions such as the possibility and extent of regulatory chill. However, the latter is more likely to be a problem in developed countries, where more effective governance systems produce laws that follow due process and address the public interest, rather than private or rent-seeking interests as in some developing countries. Yet, precisely in those developed countries, it is very hard to determine the incremental impact of investment treaty protections (especially those reinforced by the ISDS mechanism) compared to the 'chilling' effect – or, more neutrally, the 'channelling' effect – on local policy-makers resulting from developed systems of domestic public law as well as well-implemented international law disciplines such as those created by the World Trade Organization. Qualitative research on this topic, especially interviews, is probably the best way forward, triangulated

---

[71] Other known treaty-based claims by Australian companies as well as ICSID claims under investment contracts also relate to mining, including *White Industries Australia Ltd v. Republic of India* (UNCITRAL Award, 30 November 2011). For more details, see Amokura Kawharu and Luke Nottage, 'The Curious Case of ISDS Arbitration Involving Australia and New Zealand' (2018) 44(2) *University of Western Australia Law Review* 32–70.

[72] Cf. e.g. the surveys summarized by Poulsen (n. 1).

against secondary literature (including media reports) and some quantitative analysis of primary sources.[73]

The focus on government officials, in turn, involves its own challenges. Typically, they are bound directly or indirectly by strict confidentiality obligations, imposed by their own governments and/or sometimes counterparties, as occurred with the CPTPP negotiations. Wikileaks and similar sources may provide access to draft negotiating texts,[74] and potentially even other documentation related to trade and investment treaties, but this will be sporadic and likely anyway to make current officials even more reluctant to respond to requests to participate in surveys or even interviews. Politicians in charge of current projects are likely to be too busy, while those not directly involved in the field may provide little extra insight into the issues, and both may be prone to follow a party line – although discerning that may be interesting in itself. Nonetheless, such qualitative research is also interesting to explore the 'complex empirical question'[75] of whether actual or potential ISDS claims may lead to governance improvements in host states, which is highly dependent on domestic political and institutional dynamics. Although not a major focus for our project, this question impacts, for example, on the question of whether foreign investors need to and do in fact rely on investment treaty protections when sinking project funds into countries where substantive rights and legal processes do not meet contemporary international standards.

So far for our project, we have therefore conducted interviews with former officials, mostly in Australia but also those with experience in New Zealand, the United States, Vietnam and Thailand. Almost all have been in relation to past treaty negotiations and outcomes, as well as with respect to their views on investor behaviour. The challenges are that memories can fade, and times can change quite quickly. This became evident in Australia. Content analysis of coverage in major newspapers shows that debate over ISDS resurfaced suddenly and accelerated from

---

[73] Such as the analysis of Canadian regulatory developments undertaken by Côté (n. 64), and the negotiation and drafting of BITs undertaken by Poulsen (n. 1).

[74] See e.g. Mélida Hodgson, 'The Leaked TPP Investment Chapter Draft: Few Surprises ... Is that a Surprise?' (2015) 6 *Transnational Dispute Management* <transnational-dispute-management.com/journal-advance-publication-article.asp?key=579>.

[75] Kathryn Gordon and David Gaukrodger, 'Investor-State Dispute Settlement: Public Consultation 16 May–July 2012' OECD (2012) 12, <oecd.org/investment/internationa linvestmentagreements/50291642.pdf>. See also e.g. Mavluda Sattorova, *The Impact of Investment Treaty Law on Host States: Enabling Good Governance?* (Hart, 2018).

2010 in the wake of (i) the Productivity Commission's Report; (ii) Australia joining negotiations for what became the CPTPP and (iii) the Philip Morris arbitration claim. In addition, the main Australian newspapers were clearly split in their views about treaty-based ISDS. The *Sydney Morning Herald* and *Melbourne Age* (owned by the Fairfax group) are consistently opposed, whereas the *Australian Financial Review* (the main business newspaper, also owned by Fairfax) and especially *The Australian* (owned by Rupert Murdoch's Newscorp) favour ISDS.[76]

Such a novel and increasingly polarized environment for ISDS may colour respondents' views of what was intended and achieved with respect to past treaties, negotiations and consultations with business or other stakeholder groups. Nonetheless, what is striking from an Australian perspective is a sense of 'déjà vu' regarding objections to ISDS and other risks perceived with recently concluded or presently under negotiation, such as the TPP, compared to the Australia–US FTA negotiated over 2003–4.[77]

11.3.2 The Pros and Cons of Participant Observation in Public Inquiries

Similar challenges arise from a new avenue for qualitative research that has been created by the contemporary and growing interest in ISDS: parliamentary or other public inquiries. These often put on public record, even fully online, written submissions provided by various stakeholders (including government officials) as well as transcripts given by those invited to give evidence and respond to questions put by politicians at parliamentary hearings. However, this potentially rich resource for qualitative research is found primarily in more developed economies (including notably the European Union, where the European Commission concluded major public consultations in 2015).[78] Full-scale parliamentary inquiries are particularly likely in multi-House parliaments, especially where the government may not hold an absolute majority in one House (as in Australia's federal Senate under coalition governments over 2013–18).[79]

Nonetheless, even when publicly available, submissions and transcripts of evidence from officials may be limited by parliamentary rules and practices that only require or allow them to express views on the

---

[76] See Nottage (n. 7).
[77] Ibid.
[78] Cf. e.g. <trade.ec.europa.eu/consultations/index.cfm?consul_id=179>.
[79] Kurtz and Nottage (n. 6).

implementation of policy, rather than the policy itself.[80] In addition, politicians on such committees may not necessarily be expert in investment law and policy, and anyway tend to associate themselves with prevailing party positions or inclinations. The internet has also made it easier to solicit and coordinate submissions from non-expert members of the public, which parliamentary committees may have to treat instead as 'correspondence' where provided in largely identical standard form.[81]

Focusing instead on accepted submissions to parliamentary inquiries, many of these can still be very brief, albeit not straightforwardly in standard form. However, the more substantial ones are often useful for qualitative research purposes – especially for identifying core positions and supporting arguments or evidence, and identifying possible individuals or organizations to request in-depth interviews.

Nonetheless, as researchers we must first be aware that the nature and format of a parliamentary inquiry can tend to push those providing submissions towards stating their views quite strongly, and/or in response to earlier and also publicly available submissions. Having publicly expressed such views, moreover, the person or organisation will often find it difficult to change direction, especially in public but even in subsequent confidential interviews.[82] This problem is exacerbated when, as is quite often the case, for example, with respect to Australia's succession of inquiries into ISDS, those making submissions to one inquiry make similar submissions to others.[83]

---

[80] See e.g. the opening statement by the Chair of the Senate committee, when hearing evidence from Department of Foreign Affairs officials, in the 'Anti-ISDS Bill' inquiry: Luke Nottage, 'The "Anti-ISDS Bill" Before the Senate: What Future for Investor-State Arbitration in Australia?' (2015) XVIII *International Trade and Business Law Review* 245: '... the Senate has resolved that an officer of a department of the Commonwealth or of a state shall not be asked to give opinions on matters of policy and shall be given reasonable opportunity to refer questions asked of the officer to superior officers or to a minister. This resolution prohibits only questions asking for opinions on matters of policy. It does not preclude questions asking for explanations of policy or factual questions about when or how policies were adopted.' Of course, as those readers may recall who are familiar with the BBC's classic satirical series on bureaucrat–politician relations 'Yes Minister', the dividing line between policy and implementation may be difficult to determine.

[81] See e.g. Nottage (n. 7).

[82] Partly this seems due to heuristics such as the sunk cost fallacy: see generally <lifehack .org/articles/communication/how-the-sunk-cost-fallacy-makes-you-act-stupid.html> and Section 11.4 below.

[83] See some individuals and organizations cited in Nottage (n. 80); and Luke Nottage, 'Investment Treaty Arbitration Policy in Australia, New Zealand – and Korea?' (2015) 25(3) *Journal of Arbitration Studies* 185.

A second challenge for researchers is that submissions to such public inquiries tend to risk sample bias, in that submissions are more likely from those who harbour grave concerns. Those who are generally comfortable with the status quo, such as Australia's renewed policy from 2013 of including ISDS in treaties based on case-by-case assessments, will be less disposed to consume time and energy in making submissions. An exception could arise, as is increasingly the case, when an awareness emerges that the current policy may change or at least that 'silence' in the face of public consultations may be deemed to mean that the issue is unimportant.[84]

Both impediments to effective qualitative research through content analysis of parliamentary records, namely tendencies for submissions to be made quite strongly (without extensive qualifications or nuance) and to disproportionately express views challenging the status quo, also arise with respect to the subset of individuals or organizations that a parliamentary committee may invite to give evidence at public hearings based on their submissions. It is hard to reconcile from or adjust pre-stated positions, especially when politicians on the committees tend to press their own party lines or prior personal views, although some informative attempts to do so can emerge by closely analysing the transcripts of questions and answers (including subsequent, often more considered or nuanced, responses to Questions taken on Notice).

In addition, those giving evidence are often those who have already been found useful (sometimes by the very same committee) with respect to earlier inquiries. As well as risking further entrenchment of pre-stated views, this exacerbates sample bias, for researchers examining parliamentary records to discern views or experiences related to a topic such as ISDS. A further difficulty is that the parliamentarians on each committee have discretion on who to call to give oral evidence based on submissions, and may 'horse-trade' among themselves to try to generate opinions on the public record that favour their party or personal views. They

---

[84] Cf. e.g. the Productivity Commission's 2010 public inquiry into Australia's FTAs (n. 4), where the paucity of submissions from business groups especially on ISDS was taken in the majority Report as evidence that they did not see ISDS as important for protecting outbound investments. However, such groups may not have been aware of the inquiry or the focus that gradually developed on ISDS, especially from other individuals and organizations as they put in submissions, or may have assumed that Australia's then policy stance was appropriate and unlikely to change. Analysis of major Australian newspapers over 2010 certainly finds almost no mention of the Commission's ongoing inquiry with respect to ISDS: Nottage (n. 7).

are also free to ask questions during the oral hearings, which can direct the focus towards their preferred topics (such as ISDS) even if they were not a major concern expressed in prior written submissions.[85]

A final dilemma for those undertaking qualitative research into an increasingly high-profile and politicized issue is whether and how researchers should engage in parliamentary inquiries and other public debates. The pros and cons associated with 'participant observation' are the subject of long-standing methodological discussion.[86] Almost by definition, the researcher should be or will become quite expert in the field, and therefore can over-influence respondents, especially when conducting interviews. Similar problems need to be addressed if the researcher has a shared background with respondents, as with Côté in her partly qualitative study of Canadian and other officials' practices with respect to alleged 'regulatory chill'.[87]

Such risks grow if and when the researcher begins to publicly express opinions, even on a preliminary basis, especially outside academic literature. The internet now rapidly and widely diffuses such views, which may make it harder for the researcher to obtain future interviews, especially with those taking opposite views. One response is to suspend public engagement, at least in parliamentary inquiries or media commentary. However, this can be a wasted opportunity to contribute to a pressing public policy issue (which, after all, usually attracts more research funding), especially for longer-term projects.[88] In addition, universities increasingly encourage and expect their academics to engage in public policy debates or 'knowledge transfer'. Doing so may also open doors to interviews or other opportunities for qualitative research, including a well-rounded analysis of parliamentary records. On balance, the best way forward may be to have some members of the research team deliberately not engaging in wider public debates.[89]

---

[85] See e.g. questions on ISDS raised extensively in an inquiry into Australia's treaty-making processes more broadly: Nottage (n. 80).

[86] See e.g. D. Jorgensen, *Participant Observation: A Methodology for Human Studies* (Sage, 1989).

[87] Côté (n. 64), 94.

[88] On the long-standing debate among socio-legal scholars concerning the 'pull of the policy audience', see Austin Sarat and Susan Silbey, 'The Pull of the Policy Audience' (1998) 10 (2–3) *Law and Society Review* 97.

[89] In our project, Professor Leon Trakman and especially Professor Jurgen Kurtz played this role. Professor Nottage has been involved in some media commentary and parliamentary inquiries since 2014: see e.g. Nottage, above (nn. 80 and 83), and incorporating empirical evidence for the CPTPP ratification inquiry; Ana Ubilava and Luke Nottage, 'Costs,

11.4 Conclusions: Lessons from Social Psychology in Assessing and Communicating Empirical Findings

The analysis above reveals the ongoing methodological and practical challenges in conducting empirical research into investment treaties, and particularly ISDS policy and practice, whether such research is quantitative (Section 11.2) or qualitative (Section 11.3).

The shared knowledge base can be advanced by carefully mixing methodologies, reflecting on their limitations and ways to address them. This chapter has attempted to provide a solid basis for further econometric studies into the impact of varying forms of treaty-based ISDS provisions on FDI flows, as well as some preliminary results. More tentatively, it has also outlined some methodological issues arising from our unexpectedly time-consuming qualitative research, in an internet era characterized by growing accessibility of parliamentary and other public inquiries into treaty-making.

By way of conclusion, this section raises a broader concern for researchers and policy-makers that has become apparent perhaps particularly in this field of investor-state dispute resolution. Some powerful psychological issues seem to be at play, complicating the analysis in addition to geopolitics and national politics (more recently even in developed countries, such as Australia). Regulatory chill, for example, implicates an assessment of risk – whether and how much governments are going to be constrained in developing future policy. The 'cultural risk cognition' project led by Dan Kahan at Yale University has shown, through a variety of empirical studies, that how individuals perceive risks derives primarily from their basic worldviews – which can be calibrated across four main quadrants.[90] This goes against not only the notion of a 'rational risk-weigher' (assumed by most economists), but even an 'irrational risk weigher' (assumed by Cass Sunstein and other behavioural economists) whose irrational heuristics and biases about risks could be lessened by experts providing better information and guidance.[91] Kahan and others find that experts 'neutrally' providing more and better information about risks from certain vaccines, for example, in fact leads to *more* divergence in concerns expressed among individuals. Interestingly, they find that *less* divergence eventuates when a

---

Outcomes and Transparency in ISDS Arbitrations: Evidence for an Investment Treaty Parliamentary Inquiry' (2018) 21(4) *International Arbitration Law Review* 111.

[90] See <culturalcognition.net/>.

[91] Dan M. Kahan, 'The Cognitively Illiberal State' (2007) 60 *Stanford Law Review* 115.

person who recognizably shares their worldview presents the same information to each of the four subgroups.[92]

The implication for research on ISDS is that whatever results come from empirical research findings, the means of presenting them to the public will be crucial to reverse what seems to be a growing divergence in perceptions and positions.[93] Extending insights from cultural risk cognition studies, for example, the potential for empirical research findings to reduce polarization of those with divergent worldviews impacting on risk assessments will probably be greater if some demonstrable advantages of ISDS, such as some positive impact on cross-border FDI flows, are presented by representatives of a peak consumer organization in Australia, such as Choice, while some disadvantages and effective means to address them are presented by a peak business group or conservative politician. Unfortunately, however, positions have already been publicized,[94] and the debate is evolving so quickly that even this may not be feasible or effective.

Finally, even if Sunstein's 'irrational risk-weigher' approach[95] does prevail among decision-makers, other research from social psychology uncovers a disturbing array of heuristic and biases that impede rational assessments and debates. Some of these are being applied to explain empirically, for example, why and how investment treaties have been (re)negotiated.[96] Yet even more heuristics and biases are arguably now evident also in ongoing recent public debates in Australia and probably elsewhere over ISDS-backed provisions. They will be hard to counteract effectively, but the first step involves identifying which tendencies widely found in social psychology may be at work and impeding accurate assessments. These arguably include, for example:[97]

---

[92] Dan M. Kahan et al., 'Who Fears the HPV Vaccine, Who Doesn't, and Why? An Experimental Study of the Mechanisms of Cultural Cognition' (2010) 34 *Law and Human Behaviour* 501.

[93] On the threat to largely bipartisan support for foreign investment in Australia since the early 1990s, partly due to tensions over ISDS, see also Luke Nottage, 'The Evolution of Foreign Investment Regulation, Treaties and Investor-State Arbitration in Australia' (2015) 21(4) *New Zealand Business Law Quarterly* 266–76; and generally Nottage (n. 7).

[94] See further Nottage (n. 9), section 4.

[95] See e.g. Richard H. Thaler and Cass R. Sunstein, *Nudge: Improving Decisions about Health, Wealth, and Happiness* (Yale University Press, 2008).

[96] Poulsen (n. 1); Tomer Broude, Yoram Haftel and Alexander Thompson, 'Who Cares about Regulatory Space in BITs? A Comparative International Approach', in Anthea Roberts (ed.), *Comparative International Law* (Oxford University Press, 2016).

[97] For helpful summaries, including further references, see Rolf Dobelli, *The Art of Thinking Clearly* (Harper, 2013) 10–21, 31–45, 67–79, 95–7, 197–9, 209–11, 221–39, 290–2.

MIXING METHODOLOGIES IN INVESTMENT ARBITRATION   349

1. 'Availability' bias (drawing attention to high-profile events or features) and 'story' bias (building on people's attraction to narratives) is evident in the frequent references to the Philip Morris arbitration claim, in media reports and parliamentary inquiries mentioned in Section 11.3 above. 'Framing' by media commentators, or those initiating online campaigns, is also widespread.
2. The 'affect' heuristic, emphasising how initial quite emotional reactions frame subsequent reactions.
3. The 'sunk cost fallacy', which further entrenches especially publicly stated positions, was mentioned above with respect to submissions and evidence in parliamentary hearings.
4. Such entrenchment effects are also reinforced by the 'social proof' or herd instinct phenomenon, 'groupthink' which inhibits dissenting opinions, the 'false consensus' effect, and 'confirmation bias' where evidence for a particular position, such as an ISDS claim succeeding, is taken as proving the argument against ISDS; but contrary evidence is ignored or discounted, such as cases going against investors or statistics showing that they lose more often than win.[98]
5. In assessing risks of claims, 'probability neglect' (focusing instead on the *magnitude of risk* or potential liability exposure) is evident in comments on cases such as Philip Morris. A related phenomenon is 'ambiguity aversion' (a generalised reaction to *uncertainty*, which makes it difficult to delineate risks).
6. The well-known 'endowment effect' also makes people feel more attached to what they have, such as current regulation; they also suffer from 'loss aversion',[99] such as lost capacity to regulate or damages payable if had Australia lost the Philip Morris claim.
7. 'Sleeper' effects help untested or poor sources for information gain credibility over time, simply by being repeated.[100]

---

[98] On the win ratio, see e.g. UNCTAD, *World Investment Report* (2014) 126. Confirmation bias, for example, seems particularly likely to follow publication of our preliminary and nuanced results set out above in Section 11.2.

[99] See also e.g. Daniel Kahneman, *Thinking, Fast and Slow* (Farrar, Straus and Giroux, 2011).

[100] An example is the unattributed and implausible assertion that Australia spent AU\$ 50 million successfully defending the Philip Morris ISDS claim: Hepburn and Nottage (n. 5).

8. The 'not invented here' syndrome can reinforce scepticism about international law norms and processes, compared to domestic courts and legal rights for investors.
9. The 'fallacy of the single cause' leads to scape-goating, including arguably a focus on ISDS even though it is a procedural mechanism, whereas substantive rights offered under investment treaties may be far more problematic.
10. 'Domain dependence' is evident when parliamentary committees call on those expert in one field (such as intellectual property law or environmental protection) to give evidence in public hearings on another field (the broader field of public international law and ISDS) or when media commentators do the same.

Such psychological factors often help explain the growing *opposition* to ISDS, which is probably dominant in (social) media commentary now in Australia.[101] But they can also cut the other way. Those *defending* the system, such as some peak business associations or groups involved in international arbitration, also need to be conscious, for example, of reverse confirmation bias (over-emphasising cases where investors lose, rather than win) as well as social proof, groupthink and false consensus. They and government policy-makers also need to be aware of the 'overconfidence' effect (or over-optimism bias)[102] as well as 'hindsight' bias, including a ready extrapolation into the future from Australia's record in not being yet found liable in ISDS proceedings, or the capacity for treaty drafting to clearly anticipate and manage issues appropriately well into the future (related also to the 'illusion of skill'). Other psychological factors that could be at play are 'omission bias' (preferring inaction or the default option of including ISDS in treaties, over action through radical reforms) and the 'salience effect' (assuming too readily that a now-prominent feature such as ISDS is more important, say in encouraging investment flows, than more diffuse factors).[103]

---

[101] See the empirical data set out in Luke Nottage, 'International Arbitration and Society at Large', in Andrea Bjorklund, Franco Ferrari and Stefan Kröll (eds.), *Cambridge Compendium of International Commercial and Investment Arbitration* (Cambridge University Press, forthcoming).

[102] See also Lauge Poulsen and Emma Aisbett, 'When the Claim Hits: Bilateral Investment Treaties and Bounded Rational Learning' (2013) 65(2) *World Politics* 273, focusing especially on developing countries' decisions to enter into investment treaties. More generally on 'bounded rationality' impacting on investment treaty patterns, see also Poulsen (n. 1).

[103] Dobelli (n. 97), 43–5, 131–3, 242–50, 281–3.

Some or even many of these heuristics and biases may be gradually lessened through enhanced public consultation and debate, including involvement of experts of various persuasions, and they also crop up in other policy-making fields. Nonetheless, they need to be kept in mind by researchers when presenting findings in various forums, as well as in project design and implementation. In sum, broader lessons from contemporary psychology compound the already formidable difficulties of mixed-method empirical research into investment treaties and arbitration tribunals.

Statistical Appendix

Table 11.5 and Table 11.6 show the estimation results for model specification (1) and model specification (2) in Section 11.2.2 above. In both tables the FE estimates are presented in the first three columns and the PPML estimates are shown in the last three columns. For each estimator, the first column shows the baseline model without the political risk index (PRI). In the second column PRI is included. The third column in each set includes the interaction between PRI and BITs for Table 11.5, and between PRI and ISDS1 or ISDS2 for Table 11.6.

In both tables, the FE estimates show that estimated coefficients of most control variables, except the natural resource endowment differences, Nt, have expected signs. Coefficients of key control variables such as Gt, St, Kt and Lt are highly significant with expected signs, suggesting FDI flows from OECD countries are driven by the factors as predicted by the KCM. Difference in both skilled and unskilled labour ratio (Lt) has significant effects on FDI outflows. A higher unskilled labour ratio in host countries attracts more FDI flows from OECD countries. The difference in land per capita ratio has a significant impact on FDI flows, but with unexpected sign. One reason could be that certain capital exporting OECD members have a high land per capita ratio, making this proxy of this resource endowment less effective in capturing resource-seeking FDI. Moreover, there could be offsetting effects between land per capita and unskilled labour share variables as a number of recipient countries have a low level of both indicators. The PPML estimates indicate a robust and strong effect of control variables Gt, St and Kt. There is inconsistency between the FE and PPML estimates in the signs and significance of other control variables, including country-pair difference in land per capita and exchange rate. The coefficient estimate has the expected sign in FE estimation, suggesting responsiveness of FDI outflows when there is a depreciation of currency in OECD countries. The PPML estimate of exchange rate coefficient suggests an unexpected effect on FDI flows.

Turning to the key variables of interest for our project, Table 11.5 shows that a signed BIT has a positive and significant effect on FDI outflows from OECD countries. In the baseline specification, the effect is positive, significant and consistent. The estimated coefficient of a signed BIT is 0.15, equivalent to

Table 11.5 *Effects of signed BITs on FDI (FE and PPML estimators)*

Dependent variable: Log(FDI flows)

	FE estimator			PPML estimator		
	(1)	(2)	(3)	(1)	(2)	(3)
Gt	1.57***	1.56***	1.56***	1.48***	1.45***	1.45***
	(0.07)	(0.08)	(0.08)	(0.002)	(0.003)	(0.003)
St	3.78***	3.77***	3.77***	3.04***	2.97***	2.97***
	(0.3)	(0.3)	(0.3)	(0.010)	(0.010)	(0.010)
lnEXR	−0.086***	−0.091***	−0.091***	0.093***	0.097***	0.098***
	(0.02)	(0.02)	(0.02)	(0.001)	(0.001)	(0.001)
Kt	4.36***	5.01***	5.01***	1.41***	1.59***	1.59***
	(0.7)	(0.7)	(0.7)	(0.02)	(0.02)	(0.02)
Ht3	0.27***	0.31***	0.31***	0.015***	0.043***	0.046***
	(0.05)	(0.05)	(0.05)	(0.002)	(0.002)	(0.002)
Lt3	−2.17***	−2.18***	−2.18***	−6.94***	−7.03***	−7.02***
	(0.7)	(0.7)	(0.7)	(0.02)	(0.02)	(0.02)
Nt	1.14***	1.46***	1.46***	−1.05***	−1.00***	−0.97***
	(0.3)	(0.4)	(0.4)	(0.01)	(0.01)	(0.01)
Gamma	−0.044***	−0.059***	−0.059***	0.15***	0.15***	0.15***
	(0.01)	(0.01)	(0.01)	(0.0004)	(0.0004)	(0.0004)
Phi3	−0.39***	−0.41***	−0.41***	−0.72***	−0.73***	−0.73***
	(0.07)	(0.07)	(0.07)	(0.002)	(0.002)	(0.002)

Table 11.5 (*cont.*)

	FE estimator			PPML estimator		
	(1)	(2)	(3)	(1)	(2)	(3)
BIT	0.15***	0.15**	0.15	0.24***	0.23***	0.38***
	(0.06)	(0.06)	(0.3)	(0.002)	(0.002)	(0.01)
PRI		0.012***	0.012***		0.0077***	0.0081***
		(0.002)	(0.003)		(0.00008)	(0.00009)
BIT_PRI			−0.000053			−0.0020***
			(0.004)			(0.0001)
Constant	−41.9***	−42.1***	−42.1***			
	(2.0)	(2.0)	(2.0)			
R-squared	0.322	0.323	0.323			
N	25,148	24,378	24,378	43,203	40,740	40,740

Note: * $p < 0.10$, ** $p < 0.05$, ***$p < 0.01$; Standard errors are in brackets.

Source: Authors' calculation.

Table 11.6 *Effects of ISDS1 and ISDS2 (FE and PPML estimators)*

Dependent variable: Log(FDI flows)

	FE estimator			PPML estimator		
	(1)	(2)	(3)	(1)	(2)	(3)
Gt	1.57***	1.56***	1.56***	1.48***	1.45***	1.45***
	(0.07)	(0.08)	(0.08)	(0.002)	(0.003)	(0.003)
St	3.78***	3.77***	3.78***	3.03***	2.97***	2.97***
	(0.3)	(0.3)	(0.3)	(0.010)	(0.010)	(0.010)
lnEXR	−0.083***	−0.087***	−0.086***	0.094***	0.098***	0.098***
	(0.02)	(0.02)	(0.02)	(0.001)	(0.001)	(0.001)
Kt	4.45***	5.08***	5.10***	1.39***	1.56***	1.57***
	(0.7)	(0.7)	(0.7)	(0.02)	(0.02)	(0.02)
Ht3	0.26***	0.30***	0.29***	0.017***	0.046***	0.047***
	(0.05)	(0.05)	(0.05)	(0.002)	(0.002)	(0.002)
Lt3	−2.20***	−2.20***	−2.22***	−6.92***	−7.01***	−7.00***
	(0.7)	(0.7)	(0.7)	(0.02)	(0.02)	(0.02)
Nt	1.12***	1.43***	1.36***	−1.05***	−0.99***	−0.98***
	(0.3)	(0.4)	(0.4)	(0.01)	(0.01)	(0.01)
Gamma	−0.046***	−0.060***	−0.062***	0.15***	0.15***	0.15***
	(0.01)	(0.01)	(0.01)	(0.0004)	(0.0004)	(0.0004)
Phi3	−0.39***	−0.41***	−0.41***	−0.72***	−0.73***	−0.73***
	(0.07)	(0.07)	(0.07)	(0.002)	(0.002)	(0.002)

Table 11.6 (*cont.*)

	FE estimator			PPML estimator		
	(1)	(2)	(3)	(1)	(2)	(3)
bit_ISDS1	−0.14	−0.12	−0.92**	0.26***	0.26***	0.32***
	(0.09)	(0.09)	(0.4)	(0.003)	(0.003)	(0.01)
bit_ISDS2	0.30***	0.30***	0.40	0.26***	0.24***	0.33***
	(0.07)	(0.07)	(0.3)	(0.003)	(0.003)	(0.02)
PRI		0.011***	0.011***		0.0076***	0.0078***
		(0.002)	(0.003)		(0.00008)	(0.00009)
ISDS1_PRI			0.011**			−0.00079***
			(0.005)			(0.0002)
ISDS2_PRI			−0.0015			−0.0012***
			(0.005)			(0.0002)
Constant	−41.9***	−42.0***	−42.2***			
	(2.0)	(2.0)	(2.0)			
R-squared	0.322	0.324	0.324			
N	25,148	24,378	24,378	43,203	40,740	40,740

Note: * $p < 0.10$, ** $p < 0.05$, *** $p < 0.01$; Standard errors are in brackets.

Source: Authors' calculation.

an increase in FDI of about 16 per cent in FE estimation and 0.24, or 27 per cent,[104] in PPML estimation. Interestingly, the FDI effect of BITs is almost unchanged when PRI is included in the model with both estimators. Moreover, the coefficient on PRI has expected sign and is statistically significant. The coefficient on BIT becomes insignificant in FE estimation when the BIT and PRI terms are interacted. A correlation check shows that this problem is due to a very high level of correlation between BIT and the interaction term BIT_PRI, making the estimated effect of BITs insignificant in the FE estimation. In contrast, the PPML estimated coefficients of these variables are highly significant as more observations are taken into account.

Table 11.6 shows the effect of specific BIT provisions, ISDS1 and ISDS2, on FDI flows. While the FE estimation suggests that the significance of the impact of BITs on FDI flows is accounted for only by stronger ISDS clauses (ISDS2), the PPML estimation indicates a highly significant and similar impact from both types of provisions. The instability and inconsistency of the coefficient on BITs when interacted with PRI and ISDS1 or ISDS2 demonstrate the results from these models are not stable and reliable.

Sensitivity Tests

We further examined the sensitivity of our estimation results under different scenarios to provide further insight into the dynamics of FDI impact from BITs, considering the following aspects: (i) since our dataset covers a long time period, it seems useful to see if the impact of BITs on FDI has changed over different sub-periods in line with different generations of BITs; (ii) the impacts of BITs between OECD countries and different country groups might vary due to differences in the BIT design for each country group and related political and economic factors; (iii) the significance of the FDI effect of BITs might vary with characteristics of the host country's domestic business environment.

It appears that over the long period 1985–2014, annual FDI flows from OECD countries have indeed shown different trends. As shown in Figure 11.1, while the overall trend is for larger total FDI outflows over the whole period 1985–2014, there was a gradual increase in annual FDI outflows between 1985 and 2000 before a sharp drop in 2001. An average upward trend is observed between 2001 and 2014. However, the total amount of FDI outflows fluctuated markedly from 2008 to 2014 after having shown a steady growing trend in the sub-period 2001–8. Therefore, it would be possible to examine the relationship between having BITs and resulting FDI flows from OECD

---

[104] We adopt the percentage change formula: $e\beta^k -0.5\,V_k^{-1}$, as suggested e.g. by Peter Egger and Valeria Merlo 'The impact of bilateral investment treaties on FDI dynamics' (2007) 30(10) *The World Economy* 1536–49.

358   SHIRO ARMSTRONG AND LUKE NOTTAGE

countries in two sub-periods, 1985–2000 and 2001–14. Moreover, an examination of a possible structural break using the simple Chow test on the year 2000 confirms our choice.

Estimation results of the impact of BITs and its specific provisions for two periods are shown in Table 11.7. The results suggest that early BITs (signed before 2000) seem to have greater and more significant effects on FDI than the BITs of the period after 2000. This may be consistent with a trend towards improving domestic business conditions in many countries in their race to attract more FDI, including perhaps through unilateral liberalization. Again, it can be seen that ISDS1 (weaker provisions) had a stronger and significant effect on FDI flows in both sub-periods. A similar pattern is observed on the impact of BITs with the combined aspects of MFN and ISDS provisions in the period 1985–2000, as shown in Table 11.8.

Consistent with previous results, Table 11.7 suggests that weaker-form ISDS provisions have a stronger impact on FDI flows into both host developed and developing countries. It is notable that the impact of strong ISDS provisions (ISDS2) is small and insignificant in the second sub-period while significant in the first sub-period. It is similar to the impact of BITs with both strong ISDS and MFN provisions as shown in Table 11.6. This evidence of weak and insignificant impact of strong ISDS provisions in period 2001–14 in our study is consistent with the findings of previous studies.[105] However, the positive impact of ISDS2 on FDI flows becomes significant for that second sub-period for treaties that are ratified in the same year as signing, whereas it is insignificant for such treaties over 1985–2000. This progression might indicate that investors have become aware of and confident about stronger ISDS-backed commitments for treaties that are more salient due to prompt ratification after signing, as well as the growing numbers of ISDS claims being filed and publicly discussed since the turn of the century.

As for the country-specific impact of BITs, the estimation results for different host country groups are also presented in Table 11.7. It is surprising that the impact of signed BITs on FDI flows to Non-OECD destination countries is small and insignificant compared with that for OECD recipient countries. A similar finding is obtained when host countries are divided into 'developed countries' and 'less developed countries'.[106] Given that a BIT is

---

[105] See Yackee (n. 26); Busse et al. (n. 25); Berger et al. (n. 29).

[106] These terms ('DC' and 'LDC') are based on the World Bank's 2015 country classification of countries by their gross national income per capita in US dollars. DC denotes the group of high-income countries (as the World Bank has recently started to call them) with GNI per capita greater than $12,745 in the World Bank's financial year 2015 for the country data in 2013. This benchmark has changed over time, being $12,275 in the Bank's financial year 2012 for country data in 2010, although the DC country group is unchanged between these two benchmarks.

Table 11.7 *Sensitivity analysis with alternative time periods and country groups*

Variable	Whole sample	Different periods		Country group 1		Country group 2	
		1985–2000	2001–14	DC	LDC	OECD	Non-OECD
BIT (Signed)	**0.32*****	**0.37*****	**0.29**	**0.35****	**0.021**	**0.31****	**0.056**
	(0.1)	(0.10)	(0.2)	(0.2)	(0.1)	(0.1)	(0.1)
BITR (Ratified)	**0.48*****	**0.34****	**0.52****	**0.54***	**0.45**	**0.17**	**0.49****
	(0.1)	(0.2)	(0.3)	(0.3)	(0.3)	(0.2)	(0.2)
ISDS1_Signed	**0.43*****	**0.35***	**0.51****	**0.61****	**0.30***	**0.35***	**0.38***
	(0.13)	(0.19)	(0.21)	(0.3)	(0.2)	(0.2)	(0.2)
ISDS2_Signed	**0.23****	**0.33*****	**0.087**	**0.29***	**0.083**	**0.17**	**0.13**
	(0.11)	(0.099)	(0.29)	(0.2)	(0.1)	(0.2)	(0.2)
ISDSR1_Ratified	**0.42*****	**0.56****	**0.64*****	**0.29**	**0.60****	**0.45***	**0.58****
	(0.14)	(0.24)	(0.22)	(0.5)	(0.3)	(0.2)	(0.2)
ISDSR2_Ratified	**0.39****	**0.16**	**0.79***	**0.54**	**0.29**	**0.10**	**0.46***
	(0.20)	(0.18)	(0.44)	(0.4)	(0.3)	(0.3)	(0.2)

Note: * $p < 0.10$, ** $p < 0.05$, ***$p < 0.01$; Standard errors are in brackets.

Source: Authors' calculation.

360   SHIRO ARMSTRONG AND LUKE NOTTAGE

Table 11.8 *Conditional effects of MFN and ISDS in BITs over different time periods*

	1985–2014	1985–2000	2001–14
PRI	0.017***	0.014***	0.021***
	(0.003)	(0.003)	(0.007)
MFN1*ISDS1	0.54***	0.57**	0.73**
	(0.2)	(0.2)	(0.3)
MFN1*ISDS2	0.36**	0.50***	0.59*
	(0.1)	(0.1)	(0.3)
MFN2*ISDS1	0.35*	0.28	0.78*
	(0.2)	(0.3)	(0.4)
MFN2*ISDS2	0.20**	0.31**	0.057
	(0.09)	(0.1)	(0.2)

Note: * $p < 0.10$, ** $p < 0.05$, ***$p < 0.01$; Standard errors are in brackets.
Source: Authors' calculation.

expected to be a commitment enforcement device, this unexpected finding needs further research into other possible factors that might be having a stronger impact on FDI outflows from OECD countries into less developed economies. One of these factors could be a Double Taxation Treaty (DTT). However, this option is beyond our current investigation due to data availability constraints. Nevertheless, additional regressions on specific ISDS provisions suggest that both strong and (especially) weak ISDS provisions in signed treaties are still significantly effective in attracting FDI into both OECD and Non-OECD countries combined. In contrast, the FDI impact of strong ISDS provisions is smaller and insignificant when both country groups are examined separately. Table 11.7 also shows that although the impact is positive and significant from strong ISDS provisions contained in treaties ratified in the same year as signature, at least for FDI into Non-OECD countries, the effect remains stronger for weaker-form ISDS provisions. This pattern appears to be consistent with the evidence provided above.

The responsiveness of the impact of BITs with respect to alternative aspects of a host country's domestic business environment is further examined with a set of different governance indexes in addition to PRI. Covering the period 1996–2014, the World Bank's database on governance indices consists of six different indexes reflecting various aspects of a host country's governance situation: voice and accountability, political stability, government effectiveness, regulation quality, rule of law and control of corruption. Each index scales from -2.5 to 2.5 to reflect a range of a country's conditions in a relevant aspect of governance from the lowest to highest level. This scale is then

Table 11.9 *The FDI impact of PRI and alternative governance indexes*

Variable	Fixed effects estimator		Fixed-effects Poisson estimator		Two-step System GMM estimator	
	Index	BIT	Index	BIT	Index	BIT
Political risk (PRI)	0.015***	0.076	0.0080***	0.25***	0.020***	0.28**
	(0.003)	(−0.09)	(0.00009)	(−0.003)	(0.004)	(−0.1)
Voice and accountability	0.0074**	0.068	0.015***	0.29***	0.010***	0.35***
	(0.003)	(−0.09)	(0.0001)	(−0.003)	(0.002)	(−0.1)
Political stability	0.0081***	0.059	0.0045***	0.25***	0.0091***	0.29**
	(0.002)	(−0.09)	(0.00007)	(−0.003)	(0.002)	(−0.1)
Government effectiveness	0.022***	0.047	0.0055***	0.24***	0.012***	0.32***
	(0.004)	(−0.09)	(0.0001)	(−0.003)	(0.003)	(−0.1)
Regulation quality	0.024***	0.066	0.0095***	0.26***	0.014***	0.31**
	(0.003)	(−0.09)	(0.0001)	(−0.003)	(0.003)	(−0.1)
Rule of law	0.024***	0.057	0.011***	0.25***	0.0098***	0.31***
	(0.004)	(−0.09)	(0.0001)	(−0.003)	(0.002)	(−0.1)
Corruption control	0.017***	0.057	0.0069***	0.25***	0.010***	0.33***
	(0.003)	(−0.09)	(0.00009)	(−0.003)	(0.003)	(−0.1)

Note: * $p < 0.10$, ** $p < 0.05$, *** $p < 0.01$; Standard errors are in brackets; The time period covered in regressions is 1996–2014 due to the availability of data on governance indexes; With each estimator, two columns represent estimated coefficients of political risk and other governance indexes and corresponding estimated coefficients of BITs.

Source: Authors' estimation.

Table 11.10 *Countries covered by the FDI data set*

Source countries (OECD)

Australia	Estonia	Ireland	New Zealand	Spain
Austria	Finland	Israel	Norway	Sweden
Belgium	France	Italy	Poland	Switzerland
Canada	Germany	Japan	Portugal	Turkey
Chile	Greece	Korea	Slovak Republic	United Kingdom
Czech Republic	Hungary	Luxembourg	Slovenia	United States
Denmark	Iceland	Netherlands		

Host countries and economies (OECD and Non-OECD)

Albania	Cyprus	Italy	Mozambique	Sri Lanka
Argentina	Czech Republic	Jamaica	Namibia	Sudan
Armenia	Cote d'Ivoire	Japan	Nepal	Swaziland
Australia	Denmark	Jordan	Netherlands	Sweden
Austria	Ecuador	Kazakhstan	New Zealand	Switzerland
Bahrain	Egypt	Kenya	Niger	Syria
Bangladesh	El Salvador	South Korea	Norway	Taiwan
Barbados	Estonia	Kuwait	Pakistan	Tajikistan
Belgium	Fiji	Kyrgyzstan	Panama	Tanzania
Belize	Finland	Lao PDR	Paraguay	Thailand
Benin	France	Latvia	Peru	Togo
Bolivia	Gabon	Lesotho	Philippines	Trinidad and Tobago
Botswana	Gambia	Liberia	Poland	Tunisia
Brazil	Germany	Lithuania	Portugal	Turkey
Brunei Darussalam	Ghana	Luxembourg	Qatar	Uganda
Bulgaria	Greece	Macao	Romania	Ukraine
Burundi	Guatemala	Malawi	Russia	United Kingdom
Cambodia	Honduras	Malaysia	Rwanda	United States
Cameroon	Hong Kong	Maldives	Saudi Arabia	Uruguay
Canada	Hungary	Mali	Senegal	Venezuela

Central African Republic	Iceland	Malta	Serbia	Viet Nam
Chile	India	Mauritania	Sierra Leone	Yemen
China	Indonesia	Mauritius	Singapore	Zambia
Colombia	Iran	Mexico	Slovakia	Zimbabwe
Congo	Iraq	Moldova	Slovenia	
Costa Rica	Ireland	Mongolia	South Africa	
Croatia	Israel	Morocco	Spain	

converted to the 0–100 range to make them comparable with the main proxy of domestic conditions: PRI. Correlation analysis shows that these governance indexes are highly correlated with PRI. The estimation results with different estimators for the BIT coefficient and alternative indexes are presented in Table 11.9.

It can be observed that the positive FDI effect of BITs remains significant with very little changes in the magnitude with the inclusion of different governance indexes. The PPML estimates of BIT coefficients are very close to the GMM estimates. Moreover, like PRI, all governance indexes have a significant and positive effect on FDI flows to a host country, although their magnitude is smaller. This evidence confirms the essential role of a host country's domestic business environment in attracting FDI, alongside broader economic determinants and external commitments.

Summary

In general, we find evidence that BITs do have a significant and positive impact on FDI flows from OECD countries to their partner host countries. However, the effect of stronger ISDS provisions in BITs is smaller than for weaker provisions, and not robust over time and with respect to different types of host countries, despite such provisions having become dominant in treaties signed especially since the 1990s. Similar evidence is found when focusing on the MFN provisions of BITs.

One explanation for the insignificant influence of BITs with strong ISDS provisions may be some historical lack of interest from many foreign investors regarding such specific provisions. Rather, as Berger et al. suggest: 'foreign investors tend to regard BITs as a broader set of similarly important investment provisions, rather than carefully checking the multitude of BITs for specific provisions. Note also that negotiations of BITs tend to be a technical procedure conducted on the basis of ready-made model text'.[107] This situation could be linked to the fact that the rate of ISDS cases that foreign investors have successfully won against the host states is only about 25 per cent of some 365 concluded ICSID cases by the end of 2014.[108] Moreover, ISDS cases are concentrated in certain sectors where there is dominant influence of public buyers and political patronage.[109] Therefore, it would be useful to have additional empirical research on the sectoral level impact of BITs and specific provisions, particularly ISDS, on FDI flows. Unfortunately, there is limited available bilateral FDI data that is sector-specific.[110] Perhaps for this reason, there seem to have been very few studies on BIT and FDI relationships at the industry level.

[107] Berger et al. (n. 29), 262.
[108] UNCTAD, 'Recent trends in IIAS and ISDS', *IIA Issues Note*, February 2015 <unctad .org/en/PublicationsLibrary/webdiaepcb2015d1_en.pdf>.
[109] Roderick Abbott, Fredrik Erixon, and Martina Francesca Ferracane, 'Demystifying Investor-State Dispute Settlement (ISDS)', *ECIPE Occasional Paper*, No. 5/2014.
[110] The OECD database on foreign direct investments has FDI data at the industry level for a number of industries, but not dyadic data.

12

Double Jeopardy? The Use of Investment Arbitration in Times of Crisis

CÉDRIC, DUPONT* THOMAS SCHULTZ** AND
MERIH ANGIN***

12.1 Introduction

Since the mid-nineties, international investment arbitration has become a regular tool used by investors to settle disputes with host countries. Whereas its use remained almost absent from the radar from the first case in 1972 to 1995, it has since quickly risen to an average of nearly 62 known cases a year in the period 2008–2017, according to the United Nations Conference on Trade and Development.[1] It reached a record number in 2015 with 86 cases initiated.[2] According to our own data, 1,098 investment arbitration claims have been filed up to December 2018. Furthermore, the number of countries that have been targeted by arbitration is on the rise, both in the developing and developed worlds, to reach 121 countries.[3]

Filing an investment arbitration is a big decision to make. It has potentially large financial implications for the host state of the investment: in three closely related awards, an investment arbitral tribunal ordered Russia to pay over USD 50 billion in compensation to the former shareholders of the Yukos Oil Company.[4] It has significant economic consequences for the investor too: on average an investment arbitration

---

* Graduate Institute of International and Development Studies, Geneva, Switzerland.
** King's College London – The Dickson Poon School of Law; University of Geneva.
*** Assistant Professor, Koc University.
[1] UNCTAD, 'Investment Dispute Settlement Navigator', <investmentpolicy.unctad.org/investment-dispute-settlement>.
[2] Ibid.
[3] Ibid.
[4] *Yukos Universal (Isle of Man) v. Russia (UNCITRAL)*, PCA Case No. AA 227, Award, 18 July 2014; *Hulley Enterprises (Cyprus) v. Russia (UNCITRAL)*, PCA Case No. AA 226, 18 July 2014; *Veteran Petroleum (Cyprus) v. Russia (UNCITRAL)*, PCA Case No. AA 228, Award, 18 July 2014.

costs the investor USD 6 million in fees, and quite often up to USD 30 million.[5] In the aforesaid Yukos case, the claimants indicated that their costs for legal representation actually exceeded USD 80 million, while the cost of the arbitration itself (arbitrator fees, fees of the institution and other attendant costs) amounted to nearly € 8.5 million. And this does not include lost profits from the investor's future economic activity in the host state, which is typically discontinued or strongly reduced after the arbitration. As an internationally renowned investment arbitration lawyer put it in an anonymous interview, 'no-one in their right mind would want to arbitrate'.[6] In sum, investment arbitration has significant negative side effects: these costs for investors and its documented effect in restricting the policy space of states.[7]

In that sense, investment arbitration should be considered at best a means of last resort in the set of tools to remedy investment disputes. It should be used only when other means have either failed to prevent harmful state policies and decisions or to obtain compensation for them. Its use should be condoned only in patently legitimate situations. As a matter of fact, given the costs mentioned above, investment arbitration may look more like a means of destruction with potential large collateral damage. Then again, not everything is destroyed; these costs are not detrimental to everyone: in a rough estimate, investment arbitration must have generated over USD 10 billion in fees for the international bar (the lawyers and law firms who run the regime by acting as counsel and arbitrators) and probably generates nearly three quarters of a billion USD each year.[8] The question this poses, of

---

[5] Matthew Hodgson and Alastair Campbell, 'Damages and Costs in Investment Treaty Arbitration Revisited', *Global Arbitration Review*, 14 December 2017, <globalarbitrationreview.com/article/1151755/damages-and-costs-in-investment-treaty-arbitration-revisited>; David Gaukrodger and Kathryn Gordon, 'OECD Working Papers on International Investment: Investor–State Dispute Settlement: A Scoping Paper for the Investment Policy Community', *OECD Working Papers on International Investment*, 2012/03 (OECD Publishing, 2012), <dx.doi.org/10.1787/5k46b1r85j6f-en>; Wolf von Kumberg, Jeremy Lack and Michael Leathes, 'Enabling Early Settlement in Investor–State Arbitration' (2014) 29(1) *ICSID Review* 133.

[6] Interview quoted in Katharina Luz, *Bringing the Firm Back In – Investors' Choice for International Investment Arbitration* (PhD thesis, Graduate Institute of International and Development Studies, 2016), 3.

[7] Gus Van Harten and Dayna Nadine Scott, 'Investment Treaties and the Internal Vetting of Regulatory Proposals: A Case Study from Canada' (2016) 7(1) *Journal of International Dispute Settlement* 92.

[8] The calculation is based on the following figures: average party costs of USD 6,019,000 for claimants and USD 4,855,000 for respondents, thus a total of USD 10,874,000; 1,098 cases in total (which would give a total of USD 11,939,652,000 in party costs, but this figure was

course, is whether the international bar may be inclined to favour the use of investment arbitration even in situations that might be considered less than straightforwardly normatively legitimate. To take a simple example, on which this chapter eventually focuses, a pro-cyclical use of investment arbitration would not necessarily appear legitimate: that is, when it is used to hit countries that already suffer from severe economic difficulties, causing additional economic bleeding.

In this chapter, we focus on the hypothesis that investment arbitration is used as a response to the effects of two types of shocks on investors – shocks caused by severely dysfunctional governance at the national level and shocks caused by economic crises. The first type of situation, where it serves to redress or mitigate severe governance deficiencies, would be an archetype of a legitimate use. Its use in the context of economic crises, by contrast, could be viewed as a double jeopardy, in the sense that the countries' economy would be put in jeopardy twice. Investment arbitration would certainly not gain in legitimacy if it were shown that it is used in a way to hurt countries already in great difficulties. We investigate this hypothesis by testing links between governance, economic crises and investment arbitration using an original dataset. We find that bad governance, understood as corruption and lack of rule of law, has a statistically significant relation with investment arbitration claims, but economic crises do not when considered separately. Yet, bad governance and economic crises considered together are a good predictor of when countries get hit by investment arbitration claims.

The chapter is structured as follows: we begin with a brief illustration of arbitration as a response to two generically different contexts. Drawing from these cases and the literature, we develop theoretical propositions linking those two types of situation and the use of investment arbitration. We then discuss our research design, present the empirical results and conclude.

12.2 The Legitimacy of Arbitration: Two Generically Different Contexts

Context 1: In the 1990s, Banro, a Canadian company, was doing gold and tin mining in the Democratic Republic of Congo (DRC). Towards

---

roughly rounded down in the text above to account for cases that settled early); and an average of 70 new cases per year (which gives an average of USD 761,180,000). The figures for average party costs are from a study by investment arbitration counsel themselves: Matthew Hodgson and Alastair Campbell (n. 5).

the end of the decade, the government of the DRC decided to increase the share of revenues it earned from these raw materials. This decision was implemented with a series of measures that significantly reduced the value of Banro's interests in the country. Banro attempted to fight against the government through international legal channels, one of its key advisers being a lawyer named Patrick Mitchell, a US citizen working with a small legal counsel firm in Mitchell & Associates in Congo. The problem was that Mitchell & Associates were successful in advising Banro. This was not good for them. The Congolese government, upset by the presence of such competent lawyers within its territory defending foreign interests, arrested two employees and claimed that they were posing a threat to state security. Congolese authorities ransacked and sealed Mr Mitchell's offices, effectively destroying his business. Mr Mitchell, in response, filed an investment arbitration against the DRC under the aegis of the World Bank's International Center for Settlement of Investment Disputes (ICSID) in 1999. He claimed that he had been expropriated of his investment in the law firm. His employees were released after eight months of imprisonment. The use of investment arbitration in response to such a situation seemed straightforwardly legitimate – it responded to a blatant disregard for the rule of law.[9]

Context 2: After Argentina experienced eight major currency crises between the early 1970s and 1991, it introduced a radical economic plan involving reduction of trade barriers, privatization of state-owned enterprises (including those functioning in certain public utility sectors), deregulation of industries, and pegging of the Argentine peso to the US dollar. As part of this effort, the 1992 Gas Law was passed, allowing the privatization of Gas del Estado S.E., with its eight distribution and two transportation companies. Part of the shareholdings was acquired by CMS Gas Transmission, incorporated in the USA. For many years, it experienced good collaboration with the Argentine government. But then a severe economic crisis hit Argentina in January 2002: the government defaulted on its foreign debt of USD 80 billion. One measure taken by Argentina to alleviate the crisis was to unpeg the peso from the US dollar: within five months, the value of the peso dropped by 70 per cent compared to the US dollar. The government further froze all utility rates

---

[9] *Patrick Mitchell v. Democratic Republic of the Congo*, ICSID Case No. ARB/99/7. Patrick Mitchell won the initial arbitration, but the decision was subsequently annulled. Its annulment, though, does not change our argument, which relates to the contexts in which investment arbitration is used.

by putting into effect an 'economic emergency law' that disallowed privatized gas transport and distribution companies to charge tariffs calculated in US dollars, and required renegotiation of agreements under the new exchange rate regime. This resulted in CMS's filing of an investment arbitration against Argentina, invoking the provisions of the US–Argentina Bilateral Investment Treaty (BIT), just like many other foreign investors.[10] In this case, it is not quite obvious that the use of investment arbitration was legitimate: when a country is pushed by an economic crisis to default on its foreign debt, when almost everyone suffers from the crisis, should foreign investors like CMS obtain special treatment, especially treatment that further harms an already seriously jeopardized economy? The question probably deserves an intricate moral-political analysis, which is beyond the scope of this chapter. Nonetheless, our point is this: is this situation in fact typical or is it rather an exception to the norm of filing of investment arbitrations due to poor national governance?

12.3   Governance, Economic Crisis and Investment Arbitration: Conditional Legitimacy?

Properly canvassing the legitimacy of investment arbitration, in all its many dimensions, would be a Herculean task. In this chapter, we choose to take a liberal normative viewpoint, and consider that investment arbitration serves to protect parties against the vagaries of states. Specifically, we posit that its purpose is to strengthen or impose the domestic rule of law in the host state of the investment.[11] Investment arbitration is meant to guard against situations in which governments run roughshod over treaty or contract obligations, over international law or their own domestic law. Put differently, these are circumstances in which public powers are exercised by states in a way that unduly interferes with a foreign investment in plain, blunt disregard of legal obligations. Such situations correspond to a weak rule of law, in the sense that 'the rule of law is distinguished from regimes of administrative command and control, where "arbitrary" state action prevails. Law is the instrument

---

[10]   *CMS Gas Transmission Company* v. *Republic of Argentina*, ICSID Case No. ARB/01/8. The arbitral tribunal considered that Argentina had not met the requirements of the defence of necessity. Annulment proceedings were unsuccessful.

[11]   This is further discussed in Thomas Schultz and Cédric Dupont, 'Investment Arbitration: Promoting the Rule of Law or Over-Empowering Investors? A Quantitative Empirical Study' (2014) 25(4) *European Journal of International Law* 1147.

370 CÉDRIC DUPONT AND THOMAS SCHULTZ

that gives the individual power to resist the state'.[12] Investment arbitration would, then, be used to stimulate or react to the absence of 'good and orderly state administration and the protection of rights and other deserving interests', as is often claimed in the law literature.[13]

We envisage two main types of disregard of legal obligations: first, carelessness, strictly speaking, where the authority of law is simply ignored; second, simple administrative or governmental disarray, where a government is unable to enforce respect for the rule of law in its country.

We consider that such situations typically translate as poor institutional conditions. If arbitration turns out to be more likely to target states with such conditions, it would score at least decently on legitimacy from both political and economic liberal viewpoints.

Guarding against the policy vagaries of states in economic crisis is a more controversial issue. Indeed, during economic crises, governments have to react quickly in adopting policy responses that appropriately address core concerns of a large range of domestic actors who use all available institutionalized channels, including protests, in order to push for the adoption of immediate, and sometimes radical, policy responses to the crises.

Policy responses by governments have varied significantly across time and space both regarding the choice of measures and regarding their relative success in meeting domestic demands. Regarding the latter, economic crises have led to episodes of government change,[14] even to

---

[12] Kerry Rittich, *Recharacterizing Restructuring: Law, Distribution and Gender in Market Reform* (Kluwer, 2002) p. 67. A longer discussion of our understanding of the rule of law can be found in Thomas Schultz, *Transnational Legality: Stateless Law and International Arbitration* (Oxford University Press, 2014).

[13] Benedict Kingsbury and Stephan Schill, 'Investor-State Arbitration as Governance: Fair and Equitable Treatment, Proportionality, and the Emerging Global Administrative Law', *Institute for International Law and Justice, New York University Law School, Working Paper* 2009/6 (Global Administrative Law Series) 8, <dx.doi.org/10.2139/ssrn.1466980>.

[14] Recent work on the Great Recession shows that electoral processes in 30 European countries since 2008 strongly confirm the major finding of the literature on economic voting that incumbents are voted out in elections in times of economic recessions. Given that the recession was particularly severe, and in most countries clearly attributed to governments, the effect on incumbents has been particularly strong and fast. In countries with more than one electoral process since 2008 and ongoing acute economic slump, the interesting result is the tendency to choose outside main parties, including radical, 'anti-parties', or to abstain: see Hanspeter Kriesi, 'The Political Consequences of the Financial and Economic Crisis in Europe: Electoral Punishment and Popular Protest' (2012) 18(4) *Swiss Political Science Review* 518.

political regime change.[15] Regarding measures adopted, one type of reaction traverses most fault lines: market intervention.[16] Whereas such intervention may be warranted in times of economic distress, it often amounts to helping domestic interests at the expense, directly or indirectly and intentionally or inadvertently, of foreign investors' interests.[17] Furthermore, given the political dynamics that follow severe economic crises, governments have a hard time quickly reverting to 'normal' behaviour, thus continuing market intervention for too long and harming private interests, domestic and foreign.

Accordingly, in times of economic crisis investment arbitration can be seen either as a legitimate instrument when it limits the time span and the discriminatory bias of policy reactions, or as an illegitimate tool when it prevents governments from addressing justifiable domestic concerns, particularly when they are of a social nature. As a corollary, to the extent that both investors and arbitrators are likely to differentiate between the nature and type of policy reactions, we should not expect, as a departure point, any clear-cut and strong relationship between the use of arbitration and the economic situation of host countries.

One plausible hypothesis, that we will explore empirically, could be, however, that investors are inclined to attack countries during hard economic times if they have very low confidence in the type or the scope of policy reactions adopted. This is more likely to be the case when countries have a poor governance record. From this perspective, arbitration should not be merely seen as a 'vulture' instrument hurting those in a weak situation, but as an instrument used to redress poor institutional conditions and policy reactions in times when it hurts the most.

---

[15] Mark J. Gasiorowski, 'Economic Crisis and Political Regime Change: An Event History Analysis' (1995) 89(4) *American Political Science Review* 882; Andrew MacIntyre, 'The Politics of the Economic Crisis in Southeast Asia' (2001) 55(1) *International Organization* 81; Thomas B. Pepinsky, 'The Global Economic Crisis and the Politics of Non-Transitions' (2012) 47(2) *Government and Opposition* 135; Karen L. Remmer, 'Democracy and Economic Crisis: The Latin American Experience' (1990) 42(3) *World Politics* 315.

[16] See Peter A. Gourevitch, *Politics in Hard Times: Comparative Responses to International Economic Crises* (Cornell University Press, 1986) and, more recently, Nancy Bermeo and Jonas Pontusson (eds.), *Coping with Crisis: Government Reactions to the Great Recession* (Russel Sage Foundation, 2012).

[17] The 2012–13 Cypriot financial crisis is a case in point: the government bail-in measures explicitly targeted foreign, in that case, Russian, bank depositors.

12.4 Research Design

12.4.1 Dataset and Variables

Our research design proceeds as follows. We run first an ordinal logistic regression in order to investigate the relationship between arbitration claims against a given country and its economic and governance conditions. The models analyse the likelihood of a variation in the frequency of the number of arbitration claims per country per year. We then employ a negative binomial regression to test the same hypothesis with a count model.

The current study draws on a dataset of 1,098 investment arbitration claims, filed between 1972 (year the first investment claim was filed with ICSID[18]) and 2018.[19] Our unit of analysis here is 'claims' – not 'arbitral awards' since certain claims end in a negotiated agreement or are withdrawn, and not 'cases' since the meaning of that word is too imprecise.[20]

Our study relates to investment arbitration in general, also called investor–state arbitration or investor–state dispute settlement (ISDS). We thus go beyond investment *treaty* arbitration, which encompasses only investment arbitration based on an international treaty (typically a bilateral investment treaty). Our dataset therefore includes arbitration claims based on a treaty (bilateral or multilateral), or a contract between the host state and the investor, or the domestic investment law of the host state of the investment.

The study is further concerned with all types of investment arbitration in the sense that the dataset covers claims filed under the rules of all relevant arbitration institutions (mainly the World Bank's ICSID, the Permanent Court of Arbitration (PCA), the International Chamber of Commerce (ICC), the Stockholm Chamber of Commerce (SCC)) as well as ad hoc arbitrations (primarily conducted under the rules of the United Nations Commission for International Trade Law (UNCITRAL)).

Finally, the collection of our data was not limited to official sources, such as the website of the relevant arbitration institutions. We thus went

---

[18] *Holiday Inns S.A. and others* v. *Morocco*, ICSID Case No. ARB/72/1.

[19] Our statistical analysis takes a subset of this dataset and analyses claims filed between 1972 and 2012, as explained later in the chapter.

[20] A 'claim' is a request for arbitration filed by a claimant with an arbitration institution (such as ICSID), or a notification of the initiation of an arbitration sent to the respondent if no arbitration institution is involved (in ad hoc arbitrations). A 'case' is a loose term, typically designating two specific parties and a broad set of facts. A 'case' may include more than one 'claim', possibly filed with different arbitration institutions.

beyond the 'officially known' arbitration claims. The sources of the data collected were, instead, as broad as possible. The dataset includes all cases about which information was found either directly in an award, or indirectly in other datasets and reports of law firms and of specialized journalists.[21] We thus decided to focus on scope and statistical relevance, accepting a small loss in reliability and accuracy due to the use of secondary sources. Our sources of data are described in Annex I.

Based on the experience of the second author and on informal consultations with other researchers and practitioners, this universe of claims appears to be close to a complete picture of all investment arbitrations filed during that period. It seems reasonable to estimate that no more than 10 per cent of the existing investment claims are missing in our dataset, given that few arbitration cases remain entirely secret in the sense that no information about them ever leaks somehow to the public.

These 1,098 claims were coded in the dataset according to the year in which they were filed (see Annex I for a short description of dimensions that are encoded per claim).[22] Figure 12.1 shows the evolution of claims filed between 1972 and 2018. It is noteworthy that the number of claims filed annually significantly increased starting in the mid-to-late nineties – a period during which the investment arbitration system 'shifted gears', which is correlated, as we will see, to a number of significant systemic changes in investment arbitration.

Given our interest in investigating factors influencing the likelihood of arbitration claims against any given country, our choice of dependent variable is the number of arbitration claims per country per year. It is derived directly from our dataset. To make it more operational, for the logistic regression, we transform it into a categorical variable that scores 0 if either: (a) there is no claim in a given year or (b) there is only one isolated claim. An isolated claim is defined as single country/year claim without any claim in the preceding and following four years. The variable scores 1 for country/year observations with either one non-isolated claim or two claims. It scores 2 for country/year observations with three or more claims, meaning that three or more claims were filed that year against a given country.

---

[21] For more details on the specific sources, see Annex I and Schultz and Dupont (n. 11).
[22] Encoding of 1,098 claims does not mean, however, that we have been able to code fully all dimensions of those claims.

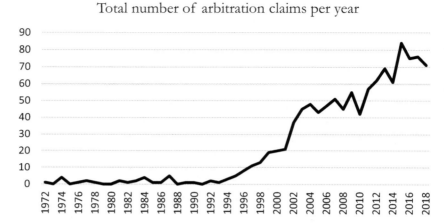

Figure 12.1 Number of investment arbitrations claims filed per year

This choice of categorical variable both captures some variation in the magnitude of the number of claims while controlling for the long tail in the distribution of the number of claims per country/year.[23]

Another specificity of the data, clearly visible in Figure 12.1, is the high concentration of claims in the period 1995–2018. Given that the preceding period includes only 34 claims over 23 years and is generally considered to be the dormant period of investment arbitration, we restrict our empirical analysis to the period 1995–2012 (the analysis does not include the years 2013–18 as we have data for ICRG scores until 2012, thus for consistency purposes the regressions are run for the other independent variables with the same time frame). The total number of observations is 2,034 with a distribution of 1,720/270/44 in the zero, one and two category respectively. We also use a further restricted dataset that removes countries targeted only once during the whole period. In such cases, the informational asymmetry noted by Elkins, Guzman and Simmons[24] may indeed be present, as well as many other idiosyncratic

---

[23] The number of claims per country/year observation is mostly one (260) with a quick decrease for two claims a year (66), three claims a year (19), four claims (15) to then drop to one or two cases of 5, 6, 7, 8, 9 and 10 claims a year. Up to 2012, there was only one observation with more claims, that is, Argentina with the record 22 claims in 2003.

[24] Zachary Elkins, Andrew T. Guzman and Beth A. Simmons, 'Competing for Capital: The Diffusion of Bilateral Investment Treaties, 1960–2000' (2006) 60(4) *International Organization* 811. In this study, the authors studied the factors that cause investment arbitrations to happen. They posited the following hypothetical: 'Why do these formal

factors. In other words, for a state to become a respondent in an arbitration once in eighteen years is something that may well just happen, just as an average driver occasionally gets a ticket, without the event telling us anything about the behaviour of the state, or the driver. This reduced dataset includes 1,368 observations. The number of countries included in the base dataset is 113 and drops to 76 in the reduced dataset. This already tends to suggest that there are only 76 countries in which something out of the plainly ordinary happened in the 1995–2012 period that triggered a reaction by investors.

12.4.2 Independent Variables

12.4.2.1 Independent Variables for Governance

As mentioned earlier, our first hypothesis suggests that investment arbitration is more likely to target countries with poor institutional conditions. We conceptualize this variable by relying on three composite indices of the Worldwide Governance Indicators (WGI).

We first assess the quality of domestic legal and judicial institutions through the WGI Rule of Law index, which 'captures perceptions of the extent to which agents have confidence in and abide by the rules of society, and in particular the quality of contract enforcement, property rights, the police and the courts'.[25] In other words, we take it to measure to what extent domestic legal institutions are able or willing to provide an independent and fair assessment, and potentially a remedy, for an interference with an investment. The index measures the perception of the quality of domestic legal institutions, rather than their objective quality. Yet, an investor that merely perceives these institutions to be deficient may also be more likely to seek remedy for any interference with his investment by presenting a claim to an international investment tribunal.

Second, we consider whether domestic institutions may interfere with an investment by design. We assess this scenario by looking at the WGI

---

dispute settlement mechanisms actually come into play [...]? Theoretically, we should expect such arbitrations to be rare, because fully informed parties should be able to settle "out of court" and avoid litigation costs.' In other words, fully informed parties would not let investment arbitration happen. And the fact that they do happen 'often', Elkins, Guzman and Simmons argued, shows that the parties were not fully informed: it 'indicates information asymmetries', they submitted. Importantly, they thought it was more likely that it was an indication of information asymmetries than an indication of 'the seriousness of the case[s]'.

[25] World Bank, 'Rule of Law', <info.worldbank.org/governance/wgi/pdf/rl.pdf>.

Regulatory Quality index, a business-friendliness measure that captures 'the ability of the government to formulate and implement sound policies and regulations that permit and promote private sector development'.[26] Rather than measuring the capacity of domestic institutions to adequately respond to an investment interference, this index would point out the likelihood of the interference itself.

Third, we look at the WGI Corruption index, which captures 'perceptions of the extent to which public power is exercised for private gain, including both petty and grand forms of corruption, as well as "capture" of the state by elites and private interests'.[27] We use all indicators without lagging their effects. We decided not to lag their effects, despite our argument that investment arbitration is the result of serious governmental misconduct in preceding years, for two reasons. First, the indicators are fairly stable. Lagging their effect does not produce any significant difference for the descriptive type of analysis performed here. Second, it is unclear to which extent past and current domestic institutional conditions respectively affect the decisions of investors to give up alternative ways to settle a dispute and use arbitration. Although poor institutional conditions in the past might have led to the dispute, ongoing poor institutional conditions are likely to continue to indicate that any deal with the government is risky.

Apart from the abovementioned indices, we also consider other prominent indicators to compare our results. The ICRG Law and Order score is a widely recognized proxy for the strength of the rule of law. It is a combination of two factors – namely, 'Law', which is an 'assessment of the strength and impartiality of the legal system', and 'Order', which is an 'assessment of popular observance of the law'.[28] The Law and Order variable ranges from 0 to 6 with lower scores indicating a less established legal system. The use of the Polity IV score (scale –10 to 10) brings a different perspective on the institutional situation in host countries. In a more authoritarian country, policy and legal changes can clearly be more sudden and swifter. This translates into potential high political risk.[29]

---

[26] Ibid.

[27] Ibid.

[28] The PRS Group, Inc., 'The International Country Risk Guide', Researcher Dataset (ICRG T3B – Political Risk, ICRG Methodology), <prsgroup.com/ICRG_Methodology.aspx>.

[29] Monty G. Marshall, 'Polity IV Project: Political Regime Characteristics and Transitions, 1800–2012', <systemicpeace.org/polity/polity4.htm>.

DOUBLE JEOPARDY? 377

12.4.2.2 Independent Variables for Economic Crises

Our second hypothesis posits that investment arbitration is more likely to target countries that have gone through severe economic hardship. In this context we use the 'Systemic Banking Crises Database' of Laeven and Valencia (2012),[30] which features three types of financial crises: systemic banking crises, currency crises, and sovereign debt crises, in order to conceptualize the economic crisis variable. Accordingly, our index is the tally of these three indicators, meaning a country facing all three types of financial crises scores 3, whereas, for instance, if there is systemic banking crisis and sovereign debt crisis it takes the value of 2.[31] Reinhart and Rogoff's prominent crisis dataset that gives us a tally measure ranging from 0 to 6 could clearly be the first candidate for measuring the scope of the economic crisis; however, unlike Leaven and Valencia's database, it leaves us with too many missing values.

Following Simmons' 2014 study that found a positive correlation between inflation and litigation, we also consider inflation rate as a measure of economic hardship. According to the results of a random-effects generalized least squares regression employed, she concludes that 'the higher the (log of) inflation, the greater the probability of arbitration is two years later'.[32] In this context, we look at percentage change in consumer price index (International Financial Statistics data) between 1995 and 2012.

12.4.3 Control Strategy

We also control for a vector of conditions or factors that may affect the relationship between our dependent and independent variables. First, we use a dummy variable to control for the existence of an ongoing International Monetary Fund (IMF) programme in the investment host country. Such programmes come with conditions that tend to severely limit the discretion of governments and tend to act as seals of guarantee of sound, market-friendly behaviour. From this perspective, one could expect that international investors may be less tempted to resort to

---

[30] For more details, see Luc Laeven and Fabian Valencia, 'Systemic Banking Crises: An Update' (2012) *IMF Working Paper No. 12/163*, <imf.org/en/Publications/WP/Issues/2016/12/31/Systemic-Banking-Crises-Database-An-Update-26015>.

[31] See Table 12.1 in Annex II.

[32] Beth A. Simmons, 'Bargaining over BITs, Arbitrating Awards: The Regime for Protection and Promotion of International Investment' (2014) 66(1) *World Politics* 30.

378 CÉDRIC DUPONT AND THOMAS SCHULTZ

international arbitration against countries that have ongoing IMF programmes. It seems reasonably plausible that countries suffering from an economic slowdown are on average softer on foreign investors if they are in an IMF programme than if they are not, because of constraints imposed by the IMF. Besides, as Broz points out, '[e]xternal monitoring by the IMF might create the transparency necessary to make a monetary commitment credible'.[33] As a matter of fact, the IMF monitoring has significant impacts regarding credible commitments. Even if a country has severe domestic economic problems, the implementation of a stability programme led and engineered by the IMF may render the country credible, as it is usually perceived as a sign that the country is on the right track, which usually avoids speculative attacks on its currency as well. The dummy variable takes the value of one if the country is borrowing from the Fund.[34]

Second, we address the issue of the alleged tendency in arbitration to target poorer countries by controlling for the level of economic development.[35] As highlighted in previous work using only descriptive statistics,[36] there is no evidence that states with low levels of economic development have been more frequently targeted than states with higher levels of economic development. In absolute numbers, states on the higher end of economic development have been respondents in more arbitrations than states on the lower end of economic development. Nevertheless, we remain to investigate whether there is some evidence of the curvilinear relationship between expropriation and the level of development, as would be suggested by earlier work on foreign direct investment. Indeed, a study examining expropriations in the 1970s found that the highest number of expropriations took place in countries with medium scores of economic development.[37] Hence, we may expect the

---

[33] Lawrence Broz, 'Political System Transparency and Monetary Commitment Regimes' (2002) 56(4) *International Organization* 884.

[34] Information available on the website <imf.org/external/country/index.htm> together with the Fund's MONA (Monitoring of Fund Arrangements) database.

[35] Muthucumaraswamy Sornarajah, 'Toward Normlessness: The Ravage and Retreat of Neo-Liberalism in International Investment Law' (2010) 2 *Yearbook of International Investment Law & Policy* 595, 618ff.

[36] Schultz and Dupont (n. 11).

[37] See David A. Jodice, 'Sources of Change in Third World Regimes for Foreign Direct Investment, 1968–1976' (1980) 34(2) *International Organization* 177. The level of economic development no longer features prominently in recent work on expropriation. For instance, Hajzler focuses on output price levels and Wellhausen – on FDI national diversity; Christopher Hajzler, 'Expropriation of Foreign Direct Investments: Sectoral

greatest number of arbitrations to take place against states in this range of economic development. We use the World Bank income level four-fold classification: low income, lower-middle income, upper-middle income and high-income countries.[38] It is based mainly on gross national income (earlier gross national product) per capita.

Third, given the large number of claims targeting Latin American and Caribbean countries, we control for a possible regional effect specific to that part of the world. We use a binary dummy variable scoring one for Latin American and Caribbean host countries, and zero for countries from the rest of world. One possible interpretation for a regional specific pattern would be a stronger influence of economic ideology on governments' reactions to economic difficulties, leading to severe strains with foreign investors. Given the high number of claims against the Bolivarian Republic of Venezuela, but also against Ecuador, Bolivia and Argentina, the economic ideology factor should be investigated and controlled for (there are 15 Latin American or Caribbean countries in our data). But this would properly require a fuller investigation, which is beyond the scope of this chapter.

Fourth, we control for a possible effect of the sector of activity of the investment to which the arbitration relates. Given recent evidence that foreign firms seem to be more vulnerable to expropriation in resource-based sectors,[39] we use a binary dummy variable that scores one for investment in the primary sector (agriculture, mining, oil, gas and petroleum).

Fifth, and last, given the high number of claims filed by investors with US nationality, we control for a possible effect of US nationality. The theoretical proposition could be that investors with US nationality may have a particularly broad set of options available to address a concern with foreign governments, given the economic power supremacy of the US. It would seem to follow that one could expect arbitration to be less likely to be used by investors with US nationality. This may particularly be true for host countries that do not belong to the high-income

---

Patterns from 1993 to 2006' (2012) 148(1) *Review of World Economics* 119; Rachel Wellhausen, 'Expropriation, Nationality and Diplomacy' (2013), Paper presented at the American Political Science Association Annual Meeting, <mail.khazar.org/bitstream/20 .500.12323/2808/1/CRRC_Wellhausen_Exprop_Diplomacy.pdf>.

[38] The distinction between lower-middle and upper-middle income was introduced in 1983; previously there was just one 'middle income' category.

[39] Hajzler (n. 37).

380 CÉDRIC DUPONT AND THOMAS SCHULTZ

category, because they are comparatively weaker against the US economic power.

12.5 Results

In this section, we summarize the statistical findings derived by testing our two hypotheses. As mentioned earlier, first an ordinal logistic regression with a categorical dependent variable (consisting of three categories for the number of arbitration claims per country per year) is employed, essentially using maximum likelihood estimation (MLE). We proceed with a baseline model regressing the primary predictor variables, and then re-run our analyses with the controls for the income, IMF loan and Latin America dummy variables (see Table 12.2 in Annex II). We again run the same models while excluding the host countries with only one arbitration claim over the whole period. The same regressions are run once again for all countries, excluding first the cases with US investors and then primary sector. We then run the regressions excluding the host countries with only one claim.

The degree of bias is strongly dependent on the number of cases in the less frequent category in maximum likelihood estimation, and since 1,720 of our 2,034 observations are coded as 0, we acknowledge the possibility of some bias. In this regard, we then employ a negative binomial regression, where the dependent variable is the total number arbitration claims a country faces, and the independent variables stay the same[40] (see Tables 12.3, 12.4 and 12.5). We first run a negative binomial regression for all countries, and then re-run the regressions this time first excluding the cases with US investors, and later the cases excluding primary sector (Table 12.4 and 12.5 respectively).

Overall, we find no strong evidence that poor institutional conditions, when measured by *polity*, are significantly associated with investment arbitration claims. Economic crisis does have a positive relation with the dependent variable, as expected, but the coefficient stays statistically insignificant in most of the models. Inflation does not have statistically significant relation with the dependent variable either. However, all WGI indicators, as well as ICRG Law & Order indicator, are statistically significant, and they all have a negative relation with investment arbitration claims, as expected.

---

[40] We employ a standard negative binomial regression model that allows for overdispersion, instead of a zero inflated Poisson (ZIP), as it fits much better than a ZIP model.

As discussed previously, we are controlling for certain variables, and in order to see if we actually get statistically significant results consistent with the literature on our control variables, we also run a basic model with regressing the control variables on our dependent variable. Consistent with our discussion, countries receiving IMF loans have a lower probability of facing investment arbitration (the indicator is statistically significant in all models when logistic regression is employed, it loses significance in some of the negative binomial count models), whereas the *income* and *Latin America* variables have a positive relation with investment arbitration claims, as expected, and they also are statistically significant in nearly all of the models.

Re-running the regressions after excluding the cases with US investors and then primary sector does not lead to a substantial change for the models with all countries; however, unsurprisingly the restricted models decrease statistical significance considerably.

As mentioned earlier, economic crisis has a positive sign, though not statistically significant. However, once we add the variables measuring institutional conditions, the coefficient of economic crisis becomes negative (stays statistically insignificant). This gives us reason to believe that the *institutional condition* variable is acting as a moderator variable. In order to analyse the relations between the dependent variable and these two indicators, we add an interaction term of economic crisis and indicators measuring institutional conditions, which, in all of the models except the one with ICRG Law & Order, yields a statistically significant coefficient with a negative sign, meaning the positive correlation between economic crisis and arbitration gets stronger when institutional conditions are poorer. This is a noteworthy finding as it implies that the countries facing a severe economic crisis face arbitration more often if they have poor institutional conditions, which might actually hurt the legitimacy of arbitration.

12.6 Conclusion

In this chapter, we investigated to which extent investment arbitration claims are related to the materialization of two types of sources of high political risk, namely severe economic situations and poor institutional conditions in host countries. We do so while explicitly keeping the predictors simple, even simplistic, and restricting the set of observations to those countries that have been targeted by investment claims more than once in the period 1995–2012. The result of our analysis is that one leg of our conceptual depiction of political risk and arbitration – namely that corruption and lack of rule of law-making dissuasion fail and thus lead to arbitrations – seems to have statistical significance. In contrast, we do not find any statistically significant link between economic crises and investment arbitration claims. Yet, when one considers countries with poor institutional conditions, economic crises tend to reinforce the likelihood for countries to be hit by arbitration claims. As discussed earlier, this implies that the countries confronting a severe economic crisis face arbitration more often if they have poor institutional conditions. Therefore, we conclude that bad governance and economic crises considered together are a good predictor of when countries get hit by investment arbitration claims. From this perspective, investment arbitration could be viewed in relatively positive terms as it is used to address worst-case scenarios: situations in which bad governance has the most adverse consequences for investors. From that perspective specifically, investment arbitration is not as illegitimate as it is sometimes said to be.

Annex I

A Few Facts about Our Database

This study is based on a data set with the following characteristics:

- Period covered: 1972–2018
- Includes 1,098 investment claims (662 until the end of 2012)
- Includes investment claims regardless of the jurisdictional basis of the arbitration:
  - investment arbitrations based on a treaty (typically a BIT, but not on multilateral treaties);
  - investment arbitrations based on a contract between the host state and the investor,
  - investment arbitrations based on the domestic legislation of the host state, when such legislation unilaterally allows the investor to file an arbitration against the government.
- Includes institutional investment arbitration (ICSID mainly, but also Stockholm Chamber of Commerce, International Chamber of Commerce, etc.) and ad hoc investment arbitration (mainly under the arbitration rules of UNCITRAL).
- Encodes the following aspects of the arbitrations:
  - Parties; case number; case status (pending/concluded/never commenced); composition of the arbitral tribunal (names of arbitrators); name of host state and home state of investor; region of the world of host state and home state of investor; year of filing; in favour of whom the initial award was rendered; arbitration rules governing the procedure; sector of the economy invested in (Agriculture, Banking and Finance, Construction, Electricity generation and distribution, Forestry, Hotels/Tourism/ Recreation, Industry (chemicals), Industry (food), Industry (metals), Industry (other light), Industry (textiles), Industry (transport and machinery), Industry (weapons), Insurance, Media and Broadcasting, Mining, Oil/gas/petroleum, Pharmaceuticals, Real Estate Development, Sales and Trade, Services, Telecom, Transportation and infrastructure, Waste Management and Utilities, Water and Sewer); type of host country action attacked; amount claimed; most recent procedural position; year of conclusion of case if applicable; years pending; if settled, phase of the

proceedings when the settlement has taken place/reason; damages awarded; percentage of the claim ultimately awarded; polity score of host state and home state (year of filing) (Polity IV Country Reports 2009); development status of host state (year of filing) (World Bank World Development Reports); number of arbitrators; nationalities of arbitrators; region of origin of arbitrators; development status of arbitrators' state of nationality; annulment proceedings (ICSID only): outcome, duration, committee members.
- Sources of information:
  - For claims submitted to ICSID: ICSID website and ICSID Reports.
  - For other claims, sources include: italaw.com; UNCTAD reports; Investment Arbitration Reporter; Oxford University Press's Investment Claims website; Kluwerarbitration.com; Westlaw database; Global Arbitration Review; NAFTA Secretariat's database; naftaclaims.com; ICC Dispute Resolution library; website of the Stockholm Chamber of Commerce; website of the Energy Charter Treaty secretariat; general newspapers; portfolios of law firms and arbitrators.

Annex II

Table 12.1 *Economic crisis variable*

Systemic banking crisis	Currency crisis	Sovereign debt crises	Tally of Financial crisis
—	—	—	0
✓	—	—	1
—	✓	—	1
—	—	✓	1
✓	✓	—	2
—	✓	✓	2
✓	—	✓	2
✓	✓	✓	3

Table 12.2 *Ordinal logistic regression results for all countries*

Model	Model 1	Model 2	Model 3	Model 4	Model 5	Model 6	Model 7	Model 8	Model 9	Model 10
Variable										
Economic crisis		0.153	−0.007	−0.524	−0.008	−0.239	0	−0.486	0.232	0.694
		(0.232)	(0.272)	(0.465)	(0.272)	(0.333)	(0.272)	(0.434)	(0.233)	(0.697)
WGI Corruption			−0.237**	−0.21**						
			(0.101)	(0.102)						
Economic crisis*WGI Corruption				−0.887*						
				(0.496)						
WGI Rule of Law							−0.244**	−0.211**		
							(0.105)	(0.106)		
Economic crisis*WGI Rule of Law								−0.874**		
								(0.443)		
WGI Regulatory Quality					−0.18*	−0.151*				
					(0.101)	(0.103)				
Economic crisis*WGI Regulatory Qual						−0.73*				
						(0.383)				
ICRG Law & Order									−0.223***	−0.214***
									(0.074)	(0.075)
Economic crisis* ICRG Law & Order										−0.136
										(0.198)

Income	0.206***	0.236***	0.345***	0.345***	0.319***	0.317***	0.356***	0.354***	0.431***	0.429***
	(0.064)	(0.065)	(0.093)	(0.093)	(0.097)	(0.097)	(0.097)	(0.097)	(0.091)	(0.091)
IMF loan	−0.394***	−0.42***	−0.411***	−0.407**	−0.388**	−0.379**	−0.416***	−0.409**	−0.441***	−0.44***
	(0.155)	(0.156)	(0.168)	0.168	(0.168)	(0.169)	(0.168)	(0.168)	(0.176)	(0.176)
Latin America	0.251*	0.334**	0.336**	0.33**	0.357**	0.354**	0.296*	0.293*	0.124	0.121
	(0.149)	(0.151)	(0.162)	0.162	(0.161)	(0.161)	(0.164)	(0.164)	(0.172)	(0.172)
Summary statistics										
Number of observations	2034	2034	1473	1473	1472	1472	1472	1472	1570	1570
Pseudo R^2	0.024	0.031	0.034	0.038	0.031	0.035	0.033	0.038	0.043	0.043

Note: Numbers in parentheses represent standard errors; *p < 0.10, **p < 0.05, ***p < 0.01.

Table 12.3 *Negative binomial regressions results for all countries*

Model	Model 1		Model 2		Model 3		Model 4		Model 5	
Variable	Coefficient	IRR	Coefficient	IRR	Coefficient	IRR	Coefficient	IRR	Coefficient	IRR
Economic crisis	0.14	1.15	−0.012	0.988	−0.533	0.587	−0.019	0.981	−0.549*	0.578
	(0.174)		(0.208)		(0.371)		(0.208)		(0.361)	
WGI Corruption			−0.274***	0.761	−0.25**	0.779				
			(0.08)		(0.08)					
Economic crisis*WGI Corruption					−0.829**	0.437				
					(0.398)					
WGI Rule of Law							−0.34***	0.712	−0.311***	0.733
							(0.081)		(0.082)	
Economic crisis*WGI Rule of Law									−0.805**	0.447
									(0.362)	
Income	0.269***	1.309	0.417***	1.518	0.417***	1.517	0.467***	1.596	0.464***	1.591
	(0.052)		(0.074)		(0.075)		(0.077)		(0.077)	
IMF loan	−0.183*	0.833	−0.176	0.839	−0.17	0.844	−0.181	0.834	−0.167	0.846
	(0.116)		(0.126)		(0.126)		(0.126)		(0.126)	
Latin America	0.7***	2.014	0.66***	1.934	0.655***	1.925	0.561***	1.753	0.553**	1.739
	(0.108)		(0.118)		(0.118)		(0.123)		(0.123)	
Summary statistics										
Log-likelihood	−1319.939		−1112.537		−1109.513		−1109.509		−1106.166	
Pearson χ^2	3328.503		2448.004		2424.394		2417.709		2406.079	
Number of observations	1926		1473		1473		1472		1472	

Note: Numbers in parentheses represent standard errors; *p < 0.10, **p < 0.05, ***p < 0.01.

Table 12.3 (cont.)

Model	Model 6		Model 7		Model 8		Model 9	
Variable	Coefficient	IRR	Coefficient	IRR	Coefficient	IRR	Coefficient	IRR
Economic crisis	−0.052 (0.21)	0.95	−0.391 (0.29)	0.676	0.210 (0.179)	1.234	0.238 (0.558)	1.269
WGI Regulatory Quality	−0.343*** (0.077)	0.709	−0.315*** (0.078)	0.73				
Economic crisis*WGI Regulatory Quality			−0.733** (0.334)	0.48				
ICRG Law & Order					−0.274*** (0.055)	0.76	−0.273*** (0.056)	0.761
Economic crisis*ICRG Law & Order							−0.008 (0.152)	0.992
Income	0.478*** (0.077)	1.612	0.475*** (0.077)	1.608	0.503*** (0.071)	1.653	0.503*** (0.071)	1.653
IMF loan	−0.134 (0.126)	0.874	−0.118 (0.126)	0.889	−0.141 (0.128)	0.868	−0.141 (0.129)	0.869
Latin America	0.621*** (0.119)	1.86	0.608*** (0.119)	1.836	0.401*** (0.128)	1.493	0.401*** (0.128)	1.493
a) **Summary statistics**								
Log-likelihood	−1,108.48		−1,105.572		−1,135.101		−1,135.1	
Pearson χ^2	2,345.49		2,333.231		2,502.092		2,502.611	
Number of observations	1,472		1,472		1,570		1,570	

Note: Numbers in parentheses represent standard errors; *p < 0.10, **p < 0.05, ***p < 0.01.

Table 12.4 *Negative binomial regressions results for all countries excluding the cases with US investors*

Model	Model 1		Model 2		Model 3		Model 4		Model 5	
Variable	Coefficient	IRR	Coefficient	IRR	Coefficient	IRR	Coefficient	IRR	Coefficient	IRR
Economic crisis	−0.254 (0.256)	0.776	−0.225 (0.264)	0.799	−0.572 (0.418)	0.564	−0.223 (0.264)	0.801	−0.599* (0.408)	0.55
WGI Corruption			−0.421*** (0.091)	0.656	−0.404*** (0.091)	0.668				
Economic crisis*WGI Corruption					−0.584 (0.45)	0.558				
WGI Rule of Law							−0.426*** (0.09)	0.653	−0.403*** (0.091)	0.668
Economic crisis*WGI Rule of Law									−0.595* (0.398)	0.551
Income	0.206*** (0.058)	1.229	0.459*** (0.081)	1.582	0.468*** (0.081)	1.58	0.477*** (0.084)	1.612	0.474*** (0.084)	1.606
IMF loan	−0.28** (0.132)	0.756	−0.242* (0.141)	0.785	−0.237* (0.141)	0.789	−0.251* (0.141)	0.778	−0.241* (0.142)	0.786
Latin America	0.582*** (0.123)	1.79	0.509*** (0.133)	1.664	0.502*** (0.133)	1.651	0.405*** (0.137)	1.5	0.396*** (0.138)	1.486
Summary statistics										
Log-likelihood	−1,083.658		−928.496		−927.441		−928.22		−926.845	
Pearson χ^2	3,425.333		2,465.235		2,444.505		2,465.935		2,457.135	
Number of observations	1,926		1,473		1,473		1,472		1,472	

Note: Numbers in parentheses represent standard errors; *p < 0.10, **p < 0.05, ***p < 0.01.

Table 12.4 *(cont.)*

Model	Model 6		Model 7		Model 8		Model 9	
Variable	Coefficient	IRR	Coefficient	IRR	Coefficient	IRR	Coefficient	IRR
Economic crisis	−0.269	0.764	−0.515	0.598	−0.212	0.809	0.431	1.539
	(0.267)		(0.349)		(0.253)		(0.673)	
WGI Regulatory Quality	−0.433***	0.648	−0.413***	0.662				
	(0.084)		(0.085)					
Economic crisis*WGI Regulatory Quality			−0.526	0.591				
			(0.364)					
ICRG Law & Order					−0.304***	0.738	−0.293***	0.746
					(0.063)		(0.064)	
Economic crisis*ICRG Law & Order							−0.205	0.814
							(0.206)	
Income	0.497***	1.643	0.493***	1.638	0.445***	1.561	0.442***	1.333
	(0.084)		(0.084)		(0.079)		(0.079)	
IMF loan	−0.188	0.829	−0.177	0.838	−0.221*	0.802	−0.213	0.808
	(0.142)		(0.142)		(0.147)		(0.147)	
Latin America	0.485***	1.625	0.475***	1.608	0.267*	1.28	0.244*	1.276
	(0.133)		(0.134)		(0.147)		(0.147)	
b) **Summary statistics**								
Log-likelihood	−926.37		−925.195		−933.178		−932.664	
Pearson χ^2	2,345.418		2,339.269		2,690.235		2,722.206	
Number of observations	1,472		1,472		1,570		1,570	

Note: Numbers in parentheses represent standard errors; *p < 0.10, **p < 0.05, ***p < 0.01.

Table 12.5 *Negative binomial regressions results for all countries excluding the cases with primary sector*

Model	Model 1		Model 2		Model 3		Model 4		Model 5	
Variable	Coefficient	IRR	Coefficient	IRR	Coefficient	IRR	Coefficient	IRR	Coefficient	IRR
Economic crisis	−0.115	0.891	−0.294	0.799	−0.821*	0.44	−0.291	0.748	−0.757*	0.469
	(0.225)		(0.273)		(0.465)		(0.273)		(0.426)	
WGI Corruption			−0.214***	0.656	−0.194**	0.824				
			(0.087)		(0.087)					
Economic crisis*WGI Corruption					−0.876*	0.416				
					(0.484)					
WGI Rule of Law							−0.224***	0.799	−0.199**	0.82
							(0.09)		(0.091)	
Economic crisis*WGI Rule of Law									−0.789*	0.454
									(0.421)	
Income	0.413***	1.511	0.527***	1.582	0.527***	1.694	0.538***	1.712	0.535***	1.707
	(0.059)		(0.084)		(0.085)		(0.087)		(0.088)	
IMF loan	−0.109	0.897	−0.091	0.785	−0.085	0.918	−0.095	0.909	−0.085	0.92
	(0.134)		(0.141)		(0.144)		(0.144)		(0.144)	
Latin America	0.563***	1.756	0.549***	1.664	0.544***	1.722	0.498***	1.645	0.492***	1.635
	(0.124)		(0.134)		(0.134)		(0.138)		(0.139)	
Summary statistics										
Log-likelihood	−1072.266		−911.394		−909.116		−911.235		−908.927	
Pearson χ^2	3,407.501		2,391.339		2,379.696		2,396.854		2,390.61	
Number of observations	1,926		1,473		1,473		1,472		1,472	

Note: Numbers in parentheses represent standard errors; *p < 0.10, **p < 0.05, ***p < 0.01.

Table 12.5 *(cont.)*

Model	Model 6		Model 7		Model 8		Model 9	
Variable	Coefficient	IRR	Coefficient	IRR	Coefficient	IRR	Coefficient	IRR
Economic crisis	−0.319 (0.275)	0.727	−0.568* (0.344)	0.567	−0.075 (0.227)	0.928	0.213 (0.665)	1.237
WGI Regulatory Quality	−0.252*** (0.087)	0.777	−0.229*** (0.088)	0.795				
Economic crisis*WGI Regulatory Quality			−0.644* (0.378)	0.525				
ICRG Law & Order					−0.255*** (0.062)	0.775	−0.25*** (0.063)	0.779
Economic crisis*ICRG Law & Order							−0.085 (0.187)	0.918
Income	0.56*** (0.087)	1.751	0.557*** (0.087)	1.746	0.63*** (0.081)	1.877	0.628*** (0.081)	1.874
IMF loan	−0.064 (0.144)	0.938	−0.053 (0.144)	0.949	−0.031 (0.146)	0.969	−0.028 (0.146)	0.973
Latin America	0.535*** (0.134)	1.707	0.527*** (0.134)	1.694	0.262* (0.146)	1.3	0.262* (0.146)	1.299
(ii) **Summary statistics**								
Log-likelihood	−910.14		−908.494		−938.7		−938.246	
Pearson χ^2	2,327.49		2,322.438		2,683.318		2,487.169	
Number of observations	1,472		1,472		1,570		1,570	

Note: Numbers in parentheses represent standard errors; *p $<$ 0.10, **p $<$ 0.05, ***p $<$ 0.01.

13

Who Has Benefited Financially from Investment Treaty Arbitration? An Evaluation of the Size and Wealth of Claimants

GUS VAN HARTEN[*] AND PAVEL MALYSHEUSKI[**]

13.1 Introduction

For their legitimacy, domestic and international adjudicative bodies are regarded as depending in part on public confidence in their role as decision-makers.[1] This question of sociological legitimacy has also arisen for investment treaty arbitration, commonly known as investor–state dispute settlement (ISDS), as it has been increasingly scrutinized and debated beyond the specialized community of ISDS practitioners and researchers.[2] By creating or consolidating ISDS as an institution of international adjudication, states allow foreign investors to bring claims for compensation directly against countries based on allegations that a state entity violated any of a variety of often-ambiguous standards of foreign investor protection. In this context of public debate, the socio-

---

[*] Professor of Administrative Law, York University Osgoode Hall School of Law.
[**] Associate, Lockyer + Hein LLP.
[1] Or Bassok, 'The Sociological-Legitimacy Difficulty' (2011) 26 *Journal of Law and Politics* 239 at 242–5; Margaret M. de Guzman, 'Gravity and the Legitimacy of the International Criminal Court' (2008) 32 *Fordham International Law Journal* 1400, at 1440–2; Harry Hobbs, 'Hybrid Tribunals and the Composition of the Court: In Search of Sociological Legitimacy' (2016) 16 *Chicago Journal of International Law* 482, 494–5; and Alba Ruibal, 'The Sociological Concept of Judicial Legitimacy: Notes of Latin American Constitutional Courts' (2008) 3 *Mexican Law Review* 343, 345–8.
[2] We refer especially to institutional aspects of the sociological legitimacy of ISDS: Richard H. Fallon, 'Legitimacy and the Constitution' (2005) 118 *Harvard Law Review* 1787 at 1828. Our use of the term sociological legitimacy also draws on Daniel Behn, Ole Kristian Fauchald and Malcolm Langford, 'How to approach "legitimacy" for the book project Empirical Perspectives on the Legitimacy of International Investment Tribunals', prepared for the August 2015 workshop of the University of Oslo's PluriCourts Project. The comments from participants in the workshop are gratefully acknowledged.

logical legitimacy of ISDS appears to depend in part on a concern that ISDS serves the interests of wealthy and powerful individuals or corporations who are able to qualify as foreign investors – by their cross-border ownership of assets – and who have the resources to finance costly ISDS litigation, at the expense of other constituencies. Proponents of new trade agreements that would expand greatly the role of ISDS – such as the EU-US Transatlantic Trade and Investment Partnership (TTIP) and the Canada–EU Comprehensive Economic and Trade Agreement (CETA) – have responded indirectly to this criticism by, for example, presenting ISDS as delivering benefits for smaller enterprises.[3]

In this chapter, we present descriptive information that may shed light on how ISDS has affected the financial position of different economic actors. We 'follow the money' in ISDS by conceptualizing it simply as a decision-making process by which financial resources are transferred from some actors to others; primarily, from some states to some foreign investors and from both states and foreign investors to professionals who earn fees from ISDS. While this approach clearly does not capture all facets of ISDS as an institution, it at least provides baseline information to assist in understanding and debating the impact of ISDS. As such, we do not aim to explain whether ISDS should have public support but rather to show how ISDS has led to transfers of financial resources.

We examined this issue of ISDS' economic impact by collecting data, up to the spring of 2015, on size and wealth of the foreign investors that have brought claims and received monetary awards due to ISDS. Our main findings are that the beneficiaries of ISDS-ordered financial transfers,[4] in the aggregate, have overwhelmingly been companies that have over USD one billion in annual revenue – especially extra-large companies with over USD 10 billion – and individuals that have over USD 100 million in net wealth.[5] ISDS has provided monetary benefits

---

[3] Suzanne Lynch, 'EU-US trade deal will benefit SMEs, says Brussels', *The Irish Times* (21 April 2015); See also Movement for Responsibility in Trade Agreements, 'Five questions SME businesses need to ask themselves about TTIP', 22 February 2015, <https://www .fair-handeln-statt-ttip.eu/kontext/controllers/document.php/34.6/2/70e91e.pdf>

[4] We do not use the term 'financial transfers' to describe ISDS orders of compensation to foreign investors in a negative way, as one participant in the PluriCourts Project workshop commented. Rather, we use the term in an effort to avoid conveying a negative or positive assessment of the legitimacy of such orders of compensation.

[5] For more information on these categories and other aspects of the methodology, see Appendix.

primarily for those companies or individuals at the expense of respondent states. Thus, we found that companies with over USD one billion in annual revenue and individuals with over USD 100 million in net wealth received about 94.5% of the aggregate compensation (93.5% if pre-award interest is included) ordered by ISDS tribunals (not including annulment proceedings under the ICSID Convention or set-aside proceedings under the New York Convention).[6] The remaining roughly 5.5% (or 6.5%) of the ordered compensation went to companies with less than USD one billion in annual revenues, unknown companies, and individuals whose net wealth appeared to be less than USD 100 million. It was evident that ISDS has also delivered substantial monetary benefits for the ISDS legal industry.

Incidentally, we also found that extra-large companies' success rates in ISDS (70.8%), measured by simple win–loss outcomes at the jurisdictional and merits stages of an ISDS claim combined, exceeded by a large margin the success rates of other claimants (42.2%). Yet the success rates of large (as opposed to extra-large) companies (44.7%) and of super-wealthy individuals (36.4%) at both of these stages combined was comparable to those of other claimants (not including large or extra-large companies or super-wealthy individuals) (42.5%). The success rate of extra-large companies at the merits stage in particular (82.9%) stood out compared to that of all other claimants (57.9%). We also found, incidentally, that forum-shopping had a major effect for US beneficiaries, whose ordered compensation increased by 70.0% after accounting for the forum-shopping, and for Netherlands' beneficiaries, whose ordered compensation decreased by 98.0%. In turn, the ordered compensation for US beneficiaries rose from a minority (39.0%) to a majority (66.7%) of the overall total.

Our analysis is descriptive in that it does not seek to predict future outcomes and does not use more complex statistical tools. One should approach all of the numbers presented here as approximate and keep in mind that variations in the experiences of different actors may be coincidental. We suggest that the most useful findings are those indicating a wide variation in these experiences and those appearing to contradict less evidence-based claims in the field.

---

[6] Three *Yukos* cases that led to a combined award of USD 50 billion are reported separately due to the sheer size of the overall order of compensation and to assist the reader in drawing his or her own conclusions.

13.2   Limitations, Dataset and Methodology

Our research and analysis focused on aggregate ordered compensation by ISDS tribunals. We did not attempt to track actual records of payment of awards or account for changes in ordered compensation due to set aside or annulment decisions. Also, there are other ways to measure claimant success in ISDS. We have moved beyond an approach based on win–loss outcomes in ISDS litigation to a somewhat more complex measure based on aggregate ordered compensation. More ambitiously, one could assess claimant success in terms of less overt and non-financial costs and benefits, such as the utility of ISDS as a tool to influence regulatory decision-making. Other forms of assessment would be more comprehensive but also less measurable numerically and more amenable, we suspect, to qualitative than quantitative tools. For these and other reasons discussed in the introduction to this chapter and below, our research and analysis generates only an approximate and descriptive picture of aspects of ISDS as a system that leads to financial transfers.

The underlying dataset for this chapter included all known and publicly available ISDS cases that led to a decision on jurisdiction, at least, as of spring of 2015. The most relevant fields in the dataset for this chapter were: claimant nationality; date and outcome of award on jurisdiction; date and outcome of award on merits; amount awarded (converted to USD as of the date of the award); and damages awarded with and without pre-award interest (calculated, where applicable, using the interest rate and date range stipulated by the tribunal). Awards were not adjusted for time value of money because our aim was to provide simple and descriptive findings supported by public data where none presently exists on the issue.

The underlying dataset was compiled by five law school students, most recently Ryan De Vries, working as research assistants over a period of seven years. Each assistant, after initial training, collected information on ISDS cases from publicly available awards and other decisions up to the relevant time cut-off. The main source of awards and other decisions was italaw.com supplemented by official websites of the International Centre for Settlement of Investment Disputes (ICSID), the Permanent Court of Arbitration (PCA), the Stockholm Chamber of Commerce (SCC) and the federal governments of Canada, Mexico, and the US. An award or decision had to be available on italaw.com and allow for verification as a treaty-based case, or the case had to be identified as treaty-based on one of the official websites just listed, in order for the case to be included in the analysis. Coding results were screened by the author (i.e. approximately half of the coding decisions were checked for errors) and past coding was checked and sometimes re-coded by another research assistant. For the data used in the present article, relevant coding rarely involved significant discretionary choices by the coder; rather, it focused on descriptive information on ISDS cases that tended to be clear in the award or other decision. Considering the extent of information collected and the absence of a comprehensive double or triple coding process, there is a risk of occasional error in data entry.

In a significant minority of cases in the dataset, roughly 15% one or more of the relevant awards or decisions were not public. Also, an unknown number of cases can be assumed to be completely confidential. For the dataset overall, there is a reasonable prospect that this confidentiality may impact the findings, especially for fields connected to arbitration forums and where one forum is more open than another. For the present analysis, in one exceptional case (*Suez & Interaguas* v. *Argentina*) public information was available up to, but not for, a known award on damages. For this case only, a non-official source (Investment Arbitration Reporter) was relied on to code the amount awarded to the claimant.

Within this ISDS case dataset, all confirmed treaty-based cases up to April 2014 were then classified for size or wealth of the claimant up to the spring of 2014 (specifically, up to posting on italaw.com as of 18 April 2014). Co-author Pavel Malysheuski – a corporate/commercial and securities lawyer with knowledge of ISDS – determined reasonable measures of the size and wealth of claimants and coded the cases for size and wealth of the claimant based on natural cut-offs. Companies were classified based on their annual revenue as small (under USD 100 million in annual revenue), medium (over USD 100 million, under USD one billion), large (over USD one billion), or extra-large (over USD 10 billion). For individuals, those with an apparent net wealth of more than USD 100 million were classified as super-wealthy; those whose net wealth was not found to exceed this threshold as other individuals.[7] Annual revenue and net wealth was examined at the time of the relevant dispute as reported in the award or decision for the ISDS case.[8]

---

[7] A more sophisticated analysis would treat annual revenue and net wealth as continuous variables; the classifications used here were simpler to code – especially in the case of net wealth – and thought sufficient to give an overall picture of past financial transfers.

[8] There were a few complicating cases, such as *PacRim* v. *El Salvador* where ownership of the claim shifted from a small to a medium company in the course of the dispute (albeit

WHO HAS BENEFITED FROM INVESTMENT ARBITRATION? 399

This approach to classification over-stated the role of small and medium enterprises and non-super-wealthy individuals in ISDS. The categories used to identify small and medium – with annual revenues under USD 100 million and USD one billion respectively – were much more inclusive than what other measures would consider a small or medium enterprise.[9] Likewise, some may consider individuals who have a net wealth below USD 100 million as still rich compared to owners of small and medium enterprises and other individuals. For these reasons, the findings may over-state the number of ISDS cases and financial transfers for small or medium-sized enterprises.

Where information was unavailable on a company's annual revenue, the company was classified as unknown. This separate category was used – instead of assuming, for example, that all such companies were small or medium – because, although some such companies appeared likely to be small or medium, others appeared to be potential holding companies where ultimate ownership could not be tracked. In contrast, where data was unavailable on an individual's net wealth, it was assumed that the individual was not super wealthy on the assumption that an individual worth USD 100 million or more would be identifiable as such using standard online sources. In any event, as will be seen below, these classification issues appeared not to impact significantly the main findings of the paper.

Where there were multiple claimant nationalities (e.g. a claim both by a foreign company and by a subsidiary in the host state), the nationality of the foreign state party under the treaty or treaties under which the ISDS claim was brought was classified as the primary nationality. In a few cases, primary nationality was divided because the claim was brought under multiple treaties. The results of the comprehensive coding allowed for incidental and approximate findings on apparent forum-shopping. That is, cases were noted as apparent forum-shopping where the largest or wealthiest owner of a claimant was based in, or (for individuals) had the nationality of, a country other than the primary nationality in the ISDS case. This was a loose approach to dealing with potential forum-shopping in that it did not ask whether the company in the foreign state

---

without affecting the findings on ordered compensation because the case is ongoing) but for the most part the issue did not raise coding challenges.

[9] See e.g., OECD, *OECD SME and Entrepreneurship Outlook: 2005*, (OECD Publishing, 2005), p. 17, citing EU definitions based on annual turnover of Euro ten million for small enterprises and Euro 50 million for medium enterprises.

party to the treaty had a substantial connection to that state or whether the ultimate owner's incorporation decision in the foreign state party was made with express intent to facilitate an ISDS claim. Instead, forum-shopping as analysed here captures: (1) situations in which multinationals brought an ISDS claim from a jurisdiction within their network of corporate nationalities that was not their historical base of operations and (2) situations in which a super-wealthy individual acquired the nationality of the foreign state party by incorporating in that state. As will be seen, the clearest finding on forum-shopping that is directly relevant to financial transfers involves US large or extra-large parent companies or US super-wealthy individuals that benefited from ISDS claims made by corporate claimants in the Netherlands.

Also, for cases involving multiple claimants, each case was classified as having a single claimant size or wealth based on precedence for the largest or wealthiest ultimate owner of a claimant in the case. To illustrate, a claim both by a domestic company of the host state and by the corporate owner of that company in the foreign state party under the treaty, where the latter was ultimately owned by an extra-large parent company in a third state, was classified as a claim by the extra-large parent company. Alternatively, a claim by a medium company owned by a super-wealthy individual was classified as a claim by that individual. In short, cases were coded based on the largest or wealthiest actor in the group of both claimants and ultimate owners of claimants. Although it did not arise in any of the cases coded here, precedence would have been given to classification as an extra-large or large company rather than as a super-wealthy individual.

In light of these assumptions for cases involving multiple claimants, the data was reviewed to identify possible misrepresentations arising from situations in which multiple claimants of different sizes or wealth brought a claim and the case was classified as having been brought by the largest or wealthiest claimant in the group. In the great majority of such cases, the claimant group consisted of multiple companies in the same corporate group; multiple companies of the same size; multiple companies with one or more unknown companies alongside a large or extra-large company and apparently falling within the larger corporate group; multiple claimants with one or more unknown companies alongside an individual; multiple individuals including a super-wealthy individual and one or more other individuals who were family members of or otherwise apparently related to the super-wealthy individual; or multiple individuals none of whom appeared super wealthy. For all of these situations, in our view the coding assumptions for cases involving multiple claimants were appropriate.

However, there was one case – *Abengoa* v. *Mexico* – where compensation was ordered and the coding assumptions appeared to risk misrepresenting the results. The claim was brought by an extra-large and an apparently unrelated large company but was coded as a claim by the extra-large company. The ordered compensation in the case was USD 40 million (USD 42 million including pre-award interest). We opted not to use an alternative coding approach – such as a 50–50 attribution of the claim between the two companies or attribution based on their relative size or ownership stake in the disputed assets – because the case had little effect on the overall findings, the alternative coding approaches also had an arbitrary quality, the coding assumptions did not otherwise appear to raise concerns about misrepresentation, and, with the present disclosure, readers are able to evaluate and adjust the findings as they see fit.

Overall, the dataset had 292 cases coded for claimant size or wealth as of the spring of 2014 with data on outcomes, including amounts awarded, up to the spring of 2015.[10] Of these 292 cases, 253 were coded as having a jurisdictional outcome, that is, a verifiable decision of the tribunal finding or not finding jurisdiction (other cases typically were ongoing or resolved before a jurisdictional outcome). Of these 253 cases, the tribunal declined jurisdiction in 52 cases and accepted jurisdiction in 201. Of these 201 cases, the tribunal did not find a violation of the treaty in 39 cases and found a violation in 162 (again, other cases typically were ongoing or had settled before a merits decision). Of these 162 cases, there were 89 in which an amount was confirmed to have been awarded (in four of these cases the amount was zero). Three of these 89 cases – the *Yukos* cases totalling USD 50 billion in ordered compensation – swamped the other results and were relatively challenging to code for size or wealth of the claimant. For these reasons, these cases were presented separately in the paper. The remaining 86 cases constitute the dataset analysed for ordered compensation due to ISDS.

---

[10] Three cases were coded as 'not applicable' (NA) for claimant size or wealth because it was difficult to identify a corporate or individual claimant based on the coding assumptions. They included cases brought by a state entity (*Kaliningrad* v. *Lithuania*), a series of irrigation districts and individuals (*Bayview Irrigation* v. *Mexico*), and a series of natural and juridical persons (*CCFT* v. *USA*). None of these cases led to a damages award: the first lacked public information and the other two were dismissed at the jurisdictional stage.

Notably, two cases that led to awards were excluded from the 86 cases. *CSOB* v. *Slovakia* was excluded because it was classified as a contract-based case although it fell close to the line and is arguably a contract-treaty hybrid. *ATA* v. *Jordan* was also excluded because it led to the remedy of an order that another arbitration could go ahead and so was difficult to quantify in terms of monetary value. Both cases involved claims by a large or extra-large company. For the record, we have provided the relevant data on the two excluded cases in Annex I. The main impact of the exclusion of these cases was to reduce the share of aggregate ordered compensation for extra-large companies from 76.8% (76.1% including pre-award interest) to 73.5% (73.3%).

For the main analysis for this paper, ordered compensation at the tribunal stage (i.e. not including annulment or set-aside decisions) was compared to claimant size and wealth in all cases to the spring of 2014. Legal outcomes at the jurisdictional, merits and combined stages of ISDS cases were also compared to claimant size and wealth. Finally, ordered compensation was compared to average ISDS costs for the disputing parties as estimated by other researchers.[11] Findings on apparent forum-shopping were also recorded, as discussed above.

13.3 Findings

13.3.1 Ordered Financial Transfers by Size or Wealth of Beneficiary

It emerged from the analysis that ISDS – approached as a process that generates ordered financial transfers – has primarily benefited extra-large or large companies and super-wealthy individuals. The great majority of ordered transfers, in the aggregate, have gone to such actors. Findings and data are outlined in the tables below. A more detailed breakdown of the dataset is appended to this chapter.

13.3.2 Apparent Forum-Shopping

The investigation of ultimate ownership of ISDS claimants brought to light some cases of apparent forum-shopping. The concept of forum-shopping here included situations where the historical base or nationality

---

[11] David Gaukrodger and Katia Gordon, 'Investor-State Dispute Settlement: A Scoping Paper for the Investment Policy Community', (2012) *OECD Working Paper on International Investment*, No. 2012/03.

Table 13.1 *Aggregate ordered compensation*

Size or wealth of beneficiary	Measure of size or wealth (company amounts are for annual revenue)	No. of cases where damages ordered	Total awarded, raw sum (USD)	% of total awarded, raw sum	Total awarded, raw sum + pre-award interest	% of total awarded, raw sum + pre-award interest
Extra-large company	>$10 billion	26	5,282 million	73.5	6,718 million	73.3
Large company	>$1 and <$10 billion	14	601 million	8.4	780 million	8.5
Medium company	>$100 million and <$1 billion	4	13 million	0.2	17 million	0.2
Small company	<$100 million	4	80 million	1.1	99 million	1.1
Unknown company	Data unavailable (DU)	13	132 million	1.8	154 million	1.7
Super-wealthy individual	>$100 million in net wealth	5	905 million	12.6	1,072 million	11.7
Other individual	<$100 million in net wealth	20	179 million	2.5	325 million	3.5

of the ultimate owner in a claimant group differed from that of the foreign state party under the relevant treaty used for the ISDS claim.

The primary finding was that this forum-shopping had a major effect for US beneficiaries; the ordered compensation increased by 70.0% after accounting for the forum-shopping. It also had a major effect for Netherlands' beneficiaries, leading to a decrease of 98.0%. In turn, the ordered compensation for US beneficiaries rose from a minority (39.0%) to a majority (66.7%) of the overall total. Accounting for this forum-shopping also modestly increased the ordered compensation for UK, German, or (in a case with a very small award) Serbian beneficiaries, whereas it modestly decreased the ordered compensation for Turkish or (for the very small award) Swiss beneficiaries.

The following table indicates the ordered transfers by country, with and without apparent forum-shopping. It also includes notes on our incidental findings on forum-shopping including a note of those situations where there was apparent forum-shopping but data was unavailable on ultimate ownership of the ISDS claim.

13.3.3 The Yukos Cases

As noted in the introduction, three *Yukos* cases that led to a combined award of USD 50 billion are reported separately from the above data due to the sheer size of the overall order of compensation and to assist the reader in drawing his or her own conclusions. For our part, we classified these cases – arising claims by the companies Yukos Universal Limited (YUL), Hulley Enterprises Limited (Hulley) and Veteran Petroleum Trust – as cases brought by a super-wealthy individual, Mikhail Khodorkovsky, on the following basis, which we have elaborated in detail in the interest of transparency.[12]

In 1997, several Russian businessmen including Mr Khodorkovsky registered an off-shore company in Gibraltar called Flaymon Limited, which was soon after re-named Group MENATEP Limited (MENATEP). When the relevant ISDS claims were filed, the share capital of MENATEP was distributed among Khodorkovsky (9.5%), Leonid Nevzlin (8.0%), Mikhail Brudno (7.0%), Platon Lebedev (7.0%),

---

[12] The detailed research on these cases case was conducted by Malysheuski based on online sources: <pca-cpa.org/en/cases/>; <en.wikipedia.org/wiki/Millhouse_Capital>; <ru.wikipedia.org/wiki/Group_MENATEP>; and <en.wikipedia.org/wiki/Bank_Menatep#Group_Menatep_Limited>; <khodorkovsky.ru/>.

Table 13.2 *Forum-shopping*[1]

Country of ISDS claim	No. of cases	No. of cases after accounting for apparent forum-shopping	Amount awarded	Amount awarded after accounting for apparent FS	Amount including pre-award interest	Amount including pre-award interest after accounting for apparent FS
USA	25.5 (1 shared with UK)	28.5	2,785 million	4,701 million	3,591 million	6,113 million
Netherlands	7	9[2]	1,946 million	1,986 million	2,551 million	2,405 million
Germany	7	7.5[3]	346 million	363.5 million	407 million	424.5 million
UK	6.5 (1 shared with USA)	7.5[4] (2 FS cases shared with Germany and Turkey)	251 million	331 million	314 million	414 million
France	5.5 (1 shared with Belgium)	5.5	625 million	NA	746 million	NA
Spain	4	4	58 million	NA	66 million	NA
Italy	3	3[5]	102 million	NA	168 million	NA
Sweden	3	3[6]	122 million	NA	162 million	NA
Belgium	2.5 (1 shared with France)	2.5	72 million	NA	108 million	NA
Argentina	2	2	7 million	NA	10 million	NA
Austria	2	2	3 million	NA	8 million	NA
Greece	2	2[7]	17 million	NA	49 million	NA
Russia	2	2	0.4 million	NA	0.4 million	NA
Switzerland	2	3	39 million	78 million	65 million	129 million
Turkey	2	3.5 (1 shared with UK)	134 million	205 million	175 million	92.5 million
Australia	1	1[8]	4.1 mill	NA	11 million	NA

Table 13.2 (*cont.*)

Country of ISDS claim	No. of cases	No. of cases after accounting for apparent forum-shopping	Amount awarded	Amount awarded after accounting for apparent FS	Amount including pre-award interest	Amount including pre-award interest after accounting for apparent FS
Barbados	1	1	46 million	NA	60 million	NA
China	1	1	0.8 million	NA	1 million	NA
Cyprus	1	1[9]	76 million	NA	76 million	NA
Finland	1	1	11 million	NA	14 million	NA
Gibraltar	1	1[10]	1.1 million	NA	1.5 million	NA
Israel	1	1	15 million	NA	45 million	NA
Malaysia	1	1	6 million	NA	7 million	NA
Moldova	1	1	498 million	NA	498 million	NA
Oman	1	1	25 million	NA	35 million	NA
Romania	0	1	NA	0	NA	0
Serbia	0	1	NA	0.4 million	NA	0.5 million

[1] Does not include Yukos cases involving apparent forum-shopping by Russian claimants via Cyprus and the Isle of Man as discussed below.

[2] Includes one case in which data was unavailable on forum-shopping, i.e. where ultimate ownership of a claimant that appeared to be a potential holding company, due to its size and a lack of public information about the company, could not be traced. See Annex 2.

[3] Includes one case in which data was unavailable on forum-shopping.

[4] Includes two cases in which data was unavailable on forum-shopping.

[5] Includes one case (and major award) in which the claimant was a dual national of the home and host state, not classified as forum-shopping.

[6] Includes one case in which data was unavailable on forum-shopping.

[7] Includes one case in which data was unavailable on forum-shopping.

[8] For this case, data was unavailable on forum-shopping.

[9] For this case, data was unavailable on forum-shopping.

[10] For this case, data was unavailable on forum-shopping.

WHO HAS BENEFITED FROM INVESTMENT ARBITRATION? 407

Vladimir Dubov (7.0%), Vasily Shakhnovsky (7.0%) and others (4.5%). The remaining 50.0% was held by a trust fund called the Special Trust Arrangement, the sole beneficiary of which was Khodorkovsky. In effect, Khodorkovsky directly and indirectly owned 59.5% of MENATEP. MENATEP owned in turn 100% of the shares of YUL, another off-shore company registered in the Isle of Man. YUL in turn owned 100% of the shares of Hulley, an off-shore company registered in Cyprus that owned 57.5% of the shares of Joint Stock Company 'NC' Yukos (another 3.5% of this company was owned by YUL directly). YUL also had another 100%-owned Cyprus-registered subsidiary, Veteran Petroleum Limited (VPL). At the time of the Yukos bankruptcy in 2005, MENATEP controlled 51.0% of Yukos shares through YUL and Hulley and an additional 10.0% through Veteran Petroleum Trust (a trust established by VPL under the laws of the state of Jersey).[13] Effectively, a group of six Russian oligarchs, including Khodorkovsky, controlled 61.6% of Yukos through the off-shore vehicles YUL, Hulley and VPL at the material times.[14] By his ownership of the largest stake, we considered Khodorkovsky, in objective terms, to be the directing or influencing mind in the Yukos group of entities.

Incidentally, these cases appear to be examples of forum-shopping whereby individuals were allowed to bring ISDS claims against their own state by using companies or other entities abroad. Khodorkovsky, Lebedev and Shakhnovsky are Russian citizens; Brudno, Nevzlin and Dubov acquired Israeli citizenship in addition to their Russian citizenship after leaving Russia for Israel in 2003, and after criminal proceedings were brought against them in Russia.

In any event, due to their size, the three *Yukos* awards were distinct from the others in the dataset and so have been reported separately. The exclusion of these cases reduced vastly – from 89.0% to 12.6% (or from 86.3% to 11.7% including pre-award interest) – the proportion of the total compensation that was ordered for super-wealthy individuals.

---

[13] In the case of *VPL*, a Swiss court found that Khodorkovsky, Lebedev, Golubovitch, Nevzlin, Doubov, Brudno and Chakhnovski were the beneficial owners of the totality of Yukos shares allegedly owned or controlled by VPL; *Veteran Petroleum Limited (Cyprus)* v. *Russian Federation*, PCA Case No. AA 228, Interim Award on Jurisdiction and Admissibility, 30 November 2009, para. 71 (E-43) and 420.

[14] Another 8.8% of Yukos was controlled by Roman Abramovich, another Russian oligarch, through his UK vehicle Millhouse Capital. The remaining approximately 38.5% of Yukos stock was held by various hedge funds, American Depository Receipts (ADRs) and minor shareholders.

408 GUS VAN HARTEN AND PAVEL MALYSHEUSKI

Table 13.3 *The* Yukos cases

Case	Claimant nationality (with apparent forum-shopping (FS) indicated)	Corp. or natural person	Claimant size or wealth	Amount awarded	Amount awarded + pre-award interest
Hulley v. Russia	Cyprus (FS: Russia)	N	Super-wealthy individual	39,972 million	39,972 million
Veteran Petroleum v. Russia	Cyprus (FS: Russia)	N	Super-wealthy individual	8,203 million	8,203 million
Yukos v. Russia	Isle of Man (FS: Russia)	N	Super-wealthy individual	1,846 million	1,846 million

13.3.4 Legal Outcomes by Size or Wealth of ISDS Beneficiary

We also compared legal outcomes in ISDS cases, at the jurisdictional, merits and combined stages of a case, to the size or wealth of claimants. The findings are outlined below.

Keeping in mind that these are descriptive statistics, the only noteworthy findings appear to be the higher success rate of extra-large companies: 70.8% combined over 48 cases with a confirmed adjudicative resolution at the jurisdictional and/or the merits stage. In contrast, the success rate of other claimants was 42.2% combined over 166 cases. However, the success rates of large (as opposed to extra-large) companies (44.7% over 38 cases) and of super-wealthy individuals (36.4% over 22 cases) was comparable to those of other claimants not including large or extra-large companies or super-wealthy individuals (42.5% over 106 cases). In particular, the success rate of extra-large companies at the merits stage (82.9% over 41 cases) was much higher than that of other claimants (57.9% over 121 cases).

13.3.5 Size or Wealth of Claimants and Ordered Financial Transfers Compared to ISDS Costs

We also compared the data on ordered compensation, classified by claimant size or wealth, to approximate legal and arbitration costs in ISDS. The estimate of costs per case was taken from an OECD survey that reported

Table 13.4 *Size of claimant*

Claimant size or wealth	Cases coded for size or wealth	Cases with con-firmed reso-lution	Out-come: juris. not found	Out-come: juris. found	Success rate: juris. (%)	Out-come: viola-tion not found	Out-come: viola-tion found	Success rate: merits (%)	Over-all success rate (%)
Extra-large company	70	48	7	54	88.5	7	34	82.9	70.8
Large company	54	38	9	39	81.3	12	17	58.6	44.7
Medium company	18	9	1	16	94.1	3	5	62.5	55.6
Small company	16	11	3	10	76.9	3	5	62.5	45.5
Unknown company	48	41	11	31	73.8	16	14	46.7	34.1
Super-wealthy individual	26	22	8	15	65.2	6	8	57.1	36.4
Other individual	57	45	13	37	74.0	11	21	65.6	46.7
Total	292	214	52	201	79.5	58	104	64.2	48.6

410 GUS VAN HARTEN AND PAVEL MALYSHEUSKI

an average of USD eight million in ISDS legal and arbitration costs per case for both sides, with some cases exceeding USD 30 million in costs.[15]

Despite the limitations noted below, the estimates are useful in evaluating tentatively whether the financial position of small or medium companies or non-super-wealthy individuals appears to have been improved due to ISDS, not only compared to larger or wealthier investors, but also in absolute terms. That is, the estimate of average ISDS costs – taken here to be USD four million per case for the claimant investor(s)[16] – suggests that many smaller investors may have spent much more on ISDS costs than they received in ordered transfers.

The estimated costs are approximate because of a lack of detailed public information on costs in ISDS awards. Also, the use of averages may skew the numbers in individual cases if costs are higher in cases brought, for example, by larger or wealthier actors. As discussed in Section 13.2, tracking of ISDS costs and ordered compensation also does not cover all potential costs and benefits of ISDS.

The estimates also do not account for cost shifting, which is ordered by the arbitrators in some but not all ISDS cases. On this point, in 196 cases with relevant data, cost shifting appeared on average per case to have favoured respondent states for nearly all but one category of claimant size/ wealth. The exception was extra-large companies, which were required to pay one-third of the costs on average per case (compared to two-thirds required to be paid by the respondent state) where cost shifting occurred.[17] The approximate data on aggregate ordered compensation, accounting for assumed ISDS costs, is outlined in table 13.5.

Within this grouping of smaller enterprises, the tentative analysis suggested that a net loss in ISDS cases for medium companies was outweighed by a net

---

[15] Gaukrodger and Gordon (n. 11), 19. The OECD analysis covered 143 available ISDS awards, of which 28 provided information on arbitral fees and legal expenses, 81 provided some information on costs, and 62 provided no such information.

[16] For instance, half of the average costs per case as estimated by Gaukrodger and Gordon (n. 11).

[17] Of the 292 cases with information on claimant size, costs were found to have been shifted in 77 of 198 cases with available data, of which 25 cases were brought by a small or medium company or a non-super-wealthy individual (with average cost allocation per case of 57.8% of costs to be paid by the claimant and 42.2% by the respondent) and 14 cases by an unknown company (57.6% by the claimant). These portions of shifted cost borne by claimants were modestly lower than in cases brought by large companies (67.8% by the claimant in 14 cases) and super-wealthy individuals (62.5% by the claimant in 10 cases) and substantially higher than in cases brought by extra-large companies (33.4% by the claimant in 14 cases).

Table 13.5 *Aggregated compensation including costs*

Claimant size or wealth	Measure of size or wealth	Cases with confirmed adjudicative resolution	Cases where received damages	Total awarded, raw sum only	Total awarded, raw sum plus pre-award interest	Total estimated ISDS legal and arbitration costs	Net gain/loss
Extra-large company	>$10 billion in annual revenue	48	26	5,282 million	6,718 million	192 million	+6,526 million
Large company	>$1 billion and <$10 billion in annual revenue	38	14	601 million	780 million	152 million	+628 million
Medium company	>$100 million and <$1 billion in annual revenue	9	4	13 million	17 million	36 million	–19 million
Small company	<$100 million in annual revenue	11	4	80 million	99 million	44 million	+55 million
Unknown company	DU for annual revenue	41	13	132 million	154 million	164 million	–10 million
Super-wealthy individual	>$100 million in net wealth	22	5	905 million	1,072 million	88 million	+984 million
Other individual	<$100 million in net wealth	45	20	179 million	325 million	180 million	+145 million

Table 13.6 *Larger cost award cases*

Case	Claimant nationality (with apparent forum-shopping indicated)	Claimant size or wealth	Amount awarded	Amount + pre-award interest if available
Siag v. *Egypt*	Italy (FS: dual national of Egypt)	Other individual	75 million	129 million
ADC v. *Hungary*	Cyprus (FS: data unavailable (DU))	Unknown	76 million	76 million
Guaracachi v. *Bolivia*	UK, US	Small	29 million	36 million
Pey Casado v. *Chile*	Spain	Other individual (and non-profit org.)	10 million	14 million
Kardassapoulos v. *Georgia*	Greece	Other individual	15 million	45 million
Fuchs v. *Georgia*	Israel	Other individual	15 million	45 million
Metalclad v. *Mexico*	US (FS: DU)	Unknown	17 million	17 million
Walter Bau v. *Thailand*	Germany	Small	41 million	50 million
Desert Lines v. *Yemen*	Oman	Other individual	25 million	30 million
Funnekotter v. *Zim*	Netherlands	Other individual	11 million	25 million
American Man. v. *Congo*	US (FS: DU)	Unknown	9 million	9 million
Unglaube v. *Costa Rica*	Germany	Other individual	3.1 million	4.1 million
Wena Hotels v. *Egypt*	UK (FS: DU)	Unknown	8.8 million	19 million
White Industries v. *India*	Australia (FS: DU)	Unknown	4.1 million	11 million
Sistem v. *Kyrgyzstan*	Turkey (FS: DU)	Unknown	8.5 million	10 million
Talsud v. *Mexico*	Argentina	Small	6 million	9 million
Alpha v. *Ukraine*	Austria	Other individual	3 million	8 million
Lemire v. *Ukraine No. 2*	USA	Other individual	8.7 million	8.7 million

WHO HAS BENEFITED FROM INVESTMENT ARBITRATION? 413

gain for small companies and non-super-wealthy individuals. For companies with unknown annual revenues, it appeared that there was a net loss.

The overall gain for smaller enterprises appeared to be concentrated in a fairly small minority of beneficiaries. At the case level, a net gain was apparent in 12 (18.5%) of 65 cases with a confirmed adjudicative resolution and not involving an extra-large or large company, an unknown company, or a super-wealthy individual. If one included unknown companies in the grouping, a net gain appeared in 18 (17.0%) of 106 cases. These were the cases in which the smaller or unknown investor received an ordered transfer exceeding the assumed average of USD four million in ISDS legal and arbitration costs. These 18 cases are listed below.

Therefore, from this tentative and limited perspective, ISDS appears to have created among smaller and unknown investors a small group of financial winners and a much larger group of financial losers. The data on ISDS costs also highlights financial benefits of ISDS for ISDS lawyers, arbitrators, experts and other actors who earn income from ISDS fees. In 214 ISDS cases with a confirmed adjudicative resolution, based on the OECD estimate of ISDS costs the total payments of fees from disputing parties to the ISDS industry would have been about USD 1.7 billion.

13.4 Concluding Summary

The purpose of this chapter was to assess claims about ISDS linked to the size and wealth of foreign investors who bring claims and obtain orders of compensation in their favour. Broadly, ISDS was approached as a system that generates financial transfers, with a focus on ordered compensation by tribunals (not including annulment or set-aside proceedings). The findings on the apparent transfers can be summarized as follows (not including the Yukos cases, see Section 13.3.3, all figures in USD):

From states to extra-large[18] companies	6,718 million in 48 cases
From states to super-wealthy individuals[19]	1,072 million in 22 cases
From states to large[20] companies	780 million in 38 cases
From states to other individuals[21]	325 million in 45 cases

[18] Over USD ten billion in annual revenue.
[19] Over USD 100 million in net wealth.
[20] Over USD one billion in annual revenue, less than US$10 billion.
[21] Under USD 100 million in net wealth. Includes both confirmed and apparent non-super-wealthy individuals.

414 GUS VAN HARTEN AND PAVEL MALYSHEUSKI

(cont.)

From states to other[22] companies	270 million in 61 cases
Total from states to foreign investors	**9,164 million in 214 cases**

From states to ISDS industry[23]	856 million
From other companies to ISDS industry	244 million
From extra-large companies to ISDS industry	192 million
From other individuals to ISDS industry	180 million
From large companies to ISDS industry	152 million
From super-wealthy individuals to ISDS industry	88 million
Total from disputing parties to ISDS industry	**1,700 million in 214 cases**

From the same perspective, net winners and losers in the aggregate emerged as follows:

Big Winners

Extra-large companies	6,526 million (136 million per adjudicated case)
ISDS industry	1,712 million (8 million per adjudicated case)
Super-wealthy individuals	984 million (45 million per adjudicated case)
Large companies	628 million (17 million per adjudicated case)

Modest Winners

Other individuals:	145 million (3 million per adjudicated case)
Small and medium companies:	36 million (2 million per adjudicated case)

Modest Losers

Companies with unknown annual revenue	−10 million (−0.2 million per adjudicated case)

---

[22] Over USD 100 million in annual revenue, less than US$1 billion. Includes companies for which annual revenues were unknown.

[23] Primarily lawyers and arbitrators but also including paid experts and arbitral institutions.

Big Losers

Respondent states	−10,020 million (−47 million per adjudicated case)

These data are not based on elaborate statistical analysis; they support descriptive findings about what has happened in ISDS but should not be taken as predictions of future outcomes. The findings may reflect coincidences and be subject to a risk of error that precludes predictive claims. The main contribution of our study is to show how ISDS has unfolded from the point of view of financial transfers based on a comprehensive review of known ISDS cases. The findings are perhaps most useful where they reveal wide variations in the experiences of different actors and where they cast doubt on claims about ISDS that are not based on comparable evidence.

Annex 1

Excluded cases

Case	Claimant nationality (with apparent forum-shopping (FS) indicated)	Corp. or natural person	Claimant size or wealth	Amount awarded (USD)	Amount awarded + pre-award interest where available (USD)
CSOB v. *Slovakia*	Czech Republic (FS: Belgium)	C	Extra-large	1,050 million	1,050 million
ATA v. *Jordan*	Turkey	C	Large	NA – non-monetary order that other arbitration can proceed	NA – non-monetary order that other arbitration can proceed

Annex 2

Breakdown of cases

Case	Claimant nationality (with apparent forum-shopping (FS) indicated)	Corp. or natural person	Claimant size or wealth	Amount awarded (USD)	Amount awarded + pre-award interest (USD)
Occidental v. *Ecuador* No. 2	US	C	Extra-large	1,770 million	2,358 million
Mobil v. *Venezuela*	Netherlands (FS: US)	C	Extra-large	1,600 million	2,067 million
EDF v. *Argentina*	Belgium, France	C	Extra-large	136 million	205 million
BG Group v.*Argentina*	UK	C	Extra-large	185 million	219 million
CMS v. *Argentina*	US	C	Large	133 million	151 million
CGE/Vivendi v. *Argentina* No. 2	France	C	Extra-large	105 million	169 million
Siemens v. *Argentina*	Germany	C	Extra-large	238 million	278 million
Enron v. *Argentina*	US	C	Extra-large	106 million	142 million
Azurix v. *Argentina*	US	C	Extra-large	165 million	186 million
Sempra v. *Argentina*	US	C	Large	128 million	171 million
Suez & *Interaguas*	France	C	Extra-large	405 million	405 million

(*cont.*)

Case	Claimant nationality (with apparent forum-shopping (FS) indicated)	Corp. or natural person	Claimant size or wealth	Amount awarded (USD)	Amount awarded + pre-award interest (USD)
CME v. *Czech Republic*	Netherlands (FS: US)	N	Super-wealthy individual	270 million	395 million
Stati v. *Kazakhstan*	Moldova	N	Super-wealthy individual	498 million	498 million
Rumeli v. *Kazakhstan*	Turkey (FS[1])	C	Large (with extra-large[2])	125 million	165 million
Micula v. *Romania*	Sweden	N	Super-wealthy individual	117 million	156 milionl
LG&E v. *Argentina*	US	C	Extra-large	57 million	57 million
Chevron v. *Ecuador No. 1*	US	C	Extra-large	78 million	96 million
Siag v. *Egypt*	Italy (FS[3])	N	Other individual	75 million	129 million
ADC v. *Hungary*	Cyprus (FS: data unavailable[4])	C	Unknown	76 million	76 million
Cargill v. *Mexico*	US	C	Extra-large	77 million	86 million
Deutsche Bank v. *Sri Lanka*	Germany	C	Extra-large	60 million	70 million
Impregilo v. *Argentina*	Italy	C	Large	21 million	28 million
El Paso v. *Argentina*	US	C	Extra-large	43 million	66 million
National Grid v. *Argentina*	UK	C	Extra-large	39 million	54 million
SAUR International v. *Argentina*	France	C	Large	40 million	60 million
Guaracachi v. *Bolivia*	UK, US	C	Small	29 million	36 million
Pey Casado v. *Chile*	Spain	N	Other individual[5]	10 million	14 million

WHO HAS BENEFITED FROM INVESTMENT ARBITRATION? 419

(cont.)

Case	Claimant nationality (with apparent forum-shopping (FS) indicated)	Corp. or natural person	Claimant size or wealth	Amount awarded (USD)	Amount awarded + pre-award interest (USD)
Eastern Sugar v. *Costa Rica*	Netherlands (FS: UK & Germany)	C	Extra-large	35 million	35 million
Occidental v. *Ecuador No. 1*	US	C	Extra-large	72 million	75 million
OKO Pankki Oyj v. *Estonia*	Finland	C	Extra-large	11 million	14 million
Kardassapoulos v. *Georgia*	Greece	N	Other individual	15 million	45 million
Fuchs v. *Georgia*	Israel	N	Other individual	15 million	45 million
RDC v. *Guatemala*	US	N	Super-wealthy individual	11 million	11 million
TECO v. *Guatemala*	US	C	Large	21 million	23 million
Abengoa v. *Mexico*	Spain	C	Extra-large	40 million	42 million
ADM v. *Mexico*	US	C	Large	34 million	37 million
Metalclad v. *Mexico*	US (FS: data unavailable)	C	Unknown	17 million	17 million
SGS v. *Paraguay*	Switzerland	C	Large	39 million	64 million
Achmea v. *Slovakia No. 1*	Netherlands	C	Extra-large	29 million	29 million[6]
Walter Bau v. *Thailand*	Germany	C	Small	41 million	50 million
Tidewater v. *Venezuela*	Barbados (FS: US)	C	Large	46 million	60 million
Desert Line Products v. *Yemen*	Oman	N	Other individual	25 million	30 million

(cont.)

Case	Claimant nationality (with apparent forum-shopping (FS) indicated)	Corp. or natural person	Claimant size or wealth	Amount awarded (USD)	Amount awarded + pre-award interest (USD)
Funnekotter v. *Zimbabwe*	Netherlands	N	Other individual	11 million	25 million
Continental Casualty v. *Arg.*	US	C	Extra-large	2.8 million	3.6 million
Saipem v. *Bangladesh* Italy		C	Extra-large	11 million	6.3 million
Goetz v. *Burundi No. 1*	Belgium	N	Other individual	3 million	3 million
Goetz v. *Burundi No. 2*	Belgium	N	Other individual	1.2 million	2.2 million
SD Myers v. *Canada*	US	C	Medium	6 million	8.3 million
MTD Equity v. *Chile*	Malaysia	C	Medium	5.9 million	7.4 million
American Man. v. *Congo*	US (FS: data unavail.)	C	Unknown	9 million	9 million
R. Unglaube v. *Costa Rica*	Germany	N	Other individual	3.1 million	4.1 million
Duke Energy v. *Ecuador*	US	C	Extra-large	5.6 million	28 million
Middle East Cement v. *Egypt*	Greece (FS: data unavail.)	C	Unknown	2.2 million	3.8 million
Wena Hotels v. *Egypt*	UK (FS: data unavail.)	C	Unknown	8.8 million	19 million
White Industries v. *India*	Australia (FS: data unavail.)	C	Unknown	4.1 million	11 million

WHO HAS BENEFITED FROM INVESTMENT ARBITRATION? 421

(cont.)

Case	Claimant nationality (with apparent forum-shopping (FS) indicated)	Corp. or natural person	Claimant size or wealth	Amount awarded (USD)	Amount awarded + pre-award interest (USD)
AIG Capital v. *Kazakhstan*	USA	C	Extra-large	6 million	9.3 million
Petrobart v. *Kyrgyzstan No. 2*	Gibraltar (FS: data unavail.)	C	Unknown	1.1 million	1.5 million
Sistem v. *Kyrgyzstan*	Turkey (FS: data unavail.)	C	Unknown	8.5 million	10 million
Nykomb v. *Latvia*	Sweden	C	Large	3 million	3.2 million
Swembalt v. *Latvia*	Sweden (FS: data unavail.)	C	Unknown	2.5 million	2.8 million
Feldman v. *Mexico*	USA	N	Other individual	1.7 million	1.7 million
Gemplus v. *Mexico*	France	C	Extra-large	4.5 million	6.4 million
Tecmed v. *Mexico*	Spain	C	Extra-large	5.5 million	7.4 million
Talsud v. *Mexico*	Argentina	C	Small	6 million	9 million
Arif v. *Moldova*	France	N	Other individual	2.8 million	2.8 million
Saar Papier v. *Poland*	Germany (FS: data unavail.)	C	Unknown	1.6 million	2.2 million
Awdi v. *Romania*	USA	N	Super wealthy individual	8.6 million	12 million
Renta 4 v. *Russia*	Spain	C	Large	2 million	2.8 million
RosInvestCo v. *Russia*	UK (FS: data unavail.)	C	Small	3.5 million	3.9 million
Sedelmayer v. *Russia*	Germany	N	Other individual	2.4 million	2.8 million
PSEG v. *Turkey*	US	C	Large	9 million	15 million

(cont.)

Case	Claimant nationality (with apparent forum-shopping (FS) indicated)	Corp. or natural person	Claimant size or wealth	Amount awarded (USD)	Amount awarded + pre-award interest (USD)
Alpha Projekt holding v. *Ukraine*	Austria	N	Other individual	3 million	8 million
Lemire v. *Ukraine No. 2*	US	N	Other individual	8.7 million	8.7 million
Pope & Talbot v. *Canada*	US	C	Medium	460,000	460000
Mitchell v. *Congo*	US	N	Other individual	750,000	1.1 million
Swisslion v. *Macedonia*	Switzerland (FS: Serbia)	C	Medium	440,000	490,000
Bogdanov v. *Moldova No. 1*	Russia	N	Other individual	280,000	280,000
Bogdanov v. *Moldova No. 2*	Russia	N	Other individual	160,000	DU
Tza Yap Shum v. *Peru*	China	N	Other individual	790,000	1 million
Maffezini v. *Spain*	Argentina	N	Other individual	410,000	490,000
AAPL v. *Sri Lanka*	UK (FS: data unavail.)	C	Unknown	460,000	610,000
Fedax v. *Venezuela*	Neth. (FS: data unavail.)	C	Unknown	600,000	760,000
Nordzucker v. *Poland*	Germany	C	Large	0	0
Rompetrol v. *Romania*	Netherlands (FS: Romania)	C	Large	0	0
Al-Bahloul v. *Tajikistan*	Austria	N	Other individual	0	0

WHO HAS BENEFITED FROM INVESTMENT ARBITRATION? 423

(cont.)

Case	Claimant nationality (with apparent forum-shopping (FS) indicated)	Corp. or natural person	Claimant size or wealth	Amount awarded (USD)	Amount awarded + pre-award interest (USD)
Biwater v. *Tanzania*	UK	C	Unknown	0	0
Total: 86 cases		**C: 61** **N: 25**	**Extra-large: 26** **Large: 14** **Medium: 4** **Small: 4** **Unknown: 13** **Super-wealthy individual:** **5** **Other individual:** **20**	**Total:** **7,191** **million**	**Total:** **9,164** **million**

[1] Forum-shopping: UK for one of two claimants.

[2] Counted as extra-large.

[3] Forum-shopping: dual national of Egypt.

[4] Data was unavailable on forum-shopping where ultimate ownership of a claimant that appeared to be a potential holding company, due to its size and a lack of public information about the company, could not be traced.

[5] And a non-profit organization.

[6] Net any tax.

14

Explaining China's Relative Absence from Investment Treaty Arbitration

FREDRIK LINDMARK[*], DANIEL BEHN[**] AND OLE KRISTIAN FAUCHALD[***]

14.1 Introduction

China has been among the top signatories of international investment agreements (IIAs) in the past two decades, and has participated actively in the international investment treaty regime since it signed its first bilateral investment treaty (BIT) with Sweden in 1982. It ranks second after Germany in terms of BITs signed, and third after Germany and Switzerland in terms of BITs that have entered into force.[1] Despite China's active participation in treaty-making, it has only been involved in a handful of investment treaty arbitration (ITA) cases. This is unusual and presents a puzzle that this chapter seeks to explore. What might best explain China's relative absence from ITA (either as a Respondent state or as Chinese Claimant-investors) despite having one of the largest and most comprehensive networks of BITs in the world and being one of the world's most significant destinations of inward and sources of outward foreign direct investment (FDI)?

Studying how China is exposed to ITA and Chinese investors use ITA is important to general legitimacy discourses due to the size of the Chinese economy, including in particular the amount of inbound and

---

[*] Legal adviser, Norwegian Industrial Property Office.

[**] Associate Professor (Senior Lecturer) of International Law, Queen Mary, University of London; Associate Research Professor, PluriCourts, University of Oslo.

[***] Professor of Law, University of Oslo, Department of Public and International Law, PluriCourts. Research for this chapter has been funded by the Norwegian Research Council through project no. 276009 – Responses to the legitimacy crisis of international investment law.

[1] According to the UNCTAD IIA Navigator, the three states with the highest number of BITs signed and in force (excluding BITs that have been replaced) are: (1) Germany with 132 signed of which 126 are in force; (2) China with 127 signed of which 107 are in force; (3) Switzerland with 113 signed of which 110 are in force. See UNCTAD IIA Navigator, <investmentpolicy.unctad.org/international-investment-agreements>.

CHINA'S ABSENCE FROM TREATY ARBITRATION 425

outbound foreign direct investment. First, being among the world's largest economies in the world and a prime source of and destination for investment, China's exposure to and use of the international investment regime is important when studying whether the regime meets standards for output legitimacy (see chapter 2). By exploring how investors use Chinese IIAs in ITA cases, we seek to explore whether China provides foreign investors adequate and effective remedies for resolving investment disputes. Secondly, Chinese IIAs have traditionally promoted domestic settlement of investment disputes, probably more so than the IIAs of any other major economy. Studying the application of Chinese IIAs therefore provides a particularly relevant opportunity to identify and consider informal and hidden effects associated with threats of ITA. For example, such characteristics of Chinese IIAs allow us to consider whether and how ITA might play a role in combating corruption – a key consideration in assessing the output legitimacy of the investment regime.

The first and most commonly referenced explanation for the low number of Chinese ITA cases relies on the fact that many of China's early BITs did not provide for investor–state dispute settlement (ISDS) or restricted its consent to ISDS to the determination of the amount of compensation in cases of expropriation (see Annexes 1 and 2, and referred to in this chapter as narrow ISDS provisions). It was only in the late 1990s that this practice changed. In 1997, China signed its eighty-seventh BIT with South Africa, and this treaty included a broad ISDS provision similar to those found in most IIAs. Starting with the signing of the BIT with the Democratic Republic of the Congo in 2000, all subsequent Chinese BITs that have entered into force (51) and six other IIAs (see Annexes 3 and 5) have included broad ISDS clauses.

Despite having so many IIAs in force, we know of only three ITA cases initiated by foreign investors against China,[2] and seven cases brought by Chinese investors against other countries.[3] Only one of the ten cases was

---

[2] *Ekran Berhad* v. *People's Republic of China*, ICSID Case No. ARB/11/15, 2011, discontinued; *Ansung Housing Co. Ltd* v. *People's Republic of China*, ICSID Case No. ARB/14/25, Award on Jurisdiction, 9 March 2017; *Hela Schwarz GmbH* v. *People's Republic of China*, ICSID Case No. ARB/17/19, 2017, pending.

[3] *Tza Yap Shum* v. *Republic of Peru*, ICSID Case No. ARB/07/6, Award, 7 July 2011; *Beijing Shougang Mining Investment Company Ltd, China Heilongjiang International Economic and Technical Cooperative Corp. and Qinhuangdaoshi Qinlong International Industrial Co. Ltd* v. *Mongolia*, PCA Case No. 2010-20, Award, 30 June 2017; *Ping An Life Insurance Co. of China, Ltd and Ping An Insurance (Group) Co. of China, Ltd* v. *Kingdom of Belgium*, ICSID Case No. ARB/12/29, Award, 30 April 2015; *Sanum Investments Ltd* v. *Lao People's*

426 FREDRIK LINDMARK ET AL.

initiated before 2010; and hence it is fair to state that there has been an increase in cases in recent years, although the total number of ITA cases remains very low.

This chapter juxtaposes China's role as a prominent party to IIAs[4] – during a period in which it has become one of the world's leading importers and exporters of FDI – with its very limited role as a participant in ITA cases. So far, many Chinese BITs have remained inaccessible to researchers. For the purpose of this chapter, we have been able to obtain the texts of all Chinese BITs that are or have been in force, with the exception of one.[5]

In the following sections, we shall first explore whether the number of cases that China has been involved in is significantly lower than should be expected given the high number of BITs to which China is a party (Section 14.2) and taking into account the volume of Chinese inbound and outbound FDI (Section 14.3). We then explore a comprehensive set of possible explanations – including factors related to corruption – as to why there have been so few ITA cases against China (Section 14.4). We conclude by considering lessons learned from the Chinese case study for the output legitimacy of investment treaty arbitration.

14.2   Chinese Participation in the International Investment Regime

China has signed IIAs with 131 countries, 18 of which have not yet entered into force and an additional two that have been terminated (see Annex 4).[6] In the following section, we shall examine the potential for the remaining 113 treaty relationships to form the basis of ITA cases from a legal perspective. We divide our analysis into two main periods: (1) the period during which China's IIA

Democratic Republic (Sanum I), PCA Case No. 2013-13, 2014, settled; *Beijing Urban Construction Group Co. Ltd v. Republic of Yemen*, ICSID Case No. ARB/14/30, 2018, settled; *Sanum Investments Ltd v. Lao People's Democratic Republic (Sanum II)*, ICSID Case No. ADHOC/17/1, 2017, pending; *Wuxi T. Hertz Technologies Co. Ltd and Jetion Solar Co. Ltd v. Greece*, ad hoc UNCITRAL arbitration, 2019, pending.

[4] IIAs are the sum of BITs and other treaties with investment provisions (TIPs) as defined in the UNCTAD IIA Navigator (n. 1). Our numbers exclude all Chinese TIPs that do not contain relevant investment protection and ISDS provisions.

[5] We have been unable to access the China–Romania BIT (1983), which was replaced by a new BIT in 1994.

[6] We derived these numbers from the UNCTAD IIA Navigator (n. 1). Note that the numbers here concern *states* with treaty relationships with China, while the numbers from UNCTAD are based on *treaties*. Several IIAs have more than two state parties.

CHINA'S ABSENCE FROM TREATY ARBITRATION 427

practice was dominated by the inclusion of no ISDS provisions or narrow ISDS provisions (1982–2006); and (2) the period during which a significant portion of Chinese IIAs includes broad ISDS provisions (from 2007).

14.2.1   The Period of Narrow ISDS Provisions (1982–2006)

Only two of the states with which China has IIAs do not include consent to ISDS – the BITs with Romania and Turkmenistan (see Annex 1). When an IIA does not include consent to ISDS, the investor will have to obtain consent from the state in question in order to proceed with an ITA case. Practice suggests that post-dispute consent to ITA is extremely rare or non-existent.[7]

Between 1982 and 1997, China pursued a consistent approach of only providing ISDS in its IIAs for disputes regarding determinations of the amount of compensation in expropriation cases.[8] This was also made clear when China joined ICSID. On 7 January 1993, one month before the ISCID Convention entered into force for China, Chinese authorities issued the following notification under Article 25(4) of the Convention: '[T]he Chinese Government would only consider submitting to the jurisdiction of the International Centre for Settlement of Investment Disputes over compensation resulting from expropriation and nationalization.' The only deviation from this policy that we have been able to trace involves eight BITs that include somewhat broader ISDS provisions that arguably extend ISDS to compensation-related issues beyond expropriation. These BITs mostly involve states in Europe and the Middle East.[9]

Hence, in the 1982–97 period China was the state that most frequently and consistently insisted on limiting the jurisdictional scope of ISDS

---

[7] PluriCourts Investment Treaty and Arbitration Database (PITAD), <jus-pitad01.uio.no/index#welcome>. There is no known ISDS case that is based on post-dispute consent. See also Anthea Roberts, 'State-to-State Investment Treaty Arbitration: A Hybrid Theory of Interdependent Rights and Shared Interpretive Authority' (2014) 55(1) *Harvard International Law Journal* 1, 7–9.

[8] Altogether, China signed 79 such treaties in this period, and an additional five treaties after it signed its first BIT containing a general ISDS clause with South Africa (1997). These figures do not include treaties signed in the period when BITs with China did not include ISDS provisions (i.e. BITs with Sweden, Thailand and Turkmenistan) and one treaty that we have been unable to obtain – the BIT with Romania (1983). See also Norah Gallagher and Wenhua Shan, *Chinese Investment Treaties: Policies and Practice* (Oxford University Press, 2009), pp. 311–19.

[9] See the Chinese BITs with the Netherlands (1985); United Kingdom (1986); Kuwait (1985); Philippines (1992); Lithuania (1993); United Arab Emirates (1993); Saudi Arabia (1996); Lebanon (1996).

428 FREDRIK LINDMARK ET AL.

provisions. The context of such provisions raises unresolved issues regarding how they should work in practice. If the foreign investor claims that there has been an act of unlawful expropriation or the host state disputes that an expropriation has taken place in a case concerning the amount of compensation, the ISDS tribunal has two alternatives. First, a tribunal could conclude that it does not have jurisdiction since the claim concerns whether expropriation has taken place in violation of the BIT and not the amount of compensation. The ISDS provisions in the early Chinese BITs generally include the option of referring a case to national courts.[10] This suggests that investors should resort to such courts to determine whether expropriation has occurred. Such an approach raises significant problems regarding fork in the road provisions.[11] The alternative – that investors could seek confirmation from national authorities that expropriation has occurred prior to bringing a case concerning the amount of compensation – seems impractical. Second, a tribunal might find that being unable to determine whether an expropriation has occurred – and requiring the investor to seek remedies in national courts – would undermine the object and purpose of the BIT or render some of its provisions ineffective. Under such a scenario, an ISDS tribunal could conclude that it has jurisdiction to determine whether the measure amounts to expropriation.

In practice, tribunals have followed both approaches. The result has depended on the wording of the ISDS provisions as well as the IIA practice of the states in question.[12] The very first ITA case involving China to deal with this question was brought by a Chinese investor against Peru (*Tza Yap Shum*, initiated 2007). In the case, Fan Jianghong, who represented China during negotiations of the China–Peru BIT, testified that:

[10] See Section 14.3.2 below.

[11] Approximately half of China's IIAs have fork-in-the-road provisions. It remains an open question as to whether an investor could limit the claim before a domestic court to the existence of expropriation, in order to be able to bring the question of amount of compensation to international arbitration. The variation in fork-in-the-road provisions in Chinese BITs indicates that China was not requesting the inclusion of such provisions during negotiations, and suggests that Chinese negotiators might have been unaware of the potential problems associated with combining such provisions with narrow ISDS provisions.

[12] See *European Media Ventures S.A.* v. *Czech Republic*, UNCITRAL, Award on Jurisdiction, 15 May 2007; *Czech Republic* v. *European Media Ventures, S.A.* [2007] EWHC 2851 (Comm), UK High Court, Judgment, 5 December 2007, as discussed in Gallagher and Shan (n. 8), 316–18. See also J. Willems, 'Investment Disputes under China's BITs. Jurisdiction with Chinese Characteristics?' in Julian Chaisse (ed.), *China's International Investment Strategy. Bilateral, Regional, and Global Law and Policy* (Oxford University Press, 2019), pp. 445–50.

CHINA'S ABSENCE FROM TREATY ARBITRATION 429

> I remember that we provided them with a clear and simple example, which we used in several negotiations: 'you can submit a dispute to arbitration without our consent if our courts decide that your investment has been expropriated and that you are owed $6, but you think that you are owed $10.' This example reflected the outer limit of China's consent to international arbitration.[13]

The tribunal concluded that it had broad jurisdiction.[14] The subsequent attempt by Peru to have the decision annulled on the basis that this interpretation of the narrow ISDS provision constituted a 'manifest excess of power' failed.[15]

In another case initiated by a Chinese investor, the *China Heilongjiang* tribunal came to the opposite conclusion as regards the interpretation of the narrow ISDS provisions in the China–Mongolia BIT. This provision contained the same wording as the China–Peru BIT, including a 'fork-in-the-road' provision. The tribunal explicitly disagreed with previous tribunals' interpretations.[16] In between these two decisions, two more tribunals – *Sanum I* and *Beijing Urban* – have dealt with the question of jurisdiction under similar provisions in Chinese BITs, both coming to the conclusion that they had broad jurisdiction over the claims.[17] In addition to these four cases, where the tribunals have issued awards, there are three more known cases based on Chinese BITs with similar narrow ISDS provisions (two pending and one discontinued),[18] bringing the total number of such cases to

---

[13] *Tza Yap Shum* (n. 3), Decisión Sobre Jurisdicción y Competencia, 19 June 2009, para. 167 (quoted from unofficial translation published by TDM in 2010). See also Amos Irwin, 'Crossing the Ocean by Feeling for the BITs: Investor-State Arbitration in China's Bilateral Investment Treaties' (2014) *GEGI Working Paper*, 17.

[14] *Tza Yap Shum* (n. 3), paras. 143–88.

[15] *Tza Yap Shum* (n. 3), Decision on Annulment, 12 February 2015, paras. 98–9. The ad hoc committee stated at para. 99: 'It is not for the Committee to replace the Arbitral Tribunal's judgment by its own. A body that had appellate jurisdiction might well find fault as a matter of law with some aspects of the Arbitral Tribunal's application of the VCLT, but an ad hoc committee does not have such powers.'

[16] *China Heilongjiang* (n. 3), Award, 30 June 2017, paras. 423–54. This decision has been challenged at the US District Court for the Southern District of New York, Civil Action No. 17 CV 7436.

[17] *Sanum I* (n. 3), Award on Jurisdiction, 13 December 2013, paras. 322–42; *Beijing Urban* (n. 3), Decision on Jurisdiction, 31 May 2017, paras. 54–109.

[18] *Sanum II* (n. 3) in which a tribunal has been constituted but no decision on jurisdiction has yet been rendered. This case is based on the China–Lao PDR BIT (1993) and raises similar issues as *Sanum I* (n. 3). *Jetion Solar* (n. 3), in which the case has been registered but no tribunal constituted. The case is based on the China–Greece BIT (1992). *Ekran Berhad* (n. 2), in which no tribunal was constituted and the case was discontinued (settlement). This case was based on China's BITs with Malaysia (1988) and Israel (1995).

430   FREDRIK LINDMARK ET AL.

seven; of which six were initiated by Chinese investors and one case brought against China (see Table 14.1 below).[19]

It may have been possible as early as 1998 – at least in theory – to bring broad ITA claims under Chinese BITs with narrow ISDS provisions by invoking the broad ISDS provision in the China–South Africa BIT through the most favoured nation (MFN) provisions of other Chinese BITs. The first decision in which an ITA tribunal permitted an investor to rely on MFN provisions in one BIT to benefit from a broader ISDS provision in another BIT came in 2000.[20] As such, we consider that it was from about this time that investors could have been expected to make use of such options. The IIAs existing during this period did therefore provide some limited potential to form the basis of ITA cases from a legal perspective. However, the use of MFN provisions to expand jurisdiction remains controversial to this day. Moreover, our reading of the relevant Chinese IIAs indicates that only 35 of the BITs with narrow ISDS provisions contain broad MFN provisions that could be used as a basis for extending jurisdiction through the China–South Africa BIT.[21] Therefore, while broadening the scope of the ISDS provisions in early Chinese IIAs was possible, the practice of ITA tribunals and the content of Chinese MFN provisions indicate that investors were unlikely to perceive this as a realistic option.

Against this background, we propose that it was not until about 2007 that investors saw the realistic and significant opportunity of bringing broad ISDS claims based on Chinese IIAs with narrow ISDS provisions. This was the year of the first finding that BITs with narrow ISDS provisions could provide jurisdiction for claims regarding whether or not an expropriation occurred.[22]

Additionally, there was no real focus on obtaining the actual texts of Chinese BITs until the publication of Gallagher and Shan's extensive analysis of Chinese BITs in 2009.[23] To this day, China figures among the states with the lowest number of available IIA texts in UNCTAD's

---

[19] *Ekran Berhad* (n. 2).
[20] *Emilio Agustín Maffezini* v. *Kingdom of Spain*, ICSID Case No. ARB/97/7, Decision on Objections to Jurisdiction, 25 January 2000, paras. 38–64.
[21] Out of the 88 BITs (of which one text is unavailable), 52 contain narrow MFN provisions. We consider these MFN clauses as 'narrow' because the MFN clause is located together with and only applies to the fair and equitable treatment provisions (and in some cases the obligation of 'protection') under these BITs.
[22] *European Media Ventures* (n. 12).
[23] Gallagher and Shan (n. 8).

CHINA'S ABSENCE FROM TREATY ARBITRATION 431

database.[24] Moreover, the period until 2007 saw very limited outward FDI from China and a relatively high degree of inward FDI.[25] Thus, it would generally be in China's interest to limit the possibility of investors to initiate ITA cases under these treaties as long as the amount of outward FDI remained insignificant.[26] Finally, China has consistently had a high number of IIAs that have not (yet) entered into force. Among the BITs China had signed by the end of 2006, fifteen still have not entered into force. At the end of 2006, an additional five BITs had not entered into force despite having been signed more than five years earlier.[27]

Overall, it seems that China's focus when signing BITs before 2007 was to build bilateral relations and promote investments in China (symbolic and political goals), while limiting the protection of investors and their investments beyond what was needed for these purposes (a material limitation). Moreover, prior to the mid-2000s there was a limited number of ITA cases among all states, not just China (see Figure 14.1). Thus, combined with a practice of only providing narrow ISDS provisions in China's early BITs, it is unsurprising that there were no ITA cases against China or brought by Chinese investors prior to 2006. These findings show that this initial period does not raise significant legitimacy issues regarding Chinese IIAs and associated ITA. The remainder of this chapter shall therefore consider the period from 2007.

14.2.2 Later Expansion: Broader ISDS Provisions (2007–19)

This subsection shall briefly consider the extent to which China is an outlier among countries in terms of number of ITA cases. The first ITA case under a Chinese IIA was initiated in 2007. Following this case, we know of six more cases brought by Chinese investors and three cases brought against China. Seven of these cases were brought under IIAs with narrow ISDS provisions[28] and three were brought under IIAs with broad

---

[24] A total of 23 BIT texts remain unavailable in UNCTAD's IIA database, including 11 BITs that have entered into force. See UNCTAD IIA Navigator (n. 1).

[25] Gallagher and Shan (n. 8), 4–14.

[26] This is based on the argument that states sign IIAs with ISDS provisions primarily to protect their own investors investing abroad.

[27] These include the BITs with Israel (signed 1995, in force 2009); Gabon (signed 1997, in force 2009); Cameroon (signed 1997, in force 2014); Republic of Congo (signed 2000, in force 2015); and Nigeria (signed 2001, in force 2010).

[28] *Ekran Berhad* (n. 2); *Tza Yap Shum* (n. 3); *China Heilongjiang* (n. 3); *Sanum I* (n. 3); *Beijing Urban* (n. 3); *Sanum II* (n. 3); *Jetion Solar* (n. 3).

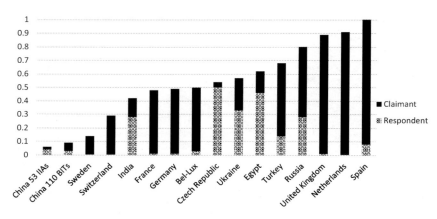

Figure 14.1 Ratio of number of ITA cases to number of BITs (up to 1 August 2019)[1]
[1] UNCTAD IIA Navigator (n. 1); PITAD (n. 7). The total numbers of ITA cases per BIT are as follows (number of cases where states were respondents within brackets): China – 3(2) ITA cases / 53 IIAs or 10(3) ITA cases / 110 BITs; Sweden – 9(0) ITA cases / 65 BITs; Switzerland – 32(0) ITA cases / 110 BITs; India – 34(23) ITA cases / 81 BITs; France – 45(1) ITA cases / 94 BITs; Germany – 52(1) ITA cases / 126 BITs; Belgium–Luxembourg – 36(2) ITA cases / 72 BITs; Czech Republic – 41(38) ITA cases / 76 BITs; Ukraine –38(22) ITA cases / 67 BITs; Egypt – 46(34) ITA cases / 74 BITs; Turkey – 49 (10) ITA cases / 72 BITs; Russia – 51(18) ITA cases / 64 BITs; United Kingdom – 84(1) ITA cases / 94 BITs; Netherlands – 87(0) ITA cases / 96 BITs; Spain – 65(5) ITA cases / 65 BITs.

ISDS provisions.[29] These ten cases represent a very limited involvement of China in the 1,069 known ITA cases initiated since 1987, constituting less than 0.5%[30]

Figure 14.1 shows the ratio of all ITA cases, including cases against the country (respondent) and cases initiated by investors of the country (claimant), relative to the number of IIAs in force for the countries in question. If we compare China to other countries that are parties to significant numbers of BITs with ISDS clauses, we find that China scores lowest in terms of frequency of ITA cases regardless of whether our estimate includes cases related to all BITs (110) or cases related to IIAs with broad ISDS clauses (see 53). However, if we only consider ITA cases where the countries are respondents, China scores higher than a significant group of European countries, including the Netherlands, Sweden

---

[29] *Ansung Housing* (n. 2); *Hela Schwarz* (n. 2); *Ping An* (n. 3).
[30] PITAD (n. 7). Calculated on the basis that each ITA case involves two distinct states – the host state and the investor's home state.

CHINA'S ABSENCE FROM TREATY ARBITRATION

Table 14.1 *Distribution of Chinese ITA cases initiated after 2006*

	China as respondent	Chinese claimant
IIA relationships with broad ISDS (53)	2	1
IIA relationships with narrow ISDS (49)	1	6

and Switzerland (with no cases), France, Germany and the United Kingdom (UK) (with one case each), as well as Belgium (two cases). The numbers of ITA cases exclude those based on the Energy Charter Treaty since neither China nor some of the other states are parties, and the Treaty is a multilateral treaty which would significantly increase the number of ISDS relationships.

The low rate of Chinese ITA cases compared to other countries could potentially be explained by the date of entry into force of the Chinese BITs. It generally takes time from the entry into force of a treaty until investors initiate ITA cases, essentially depending on the extent to which investors of the treaty parties have been engaged in disputes previously. On average, Chinese IIAs with broad ISDS provisions have been in force for more than ten years.[31] Moreover, China has concluded such treaties mostly with states categorized as high income states by the World Bank Income Groups (WBIGs),[32] and much less with low, lower middle and upper middle income states.[33] Altogether, the states with which China has broad ISDS provision IIAs have been involved in 812 ITA cases, on

---

[31] See Annex 5.

[32] The WBIGs are used to determine states' lending eligibility. They are calculated using the World Bank atlas method, essentially a way of smoothing out the impact of fluctuations in prices and exchange rates on the state-year estimates. In practice, the World Bank applies a conversion factor that averages a state's exchange rate for a given year and the two preceding years, while adjusting for differences in rates of inflation between the state and a basket of developed economies. Economies are split into four categories: (1) low income; (2) lower middle income; (3) higher middle income and (4) high income. See <datahelpdesk.worldbank.org/knowledgebase/articles/906519>.

[33] The WBIG breakdown of China's treaty partners with IIAs that include broad ISDS provisions: high income states (23), corresponding to 44% of the total number of states in this group; upper middle income states (13), corresponding to 25% of states in this group; lower middle income states (11), corresponding to 21% of states in this group; and low income states (5), corresponding to 10% of states in this group.

average 16 per state.[34] These factors clearly indicate that the three ITA cases initiated under Chinese IIAs with broad ISDS provisions is a remarkably low number.[35] Any way that one looks at it, there appears to be a surprisingly small number of ITA cases involving China, considering both its extensive IIA practice, and in comparison with other states with a significant number of IIAs in force (Figure 14.1). If we distribute Chinese ITA cases according to categories of ISDS provisions as well as cases initiated against China and by Chinese investors (Table 14.1), we find no reason to question these findings. The only exception is the relatively high number of cases initiated by Chinese investors under IIAs with narrow ISDS clauses. Against this background, the main questions in the following are why foreign investors have initiated only one case against China under IIAs with broad ISDS clauses since 2007, and what this, combined with China's involvement in IIAs with a broad variety of ISDS clauses, can tell us about legitimacy issues regarding ITA.

14.3 Patterns of Chinese Inward FDI from 2007: Further Adding to the Puzzle?

14.3.1 Amounts of FDI

Juxtaposing the Chinese IIAs that are in force with data on FDI between China and its IIA partners, this section analyses the extent to which inward Chinese FDI stocks are under the protection of Chinese IIAs. Figure 14.2 indicates that inward stocks of FDI have had a stable and significant increase over the period. It also shows that outward stocks of FDI started from a significantly lower level in 2007 but have eventually caught up with inward stocks.

In Table 14.2, we have identified the percentage of China's stocks of inward FDI in 2012 from states that have IIAs with China that include broad, narrow or no ISDS provisions.[36] This provides a general

---

[34] UNCTAD IIA Navigator (n. 1); PITAD (n. 7).

[35] *Hela Schwarz* (n. 2); *Ansung Housing* (n. 2); *Ping An* (n. 3).

[36] We have been unable to identify more recent data that provide a comparable level of detail on sources of Chinese FDI. Arguably, data from 2012 should be a relatively good proxy for the average distribution of Chinese FDI in the period since 2007, partly because data from 2012 is midway through the period, and partly because the increase in stocks of inward FDI is relatively linear throughout the period.

Table 14.2 *Chinese inward FDI stocks in 2012*[1]

Access to ISDS	IIAs	USD (million)	% inward FDI	% inward FDI (ex. Hong Kong)
Broad	53	279,512	20.8%	37.2%
Narrow or none	62	26,706	2.0%	3.6%
No IIA in force	48	917,927	68.3%	43.3%
Unspecified[2]	NA	119,415	8.9	15.9%

[1] UNCTAD 2014 Bilateral FDI Statistics <unctad.org/en/Pages/DIAE/FDI%20Statistics/FDI-Statistics-Bilateral.aspx>. There is a very significant discrepancy between the total FDI stock reported here (USD 1,343,559 million) and the total FDI stock in 2012 reported in UNCTAD's data centre (USD 832,882 million, a discrepancy of USD 511 billion). This may possibly be due to the fact that the inward FDI stock reported here is based on accumulated FDI inflows into China.

[2] 'Unspecified' refers to FDI for which the state of origin is unknown. Such investment might belong to any of the three categories.

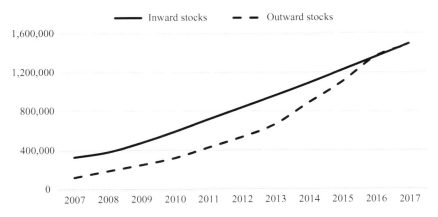

Figure 14.2 Stocks of Chinese inward and outward FDI 2007–17 (US$ million)[1]

[1] UNCTAD <unctadstat.unctad.org/EN/Index.html>.

indication of distribution of the sources of inward FDI stocks according to category of ISDS provisions.

A very significant share of FDI stocks in China are from Hong Kong (USD 592 billion in 2012). FDI coming from Hong Kong may be made by purely Hong Kong-based entities, but also by mainland Chinese entities (through so-called round tripping) and foreign entities. On the one hand, it has been estimated that round tripping investment accounts for in total 25% to 40% of the total FDI into China.[37] On the other hand, it is also likely that a substantial part of the FDI flowing into China from Hong Kong is originating from other countries. Hong Kong has 18 IIAs with other states, but no IIA with ISDS clause with China. Whether investment entering China through Hong Kong could enjoy protection under a Chinese IIA would depend on the facts of the specific case. The data provides only a general indication on the amount of FDI stocks under the protection of Chinese IIAs. We also concede the lack of correspondence between criteria for determining the origin of FDI for statistical purposes and for determining the scope of protection under IIAs.

Despite these weaknesses in the data, we conclude that the amount of FDI is significantly lower from states with which China has IIAs with narrow ISDS than from states with IIAs with broad ISDS provisions. Our snapshot of the distribution of Chinese inward FDI stocks therefore indicates support for two hypotheses: (1) We should expect more ITA cases under IIAs with broad ISDS provisions than under IIAs with narrow provisions since the former IIAs cover significantly higher amounts of FDI. (2) The higher amount of inward FDI stocks into China compared to outward FDI stocks from China during the period (Figure 14.2) indicates that we should expect more ITA cases initiated against China than by Chinese investors against other states. Contrary to these expectations, most ITA cases initiated under Chinese IIAs to date have been under IIAs with narrow ISDS provisions, and mostly by Chinese investors (Table 14.1). These findings indicate that China's limited ITA practice cannot be explained by the amount of FDI.

14.3.2   FDI by Sectors

Moving from amount of FDI and types of IIAs, we will look closer at the relationship between economic sectors, FDI flows and ITA disputes in relation to China. We identify which economic sectors have been most prone to ITA cases and consider whether the structure of China's inward

---

[37] Kelly Liu and Kevin Daly, 'Foreign Direct Investment in China Manufacturing Industry: Transformation from a Low-Tech to a High-Tech Manufacturing' (2011) 6(7) *International Journal of Business and Management* 6, 21. See also Ken Davies, 'China Investment Policy: An Update' (2013) *OECD Working Papers on International Investment* 2013/01, 11.

CHINA'S ABSENCE FROM TREATY ARBITRATION 437

Table 14.3 *Chinese inward FDI flows by economic sector*[1]

	1999	2004	2009	2014	All ITA disputes
Primary Sector (Agriculture)	3.1%	2.7%	2.1%	1.7%	5.1%
Secondary Sector (Manufacturing)	57.9%	71.0%	52.0%	33.4%	48.4%
Tertiary Sector (Services)	38.9%	26.3%	45.9%	64.9%	46.5%
FDI (billion USD) / Number of ITA disputes	403	606	900	1,195	1,069

[1] National Bureau of Statistics of China, <stats.gov.cn/english/statisticaldata/AnnualData>; PITAD (n. 7).

FDI flows correlate with the economic sectors in which there are a high incidence of ITA disputes (considering the entire caseload of 1,069 ITA cases).

To our knowledge, there is no conclusive data on the *stocks* of Chinese inward FDI registered delineated by economic sectors. Hence, we use data on *flow* of inward Chinese FDI in four selected years. As we can see from Table 14.3, a very significant share of China's inward FDI flows goes into the manufacturing sector, although such FDI has declined in recent years. Meanwhile, FDI into the services sector has increased significantly in the last two decades. China has historically had very low inward FDI flows in the agricultural sector, a tendency which has remained stable. Looking at the characteristics of Chinese inward FDI flows, there is no stark deviation between the percentage of ITA disputes in these three broad economic sectors and the amount of inward Chinese FDI in those sectors. In other words, our data does not appear to support any conclusion that the distribution of inflow of FDI into the three broad sectors can explain China's low exposure to ITA cases.

14.4 Understanding China's Relative Absence from ITA

14.4.1 Introduction

Based on our preliminary findings in Sections 14.2 and 14.3, we shall proceed to consider other factors that might explain the following two puzzles:

438   FREDRIK LINDMARK ET AL.

1. Why have there been so few ITA cases against China under IIAs with broad ISDS clauses since 2007?
2. Why have there been more ITA cases under Chinese IIAs with narrow than broad ISDS provisions?

Exploring the reasons why a phenomenon is absent raises very significant methodological problems. In this case, a key problem is that we do not know anything about the investors that have or could have considered bringing an ITA case. This study might therefore be seen as a preliminary and incomplete attempt at contributing to expanding the scope of empirical legal studies to fields that have so far received little attention.

Based on Figure 14.1, an initial question is why we would not expect China to be able to join the group of European countries that have hardly been respondents in any cases despite having very high exposure to such disputes. As we shall return to below, the main reason why we would not expect China to be comparable to these countries is the characteristics of the Chinese domestic judiciary.

The main challenge when trying to explain the absence of a phenomenon is to narrow down and structure the list of explanatory factors. The first step we have taken is to establish the assumption that there has been an actual need for dispute settlement among foreign investors and Chinese authorities commensurate with the amount and characteristics of inward investment. This assumption might not be valid due to the broad variety of reasons why investors might choose not to pursue a claim. Such decisions by investors are based on more or less well-informed benefit–cost analyses, for example that the cost to foreign investors of bringing a case against Chinese authorities is so high that they accept the treatment offered, or that Chinese authorities generally offer benefits to dissatisfied foreign investors that make them abandon their claims. For the purpose of this chapter, it has not been possible to enter into any detailed exploration of all such explanatory factors.

We have chosen to focus on mechanisms available to the two parties to a dispute to prevent its escalation into a full-blown ITA case. Accordingly, we first study the type of pre-ITA mitigation measures that states have integrated into their IIAs, including requirements that investors must first attempt domestic administrative review procedures, accept a 'cooling off' period, and bring the claim within a certain deadline (Section 14.4.2).[38] Thereafter,

---

[38] August Reinisch, 'How Narrow are Narrow Dispute Settlement Clauses in Investment Treaties?' (2011) 2(1) *Journal of International Dispute Settlement* 115, 116; and Catherine

we proceed to explore the extent to which other mechanisms for dispute settlement are preferred over ITA in the Chinese context (Section 14.4.3). We have identified domestic courts and contract-based commercial arbitration as the two most likely alternatives to ITA. Finally, we shall proceed to explore the role of corruption based on the argument that Chinese authorities and foreign investors might have a joint interest in finding a way of settling disputes informally (Section 14.4.4).

14.4.2 Pre-dispute Mitigation

14.4.2.1 Administrative Review Procedures

Almost all China's IIAs with broad ISDS provisions provide for foreign investors to resort to an 'administrative review procedure' (ARP) before bringing an ITA case against China. It has been argued that the purpose of such procedures is not to prevent or limit investors' access to arbitration, but rather to establish whether official Chinese authorities acted in accordance with the law.[39] In this sense, the procedures could contribute to improving Chinese authorities' handling of foreign investors and investments, and thereby not only solve the present dispute, but also prevent the emergence of future disputes. However, it has also been claimed that it is unlikely that the ARP has any potential to reduce the possibility of ultimately bringing an ITA case.[40]

This subsection explores in more detail the potential effects that the ARP may have for the frequency of ITA. The ARP is a mechanism under Chinese law that is used broadly for administrative complaints of all types, and which may form the basis of both rights and obligations. In this sense, the ARP clearly has legal implications beyond determining the legal conduct of administrative agencies under Chinese law.[41]

With only two exceptions,[42] the ARP is included in all Chinese IIAs with broad ISDS provisions. It was omitted temporarily in IIAs with

---

Kessedjian et al., 'Mediation in Future Investor-State Dispute Settlement', Academic Forum on ISDS Concept Paper 2020/16, 5 March 2020..

[39] Axel Berger, 'China's New Bilateral Investment Treaty Programme: Substance, Rational and Implications for International Investment Law Making', presented to the ASIL Economic Law Interest Group conference in Washington DC, November 2008, 11.

[40] Ibid; Stephan W. Schill, 'Tearing down the Great Wall: The New Generation of Investment Treaties of the People's Republic of China' (2007) 15 *Cardozo Journal of International and Comparative Law* 73, 92.

[41] For contrary opinions, see Berger (ibid.) and Schill (ibid.).

[42] China's BITs with Iran (2000) and Nigeria (2001).

440 FREDRIK LINDMARK ET AL.

narrow ISDS provisions signed after 1990, but was reintroduced in China's BIT with South Africa in 1997.[43] The almost complete correlation between IIAs with broad ISDS provisions and the inclusion of the ARP strongly suggests that the inclusion of these procedures is a strategic policy of China in order to control potential effects of extending ISDS to all substantive obligations under its IIAs. There are several varieties of the provisions on the ARP in IIAs, including in particular:

- provisions stating that the host state 'may require the investor concerned to exhaust the domestic administrative review procedures',[44]
- provisions stating that the investor 'shall go through the domestic administrative review procedures as specified by the laws and regulations of the disputing Contracting Party' with a maximum duration of four months,[45] and
- provisions stating that China's IIA partner 'takes note of the statement' that China 'requires that the investor concerned exhausts the domestic administrative review procedure' specified in its legislation, as well as China's declaration that the 'procedure will take a maximum period of three months'.[46]

The ARP refers to a system of administrative reconsideration (*Xingzheng Fuyi*) under China's Administrative Reconsideration Law of 1999,[47] whereby 'administrative organs of a higher level [can] review any specific administrative acts of lower-level organs for legality and propriety'.[48] Pursuant to Articles 6–8 of the Reconsideration Law, citizens, legal

---

[43] Some of China's older BITs also contain references to comparable procedural requirements. China's BIT with Pakistan (1989) states that the investor 'may file complaint with the competent authority' in the host state. If the complaint is not 'solved within one year after the complaint', the investor may bring the dispute to ITA: see China–Pakistan BIT (Article 10). Similar provisions can be found in China's BITs with Poland (1988, Article 10) and Malaysia (1988, Article VII).

[44] China–Trinidad and Tobago BIT (2002, Article 10.2(b)).

[45] China–Mexico BIT (2008, Annex C).

[46] China–Netherlands BIT (2001, Protocol, ad Article 10).

[47] See Administrative Reconsideration Law of the People's Republic of China, promulgated 9 April 1999, in force as of 1 October 1999, <http://www.npc.gov.cn/zgrdw/englishnpc/Law/2007-12/11/content_1383562.htm>; Elodie Dolac, 'Chinese Investment Treaties: What Protection for Foreign Investment in China?' in Micheal Moser (ed.), *Dispute Resolution in China* (JurisNet, 2012), pp. 237, 295.

[48] Wenhua Shan, 'China and International Investment Law' in Leon Trakman and Nicola Ranieri (eds.), *Regionalism in International Investment Law* (Oxford University Press, 2013), pp. 214, 248.

persons and organizations, including foreigners, may file an application for administrative reconsideration for most types of executive actions, including specific provisions and sanctions issued by authorities. Most, but not all, administrative acts will fall under the auspices of the Reconsideration Law. In addition, the Administrative Procedure Law contains provisions for administrative litigation (*Xingzheng Susong*).[49] An administrative reconsideration decision may be appealed to a people's court. Administrative reconsideration is usually not compulsory before accessing administrative litigation.[50]

There has been a significant increase in the number of cases initiated under the two procedures, from 74,448 administrative reconsideration cases and 85,760 administrative litigation cases in 2000 to respectively 149,222 and 141,880 such cases in 2014. Compared to the amount of cases handled by Chinese courts, however, the total number of the ARP cases is negligible: the courts accepted approximately 9.5 million cases in 2014 (of which approximately 8.3 million were civil proceedings),[51] and the total number of administrative review cases was a mere 291,102.[52]

Despite the relatively even application of the two administrative review mechanisms, none of China's IIAs mention administrative litigation in the context of the ARP provisions.[53] Moreover, the Reconsideration Law only applies to the review of administrative acts as listed in its provisions, but it does not exclude the possibility that a foreign investor may be required under an IIA to resort to the ARP for administrative acts *not* mentioned in the Law. Additionally, if a *non*-administrative act is the basis for the IIA claim – for instance a court decision that violates an investor's rights under an IIA – Chinese IIAs do not set out how the investor is supposed to resort to the ARP. The dynamics between the

---

[49] Ibid; Gallagher and Shan (n. 8), 367; Administrative Procedure Law of the People's Republic of China, promulgated at the National People's Congress, 4 April 1989, <http://english.mofcom.gov.cn/aarticle/lawsdata/chineselaw/200211/20021100053380.html>.

[50] Weidong Yang, 'Can the Introduction of Administrative Reconsideration Committees Help Reform China's System of Administrative Reconsideration?' (2018) 13(1) *University of Pennsylvania Asian Law Review* 107, 109–10.

[51] China Statistical Yearbook (2014), National Bureau of Statistics of the PRC <www.stats.gov.cn/tjsj/ndsj/2015/indexeh.htm>.

[52] Yang (n. 50), 112 and 123 (with further references to the Law Yearbook of China from 2000–14 in n. 16 and n. 42).

[53] The English versions of Chinese BITs use the more ambiguous wording 'administrative review procedure' but the Chinese versions clearly refer to 'administrative reconsideration'.

442   FREDRIK LINDMARK ET AL.

requirements regarding the ARP in Chinese IIAs and the provisions in the Reconsideration Law and Administrative Procedure Law remain somewhat unclear. Until foreign investors in China with first-hand experience provide information on how such cases are handled, the interplay between the ARP and ITA is likely to remain 'unknown territory'.[54]

We would expect that if an investor initiates the ARP *together with or subsequent to* the notification and registration of the ITA case, we should have known of most of these cases. Under these circumstances, the ARP as such could not have explained the low number of ITA cases. However, it is likely that foreign investors would prefer to use the ARP *prior to* notifying and registering the case. We do not know to what extent foreign investors actually use the ARP to seek review of administrative acts.[55] It seems to have been rare for foreign investors in China to use these administrative remedies.[56] Three relatively recent cases that received public attention in China illustrate the complex nature of the ARP.[57] One of these, the *Beijing Jialilai Case*, resulted in one decision under administrative reconsideration followed by two lawsuits under administrative litigation and one commercial arbitration award rendered by China International Economic and Trade Arbitration Commission (CIETAC) before the case was ultimately settled.[58]

As has been made clear in a number of Chinese IIAs, China can forgo the option of requiring the ARP and permit the investor to proceed directly to arbitration.[59] For example, the *Hela Schwarz Case* was initiated under the China–Germany BIT, which requires the exhaustion of the ARP before accessing ITA.[60] In a letter to the claimant-investor, China has asserted that

---

[54] Dolac (n. 47), 297.

[55] To our knowledge, there are no official statistics on the involvement of foreign investors using the ARP. The Law Yearbook of China (in Chinese) contains statistics on administrative reconsideration but does not have information of the nationality of the complainants. The China Statistical Yearbook contains statistics on administrative litigation but does not have information on the nationality of the parties.

[56] Gallagher and Shan (n. 8), 371.

[57] The *Beijing Jialilai Case,* the *Changchun Huijin Case* and the *Fuzhou Xinyuan Case,* discussed in Gallagher and Shan (n. 8), 371–6.

[58] Ibid.

[59] Norah Gallagher, 'China's BITs and Arbitration Practice: Progress and Problems', in Wenhua Shan with Junyuan Su (eds.), *China and International Investment Law. Twenty Years of ICSID Membership* (Brill, 2015), pp. 180, 201.

[60] The China–Germany BIT (2003, Protocol, ad Article 9) requires the investor to refer the issue to ARP according to Chinese law and that the dispute must still exist after three months from the initiation of the review procedures.

the claimant 'did not ... apply for administrative review'.[61] This clearly shows that China is not unwilling to argue that an investor has failed to fulfil the pre-dispute ARP requirement in order to avoid ITA. However, we do not know whether and to what extent this case is representative of China's stance on such procedures. In any case, we find it likely that Chinese authorities may also be using the ARP as a means to enter into negotiations with the investor to resolve the dispute before it escalates to ITA.

In our view, resorting to the ARP may in many cases be beneficial to the investor. First, the ARP is free[62] and a relatively expedient mechanism. Both the system under the Reconsideration Law and some of the Chinese IIAs set a brief time limit for the ARP, usually three months.[63] Second, the ARP provides the investor an opportunity to discuss the dispute with a high-level administrative organ under a procedure that is much less confrontational than formal litigation or arbitration. Finally, the time with which the ARP procedure would delay arbitration proceedings is generally consumed by the cooling-off period required under most IIAs and it might therefore not delay the ITA case at all (see Section 14.4.2.2). Hence, if the investor is satisfied with the result of the ARP, it may be the most efficient way to resolve the dispute.

On the other hand, the ARP gives Chinese authorities significant room for promoting other means of dispute resolution that could be less attractive to the investor.[64] Depending on the wording of each IIA, there may be a twilight zone between the requirement of exhaustion of the ARP in Chinese IIAs and the way that the ARP is implemented.[65] Does the ARP requirement mean that the foreign investor must await a final decision before accessing ITA? What if an opponent or a third party appeals the decision to domestic courts? Many of the IIA provisions requiring the ARP set no time limits for the procedure. The *Beijing Jialilai Case* illustrates that the ARP might be unpredictable and time-consuming. In this case, the domestic party in the joint venture brought

---

[61] *Hela Schwarz* (n. 2), Procedural Order No. 2, 10 August 2018, para. 39.

[62] See Article 39 of the Administrative Reconsideration Law (n. 47).

[63] Ibid, Article 26. Some IIAs have a longer time limit: see the China–Mexico BIT, which allows the ARP to take up to four months.

[64] One example relates to Chinese IIAs with fork-in-the-road provisions, under which investors could be prevented from initiating an ITA claim if the result of reconsideration is appealed.

[65] Some BITs contain clear obligations. For instance, Annex C in the China–Mexico BIT states that if the ARP is not completed within four months, the procedures are considered as complete and 'the investor may proceed to an international arbitration'.

444   FREDRIK LINDMARK ET AL.

the Chinese ministry's administrative reconsideration decision to administrative litigation. Thereafter, the ministry appealed the court's decision.[66] The procedure gives Chinese authorities time and opportunity to assess the risk of ITA. During the time a foreign investor is initiating the ARP, and any subsequent appeals, the Chinese authorities have ample time to negotiate. Since the ARP is a complete review of the legality and propriety of an organ's actions, the ARP also provides a basis for assessing all aspects of the foreign investor's case. This could allow Chinese authorities to separate the potential ITA cases from the cases that are unlikely to progress to that level.

In conclusion, we find that the ARP requirements of Chinese IIAs with broad ISDS provisions may constitute a significant explanatory factor for why there have been few ITA cases against China. Its direct importance flows from the fact that it forces the investor to enter into a dialogue with Chinese administrative authorities at a clearly defined stage in the process. While there is the argument that such a dialogue is very likely to have taken place at an earlier stage, the formalization of a dialogue between the investor and Chinese authorities when the dispute has come to a point where ITA is the next step is likely to constitute an important additional incentive for the parties to find a solution. The involvement of higher levels of Chinese authorities through the ARP procedures might change the dynamics of ongoing or past negotiations.

14.4.2.2   Cooling-Off Periods

In general, requirements concerning cooling-off periods have been given vastly different meaning by tribunals, with some tribunals viewing them as 'mere exhortations' to attempt conciliation, others as 'conditions precedent' to jurisdiction, and some as 'contractual obligations, breach of which results not in lack of jurisdiction ..., but in damages or injunctive relief.[67] This indicates that compliance with and effects of cooling-off provisions depend on characteristics of host states, including internal rules and practices, and are likely to vary significantly among states.

Among the 53 states with which China has IIAs with broad ISDS provisions, 85% require a cooling-off period of six months.[68] The

---

[66] Gallagher and Shan (n. 8), 371–3.

[67] Aravind Ganesh, 'Cooling Off Period (Investment Arbitration)' (2017) *MPILux Working Paper No. 7*, 3.

[68] Two IIAs require three-month cooling-off periods, three require four months, 45 require six months, and one requires nine months.

cooling-off period begins upon notification of the claim. In most cases, the cooling-off period will continue to prevent the ITA cases from moving forward until after the ARP has ended. It is hard to assess to what extent negotiations during the cooling-off period and beyond the ARP period are effectively preventing ITA cases from moving forward. The parties involved generally keep confidential documents exchanged during negotiations, the outcome of the negotiations, and even the fact that negotiations have taken place.[69]

Nevertheless, the nature of the cooling-off period, namely that it starts upon the notification and registration of an ITA case, means that we should have knowledge of most ITA cases to which the cooling-off period was applied. Hence, the key question here is whether the requirement of a cooling-off period provides any significant additional incentive for investors to drop ITA cases before they are formally registered. This must be considered not only in light of the ARP requirements, but also in light of the extent to which there exist other incentives to resolve the case before such registration. Traditionally, China has favoured conciliation and mediation and avoided formal dispute settlement mechanisms 'because they associate litigation with penal codes and punishment;' a tradition that 'may be traced back to the Legalists'.[70] The tradition-based preference for conciliation and mediation has followed China through the ages.[71] This has also been a prominent feature of the Chinese legal system and legal culture after the overthrowing of the Qing Dynasty in 1911, after the founding of the Peoples' Republic of China in 1949,[72] after the Cultural Revolution, and during China's 'opening up'. From 2006 to 2012, there was a push by the central government in this direction through a 'renewed emphasis' on conciliation and mediation by sending instructions to 'all legal institutions to prioritize mediation over litigation'.[73] Conciliation or mediation is an intrinsic part of dispute resolution in China, with deep-rooted traditions of utilizing it at all stages

---

[69] Esmé Shirlow, 'The Rising Interest in the Mediation of Investment Treaty Disputes, and Scope for Increasing Interaction between Mediation and Arbitration', *Kluwer Arbitration Blog*, 29 September 2016.

[70] Sally L. Ellis and Laura Shea, 'Foreign Commercial Dispute Settlement in the People's Republic of China' (1981) 6 *Maryland Journal of International Law* 155, 156.

[71] Stanley Lubman, 'Mao and Mediation: Politics and Dispute Resolution in Communist China' (1967) 55 *California Law Review* 1284, 1286.

[72] Ibid.

[73] Jerome A. Cohen, 'Settling International Business Disputes with China: Then and Now' (2014) 47 *Cornell International Law Journal* 555, 560 (with further references in fn. 22).

446 FREDRIK LINDMARK ET AL.

of a dispute; by lawyers, judges and even arbitrators.[74] More specifically, many of China's laws and regulations on foreign investment and trade adopted after China's 'opening up' strongly encourage or may even require conciliation or mediation before arbitration or litigation can be initiated.[75] Against this background, we find it highly likely that Chinese authorities would undertake serious efforts at reaching settlements prior to the cooling-off period, and that foreign investors interested in continuing their operations in China will partake in such efforts in good faith.

In the *Ekran Berhad* case, the proceedings were halted in July 2011 and discontinued by agreement in May 2013.[76] We have been unable to access information on the outcome of this case, but it seems likely that the investor and Chinese authorities reached a settlement.[77] This case is illustrative of the problems regarding access to information when researching the effects of mandatory cooling-off periods. Moreover, it shows that we are likely have knowledge about ITA cases in which cooling-off periods apply.

The Chinese traditions regarding alternative dispute resolution and the ARP requirement are likely to represent significant incentives for foreign investors to resolve disputes before notifying and registering an ITA case. It seems unlikely that the relatively short cooling-off periods in Chinese IIAs – mostly limited to six months – would constitute any significant additional incentive. We therefore conclude that the cooling-off periods are unlikely to contribute significantly to lowering the number of ITA cases involving China as host state.

---

[74] For an overview on the use of conciliation in China in recent years, see ibid., 558–61.

[75] This started with the Law of the People's Republic of China on Chinese-Foreign Equity Joint Ventures, Article 15, promulgated at the 5th National People's Congress, 1 July 1979 <china.org.cn/english/DAT/214773.htm>. See also Law of the People's Republic of China on Economic Contracts Involving Foreign Interests, Article 37, promulgated at the 6th National People's Congress, 21 March 1985 <asianlii.org/cn/legis/cen/laws/ ecifi457>; Law of the People's Republic of China on Sino-Foreign Cooperative Enterprises, Article 25, promulgated an the 7th National People's Congress, 13 April 1988, <english.mofcom.gov.cn/aarticle/policyrelease/internationalpolicy/200705/ 20070504715781.html>; Economic Contract Law of the People's Republic of China, Article 42, promulgated at the 8th National People's Congress, 2 September 1993, <english.mofcom.gov.cn/aarticle/lawsdata/chinese law/200211/20021100053738.html>.

[76] *Ekran Berhad* (n. 2).

[77] See Gallagher (n. 59), 183, fn. 12.

14.4.2.3 Temporal Jurisdictional Limitations

A further factor that could significantly affect notification and registration of ITA cases is temporal jurisdiction limitations, since requirements that a case be submitted within a brief deadline after an alleged violation of a BIT could prevent such cases from moving forward. Such limitations occur more frequently in Chinese IIAs with broad ISDS provisions than in the IIAs of other countries. We find such limitations in Chinese IIAs with 19 states (37%),[78] while UNCTAD's coding project had identified such provisions in 182 of 2,572 IIAs (7%).[79] The Chinese clauses require that an ITA case be brought within three years from the date on which the investor first acquired or should have acquired knowledge of the events that gave rise to the dispute. The only deviation is the China–Cuba BIT as amended in 2007, in which the deadline is two years.

Temporal jurisdiction limitations may prevent a foreign investor from getting a case registered as an ITA case. In this sense, temporal jurisdiction limitations are more likely to contribute significantly to lowering the number of ITA cases involving China as host state than requirements in IIAs regarding ARP and cooling-off periods which apply only after the case has been notified or registered. On the other hand, both the North American Free Trade Agreement (NAFTA) and the Central American Free Trade Agreement (CAFTA-DR) include temporal jurisdictional limitations, and these two agreements have spawned nearly 100 ITA cases. This indicates that we should be careful not to overstate the importance of such limitations. Moreover, we are aware of only a low number of ITA cases in which temporal jurisdictional limitations have been invoked.[80]

Against this background, we find that the inclusion of temporal jurisdiction limitations in Chinese IIAs with broad ISDS provisions is more likely than not a contributory factor for the low number of ITA cases under these IIAs. However, we do not believe it to be an important contributor, since the deadline for bringing cases is fairly long and in light of the limited resort to temporal limitation clauses in ITA practice.

---

[78] See China's BITs with South Korea (2007); Cuba (2008); Mexico (2009); Uzbekistan (2011); Colombia (2013); Tanzania (2014); and IIAs with ASEAN (2010); South Korea and Japan (2014); New Zealand (2008), Canada (2014) and South Korea (2015).

[79] Data from UNCTAD's IIA Mapping Project as of December 2017. For relevant coding, see <investmentpolicy.unctad.org/international-investment-agreements/iia-mapping>.

[80] PITAD (n. 7).

448   FREDRIK LINDMARK ET AL.

14.4.3   Alternatives to ITA

14.4.3.1   International Commercial Arbitration

There are also factors less directly related to IIAs that are likely to affect the number of ITA cases, including in particular investors' use of commercial arbitration and domestic courts as alternatives to ITA. Commercial arbitration has become hugely popular among Chinese and foreign companies in China, with Chinese arbitral institutions deciding 113,600 cases in 2014.[81] China has a relatively recent and modern arbitration law, but has not adopted the UNCITRAL Model Law.[82] Chinese courts support the independence and autonomy of arbitration and do not get involved as they accept that they have no jurisdiction to adjudicate if the contracting parties have an arbitration agreement.[83] They are generally compliant with enforcing arbitral awards when asked.[84] Commercial arbitration therefore seems to be a trusted form of dispute resolution in China.

China acceded to the New York Convention in 1987.[85] This made foreign awards enforceable in China and Chinese awards enforceable in other contracting states. However, China listed the following reservation to the Convention: 'The People's Republic of China will apply the Convention only to differences arising out of legal relationships, whether contractual or not, which are considered as commercial under the national law of the People's Republic of China.' In April 1987, the Supreme People's Court of China issued a judicial interpretation clarifying the reservation, which contains an exhaustive list of the relationships exempted. It makes an explicit reference to all 'disputes between foreign investors and the host government'.[86]

---

[81] Wei Sun and Melanie Willems, *Arbitration in China: A Practitioner's Guide* (Kluwer, 2015), pp. xix–xx.

[82] UNCITRAL Model Law on International Commercial Arbitration of 1985, revised in 2006, 24 ILM 1302; Arbitration Law of the People's Republic of China, 31 August 1994, <npc.gov.cn/englishnpc/Law/2007-12/12/content_1383756.htm>.

[83] See Mo Zhang, 'International Civil Litigation in China: A Practical Analysis of the Chinese Judicial System' (2002) 25 *Boston College International and Comparative Law Review* 59.

[84] Meg Utterback et al., 'Enforcing Foreign Arbitral Awards in China: A Review of the Past Twenty Years', *King and Wood Mallesons*, 15 September 2006, <kwm.com/en/cn/know ledge/insights/enforcing-foreign-arbitral-awards-in-china-20160915>.

[85] New York Convention on the Recognition and Enforcement of Foreign Arbitral Awards (New York Convention), 330 UNTS 3, 4 ILM 532 (1958).

[86] Notice of the Supreme People's Court on Implementing the Convention on the Recognition and Enforcement of Foreign Arbitral Awards Acceded to by China, Article II, 10 April 1987.

CHINA'S ABSENCE FROM TREATY ARBITRATION 449

We find that commercial arbitration (i.e. non-ICSID contract-based arbitration involving a state or state entity) most likely has limited potential to replace ITA cases against China for three main reasons. First, commercial contract-based arbitration, unlike treaty-based arbitration, would always require a relationship in privity with the Chinese state or a Chinese state entity. The Chinese reservation to the New York Convention indicates that these type of contract-based arbitrations would not be enforceable in China. Unlike the *Ekran Berhad* and *Ansung Housing* cases, which both concerned the lawfulness of acts taken by local Chinese government officials and were both ICSID treaty-based arbitrations, any non-ICSID contract-based dispute.[87] Dispute between China and a foreign investor brought before an arbitral tribunal in any jurisdiction, China would most likely invoke its commercial reservation and refuse to recognize or enforce an award if it was made against China as 'the host government'.[88] Second, China has a policy of avoiding direct contractual relationships between public authorities and foreign investors. Finally, even if the Chinese authorities have concluded an arbitration agreement, it may not be possible to bring such disputes to arbitration under Chinese law.[89]

14.4.3.2 Foreign Investors in Chinese Courts

This sub-section considers foreign investors' use of Chinese courts as a potential alternative to ITA. As a key aspect of this issue, it discusses the role that corruption may play when investors decide on whether to bring a case to the domestic judiciary. As a starting point, it is reported that Chinese courts, were considered a 'total black box and an unacceptable risk' to foreign investors in the early 1970s.[90] Even today, Chinese courts continue to provide insufficient reassurance for foreign investors. Tao, for example, argues that the more 'fundamental malignancies evident in the Chinese legal system' are owed to 'the dearth of jurisprudence; an inexperienced and/or generally ill trained judiciary; a lack of established and uniform procedural rules, or at least deficiencies in their universal application; and rampant local protectionism.'[91]

---

[87] See n. 2.

[88] This view is held also by the Supreme People's Court (SPC), <supreme peoplescourtmonitor .com/2018/03/11/update-on-chinas-international-commercial-court/>.

[89] See Jingzhou Tao, *Arbitration Law and Practice in China,* 3rd edition (Kluwer, 2012), pp. 9–10.

[90] Cohen (n. 73), 557.

[91] See Tao (n. 89), xvi–xvii.

450   FREDRIK LINDMARK ET AL.

Together, these shortcomings supposedly make it a 'kiss of death' to bring Chinese authorities before domestic courts.[92] Nevertheless, Chinese courts are *de facto* an important institution for dispute settlement – including foreigners – and their role should not be underestimated.[93] From 2013 to 2015, Chinese courts considered over 100,000 civil, commercial and maritime cases involving at least one foreign party, a 10% increase from the 2010 to 2012 period. Of these cases, approximately half involved parties from Hong Kong, Macau and Taiwan.[94] We cannot assume that these numbers mean that Chinese courts are a popular venue for foreign investors involved in disputes with Chinese authorities, as we have no statistics on how frequently they are involved in such litigation. Nevertheless, the numbers show that Chinese courts are relatively popular as a venue for disputes involving foreigners, despite the criticism they receive.

Among the various factors that might affect foreign investors' use of Chinese domestic courts, we have explored corruption as a key proxy for their independence and impartiality. While other indicators could have been used, such as independence of the judiciary and enforcement, we have made this choice because corruption covers the relationship between courts and both parties to a case, and makes it possible to distinguish between the relationship between courts and local and central authorities. Moreover, this choice makes it possible to explore how ITA may relate to domestic corruption. Historic trends in corruption in China have been mapped as part of the Varieties of Democracy project (V-Dem).[95] Their data make it possible for us to acquire some knowledge about how foreign investors have considered the potential use of Chinese domestic courts. It provides a general picture of how such corruption has evolved in China compared to the average of all other states for which data exist, as well as two groups of states that clearly differ in terms of corruption levels: least developed countries (LDCs) and OECD member states. Figure 14.3 indicates that Chinese courts have been percieved as much more corrupt than the world average since the early 1990s, and

---

[92] François Godement and Angela Stanzel, 'The European Interest in an Investment Treaty with China', *European Council on Foreign Relations* 19 February 2015, <https://ecfr.eu/publication/the_european_interest_in_an_investment_treaty_with_china332/>, 6.

[93] See Zhang (n. 83).

[94] Y. Zhang, Courts See More Foreign Legal Disputes, China Daily, 6 January 2016, <chinadaily.com.cn/china/2016-01/06/content_22946797.htm>.

[95] V-Dem, <v-dem.net/en>.

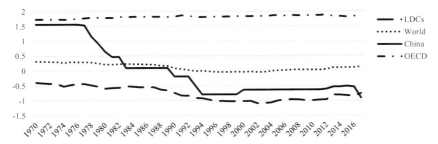

Figure 14.3 Judicial corruption in China 1970–2017 based on V-Dem data[1]

[1] V-Dem Codebook V8 (July 2018), section 3.7.7. Judicial corruption decision: 'How often do individuals or businesses make undocumented extra payments or bribes in order to speed up or delay the process or to obtain a favourable judicial decision?'

they have recently deteriorated further to being perceived as even more corrupt than the average of the LDCs (the scale runs from −3 to +3, where −3 represents the highest level of corruption).

The presence of corruption in the Chinese judiciary raises doubts as to the impartiality and quality of these courts. In general, we assume that this makes Chinese courts less attractive as an alternative to ITA.

Although IIAs allow investors to remove politically sensitive disputes from domestic courts,[96] it is likely that Chinese courts have solved some potential ITA cases. Given the recent efforts within China to prevent and prosecute corruption,[97] we assume that those involved in corruption have a strong and joint interest in avoiding exposure through the publicity of ITA proceedings. Hence, to the extent that there has been corruption between the foreign investor and Chinese authorities prior to the dispute, foreign investors and public authorities are likely to find it beneficial to seek dispute resolution through corrupt domestic courts rather than through ITA.

Foreign investors involved in corruption are likely to avoid ITA for two main reasons. First, investor misconduct, in particular linked to corruption, could limit or eliminate an investor's chances of a successful ITA claim. The vast majority of China's IIAs includes a requirement that the investment is made 'in accordance with the laws and regulations' of

---

[96] See generally Marco Bronckers, 'Is Investor-State Dispute Settlement (ISDS) Superior to Litigation before Domestic Courts? An EU View on Bilateral Trade Agreements' (2015) 18(3) *Journal of International Economic Law* 655.
[97] See e.g. Tony C. Lee, 'Pernicious Custom? Corruption, Culture, and the Efficacy of Anti-Corruption Campaigning in China' (2018) 70(3) *Crime Law and Social Change* 349.

452 FREDRIK LINDMARK ET AL.

the host state. Investor misconduct may occur during the FDI approval process, whereby authorities approve a foreign investment on a case-by-case basis at their discretion. Such processes could allow officials to demand illegal payment to grant an approval.[98] Moreover, tribunals have rejected protection under IIAs in some cases of serious misconduct of investors (sometimes referred to as the 'clean hands doctrine'). Relevant misconduct includes, *inter alia,* corruption[99] and fraud.[100] These features of Chinese IIAs mean that it is likely that China as respondent in ITA cases will make use of opportunities to argue that corruption or other forms of investor misconduct prevent foreign investors from benefiting from protection under IIAs. Second, bringing an ITA case could sever important ties with authorities and make it difficult for the investor to continue operations. Many foreign businesses in China seek long-term return on their investments. This necessitates a strategic approach to disputes. The fallout from initiating an ITA case may be too risky as it may permanently damage the relationship between the investor and Chinese authorities. In the early days after China's 'opening up', investors 'were consistently met with the refrain that arbitration is a very unfriendly act and were warned that insistence on invoking ... [commercial] arbitration ... could terminate their cooperation with China'.[101] Correspondingly, Chinese authorities that have been involved in corruption – in particular those at the local and regional level as well as central authorities at a low level – are likely to avoid exposure of their practices through ITA proceedings that would involve high-level central authorities.

Accordingly, foreign investors involved in corruption within China can assume that potential future disputes with Chinese authorities are unlikely to increase the risk that corruption will be exposed. Hence, their preference is most likely to resolve such disputes by non-transparent

---

[98] Like in most states, approvals with vague requirements could allow for discretionary decisions by executive branches. For instance, a joint venture contract requires an approval from MOFCOM before the contract enters into force. Such approval will not be granted if the joint venture is considered to be detrimental to Chinese State sovereignty, against Chinese law, or incompatible with the needs of China's economic development: see Gallagher and Shan (n. 8), 237.

[99] See e.g. *World Duty Free Company Ltd* v. *Republic of Kenya*, ICSID Case No. ARB/00/7, Award, 4 October 2006.

[100] See e.g. *Inceysa Vallisoletana, S.L.* v. *Republic of El Salvador*, ICSID Case No. ARB/03/26, Award, 2 August 2006.

[101] Cohen (n. 73), 557.

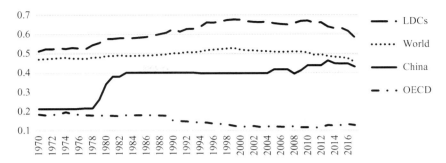

Figure 14.4 Executive corruption in China 1970–2017 based on V-Dem data[1]

[1] V-Dem Codebook V8 (July 2018), section 4.0.23. Executive corruption index: 'How routinely do members of the executive, or their agents grant favours in exchange for bribes, kickbacks, or other material inducements, and how often do they steal, embezzle, or misappropriate public funds or other state resources for personal or family use?'

procedures (e.g. negotiations or the ARP) with relevant authorities or by resort to domestic courts with low risk of exposure. In contrast, foreign investors with 'clean hands' are likely to prefer ITA if a dispute cannot be resolved to their satisfaction through negotiations or the ARP due to the perception of Chinese courts. Similarly, in light of the attempts by central authorities to combat corruption, Chinese authorities that have not been involved in such activities may have an interest in promoting exposure of corrupt practices among other authorities. The significant scepticism that has existed towards Chinese domestic courts as well as their high level of corruption is likely to lead such investors and public authorities to prefer ITA. However, the extent to which ITA substitutes domestic courts in such situations remains somewhat unclear.[102]

Against this background, we shall further explore levels of corruption among Chinese authorities as mapped through relevant V-Dem corruption indexes. One important group of public officials is members of the executive who have decision-making power in individual cases. Figure 14.4 traces executive corruption based on how often members of the executive or their agents are involved in corruption. The data indicates that Chinese corruption increased at the end of the Cultural

---

[102] See Thomas Schultz and Cédric Dupont, 'Investment Arbitration: Promoting the Rule of Law or Over-empowering Investors? A Quantitative Empirical Study' (2014) 25(4) *European Journal of International Law* 1147, 1161–2.

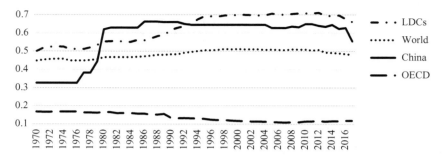

Figure 14.5 Public sector corruption in China 1970–2017 based on V-Dem data[1]

[1] V-Dem Codebook V8 (July 2018), section: 4.0.33. Public sector corruption index: 'To what extent do public sector employees grant favours in exchange for bribes, kickbacks, or other material inducements, and how often do they steal, embezzle, or misappropriate public funds or other state resources for personal or family use?'

Revolution and stayed relatively unchanged throughout the following two decades, with a slight increase since 2000. According to these data, executive corruption in China remains slightly lower than the world average. Against this background, our starting point is that corruption does not seem to be of above average concern in the Chinese context, and to the extent that it has been a concern, it has not varied much over the period that we are studying here.

V-Dem also provides data on corruption among a broader group of public sector employees. Since there is extensive deferral of decision-making power to the provincial and local levels in China, we may assume that it is important to examine corrupt practices among this group. Moreover, such authorities are likely to be particularly interested in avoiding exposure of corrupt practices through ITA as they are vulnerable to sanctions by superior or central authorities. The level of corruption for public sector employees (Figure 14.5) stands in some contrast to that for executive corruption as it reached a high level after the Cultural Revolution and has stayed significantly above the world average in the following period. It has been relatively stable after 1980, but seems to have dropped sharply since 2016.

It seems reasonable to conclude that during the period since 2007, there would have been a significant potential for ITA to contribute to raise the risk of exposure of corruption involving public authorities and foreign investors in China. In essence, the above data is based on expert assessments. Quantitative research on the tendency to make illegal payments is scarce, and it is therefore difficult to get exact numbers on how

CHINA'S ABSENCE FROM TREATY ARBITRATION

often foreign investors are involved in corruption in China. Nevertheless, some Chinese studies are of interest. In a 2014 market intelligence poll where 2,293 executives responded, 35% of the executives responded that they 'have to pay bribes, unofficial fees or make gifts to operate'.[103] The poll included executives from both state-owned and privately owned companies and covered companies with ownership from mainland China, Hong Kong and foreign companies. Among executives of *foreign-owned* companies, 37% reported that such payments were required,[104] indicating that foreign investors were slightly more involved in corruption than were domestic investors.

14.5 Concluding Remarks

Saving and gaining 'face' is still an important part of contemporary Chinese culture; and extensive loss in ITA cases would likely be detrimental to China's self-perceived image. Some commentators have theorized that avoidance of humiliation is key to understanding China's aversion to confrontational dispute settlement. Pan has described the phenomenon succinctly:

> The traditional Chinese preference for consultation, mediation, and conciliation over formal methods of dispute resolution has its origins in Confucian philosophy, which views social conflicts as shameful aberrations from *Li*, that is, from the natural order of social life. In the ideal Confucian world, a person would know the difference between right and wrong. If his claim is spurious or questionable, he would feel too ashamed to raise it. ... Based on such a legal culture, it was common to regard adjudication as a kind of humiliation. ... Hence, even if modern Chinese now have some trust in courts and judges, they still give preference to more informal methods of dispute resolution.[105]

Against this background, a relationship-oriented strategy to dispute settlement resonates more with traditional Chinese legal culture than more confrontational mechanisms involving third parties. Any engagement in ITA, or worse yet, losing in arbitration to a foreign investor, would be contrary to the Confucian values of non-confrontational

---

[103] Craig Charney and Shehzad Qazi, 'Corruption in China: What Companies Need to Know', Charney Research, <charneyresearch.com/wp-content/uploads/2015/01/White-Paper-Corruption-in-China-FINAL-v10.pdf>.

[104] Ibid.

[105] Junwu Pan, 'Chinese Philosophy and International Law' (2011) 1(2) *Asian Journal of International Law* 233, 237–8.

456   FREDRIK LINDMARK ET AL.

handling of disputes, the value of which should not be underestimated in today's China.[106]

However, it is also clear that China is about to leave elements of this tradition behind, at least in the context of international economic relations. Chinese investment abroad generates many disputes, and, as evidenced by the emerging ITA case law involving China, Chinese investors have relatively frequently brought ITA claims against other states, even based on BITs with narrow ISDS provisions. Moreover, within the brief period that China has been party to the WTO it has become its third most frequent user of its dispute settlement mechanism. Even though this position is more the result of being sued than suing others, China remains a staunch supporter of the WTO dispute settlement mechanism.[107]

Moreover, as an element of its opening up to international trade and foreign investment, including in particular liberalization of legal services, as well as its promotion of Chinese investment abroad, Chinese authorities have launched several initiatives to become a host to international dispute settlement, including commercial arbitration. This has been ongoing since the early 1980s;[108] and is illustrated more recently by the adoption of the 2017 CIETAC Investment Arbitration Rules and the 2019 draft International Investment Arbitration Rules from the Beijing Arbitration Commission.[109]

Our study has considered the reasons why there have been few ITA cases against China since 2007. We have found that Chinese exposure to ITA has remained exceptionally low during a period in which the risk that investors bring cases has increased through IIAs with broad ISDS

---

[106] On the Confucian preference for conciliation, see also Jerome Alan Cohen, 'Chinese Mediation on the Eve of Modernization' (1966) 54(3) *California Law Review* 1201, 1206–9.

[107] See WTO, <wto.org/english/tratop_e/dispu_e/dispu_by_country_e.htm> and the Chinese interventions in favour of the Appellate Body during the current crisis regarding appointment of new Appellate Body members, WTO doc. WT/GC/M/172 agenda item 4.

[108] One early example is the South China International Economic and Trade Arbitration Commission, which was established in 1983 in the Shenzhen Special Economic Zone to resolve contract and property rights disputes involving, inter alia, foreign investors: see <sccietac.org>.

[109] CIETAC Investment Arbitration Rules, <www.cietac.org/index.php?m=Page&a=index&id=390&l=en>. Draft BAC Rules, <arbitrationblog.kluwerarbitration.com/2019/03/20/new-2019-bac-rules-for-international-investment-arbitration-a-chinese-approach-to-the-concerns-over-investment-arbitration-regime>.

clauses and increased stocks of foreign investment. On the one hand, we have shown that factors such as the amount and characteristics of FDI and cooling-off periods in IIAs, are unlikely to explain the low number of ITA cases. On the other hand, we have found that the inclusion of mandatory administrative review procedures and temporary jurisdictional limitations in IIAs and the negotiations that will ensue after a claim has been notified, and to a very limited extent the emergence of commercial arbitration as an alternative to ITA, may constitute explanatory factors. Our findings indicate that China's current regime for investment treaty arbitration remains insignificant as a means for foreign investors to resolve investment disputes. We also find that commercial arbitration has significant weaknesses in the Chinese context as an alternative to ITA.

Our analysis of the role of the domestic judiciary and of corruption in courts, public authorities and among foreign investors, indicates that high levels of corruption are likely to push dispute settlement away from ITA and in the direction of less transparent and formalized dispute settlement mechanisms. Such mechanisms include consultations and negotiations, administrative review procedures, as well as weak or corrupt national courts. We therefore propose that high levels of corruption among public authorities and within the judiciary is likely to contribute to low numbers of ITA cases. However, we would argue that this proposal does not apply under all circumstances. We suggest that two features are of particular importance: a complex administrative decision-making structure with significant delegation of authority; and a significant risk of negative sanctions linked to exposure of corrupt practices.

The data on judicial corruption in China does not show any sign that access to ITA in the Chinese context has contributed to lower levels of corruption in the judiciary. Nevertheless, we have identified significant relationships between ITA, Chinese courts and corruption. While our case study does not answer whether increased access to ITA will lead to reduced levels of corruption, it seems clear to us that ITA could have such effects due to the transparency of ITA procedures and involvement of high-level public officials during proceedings. If IIAs and ITA were to have such effects, we would suggest that China consider abandoning requirements regarding use of administrative review procedures. The main reason is that such procedures are likely to facilitate resolution of investment disputes where pubic officials and foreign investors have joint interest in keeping unlawful activities out of sight of central authorities and the public.

The low number of cases against China suggests an unequal power relationship between foreign investors and Chinese authorities. This is arguably part of a broader legitimacy concern within international investment law – ITA is an effective tool for powerful investors against less powerful countries, but a less potent means for securing investors' interests against powerful countries – in particular where such countries also score low in terms of rule of law standards. In terms of output legitimacy, the Chinese case study thereby raises the less frequently discussed topic of whether the regime provides sufficient protection to foreign investors. One could argue that the Chinese IIAs are designed to benefit Chinese authorities and investors in terms of outbound investment while minimizing the protection of inbound investment. This is a phenomenon that we can observe among a number of countries seeking to revise their IIAs. However, what distinguishes China from other countries in this respect, is that China's IIAs continue to contain broadly phrased investment protections. The requirements of administrative review procedures is likely to significantly reduce the real protection of inbound investment, but there are also other factors that are likely to be important, including China's economic power and resistance to confrontational handling of disputes. As to protection of Chinese outbound investment, China's approach raises significant issues regarding hidden effects associated with threats of ITA. The low number of cases initiated by Chinese investors under IIAs with broad ISDS clauses indicate that this is an important issue in need of more research.

Annex 1

Chinese BITs with No ISDS Provisions

Listed according to year of entry into force:

1. Sweden (1982, amended to include ISDS clause in 2004)
2. Romania (1983, the same applies to the new BIT that entered into force in 1995)
3. Thailand (1985, a relevant ISDS clause applies between China and Thailand in the China–ASEAN IIA)
4. Turkmenistan (1992).

Annex 2

Chinese BITs with Narrow ISDS Provisions

In alphabetical order:

1. Albania	16. Denmark	31. Kuwait	46. Serbia
2. Algeria	17. Ecuador	32. Kyrgyzstan	47. Slovakia
3. Argentina	(terminated 2018)	33. Lebanon	48. Slovenia
4. Armenia	18. Egypt	34. Lithuania	49. Sri Lanka
5. Austria	19. Estonia	35. Macedonia	50. Sudan
6. Azerbaijan	20. Ethiopia	36. Mauritius	51. Syria
7. Bahrain	21. Gabon	37. Moldova	52. Tajikistan
8. Bangladesh	22. Georgia	38. Mongolia	53. Turkey
9. Belarus	23. Ghana	39. Morocco	54. Ukraine
10. Bolivia	24. Greece	40. Norway	55. United Arab
11. Bulgaria	25. Hungary	41. Oman	Emirates
12. Cameroon	26. Iceland	42. Papua New	56. United
13. Cape Verde	27. Israel	Guinea	Kingdom
14. Chile	28. Italy	43. Poland	57. Uruguay
15. Croatia	29. Jamaica	44. Qatar	58. Yemen
	30. Kazakhstan	45. Saudi Arabia	59. Zimbabwe

Annex 3

Chinese TIPs with ISDS Provisions

Listed according to year of entry into force:

1. FTA between the Government of the Islamic Republic of Pakistan and the Government of the People's Republic of China (chapter IX, 2006)
2. FTA between the Government of New Zealand and the Government of the People's Republic of China (chapter 11, 2008)
3. Agreement on Investment of the Framework Agreement on Comprehensive Economic Co-operation between the People's Republic of China and the Association of Southeast Asian Nations (treaty parties: Brunei Darussalam, Cambodia, Indonesia, Laos, Malaysia, Myanmar, Philippines, Thailand, Singapore, and Viet Nam, 2010)
4. Agreement among the Government of Japan, the Government of the Republic of Korea and the Government of the People's Republic of China for the Promotion, Facilitation and Protection of Investment (2012)
5. FTA between the Government of Australia and the Government of the People's Republic of China (chapter 9, 2015)
6. FTA between the Government of the People's Republic of China and the Government of the Republic of Korea (chapter 12, 2015).

Annex 4

Chinese IIAs Signed but Not in Force/Terminated

Listed according to year of signature:

1. Zambia (signed 1996)
2. Ecuador (in force 1997–2018)
3. Botswana (signed 2000)
4. Sierra Leone (signed 2001)
5. Kenya (signed 2001)
6. Jordan (signed 2001)
7. Ivory Coast (signed 2002)
8. Djibouti (signed 2003)
9. Benin (signed 2004)
10. Uganda (signed 2004)
11. Namibia (signed 2005)
12. Guinea (signed 2005)
13. Vanuatu (signed 2006)
14. India (in force 2007–18)
15. Seychelles (signed 2007)
16. Costa Rica (signed 2007)
17. Bahamas (signed 2009)
18. Chad (signed 2010)
19. Libya (signed 2010)
20. DRC (signed 2011, first treaty signed 1997 but did not enter into force)

Annex 5

Chinese IIAs Containing Broad ISDS Provisions

Listed according to year of signature, year in parentheses is year of entry into force, classification of states according to World Bank income groups as of January 2019:

1. South Africa (1997), Upper middle income
2. Barbados (1998), High income
3. Cyprus (2002), High income
4. Mozambique (2002), Low income
5. Myanmar (2002), Lower middle income
6. Guyana (2004), Upper middle income
7. Netherlands (2004), High income
8. Sweden (2004), High income
9. Trinidad and Tobago (2004), High income
10. Bosnia and Herzegovina (2005), Upper middle income
11. Germany (2005), High income
12. Iran (2005), Upper middle income
13. North Korea (2005), Low income
14. Czech Republic (2006), High income
15. Equatorial Guinea (2006), Upper middle income
16. Finland (2006), High income
17. India (2006, terminated 2018)
18. Latvia (2006), High income
19. Tunisia (2006), Lower middle income
20. Costa Rica (2007), Upper middle income
21. Madagascar (2007), Low income
22. Pakistan (2007), Lower middle income
23. South Korea (2007), subsequent treaties in force in 2014 and 2015, High income
24. Cuba (2008), Upper middle income
25. Mexico (2008), Upper middle income
26. New Zealand (2008), High income
27. Portugal (2008), High income
28. Spain (2008), High income
29. Belgium (2009), High income
30. Luxembourg (2009), High income
31. Mali (2009), Low income
32. Malta (2009), High income
33. Russia (2009), Upper middle income
34. Brunei (2010), High income
35. Indonesia (2010), Lower middle income
36. Laos (2010), Lower middle income
37. Nigeria (2010), Lower middle income
38. Viet Nam (2010), Lower middle income
39. Cambodia (2010), Lower middle income

(cont.)

40. Philippines (2010), Lower middle income
41. France (2010), High income
42. Peru (2010), Upper middle income
43. Thailand (2010), Upper middle income
44. Singapore (2010), High income
45. Switzerland (2010), High income
46. Malaysia (2010), Upper middle income
47. Uzbekistan (2011), Lower middle income
48. Colombia (2013), Upper middle income
49. Canada (2014), High income
50. Tanzania (2014), Low income
51. Japan (2014), High income
52. Republic of Congo (2015), Lower middle income
53. Australia (2015), High income

PART IV

Legitimation Strategies

15

Does International Arbitration Enfeeble or Enhance Local Legal Institutions?

CATHERINE A. ROGERS* AND CHRISTOPHER R. DRAHOZAL**

15.1 Introduction

One of the more serious critiques of investment arbitration is that it undermines the development of local legal institutions and the domestic rule of law.[1] Critics argue that by providing foreign investors a forum that is separate from local courts, investment arbitration removes any incentive for foreign investors to promote the development of local legal

---

* Full Professor of Law at Bocconi University; Professor of Ethics, Regulation and the Rule of Law at Queen Mary University of London. Some of the ideas in this chapter were initially developed in Catherine A. Rogers, 'International Arbitration, Judicial Education, and Legal Elites' (2015) *Journal of Dispute Resolution* 71, and through various capacity-building activities in various developing and emerging economies.
** John M. Rounds Professor of Law, University of Kansas School of Law. Thanks to participants in the Empirical Workshop on the Legitimacy of International Investment Tribunals; our commentator, Alec Stone Sweet; the editors; and Samantha Zyontz for helpful comments. Special thanks to Tom Ginsburg and to Daniel Behn, Tarald Laudal Berge and Malcolm Langford for sharing data with us.
[1] Susan D. Franck, 'Foreign Direct Investment, Investment Treaty Arbitration, and the Rule of Law' (2007) 19 *Pacific McGeorge Global Business and Development Law Journal* 337, 365: 'While speculative, a debate is emerging about whether investment treaty arbitration creates an enclave that prevents domestic development of the rule of law.' Other related debates consider whether investment arbitration *substitutes* for the domestic rule of law by providing recourse for investors in States with unstable political and legal structures, and whether it strengthens the *international* rule of law by providing a forum where the rules are applied in a cognitively reliable way through competent and impartial adjudication. See Thomas Schultz and Cédric Dupont, 'Investment Arbitration: Promoting the Rule of Law or Over-Empowering Investors? A Quantitative Empirical Study' (2014) 25 *European Journal of International Law* 1147, 1164–5, finding modest statistical support for the former before the 1990s, and support for the hypothesized implications of the latter; see also Susan Franck (ibid.), 370: '[T]he existence of robust national court systems, which adhere to the rule of law, supports the fair resolution of investment disputes.' While not wholly unrelated, these debates about investment arbitration and the rule of law are beyond the scope of this chapter.

468   CATHERINE A. ROGERS & CHRISTOPHER R. DRAHOZAL

institutions and, hence, the domestic rule of law.[2] This critique is particularly troubling because an implicit promise of investment arbitration is that it will not only provide protection for foreign investors, but also foster good governance in developing and emerging economies.[3] If instead the investment regime hampers local legal institutions and undermines the rule of law, it would seem more like a vampiric parasite than a guardian of development.[4]

In response to this criticism, some commentators have suggested that instead the opposite may be true. For example, Franck has explained:

> Arbitration does not occur in a vacuum, and the existence of investment treaty arbitration does not eliminate the need to encourage the development of a court system where rights are adjudicated in an impartial, fair, and predictable manner. Investment treaty arbitration and national courts have a symbiotic relationship. Fostering the development of the rule of law in national courts not only develops local judicial institutions, but it also promotes confidence in the overall process of resolving investment disputes.[5]

---

[2] The debate about the relationship between the rule of law and investment arbitration is predicated on the definition of the rule of law and on the impetus behind efforts to promote it in developing and emerging economies. See John C. Reitz, 'Export of the Rule of Law' (2003) 13 *Transnational Law and Contemporary Problems* 429, 436: 'The rule of law is "a notoriously contested concept," and its precise meaning is subject to much debate.' (Internal footnotes omitted, discussing range of definitions.) This chapter does not weigh in on larger debates about the meaning and value of the rule of law, but instead takes as a starting point the basic ideal underlying most definitions, namely that 'the exercise of all power, public or private, [should] be subject to limitation by law' (ibid.), 436. In his various works on this topic, Reitz argues persuasively that, despite debates and linkage of the concept to neoliberalism, the core notions of the rule of law are compatible with a broad spectrum of political ideologies. See also Schultz and Dupont (n. 1), 1163–4, defining 'rule of law' to mean 'formal legality' and to require 'rules be formulated in general terms . . . be accessible and understandable by their addressees, and . . . be applied coherently, consistently, competently, and impartially' to all.

[3] Another strain of this debate examines the relationship between foreign investment inflows on the one hand, and local legal institutions and the rule of law on the other. See Tamara Lothian and Katharina Pistor, 'Local Institutions, Foreign Investment and Alternative Strategies of Development: Some Views from Practice' (2003) 42 *Columbia Journal of Transnational Law* 101, 101–2, identifying that 'there is much more empirical support for the claim that law matters for foreign investment', but critiquing both the methodology of such studies and the 'problematic' policy implications that are drawn from these studies. This debate also is beyond the scope of this chapter.

[4] Christopher J. Borgen, 'Transnational Norms and the Transmission of Norms: The Hegemony of Process' (2007) 39 *George Washington International Law Review* 685, 685.

[5] Franck (n. 1), 365.

Under this view, investment arbitration and local courts work in tandem, complementing each other. While this account is more optimistic, it has also been challenged for failing to specify the precise contours of the described symbiotic relationship.[6]

This chapter develops a new theory of the relationship between investment arbitration – and commercial arbitration more generally – and local legal institutions. It then tests that theory empirically. Our theory is founded on two basic propositions. These propositions originated from first-hand observations while doing international-arbitration-related work in various developing and emerging economies.

The first proposition is that international arbitration – not only investment arbitration but also international commercial arbitration – creates unique and potentially valuable international professional opportunities for local legal elites.[7] To access these professional opportunities, local elites demonstrate their understanding of and support for international arbitration by introducing into their local legal systems reforms that benefit international arbitration. These reforms, however, also indirectly transmit the rule-of-law norms on which those reforms are based.

The second proposition is that international arbitration provides these elites with a ready-made toolkit that includes international conventions, model laws, rules and soft law. At the urging of local elites, these sources are readily adopted in local legal reforms and through local arbitral institutions and organizations seeking to bring their local legal systems into compliance with international standards and best practices.

Importantly, for two reasons this process of engaging elites and supplying them with ready-made rule-of-law toolkits differs from some historically less successful, legal transplants and rule-of-law initiatives for a few important reasons.[8] First, this process does not rely on civil

---

[6] Ibid.

[7] This chapter uses the term 'legal elites' to refer to those members of society who wield significant power in local legal institutions. For a related definition of 'legal elites' in emerging economies, see David B. Wilkins and Mihaela Papa, 'The Rise of the Corporate Legal Elite in the BRICS: Implications For Global Governance' (2013) 54 *Boston College International and Comparative Law Review* 1149, 1151, defining 'legal elites' as 'lawyers who work in law firms based in [emerging economies] that serve a clientele composed primarily of foreign and domestic corporations, and lawyers who work in the internal legal departments of the growing number of corporations based in [these jurisdictions]'.

[8] Amichai Magen, 'The Rule of Law and Its Promotion Abroad: Three Problems of Scope' (2009) 45 *Stanford Journal of International Law* 51, providing an overview of the billions of dollars and euros invested to improve local rule of law and challenges in empirically assessing the effects. For an overview of historic rule-of-law initiatives and their

society and external reformers, but instead on the enlightened self-interest of legal elites who are well positioned to successfully implement legal reforms.[9] In this respect, the process we identify is consistent with other rule-of-law initiatives that succeed by 'identify[ing] and promot[ing] key individuals through direct education, professional training programs, professional development opportunities, and work experience'.[10]

Second, international-arbitration-inspired reforms include a combination of structural legal frameworks and detailed rules and standards that are tied to the nature and quality of international adjudication, but only seek limited direct support from local legal institutions.[11] Because they are not directly seeking to modify rules, norms and practices that apply to domestic litigation, international arbitration reforms do not aim to modify domestic legal practices. Consequently, arbitration-related reforms do not confront some of the challenges that may be involved in efforts to directly and explicitly reform domestic court practices.[12]

This chapter proceeds as follows. Section 15.2 describes the literature criticizing investment arbitration as undermining the development of the rule of law, including the existing empirical studies on that issue. Section 15.3 sets out in greater detail our alternative account, including the testable hypotheses that follow from it. Section 15.4 describes our sample and data, and Section 15.5 presents our empirical results. We find that (1) the number of bilateral investment treaties (BITs) and the number of investment arbitration proceedings to which a country is a party are negatively related to measures of rule of law in the country; but (2) the presence of an indicator of support for international commercial

---

shortcomings, see generally David M. Trubek, 'The "Rule of Law" in Development Assistance: Past, Present, and Future,' in David M. Trubek and Alvaro Santos (eds.), *The New Law and Economic Development: A Critical Appraisal* (Cambridge University Press, 2006), pp. 74, 80–1; and Thomas Carothers, *Promoting the Rule of Law Abroad: In Search of Knowledge* (Carnegie Endowment for International Peace, 2006).

[9] See section 15.3.1. Future empirical research might seek to measure this anticipated difference by, for example, comparing the relationship between rule of law and, on the one hand, investment in traditional rule-of-law initiatives, and, on the other, international arbitration reforms. We do not, in this chapter, undertake this research.

[10] M. Margaret McKeown, 'The ABA Rule of Law Initiative: Celebrating 25 Years of Global Initiatives' (2018) 39(1) *Michigan Journal of International Law* 117, 142.

[11] See section 15.3.1.

[12] For one of the first and most potent critiques of external efforts to promote domestic rule of law in developing countries, see David Trubek and Marc Galanter, 'Scholars in Self-Estrangement: Some Reflections on the Crisis in Law and Development Studies in the United States' (1974) 4 *Wisconsin Law Review* 1062.

15.2 The Effect of Investment Arbitration on the Domestic Rule of Law

arbitration – adoption of the UNCITRAL Model Law on International Commercial Arbitration – at least partially offsets that negative relationship. We conclude by offering an agenda for future research in this area.

15.2 The Effect of Investment Arbitration on the Domestic Rule of Law

Several scholars have hypothesized that investment arbitration undermines development of the domestic rule of law and local legal institutions in countries that adopt BITs. One of the first to promote this view was Ginsburg. He argued that 'the decision to bypass domestic courts [by going to investment arbitration] may reduce courts' incentives to improve performance by depriving key actors from a need to invest in institutional improvement'.[13] Ginsburg's view is part of a broader contention that investment arbitration 'inhibits the development of the rule of law in national courts by creating a regime that provides a privilege to foreign investors and removes investment disputes from local courts'.[14]

Under this view, 'foreign investors rationally refrain from championing good and generalized law reforms in the developing state, preferring instead to protect their interests by relying on the BIT rule of law enclave'.[15] Other scholars have gone even further, arguing 'that BITs enfeeble host state governments and, in sharp contrast to the claims made by supporters of BITs, will end up discrediting the normative legitimacy of the BIT as a rule of law demonstration project'.[16]

---

[13] Tom Ginsburg, 'International Substitutes for Domestic Institutions: Bilateral Investment Treaties and Governance' (2005) 25 *International Review of Law and Economics* 107, 119.

[14] Franck (n. 1), 365, summarizing but disagreeing with this view.

[15] Ibid., 366. Sergio Puig and Gregory Shaffer, 'Imperfect Alternatives: Institutional Choice and the Reform of Investment Law' (2018) 112 *American Journal of International Law* 361, 397, arguing that because 'ISDS discourages a relationship of complementarity with domestic courts, it can reduce the pressure for domestic rule-of-law reforms . . . and thus tends to promote exit (from domestic legal systems) over voice (in domestic law reform debates)'.

[16] Ronald J. Daniels, 'Defecting on Development: Bilateral Investment Treaties and the Subversion of the Rule of Law in the Developing World' (University of Toronto, Draft dated 23 March 2004), p. 2, describing BITs as creating a 'stand alone enclave' that allows 'foreign investors [to be] largely insulated from the legal and political risks of contracting in the home state and relying on its institution'. For more generalized critiques of the relationship, see Benedict Kingsbury and Stephan W. Schill, 'Investor-State Arbitration as Governance: Fair and Equitable Treatment, Proportionality and the Emerging Global Administrative Law', in Kingsbury et al. (eds.), *El Nuevo Derecho Administrativo Global En America Latina* (Rap, 2009), p. 221; Gus van Harten, 'Five Justifications for

472   CATHERINE A. ROGERS & CHRISTOPHER R. DRAHOZAL

In a similar vein, other scholars critique the lack of 'institutional complementarity' as a 'central consideration of the international investment regime' to promote domestic rule of law.[17] Under this view, complementarity avoids substituting international processes for domestic processes, and thereby necessarily assures greater domestic government accountability, and hence increased enhanced domestic rule of law.[18]

Empirical studies to date have supported, or at least not contradicted, these criticisms. For example, Ginsburg examined the relationship between a country's adoption of a BIT (in 1996) and subsequent changes in its World Governance Indicator (WGI) Rule-of-law rating. He found that 'for the Rule of Law variable in particular, BIT adoption leads to subsequent declines in quality, controlling for other factors'.[19]

Meanwhile, Sasse, using a panel data model with the WGI rule-of-law rating as the dependent variable, found 'no signs at all of a potential positive impact of BITs on institutional quality'.[20] According to Sasse, however, 'a negative impact of BITs was only detected in few regressions and was virtually never robust to the inclusion of time fixed effects and/ or model specifications'.[21] He concluded: 'Nevertheless, the consistent negative sign of the BIT variable and the (yet small) significance in some specifications is troubling and calls for future research.'[22]

In another study, Aranguri focused instead on the relationship between the rule of law and 'enforcement events' – the number of investment arbitrations filed and the dollar amount of awards issued against a host state.[23] He found that the number of arbitrations filed and awards made against a country 'exerted a statistically significant negative effect' on the rule-of-law rating and that the number of

---

Investment Treaties: A Critical Discussion' (2010) 2 *Trade, Law and Development* 1; Office of the High Commissioner for Human Rights (OHCHR), 'Investor-State Dispute Settlement Undermines Rule of Law and Democracy, UN Expert Tells Council of Europe' (19 April 2016), <ohchr.org/EN/NewsEvents/Pages/DisplayNews.aspx?NewsID=19839& LangID=E>.

[17] Puig and Shaffer (n. 15), 397.

[18] Ibid., 389, arguing that increased complementarity will enable domestic institutions to 'develop expertise and a professional ethos and reputation' and thus 'be accepted as [more] legitimate venues for resolving claims than a remote international body'.

[19] Ginsburg (n. 13), 121.

[20] Jan Peter Sasse, *An Economic Analysis of Bilateral Investment Treaties* (Gabler Verlag, 2011), p. 175.

[21] Ibid.

[22] Ibid.

[23] Cesar Aranguri, 'The Effect of BITs on Regulatory Quality and the Rule of Law in Developing Countries' (NYU Investment Law Forum, Spring 2011), 25.

investment treaties signed had no statistically significant relationship with the rule-of-law rating.[24]

The Ginsburg and Sasse studies examined the relationship between adoption of a BIT and the rule of law in a country. Aranguri added consideration of the frequency of investment arbitration claims and magnitude of investment arbitration awards under a BIT. To date, no studies have examined whether and to what extent the legal support for international commercial arbitration more generally and in combination with investment arbitration affects the domestic rule of law.

15.3 An Alternative Account: International Arbitration and the Domestic Rule of Law

International arbitration is favoured by investors and commercial actors because it is perceived as providing a reliable means of enforcing investor and commercial rights, even when local legal systems are not considered to be up to the task.[25] To date, the debate over whether investment arbitration weakens local legal institutions does not take into account the potential for a similar effect by international commercial arbitration. As noted in the introduction, whatever effect investment arbitration has on local legal institutions would arguably be even greater for international commercial arbitration because the latter annually syphons off many more cases from national courts than investment arbitration, and it resolves cases similar to the domestic contract disputes that are the bread and butter of domestic courts.[26] This section offers an alternative account

---

[24] Ibid., 30.

[25] Some commentators argue that investment arbitration is not necessary in developed economies that already have robust and effective local court systems, which can competently and fairly address foreign investor claims. See William S. Dodge, 'Investor-State Dispute Settlement between Developed Countries: Reflections on the Australia-United States Free Trade Agreement' (2006) 39 *Vanderbilt Journal of Transnational Law* 1, 5–8. But see Mary Hallward-Driemeier, 'Do Bilateral Investment Treaties Attract Foreign Direct Investment? Only a Bit – and They Could Bite', World Bank Policy Research Working Paper, June 2003, <documents.worldbank.org/curated/en/113541468761706209>.

[26] See Stacie I. Strong, 'Realizing Rationality: An Empirical Assessment of International Commercial Mediation' (2016) 73 *Washington and Lee Law Review* 1973, 1979, noting that 'the frequency of international commercial arbitration far outweighs that of investment arbitration, as reflected by the number of proceedings that are filed annually (between twenty and fifty per year in the investment realm as compared to well over 5,000 per year in the international commercial context).' Some international commercial cases strongly resemble investment arbitration cases, for example if they involve states or

474 CATHERINE A. ROGERS & CHRISTOPHER R. DRAHOZAL

that considers how international arbitration taps into the self-interest of legal elites in local contexts, and how cultivating that self-interest can be a catalyst for positive reforms that promote the rule of law.

As our alternative account is not limited to investment arbitration, it is worth noting at the outset that the field of practitioners and arbitrators in investment arbitration overlaps significantly with the field of practitioners and arbitrators in international commercial arbitration. These overlapping fields involve both international and local legal (and, indirectly, business[27]) elites who have an interest in political stability and national legal institutions that support the success of international arbitration.

Local elites have incentives, influence and resources to ensure that international arbitration reforms are enacted and adhered to in their legal systems. Unlike, for example, human rights reforms, there is no need to rely on members of civil society who are committed to the substantive goals but may be disempowered and thus unable to force change.

At a more substantive level, arbitration-related reform efforts may also be easier to introduce than other types of rule-of-law reforms. As detailed below, there is a wealth of existing sources that specify broad structural norms, detailed rules for implementing those norms, and professional conduct standards that complement those norms. While these sources are initially grafted onto local legal systems to support international arbitration, once domesticated they are more easily internalized into local legal systems.

15.3.1 Elites Implementing Arbitration Reforms

Like other areas of international or transnational legal practice,[28] international arbitration can be a means by which local elites access future professional and economic opportunities.[29] To effectively develop these

---

state-owned enterprises as parties. Other international arbitrations more closely resemble typical domestic commercial disputes. This distinction is largely irrelevant to our hypothesis, which considers the effects of international commercial and investment arbitration together because both have the same effect of removing disputes involving foreign investors from local courts.

[27] Luciana Gross Cunha et al., 'Globalization, Lawyers, and Emerging Economies', in Luciana Gross Cunha et al. (eds.), *The Brazilian Legal Profession in the Age of Globalization: The Rise of the Corporate Legal Sector and Its Impact on Lawyers and Society* (Cambridge University Press, 2018).

[28] Wilkins and Papa (n. 7), 1179.

[29] See Christopher R. Drahozal, 'Arbitrator Selection and Regulatory Competition in International Arbitration Law', in Christopher R. Drahozal and Richard W. Naimark

DOES ARBITRATION ENFEEBLE LOCAL INSTITUTIONS? 475

opportunities, local legal elites must both demonstrate a professional facility with the rules, norms and practices of international arbitration, and use their influence to introduce them into national legal systems. In this respect, the purpose, means and effect of international arbitration reforms indirectly promote domestic rule of law.

The *purpose* of introducing international arbitration laws, norms and practices to local legal systems is to strengthen national legal institutions that support international (and, indirectly, often also domestic) arbitration. The *means* for introducing these laws, norms and practices to local legal systems most directly include legislative reforms, such as ratification of the New York Convention or adoption of the UNCITRAL Model Law. They might also include training for judges on how to interpret and apply those sources in a manner that is consistent with international approaches,[30] and introduction of educational reforms such as new law classes on international arbitration in local law school curricula, promoting interest in foreign legal degrees and other credentials, and sponsoring law student participation in international arbitration moot competitions.[31]

(eds.), *Towards a Science of International Arbitration: Collected Empirical Research* (Kluwer Law International, 2005), pp. 167–68, finding that enactment of a new international arbitration statute 'benefits local arbitrators not only by increasing the number of proceedings in the country, but also by increasing the rate at which local arbitrators are selected in those proceedings'; Luke Nottage, 'The Vicissitudes of Transnational Commercial Arbitration and the Lex Mercatoria' (2000) 16 *Arbitration International* 53, 56: 'Although arbitral institutions stand to gain from additional fees for more arbitrations administered by them, and local lawyers even more so (subject, however, to the trend towards allowing representation also by foreign lawyers), the major beneficiaries [of new arbitration laws] are good local arbitrators.'

[30] See e.g., Joshua Briones and Ana Tagvoryan, 'Is International Arbitration in Latin America in Danger?' (2010) 16 *Law and Business Review of the Americas* 131, 134: 'To improve the local judiciary's level of knowledge, the International Chamber of Commerce (ICC) has organized a six-month arbitration training course for Mexico's judges.'

[31] It is beyond the scope of this chapter to examine the effect of legal education on the development of rule of law generally, or arbitration more specifically. It bears noting, however, that the Willem C. Vis Moot Competition undoubtedly has a role to play. The 'Vis', as it is affectionately called, annually draws over 300 teams from around the world. Students who compete in the Vis take their knowledge and skills with them into their professional careers. See Eric E. Bergsten, 'The William C. Vis International Commercial Arbitration Moot and the Teaching of International Commercial Arbitration' (2006) 22 *Arbitration International* 309; Jack M. Graves and Stephanie A. Vaughan, 'The Willem C. Vis International Commercial Arbitration Moot: Making the Most of an Extraordinary Educational Opportunity' (2006) 10 *Vindobona Journal of Comparative and International Law* 173.

Finally, the *effect* of introducing these rules, norms, and practices is that they are internalized into local legal systems. For example, a judge trained to accurately interpret and faithfully apply arbitration laws and treaties does not easily set aside those skills when the law being applied is domestic, not international arbitration law, or is law unrelated to arbitration altogether. Meanwhile, attorneys and arbitrators trained in international standards for conflicts of interest are less likely to accept much lower standards in domestic arbitration or in national court litigation. As has been observed in other contexts,[32] rule of law reforms are more 'sticky' when there is buy-in by specific individuals through training and professional opportunities. In sum, we hypothesize that international arbitration reforms might concretely contribute to improve, rather than detract from, local legal institutions. Moreover, if this hypothesis holds, the relationship between international arbitration reforms and national court-related indicators might be expected to be stronger than their relationship with more generalized rule-of-law indicators.[33]

In a related vein, many reforms to promote international arbitration are based on pre-established international hard law and soft law sources. These sources have been developed both to codify and harmonize international arbitration best practices.[34] They provide both broad legal frameworks (such as the New York Convention and the UNCITRAL Model Law) and more detailed guidance (such as the International Bar Association (IBA) Guidelines on Conflicts of Interest in International Arbitration,[35] the IBA Rules on the Taking of Evidence in International

---

[32] McKeown (n. 10), 142.

[33] This hypothesis arguably raises broader questions about how international norms and standards are generated, though such questions are beyond the scope of this chapter.

[34] See Christopher R. Drahozal, 'Diversity and Uniformity in International Arbitration Law' (2017) 31 *Emory International Law Review* 393: 'Uniformity of legal rules clearly has benefits, and widespread adherence to the New York Convention and adoption of the UNCITRAL Model Law have been beneficial to individual States and the international community as a whole.' See also Drahozal (n. 29), 113: 'The Model Law offers a low-cost way for countries without well-developed legal regimes governing international arbitration to update their arbitration laws.' Notably, while acknowledging the benefits of uniformity from the New York Convention and Model Law, Drahozal also cautions that harmonization should not be blindly pursued without regard to the benefits that can come from rules tailored to specific contexts and legal innovation more generally. See Drahozal, 'Diversity and Uniformity', 414.

[35] International Bar Association (IBA), 'IBA Guidelines on Conflicts of Interest in International Arbitration' (2014), <ibanet.org/Document/Default.aspx?DocumentUid=E2FE5E72-EB14-4BBA-B10D-D33DAFEE8918>.

Arbitration, the Prague Rules on the Efficient Conduct of Proceedings in International Arbitration,[36] and the Report of the Task Force on Third-Party Funding in International Arbitration[37]). These international sources introduce opportunities for local elites to interact with international arbitration specialists by participating in their development, which is often through multi-national task forces and working groups that strive to include geographically- and stakeholder-diverse representation. Such opportunities in turn create an expectation that local arbitration specialists will buy into and actively promote international norms that they help establish in these sources.

Increasingly, these reforms are accompanied by the founding of new private arbitral institutions to administer locally seated arbitrations. These centres often borrow from leading arbitral institutions to craft their rules and administrative procedures. Adopting established arbitral rules saves time, but also ensures that the terms and standards of new arbitral institutions are familiar to international practitioners. Borrowing rules and practices from a leading institution is also a means of establishing an informal link with a more established institution in the hope of benefiting indirectly from its prominent reputation.[38]

Finally, local legal elites seeking the benefits of participation in the field of international arbitration often host international arbitration events, such as 'Arbitration Days'. These designated days (or weeks) are organized to showcase the local venue, including the skill of its arbitral institutions and related organizations, the effectiveness of its courts in enforcing arbitration

---

[36] The Prague Rules on the Efficient Conduct of Proceedings in International Arbitration, <praguerules.com/prague_rules/>.

[37] ICCA-Queen Mary Task Force Report on Third-Party Funding in International Arbitration (April 2018), <arbitration-icca.org/publications/Third-Party-Funding-Report.html>.

[38] For example, when the ICC Palestine and the ICC Israel collaborated to establish an arbitration centre for resolution of commercial disputes between Palestinians and Israelis, rather than start from scratch, they modelled the rules for the Jerusalem Arbitration Center (JAC) after the famed ICC International Court of Arbitration in Paris. By adopting the ICC model, and expressly involving the ICC in the venture, the JAC not only ensured that its rules would have time-tested functionality and efficacy, it also ensured that the ICC was actively involved in the process of creating and promoting the JAC. Similarly, the *Centro de Arbitraje de México* (CAM) based its arbitral rules on those of the ICC. See Global Arbitration Review, 'Guide to Regional Arbitration' (2017), <globalarbitrationreview.com/insight/guide-to-regional-arbitration-volume-5-2017/1070162/worth-a-closer-look-latin-america-and-the-caribbean>, describing CAM as 'a strong and well-run organisation with well-drafted rules, based on the 1998 ICC Rules of Arbitration' and comparing the role of CAM's council as 'similar to the ICC's Court'.

478   CATHERINE A. ROGERS & CHRISTOPHER R. DRAHOZAL

agreements and awards, and the skills and experience of local arbitration specialists. International arbitration events also provide an occasion for local arbitration specialists to exchange ideas and form professional relationships with foreign arbitration specialists, who may eventually provide them with future arbitration business and professional opportunities, including potential recruitment or formal professional affiliation.[39]

15.3.2   Existing Theories

Our account of the relationship between international arbitration and the rule of law is consistent with and builds on existing theories, both about how international norms are incorporated into local legal systems and about the role of transnational lawyers and other legal elites in that process.

For example, Slaughter, our thesis is premised on the inextricable linkage between domestic and international legal realms, and the existence of professional networks.[40] The fact that these networks require transnational attorneys and local legal elites to work collaboratively in an international adjudicatory regime may, in turn, accelerate transmission of norms. For local attorneys, an understanding of and facility with transnational procedural norms can be a professional credential that enables them to access the potentially lucrative practice of international arbitration, including both investment and commercial arbitration.[41] Once these norms are internalized, lawyers and litigants may come to expect similar standards in domestic proceedings, particularly domestic

---

[39] It is beyond the scope of this chapter to explore in depth the role of multi-national law firms in spreading and perpetuating the rule of law, though such firms undoubtedly supplement and reinforce international arbitration through the dynamics we identify. See Yves Dezalay and Bryant G. Garth, *The Internationalization of Palace Wars: Lawyers, Economists and the Contest to Transform Latin American States* (University of Chicago Press, 2002), p. 50, identifying how increased contact with foreign law firms 'substantially increased the value of US law degrees in all the countries' in the study; Catherine A. Rogers, 'When Bad Guys Are Wearing White Hats' (2013) 1 *Stanford Journal of Complex Litigation* 487, 491, analysing multi-national law firms' risk management policies as a prophylactic against local legal corruption in cases in which they are involved.

[40] Anne-Marie Slaughter, 'A Liberal Theory of International Law' (2000) *94 American Society of International Law Proceedings* 240, 241.

[41] See David M. Trubek et al., 'Global Restructuring and the Law: Studies of the Internationalization of Legal Fields and the Creation of Transnational Arenas' (1994) 44 *Case Western Reserve Law Review* 407, 461; Borgen (n. 4), 718; see also Wilkins and Papa (n. 7), 1159–60, advancing similar arguments regarding how corporate lawyers contribute to global governance.

DOES ARBITRATION ENFEEBLE LOCAL INSTITUTIONS? 479

arbitration that is administered by the same institutions, presided over by the same arbitrators, and involves the same attorneys.[42]

Our thesis is also largely consistent with Koh's theory that one of the three ways international norms can be internalized is through conformity, compliance, and eventually obedience.[43] Our theory is also consistent with other theories that have built on Koh's work, such as the work of Jinks and Goodman and the work of Borgen. Jinks and Goodman identify different socialization processes that can lead to incorporation of norms,[44] including both norms internalized by persuasion and norms internalized by acculturation:

> [P]ersuasion requires acceptance of the validity or legitimacy of a belief, practice, or norm—acculturation requires only that an actor perceive that an important reference group harbors the belief, engages in the practice, or subscribes to the norm.[45]

Local legal elites appear to adopt international arbitration reforms both because they are persuaded about their validity and because of a desire to acculturate into the international arbitration community. Also building on Koh's theory, Borgen has identified the special role of adjudication in norm transference:

> As a profession, lawyers tend to approach problems with certain common techniques: elucidating rules, codifying law, and citing to sources that support a position. The act of adjudication itself ... often relies on certain common techniques such as interest balancing (which requires the jurist to endeavor to understand and weigh the interests of each of the parties, foreign or domestic) and attempting to treat 'like cases alike'.[46]

We leave to future work a more detailed parsing of these works' relationship to international arbitration. There are, however, two important distinctions that bear noting.

---

[42] Wilkins and Papa (n. 7), 1160. In some national contexts, particularly in wealthier countries that have a larger legal profession, international practice is more likely to be a distinct specialization. In smaller and developing contexts, greater overlap and interaction would be expected among international and domestic legal experts.

[43] Harold Honju Koh, 'Bringing International Law Home' (1998) 35 *Houston Law Review* 623, 625–6 (internal citations omitted); see also Harold Honju Koh, 'How Is International Human Rights Law Enforced?' (1999) 74 *Indiana Law Journal* 1397, 1400, describing the spectrum from coincidence to conformity to compliance to obedience.

[44] Ryan Goodman and Derek Jinks, 'How to Influence States: Socialization and International Human Rights Law' (2004) 54 *Duke Law Journal* 621, 642.

[45] Ibid., 643.

[46] Borgen (n. 4), 715.

First, the theories identified above seek primarily to explain national reception of *public international law norms* as *law*. Our thesis, by contrast, seeks to explain reception of *private international law norms*, which may be an easier guise under which to adopt standards that can also have public international law status. For example, as noted above, the norms that govern international arbitration processes do not all have the status of law. Many of the norms transmitted, particularly those transmitted through soft-law instruments and professional codes of practice, are by design flexible enough to accommodate differences in national legal cultures. This distinction may make it easier to transmit what in international arbitration parlance are called 'best practice norms' for fair and effective proceedings. In public international law parlance, the more typical term might be 'international norms of due process'.[47]

A second, related distinction is that in contrast to international law theories above, which focus primarily on how *substantive* international norms are internalized, our thesis focuses on the processes by which *procedural* international norms are internalized. This distinction has important implications for how a particular norm is internalized. For example, a state's functionaries may be persuaded, acculturated, or may learn to follow international norms against torturing political rivals. However, they do not learn those norms from the process of torturing or refraining from torturing. In other words, the process for internalization is separate from the norm being internalized.

By contrast, the learning, persuasion, or acculturation of international due process norms occurs through professional use of those norms in international arbitration.[48] For example, an attorney may be inherently

---

[47] Robert B. Ahdieh, 'Between Dialogue and Decree: International Review of National Courts' (2004) 79(6) *New York University Law Review* 2029, 2124–5 and fn. 451, distinguishing between 'international norms of due process' and 'international due process norms'. While Ahdieh drew an important distinction, here we use the terms interchangeably as we are referring both to norms employed in international proceedings and norms that are common to both international and domestic proceedings.

[48] As Borgen has explained with respect to rule-of-law reforms, 'the crucial issue is not so much how to change the "black letter law," but rather how to change attitudes, habits, and expectations'. More traditional rule-of-law projects 'are often designed without regard to the specific norms of a society on an assumption that "best practices" are readily able to be transplanted' even if those norms are inconsistent with those of the receiving legal system: Borgen (n. 4), 715–16. For a discussion of this phenomenon in the human rights context, see Tori Loven Kirkebø and Malcolm Langford, 'The Commitment Curve: Global Regulation of Business and Human Rights' (2018) 3 *Business and Human Rights Journal* 157.

sceptical about the objectionability of arbitrator conflicts of interest. That attorney, however, may be persuaded, learn about, or become acculturated to international conflicts standards after being required to make certain disclosures or being involuntarily disqualified from serving as an arbitrator.[49]

This conflation of the process for internalizing with the norm being internalized arguably amplifies and accelerates the process for transmitting norms. Moreover, as noted above, professional and procedural norms are transmitted to local elites who are both well-positioned and incentivized to propagate those norms in the local legal culture, even beyond matters dealing with international arbitration.

15.3.3 Republic of Georgia as a Case Study

Our thesis was initially inspired by on-the-ground experiences working with local legal elites in a range of jurisdictions. A brief case study, therefore, provides more concrete and detailed observed examples to complement our theory and empirical analysis. We have chosen to focus on the Republic of Georgia for this purpose.

In recent years, Georgia has undertaken several reforms to promote and advance international arbitration in the country. As Austermiller explains, instead of being 'an unwelcome Western transplant that international players have imposed', those reforms were initiated by local legal elites who regarded international arbitration as 'a useful tool for economic and social development'.[50] Prior to recent reforms, Georgia had a 'disastrous' statutory arbitration regime.[51] Although Georgia had ratified the New York Convention, courts were generally unaware of it. When asked to enforce an arbitral award, Georgian courts typically looked either to the Minsk Convention, which applies only to foreign court judgments not arbitral awards, or to Georgian private international

---

[49] For an excellent article reviewing the literature and presenting a compelling argument for how the process of adjudication works to transmit substantive international norms, see Borgen (n. 4), 687–8, arguing that the process of adjudication transmits substantive international norms because it 'establishes certain methods of asking and answering legal and policy questions and consequently certain results are reached time and again and also certain expectations as to substantive ends arise'.

[50] Steven Austermiller, 'Rescuing Arbitration in the Developing World: The Extraordinary Case of Georgia' (2015) 32 *Arizona Journal of International and Comparative Law* 671, 674.

[51] Ibid., 683.

law.[52] Meanwhile, often-unreliable arbitral institutions proliferated and operated to attract and preference large, institutional clients rather than provide for neutral administration of disputes. In sum, the 'arbitral environment was a toxic mix of opportunism, lack of education, absent ethical norms, and *laissez faire* oversight'.[53] In this context, arbitration could be used to 'purloin the property of third parties':[54]

> The scheme worked as follows: two parties would fabricate a dispute over the ownership of property that was actually owned by a third person. The parties would engage an arbitration provider to resolve the contrived dispute. The [arbitration] provider would issue an order awarding the prevailing party the property and the Enforcement Bureau would execute that order, as legally mandated. The third party would then lose the property, without notice.[55]

On occasion, the original property owner could challenge the award, but even that process was 'cumbersome and time consuming'.[56]

This problematic regime existed within a legal system that enjoyed low levels of public trust. For example, a survey of Georgian business leaders revealed that only 26 per cent of businesses were willing to take a dispute to court in Georgia. Business leaders believed that the courts were presided over by judges who had an 'ignorance of commercial law' and that legal procedures were problematically slow.[57]

In 2009, as part of a general overhaul of its entire arbitration regime, Georgia adopted the new Law of Georgia on Arbitration (LOA), which was based on the UNCITRAL Model Law and has been subsequently further amended.[58] As a comprehensive, off-the-shelf statutory regime, the Model Law ensured that Georgia's new statutory arbitration regime was consistent with international standards. More importantly for our

---

[52] Ibid., 683–4, citing the Minsk Convention on Legal Assistance and Legal Relations in Civil, Family and Criminal Matters, Unified Register of Legal Acts and Other Documents of the Commonwealth of Independent States, adopted on 22 January 1993.

[53] Ibid., 685.

[54] Ibid., 704: 'The [new Law of Georgia on Arbitration] brings Georgia into consonance with current international norms. It follows the Model Law almost word for word on the rules of recognition and enforcement of awards.'

[55] Ibid.

[56] Ibid., 683.

[57] Ibid., 678–9, citing Caucasus Research Resource Centers, 'Attitudes to the Judiciary in Georgia: Assessment of General Public, Legal Professionals and Business Leaders' (May 2014), 29.

[58] Law of Georgia on Arbitration, No. 1280-IS, adopted on 19 June 2009, <matsne.gov.ge/ru/document/download/89284/5/en/pdf>.

purposes, because the Georgia LOA governs both domestic and international arbitration, by updating its international arbitration law, Georgia also implemented reforms that could counter some of the worst defects in domestic arbitration.

The statutory reform was accompanied by several institutional reforms. In recent years, a new Georgia Arbitration Association (GAA) was founded as a body to bring together the leading providers of domestic arbitration.[59] Those providers are also among those most interested in and integrated with international commercial activities and international commercial disputes. The GAA now serves as a form of private, informal regulation of the once questionable standards for arbitral institutions.

Efforts to develop and fortify local arbitration, predictably, have Georgia turning to international sources for guidance.[60] In October of 2014, the new Georgian International Arbitration Centre (GIAC) adopted arbitration rules that 'reflect best international practices and include many innovations from the recent ICC and London Court of International Arbitration (LCIA) arbitration rules, [and that] firmly establish GIAC as the leading dispute resolution institution in the Caucasus – Black Sea – Caspian Region'.[61]

In addition to these efforts, the GAA adopted in 2014 a new code of ethics for arbitrators (subsequently amended in 2017), which is based largely on the American Bar Association (ABA) and American Arbitration Association's (AAA) Code of Ethics for Arbitrators in Commercial Disputes.[62] This new Code introduced new ideas about what constitutes a conflict of interest for arbitrators in concrete terms that had been lacking under the previous law and practice of arbitration.[63]

---

[59] Detailed information about the Georgian Arbitration Association's activities is available on its website, <gaa.ge/gaa-siaxleebi/Arbitration-news-and-Association-events/>. Those activities include projects to introduce disciplinary procedures, consideration of the new Prague Rules (cited above), and various educational initiatives.

[60] For example, in confirming party autonomy to select applicable substantive law, the LOA was amended in 2015 to change from its original term 'law' to conform with the Model Law's term 'rules of law' to emphasize that parties are free to select rules from more than one legal system. See Austermiller (n. 50), 701 and fn. 207.

[61] See Archil Giorgadze, Timothy Lindsay and Nicola Mariani, 'Georgian International Arbitration Centre Adopts New Arbitration Rules' (JD Supra, October 2014), <jdsupra .com/legalnews/georgian-international-arbitration-centr-03749/>.

[62] American Bar Association, 'Code of Ethics for Arbitrators in Commercial Disputes' (2014), <americanbar.org/groups/dispute_resolution/resources/Ethics/Code_Ethics_ Com_Arb_Ann/>.

[63] The Code is available at <gaa.ge/gaa-saxelmdzgvanelo/resursebi-da-masalebi/>. This Code is regarded as part of Georgia's broader efforts to 'secure its place on the map of

The reliance on international sources and the integration of local elites into the international arbitration community also facilitate ongoing monitoring of the effectiveness of such reforms. Leading local elites often critique local legal developments against international standards. For example, in response to such critiques,[64] amendments were made to the Georgian LOA to bring it into compliance with international standards.[65]

Such critiques earn local elites' recognition in the international arbitration community. These efforts are also facilitated by the numerous professional exchanges local elites engage in with foreign international arbitration practitioners. For this reason, it is no surprise that in 2014 GIAC inaugurated Georgia Arbitration Days, an annual event in which speakers from around the world join local arbitration experts in discussing international developments and their implications for arbitration in Georgia.[66] Since then, Georgia has continued these and related efforts to improve the effectiveness of international arbitration in the region.[67]

While it is too soon to evaluate the effects of these arbitration reforms on the rule of law in Georgia, early indications are promising. One particularly illustrative anecdote comes from the conference that was organized to launch the new Code of Ethics. At the conference, a Georgian appellate court judge stood up and said something to the effect that if the GAA was going to raise the standards for conduct for arbitrators, it would put pressure on judges also to raise their standards of conduct.[68]

---

international arbitration'. Sophie Tkemaladze, 'The Supreme Court of Georgia Affirms the Authority of the Georgian Courts to Issue Interim Measures in Support of Foreign Arbitral Proceedings' (2015) 20 *IBA Arbitration News* 33.

[64] Sophie Tkemaladze and Inga Kacevska, 'Procedure and Documents under Articles III and IV of New York Convention on Recognition and Enforcement of Arbitral Awards: Comparative Practice of Latvia and Georgia' (2013) 1 *Eurasian Multidisciplinary Forum* 7, 7–8, criticizing a requirement for international award enforcement introduced by the Georgia Supreme Court as potentially harmful to Georgia's international reputation.

[65] See Austermiller (n. 50), 702–4.

[66] More information about Georgian Arbitration Days is available at <giacarbitrationdays .ge/>.

[67] For a detailed summary, see Georgian International Arbitration Centre, 'Report on GIAC Activities Importing International Arbitration into the Region' (2018), <giac.ge/wp-content/uploads/2018/08/Report-on-GIAC-Activities-Importing-International-Arbitration-into-the-Region1.pdf>.

[68] This characterization is based on Rogers' observations as a participant at the conference. Notably, Rogers was also involved as part of a USAID initiative in the drafting and implementation of the Code.

Other national reforms and activities suggest that the Georgian case study is not an isolated example of international arbitration providing an impetus for bottom-up reforms that indirectly support the rule of law. For example, an ill-advised amendment to the 2012 rules of the Chamber of Commerce and Industry of Romania (CCIR) provided that all arbitrators would thereafter be appointed by the president of the CCIR, and that the president would receive a substantial fee for such appointments.[69] This regime was internationally criticized as a 'worst-case scenario for institutional appointment' of arbitrators and as having the whiff of biased and potentially corrupt incentives for the president to make arbitrator appointments.[70]

In response to these critiques, three prominent, internationally recognized arbitration specialists resigned from the CCIR.[71] Within a few short years, the offending provision was reversed. Amendments introduced in early 2014 provided that the CCIR 'does not have the right, through its organisation and administration of the arbitration, to intervene in the resolution of the dispute or to influence in any way the arbitral tribunal'.[72]

It is also reported that, in an interview, the President of CCIR insisted that today 'the CCIR prides itself with the very hands-off approach to all of the Court's operations'.[73] Further revisions were implemented in 2018. As one commentator noted, the 2018 revisions bring CCIR rules much more in keeping with prevailing international standards.[74]

The experiences in Georgia and other countries provide some concrete illustrations of how international arbitration standards and norms get incorporated into local legal regimes, and how local legal elites are involved in that process. As such, these illustrations provide more granular details about how the positive relationship we hypothesize between

---

[69] See Cornel Marian, 'Party-Appointed Arbitrators: The Lesser of Two Evils?' Kluwer Arbitration Blog (22 February 2012), <arbitrationblog.kluwerarbitration.com/2012/02/22/party-appointed-arbitrators-the-lesser-of-two-evils/>.

[70] Ibid.

[71] Ibid.

[72] Ibid.

[73] A summary of these updates was provided to the authors by Romanian attorney and arbitration specialist Adrian Hodis (22 June 2018, email on file with the authors).

[74] Stocica and Associatii – Attorneys at Law, 'The New Rules of Arbitration Established by the Court of International Commercial Arbitration Attached to the CCIR', British–Romanian Chamber of Commerce (2 February 2018), <brcconline.eu/new/the-new-rules-of-arbitration-established-by-the-court-of-international-commercial-arbitration-attached-to-the-ccir/>.

international arbitration reforms and rule of law may function in practice.

15.3.4 Testable Hypotheses

Our alternative account, articulated above and illustrated in the specific national examples, suggests three main hypotheses that can be tested empirically.

First, this alternative account suggests that investment arbitration might, to some extent at least, have a positive effect on the rule of law in a country. If the effect is sufficiently strong, it would outweigh the possible negative effects identified by others. If not, it might reduce those negative effects, even if the net effect of investment arbitration on the rule of law remains negative. The latter proposition is not one we are able to test in this chapter.

Second, the involvement of a country in international commercial arbitration reforms is a central consideration under our alternative account and is predicted to be positively correlated with the country's rule-of-law rating. Whether involvement in international arbitration reform itself is sufficient to enhance the rule of law in a country or whether it works in combination with investment arbitration (or both) can be tested empirically.

Third, this alternative account suggests a focus on domestic courts and on local legal communities rather than on more general measures or ratings of the rule of law. National courts are the local legal institutions most directly involved with international commercial arbitration. Thus, it may be that any effect of international arbitration reforms can only be observed on the court system rather than on the rule of law in a country more generally.

15.4 Sample and Data

15.4.1 Sample

The sample consists of an unbalanced panel of countries for which data are available from 1994 to 2014. Consistent with prior research,[75] we

---

[75] Sasse (n. 20), 162, excluding from his analysis countries defined as 'rich' by the World Bank, and explaining that 'it does not seem unreasonable to assume that the effect of BITs on institutional quality, if existent, mainly affects low and middle income countries'.

generally exclude countries defined as high income by the World Bank (although we use all countries in the sample for some simple replications of Ginsburg's work).[76] The full sample consists of 190 countries, with data for varying numbers of years. After excluding high-income countries, the sample consists of 130 countries. Not all countries have data available for all variables.

15.4.2 Rule of Law (Dependent) Variables

We use two different measures of the rule of law in a particular country. First, like prior studies of the issue, we use the Worldwide Governance Indicator's (WGI) rule-of-law ratings.[77] The WGI rule-of-law rating 'captur[es] perceptions of the extent to which agents have confidence in and abide by the rules of society, and in particular the quality of contract enforcement, property rights, the police, and the courts, as well as the likelihood of crime and violence'.[78] The score ranges from roughly –2.5 to 2.5, with higher numbers meaning more favourable perceptions of the rule of law.[79] Data are available annually beginning in 1994.[80]

Second, we also use component ratings from the Fraser Institute's economic freedom rankings for judicial independence, court impartiality, contract enforcement, and legal integrity.[81] The ratings range from zero to ten, with ten being the highest. The data for these court-related component ratings are available less consistently than the WGI ratings and for different countries at different times. Indeed, the number of observations in our sample with data from the economic freedom rankings is generally less than half the number of observations with data from

[76] World Bank, 'Country Lending Groups', <datahelpdesk.worldbank.org/knowledgebase/articles/906519-world-bank-country-and-lending-groups>; see Sasse (n. 20), 162.

[77] World Bank, 'Worldwide Governance Indicators', <datacatalog.worldbank.org/dataset/worldwide-governance-indicators> ('download full dataset').

[78] Daniel Kaufmann et al., 'The Worldwide Governance Indicators: Methodology and Analytical Issues' (Brookings Institution and World Bank Draft Policy Research Working Paper, September 2010), p. 4. As the description suggests, 'the WGI project is based exclusively on subjective or perceptions-based measures of governancep. , taken from surveys of households and firms as well as expert assessments produced by various organizations' (ibid.), 18. For justifications for, and limitations of, that approach, see ibid., 18–20.

[79] Ibid., 12.

[80] For information on the sources used, see World Bank (n. 77) ('Rule of Law').

[81] Fraser Institute, 'Economic Freedom: Filter and Download Dataset', <fraserinstitute.org/economic-freedom/dataset?geozone=world&page=dataset&min-year=2&max-year=0&filter=0>.

the WGI rule-of-law rankings. The advantage of the economic freedom rankings is that they provide ratings addressing the court system of a country only, unlike the more general rule-of-law rating. Some of the ratings are based on perceptions (like the WGI rule-of-law rating), while others (most notably the contract enforcement measure) are based on more objective measurements.[82]

Neither the WGI rule-of-law rating nor the Fraser Institute's economic freedom rankings expressly include as a component the country's legal framework governing international arbitration.[83] While changes in a country's international arbitration law might affect some perception-based subcomponents of the rankings, the broad range covered by those components and subcomponents – particularly in the WGI rule-of-law rating – makes the possible influence of a country's international arbitration law as a component of the rating extremely limited. We also lagged the independent variables by one year, further mitigating any concerns about endogeneity in our regression models.

15.4.3 Arbitration Variables

We use a variety of arbitration-related variables to test our hypotheses. For investment arbitration, we generally use the cumulative number of BITs entered into by the country,[84] the cumulative number of investment arbitration proceedings initiated against the country,[85] and the cumulative number of awards made in those arbitrations – in favour of the state (on jurisdiction or the merits) or in favour of the claimant,[86] all lagged by

---

[82] For a description of the sources for the data underlying the rankings, see James Gwartney et al., 'Economic Freedom of the World: 2014 Annual Report' (Fraser Institute, 2014), 233–4.

[83] World Bank, 'Rule of Law', <info.worldbank.org/governance/wgi/pdf/rl.pdf>; Gwartney ibid.

[84] United Nations Conference on Trade and Development (UNCTAD), 'Investment Policy Hub, International Investment Agreements (IIA) Navigator', <investmentpolicy.unctad .org/international-investment-agreements>. We also used a dummy/indicator variable equaling 1 if the International Centre for Settlement of Investment Disputes (ICSID) Convention was in force in the country in a given year. ICSID, 'Database of ICSID Member States', <icsid.worldbank.org/en/Pages/about/Database-of-Member-States .aspx>. Variable was omitted from the regressions due to collinearity.

[85] UNCTAD, 'Investment Dispute Settlement Navigator', <investmentpolicy.unctad.org/ investment-dispute-settlement>.

[86] We use data from Daniel Behn, Tarald Laudal Berge and Malcolm Langford, 'Poor States or Poor Governance? Explaining Outcomes in Investment Treaty Arbitration' (2018) 38 *Northwestern Journal of International Law and Business* 333.

one year. We also sometimes use as independent variables a dummy/indicator variable equaling one if the country had a BIT in force during the prior year and zero otherwise; and a dummy/indicator variable equaling one if the country had an investment arbitration filed against it in the prior year and zero otherwise. Note that we use the date that the BIT entered into force (rather than the date of signature) for characterization.[87]

The standard theory predicts that the coefficient on these variables will be negative – that investment arbitration is associated with a reduced rule-of-law rating in the countries studied. Alternatively, a strong form of our alternative account – that the filing of investment arbitration claims or the issuance of awards in favour of claimants is likely to be related to improvements in the rule of law – would predict that the coefficient on these variables would be positive.[88]

We use two variables as proxies for the extent of international commercial arbitration reforms. The first is a dummy/indicator variable equalling one if the New York Convention was in force in the country[89] and the second is a dummy/indicator variable equalling one if the UNCITRAL Model Law was in force in the country.[90] We view these variables as proxies for the extent of international arbitration reform activity in the country.[91] Our alternative account would predict that the coefficients of these variables would be positive. Of the two we expect the

---

[87] We excluded from our counts the handful of BITs identified by UNCTAD as not including dispute settlement provisions. See UNCTAD, 'IIA Mapping Project', <investmentpolicy .unctad.org/international-investment-agreements/iia-mapping#iiaInnerMenu> ('Investor-State Dispute Settlement (ISDS); ISDS included; No'). We do not subtract terminated treaties from our treaty count because a country's termination of an investment treaty does not necessarily have the exact opposite effect on its rule-of-law rating as the country's entry into an investment treaty.

[88] A variation would be to consider the relationship between the number of investment arbitrations brought by investors from a country and changes in the rule-of-law rating in that country. That variation is worth further research but is beyond the scope of this chapter.

[89] United Nations Commission on International Trade Law (UNCITRAL), 'Status: Convention on the Recognition and Enforcement of Foreign Arbitral Awards (New York, 1958)', <uncitral.un.org/en/texts/arbitration/conventions/foreign_arbitral_ awards/status2>.

[90] UNCITRAL, 'Status: UNCITRAL Model Law on International Commercial Arbitration (1985), with Amendments as Adopted in 2006', <uncitral.un.org/en/texts/arbitration/ modellaw/commercial_arbitration/status>.

[91] An alternative measure could be the total number of international commercial arbitration proceedings held in a country each year, but reliable data on those totals are not available.

490 CATHERINE A. ROGERS & CHRISTOPHER R. DRAHOZAL

UNCITRAL Model Law variable to be the better measure of international arbitration reform because it is less common for countries to adopt the UNCITRAL Model Law than to accede to the New York Convention.

Finally, we include an interaction variable equaling zero if the UNCITRAL Model Law is not in force in the country and equaling the cumulative number of investment arbitration proceedings if the UNCITRAL Model Law is in force.[92] This variable tests for the interaction of investment arbitration and international commercial arbitration in the country. As both the number of investment arbitration proceedings increases and the country engages in international arbitration reform activity, we expect the country's rule-of-law rating to increase.

15.4.4 Control Variables

We use most of the same controls in our multivariate analysis as Sasse: gross domestic product (GDP) per capita (we expect a positive coefficient on the view that wealthier countries will have higher rule-of-law ratings); population (we expect a negative coefficient on the view that enhancing the rule of law is more costly in larger countries); foreign direct investment, imports as a percentage of GDP, and foreign aid as a percentage of gross national income (GNI) (which might be positively or negatively related to the rule of law); and a democracy/autocracy rating (we expect a higher democracy rating to be positively related to the rule-of-law score).[93]

For control variables other than percentages and ratings we used log transformations. All data come from the World Bank,[94] except for the democracy/autocracy measure, which comes from the Center for Systemic Peace.[95] Summary statistics for these variables are reported in Table 15.1.

---

[92] That is, the interaction variable equals the value of the UNCITRAL Model Law interaction/dummy variable (0 or 1) multiplied by the cumulative number of investment arbitration proceedings filed against the country.

[93] Sasse (n. 20), 164. Ginsburg (n. 13), uses similar controls, albeit adding a country's WGI political stability score as an independent variable. Sasse (n. 20), 162–3 treats the political stability score as a possible dependent variable, rather than an independent variable, and we likewise do not consider it as an independent variable.

[94] World Bank, 'Data: By Indicator, All Indicators', <data.worldbank.org/indicator> (GDP per capita (NY.GDP.PCAP.CD); Total population (SP.POP.TOTL); Foreign direct investment net inflows (BX.KLT.DINV.CD.WD); Imports of goods and services as a percentage of GDP (NE.IMP.GNFS.ZS); Net official development assistance (DT.ODA.ODAT.GN.ZS)).

[95] Center for Systemic Peace, 'The Polity Project', <systemicpeace.org/polityproject.html>.

Table 15.1 *Summary statistics*

	Obs.	Mean	Std. Dev.	Min.	Max.
World Governance Indicator Rule-of-law rating	1,940	-0.532	0.643	−2.230	1.379
Fraser Institute Judicial Independence rating	879	3.884	1.661	0.167	8.183
Fraser Institute Court Impartiality rating	1,163	4.054	1.260	0	8.016
Fraser Institute Contract Enforcement rating	984	3.924	1.673	0	10
Fraser Institute Legal Integrity rating	993	5.075	1.811	0	10
BIT in force (t-1)	2,672	0.836	0.370	0	1
Cumulative BITs (t-1)	2,672	12.527	17.193	0	117
ISDS arbitration filed (t-1)	2,672	0.080	0.272	0	1
Cumulative ISDS cases (t-1)	2,672	0.801	2.288	0	23
Cumulative State wins, on jurisdiction	2,672	0.064	0.324	0	5
Cumulative State wins, on merits	2,672	0.110	0.511	0	5
Cumulative State losses	2,672	0.151	0.626	0	9
New York Convention (t-1)	2,672	0.582	0.493	0	1
UNCITRAL Model Law (t-1)	2,672	0.168	0.374	0	1
Interaction: UNCITRAL * Cumulative ISDS (t-1)	2,672	0.392	1.833	0	23
GDP per capita (log) (t-1)	2,621	7.151	1.099	4.171	9.604
Population (log) (t-1)	2,672	15.577	2.068	9.134	21.029
Foreign direct investment (log) (t-1)	2,419	18.905	2.773	2.303	26.575
Imports as % of GDP (t-1)	2,507	45.985	22.080	6.962	193.469
Foreign aid as % of GNI (t-1)	2,486	8.702	11.726	−2.612	181.187
Net democracy/autocracy (polity2) rating (t-1)	2,253	1.991	6.032	−10	10

15.5 Empirical Results

We begin with simple tests that track some of the tests done by Ginsburg, albeit with updated data over a longer time frame. We then present our multivariate regression results, which differ from those previously done in two main respects. First, and central to our alternative account of the

492 CATHERINE A. ROGERS & CHRISTOPHER R. DRAHOZAL

relationship between international arbitration and the rule of law, we focus on the involvement of countries in international commercial arbitration reforms in addition to BITs and investment arbitration. Second, while examining countries' general rule-of-law ratings, we also look at narrower measures that focus on the court system, which may be most likely to be affected by arbitration-related activities.

15.5.1 Replicating Ginsburg

We start with simple univariate regression models that replicate to some degree the empirical tests done by Ginsburg.[96] In doing so, we focus solely on the relationship between investment treaties and the rule of law. In the next section, we expand our analysis to include the arbitration-related variables described above as well as various controls.

The dependent variable is the change in the WGI rule-of-law rating between 1996 and 1998, 1998 and 2000, and 2000 and 2002 (to track the Ginsburg analysis), as well as between 1996 and 2010 and between 1996 and 2013 (to trace changes over a longer period). The independent variables are (1) a dummy variable equaling one when a BIT took effect in a country in either 1995 or 1996 and zero otherwise (again, to track Ginsburg), and (2) a dummy variable equaling one when at least one BIT was in force in the country in 1996 and zero otherwise (again, to trace effects over a longer period). We use both the full sample (including high-income countries) and a subsample (excluding high-income countries), although the results are largely consistent regardless of the sample used.

The results are summarized in Table 15.2 (with standard errors in parentheses). The coefficients reported in the second column in table 15.2 are the ones that most closely follow the Ginsburg methodology. Indeed, the coefficients for the change in rule of law between 1996 and 1998 and between 1998 and 2000 are very similar to those found by Ginsburg.[97] The results thereafter depart from Ginsburg's (at least in part because of changes in how the WGI rule-of-law ratings are calculated since Ginsburg published his article[98]) and show no statistically significant

---

[96] Ginsburg (n. 13), 120–1. Thanks to Alex Stone Sweet for this suggestion.

[97] Ibid., 121, reporting coefficient of 0.03 on change in rule of law between 1996 and 1998 and –0.07 on change in rule of law between 1998 and 2000.

[98] See Daniel Kaufmann et al., 'Governance Matters III: Governance Indicators for 1996, 1998, 2000, and 2002' (2004) 18 *World Bank Economic Review* 253, 270 (changes made

Table 15.2 *Linear regression models with change in WGI rule-of-law rating as dependent variable*

	Full sample		Excluding high-income countries	
	New BIT in 1995 or 1996	BIT in effect 1996 or before	New BIT in 1995 or 1996	BIT in effect 1996 or before
Change in rule-of-law rating – 1996–98	0.026 (0.025)	0.070** (0.029)	0.014 (0.034)	0.096** (0.038)
Change in rule-of-law rating – 1998 to 2000	−0.056** (0.028)	−0.021 (0.034)	−0.053 (0.041)	0.009 (0.047)
Change in rule-of-law rating – 2000–02	0.046* (0.272)	0.056* (0.032)	0.068* (0.035)	0.081** (0.040)
Change in rule-of-law rating – 1996 to 2010	0.052 (0.062)	0.166** (0.073)	0.043 (0.085)	0.224** (0.094)
Change in rule-of-law rating – 1996 to 2013	0.054) (0.064)	0.154** (0.076)	0.066 (0.087)	0.230** (0.098)
Observations	186	186	123	123

* Statistically significant at 0.10 level; ** Statistically significant at 0.05 level;
*** Statistically significant at 0.01 level.

relationship between a BIT taking effect in 1995 or 1996 (as distinct from having entered into a BIT in 1995 or 1996) and long-term changes in the rule of law. By comparison, the fact that a country has at least one BIT in force in 1996 has a positive correlation with changes in rule-of-law rating, both in the short term and in the long term. But, of course, this analysis neither controls for confounding variables nor examines the arbitration-related variables of interest here. We consider those complicating factors in the next section.

retroactively to prior years' data). Another difference is that we coded BITS based on the date they took effect rather than the date they were signed.

15.5.2   Multivariate Regression Results

In this section, we add in consideration of various arbitration-related variables and controls. We estimate fixed-effects models (controlling for both country and year fixed effects) with robust standard errors clustered by country,[99] using several measures of the rule of law as dependent variables. Consistent with Sasse, all independent variables are lagged one year.[100]

Our regression results appear in Tables 15.3 and 15.4. As for the control variables, the GDP per capita variable is of the expected sign and strongly statistically significant. The coefficient on the foreign direct investment variable has a positive sign and is statistically significant, as is the coefficient on the democracy/autocracy variable (that is, more democratic countries are associated with higher rule of law scores). The coefficients on the remaining control variables were not statistically significant.

Our central empirical findings are the following:

1. In the regressions using the WGI rule-of-law index as the dependent variable (see Table 15.3), the coefficients on the variables for the cumulative number of BITs and the cumulative number of investment arbitration proceedings are negative and statistically significant in most of the models estimated. These findings are consistent with those of prior studies that BITs and investment arbitration proceedings, by themselves, are negatively related to the rule of law in a country. These findings are also inconsistent with a strong form of our alternative account.[101] Interestingly, the number of State wins on jurisdiction in

---

[99] Sasse (n. 20), 161; see A. Colin Cameron and Douglas L. Miller, 'A Practitioner's Guide to Cluster-Robust Inference' (2015) 50 *Journal of Human Resources* 317.

[100] Sasse (n. 20), 164. The variable for the cumulative number of BITs also provides a lagged effect, to some extent at least.

[101] UNCTAD has made available partial data identifying those BITs that require exhaustion of local remedies before a party can proceed in arbitration. See UNCTAD (n. 87) (Investor–State Dispute Settlement (ISDS); Forums; Relationship between forums; Local remedies first). In results not reported here, we included as a variable the cumulative number of BITs that required resort to local remedies first in force in a country (lagged one year) and found no statistically significant positive relationship between that variable and the rule-of-law rating in the country. The UNCTAD data are incomplete, however, and so this possible relationship is one that needs to be pursued in future research. See UNCTAD, 'New Database – UNCTAD University Project Maps over 1,400 IIAs' (1 July 2016), <investmentpolicy.unctad.org/news/hub/506/20160701-new-database-unctad-university-project-maps-over-1-400-iias>: 'The IIA Mapping Project is an ongoing effort that aims to map all IIAs for which texts are available (about 2,700)', with over 1,400 IIAs mapped at the time of the report.

Table 15.3 *Fixed-effects models with WGI rule-of-law rating as dependent variable*

Arbitration variables	(1)	(2)	(3)	(4)
BIT in force (t-1)	0.0752			
	(0.0935)			
ISDS arbitration	−0.0543*			
filed (t-1)	(0.0314)			
Cumulative		−0.0050**	−0.0057***	−0.0059***
BITs (t-1)		(0.0024)	(0.0021)	(0.0022)
Cumulative ISDS		−0.0253***	−0.0207**	−0.0135
cases (t-1)		(0.0082)	(0.0085)	(0.0086)
Cumulative ISDS State		0.0455**	0.0287	
wins, on		(0.0222)	(0.0224)	
jurisdiction (t-1)				
Cumulative ISDS State		−0.0125		
wins, on merits (t-1)		(0.0338)		
Cumulative ISDS State		0.0395	0.0347	
losses (t-1)		(0.0268)	(0.0236)	
New York Convention	0.0565	0.0564		
(t-1)	(0.0571)	(0.0552)		
UNCITRAL Model Law	0.107**	0.0849*	0.0750	0.0709
(t-1)	(0.0459)	(0.0458)	(0.0465)	(0.0463)
Interaction: UNCITRAL *		0.0202**	0.0178*	0.0205**
Cumulative ISDS (t-1)		(0.0093)	(0.0095)	(0.0096)
Control variables				
GDP per capita	0.272***	0.303***	0.242***	0.240***
(log) (t-1)	(0.0577)	(0.0588)	(0.0499)	(0.0511)
Population	0.371	0.279	0.0590	0.0606
(log) (t-1)	(0.364)	(0.387)	(0.333)	(0.333)
FDI (log) (t-1)	0.0184**	0.0193**	0.0282***	0.0275***
	(0.0088)	(0.0079)	(0.0079)	(0.0078)
Imports as %	0.0023	0.0026		
of GDP (t-1)	(0.0017)	(0.0017)		
Foreign aid as %	0.0023	0.0022		
of GNI (t-1)	(0.0016)	(0.0016)		
Net democracy/autocracy	0.0104**	0.0093*	0.0124**	0.0124**
rating (t-1)	(0.0052)	(0.0052)	(0.0054)	(0.0054)
Observations	1,430	1,430	1,522	1,522
No. of countries	108	108	110	110
R-squared (within group)	0.1514	0.1733	0.1441	0.1383

* Statistically significant at 0.10 level; ** Statistically significant at 0.05 level;
*** Statistically significant at 0.01 level. All models estimated with both country and year fixed effects.

496 CATHERINE A. ROGERS & CHRISTOPHER R. DRAHOZAL

Table 15.4 *Fixed-effects models with Fraser Institute Legal System Component Ratings as dependent variables*

Arbitration Variables	Independent judiciary	Impartial courts	Contract enforcement	Legal integrity
Cumulative BITs (t-1)	−0.0102	−0.0178	0.0038	0.0044
	(0.0117)	(0.0113)	(0.0082)	(0.0124)
Cumulative ISDS cases (t-1)	0.0718**	0.0163	0.0061	−0.0128
	(0.0303)	(0.0248)	(0.0158)	(0.0401)
Cumulative ISDS State wins, on jurisdiction (t-1)	0.109	0.149**	0.0228	−0.287
	(0.174)	(0.0730)	(0.0634)	(0.183)
Cumulative ISDS State wins, on merits (t-1)	−0.0114	−0.0078	−0.0093	−0.165
	(0.107)	(0.0831)	(0.0578)	(0.130)
Cumulative ISDS State losses (t-1)	−0.0374	0.0187	0.0413	−0.0985
	(0.116)	(0.0654)	(0.0408)	(0.124)
New York Convention (t-1)	−0.273	−0.213	0.0728	−0.234
	(0.423)	(0.228)	(0.0787)	(0.297)
UNCITRAL Model Law (t-1)	−0.0117	0.310*	0.410***	−0.328
	(0.184)	(0.167)	(0.150)	(0.339)
Interaction: UNCITRAL * Cumulative ISDS (t-1)	−0.0435	−0.0329	−0.0319	0.0949*
	(0.0408)	(0.0284)	(0.0284)	(0.0568)
Control variables				
GDP per capita (log) (t-1)	0.353	0.465**	0.110	−0.448
	(0.313)	(0.230)	(0.142)	(0.340)
Population (log) (t-1)	−2.749***	−0.687	2.292**	−0.938
	(0.983)	(0.647)	(1.065)	(1.658)
FDI (log) (t-1)	0.0126	0.0273	−0.0371	0.0162
	(0.0482)	(0.0264)	(0.0188)	(0.0549)
Imports as % of GDP (t-1)	0.0049	−0.0006	−0.0074	−0.0153**
	(0.0046)	(0.0041)	(0.0048)	(0.0073)
Foreign aid as % of GNI (t-1)	0.0065	−0.0073*	−0.0011	−0.0136
	(0.0114)	(0.0041)	(0.0035)	(0.0123)
Net democracy/autocracy (polity2) rating (t-1)	0.0270	−0.0096	−0.0039	0.0543**
	(0.0287)	(0.0139)	(0.0084)	(0.0260)
Observations	786	1,027	880	900
No. of countries	81	90	90	78
R-squared (within group)	0.1111	0.1861	0.1512	0.0824

* Statistically significant at 0.10 level; ** Statistically significant at 0.05 level; *** Statistically significant at 0.01 level. All models estimated with both country and year fixed effects.

investment arbitrations is positively associated with the rule of law in one of the models estimated. But none of the other outcomes variables has any statistically significant relationship with the WGI rule-of-law rating.

2 The coefficient on the NY Convention dummy/indicator variable for the regressions using the WGI rule of law index as the dependent variable (also see Table 15.3) is positive but not statistically significant. The coefficient on the UNCITRAL Model law dummy/indicator variable is also positive and is statistically significant in some of the models estimated. These findings provide mixed but weak support for our alternative account in that international arbitration reforms, holding constant the number of BITs and investment arbitration proceedings, are sometimes positively related to the domestic rule of law.

3 The coefficient on the UNCITRAL Model Law/investment arbitration interaction variable (also see Table 15.3) is positive and statistically significant at the 0.10 and 0.05 significance levels. This result is consistent with our alternative account: that, when combined, investment arbitration and international commercial arbitration reforms are associated with improvements in the rule of law. On net, the amount of the improvements at least partially offsets the negative effect of BITs and investment arbitration alone on the rule of law.

4 The regression results for the four court-related components of the Fraser Institute ratings (see Table 15.4) [42]vary widely. The cumulative number of investment arbitration cases is positively related to 'judicial independence' but none of the other ratings. The UNCITRAL Model Law dummy/ indicator variable is positively related to 'contract enforcement' and 'court impartiality', both of which findings are consistent with our alternative account, but is not related to the 'independent judiciary' or 'legal integrity' ratings. Finally, for the 'legal integrity' rating, the coefficient on the UNCITRAL Model Law/investment arbitration interaction variable is positive and statistically significant at the 0.10 significance level, but none of the other arbitration variables is statistically significant.

It is difficult to draw any definitive conclusions from the models using the Fraser Institute ratings because of the widely disparate results, data uncertainties, and the fact that the regression results are quite weak – that is, the model as a whole has little explanatory power.[102] That said, these

---

[102] Note that the results in Table 15.4 are not directly comparable to those in Table 15.3 because of differences in the sample: the results in Table 15.4 are based on a smaller group of countries and different years.

498 CATHERINE A. ROGERS & CHRISTOPHER R. DRAHOZAL

results do reinforce the idea that empirical results from ratings based on narrower characteristics of the court systems may differ from empirical results based on broader rule-of-law ratings.

15.5.3 Implications

As discussed above, our alternative account of the relationship between investment and international commercial arbitration and the domestic rule of law gives rise to three testable hypotheses. Our empirical results in this – particularly those derived from our multivariate regressions – provide support for some, but not all, of those hypotheses.

First, we find a negative relationship between both the cumulative number of BITs and the cumulative number of investment arbitration proceedings and a country's WDI rule-of-law rating. Those findings are consistent with the traditional theory and inconsistent with a strong form of our alternative account, which predicts a net positive relationship. These results are not, however, necessarily inconsistent with a weaker form of our alternative account. It may be that the relationship between investment arbitration and the domestic rule of law would be even more negative but for the reasons we identify here. Moreover, as discussed in the next paragraph, the positive relationship between a country's international arbitration reforms and the domestic rule of law offsets this negative relationship at least in part.

Second, we find a positive but inconsistent relationship between adoption of the UNCITRAL Model Law on International Commercial Arbitration and a country's WGI rule-of-law rating, and a positive and more consistent relationship between a country's rule-of-law rating and a variable interacting adoption of the UNCITRAL Model Law with the cumulative number of investment arbitration proceedings filed against the country. This latter relationship suggests that, when combined, both adoption of international arbitration reforms and involvement in investment arbitration proceedings has a positive relationship with the domestic rule of law, as predicted by our alternative account.

Third, and finally, our results using the more fine-grained economic freedom rankings are too inconsistent to provide much insight into our alternative account, although the varying estimates do indicate that the choice of rule-of-law measure matters.

15.6 Agenda for Future Research

This chapter sets out an alternative account of the relationship between international arbitration – both investment and commercial arbitration – and local legal institutions. We propose that local legal elites, who stand to benefit from participation in international arbitration cases, use their influence to strengthen national legal institutions that support international (and indirectly often also domestic) arbitration. Some of these efforts, such as legislative reforms, judicial training, reforms in legal education, and attorney training, have ancillary or spillover benefits for the domestic rule of law in the country that counteract, either in whole or in part, negative effects on the rule of law that otherwise might result from diversion of national litigation to international arbitration. We describe a case study from Georgia that is consistent with our theory and present empirical results that provide at least provisional support as well.

Nonetheless, both the theory and empirical work could undoubtedly benefit from further research. Such research might aim, for example, to introduce more specific markers beyond simply adoption of the UNCITRAL Model law as a measure of the degree to which countries are entering the international arbitration regime.

Future research might also work to disaggregate further and more precisely measure the behaviour of courts. Empirical research on judicial independence and adjudication is notoriously tricky because it is virtually impossible to control for the 'right outcome'.[103] Political scientists are developing increasingly sophisticated means of measuring the phenomenon that may allow more targeted research.[104]

Finally, further inquiry should also seek to identify whether there are exceptions to our general theory about the positive relationship between international commercial arbitration and the domestic rule of law. It is possible that, in some circumstances, international arbitration may be abused to undermine the rule of law.[105] Meanwhile, by providing

---

[103] For a discussion on the challenges of empirical research on judicial and arbitral decision-making, see generally Catherine A. Rogers, 'The Politics of Investment Arbitrators' (2013) 12 *Santa Clara Journal of International Law* 223.

[104] See e.g., Mila Versteega and Tom Ginsburg, 'Measuring the Rule of Law: A Comparison of Indicators' (2017) 42 *Law and Social Inquiry* 100; Svend-Erik Skaaning, 'Measuring the Rule of Law' (2010) 63 *Political Research Quarterly* 449; Julio Ríos Figueroa and Jeffrey K. Staton, 'Unpacking the Rule of Law: A Review of Judicial Independence Measures' (CELS 2009 4th Annual Conference on Empirical Legal Studies, Paper, 26 April 2009), <people.bu.edu/jgerring/Conference/MeasuringDemocracy/documents/RiosStaton2009.pdf>.

[105] For a thoughtful reflection on how international arbitration might be misused by authoritarian regimes, see Mark Fathi Massoud, 'International Arbitration and Judicial Politics in Authoritarian States' (2014) 39 *Law and Social Inquiry* 1, 3: 'For international lawyers who promote international arbitration as an alternative to litigation, not paying heed to the side effects of their model can unwittingly help illiberal regimes continue to repress domestic judiciaries and curtail both the rule of law and human-rights-promotion activities.'

potential professional benefits for elites, international arbitration may reinforce hierarchies within national legal professions and entrench legal elites in a monopolistic position within local legal environments. Such developments might in turn hamper rule-of-law developments outside the narrow category of international arbitration reforms that benefit these elites. Future study should seek to investigate these potential concerns, as well as measures that may be taken to reduce or eliminate such potential concerns.

16

Learning from Investment Treaty Law and Arbitration: Developing States and Power Inequalities

MAVLUDA SATTOROVA[*] AND OLEKSANDRA VYTIAGANETS[**]

16.1 Introduction

The interaction of developing states with investment treaty law and arbitration constitutes an important, albeit often less visible, part of the ongoing debate about the legitimacy of the investment treaty regime and its dispute settlement mechanisms. Even a cursory overview of the literature on legitimacy of international investment law reveals that developing states and their concerns are frequently lumped together under the broader rubric of investment treaty law as a threat to national sovereignty and a constraint on state capacity to regulate in the public interest. By focusing on the formal equality between contracting state parties and the reciprocal nature of international investment agreements (IIAs), such narratives tend to mask the presence of power disparities, which considerably shape the involvement of developing states in the creation, diffusion and internalization of investment treaty law.[1]

This chapter seeks to counter these narratives by drawing on new empirical data to expose a range of structural, normative and institutional power inequalities that currently shape the various stages of

---

[*] Reader in International Economic Law, University of Liverpool, Liverpool Law School.
[**] Doctoral Research Fellow, Birmingham City University, School of Law.
[1] See e.g. Stephan W. Schill, 'Enhancing International Investment Law's Legitimacy: Conceptual and Methodological Foundations of a New Public Law Approach' (2011) 52(1) *Virginia Journal of International Law* 57; Armand de Mestral and Céline Lévesque (eds.), *Improving International Investment Agreements* (Routledge, 2012); Jürgen Kurtz, 'Building Legitimacy through Interpretation in Investor-State Arbitration: On Consistency, Coherence and the Identification of Applicable Law', in Douglas, Pauwelyn and Viñuales (eds.), *The Foundations of International Investment Law: Bringing Theory into Practice* (Oxford University Press, 2014) 257.

developing states' participation in the international investment regime. By using the optics of power and focusing on how developing states learn from and internalize investment treaty law, we peer behind the formal structures of investment treaties and investor–state arbitration so as to identify the underlying processes and actors and to question the legitimacy of the prevailing norms and institutional arrangements. Our principal argument is that a meaningful reform of investment treaty law is impossible without addressing power inequalities in negotiating the norms constituting a global investment treaty regime.

Why these empirical case-studies and why now? The international investment regime is at a crossroad. On the one hand, as acknowledged in a recent UNCTAD report, investment remains a primary driver of economic growth and mobilising investment to achieve sustainable development objectives is a priority for all countries and for developing countries in particular.[2] On the other hand, studies show that foreign investors have a considerable impact on host states because of their ability to make decisions that affect people's lives.[3] Since the international investment regime empowers foreign investors by providing them with an array of substantive and procedural legal privileges, it has attracted scathing criticism for creating a framework that operates to the advantage of foreign investors, often at the expense of states' ability to pursue social and economic policies in the public interest.[4] Recent studies also suggest that developing countries are more likely to bear the brunt of adverse awards in investor–state arbitration.[5] Faced with the significant sums awarded to investors and the high cost of arbitration process, developing states may often find themselves particularly vulnerable due to the detrimental financial impact of the awards on a country's budget.[6]

As developing countries represent a major destination for foreign direct investment, the crucial question is how their new and revised investment agreements – the product of the ongoing reform – can embody learning from the past experience. Using an empirical lens to

---

[2] UNCTAD, *Investment Policy Framework for Sustainable Development* (2015) 10.
[3] See Moshe Hirsch, 'The Sociology of International Investment Law', in Douglas, Pauwelyn and Viñuales (n. 1) 146.
[4] See e.g. David Schneiderman, *Constitutionalizing Economic Globalization: Investment Rules and Democracy's Promise* (Cambridge University Press, 2008).
[5] UNCTAD, *Investor-State Disputes Arising from Investment Treaties: A Review* (2004) 24.
[6] UNCTAD, *Best Practices in Investment for Development. How to Prevent and Manage Investor-State Disputes: Lessons from Peru*, Investment Advisory Series, Series B, number 10 (2011) 7.

examine the recent evolution of investment treaty law provides the opportunity for a deeper, more evidence-based engagement with a broad array of issues underpinning the interaction between international investment law and host states, with particular focus on developing countries. It also invites us to re-engage critically with the recent discourse on the reform of international investment law by identifying the areas and issues where the present configurations of the investment treaty regime are adversely affecting stakeholders in developing countries and generating discontent. This chapter argues that unless investment treaty law and its core mechanisms are redesigned to cater for interests of developing host states and their communities, the ongoing efforts to address concerns about the legitimacy of the investment treaty regime are likely to remain futile.

The chapter will proceed as follows. Section 16.2 will set out our methodology and introduce new empirical case studies that illuminate how developing states learn from their encounter with investment treaty law. Drawing on the findings from the empirical case studies, Section 16.3 will argue that awareness about international investment law is a form of power and the lack thereof is a significant barrier to a meaningful participation of developing states in the investment treaty regime. Following an overview of existing theories on the role of awareness and internal capacity in host state learning from prior experience, Section 16.3.2 will present and analyse the novel empirical data elucidating low levels of awareness about investment treaty law among government officials in developing countries. The empirical findings suggest that even in cases where some awareness has been found, it does not always translate into learning. Section 16.3.3 will critically analyse power disparities that affect governments of developing states to learn from their previous encounters with investment arbitration with a view to optimizing their domestic and international responses. Section 16.3.4 will examine the emerging qualitative insights into why developing state governments are limited in their capacity to introduce changes into new and existing investment treaties to ensure these treaties better reflect their needs. As power asymmetries appear to play a vital part in shaping the input by developing states into the making and change of the investment treaty regime, Section 16.4 will interrogate the lack of power-levelling opportunities within the structures and norms of investment treaties and investment arbitration. Building on the empirical data, the analysis will focus on what to avoid in future efforts to redress the existing power inequalities and to help developing states to build their own capacity.

16.2 Setting the Scene: Participation in the Investment Treaty Regime as a Form of Learning

'Learning lessons' is one way in which the participation of developing states with the international investment regime is often conceptualised. To some, the signing of investment treaties and subsequent involvement as a respondent in investor–state arbitration cases is a process whereby developing host states learn 'what a proper, international and universal standard of governance is' and what benchmarks should guide domestic legal and bureaucratic processes.[7] Other scholars argue that by undertaking investment treaty commitments and facing claims from investors, developing states learn how to transform their legal systems into 'ones that are conducive to market-based investment activities and provide the institutions necessary for the functioning of such markets'.[8] And for yet others, the international investment regime is a laboratory[9] where contracting state parties, having acquired information about the consequences of their investment treaty commitments, learn how to renegotiate and change their treaty practices.[10] Such learning – and necessary adjustments – are said to be warranted because the scope and practical implications of investment treaties were poorly understood at the time of their original diffusion.[11] Learning can manifest itself in states withdrawing or scaling back their investment treaty commitments, or it can serve to support the existing treaties, such as in cases where states incorporate more provisions for social and economic policy objectives into their revised treaty templates.[12]

As a growing number of states are increasingly concerned about the effects of investment treaties, the international investment regime is

---

[7] Thomas W. Wälde, 'The "Umbrella Clause" in Investment Arbitration: A Comment on Original Intentions and Recent Cases' (2005) 6 *Journal of World Investment and Trade* 183, 188.

[8] Stephan W. Schill, *The Multilateralization of International Investment Law* (Cambridge University Press, 2009) 377.

[9] Yoram Z. Haftel and Alexander Thompson, 'When Do States Renegotiate Investment Agreements? The Impact of Arbitration' (2018) 13(1) *The Review of International Organizations* 25, 26.

[10] Ibid.

[11] Ibid. 28; see also Lauge N. Skovgaard Poulson and Emma Aisbett, 'When the Claims Hit: Bilateral Investment Treaties and Bounded Rational Learning' (2013) 65 *World Politics* 273.

[12] See e.g. James McIlroy, 'Canada's New Foreign Investment Protection and Promotion Agreement: Two Steps Forward, One Step Back?' (2004) 5 *Journal of World Investment and Trade* 621.

undergoing a period of intensive learning and reform.[13] While policy-makers can draw lessons from the experience of other actors on the international investment law stage, scholars tend to concur that the most important learning occurs following a host state's direct encounter with investment arbitration in a respondent capacity.[14] Thus, the primary site of learning is the practice of investment arbitration[15] and primary learning effects are lessons on how to (1) prevent foreign investment disputes,[16] and (2) approach treaty-making with more caution and scrutiny[17] and sign treaties that better reflect their interests.[18]

How precisely do developing states learn from encounters and interactions with the investment treaty regime? Do such encounters compel host state governments to re-think and improve their ways of dealing with commercial/business actors?[19] Does exposure to investment arbitration lead governments of developing states to alter their investment treaty policies and treaties to better serve their needs? The existing literature on the investment treaty regime and developing states is primarily confined to legal-doctrinal and normative expositions exploring how the regime is, or should be, addressing development concerns both in treaty-making and the practice of investment arbitration.[20] There is, however, a limited but fledgling body of empirically orientated scholarship that sheds light on the interactions between developing state governments on the one hand and actors and processes of investment treaty law on the other.[21]

---

[13] UNCTAD, 'Reform of the IIA regime: Four Paths of Action and a Way Forward' (2014) *IIA Issues Note No. 3*, 2.

[14] See Poulsen and Aisbett (n. 11); see further G. Sampliner, 'Arbitration of Expropriation Cases under U.S. Investment Treaties – A Threat to Democracy or the Dog That Didn't Bark?'(2003)18(1) *ICSID Review* 1.

[15] Haftel and Thompson (n. 9) 29.

[16] UNCTAD (n. 6).

[17] Anne van Aaken, 'International Investment Law between Commitment and Flexibility: A Contract Theory Analysis' (2009) 12 *Journal of International Economic Law* 507.

[18] Mark S. Manger and Clint Peinhardt, 'Learning and the Precision of International Investment Agreements' (2017) 43 *International Interactions* 920.

[19] See e.g. Roberto Echandi, 'What Do Developing Countries Expect from the International Investment Regime?' in Alvarez and Sauvant (eds.), *The Evolving International Investment Regime: Expectations, Realities, Options* (Oxford University Press, 2011) 13.

[20] See e.g. various contributions to Stephan W. Schill, Christian J. Tams and Rainer Hofmann (eds.), *International Investment Law and Development: Bridging the Gap* (Edward Elgar, 2015).

[21] See, for instance, Lauge N. Skovgaard Poulsen, *Bounded Rationality and Economic Diplomacy: The Politics of Investment Treaties in Developing Countries* (Cambridge University Press, 2015); Taylor St John, *The Rise of Investor–State Arbitration: Politics, Law, and Unintended Consequences* (Oxford University Press, 2017); Christine Côté, 'A

While drawing on the existing empirical studies, this chapter will offer new qualitative data to unveil the hitherto underexplored patterns of learning on the part of developing states. Our analysis builds upon the empirical insights from new case studies we conducted in Kazakhstan, Kyrgyzstan, Georgia, Jordan and Ukraine, as well as the previously reported case studies examining the governance spill-overs of investment treaty law for Nigeria, Turkey and Uzbekistan.[22] The qualitative data has been obtained through semi-structured qualitative interviews carried out with government officials who work or have worked in the ministries and agencies involved, directly or indirectly, in investment treaty-making and investment dispute settlement, as well as government officials who interact with foreign investors outside the context of investment treaty law and investment dispute settlement, that is in the process of making, implementing and otherwise applying investment-related national laws in domestic, not international, settings.[23] The latter category of respondents were included in our sample due to the importance of awareness and learning among the government cadre that deals with foreign investors in a day-to-day context: statistical analyses of the International Centre for the Settlement of Investment Disputes (ICSID) caseload suggest that the majority of government decisions that lead to investment arbitrations are associated with actions taken by the executive branch and that, beyond ministries, it was the conduct of subnational actors such as provincial, state and municipal authorities and agencies that eventually led to investment disputes.[24]

The respondents were drawn from a variety of agencies and ministries responsible for foreign affairs, investment promotion, economic development, municipal administration, state prosecution and internal affairs, anti-corruption, public health, innovation, as well as legislature and the

---

Chilling Effect? The Impact of International Investment Agreements on National Regulatory Autonomy in the Areas of Health, Safety and the Environment', PhD thesis, The London School of Economics and Political Science (LSE, 2014).

[22] These case studies were published in Mavluda Sattorova, Mustafa Erkan and Ohio Omiunu, 'How Do Host States Respond to Investment Treaty Law? Some Empirical Observations' in Rasulov and Haskell (eds.), *International Economic Law: New Voices, New, Perspectives* (2020) *European Yearbook of International Economic Law* 133.

[23] In total, 41 interviews were conducted in 2017 and 2018.

[24] Jeremy Caddel and Nathan M. Jensen, 'Which Host Country Government Actors Are Most Involved in Disputes with Foreign Investors?' *Columbia FDI Perspectives No. 120*, 28 April 2014, <ccsi.columbia.edu/files/ 2013/10/No-120-Caddel-and-Jensen-FINAL-WEBSITE-version.pdf>.

judiciary. The interviews were conducted in 2017 and 2018 using a snowball sampling method whereby some of the initially approached respondents referred us onto other participants.[25] Despite its limitations, this methodology allowed access to government officials whose experiences would have otherwise been excluded.[26] The case studies were complemented by the analysis of national legislation and policy documents so as to provide a broader and more nuanced understanding of the interplay between international investment law and national realities.

As is the case in scholarly studies comprising a significant empirical component, a disclaimer is due. We acknowledge that a comprehensive analysis of how developing states learn necessitates a large-scale, longitudinal qualitative and quantitative examination covering a large number of host states. As empirical scholars of international investment law have conceded, '[j]ust as there are perils with quantitative research, qualitative methods involve their own pitfalls'.[27] Respondents may be biased in their portrayal of realities to reflect their individual or institutional preferences.[28] To address this problem, individual responses have been corroborated with the data emerging from other developing states. Furthermore, our study builds on the analysis of national legislation and policy documents as well as other published empirical studies so as to complement the interviews and provide a broader and more accurate picture.

This chapter is premised on a belief that, despite their shortcomings, findings from smaller-scale empirical case studies can be valuable insofar as they enable us to go beyond analysing the formal characteristics of the investment treaty regime and to examine the practical experiences of governments in developing countries. The findings from our case studies do not paint a representative picture of the overall experience of the broad and diverse range of developing countries, but rather to offer new novel insights into the experiences of some of those that have been involved in investment treaty-making, investment arbitration and dealing with foreign investors on a day-to-day basis. Although the empirical findings analysed in this chapter reflect unique experiences of the host

---

[25] W. Paul Vogt, *Dictionary of Statistics and Methodology: A Nontechnical Guide for the Social Sciences* (Sage, 1999).

[26] Steven K. Thomson, 'Adaptive Sampling in Behavioural Surveys', *NIDA Research Monograph* (1997) 296.

[27] Poulsen (n. 21) 23.

[28] Ibid.

states in the case study sample, they also help shed light on the hitherto less visible effects of the investment treaty regime on a wider array of developing states sharing similar characteristics. The overarching aim of this contribution is to capture some important elements of interactions between the investment treaty regime and developing states. By doing so – with the aid of the power optic – the chapter seeks to unmask some of the enduring structural forces and processes of investment treaty law and arbitration that presently determine the ability of developing states to shape their fates and their futures.[29]

16.3 Power Disparities and Limits of Learning

Power is 'a disposition that depends on knowledge'.[30] States learn by using knowledge to specify causal relationships in new ways so that the result affects the content of their new policies.[31] Our contention is that power disparities prevent developing states from being able to effectively navigate the complex web of international investment treaties and investment arbitration jurisprudence. In particular, for developing states the lack of capacity denotes limited awareness of the meaning and implications of investment treaties and limited opportunities to learn. In order to be able to effectively use investment treaties to their advantage – and to shield themselves from the financial consequences of sanctions for noncompliance with investment treaty prescriptions – developing state governments must possess full awareness and understanding of how such treaties work. Internal capacity to maintain the requisite levels of awareness and understanding is a key factor in enabling the effective participation by developing states in the investment treaty regime. To quote a recent UNCTAD study, for developing countries to learn from their encounters with investment treaty law, it is essential that 'all levels of government and agencies that interact with foreign investors understand the scope and consequences of the commitments under investment treaties and the practical implications for their day-to-day activities'.[32]

---

[29] Michael Barnett and Raymond Duvall (eds.), *Power in Global Governance* (Cambridge University Press, 2004) 3.

[30] Emanuel Adler and Steven Bernstein, 'Knowledge in Power: The Epistemic Construction of Global Governance', in Barnett and Duvall, ibid. 294.

[31] Ernst B. Haas, *When Knowledge Is Power: Three Models of Change in International Organizations* (University of California Press, 1990) 24.

[32] UNCTAD (n. 6) 11.

16.3.1 How Do States Learn? The Role of Awareness and Internal Capacity

It is by now fairly uncontested that investment treaties were poorly understood during the 1990s when many developing states signed such treaties in great numbers. One of the recent major studies into investment treaty-making shows that governments of developing countries had been mostly unaware of the far-reaching scope and implications of bilateral investment treaties until well after the first claim was filed against their country.[33] Through an illuminating analysis of archive trails and interviews, Poulsen reveals that 'developing countries were not as rigorous and careful when negotiating investment treaties as have been assumed in previous accounts of the international investment regime'.[34] Policy-makers signing treaties exhibited bounded rationality, making their decisions subject to cognitive constraints and prone to mistakes.[35] Poulsen shows that national policy-makers in developing states may well be rational in the broadest sense of the word but instances of their decision-making (such as signing treaties which hurt them) may often be a product of narcissistic learning and biased by cognitive shortcuts: 'although governments may have tried to pursue their own preferences when using investment treaties to compete for capital, systematic information processing biases among policy-makers could have resulted in predictably irrational behaviour both in terms of adoption patterns and treaty designs'.[36]

Even after the information about investment treaties and their liability implications became available, decision-makers in many developing countries tended to ignore the experience of other countries and neglected to take investment treaties seriously until their first exposure to an investment arbitration claim in a respondent capacity.[37] Poulsen hypothesises whether higher levels of administrative capacity in developed states makes them less prone to bias in learning about design, content and implications of investment treaties compared with developing countries where such capacity is considerably lacking. He argues that lack of expertise within the relevant government agencies in developing states contributes to the status quo bias, whereby bureaucrats are less

---

[33] See Poulsen (n. 21) 17.
[34] Ibid. 70.
[35] Ibid. 17.
[36] Ibid. 45.
[37] Poulsen and Aisbett (n. 11) 282.

likely to opt out of default treaty designs adopted by their predecessors.[38] This hypothesis finds support in more recent studies which show that while developing countries learn primarily from their own experience, developed states are likely to learn more broadly, including from cases in which they are not a participant.[39]

Critics of international investment law have warned that if government decision-makers remain unaware of international investment law and the standards of behaviour it imposes on states, such decision-makers are unlikely to internalize these standards not only when evaluating the adoption of new governmental measures but also in exercising their day-to-day decision-making powers vis-à-vis foreign investors.[40] The question is whether government officials in developing states possess the requisite levels of awareness to enable them to effectively negotiate, implement and change international investment treaties and their concrete prescriptions.

16.3.2 Lack of Awareness (and Limited Learning): Insights from Empirical Case Studies

While learning is often presented as a positive (and unintended) benefit of the investment treaty regime, the emerging qualitative data suggests that lack of awareness about investment treaty law and its implications significantly hinders the capacity of developing states to meaningfully partake in the shaping of investment treaty norms and practices. The major shortcoming of the existing treaty framework is that it does not envisage any mechanisms that would enable and facilitate the internalization of investment treaty norms by host governments. Nor does the regime offer any systemic solutions to redress the disparities in capacity and to improve awareness in developing states.

Consider, for instance, the earlier empirical studies in Nigeria, Turkey and Uzbekistan have revealed a limited awareness among government officials about international investment law and its concrete liability

---

[38] Poulsen (n. 21) 45.

[39] Manger and Peinhardt (n. 18) 937.

[40] See e.g. Jack Coe Jr and Noah Rubins, 'Regulatory Expropriation and the *Tecmed* Case: Context and Contributions', in Weiler (ed.), *International Investment Law and Arbitration: Leading Cases from the ICSID, NAFTA, Bilateral Treaties and Customary International Law* (Cameron May, 2005) 599; also Sergio Puig, 'No Right without a Remedy: Foundations of Investor-state Arbitration', in Douglas, Pauwelyn and Viñuales (n. 1) 235.

implications.[41] The data suggest some learning in developing host states tends to occur primarily after the respective governments had their first experience of defending themselves in an investment arbitration case. It has also transpired that such learning tends to remain confined to those who were involved, directly or indirectly, in the process of responding to investment treaty claims.[42] These are usually the ministries of justice, national foreign investment agencies and other similar bodies tasked with the representation and defence of the state interests in international disputes. Government officials in other ministries or agencies showed very limited or no awareness of investment treaty law even after the respective governments were hit by investment arbitration disputes on more than one occasion.[43]

These earlier findings are by and large corroborated by the data emerging from the interviews more recently completed in Georgia, Kazakhstan, Kyrgyzstan, Jordan and Ukraine. Georgia has signed 54 IIAs and was a respondent in at least 15 investment arbitration disputes, four of which were concluded in favour of claimant-investors and two cases settled[44] (the state successfully defended itself in two cases, one case was discontinued, and seven are pending). The total amount of damages awarded against the state in the four cases lost exceeds US$63 million (in 2018 dollars).[45] In view of the sheer scale of liabilities sustained by the government in investment arbitration disputes, one would expect a relatively high level of awareness among government officials about the meaning and effects of Georgia's investment treaty commitments. In line with the earlier studies, however, even a decade after the first award was rendered against Georgia, such awareness and knowledge of investment treaty law still remains confined within the agencies directly involved in representing and defending the government in international disputes. As one interview respondent explained, some steps were being undertaken to pass the knowledge about IIAs and investment arbitration to other 'line ministries', including through seminars led by experts from the Ministry of Justice.[46]

---

[41] See Sattorova, Erkan and Omiunu (n. 22).

[42] Ibid.

[43] Ibid.

[44] Although not exclusively the case, investment arbitrations ending in settlement tend to favour the claimant-investor in some way; and, thus, might be considered at least a partial win.

[45] Data from PluriCourts Investment Treaty and Arbitration Database (PITAD) at 1 July 2019, <pitad.org/index#welcome>.

[46] Interview JMN.

Similar findings emerge from the interviews in Kazakhstan, which is an interesting case in point, primarily due to its long-standing involvement in the signing of IIAs and in responding to investment disputes against it (the first investment arbitration in Kazakhstan dates to 1996[47]). Kazakhstan is a signatory to at least 62 IIAs, and acted as a respondent in at least 23 investment arbitration cases, of which eight cases were decided in favour of the claimant-investor and two settled (nine are pending and the state successfully defended itself in four cases). The total amount awarded against Kazakhstan amounted to some US$835 million (in 2018 dollars) in damages.[48] The extent of Kazakhstan's liabilities under investment arbitration awards to date should arguably have led to a dramatic rise in the levels of awareness among government officials about Kazakhstan's investment treaty commitments and their liability implications. However, only a quarter of the interviewed officials showed awareness of the international investment regime and its arbitration mechanism.[49] These officials were affiliated with one of the key government agencies tasked with the promotion and protection of foreign investment in Kazakhstan. One high-ranking government official opined that investment arbitration disputes often arise due to the lack of awareness in the lower-tiers of the government as well as the ministries that are not directly responsible for investment promotion and protection.[50]

Kyrgyzstan has also been an active long-standing actor and participant in the international investment regime, having signed at least 56 IIAs and acted as a respondent in 14 investment arbitration disputes, of which six were decided in favour of the claimant-investor and two cases settled (two were discontinued, three are pending, and the state has not successfully defended itself once). Investors were awarded US$167 million (in 2018 dollars) in damages. Strikingly, Kyrgyzstan has not been able to successfully defend itself in investment arbitration cases brought against it. The Kyrgyz case study is an outlier in the sense that the overwhelming majority of respondents in our limited sample had at least some awareness of investment treaty law and arbitration due to the participant pool all being directly affiliated with the government agencies that are

---

[47] *Biedermann International, Inc.* v. *Republic of Kazakhstan and Association for Social and Economic Development of Western Kazakhstan 'Intercaspian'*, SCC Case No. 97/1996, Award, 2 August 1999.
[48] PITAD (n. 45).
[49] Interviews IDM1, IDM2.
[50] Interview IDM1.

responsible for drafting and expertise of IIAs and the representation of the state interests before international courts and tribunals. However, despite such affiliation resulting in increased *awareness*, the majority of respondents (six out of eight) demonstrated a somewhat limited *understanding* of the actual content and reach of investment treaty prescriptions. The respondents showed their awareness of investment arbitration as a tool the foreign investors would wield when experiencing disagreements with the host government; however, they also acknowledged the absence of a government cadre with deeper knowledge of investment treaty law and the growing need to rely on external, foreign experts.

Jordan has reportedly signed 66 IIAs and was involved in a respondent capacity in at least 11 investment arbitration disputes, one of which has been decided in favour of claimant investors, two in favour of the state, five settled, two discontinued and one pending (amount of damages unknown).[51] Of eight interview respondents, two showed some awareness of investment treaty law; two further respondents – representing one of the key investment agencies – demonstrated a very good knowledge of both investment treaty practice and investment arbitrations. Other respondents, although affiliated with key business-facing ministries and agencies, reported limited to no knowledge of investment treaty law and arbitration. The respondents tended to conflate settled cases with those where damages awards were rendered. The data suggests that the real awareness of the actual extent of Jordan's liabilities under investment arbitration awards is still limited and some officials do not have a full and accurate picture of the government's experience with international investment law and its institutions.

Ukraine has been actively involved in both signing investment treaty instruments and engaging with investment arbitration. It is currently signatory to 76 IIAs[52] and has been named as a respondent in at least 30 investment arbitration disputes (eight pending, four settled, three discontinued, seven investor wins, seven state wins).[53] Although Ukraine has successfully deflected the majority of investment arbitration claims brought against it, there have still been significant losses. In a recent case, the claimant-investor succeeded in obtaining a damages

---

[51] PITAD (n. 45).
[52] Ibid.
[53] Ibid.

award amounting to US$8.7 million,[54] and that brought the overall total that the government has had to pay to more than US$143.7 million.[55] Furthermore, even in cases where Ukraine succeeds in its defence, there is the inevitable economic loss that comes in the form of arbitration costs as well as its own legal costs and expenses. Only in 2017, the Ministry of Justice offered circa US$5 million for procurement of legal services for representing Ukraine in its investment arbitration disputes.[56] In spite of its track record of close engagement with investment treaty law and arbitration, our interviews with Ukrainian government officials point to a prevailing lack of awareness about the international investment regime. Only four interview respondents were aware of the extent of Ukraine's investment treaty commitments and its involvement in investor–state arbitration. These respondents gained their awareness through their work in the departments that were involved in representing Ukrainian interests in investment arbitration.[57] One further respondent admitted to having heard of an arbitration case recently resorted to by a foreign corporation (the case was mentioned at a reception organized by the embassy of Spain in Ukraine). This interviewee was not certain whether the case was or was not an investment treaty arbitration.[58] Despite their regular dealings with foreign investors, other interview respondents reported no real awareness of investment treaty law and its arbitration mechanism. Notably, even those affiliated with a newly established investment promotion agency showed no real awareness of investment treaties and investor–state arbitration and their implications for the government.[59]

The overarching conclusion to be drawn from these empirical insights resonates with previously published findings[60] about the overall low levels of awareness among government officials about what investment treaty law entails for host states in terms of standards of treatment it imposes and sanctions meted out through its investment arbitration mechanism.[61]

---

[54] *Joseph Charles Lemire* v. *Ukraine*, ICSID Case No. ARB/06/18, Award, 28 March 2011.
[55] 'Ukraine as Respondent State', <investmentpolicy.unctad.org/investment-dispute-settlement>.
[56] *Prozorro: Публічні закупівлі*, 2019, <prozorro.gov.ua>.
[57] Interviews MUL, MUT.
[58] Interview MPU.
[59] Interview IU1.
[60] Sattorova, Erkan and Omiunu (n. 22).
[61] While limited awareness has been relatively common to all countries in our case study sample, the empirical data shows a variation in the ways the respective governments have

Where awareness has been shown, it tended to be confined to a small number of officials who have been directly involved in defending the states' interests in international disputes as well as the officials who have been involved in drafting and negotiating IIAs. The fact that many government officials in the reported case studies have shown insufficient and at times no knowledge of international investment law – even after encountering foreign investor claims – suggests that the opportunities to learn from such encounters are limited and not fully utilized.

Of course, it could be argued that, with a few exceptions, awareness might be similarly lacking among the government officials in many developed states. Indeed, this phenomenon warrants a fresh empirical investigation, and is therefore outside the scope of this chapter. It is equally imperative to stress that the aim of this chapter is not to criticize developing states for low levels of awareness about the international investment regime, but rather to highlight that limited awareness is an obvious factor, as well as a cause, impeding the ability of states to learn from experience. While better awareness and learning could indeed alter the ways in which developing states make and implement their investment treaty commitments, the existing treaty framework does not envisage any solutions to improve awareness and to redress other systemic barriers to internal capacity building.

16.3.3   Lack of Capacity as a Barrier to Learning

For Aristotle, power was synonymous with potency, which has three aspects: as a source of change, as a capacity for performance, or as a condition making a thing unchangeable.[62] Internal capacity, although an important aspect of power disparities which shape the involvement of developing states in the investment treaty regime, is often neglected in the mainstream scholarship on the regime's legitimacy. Our empirical findings point to a vital role of domestic capacity for purposes of improving awareness and learning from previous encounters with investment treaty law and investment arbitration. Not only does the level of awareness about investment treaty law transpire to be low but the empirical data also suggests that, even after going through a number of

---

responded to their encounter with the regime. This is discussed in more detail in Mavluda Sattorova, *The Impact of Investment Treaty Law on Host States: Enabling Good Governance?* (Hart Publishing, 2018) ch. 3.

[62] Keith Dowding (ed.), *The Encyclopedia of Power* (Sage Publications, 2011) 30.

investment arbitration disputes, governments in developing countries are limited in their capacity to learn from their experiences.[63] For host states, this lack of learning denotes a missed opportunity for the relevant government agencies to meaningfully participate in the processes of revising and reforming the country's international investment agreements and utilising such agreements to effectuate changes in the domestic arena.

The interview responses from our case studies suggest that the reasons for the persistent lack of learning are manifold. Among other factors, the interview respondents noted a lack of institutional memory due to a high turnover in government agencies, limited or at times non-existent inter-agency coordination and dialogue – or 'working in silos', and lack of financial and institutional support for building and sustaining local capacity. According to one respondent, from Jordan, the lack of awareness – and limited learning from prior experience – persists because 'the government has no single brain . . . its capacity is limited and scattered'.[64] Although awareness seems to be gradually growing, at least in some segments of the government, lessons from investment arbitration are not being spread due to 'poor coordination of the overall government machinery' and lack of engagement between the executive and law-making branches of the government.[65] This echoes findings from the previous case studies where respondents remarked about the absence of 'shared vision' between officials in central government agencies and regional/municipal authorities.[66]

Other responses point to the lack of material incentives to learn. Contrary to the assumption that investment treaty rules and their arbitration mechanisms 'exert considerable pressure on states to bring their domestic legal orders into conformity with their investment treaty obligations'[67] and thereby 'contribute greatly to institutional quality in host countries',[68] none of the countries in these case studies appear to have been motivated to adopt a systemic measures to raise the levels of

---

[63] The existing studies suggest developed states with higher administrative capacity tend to learn better. See e.g. above nn. 38–9 and accompanying text.

[64] Interview IAJM.

[65] Interviews DPSK, EGK.

[66] See Sattorova (n. 61) 70.

[67] Stephan W. Schill, 'System Building in Investment Treaty Arbitration and Lawmaking' (2001) 12 *German Law Journal* 1083, 1085.

[68] Kenneth J. Vandevelde, 'Model Bilateral Investment Treaties: The Way Forward' (2012) 18 *Southwestern Journal International Law* 313.

awareness about investment treaty law and to learn from their experience as respondents in investment arbitration cases. A view shared by many interviewees was neatly captured in one response: 'the government rarely goes deep into questioning what's just happened'.[69] Lack of feedback from those involved in defending the government was also mentioned among the factors that hamper the transposition of lessons from arbitration into concrete changes in national and international commitments.

Finally, the respondents also pointed to the limited involvement of local law firms in representing governments in investment arbitration cases. In the words of one respondent, 'national experts are being largely rejected'.[70] Even though some governments have been reported to insist on joint bidding by international and local law firms in tendering legal services,[71] a number of respondents across three case studies pointed out the tendency for international law firms to dominate in the investment arbitration market and the limited opportunity for the local legal cadre to gain exposure to investment arbitration practice and to act as conduits of knowledge in the domestic legal arena.

The recent trends in investment treaty-making and arbitration outcomes show that developing states remain the rule-takers and have so far heralded limited changes in their treaties,[72] while also bearing the brunt of damages awards in investment arbitration disputes.[73] When examined in conjunction with these trends, our empirical findings strongly suggest that lack of internal capacity is one of the principal barriers hampering the ability of developing state governments to gain, internalize and utilize knowledge about investment treaty law and arbitration. An important factor beneath levels of awareness – and subsequent learning – is the nature of the international investment regime itself, in particular its broadly framed and rapidly evolving rules, and a complex institutional

---

[69] Interview MPU.

[70] Interview PLU.

[71] Ibid.

[72] With the exception of some South–South treaty arrangements: see further Wolfgang Alschner and Dmitriy Skougarevskiy, 'Mapping the Universe of International Investment Agreements' (2016) 19 *Journal of International Economic Law* 561.

[73] See Daniel Behn, Tarald Laudal Berge and Malcolm Langford, 'Poor States or Poor Governance? Explaining Outcomes in Investment Treaty Arbitration' (2018) 38(3) *Northwestern Journal of International Law & Business* 333 (explaining why relatively wealthy respondent states fare better in investment arbitration than lower-income developing states). For statistical data showing investment arbitration outcomes for developing states, see e.g. UNCTAD, 'Investor–State Dispute Settlement: Review of Developments in 2017' (2018) IIA Issue Note No. 2.

landscape, which often leave host states unsure as to how their governmental measures would be evaluated by arbitrators.[74] Even high-capacity governments are likely to find it difficult to anticipate the consequences of IIAs and outcomes of investment arbitration cases. For a cash-strapped government of a developing state, such complexity constitutes a significant barrier in the way of learning from its own encounters with the investment treaty regime as well as acquiring and processing information about broader trends in investment treaty policy and jurisprudence. The 'learning effect' of investment arbitration may well have allowed some states to approach investment treaties with more scrutiny and caution,[75] while also delimiting their exposure to liability through more sophisticated litigation tactics and improved strategies in arbitrator appointment choices.[76] But lack of internal capacity is likely to prevent developing state governments from benefiting from such learning effects to their advantage.

In the rare cases where developing host states have taken active measures to improve internal awareness about their investment treaty commitments, such measures have been aided by international donor organizations,[77] and in some cases private law firms and arbitration bodies.[78] Such was the case, for example, in Peru and Colombia where national regulatory frameworks have been put in place to facilitate the learning about investment treaty law and the prevention of investment arbitration disputes.[79] The question one might ask is whether the involvement of international institutions empowers developing states. While the answer to this question warrants a separate analysis, a preliminary conclusion that can be safely drawn from the empirical data discussed above is that developing states are presently disadvantaged due to their limited capacity to learn from experience as well as from the broader international developments in investment treaty policy and arbitration practice. The crucial shortcoming of the investment treaty regime is that it does not provide for any power-levelling possibilities for weaker states.

---

[74] Haftel and Thompson (n. 9) 29.

[75] Ibid. 30.

[76] Behn, Berge and Langford (n. 73) 365.

[77] This appears to be the case in Kazakhstan where the respondents mentioned UNCTAD and World Bank-sponsored initiatives.

[78] The Georgian case study reveals a growing interest of arbitrators and counsel from international law firms in 'raising awareness' on the ground. See further Section 16.4 below.

[79] For more detail, see Sattorova (n. 61) 80–2.

16.3.4 Lack of Capacity as a Barrier for Effectuating Change in Investment Treaty Practice

Power could also be understood as 'the production, in and through social relations, of effects that shape the capacities of actors to determine their own circumstances and fate'.[80] Historically, the attempts by developing states to shape their own fate through engaging with the international economic order have been fraught with considerable difficulties. Besides political resistance from powerful states, developing countries have frequently found themselves at a disadvantage due to lack of capacity to assert their own stance. Even at a time when investment treaty law is undergoing a significant recalibration – as manifested in the successive changes made to treaty models of developed states – developing countries continue to be minimally involved in the process.[81] With the exception of a few countries that have announced their withdrawal from the investment treaty regime or major modification of their investment treaties,[82] the majority of developing states have so far introduced only minor, if any, changes to their investment treaties.

The empirical data from our case studies points to power inequalities and to limited capacity as a shared concern in interviewees' views about the negotiation, drafting and modification of international investment agreements. These concerns can be grouped into three different categories highlighting distinct forms in which power and capacity can manifest themselves in investment treaty practice.

Lack of negotiating power: Developing states appear to be afflicted by lack of bargaining power to negotiate treaties that serve their interests. Some of the interviewed officials (those directly involved in negotiating and signing investment treaties) reported their concerns about the scope of investment treaty protections and in particular the scope and effects of investment arbitration clauses included in the overwhelming majority of their treaties. Furthermore, an overwhelming number of respondents (those aware of how investment treaty law works) considered the investment arbitration clauses to be inescapable and the treaties containing them immutable. A cross-section of respondents from three countries in

---

[80] Barnett and Duvall (n. 29) 8.

[81] For a critique, see Antonius Hippolyte, 'Aspiring for a Constructive TWAIL approach towards the International Investment Regime', in Schill, Tams and Hofmann (n. 20) 197.

[82] For instance, India, Indonesia and South Africa have announced a radical overhaul of their investment treaties, while Venezuela and Ecuador denounced their investment treaty commitments.

the study expressed their concerns over being unable to depart from the drafts put in front of them by a negotiating developed country partner. For instance, one respondent commented positively on international donor support for designing the country's own model treaty but also pointed to its limited relevance in negotiating with developed states: 'many states have their own models so they often tend to insist on using theirs ... it does not always make sense to insist on our own model'.[83] Another respondent referred to the recently signed investment treaty with Japan: 'some countries, such as Japan, insist on signing a BIT before Japanese companies invest in a big project, and we have to use their model draft'.[84] Two further respondents lamented the futility of even attempting to influence the negotiation of a treaty.[85]

Lack of negotiating capacity: Government officials in developing states tend to be disadvantaged due to inequalities of power in the sense of lack of parity in institutional and human capacity. For instance, an interview with an experienced investment law expert from another state revealed her frustration over lack of financial and informational support to develop a coordinated, inter-agency approach to negotiating investment treaties: 'I am on my own and it takes time to prepare for a negotiation whilst also dealing with numerous other responsibilities.'[86] An officer involved in defending the host state expressed similar concerns over the impact of workload on her inability to pass her knowledge to other relevant agencies involved in signing new and revised investment treaties.[87] Other interviewees again pointed to the frequent rotations as well as the government's inability to provide sufficient material incentives to retain highly trained staff.[88]

Quasi-coercive effect: Although developing countries may not have been *directly* coerced into concluding investment treaties, a number of recent studies reveal that dependence on debt relief and aid rendered them vulnerable to directives emanating from international financial

---

[83] Interviews IDM1 and FIK.

[84] Interview IDM2.

[85] Interviews FIK and MEK2. A similar concern was expressed by a respondent whose role involved expert evaluation of investor–state contracts: 'we cannot ask for a better arbitration clause to be included in a contract in cases where funding for the project comes from an international lender ... we have to accept what they insist on including in the contract' (interview MEK1).

[86] Interview IVJM.

[87] Interview DPSK.

[88] Interviews MJU2, FIK.

institutions. For example, the Multilateral Investment Guarantee Agency (MIGA) and the World Bank took an active part in promoting investment treaties through their exercise of policy-advisory functions, including guidelines proposing the incorporation of specific investment protections in national laws and prompting states to sign investment treaties as part of domestic legal reform.[89] The interviews from our case studies also echo the by now famous scholarly account of how the negotiation of US investment treaties often took the shape of 'an intensive training seminar conducted by the United States, on US terms, on what it would take to comply with the US draft'.[90] While the doctrinal accounts continue to emphasize state consent and formal equality of contracting state parties entering into investment agreements, the empirical data reminds us about crude imposition that may often lie behind the emergence of a new norm.[91]

These findings highlight significant structural impediments that presently hinder the ability of developing state governments to learn from their experience and apply such learning in the process of creation and modification of investment treaty rules. The previous studies have shown that, when it comes to the formation and evolution of investment treaty norms, developing countries often act as rule-takers, rather than rule-makers.[92] For instance, Poulsen highlighted a lack of meaningful participation by developing countries in the drafting and negotiation of their investment treaties.[93] There is ample evidence to show that developing country governments more often than not follow blueprints supplied by their developed country counterparts or advocated by international organizations.[94] Although Poulsen dismisses the idea that developing countries were coerced into signing bilateral investment treaties, his empirical accounts supply numerous examples of developing states accepting the drafts proffered by their developed state co-signatories.[95]

---

[89] Poulsen (n. 21) 76, 79.

[90] Jose Alvarez, 'Remarks' (2012) 86 *ASIL Proceedings* 550, 552.

[91] Andrew Hurrell, 'Power, institutions, and the production of inequality', in Barnett and Duvall (n. 29) 40.

[92] See, for instance, Wolfgang Alschner and Dmitriy Skougarevskiy, 'Rule-takers or Rule-makers? A New Look at African Bilateral Investment Treaty Practice' (2016) 4 *Transnational Dispute Management*.

[93] Poulsen (n. 21) 93, 109. See also Alschner and Skougarevskiy (n. 72) 561, revealing that most of the United Kingdom's IIAs are very similar in content, whereas a developing state such as Burundi is a signatory to treaties that are vastly different in content and scope.

[94] Poulsen (n. 21) 109.

[95] Ibid. 68–79.

522   MAVLUDA SATTOROVA AND OLEKSANDRA VYTIAGANETS

Our empirical findings also resonate with Poulsen's study in the sense that career rotations, high staff turnovers in ministries, and lack of inter-agency coordination appear to militate against the emergence of a sufficiently robust class of national investment treaty negotiators.[96]

What lessons do governments of developing states learn from negotiating investment treaties? As the empirical findings suggest, one such lesson is that international investment law is highly unequal. It is widely acknowledged that 'unequal economic powers among negotiating states will in more cases than not lead to treaty clauses that, though on their surface reciprocal, have in fact been imposed by the economically stronger state'.[97] Existing studies have also shown that as 'rule takers' in investment treaty negotiations, developing states are left with much more diversity and inconsistency among their treaties than developed states whose investment treaties are fairly uniform in content and scope.[98] As a consequence, developing states may be disadvantaged by provisions of the investment treaties they have ratified.[99]

A view commonly shared among many critics of the investment treaty regime is that investment treaties owe their origin to power asymmetries among negotiating parties, with developed states seeking to impose strong investor protection obligations on developing states.[100] What is problematic in our view is that the practice of investment arbitration tends to disregard these inequalities when dealing with investor–state disputes. To many arbitrators, such inequalities are irrelevant and should have no bearing on the issue of state responsibility. As captured in a statement of one eminent practitioner:

> it is no good States complaining afterwards about the results that come out of the application of their treaties if they negotiated bad treaties in the first place. The responsibility for what goes into the text of a treaty is that of the negotiating parties and if, for example, a State decides to accept a

---

[96] Ibid. 195: 'Frequent rotation of developing country bureaucrats is common, and it undermines their ability to gain sufficient knowledge of the intricacies and complexities of investment treaty arbitration.'

[97] Jorun Baumgartner, *Treaty Shopping in International Investment Law* (Oxford University Press, 2016) 37.

[98] Behn, Berge and Langford (n. 73) 346; see further Alschner and Skougarevskiy (n. 72) 561, providing the example that most of the United Kingdom's (UK) investment treaties are very similar in content, while the majority of Burundi's investment treaties are vastly different and divergent in content and scope.

[99] Behn, Berge and Langford (n. 73) 346.

[100] Emma Aisbett et al., *Rethinking International Investment Governance: Principles for the 21st Century* (2018) 25.

LEARNING FROM INVESTMENT LAW

particular clause proposed to it in a treaty without discussion, that is
something which has its consequences – namely, that the clause will be
interpreted and applied in accordance with its terms. A central purpose of
international law is to protect the sanctity of treaties and treaties must be
taken to mean what they say.[101]

One might argue that analysis of power inequalities may indeed be
outside the scope of legal doctrinal analysis used in determining the
validity of treaty provisions.[102] However, a growing recognition of the
inequalities in the making and changing of international investment law
also highlights the importance of engaging in a moral and policy analysis
to address the existing asymmetries. As a species of global governance,
the investment treaty regime 'rests on material capabilities and knowledge, without which there is no governance, and legitimacy and fairness,
without which there is no moral governance'.[103] Legitimacy of investment treaty law is currently compromised by its limited capacity to
counterbalance acts of the powerful actors, such as developed country
negotiators and international lending institutions.

By casting light on the inherent power and capacity asymmetries
underpinning the investment treaty regime, insights from the empirical
case studies also invite us to re-evaluate some of the conventional explanations of a variation in the content and scope of the treaties signed by
developing states. The majority of prevailing conceptualizations of
investment treaty design are based on the so-called credible commitment
premise: since many developing states seeking inward investment cannot
credibly commit ex ante to respecting such investment over the long term
(e.g. due to weak governance and other related factors), investors tend to
be reluctant to invest in such countries (owing to poor governance track
record).[104] Investment treaties arguably address the lack of credibility
problem by encapsulating strong (and credible) procedural and substantive protections which investors could enforce in cases where the

---

[101] Franklin Berman, 'Evolution or Revolution?' in Chester Brown and Kate Miles (eds.),
Evolution in Investment Treaty Law and Arbitration (Cambridge University Press,
2011) 658, 670.
[102] Baumgartner (n. 97) 37.
[103] Adler and Bernstein (n. 30) 294.
[104] Todd Allee and Clint Peinhardt, 'Evaluating Three Explanations for the Design of
Bilateral Investment Treaties' (2014) 66(1) *World Politics* 47, 58; see also Alan Sykes,
'Public Versus Private Enforcement of International Economic Law: Standing and
Remedy' (2005) 34 *Journal of Legal Studies* 631, 644.

government reneges on its promise made at the time an investment was made.[105]

Yet the credible commitment rationale does not explain the variety in design of treaties signed, for instance, by Kyrgyzstan. Do its treaties with various state parties vary because the successive Kyrgyz governments have tied their own hands the tightest by including the strongest investment protections in a deliberate and self-interested manoeuvre to attract more inward foreign investment? Or can the variation be explained by the signatory developed government's insistence on stronger investment protections as well as a greater relative ability of the developed states to achieve the desired negotiation outcomes – regardless of the credibility of host state partners?[106] Empirical evidence suggests it is the latter. The interview responses show that, unlike in multilateral settings, in bilateral treaty negotiations a developing country such as Kyrgyzstan is less likely to be able to counterbalance the superior power of a more economically powerful party such as Japan. As Garcia observed in his critique of the the historically asymmetric nature of investment treaty negotiations, 'bilateral negotiations maximize leverage on the part of the more powerful partner, resulting in agreements that are unbalanced in terms of the ultimate negotiated concessions ... individual host states face serious collective action problems in presenting a united front in terms of negotiation positions and investment policy frameworks'.[107] These power disparities need to be addressed, yet the recent reform agenda does little to acknowledge the problem.

16.4   How Not to Build Capacity: Inadequacy of Existing Approaches to Power Inequalities

A pertinent question is whether a different normative and institutional framework is warranted to help tackle the existing power asymmetries and to enable the emergence of investment treaties reflecting the needs and preferences of developing state signatories to a greater extent than they do now. Yet, despite the growing salience of issues relating to

---

[105] Allee and Peinhardt, ibid. 59.

[106] Ibid.

[107] See also Frank J. Garcia, *Global Justice and International Economic Law: Three Takes* (Cambridge University Press, 2014) 240–51, also Zeng Huaqun, 'Balance, Sustainable Development and Integration: Innovative Path for BIT Practice' (2014) 17 *Journal of International Economic Law* 299.

developing countries' capacity to meaningfully learn about the precepts of international investment law and to internalize such precepts, so as to partake meaningfully in the contestation and innovation of the relevant norms, capacity building and its role in the ongoing investment law reform globally still retains a relatively marginal space in investment treaty scholarship and the agenda of key international actors.[108]

Even those who have recently welcomed reform efforts that help states build the capacity seem to place responsibility squarely on the shoulders of developing states. For instance, Sharpe correctly notes 'the legitimacy (and utility) of the system rests in part upon states' ability to understand and comply with their legal obligations, effectively defend against investor claims, and keep the law on a sensible track'.[109] Yet, he also suggests 'that every state active in investment arbitration needs to take steps to closely monitor investment disputes; to participate actively as a respondent state; to intervene where appropriate as a non-disputing party; and to adapt its investment treaty negotiations to reflect fast-changing developments in international arbitration'.[110] Furthermore, while acknowledging the need for capacity building, this view not only somewhat obscures the nature of developing states' participation in investor–state arbitration, but it also hints at developing states' responsibility to create and maintain effective mechanisms for managing and preventing investment disputes. Given the significant costs associated with the creation of internal dispute monitoring and management mechanisms, as well as weaknesses in the domestic legal and bureaucratic culture and lack of human and institutional capacity, host governments are frequently unable to effectively prevent their exposure to investment arbitration awards and expensive settlements. Crucially, such lack of capacity is not taken into consideration either by arbitrators in the process of determining state responsibility in investor–state disputes or by policy-makers in the process of drafting and negotiating new and revised investment treaties.

---

[108] For instance, reports from the meetings of the UNCITRAL Working Group III on the Reform of Investor–State Dispute Settlement highlight the narrow mandate of the group. See further Malcolm Langford and Anthea Roberts, 'UNCITRAL and ISDS Reforms: Hastening slowly', *EJIL: Talk!* 29 April 2019.

[109] Jeremy K. Sharpe, 'Control, Capacity, and Legitimacy in Investment Treaty Arbitration' (2018) 112 *American Journal of International Law Unbound* 261, 265.

[110] Ibid.

The empirical insights presented in this chapter shed an important light on this subject, in particular by exposing the pitfalls and shortcomings of capacity building initiatives to which developing countries have been exposed in recent years. When queried about the ways awareness is generated and capacity built on the subject of international investment law, one interview respondent pointed, with a degree of pride, to conferences regularly held with government stakeholders and led by 'the sharks of international arbitration community'.[111] Yet, whilst being apparently awe-inspiring for some, the involvement of counsel from leading law firms in the delivery of capacity-building initiatives can also be received with considerable mistrust and the corresponding reluctance to engage by government officials. While commenting on the dire need for experts in investment treaty law and the government's lack of resources to build internal capacity, one of our respondents deplored the prevalence of international legal counsel in delivering the externally sponsored training and capacity-building programmes: '[h]ow can I possibly ask important legal questions and express my views if the expert delivering the training is a lawyer well-known for his involvement in investment arbitration cases and representing investor-claimants? ... Anything I say might be used against my government in a future case with the same lawyer representing an investor'.[112] A number of respondents concurred in expressing mistrust towards externally driven capacity-building initiatives, highlighting the importance of addressing the conflict of interest issues and its negative impact on the emerging efforts to address the lacunae in local knowledge and expertise.

Last but not least, the interviews overwhelmingly suggest that any efforts to create and nurture local capacity are likely to be significantly hampered by the preponderant deference to foreign experts in the design and delivery of training programmes and initiatives. The interviews in Georgia, Kazakhstan, Kyrgyzstan and Ukraine all highlight a tendency for foreign lawyers to be presented as possessing superior (and insuperable) knowledge and expertise. An example of such tendency can be found in the reported avowal by the respective governments to appoint foreign experts as judges and arbiters at the newly sprouting national quasi-judicial bodies for resolving investment disputes. As one respondent explained, 'the emphasis is on the brand' and 'foreign experience' of

---

[111] Interview JMN.
[112] Interview DPSK.

the appointee.[113] By entrenching a belief in superiority and effectiveness of foreign experts, the capacity-building initiatives of such nature are unlikely to meaningfully support the building of domestic capacity. Instead, they are likely to have an emasculating effect on national actors and institutions, hindering the emergence of local cadre and expertise. Emerging empirical data also shows that, owing to the by now established tradition of legal reforms being externally initiated, staffed and sponsored, there is a pervasive sense of dependence on an external 'helping hand', and a growing sense of indispensability of external, foreign expertise.[114]

These findings echo the critiques familiar to law and development scholars. Legal capacity-building reforms in developing countries have long been criticized for being driven less by the aim to ensure the welfare of their citizenry and more by the desire 'to create new ties with the West' – as 'an affirmation of Western knowledge, legal theory and practice'.[115] It has been acknowledged that Western legal advisers were not only in an intense competition with one another and strove for 'supremacy' in host states, but they also paid little attention to participation of the people in their own government.[116] Donor-driven legal technical assistance projects were condemned for privileging foreign experts.[117] Recent reform initiatives, including the meetings of the UNCITRAL Working Group III on investor–state dispute settlement (ISDS), reveal a similar lack of action to ensure genuine inclusivity: while a number of developing states were for the first time invited to present their views on the future of investment arbitration, the presence of numerous delegations from the global South 'does not mean that all of them are likely to be actively involved in the formulation of reforms and compromise deals'.[118] As commentators have rightly noted, well-resourced delegations are likely to benefit from the working group

---

[113] Interview AFM1.

[114] See further Sattorova (n. 61) 86–7.

[115] J. J. Deppe, 'Comments on Lawmaking and Legal Reforms in Central Asia', in Arnscheidt, Rooij and Otto (eds.), *Lawmaking for Development: Explorations into the Theory and Practice of International Legislative Projects* (Leiden University Press, 2008) 220–1.

[116] Ibid. 228.

[117] Scott Newton, 'Law and Development, Law and Economics and the Fate of Legal Technical Assistance', in Arnscheidt, Rooij and Otto (n. 115) 27.

[118] Anthea Roberts and Taylor St John, 'UNCITRAL and ISDS Reforms: The Divided West and the Battle by and for the Rest', *EJIL: Talk!* 30 April 2019.

meetings more than their counterparts of developing states, the latter being frequently represented by officers from the local embassy rather than experts from the relevant agency.[119]

Some international actors have been increasingly expanding their policy portfolios to include capacity building regionally and locally,[120] and such initiatives – coupled with greater oversight by and involvement of civil society – might help redress power asymmetries that are currently preventing developing states from influencing investment treaty designs. However, as transpires from the studies of a wider field of international economic policy, developing states are often left to the mercies of transnational civil society and international organizations. Although their input in redressing the lack of capacity in the global South through training and technical assistance can be invaluable, the ultimate long-term effects can be questionable, not least because of the role of powerful developed economies in funding civil society groups and influencing the agenda of international organizations.[121] Furthermore, as the insights from our case studies suggest, assisting developing states with ready-made treaty blueprints – however sophisticated – is clearly not enough. To enable a more meaningful participation by developing countries in the making of investment treaty law, and thus enhance legitimacy and credibility of the latter, we need to look into ways to encourage the shaping of nationally felt approaches, facilitated by greater awareness and sustained home-grown legal and policy capacity within such countries. Unless the currently prevailing approaches to legal capacity building are overhauled and re-imagined, the international investment law regime and its epistemic communities are unlikely to be able to generate positive governance spill-overs for host communities in developing states. If inequalities of power and capacity remain ignored in the ongoing reform efforts, the regime and its 'agents of change' will

---

[119] Ibid.

[120] See, for instance, an overview of UNCTAD capacity building programmes: 'International Investment Agreements: Benefiting from Investment Agreements for Development', <unctad.org/en/PublicationChapters/tc2015d1rev1_S03_P09.pdf>. Of note is the fact that since recently capacity building on investment treaty law has also been sponsored by the World Health Organization. See e.g. World Health Organization, 'Key Considerations for the Use of Law to Prevent Noncommunicable Diseases in the WHO European Region', Report of an intensive legal training and capacity-building workshop on law and noncommunicable diseases, Moscow, 30 May–3 June 2016, <euro .who.int/__data/assets/pdf_file/0009/333954/Moscow-report.pdf>.

[121] Adler and Bernstein (n. 30) 315.

16.5 Conclusion

Legitimacy rests 'on the degree to which the structures of global governance are contaminated by preferences and special interests of the powerful'.[122] By drawing on new empirical data and situating it within the emergent body of qualitative scholarship on state learning in investment treaty law, this chapter has sought to unveil an array of structural, normative and institutional power inequalities that bear upon developing states' participation in the investment treaty regime. While our empirical findings may not be truly representative of all the reality in the global South, they nevertheless bring to the fore important elements of everyday experiences of some developing states, enabling us to raise new and more nuanced questions about the legitimacy of the investment treaty regime. The two crucial aspects of the emerging picture are: (1) the pervasive deficits of capacity on the part of developing states to acquire, process and utilize information about investment treaties so as to ensure such treaties better serve their needs; and (2) the absence of any power-levelling possibilities for weaker states within the normative and institutional frameworks governing investment treaty practice and arbitration.

Power inequalities 'need active policies, not merely time, to be solved'.[123] Interrogating the inequalities of power and unmasking the role of investment treaty law and investment arbitration in entrenching them is particularly important at a time when investment treaties are undergoing a dramatic overhaul as part of what appears to be a global move towards a different, more legitimate international investment governance. It is telling that the very process of investment treaty reform has so far been largely driven by the growing dissatisfaction by developed states with being drawn into investment disputes in a respondent capacity. Major developed economies have been altering the content of their treaties to 'to avoid outcomes that contradict their interests'.[124] At the

---

[122] Hurrell (n. 91) 56.

[123] Erin Hannah, Holly Ryan and James Scott, 'Power, Knowledge and Resistance: Between Co-optation and Revolution in Global Trade' (2017) 24 *Review of International Political Economy* 757.

[124] Manger and Peinhardt (n. 18) 920.

opposite end of the spectrum there is a new generation of investment treaty models adopted by developing countries, as exemplified by the international investment agreement between Nigeria and Morocco and the Investment Agreement for the COMESA Common Investment Area, both of which feature provisions that seek to mitigate, albeit tentatively, the burden of responsibilities and obligations on developing host states. However, said agreements have so far been signed only between developing countries. The extent to which the newly emerging drafting patterns from the global North would reflect the interests of the global South is open to question. To paraphrase Anghie: even when it innovates, investment treaty law follows the familiar pattern of the division between the developed and the developing, a division it seeks to define and maintain 'using extraordinarily flexible and continuously new techniques'.[125] The process of shaping international investment norms is where international law is at its most helpless – 'unable to constrain a powerful state on its own'.[126] Investment treaty reform so far does little to address the impact of economic and political power disparities between developing and developed states.[127] A meaningful transformation of international investment law and its dispute settlement mechanisms requires acknowledging and addressing power inequalities in negotiating the norms constituting a global investment treaty regime.

[125] Antony Anghie, *Imperialism, Sovereignty and International Law* (Cambridge University Press, 2007) 244.

[126] Nico Krisch, 'International Law in Times of Hegemony: Unequal Power and the Shaping of the International Legal Order' (2005) 16 *European Journal of International Law* 369, 370.

[127] With the exception of proposals to establish an advisory centre, see e.g. Eric Gottwald, 'Levelling the Playing Field: Is It Time for a Legal Assistance Center for Developing Nations in Investment Treaty Arbitration?' (2007) 22 *American University International Law Review* 237; see also Robert W. Schwieder, 'Legal Aid and Investment Treaty Disputes: Lessons Learned from the Advisory Centre on WTO Law and Investment Experiences' (2018) 19 *Journal of World Investment and Trade* 628.

17

Legitimation through Modification: Do States Seek More Regulatory Space in Their Investment Agreements?

TOMER BROUDE*, YORAM Z. HAFTEL** AND
ALEXANDER THOMPSON***

17.1 Introduction

Dissatisfaction with the global investment regime (henceforth: the Regime) is on the rise, leading to shifts in treaty-based investment protection policies and attempts by some governments to extricate themselves from the system. Much of this backlash has focused on the impact of binding arbitration, specifically the investor–state dispute settlement (ISDS) provisions found in most bilateral investment treaties (BITs) and other investment agreements.[1] Critics complain that arbitrators produce

---

* Professor and Bessie & Michael Greenblatt, Q.C., Chair in Public and International Law, Faculty of Law and Department of International Relations, Hebrew University of Jerusalem.
** Professor and Giancarlo Elia Valori Chair in the Study of Peace and Regional Cooperation at the Department of International Relations, Hebrew University of Jerusalem.
*** Professor of Political Science and Senior Faculty Fellow of the Mershon Center for International Security Studies at Ohio State University.
  The authors' names appear in random order and indicate equal authorship. This research was supported by a Marie Curie FP7 Integration Grant within the 7th European Union Framework Programme and an Israel Science Foundation research grant (1117/17). The authors are grateful for comments received from presentations at the University of Oslo, the University of Virginia, the Hebrew University of Jerusalem, the University of California, Los Angeles, the University of Arizona, Freie Universität Berlin, King's College London; and individually from Anne van Aaken, Jürgen Kurtz and the editors of this volume. We also thank Elisabeth Tuerk and UNCTAD for kindly sharing and assisting with their Mapping Guide. Yulia Arport, Or Avrahami, Alex Fischer, Moshe Goldman, Lea Gutowicz, Avigaelle Halevy-Goetschel, Liza Holodovsky, Morr Link, Shirley Lukin, Maayan Morali and Keren Sasson provided valuable research assistance. Any errors are solely those of the authors.
[1] Michael Waibel et al. (eds.), *The Backlash Against Investment Arbitration: Perceptions and Reality* (Wolters Kluwer, 2010).

inconsistent and conflicting decisions, or worse, that they are biased towards the interests of investors and interpret treaty provisions in ways that constrain host governments excessively. This has provoked concerns of a 'legitimacy crisis' in investment arbitration and calls for reform to establish more regulatory space for host states, especially in the areas of economic and social policy.[2]

We explore how states have reacted to their experiences with the Regime, and to the controversy surrounding investment arbitration, by analysing the content of international investment agreements (IIAs) over time. If certain aspects of IIAs are deemed undesirable or even illegitimate, this should be reflected in changes to the content of IIAs over time. In particular, if ISDS is increasingly and widely viewed as politically unpopular and an impingement on state sovereignty, we should see a systematic effort by states to address these concerns when they negotiate new treaties and when they modify their existing treaty obligations. Using an original dataset on the degree of state regulatory space (SRS) reflected in IIA provisions, we investigate whether these patterns are indeed evident in the design of provisions related to ISDS. Focusing on such provisions is especially valuable because they relate directly to the legitimacy debate and because the rules governing investor–state arbitration shape the legal consequences of all substantive obligations, thus they have a direct and profound effect on the balance between investor rights and SRS.

The emphasis of this chapter is on the formal treaty rules that govern ISDS, not on arbitration practice or on the identification of the arbitrators themselves. In terms of the introductory chapter to this volume,[3] we are interested in a key aspect of 'process' legitimacy: the process for establishing and changing the rules. If the underlying rules lack legitimacy, there is little hope that arbitration itself will produce substantive outcomes that are deemed legitimate. The relevant actors for us are governments of host states (where investments are located) and home states (where the senders of such investment are located). Governments are in a position to accept, reject or amend IIA provisions

---

[2] Susan D. Franck, 'The Legitimacy Crisis in Investment Treaty Arbitration: Privatizing Public International Law through Inconsistent Decisions' (2005) 73(4) *Fordham Law Review* 1521; UNCTAD, *Investment Policy Framework for Sustainable Development* (United Nations, 2012).

[3] See also Daniel Behn, Ole Kristian Fauchald and Malcolm Langford, 'How to Approach "Legitimacy"', *PluriCourts Investment, Internal Working Paper* 1/2015, <jus.uio.no/plur icourts/english/topics/investment/documents/1-2015-legitimacy-book-project.pdf>.

and their participation is absolutely necessary to maintain the viability of the Regime.

Our empirical analysis of SRS looks at the evolution of IIAs from four different perspectives. First, we look at trends over time in average levels of SRS across the landscape of IIAs. Second, we look at the content of 'model BITs' that many states use to guide negotiations and that reflect their prevailing policy preferences. Third, we address the revealing phenomenon of treaty renegotiation to see how states alter their ISDS provisions when they choose to revise existing IIAs. Finally, we look at the practice of treaty termination and its relationship to concerns over ISDS. In each of these cases, the analysis is used to shed light on whether, when and how states adjust their treaties to address concerns over regulatory space. We find that, since the late 2000s, states have used these policy tools systematically to increase levels of SRS and to rebalance ISDS provisions in a way that favours host states. At the same time, it appears that IIA termination is still not widespread and that most states prefer to adjust their international obligations through new or renegotiated IIAs rather than to scrap them. Thus, even if the Regime's crisis of legitimacy is indeed reflected in the changing content of IIAs, current developments point to a process of gradual adjustment rather than a sharp break from the existing rules or wholesale rejection of the Regime.

The remainder of this chapter proceeds as follows. In Section 17.2 we introduce the concept of state regulatory space and explain how we measure it in the context of ISDS provisions. In Section 17.3 we present our data analysis, looking at trends in signed IIAs, model BITs, renegotiated IIAs and terminated IIAs. Section 17.4 concludes, with forward-looking thoughts on the implications of the empirical analysis for the legitimacy of the international investment arbitration system.

17.2   Capturing State Regulatory Space in Treaty Design

A comparison of treaty texts can cast light on governments' perspectives regarding their legal obligations. While the intentions of policy-makers and negotiators are not always discernable, the content of agreements, as a 'revealed preference', provides an indirect measure of the interests motivating them. In this section, we elaborate on our approach to capturing and comparing IIA content, which is grounded in the concept of SRS. We utilize a measure based on this concept to explore how states have designed and adjusted the level of SRS in ISDS provisions, a measure we label *SRS ISDS*. Changes in *SRS ISDS* can be used to gauge

534 TOMER BROUDE ET AL.

the level of concern states have with respect to the impact of ISDS on their regulatory autonomy.

SRS refers to the extent of the ability of governments to freely legislate and implement regulations in given public policy domains.[4] Thinking of SRS as a continuum, at one extreme states have a great deal of flexibility to pursue policies they see fit, and are thus insulated from external pressure or influence attempts (in the present context, pressure from foreign investors utilizing ISDS). At the other extreme, governments have little room to manoeuvre and are highly constrained by the ability of foreign investors to challenge their policies under IIAs and ISDS, even if they are not challenged in practice or even if actual challenges are ultimately unsuccessful (a phenomenon sometimes labelled 'regulatory chill').[5] The flipside of lower regulatory space is often better treatment and greater protection of foreign investors,[6] but this is not necessarily the case and we make no distinct claims in this respect. We also do not view more or less SRS as inherently more legitimate. Our sole interest here is in capturing and understanding governmental positions on *SRS ISDS* as reflected in their international treaties.

To measure SRS, we build on UNCTAD's IIA Mapping Project (henceforth IIAMP).[7] This scheme examines the most important substantive and procedural provisions of IIAs and codes them on the inclusion or exclusion of various elements. The IIAMP was designed for comparative purposes, not with SRS in mind; indeed, it can be used for a variety of comparative research goals. As we explain later, in some parts of the analysis we used UNCTAD's own coding, but in others we coded treaties ourselves, based on the IIAMP codebook. Either way, we transformed the coding in various selected categories into measures that indicate, in our estimation, more or less SRS. While we have done this for

[4] We thus use the term regulation broadly to mean 'rules issued for the purpose of controlling the manner in which private and public enterprises conduct their operations': see Giandomenico Majone, *Regulating Europe* (Routledge, 1996), 9.

[5] Lorenzo Cotula, 'Do Investment Treaties Unduly Constrain Regulatory Space?' (2014) 9 *Questions of International Law* 19; Stephan W. Schill, 'Do Investment Treaties Chill Unilateral State Regulation to Mitigate Climate Change?' (2007) 24(5) *Journal of International Arbitration* 469.

[6] Suzzane A. Spears, 'The Quest for Policy Space in a New Generation of International Investment Agreements' (2010) 13(4) *Journal of International Economic Law* 1037; Daniel J. Blake, 'Thinking Ahead: Time Horizons and the Legalization of International Investment Agreements' (2013) 67(4) *International Organization* 797.

[7] See UNCTAD IIA Mapping Project, <https://investmentpolicy.unctad.org/international-investment-agreements/iia-mapping>.

LEGITIMATION THROUGH MODIFICATION

the entire coding scheme, in this chapter we present only data related to ISDS provisions.

ISDS provisions are important because they give the rest of the legal obligations 'teeth', they have elicited so much debate among practitioners and politicians, and they exhibit substantial and consequential variation.[8] To be sure, we are fully aware that ISDS procedures should not, ideally, be detached from substantive investment law. States' positions on ISDS, as a procedural matter, may be affected by the content of their substantive commitments and changes in them. No less importantly, however, they do provide us with information on how states view ISDS as a method of settling investment disputes, arguably the most politically contentious aspect of the Regime.

Employing the IIAMP as a point of departure, we have classified ISDS provisions in nine categories that are related to SRS, listed in Table 17.1 and described immediately below.[9] The coding of each category ranges from zero (0), for limited SRS (less policy space), to one (1), for a greater extent of SRS (more policy space). In this context, along the spectrum of SRS, treaties with no ISDS at all score one in each category. The cumulative measure is then standardized to vary from zero to one, with each of the nine categories weighted equally.[10] Thus, the maximum value of *SRS ISDS* is one, reflecting the lowest impact of IIAs upon policy space. In contrast, IIAs that include ISDS with no qualifications or limitations on the capacity of foreign investors to file investment claims score zero, the highest degree of IIA constraints on SRS. Below is a description of the nine categories and a justification of our coding choices. Some categories are 'ordinal' in that the value of SRS is determined according to whether one or more thresholds have been met. Other categories are 'cumulative' in that the SRS value is determined by the presence of multiple provisions, which are added together to determine the value.

---

[8] Todd Allee and Clint Peinhardt, 'Delegating Differences: Bilateral Investment Treaties and Bargaining over Dispute Resolution Provisions' (2010) 54(1) *International Studies Quarterly* 1; Joachim Pohl, Kekeletso Mashigo and Alexis Nohen, 'Dispute Settlement Provisions in International Investment Agreements: A Large Sample Survey', *OECD Working Papers on International Investment* 2012/02, <dx.doi.org/10.1787/5k8xb71nf628-en>.

[9] We have not included reference to state-to-state dispute settlement under IIAs, given the rarity of such procedures and their distinct political and legal implications.

[10] One might argue that the categories should be weighted differently. We address this concern, both conceptually and methodologically, elsewhere: see Alexander Thompson, Tomer Broude and Yoram Z. Haftel, 'Once Bitten, Twice Shy? Investment Disputes, State Sovereignty and Change in Treaty Design' (2019) 73 *International Organization* 859.

536 TOMER BROUDE ET AL.

Table 17.1 *Categories and values of SRS ISDS*

Category	Type	Indicator	Value
Alternatives to arbitration	Ordinal	No clause (compulsory ISDS)	0
		Voluntary recourse to alternatives	0.25
		Mandatory recourse to alternatives	0.75
		No ISDS	1
Scope of claims	Ordinal	Any dispute relating to investment	0
		Listing specific basis of claim beyond treaty	0.33
		Limited to treaty claims	0.66
		No ISDS	1
Limitation on provisions subject to ISDS	Ordinal	No limitations	0
		Limitation of provisions subject to ISDS	0.75
		No ISDS	1
Limitation on scope of ISDS	Cumulative	Exclusion of policy areas from ISDS	0.33
		Special mechanism for taxation or prudential measures	0.33
		No ISDS	1
Type of consent to arbitration	Ordinal	Expressed or implied consent	0
		Case-by-case consent or no ISDS	1
Forum selection: domestic courts	Ordinal	No mention of domestic courts or investor's choice	0
		Domestic court a pre-condition for ISDS	0.5
		No ISDS	1
Particular features of ISDS	Cumulative	Limitation period	0.25
		Provisional measures	0.25
		Limited remedies	0.25
		No ISDS	1
Interpretation	Cumulative	Binding interpretation	0.25
		Renvoi	0.25
		Rights of non-disputing contracting party	0.25
		No ISDS	1
Transparency in arbitral proceedings	Cumulative	Making documents publicly available	0.25
		Making hearings publicly available	0.25
		Amicus curiae	0.25
		No ISDS	1

1 *Alternatives to Arbitration* – ordinal: even in the shadow of binding investment arbitration, parties always have the option to choose alternative (non-arbitral) dispute resolution procedures, such as conciliation or mediation. There is, however, a qualitative difference between: (1) IIAs in which such procedures are a mandatory requirement before turning to international arbitration, in which case states have greater opportunity to defend regulatory policies in the face of investor complaints; (2) IIAs in which such procedures are not mandatory but explicitly noted as preferable or otherwise desirable; and (3) IIAs in which such procedures are not mentioned at all. We consider the first option as most conducive to SRS (other than no ISDS at all), with some difference between the second and third alternatives.

2 *Scope of ISDS Claims* – ordinal: jurisdiction of ISDS under IIAs varies from the very broad (any dispute relating to investment), through specifically enumerated non-treaty bases of jurisdiction (e.g. contract claims), to strict limitation to treaty-based claims, and, ultimately, no ISDS at all (least SRS-restrictive). We consider broader jurisdiction to be more restrictive of SRS and narrower scope to be less restrictive.

3 *Limitations on ISDS Scope – Limited provisions subject to ISDS* – ordinal: some IIAs delimit the scope of the provisions that may be subject to ISDS, either by prescription or by exclusion. IIAs that do not include any such limitations are potentially the most restrictive of SRS. IIAs that prescribe some substantive provisions as bases for ISDS are less SRS restrictive. IIAs that restrict ISDS to very particular areas (such as the calculation of monetary compensation) are least SRS restrictive, other than IIAs that do not include ISDS at all.

4 *Limitations on ISDS Scope – Exclusion of Policy Areas from ISDS* – cumulative: some IIAs exclude defined policy areas from ISDS coverage with the effect of preserving SRS. Such exclusions come in two broad forms: they may relate to particular sectors or issues (e.g. security), or they may provide special mechanisms for taxation or prudential concerns.[11] We assess such exclusions cumulatively and give equal weight to each of these two categories. This is for measurement purposes only and should not be construed as reflecting the relative normative importance of such exclusions.

---

[11] Some IIAs include more general exceptions related to sensitive sectors and policy areas. They are more relevant to SRS in substantive provisions and are therefore not discussed here. See ibid. for more detail.

5 *Type of Consent to ISDS* – ordinal: where consent to ISDS is expressed or implied to the point of automaticity, state exposure to investment arbitration (and hence SRS restriction) is maximal. Where case-by-case consent or future consent is required, we assess a much lower degree of SRS restriction, tantamount to an absence of ISDS.

6 *ISDS Rules – Forum Selection (Domestic Courts)* – ordinal: where the default dispute settlement procedure is international arbitration, or where investors have an explicit option to prefer it, we presume that SRS is potentially and more significantly restrained, in comparison to a requirement to start with domestic courts before pursuing international arbitration.

7 *Particular Features of ISDS* – cumulative: we consider three particular features of ISDS included in the IIAMP as relevant to SRS. Where investment claims are restricted in time through a type of statute of limitations, SRS is less restricted. Likewise, when provisional measures are not entertained, and when ultimate remedies are restricted to those specifically enumerated in the agreement.

8 *Interpretation* – cumulative: some IIAs authorize parties to be pro-actively involved in the interpretation of IIA provisions, in ways that may expand SRS. Some IIAs allow parties to issue a joint interpretative guidance that may be binding upon arbitral tribunals addressing issues under the same treaty. Other treaties refer certain questions to inter-pretation by the parties as *renvoi*, or permit interpretative interven-tions by parties to the IIA that are not the respondent party. We consider these cumulatively, with every opportunity that IIA parties have to influence the interpretation of their obligations considered as enhancing SRS.

9 *Transparency in Arbitral Proceedings* – cumulative: arbitral proceed-ings under IIAs are usually not transparent to the public, with closed written and oral proceedings, and an absence of public interventions in the form of *amicus curiae* briefs. We take the view that such lack of transparency constrains SRS, primarily by making state regulation more susceptible to adverse international arbitral intervention. Thus, we cumulatively reduce the SRS rating of an IIA according to the existence of open written pleadings, oral hearings or *amicus* briefs.

17.3 The Changing Landscape of IIAs and Their Content

To understand how the IIA regime has evolved in response to its legitimacy crisis, in this section we examine several key trends in the design of ISDS provisions. We conduct this exercise using a large sample of IIAs as well as national treaty templates, commonly known as 'model BITs'. We begin by analysing trends over time in levels of *SRS ISDS* in all signed treaties, followed by a look at model BITs. Next, we zero in on the phenomenon of IIA renegotiation and ask how SRS has changed from the original to the renegotiated treaties. Finally, we look at the recent trend of IIA terminations.

The picture that emerges from the analysis is rather consistent: since the late 2000s, states have designed model BITs and concluded IIAs with greater *SRS ISDS*. They have also increased *SRS ISDS* when they renegotiated, and, of course, terminated their IIAs.[12] At the same time, it appears that IIA termination is still not widespread and that most states prefer to adjust their international obligations through new or renegotiated IIAs rather than abrogate them. Thus, even if the Regime's crisis of legitimacy is indeed reflected in the changing content of IIAs, current developments point to a process of gradual adjustment rather than a sharp break from the existing rules.

17.3.1   SRS ISDS *in Signed IIAs*

With our measure of *SRS ISDS* in hand, we first examine trends in a large sample of IIAs. The data set includes 2,785 IIAs from 1959, the year in which the first BIT was signed, to 2016, the most recent year for which information on treaty design is available.[13] The coding of most IIAs relies on UNCTAD's records and mapping, which was made public in 2017. After obtaining it from UNCTAD, we transformed the raw data into SRS, according to the procedure described above. UNCTAD's data base has 2,572 mapped IIAs available. To those, we added 213 IIAs we coded ourselves in related projects[14] for a total of 2,785 IIAs.

Figure 17.1 charts the average annual *SRS ISDS* from 1959 to 2016. It suggests that different time periods are associated with distinct

---

[12] In addition, states have also signed and ratified far fewer IIAs in the 2010s, compared to the two previous decades. This trend is well documented in UNCTAD periodical reports (see e.g. UNCTAD, *Investment Policy Monitor* (2018) No. 20 (December)), so we do not elaborate on this matter here.

[13] This is out of 3,324 IIAs in existence by the end of 2016, according to UNCTAD's *World Investment Report*.

[14] Tomer Broude, Yoram Z. Haftel and Alexander Thompson, 'The Trans-Pacific Partnership and Regulatory Space: A Comparison of Treaty Texts' (2017) 20(2) *Journal of International Economic Law* 391; Thompson, Broude and Haftel (n. 10).

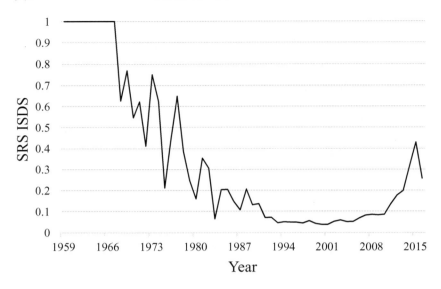

Figure 17.1 Average annual SRS ISDS in 2,785 IIAs, 1959–2016

approaches to ISDS provisions. The marked divergence between these periods points to four 'waves' in the development of the Regime, thereby substantiating previous studies that document similar patterns.[15] Specifically, it illustrates the reality that the early BITs, most of them signed by Western European countries such as Germany, France and Switzerland, did not include any reference to ISDS (although they did have state-to-state dispute settlement). These treaties, most of them signed in the 1960s, did not provide foreign investors with access to binding international investment arbitration, thereby minimizing the exposure of host states to associated risks. In the 1970s and the 1980s, ISDS provisions become more common, but many of them were limited in scope.[16] Communist countries, such as Romania, the Soviet Union and China, in particular, concluded BITs with binding ISDS only with respect

---

[15] Srividya Jandhyala, Witold J. Henisz and Edward D. Mansfield, 'Three Waves of BITs: The Global Diffusion of Foreign Investment Policy' (2011) 55(6) *Journal of Conflict Resolution* 1047; Lauge Skovgaard Poulsen and Emma Aisbett, 'When the Claim Hits: Bilateral Investment Treaties and Bounded Rational Learning' (2013) 65(2) *World Politics* 273.

[16] The first BIT to include ISDS was signed between the Netherlands and Indonesia in 1968.

to the amount of compensation. Overall, we see significant variation over the years but a steady decline in *SRS ISDS* during this period.

The third time period runs from the early 1990s to the mid 2000s, and largely corresponds to the building stage of the 'legitimacy crisis' identified by the Editors of this volume. During this decade-and-a-half, IIAs became ubiquitous, with many hundreds of new BITs signed by almost all countries around the world. As Figure 17.1 makes clear, this generation of treaties is characterized by broad ISDS provisions that offer foreign investors a rather unrestricted access to arbitration, thereby leaving host countries with very limited regulatory space. Finally, in the fourth period, one begins to observe increasing levels of *SRS ISDS*. Responding to the growing number and significance of investment claims, governments begin to seek ISDS provisions with greater SRS.[17] The rise in SRS is especially notable from the early 2010s and peaks in 2015 with an average *SRS ISDS* value of 0.43, compared to 0.038 in 2000, the year with the lowest value on this measure. Thus, the average value of *SRS ISDS* increased more than tenfold in fifteen years. This is a dramatic increase, to be sure, although SRS has not returned to the much higher levels of the Regime's early years.

17.3.2   SRS ISDS *in Model BITs*

With the increasing ubiquity of IIAs in the 1990s, states began to draft and publish template agreements, often labelled 'Model BITs'. These documents are important insofar as numerous governments use them as a starting position for negotiations over the actual agreements,[18] thereby representing a particular country's 'ideal point' over the regulation of foreign investment. As Brown explains,[19] Model BITs are 'an expression of a State's investment policy, its negotiating position on the protection of foreign investment, as well as (in some cases) its reaction to the jurisprudence emanating from arbitral tribunals'. Although not all

---

[17] See Yoram Z. Haftel, Tomer Broude and Alexander Thompson, 'Ulysses Bound, More or Less? Democracy, Globalization and the Design of Investment Agreements' (2021) unpublished manuscript.

[18] Stephan W. Schill, *The Multilateralization of International Investment Law* (Cambridge University Press, 2009).

[19] Chester Brown, 'Introduction: The Development and Importance of the Model Bilateral Investment Treaty', in Chester Brown (ed.), *Commentaries on Selected Model Investment Treaties* (Oxford University Press, 2013), 2.

countries have a Model BIT, UNCTAD lists, but has not yet mapped, more than seventy such documents. The countries with their own Model BIT include some of the largest economies in the world, such as the United States, Germany and India, as well as smaller countries, such as Austria, Israel, Kenya and Peru.

Using UNCTAD's coding rules, we mapped most of these documents and then transformed the raw values into SRS. The data are very much consistent with our expectations: the *SRS ISDS* mean value of forty-six Model BITs drafted between 1991 and 2004 is 0.06, but the corresponding value for twenty Model BITs drafted between 2005 and 2017 is 0.23.[20] Thus, template agreements drafted in recent years restrict foreign investors' access to ISDS to a much greater extent than earlier ones. In an extreme case, the 2015 Brazilian model excludes ISDS altogether. Arguably, these recent models are especially informative, as they are likely to be harbingers of future trends in ISDS provisions.

Another way to illustrate this trend is to compare templates of the same country at different points in time. Figure 17.2 reports *SRS ISDS* for four countries that have revised their models at least once: India, the Netherlands, the United States and Germany.[21] As one can see, three out of the four countries substantially increased *SRS ISDS* in the models drafted in the late 2000s and the 2010s. For example, in 2018 the Netherlands, which was known for its investor-friendly IIAs, published a Model BIT that substantially increases SRS. With respect to ISDS, the new model excludes debt restructuring from ISDS, limits the time period within which investors can file a complaint, and requires transparency in arbitral proceedings (among other things).[22] For its part, India's 2015 model requires that an investment claim first be submitted to a domestic court before ISDS is allowed. The German case seems to buck this trend, however. The only difference between its 2008 model and those drafted in the 1990s is a reference to conciliation proceedings (Article 10(1)).

---

[20] The number of coded texts is too small to produce a meaningful comparison of annual means. In addition, the drafting year is not available for two of the models in the sample.

[21] To be clear, these are not the only countries that updated their Model BITs. We selected these four to illustrate current trends as well as for their intrinsic importance.

[22] For a detailed analysis, see Bart-Jaap Verbeek and Roeline Knottnerus, 'The 2018 Draft Dutch Model BIT: A Critical Assessment', Investment Treaty News (30 July 2018) <iisd .org/itn/2018/07/30/the-2018-draft-dutch-model-bit-a-critical-assessment-bart-jaap-ver beek-and-roeline-knottnerus/>.

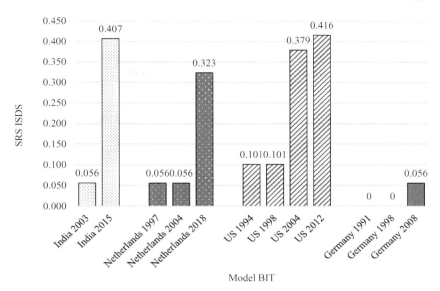

Figure 17.2 SRS ISDS in Model BITs of India, the Netherlands, the United States and Germany

17.3.3 SRS ISDS in Renegotiated IIAs

Alongside drafting new models and concluding new IIAs, states can also renegotiate existing treaties (which may or may not be based on newer models) in order to adjust their international investment commitments to new realities.[23] Thus, renegotiation can translate dissatisfaction with the Regime into concrete decisions by governments to recalibrate their treaty obligations, perhaps rendering them more legitimate.

We define a renegotiated IIA as a signed *and* ratified treaty that replaces an existing mutually ratified IIA or a signed (and where relevant, ratified) amendment to an existing mutually ratified IIA. This definition excludes investment treaties that were signed and then renegotiated before entry into force. In such instances the original treaty is not legally binding and does not require the two countries to adhere to its provisions.[24] Among

---

[23] Yoram Z. Haftel and Alexander Thompson, 'When Do States Renegotiate Investment Agreements? The Impact of Arbitration' (2018) 13 *The Review of International Organizations* 25.

[24] Yoram Z. Haftel and Alexander Thompson, 'Delayed Ratification: The Domestic Fate of Bilateral Investment Treaties' (2013) 67(2) *International Organization* 355.

IIAs in force, their renegotiation can take three different forms. First, governments may keep the old treaty in place but amend it with a new protocol. In such cases, the changes to the treaty commonly address a small number of specific issues (which may nevertheless be quite important to the parties). Second, the parties to an existing IIA may sign a new investment treaty and add a clause that terminates its precursor.

Third, the parties may substitute an IIA with a free trade agreement (FTA) that includes an investment chapter. Here we include only FTAs that explicitly terminate and replace the IIA, such as the US–Morocco and the Taiwan–Nicaragua FTAs. We thus exclude more ambiguous instances in which parties sign an FTA with an investment chapter but do not terminate an existing IIA.[25] Insofar as these IIAs coexist and have competing rules, at least potentially, it is not entirely clear which govern. It is therefore difficult to conceive the later IIA as a replacement of the earlier one.[26]

With these criteria, we identified 226 renegotiated IIAs through the end of 2017. The earliest instances of renegotiation on record are the 1965 Netherlands–Côte d'Ivoire BIT and the 1963 France–Tunisia BIT, which were renegotiated in 1971 and 1972, respectively. The most recent cases in the data set are a 2016 amending agreement to the 2003 Australia–Singapore FTA and a 2016 amending protocol to the 1997 Croatia–Ukraine BIT. With respect to the different forms of renegotiations, about 53 per cent are new investment treaties, 37 per cent are amending protocols, and the remaining 10 per cent are FTAs with investment chapters.

Figure 17.3 presents the annual number of renegotiations, broken down by type. It indicates that this trend took off only in the mid 1990s with the renegotiation of five treaties in 1994 and four treaties in 1995. The number of renegotiated treaties increased steadily over the next fifteen years, peaking in 2010, which saw twenty-five new cases of renegotiation. This was followed by a sharp decline in renegotiations in

[25] For example, China and South Korea have signed and ratified two IIAs, the 2012 China–South Korea–Japan Tripartite Investment Agreement, and a 2015 FTA, without terminating their 2007 BIT. In another example, in 2009 Malaysia and New Zealand signed a bilateral FTA with an investment chapter as well as the ASEAN–Australia–New Zealand FTA, which also includes an investment chapter. Both agreements entered into force in 2010.

[26] For more on the consequences of overlap and potential conflicts among IIAs, see UNCTAD, 'Phase 2 of IIA Reform: Modernizing the Existing Stock of Old-Generation Treaties' (2017) *IIA Issues Note*, Issue 2.

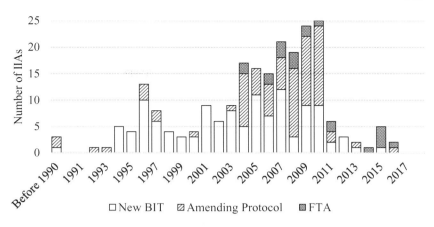

Figure 17.3 Annual number of renegotiated IIAs, 1971–2017

the 2010s. In addition, it appears that renegotiating parties preferred to sign an FTA with an investment chapter rather than a stand-alone BIT. This is significant insofar as investment chapters in FTAs tend to have higher *SRS ISDS* compared to BITs. In the entire sample of 2,785 IIAs, the values on *SRS ISDS* are 0.23 for stand-alone BITs and 0.45 for FTAs with an investment chapter.

While Figure 17.3 appears to suggest that renegotiation is becoming outmoded, a closer look at recent developments indicates that such a conclusion is unwarranted. After several years during which states have paused, appraised and reformed their approach to IIAs, at least in part due to the growing criticism of the Regime, at the time of this writing renegotiation is gaining traction again. In one important example, the European Commission took over investment policy in 2012, not without controversy, and developed a common EU approach to IIAs over several years. Its investment agreement with Singapore, signed in October 2018, will replace twelve existing BITs between Singapore and EU countries, once it enters into force.[27] The European Union is in the process of negotiating IIAs with several additional countries, such as Mexico and China, which may lead to additional replacements. In other examples, Indonesia denounced its BIT with Singapore in 2016, only to renegotiate and sign a new BIT in late 2018, and Australia replaced its BITs with

[27] UNCTAD (n. 12).

Mexico and Vietnam with the Comprehensive and Progressive Agreement for Trans-Pacific Partnership (CPTPP) in late 2018 and early 2019. In yet another significant example, the United States–Mexico–Canada Agreement (USMCA), also signed in late 2018, is a renegotiation of NAFTA. We thus expect another wave of renegotiations in coming years.

We now turn from overall trends in renegotiation to a more specific analysis of change in *SRS ISDS* from the original to the renegotiated IIA. Here, we should note that renegotiation per se does not necessarily reflect discontent with the Regime and should not always result in greater SRS. Rather, governments have various reasons to renegotiate and update ISDS provisions in their agreements. In some instances, they may want to constrain the ability of investors to take them to international arbitration and to narrow the legal basis for investment claims (i.e. making their IIAs less 'investor friendly' or reducing state exposure to arbitration), perhaps as a lesson learned from actual ISDS experience.[28] In other instances, however, governments view ISDS as a valuable mechanism to resolve disputes in an impartial and efficient manner and will thus work to promote treaties with greater protection of foreign investors. Anecdotal evidence reveals that both logics are at work in cases of renegotiation.

To cast more light on this issue, we collected and coded, based on IIAMP, all IIAs for which both texts (the original and the renegotiated) were available in languages we were able to decipher up until 2015.[29] This sample includes 181 IIA pairs. The analysis here focuses on the difference between the *SRS ISDS* values of the original and the new IIAs, labelled *Delta SRS ISDS*. This variable ranges from 1 to –1, with positive values indicating an increase, negative values indicating a decrease, and zero indicating no change in *SRS ISDS*.

Figure 17.4 depicts the average annual *Delta SRS ISDS* as a result of renegotiation. It suggests that the first wave of renegotiations, which lasted from the mid 1990s to the mid 2000s, mostly increased foreign investors' access to ISDS at the expense of states' regulatory space. Many of the renegotiations during these years were instances in which the original BIT did not include ISDS at all (revisit Figure 17.1) and the new treaty adds this crucial component, or in instances in which the original BIT provided for automatic ISDS only with respect to the

---

[28] Haftel and Thompson (n. 23); Thompson et al. (n. 10).
[29] See Thompson et al. (n. 10) for further information on the coding and sample.

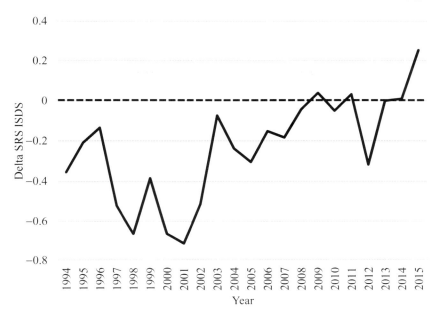

Figure 17.4 Average of SRS ISDS change in renegotiated IIAs, 1994–2015

amount of compensation. This category includes some of the earliest BITs from the 1960s and 1970s, signed by Western European countries, most prominently Germany, as well as BITs that were signed by then-communist countries in the 1980s. Examples of the former include the first ever BIT between Germany and Pakistan as well as the 1982 Sweden–China BIT and the 1968 Denmark–Indonesia BIT. Examples of the latter are the 1982 Romania–Malaysia BIT and the 1984 Netherlands–China BIT. These renegotiations are hardly a testament to the illegitimacy of ISDS in the eyes of policy-makers. Rather, they suggest that investors in capital exporting countries realized that the increasingly used instrument of ISDS was unavailable to them in some instances and pushed governments to include them in IIAs.

This trend begins to reverse in the second half of the 2000s, and in 2009 *Delta SRS ISDS* reaches positive territory for the first time, reflecting the reality that more and more renegotiations result in a higher *SRS ISDS*, thus reclaiming national sovereignty and restricting foreign investors' ability to use ISDS against states. This tendency appears to continue into the 2010s. Most IIAs renegotiated in this time-period were signed in the

1990s and many of them include at least one country from the Western Hemisphere, most notably Canada's BITs, but also recent US FTAs and Latin American IIAs. Others involve Latin American–Asian and intra-Asian FTAs, for example the 2003 South Korea–Chile and the 2008 Malaysia–Pakistan FTAs. These agreements contain many limitations and qualifications on the ability of investors to use ISDS, from the exclusion of sensitive policy areas, to time limitations, to the transparency of legal proceedings.

In sum, Figure 17.4 illustrates states' recent concern with the negative impact of IIAs on their regulatory space and perhaps their doubts about the merits and legitimacy of the ISDS system. Nonetheless, the fact that states devote so much time and energy to revising and updating their treaties, rather than simply terminating them (see the next section), suggests that most are not inclined to reject their current stock of IIAs. Rather, they prefer to modify and rebalance investor protection and SRS. From this perspective, renegotiation is an important mechanism to address the Regime's legitimacy crisis.

17.3.4   SRS ISDS *and IIA Termination*

Instead of renegotiation, parties may choose to terminate their investment treaties. Here, there are two main possibilities. First, governments can terminate their treaty by mutual agreement or allow it to expire. Second, one government can denounce the treaty, usually when its term is up for renewal. Thus far, governments have used both methods rather sparsely, but the number of such instances is on the rise. According to the UNCTAD International Investment Agreements Navigator,[30] 115 terminations of IIAs took place by the end of 2018, of which twenty-six were terminated by mutual consent and eighty-nine were unilaterally denounced.[31] This trend started in earnest in 2008, with only a handful of terminations before then.[32] Moreover, as Figure 17.5 shows, even as the number of mutually consensual terminations remained relatively constant, the number of unilateral denunciations shot up after 2012, peaking

---

[30] Available at <investmentpolicy.unctad.org/international-investment-agreements>.

[31] In this section we only examine trends in the number of terminations, rather than *SRS ISDS*. Given that termination always results in the maximum value of one on this variable, *Delta SRS ISDS* is always positive.

[32] The denunciation of the Norway–Indonesia BIT in 2001 is the earliest instance of termination on record.

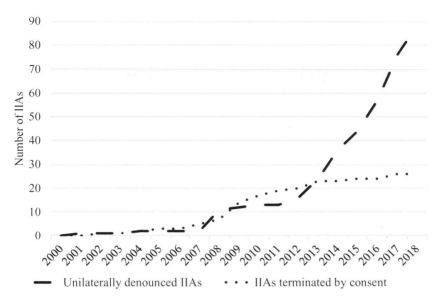

Figure 17.5 The cumulative number of IIA terminations, 2000–18

in 2017, with nineteen new terminations. Unsurprisingly, this sharp rise in the denounced IIAs corresponds to the introductory chapter's demonstration of growing criticism of the Regime and its legitimacy from the late 2000s.

A closer look at the parties that terminated the treaties suggests distinct logics to consensual termination and denunciation. With respect to the former, most agreements involve at least one state that has joined the European Union in the 2000s, most commonly with another EU member. Governments as well as the European Commission have been concerned about the incompatibility of their legal obligations when bilateral treaties overlap with EU treaties and internal EU rules. This trend is likely to continue apace as EU members harmonize and streamline their foreign investment policies.[33] It is unlikely that these terminations reflect broader dissatisfaction with the rules of the Regime, but instead reflect a change in political and legal circumstances for the states involved and an effort to accommodate them.[34]

---

[33] UNCTAD, *World Investment Report* (United Nations, 2016), 102. In 2020 EU members agreed to terminate all intra-EU BITs, a decision that is being implemented gradually.

[34] Haftel and Thompson (n. 23).

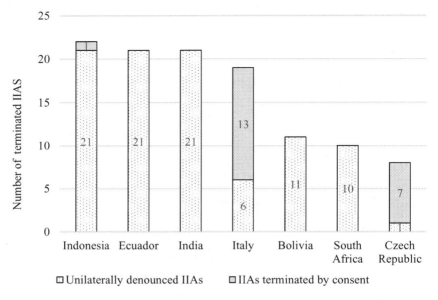

Figure 17.6 Number of terminated IIAs for the top seven terminating countries, 2000–2018

The list of denounced IIAs, on the other hand, is dominated by only five countries: Ecuador, Bolivia, South Africa, Indonesia and India. As depicted in Figure 17.6, together, they were involved in eighty-two instances of unilateral denunciation.[35] All five countries were hit by investment claims, which led their governments to doubt the benefits and even legitimacy of these agreements and to gradually undo their programmes.[36] For example, India announced its intention to terminate dozens of BITs, as it 'faces a record number of claims from foreign investors seeking billions of dollars in compensation for the alleged violation of existing investment treaties'.[37] The decision to terminate or

---

[35] Two of these BITs were between Bolivia and Ecuador and between India and Indonesia, respectively. It is not entirely clear which side initiated the termination, so they are double counted.
[36] To be sure, not all countries hit by multiple investment claims denounced their IIAs. See, for example, Argentina's behaviour to the contrary: see Yoram Z. Haftel and Hila Levi, 'Argentina's Curious Response to the Global Investment Regime: External Constraints, Identity, or Both?' (2020) 23(4) *Journal of International Relations and Development* 755.
[37] Kavaljit Singh and Burghard Ilge, 'India Overhauls Its Investment Treaty Regime', *Financial Times*, 15 July 2016, <ft.com/content/53bd355c-8203-34af-9c27-7bf990a447dc>.

denounce a BIT may be risky insofar as it signals to international investors a rejection of the investor-protection regime, while providing limited legal benefits in terms of potentially avoiding arbitration and liability.[38]

Even when unilaterally denouncing IIAs, however, states are not always interested in a complete disengagement from the Regime. In some cases, this is part of a strategy to update and reform their IIA programme. Indonesia made it clear that it terminates its older BITs in order to sign new, more progressive agreements. As mentioned in the previous section, it already signed a new BIT with Singapore and an FTA with an investment chapter with Australia. India, too, stated explicitly that it intends to negotiate new IIAs, based on its most recent model, with partners with which it had agreements previously.[39] Whether this strategy is successful remains to be seen, as potential partners find *SRS ISDS* too high. For example, one news report suggests that 'Foremost among [negotiating partners'] concerns are a requirement for investors to fight any case in the Indian courts for at least five years before going for international arbitration, and other provisions narrowing the scope for companies to make claims.'[40] Even Ecuador, one of the first countries to challenge the established rules, drafted a new model agreement in 2018 and is trying to negotiate new IIAs, based on this model, with many of the same countries with which it signed BITs in the past and later denounced.[41] These developments underscore the reality that the distinction between termination and renegotiation is not always clear-cut and that different countries take divergent paths in their effort to reform their foreign investment policies and to recalibrate their IIAs.

---

[38] Federico M. Lavopa, Lucas E. Barreiros, M. Victoria Bruno, 'How to Kill a BIT and Not Die Trying: Legal and Political Challenges of Denouncing or Renegotiating Bilateral Investment Treaties' (2013) 16(4) *Journal of International Economic Law* 869.

[39] Deepshikha Sikarwar, 'India Seeks Fresh Treaties with 47 Nations', *The Economic Times*, 27 May 2016, <economictimes.indiatimes.com/news/economy/foreign-trade/india-seeks-fresh-treaties-with-47-nations>.

[40] Aditi Shah, 'India's Proposed Investment Treaty Terms Leave Foreign Partners Cold', *Reuters*, 16 January 2018, <reuters.com/article/india-investment-treaty/indias-proposed-investment-treaty-terms-leave-foreign-partners-cold-idUSL4N1P72N1>.

[41] 'Ecuador proposes new investment agreements that protect the country and defend human rights', *Ministerio de Relaciones Exteriores y Movilidad Humana*, 8 May 2018, <cancilleria.gob.ec/en/ecuador-proposes-new-investment-agreements-that-protect-the-country-and-defend-human-rights/>.

17.4 Conclusions and Prospects

There is nothing inherently illegitimate about IIAs and the obligations they impose on states, including provisions for dispute settlement. They are arrived at through a traditional process of negotiation, signature and ratification, and formal treaties remain the gold standard for ensuring state consent to international law.[42] They serve purposes considered legitimate by the agents of the parties at the time of their execution, recurring over time and space.

However, rule systems must change with circumstances to remain effective and legitimate. As Ostrom famously noted,[43] successful and robust institutions should have built-in mechanisms for adjustment so that rules remain appropriate to prevailing conditions. This is an important challenge for IIAs, as the investment environment and the legal regime itself – including the interpretation of rules and the practice of arbitration – have evolved over time,[44] sometimes in ways that were impossible to predict by negotiators with little experience relating to the practical implications of the agreement. In this context, modifications to the Regime, such as renegotiation, are essential for its long-term viability and especially to maintain the legitimacy reflected in its rules. Fortunately, although IIAs are designed to enable long-term commitments, the Regime does have features that are conducive to more flexible adjustment. First, the vast majority of IIAs are bilateral. Being part of a dyadic network of parties makes renegotiation by mutual consent easier to accomplish than in a multilateral, veto-based, system, as it allows for more low-risk experimentation. Second, almost all IIAs are of limited duration, allowing dissatisfied states to more easily update or terminate them after the initial period has expired. Finite duration provisions are a key source of flexibility for international agreements.[45]

---

[42] Duncan B. Hollis, 'Why State Consent Still Matters: Non-State Actors, Treaties, and the Changing Sources of International Law' (2005) 23(1) *Berkeley Journal of International Law* 137.

[43] Elinor Ostrom, *Governing the Commons: The Evolution of Institutions for Collective Action* (Cambridge University Press, 1990).

[44] Jose E. Alvarez and Karl P. Sauvant (eds.), *The Evolving International Investment Regime: Expectations, Realities, Options* (Oxford University Press, 2011); Chester Brown and Kate Miles (eds.), *Evolution in Investment Treaty Law and Arbitration* (Cambridge University Press, 2011); Schill (n. 18).

[45] Barbara Koremenos, 'Contracting around International Uncertainty' (2005) 99(4) *American Political Science Review* 549.

Our analysis focuses on changes to the ISDS provisions of IIAs. Given how much variation exists in dispute settlement provisions, across time and across IIA parties,[46] it is clear that states are making conscious choices about the design of ISDS. If they are dissatisfied with the effects of investment arbitration, this should be reflected in modifications over time to the relevant treaty provisions and, in particular, we should see a trend towards designs that provide more policy autonomy for host states. Based on a coding scheme devised to capture the degree of SRS reflected in treaty provisions, we use our data to explore trends over time across the landscape of IIAs and in the content of model BITs, as well as changes resulting from treaty renegotiation and termination.

We find that, over the last few years, states have systematically reclaimed levels of SRS and sought to re-balance ISDS provisions in a way that favours host states. At the same time, it appears that IIA termination is still not widespread and that most states prefer to adjust their international obligations through new or renegotiated IIAs rather than abandon them. Thus, even if the Regime's crisis of legitimacy is indeed reflected in the changing content of IIAs, current developments point to a process of gradual adjustment, not a wholesale rejection of the Regime. The relationship between these policy approaches and legitimacy is important. When states use new and renegotiated treaties to address their concerns with the investment regime, it constitutes a productive effort to maintain the Regime's viability. Rather than being rigid and fatally flawed, the Regime as a whole is flexible enough to withstand and respond to many of its legitimacy challenges.

Recent debates and policy trends show signs of a more thoughtful approach to IIAs, and to investment arbitration in particular, that addresses many of the controversies surrounding existing agreements and institutions. Some newer IIAs leave out ISDS entirely and others significantly limit its application (for example, the USMCA that replaced NAFTA). However, most recent agreements continue to provide for ISDS, though with a variety of reform elements.[47] Some stakeholders are focused on reform at the multilateral level that would go beyond particular IIAs. For example, the procedures governing arbitration at the International Centre for Settlement of Investment Disputes, the most important forum for ISDS, are being reconsidered with an eye towards

---

[46] Pohl, Mashigo and Nohen (n. 8).

[47] UNCTAD, 'Reforming Investment Dispute Settlement: A Stocktaking' (2019) *IIA Issue Note, No. 1*.

enhancing their fairness and efficiency.[48] A wider variety of issues are being discussed by the inter-governmental Working Group III of the UN Commission on International Trade Law, which has a broad mandate to identify concerns regarding ISDS and to propose solutions. Among the most ambitious proposals, the EU favours the creation of a permanent Multilateral Investment Court, arguing that it would provide more coherence and independence than the current patchwork of tribunals. In the future, we are likely to see a combination of incremental reforms implemented treaty-by-treaty and more dramatic, systemic reforms at the multilateral level.[49]

These debates and innovations have the potential to produce a set of more balanced obligations and dispute settlement procedures, ones that provide investor protection while preserving sufficient policy space for governments to address other goals and political demands at the domestic level. Given the range of preferences regarding FDI, and the variation in domestic political and legal circumstances across countries, one-size-fits-all solutions are unlikely to work.[50] The careful calibration of provisions in new and renegotiated treaties, and their modification over time, will be important for maintaining a robust and legitimate investment regime in the future.

[48] ICSID, 'Proposals for Amendment of the ICSID Rules' (2019) Working Paper No. 2, Vol. 1.

[49] Anthea Roberts, 'UNCITRAL and ISDS Reform: Moving to Reform Options … the Politics', *EJIL: Talk!* 8 November 2018, <ejiltalk.org/uncitral-and-isds-reforms-moving-to-reform-options-the-politics/>.

[50] Sergio Puig and Gregory Shaffer, 'Imperfect Alternatives: Institutional Choice and the Reform of Investment Law' (2018) 112(3) *American Journal of International Law* 361.

INDEX

access to ISDS, 44, 47–9, 74, 171, 208, 212, 322, 340, 436, 439, 444, 457, 469, 474, 478, 540–2, 546
accountability, 27, 208, 360–1, 472
ad hoc arbitration, 34, 58, 372
adjudicative, 14, 19, 24, 28, 30, 32, 199, 206–7, 212, 233, 235, 254, 292, 394, 408, 411, 413, 478
adjudicatory
  authority, 32, 233, 254
  roles, 235
admissibility, 74, 147–8
agency, 93, 117, 120, 205, 254–5, 262, 514, 528
agent, 13, 125, 133, 375, 453, 456, 487, 528, 552
amicus curiae, third parties, 18, 27, 145–6, 149, 151, 153, 155, 161, 443, 455, 482, 538
appeals mechanism, 74, 173, 178–80, 187–8, 200, 212
  Appellate Body, WTO, 163, 456
applicable law, 175, 205, 231, 237–8, 243
appointment and selection
  adjudicator, 29, 31, 74, 79–80, 90, 92, 98, 104–5, 112, 120, 122, 124–5, 127, 134, 141, 143, 145–9, 153, 156, 161, 164, 168, 232–4, 236, 239, 244, 269, 284–6, 289, 291, 293, 295–6, 299, 313, 338, 456, 485, 518
  arbitrator, 79–80, 92, 104, 111, 122, 124–5, 127, 134, 143, 145–9, 153, 156, 161, 164, 269, 284–6, 289, 291, 293, 295–6, 299, 313, 456, 485, 518

chair, 75, 110, 122, 126, 140, 152, 160–2, 164, 166–8, 265, 269, 272, 289, 311, 485
party-appointed, 4, 21, 30, 68, 160–5, 167–8, 311
Arab Investment Agreement, 42, 73
arbitration rules, 135, 161, 383, 483
  CIETAC, 442, 456
  GIAC, 483–4
  ICC, 57–8, 69, 107, 137, 143, 147–8, 158, 161, 210, 266, 372, 384, 475, 477, 483
  ICSID, 2, 5, 7–9, 20, 23, 40, 53, 56–8, 63–6, 69–71, 73–4, 77, 80–1, 93, 95, 101–2, 104, 106–12, 136–7, 139, 141–7, 149, 151–2, 154–5, 157–8, 161, 165, 171–2, 175–6, 182–8, 190, 193, 199–200, 202, 215, 217, 220, 222, 224–5, 227, 229, 234–5, 237–8, 245, 250, 253, 257, 260, 264, 266, 268, 270, 277–80, 285–9, 294–5, 297, 301, 307–8, 310, 316, 326, 340–1, 363, 365, 368–9, 372, 383–4, 397, 425, 427, 430, 442, 452, 488, 505–6, 510, 514, 554
  LCIA, 58, 61, 69, 109, 147, 260, 277, 280, 483
  UNICTRAL, 7, 11, 28, 36, 40, 58, 63–6, 69, 74, 77, 81, 86, 106–10, 137, 139, 143, 145–6, 148–9, 152, 156, 158, 161, 173, 175, 185, 194, 202, 205, 216–17, 219, 221, 224, 230–2, 236, 238, 250–1, 254, 260, 271, 273, 277–80, 284, 286, 341, 372, 383, 426, 428, 448, 470, 475–6, 482, 489, 491, 495–9, 525, 527, 554

555

INDEX

ASEAN, 43, 317, 447
ASEAN investment agreement, 43

backlash, 18, 39, 61, 256, 531
bilateral investment treaty (BIT), 2,
39–40, 45, 47, 53, 64, 67, 69–70,
73, 75, 77, 93, 107–9, 150–1, 154,
156, 205, 218, 225, 238, 242,
245–8, 250, 262, 266, 270, 272,
319–26, 330, 332–3, 336, 338, 352,
354, 357–9, 363–4, 369, 372, 383,
424–31, 433, 439–40, 442–3, 447,
459, 471–2, 489, 491–3, 495,
520–1, 524, 539–40, 542, 544–6,
548, 551
binding treaty interpretations, 255, 264
bounded rational learning, 318, 350, 509

causation, 23
citation networks, 31, 246
coercion, 27, 273–4
coherence, 107–8, 230, 233, 287, 554
commercial arbitration, 36, 68, 90, 95,
266, 287, 289, 292, 439, 442, 449,
456–7, 469, 471, 473–4, 478, 486,
489–90, 492, 497–9
committee, treaty, 56, 137, 255, 260,
270–1, 274–5, 287–9, 297, 344–5,
350, 384, 429
compensation, 54, 59, 71, 93, 154, 199,
307, 326, 365–6, 394, 396–7, 399,
401–4, 407–8, 410, 413, 425,
427–8, 537, 541, 547, 550
interest, 396–7, 401–5, 407, 411,
416–23
compliance, 79, 508
Comprehensive Economic and Trade
Agreement, EU-Canada (CETA),
64, 256, 274–5, 395
computational, xii–xiii, xvii, 10, 17,
23–4, 41, 114, 304, 320
confidentiality, 20, 136, 160, 287, 340,
342, 398
convergence, xviii, 25, 108, 258
costs, 11, 27, 32, 34, 59, 68, 79, 86, 92,
94–6, 98, 163, 165–6, 188, 210,
305, 315–16, 325, 327, 366, 375,
397, 402, 408, 410, 413, 514, 525

allocation of costs, 28, 94, 96, 98, 410
arbitration costs, 366, 408, 411, 413,
514
Court of Justice of the EU (CJEU), 47,
79

decentralisation, 4, 12, 15, 20, 39, 79,
257–8, 260–1, 271–3
delegation, 27, 233, 255, 276, 457
developing country, 19, 25–6, 36, 61,
68, 88, 92, 243, 285, 289, 318, 341,
350, 358, 470–1, 501–10, 515,
517–29
diffusion, 36, 374, 501, 504
diplomatic protection,
174
discrimination, 274, 338
non-discrimination, 273
dispute
state-state, 2, 535, 540
trade, 79, 456
dispute settlement mechanism, xiv, xvii,
1, 4, 39–40, 62, 87, 90, 100, 107,
173, 230–1, 283–4, 322, 372, 375,
394, 425, 438, 445, 450, 455–7,
489, 501, 506, 527, 530–1, 535,
538, 540, 552–4
divergence, 16, 25, 258, 273, 347–8,
540
domestic
court, 15, 31, 36, 79, 171–84, 186–8,
192, 195–6, 198–209, 211–12, 214,
227, 350, 428, 439, 443, 449–50,
453, 467, 469–71, 473–4, 486, 536,
538, 542
dispute settlement, 174, 197, 199,
204–5
law, 174, 193, 205, 208, 369, 471

Economic Community of West African
States (ECOWAS), 43, 45
Supplementary Act on Investments,
43, 45
economic integration, xiv
empirical methods
computational, xiii, xvii, 10, 17, 23–4,
41, 56, 114, 304, 320
empiricism, 87

INDEX

interview, 10, 17, 21, 24, 100, 131, 180, 304, 338–42, 344, 346, 366, 485, 506–7, 509, 511–14, 516, 520–1, 524, 526
network analysis, 24, 104, 113–17, 119, 131, 494
qualitative, 10, 17, 22–6, 28, 32–3, 39–40, 87, 241, 259, 304, 316, 324, 335, 338–40, 342–7, 397, 503, 506–7, 510, 529, 537
quantitative, xix, 10, 16–17, 22–5, 28, 32, 40–1, 87, 113, 116, 241, 259, 304, 316–17, 319, 324, 337, 342, 347, 397, 454, 507
regression, 23, 25, 287, 308–9, 311, 313, 372–3, 377, 380–1, 386, 488, 491, 493–4, 497
Energy Charter Treaty (ECT), 8, 42, 44, 46–7, 59, 65, 68, 73, 77, 183, 204, 224, 233, 245–6, 248, 251, 307–8, 310, 384, 433
enforcement, 18, 21, 69, 103, 172, 175, 331, 360, 375, 472, 482, 484, 487, 496–7
epistemic community, 39
establishment, 11, 46, 53, 147, 171, 334
European Court of Human Rights (ECtHR), 22, 180, 206, 208, 234, 314
European Union (EU), xv, 47, 64, 72, 75–6, 79, 173, 176, 181, 185, 188, 200–1, 204, 206, 209, 211, 225, 256, 274, 314, 343, 399, 451, 531, 545, 549, 554
Commission, 173, 181
investment court, ICS, MIC, 76, 213, 314
Parliament, 181
exception, 147, 176, 183, 197, 202–3, 309, 338, 345, 369, 410, 426, 517, 519, 530
exit, 47, 77, 471
expropriation, 22, 80, 199, 270, 326, 378–9, 425, 427–8, 430

fair and equitable treatment (FET), 22, 31–2, 193, 199, 250, 256–66, 268–75, 277, 334, 430

fork-in-the-road clause (FITR) clause, 172, 174, 177, 203–5, 428, 443
free trade agreement (FTA), 42, 76, 218, 317, 323, 326, 343, 461, 544
investment chapter, 42, 59, 64, 72, 75–6, 176, 317, 323, 326, 544
Free Trade Commission (NAFTA), 65, 264
full protection and security (FPS), 23, 264, 266, 274

general principles of law, 109
Georgian International Arbitration Centre (GIAC), 483–4
graph analysis, 57, 114–15, 246

home state, 18–19, 60, 291, 293, 311, 331, 339–40, 383, 432, 471, 532
host state, 18, 31–3, 52, 59, 164, 263, 265–6, 287, 305, 312, 315–16, 322, 336–9, 341–2, 363, 365, 369, 372, 383, 399–401, 426, 428, 432, 436, 440, 444, 447, 452, 456, 471–2, 502–5, 507–8, 511, 514, 516, 518, 520, 524, 527, 530, 532–3, 540, 553

implementation, 331, 339, 344, 351, 378, 484
institutional memory, 516
insurance, 321, 338
International Centre for Settlement of Investment Disputes (ICSID), 2, 5, 7–9, 20, 23, 40, 53, 56–8, 63–6, 69–71, 73–4, 77, 80, 95, 101–2, 104, 107–12, 136–7, 139, 141–7, 149, 151–2, 154–5, 157–8, 161, 165, 171–2, 175–6, 182–8, 190, 193, 199–200, 202, 215, 217, 220, 222, 224–5, 227, 229, 234, 236–7, 245, 250, 253, 257, 260, 264, 266, 268, 270, 277–80, 285–9, 294–5, 297, 301, 307–8, 310, 316, 326, 340–1, 363, 365, 368–9, 372, 383–4, 397, 425, 427, 430, 442, 452, 488, 505–6, 510, 514, 554
Administrative Council, 143–5, 151, 154, 161

INDEX

International Centre for Settlement of
Investment Disputes (ICSID) (cont.)
  Arbitration Rules, 95
  Convention, 40, 64, 70, 107, 109–11,
    137, 143, 145, 147, 171, 236, 270,
    288, 307, 488
  Tribunals, 157, 234, 236, 270
International Chamber of Commerce
    (ICC), 39, 58, 69, 107, 137, 143,
    147–8, 158, 161, 210, 266, 372,
    383–4, 475, 477, 483
International Court of Justice (ICJ), xvi,
    89, 133, 157, 180, 235, 266, 270,
    285, 314
international economic law, xiii–xiv,
    xix, 24
interpretation, 14, 19, 25, 32, 65, 88,
    108, 231–3, 236–8, 243, 245,
    250–1, 254, 256, 259–62, 264–9,
    271–5, 292, 316, 330, 379, 429,
    448, 536, 538, 552
  expansive, 67
investment
  protection, 2, 43, 50, 205, 340, 426,
    521, 524, 531
investment court
  Multilateral Investment Court,
    (MIC), 206–8, 210
  System, 76, 150
investment court, 76, see also
    Multilateral Investment Court
    (MIC)
investment legislation, 28, 50
investment treaty
  design, 9, 33, 41–2, 236, 238, 250–4,
    284, 357, 509–10, 520, 523–4, 528,
    532, 539, 552–3
investor–state
  arbitration, xii, xix, 1, 9, 70, 88,
    136–9, 141, 171, 185, 232, 239,
    285–8, 295, 304, 322, 372, 502,
    504, 514, 525, 532
investor–state dispute settlement
    (ISDS), xii, xix, 1–2, 9, 70, 87–8,
    100, 107, 136–9, 141, 143, 171,
    173, 205, 230, 232, 283, 285–6,
    288, 295–6, 304, 313, 347, 372,
    394, 425, 501–2, 504, 513, 519–20,
    522, 528, 531–2

reform, 8, 31, 230–1, 233–4
tribunals, 22, 27, 32, 68, 72, 79, 232,
    234, 237, 241, 251–2, 261, 267,
    274–5, 289, 294, 396–7, 538, 541

jurisprudence, 3, 6, 22, 67, 80, 104, 107,
    113, 234–5, 248, 449, 508, 518, 541

least developed countries (LDCs),
    358–9, 450
legitimacy
  crisis, 4, 7, 11, 13, 22, 39–40, 61–2,
    64, 67–8, 72, 77–8, 100–1, 230,
    232, 298, 424, 532, 538, 548
  normative, 12, 14–16, 19, 27, 32, 72,
    207–9, 471
  sociological, 13, 15–17, 19, 28, 314,
    394
liberalisation, 43, 322–4, 334, 358, 456
London Court of International
    Arbitration (LCIA), 58, 69, 109,
    147, 260, 277, 280, 483

market access, 319
model BIT, 77, 108, 533, 539, 553
most-favoured-nation treatment
    (MFN), 322, 334–5, 358, 360, 363,
    430
most-favoured-nation treatment, MFN,
    23
Multilateral Agreement on Investment
    (MAI), 8, 36, 66
Multilateral Investment Court (MIC),
    8, 76, 173, 206–8, 210, 213, 284,
    314, 554

national treatment, 322
network analysis, xix, 1–2, 10, 24, 29,
    39, 42, 66, 101–2, 104–6, 112,
    114–20, 122–3, 125–6, 128, 130–1,
    233, 242, 244, 246–7, 287, 400,
    552, see also empirical
    methods
non-governmental organization
    (NGO), 19, 209
normative, 8, 11–17, 19, 27–9, 32, 36,
    38, 52, 72, 85, 172, 174, 206–9,
    213, 257, 259, 290, 369, 471, 501,
    505, 524, 529, 537

INDEX

North American Free Trade Agreement (NAFTA), 4, 41–2, 59, 64–6, 68, 73, 75–6, 146, 149, 174, 182, 185, 188, 190, 197, 203, 205, 208, 215, 217, 219, 221–2, 233, 242, 244–9, 251, 254, 260, 264, 268, 271, 278–9, 308, 310, 339, 384, 447, 510, 546, 553
 Chapter 11, 4, 65, 75, 174, 185, 188, 208, 339

object and purpose, treaty, 428
objections, 305, 343
Organisation for Economic Co-operation and Development, (OECD), 1, 8, 36, 66, 73–4, 121, 317, 320, 323, 328, 330–1, 334, 336–9, 342, 352, 357–9, 362–3, 366, 399, 402, 408, 413, 436, 450, 535
Organisation of the Islamic Cooperation (OIC), 42, 45, 47, 59, 73

party autonomy, 483
Permanent Court of Arbitration (PCA), 57–8, 63, 69, 73–4, 133, 135–9, 141, 150, 155, 161, 184, 194, 219, 221, 223, 250, 273, 277, 279–80, 372, 397, 407, 425
PluriCourts Investment Treaty and Arbitration Database (PITAD), 1–2, 12, 20, 30, 50, 56–7, 65, 68, 70, 101–2, 104–5, 113, 285–7, 289, 304–5, 427, 432–4, 439, 448, 511, 513
positivism, legal, 292
precedent, 31, 232–8, 244–6, 248–55, 257–62, 269–73, 276, 444
predictability, 31, 231–2, 237, 266
pre-establishment, 322, 324, 334
principal, 37, 78, 88, 292, 323, 502, 517, *see also* principal–agent theory
principal–agent theory, 233, 254, *see also* agency

rational choice, 235
regulatory chill, 52, 68, 315, 338–9, 341, 346, 534

remedies, 32, 35, 70, 74, 172, 174, 177–9, 183, 197, 199–200, 203, 206, 209–10, 212, 224, 304, 425, 428, 442, 494, 536, 538
resolution of investment disputes, xv, 35, 135, 142, 164, 262, 269, 347, 443, 445–6, 448, 451, 455, 483, 537
responsiveness, 79, 352, 360
rule of law, 19, 34–5, 37, 42, 181, 208, 237, 360, 367–70, 376, 382, 458, 467–72, 474–6, 478, 484, 486–7, 489–90, 492, 494, 497–9

services, 127, 164, 263, 266, 294, 319, 341, 437, 456, 490, 514, 517
Southern African Development Community (SADC), 43, 45
sovereignty, 36, 208, 210, 452, 501, 530, 532, 547
spill-over, 499
standard of review, 138, 145
stare decisis, 32, 234, 236, 257, 259, 261, 270, 272–3
Stockholm Chamber of Commerce (SCC), 57, 107, 143, 146, 372, 383–4, 397
substantive rules, 7, 292

trade, ii, 6, 24, 41–3, 65, 70, 74, 79, 103, 171, 176, 190, 205, 216, 235–6, 255–7, 274, 284, 315–16, 319, 322, 344, 372, 383, 395, 451, 456, 472–3, 489, 494, 504, 530, 554
 agreement, 41, 131, 176, 395
Transatlantic Trade and Investment Partnership (TTIP) Agreement, 64, 75, 256, 274, 395
transfer, 346, 413
Transpacific Partnership Agreement (TPP), 42, 64, 76, 256, 317, 342–3
transparency, 5, 19, 27, 58, 65, 74, 86, 90, 108, 136, 207, 256, 265, 273–4, 340, 378, 404, 538, 542, 548
treaty
 context, 243
 object and purpose, 428

560 INDEX

United Nations Commission on
International Trade Law
(UNCITRAL), 1, 7, 9, 11, 20, 28,
36, 40–2, 44, 46, 49–50, 56, 58,
63–6, 69, 74, 77, 81, 86, 106–10,
137, 139, 143, 145–6, 148–50, 152,
156, 158, 161, 172–3, 175, 185,
194, 202–3, 205, 207, 216–17, 219,
221, 223–4, 230–2, 236, 238, 240,
244, 250–1, 254, 260, 271, 273,
277–80, 284, 286, 317–18, 320,
325, 338, 341, 349, 364–5, 372,
383–4, 424, 426, 428, 430, 433–4,
436, 439, 447–8, 470, 475–6, 482,
488–9, 491, 494–9, 502, 505, 508,
517–18, 525, 527–8, 531–2, 534,
539, 542, 544–5, 548–9, 553–4
Arbitration Rules, 40
Working Group III, 7, 108, 173, 230,
284, 525, 527, 554
United Nations Conference on Trade
and Development (UNCTAD)

International Investment
Agreements Navigator, 488, 548

Vienna Convention on the Law of
Treaties (VCLT), 43, 134, 243, 429
Article 31, 243
voice, 30, 160, 360, 471

World Bank, 9, 19, 48, 50, 93, 145, 289,
328–9, 339, 358, 360, 368, 372,
375, 379, 384, 433, 463, 473, 487,
490, 492, 518, 521
income groups, 48–51, 60–1, 289,
308, 433, 463
World Trade Organisation (WTO),
2–3, 6, 24, 65–6, 79, 163, 235, 314,
324, 341, 456, 530
dispute settlement mechanism, 40,
107, 456
Dispute Settlement Understanding
(DSU), 2–3
panel(s), 6, 164, 205, 299, 306, 308, 310